Translations of Chaucer and Virgil

The Cornell Wordsworth

General Editor: Stephen Parrish
Associate Editor: Mark L. Reed
Assistant Editor: James A. Butler

Coordinating Editor: Jared Curtis

Advisory Editors: M. H. Abrams, Geoffrey Hartman, Jonathan Wordsworth

---

Early Poems and Fragments, 1785–1797, edited by Carol Landon and Jared Curtis
An Evening Walk, edited by James Averill
Descriptive Sketches, edited by Eric Birdsall
The Salisbury Plain Poems, edited by Stephen Gill
The Borderers, edited by Robert Osborn
The Ruined Cottage and *The Pedlar,* edited by James Butler
Lyrical Ballads, and Other Poems, 1797–1800, edited by James Butler and Karen Green
Peter Bell, edited by John Jordan
The Prelude, 1798–1799, edited by Stephen Parrish
Home at Grasmere, edited by Beth Darlington
The Thirteen-Book *Prelude,* edited by Mark L. Reed
Poems, in Two Volumes, and Other Poems, 1800–1807, edited by Jared Curtis
Benjamin the Waggoner, edited by Paul F. Betz
The Tuft of Primroses, with Other Late Poems for *The Recluse,* edited by Joseph F. Kishel
The White Doe of Rylstone, edited by Kristine Dugas
Translations of Chaucer and Virgil, edited by Bruce E. Graver
Shorter Poems, 1807–1820, edited by Carl H. Ketcham
The Fourteen-Book *Prelude,* edited by W. J. B. Owen

CENTER FOR
SCHOLARLY EDITIONS
AN APPROVED EDITION
MODERN LANGUAGE
ASSOCIATION OF AMERICA

Translations of Chaucer and Virgil

by William Wordsworth

Edited by

Bruce E. Graver

CORNELL UNIVERSITY PRESS

ITHACA AND LONDON

PUBLICATION OF THIS BOOK WAS ASSISTED BY GRANTS FROM THE PROGRAM FOR EDITIONS OF THE NATIONAL ENDOWMENT FOR THE HUMANITIES, AN INDEPENDENT FEDERAL AGENCY.

First published 1998 by Cornell Univeristy Press.

Printed in the United States of America.

Cornell University Press strives to utilize environmentally responsible suppliers and materials to the fullest extent possible in the publishing of its books. Such materials include vegetable-based, low-VOC inks and acid-free papers that are either recycled, totally chlorine free, or partly composed of nonwood fibers.

Library of Congress Cataloging-in-Publication Data

Wordsworth, William, 1770–1850.
Translations of Chaucer and Virgil / by William Wordsworth;
edited by Bruce E. Graver.
p. cm. — (The Cornell Wordsworth)
Includes bibliographical references and index.
ISBN 0-8014-3452-1 (alk paper)
1. English poetry—Middle English, 1100-1500—Modernized versions. 2. Latin poetry—Translations into English. 3. Virgil—Translations into English. I. Graver, Bruce Edward. II. Chaucer, Geoffrey, d. 1400. Selections. III. Virgil. Selections. English. IV. Title. V. Series: Wordsworth, William, 1770-1850. Selections. 1975.
PR5852.G73 1998
821'.7—dc21 97-47787

Cloth Printing 10 9 8 7 6 5 4 3 2 1

TO MARGARET

The Cornell Wordsworth

The individual volumes of the Cornell Wordsworth series, some devoted to long poems, some to collections of shorter poems, have had two common aims. The first has been to bring the early Wordsworth into view. Wordsworth's practice of leaving his poems unpublished for years after their completion and his lifelong habit of revision—Ernest de Selincourt called it "obsessive"—have obscured the original, often thought the best, versions of his work. These original versions are here presented in the form of clean, continuous "reading texts" from which all layers of later revision have been stripped away. In volumes that cover the work of Wordsworth's middle and later years, bringing the "early Wordsworth" into view means simply presenting as "reading texts," wherever possible, the earliest finished versions of the poems, not the latest revised versions.

The second aim of the series is to provide, for the first time, a complete and accurate record of variant readings, from Wordsworth's earliest drafts down to the final lifetime (or first posthumous) publication. The most important manuscripts are shown in full transcription; on pages facing the most complex and interesting transcriptions, photographs of the manuscript pages are also provided. Besides transcriptions and the photographs, on which draft revisions may be seen, and an *apparatus criticus* in which printed variants are collected, a third device for the study of revisions is adopted: when two versions of a work match sufficiently well, they are arrayed on facing pages so that the steps by which one was converted into the other become visible.

Volumes in the series are unnumbered, but upon publication their titles are inserted into the list of volumes in print in the order in which the works were written. A more detailed introduction to the series may be found in the first volume published, *The Salisbury Plain Poems,* edited by Stephen Gill.

S. M. Parrish

Ithaca, New York

Contents

Appendixes

Preface

The present volume offers the first full account of Wordsworth's two most extensive translation projects: his modernizations of Chaucer and his unfinished translation of Virgil's *Aeneid*. This account makes possible an accurate assessment of Wordsworth's methods and achievement as a translator. Although he did not translate as regularly or extensively as John Dryden or Alexander Pope, Wordsworth nevertheless turned to translation throughout his career, often at key transitional periods. A better understanding of when and why he translated, and his methods of doing so, offers new and important insights into his creative process. The translations of Chaucer and Virgil are especially significant in this regard, for they are the most direct records of Wordsworth's encounter with two of the most important poets in the Western tradition. How he read and understood them, and what relation their works had to his original poetry, can best be revealed by a study of his translations.

In this volume I also make a modest attempt to place Wordsworth's translations in context with other English translations of Virgil. The history of these translations is in many ways a history of English poetry. Virgil was one of the first poets schoolboys read; Latin poetry composed in the schools was largely a cento of Virgilian, Ovidian, and Horatian half-lines; and the conventions of schoolboy translation of classical authors deeply informed the language of English poetry. It is also clear from the translations themselves, and especially their prefaces, that translators considered translation of Virgil to be the proving ground for the poetical power of the English language. In this respect, translation is not the derivative, secondary kind of creation it is so often thought of as being, but one of the chief means by which a language can discover and establish its own poetic idiom and range of expression. Wordsworth's borrowings from his predecessors, and his departures from them, necessarily shed new light on his understanding of the possibilities for poetic expression in English.

Most important of all, an understanding of Wordsworth's methods of translation and his place in the history of English translation at last makes possible a thorough examination of Wordsworth's uneasy relations with the greatest English translator, and one of his most important neoclassical predecessors, John Dryden. Dryden translated both Chaucer and Virgil, and Wordsworth's opinions of Dryden's successes and failures are well known. Yet Wordsworth's actual practice as a translator, including both his differences and his borrowings from Dryden, has rarely been considered even by those interested in the relation of his poetry to English neoclassicism. We know from the Grasmere journals that the Wordsworths had been reading Dryden's modernizations of Chaucer in 1801, as his own translations were being composed. And we know that Dryden's works were in Robert Anderson's *Works of the British Poets* (Edinburgh, 1792–1795), as were the texts of Chaucer from which Wordsworth translated. From his own admission we know further that he borrowed freely from Dryden when composing his *Aeneid* in 1823–1824. Wordsworth's translations of Chaucer and Virgil thus constitute a self-conscious dialogue with Dryden, as well as a competition with his achievement. The present edition of Wordsworth's translations supplies crucial evidence for a major reassessment of Wordsworth's attitudes toward John Dryden; from this evidence emerges a more complicated and vexed picture of the relation of his poetry to British neoclassicism.

It gives me great pleasure to acknowledge the generous assistance of so many scholars, libraries, foundations, and academic institutions in the preparation of this volume. To my co-editors of the Cornell Wordsworth, especially Paul F. Betz, Eric Birdsall, Beth Darlington, Stephen Gill, Karen Green, and Carol Landon, I am indebted for advice of many kinds and their unflagging support as the edition was being prepared. I wish that the late Carl Ketcham, who showed such a lively interest in my work, and whose own volume is one of the great achievements of the series, were alive to see this edition published. I am especially grateful to the general editors of the series, whose contributions to this volume make them its virtual co-authors: to Stephen M. Parrish, who tirelessly checked, corrected, and reviewed every word of the volume, and urged it on to completion; to Mark L. Reed, under whose guidance I first began the study of Wordsworth's poetry, and whose standards of precision and thoroughness are my most important scholarly influence; to Jared Curtis, who supervised the work in its early stages and whose computer expertise made publication considerably easier than it would have been otherwise; and to James Butler, who carefully read proof and offered many suggestions along the way. I am also grateful to many other scholars: to Jonathan Wordsworth, who has supported this project from the first, and who has permitted me to study and copy manuscripts both in the Wordsworth Library and in his own possession; to Robert Woof, who has helped me navigate my way through the holdings of the Wordsworth Library, and has offered advice and counsel on numerous matters of detail that only he could help with; to Pamela Woof, whose knowledge of Dorothy Wordsworth's Grasmere journals was especially helpful; to Alan G. Hill, who generously responded to my questions when our paths crossed in Grasmere; to Richard W. Clancey, who shared his knowledge of Wordsworth's classical education, and whose kindness and generosity are a model of scholarly collegiality; and to Betsy Bowden, R. A. Foakes, David Garcia, Alexander Gourlay, Karen Hodder, William Keach, Robert Kirkpatrick, Sara Mack, Peter Manning, Thomas McFarland, Richard Noble, Brennan O'Donnell, the late Harold Shapiro, Arthur Sherbo, Thomas Stumpf, Joseph Viscomi, Eric Walker, and Duncan Wu for advice on various matters. I am also grateful to my colleagues in the

Department of English at Providence College for aiding and abetting my work at every stage, especially to the Chaucerian Rodney K. Delasanta and to J. T. Scanlan, scholar of Edmond Malone. Finally, I am happy to acknowledge the work of the late William Frost, whose lifelong study of Dryden's achievement as a translator was, in so many ways, an inspiration for this volume.

The staffs of numerous libraries have provided valuable assistance: the Bodleian Library, Oxford; the British Library; the Cumbria County Record Office, Carlisle; the John Hay Library, Brown University; the Wren Library, Trinity College, Cambridge; Cornell University Library; the Folger Shakespeare Library; the Houghton Library, Harvard University; the Huntington Library; the Berg Collection, New York Public Library; the Pierpont Morgan Library; Phillips Memorial Library, Providence College; Alderman Library, University of Virginia; Dr. Williams's Library, London; the Beinecke Rare Book and Manuscript Library, Yale University. I am especially grateful to Jeffrey Cowton and the staff of the Wordsworth Library, Grasmere, who made my numerous stays in Grasmere so pleasurable and productive.

I thank Jonathan Wordsworth and the Trustees of the Wordsworth Trust for permission to publish or quote from Wordsworth's manuscripts and books that are in their possession. Thanks are also due to the following for permission to consult, publish, or quote from printed books and manuscript materials in their possession: Paul F. Betz; The Bodleian Library, Oxford; The British Library; the Cumbria County Record Office, Carlisle (letters from Wordsworth to Lord Lonsdale, published with permission of the Lonsdale Estate Trust, in whom copyright resides); Cornell University Library; Mark L. Reed; John Spedding; the Master and Fellows of Trinity College, Cambridge (manuscript notebooks of Christopher Wordsworth and Christopher Wordsworth, Jr.); Jonathan Wordsworth.

Work on this volume was made possible by grants of various kinds: from the Research Committee of Delta State University (1984–1985); from the American Philosophical Society (1986); from the American Council of Learned Societies (1987); and from the National Endowment for the Humanities (1987, 1990). I am grateful to all of them for their generous assistance. My special thanks are reserved for the Committee to Aid Faculty Research at Providence College, which provided me with four grants, covering such items as computer hardware and software, photographs of manuscripts, and travel. I am especially grateful to James McGovern, former Associate Vice President for Academic Administration; Fr. Thomas McGonigle, O.P., former Vice President for Academic Administration; and Fr. John F. Cunningham, O.P., former President of Providence College.

Finally, my deepest thanks are due to Margaret R. Graver, who first convinced me that Wordsworth's translations were worth studying, and whose knowledge of classical languages and culture has been invaluable to me in all my scholarly endeavors. To her this volume is dedicated.

Bruce E. Graver

Providence, Rhode Island

Abbreviations

Listed at the end of the Editorial Procedure are abbreviations used in transcriptions, those employed to record textual variants and editions in the *apparatus criticus* and notes, and those used to indicate Wordsworth's classifications of his poems. The Manuscript Census lists short titles of manuscripts.

Alderson	William Alderson and Arnold Henderson, *Chaucer and Augustan Scholarship* (Berkeley, 1970).
BF	Barron Field.
BL	British Library.
Blainey	Ann Blainey, *The Farthing Poet: A Biography of Richard Hengist Horne, 1802–84* (London, 1968).
Bowden	*Eighteenth-Century Modernizations from the Canterbury Tales,* ed. Betsy Bowden (Rochester, N. Y., 1991).
British Poets	*The Works of the British Poets,* ed. Robert Anderson (13 vols.; Edinburgh, 1792–1795; vol. 14 issued 1807) *Browning Correspondence The Browning Correspondence,* ed. Philip Kelley and Ronald Hudson (11 vols.; Winfield, Kans., 1984–1994).
Chronology: MY	Mark L. Reed, *Wordsworth: The Chronology of the Middle Years, 1800–1815* (Cambridge, Mass., 1975).
CL	Charles Lamb.
CM	*The Poems of Geoffrey Chaucer, Modernized,* ed. R. H. Horne (London, 1841).
Conran	Anthony E. M. Conran, "The Dialectic of Experience: A Study of Wordsworth's *Resolution and Independence,*" *PMLA* 75 (1960), 66–74.
Cuckoo	*The Cuckoo and the Nightingale.* Wordsworth's modernization of a Middle English poem, once thought to be Chaucer's.
CW	Christopher Wordsworth.
CW, Jr.	Christopher Wordsworth, Jr.
DC	Dove Cottage.
DCP	Dove Cottage Papers; unnumbered manuscript.
DNB	*Dictionary of National Biography.*
Dora W	Dora Wordsworth.
Dowden	Edward Dowden, "Wordsworth's Selections from Chaucer Modernised," in *Wordsworthiana: A Selection from Papers*

	Read to the Wordsworth Society, ed. William Knight (London, 1889), 19–28.
Dryden	John Dryden; or his translation of Chaucer or of Virgil (the specific editions that Wordsworth used are not known).
DW	Dorothy Wordsworth.
1820RD	William Wordsworth, *The River Duddon, A Series of Sonnets; Vaudracour and Julia: and Other Poems* (London, 1820).
EQ	Edward Quillinan.
EY	*The Letters of William and Dorothy Wordsworth: The Early Years, 1787–1805,* ed. Ernest de Selincourt (2d ed., rev. Chester L. Shaver; Oxford, 1967).
Fables	John Dryden, *Fables, Ancient and Modern* (London, 1700).
GGW	Gordon Graham Wordsworth, grandson of William Wordsworth.
Grasmere Journals	Dorothy Wordsworth, *The Grasmere Journals,* ed. Pamela Woof (Oxford, 1991).
Graver, *SP*	Bruce Graver, "Wordsworth and the Language of Epic: The Translation of the *Aeneid,*" *Studies in Philology* 83, 3 (Summer 1986), 261–285.
Grosart	*The Prose Works of William Wordsworth,* ed. Alexander B. Grosart (3 vols.; London, 1876).
H at G	*Home at Grasmere: Part First, Book First, of "The Recluse" by William Wordsworth,* ed. Beth Darlington (Ithaca, 1977).
HCR	Henry Crabb Robinson.
Healey	George Harris Healey, *The Cornell Wordsworth Collection* (Ithaca, 1957).
Hodder	Karen Hodder, "Chaucer and Wordsworth: The Growth of a Poet's Responsibility," unpublished manuscript.
IF	Isabella Fenwick.
JC	John Carter, Wordsworth's secretary at Rydal Mount.
JCH	Julius Charles Hare.
LB, 1797–1800	*"Lyrical Ballads," and Other Poems, 1797–1800,* ed. James Butler and Karen Green (Ithaca, 1992).
Legouis	Émile Legouis, *The Early Life of William Wordsworth, 1770 – 1798: A Study of "The Prelude,"* trans. J. W. Matthews (London, 1897).
Lipscomb	*The Canterbury Tales of Chaucer, completed in a Modern Version,* ed. William Lipscomb (3 vols.; London, 1795).
Lucas	*The Letters of Charles and Mary Lamb,* ed. E. V. Lucas (3 vols.; New Haven, 1935).
LY, I, II, III, IV	*The Letters of William and Dorothy Wordsworth: The Later Years, 1821–1850,* ed. Ernest de Selincourt (4 vols.; 2d ed.; rev., arranged, and ed. Alan G. Hill; Oxford, 1978, 1979, 1982, 1988). Roman numerals in citations refer to volumes.
Manciple	*The Manciple's Tale* by Geoffrey Chaucer, as modernized by Wordsworth.
Memoirs	Christopher Wordsworth, Jr., *Memoirs of William Words-worth* (2 vols.; London, 1851).
Manning	Peter Manning, "Cleansing the Images: Wordsworth, Rome, and the Rise of Historicism," *Texas Studies in Literature and Language* 33, 2 (Summer 1991): 271–326.
MH	Mary Hutchinson.

Minellius	*Publii Virgilii Maronis opera omnia cum annotationibus J. Minelli* (Hafnia, 1740). Wordsworth's copy, Cornell Wordsworth Collection.
MW	Mary Wordsworth.
MWL	*The Letters of Mary Wordsworth, 1800–1855*, ed. Mary Burton (Oxford, 1958).
MY, I, II	*The Letters of William and Dorothy Wordsworth: The Middle Years, 1806–1820*, ed. Ernest de Selincourt (2 vols.; 2d ed. Part I, 1806–1811, rev. Mary Moorman, Oxford, 1969; Part II, 1812–1820, rev. Mary Moorman and Alan G. Hill, Oxford, 1970). Roman numerals in citations refer to parts.
OED	*Oxford English Dictionary.*
Ogle	*The Canterbury Tales of Chaucer, Modernis'd by several Hands*, ed. George Ogle (3 vols.; London, 1741).
Ogilby (1650)—WL	*The Works of Virgil*, trans. John Ogilby (London, 1650). Wordsworth's copy, in the Wordsworth Library, Grasmere.
PBSA	*Publications of the Bibliographical Society of America.*
PELY	William Wordsworth, *Poems, Chiefly of Early and Late Years* (London, 1842).
Pitt	Christopher Pitt, translator; or his translation of Virgil (the specific edition that Wordsworth used is not known).
PM	*The Philological Museum.*
Poems, 1800–1807	*"Poems, in Two Volumes," and Other Poems, 1800–1807*, ed. Jared Curtis (Ithaca, 1983).
Poems, 1807–1820	*Shorter Poems, 1807–1820*, ed. Carl H. Ketcham (Ithaca, 1989).
Prioress	*The Prioress's Tale* by Geoffrey Chaucer, as modernized by Wordsworth.
Prose	*The Prose Works of William Wordsworth*, ed. W. J. B. Owen and Jane Smyser (3 vols.; Oxford, 1974).
PW	*The Poetical Works of William Wordsworth*, ed. Ernest de Selincourt and Helen Darbishire (5 vols.; Oxford, 1940–1949; rev. 1952–1959).
RHH	Richard Henry [or Hengist] Horne.
Ruæus	*Publii Virgilii Maronis opera interpretatione et notibus illustravit Carolus Ruæus ad usum Delphini* (London, 1725).
Scattergood	*The Works of Sir John Clanvowe*, ed. V. J. Scattergood (Cambridge, 1975).
SH	Sara Hutchinson.
Shaver	Chester L. Shaver and Alice C. Shaver, *Wordsworth's Library: A Catalogue* (New York, 1979).
SHL	*The Letters of Sara Hutchinson, from 1800 to 1835*, ed. Kathleen Coburn (Toronto, 1954).
Skeat	*The Complete Works of Geoffrey Chaucer*, ed. Walter W. Skeat (7 vols.; Oxford, 1894).
Speght	*The Works of our Ancient, Learned, & Excellent English Poet, Jeffrey Chaucer: As they have lately been Compar'd with the best Manuscripts; and several things added, never before in Print*, ed. Thomas Speght (London, 1687).
Spurgeon	Caroline F. E. Spurgeon, *Five Hundred Years of Chaucer Criticism and Allusion, 1357–1900* (vols.; New York, 1960).
STC	Samuel Taylor Coleridge.

STCBL	*The Collected Works of Samuel Taylor Coleridge, Biographia Literaria,* ed. James Engell and W. Jackson Bate (2vols.; Princeton, 1983).
STCL	*Collected Letters of Samuel Taylor Coleridge,* ed. E. L. Griggs (6 vols.; Oxford, 1956–1971).
Thynne	*The workes of Geffray Chaucer newly printed, with dyuers workes which were neuer in print before,* ed. William Thynne (London, 1532).
TPP	Thomas Powell Papers, in the Wordsworth Library, Grasmere.
Trapp	Joseph Trapp, translator; or his translation of Virgil (the specific edition that Wordsworth used is not known).
Troilus	*Troilus and Cresida. An Extract.* Wordsworth's modernization of a passage from Chaucer's poem.
Tuft	*"The Tuft of Primroses," with Other Late Poems for "The Recluse,"* ed. Joseph F. Kishel (Ithaca, 1986).
Tyrwhitt	*The Canterbury Tales of Chaucer,* ed. Thomas Tyrwhitt (5 vols.; London, 1775–1778).
Urry	T*he Works of Geoffrey Chaucer, compared with the Former Editions and many valuable MSS.,* ed. John Urry (London, 1721).
WL	Wordsworth Library, Grasmere.
WW	William Wordsworth.

Manuscript Census

***British Poets*—Folger** STC's copy of *British Poets.* Vol. VIII of the set is lacking. Vol. I contains marginalia in WW's autograph connected with his modernizations of Chaucer. Folger Shakespeare Library, Washington, D.C.

***British Poets*—WL** WW's copy of *British Poets.* Vol. I contains marginalia connected with his modernizations of Chaucer and his corrections of R. H. Horne's modernizations. WW 14 (AND), WL.

Calvert MS. The opening stanza of *Cuckoo.* One sheet, small quarto. Signed "Wm Wordsworth Nov[br] 27th / 1819." At page foot is written by an unidentified hand: "M[rs] Calvert upon requesting M[r] Wordsworth for a few lines in his own hand writing—received the above." The paper has been folded. Private collection.

Cornell MS. (Healey 2277) The opening stanza of *Cuckoo* . Half sheet wove paper, 18.5 by 12.1 cm., irregularly trimmed. Signed "W[m] Wordsworth / London. 1820." The manuscript has been folded, as if for mailing, and was pasted onto green paper, perhaps in an album. Cornell Wordsworth Collection, Kroch Library, Cornell University.

DC MS. 13 Described *LB, 1797–1800.* Contains *Prioress,* ll. 149–end, in DW's and WW's autographs, with revisions by DW, WW, and MW; *Cuckoo* , ll. 1–260, in WW's and MW's hands, with revisions by MW, WW, and John Carter; *Manciple,* in hands of MW and WW, with revisions by MW, WW, and Dora W. See *Chronology: MY,* pp. 132–134, for conjectures on the order in which they were entered.

DC MS. 24 Described *Poems, 1800–1807* and *LB, 1797–1800.* Contains *Troilus,* ll. 47–98, in WW's and MW's autographs, and two quotations concerning Chaucer from Milton and Drayton.

DC MS. 35 A single sheet of laid paper, 29.2 by 31.1 cm., watermarked with a crowned medallion with Britannia and countermarked 1799; chain lines appear at intervals of 2.6 cm. The paper has been divided into three columns of about 9.8 cm. Contains fair copy of *Prioress* in MW's autograph, complete but for ll. 138, 180, 212, and 221. The fair copy begins about a fifth of the way down the middle column of the recto. At bottom of left-hand column, recto, upside down, appears the note "Before I begin to write tonigh" in ?DW's autograph. The paper has been folded several times, as if to be mailed.

DC MS. 36 A bifolium of laid paper, 31.1 by 39.1 cm., watermarked 1799; chain lines appear at intervals of 2.6 cm. The paper has been divided into two columns of about 15.5 cm. Contains fair copy of *Manciple,* ll. 1–86, in MW's autograph. DW seems to have been practicing her signature on verso. The paper has been folded twice, as if to be mailed.

DC MS. 89 Described *Tuft,* p. 72. Contains quotations concerning Chaucer from Milton and Drayton (see p. 145), stubs of *Cuckoo* and *Troilus,* draft of *Manciple (from the Prologue),* fair copy of *Manciple,* and complete drafts of the *Aeneid.* For foliation, see pp. 151, 331.

DC MS. 101A A handmade notebook, bound in marble boards with a green cloth spine; the title "Virgil" has been written on a slip of paper, pasted on the front cover. The notebook contains *Aeneid,* Books I, II, and III, ll. 409–720, each book of which is sewn separately. Book I is in MW's hand, with ink and pencil revisions by MW, WW, and DW. It is written on wove paper, 20.3 by 24.9 cm., watermarked C WILMOT / 1822, and consists of a gathering of 14 bifolia, sewn in the middle, of which 26 leaves and 2 stubs remain. Book II is in MW's hand, with ink and pencil revisions by MW, WW, and CW, Jr. It is written on wove paper, averaging 20 by 24.5 cm., watermarked C WILMOT / 1821, and consists of a gathering of 12 bifolia, sewn in the middle. Book III is in DW's hand with ink and pencil revisions by DW and WW. It is written on wove paper, 19.3 by 25.2 cm., watermarked J BUDGEN / 1823, and consists of a gathering of 5 bifolia, sewn consecutively, of which 9 leaves and one stub remain. Leaf 10 contains an early version of WW's *Ode Composed on a May Morning* and *To May,* written before they had been divided into two separate poems.

DC MS. 101B Two notebooks in wrappers; one contains *Aeneid,* Book I, in DW's hand, an "Advertisement" in MW's hand, ink revisions by DW and WW, and pencil and ink markings and notes by STC; the other contains *Aeneid,* Book II, in DW's hand with ink revisions by DW, WW, and CW, Jr., a pasteover by DW, and interleaves containing revisions in CW, Jr.'s hand. The wrapper of the notebook containing Book I is made of wove paper, watermarked C WILMOT / 1822 and stamped G. Roake, 83 Strand, Bath; inside the wrapper is a gathering of 13 bifolia, sewn consecutively, of which 22 leaves and 4 stubs remain. These bifolia are made up of wove paper, 18.5 by 22.8 cm., watermarked HAGAR CO. / 1822 (through leaf 21), SIMMONS / 1820 (leaves 22–23), and SIMMONS / 1821 (leaves 24–27). The wrapper of the notebook containing Book II is made of wove paper, watermarked SIMMONS / 1820 and stamped G. Roake, 83 Strand,

Bath; inside the wrapper is a gathering of 13 bifolia, sewn consecutively, of which 24 leaves and 2 stubs remain. These bifolia are made up of wove paper, 18.5 by 22.8 cm.; leaves 1–10 and 15–26 are watermarked SIMMONS / 1820; leaves 11–14 are watermarked HAGAR CO. / 1822. There is also a pasteover on 2ᵛ, made of laid paper 7–7.3 by 18.5 cm., with chain lines at intervals of 2.5 cm.; there is no visible watermark. The entire notebook is interleaved; the interleaves are written on laid paper, 18.5 by 15.2 cm., with chain lines 2.6 cm. apart, watermarked with a crown surmounting a quartered shield containing a bear, a lion rampant, a harp, and a unicorn, and countermarked WP / 1815. On the back of the wrapper WW has written in ink: "To be sent to Lady Beaumont / Grosvenor Square—before, [?] or / on Saturday Sennight / 20th April."

DC MS. 101C A bound exercise book, containing *Aeneid*, Book III, ll. 1–816, in MW's hand, with ink and pencil revisions by MW, WW, and DW, and a note by STC. The wrapper measures 19.6 by 26.4 cm. and is not watermarked; on the front is a woodcut portraying a mother reading to a child, below which are printed five "Divine Precepts"; on the back are three cartoon-like woodcuts, probably illustrating William Cowper's *John Gilpin*. This notebook contains a gathering of 12 bifolia, of which 23 leaves and one stub remain. It is made up of wove paper, 20 by 25.1 cm., watermarked C WILMOT / 1821.

DC MS. 101D One bifolium and one leaf (a bifolium torn at the fold) of laid paper, 22.5 by 37.5 cm., with chain lines 3.9 cm. apart, watermarked A COWAN / 1822. Contains STC's notes to WW's translation of *Aeneid*, Book I, with "Coleridge's Remarks on Virgil" in DW's hand on 3ᵛ. Folds and pinholes suggest that it may have been pinned in DC MS. 89 with the drafts of the *Aeneid* translation, where similar pinholes can be found.

DC MS. 151 A collection of manuscripts, in various hands and on various kinds of paper, used in preparation of *PELY* (1842). Its materials may be divided according to original function into three classes, each of which suggests its own internal logic of ordering. WW began work toward a collective volume of early and late poems in early 1841. The principal manuscript result of that work was a large number of fair copies by MW of earlier and recent poems in DC MS. 143. Few of the poetic manuscripts in DC MS. 151 seem likely to date before late July 1841, when, after returning from a long trip, WW appears to have embarked on a prolonged endeavor of writing out new copies of poems then available in MS. 143, and still other works from other sources, for reasons that probably included: (1) convenience in arranging and rearranging materials as he developed the plan of final order of the projected volume, (2) need for legible fair copies of works that he had revised heavily (most such revision being work of 1841), and (3) preparation of printer's copy. This work continued into early 1842. The logistical plan of the late 1841–early 1842 work appears to have included use principally of two kinds of paper: (1) bifolium sheets of cream wove paper, 22.9 by 18.9 cm., embossed LONDON SUPERFINE, and (2) bifolium sheets of blue wove paper, 25.1 by 20.3

cm., without watermark. In general, the cream paper was used for copies for home use and recordkeeping, the blue for printer's copy, but some of each became employed for the other purpose, and many other papers were used incidentally, especially for the home manuscripts. In the renumbering of the various materials found in the eight separate folders of the previous arrangement, the three classes mentioned above are designated as MSS. 151.1, 151.2, and 151.3, with foliation following the numbers "1.," "2.," and "3.," respectively. The first section is of manuscripts retained at home, the second of printer's copies actually sent, and the third of printer's proofs. The second and third groups stand in sequences that were in general the result of careful intrinsic ordering or the necessary result of the process of printing. The first group was never put into a finished and secured physical sequence. Some of its sheets were used for poems or prose items that stood widely separated in the volume as published, and many, having first been used for fair copy, were used for later draft work without any final fair copy of the results having been prepared for keeping and, in the case of poems in series, without clear designation of the series numbers of the poems. In the absence of a clearly formed intrinsic ordering in this first group, the ordering of the published book appears the most sensible basis for a general listing. Normally, where more than one draft or copy of a particular work or passage is present, the order given is in sequence from latest work through earlier, but the object of revealing the interconnections of main use of the materials appears best served, at some points, by alternate arrangements. In general, though with many exceptions, old numbers 151/1, 151/2, 151/3, 151/4, and 151/8 fall into the first group; 151/5 and 151/6 make up the second; and 151/7 becomes the third.

DC MS. 151.2, formerly 151/6 (1) MS. 151.2.69–77. Eight leaves and a scrap of a ninth, pp. 37–53 of *CM* (1841), and containing *Cuckoo,* as returned from the printer of *PELY* (1842). These may originally have been printer's proofs of *CM,* and have been cut or torn apart. The text has been corrected in ink by Mary and Dora Wordsworth, and on p. 37 the following note appears in Mary's hand: "(To the Printer / This Poem to follow the / Memorials of a Tour in Italy)." The leaves have been irregularly trimmed; the first seven are approximately 9.0 by 12.0 cm., the eighth is 9.5 by 12.0 cm., and the ninth is approximately 8.5 by 6.0 cm. The paper has no watermark. (2) MS. 151.2.105–107. Three sheets, filled on both sides, numbered 38–43 and 1–6 in ink, containing a fair copy of *Troilus* in the autograph of MW, as returned from the printer of *PELY* (1842) with "P 209" marked in ink on 106^{r} above l. 57. The sheets are of blue-tinted paper, 20.2 by 12.5 cm., and are not watermarked.

DC MS. 151.3, formerly 151/7 Described *LB, 1797–1800.* Printer's proofs of *PELY,* including *Cuckoo,* ll. 231–end (MS. 151.3, pp. 162–165), and *Troilus,* ll. 57–end (MS. 151.3, pp. 209–214), with notes and corrections in the autographs of MW, WW, and JC.

MS. 1836/45 Described *Poems, 1800–1807* and *LB, 1797–1800.* Revisions in various hands in the copy of *Poetical Works* (1836), which WW used when preparing the editions of 1838, 1840, and 1845. The only relevant revision is to *Prioress,* especially to WW's headnote. Royal Library, Windsor Castle.

MW to EQ, November 12, 1823. Contains MW's fair copy of WW's translation of *Georgics,* Book IV, ll. 511–515, written at the head of a letter to EQ, following accounts in DW's autograph. A bifolium of laid paper, 31 by 40.2 cm., with chain lines at intervals of 2.6 cm. The paper is watermarked with a crowned medallion with Britannia and countermarked J & T JELLYMAN / 1821. WL.

WW to CW and CW, Jr., c. November 30, 1827. Contains alternate versions of three passages from *Aeneid,* Book II, which WW and CW, Jr., probably had revised the previous summer. A bifolium of laid paper, 22.8 by 36.6 cm., with chain lines at intervals of 2.3 cm. The paper is watermarked with a crowned medallion. Add. MS. 46136, BL.

Editorial Procedure

This volume presents the textual history of Wordsworth's two most extensive translations: his modernizations of selected poems by Geoffrey Chaucer and his partial translation of Virgil's *Aeneid.* As with other volumes in this series, two kinds of texts are provided: (1) reading texts, together with variant readings in the manuscripts and published versions of these poems; and (2) transcriptions and photographic reproductions of manuscripts that are especially interesting or are too complex to reduce clearly to a critical apparatus. Also included are manuscript notes to Book I of the *Aeneid* translation, written by Samuel Taylor Coleridge at Wordsworth's request, a record of Wordsworth's possible borrowings from earlier translators of Virgil, excerpts from Wordsworth's letters to Lord Lonsdale in which he discusses the *Aeneid* translation, and the text of the extract from Book I of the *Aeneid* published by Julius Charles Hare in his journal, *The Philological Museum* (1832).

The reading texts in this volume represent either the first form of the poem published under Wordsworth's supervision or, in the case of unpublished poems, the earliest finished version of the poem. Thus, the reading text of *The Prioress's Tale* is the version published in *The River Duddon . . . and Other Poems* (1820), and the reading texts of *The Cuckoo and the Nightingale* and *Troilus and Cresida. Extract from Chaucer* are those published in *Poems, Chiefly of Early and Late Years* (1842). The text of *Poems, Chiefly of Early and Late Years* is preferred to the earlier text of *The Poems of Geoffrey Chaucer, Modernized* (1841) because publication of the latter volume was supervised by R. H. Horne and Thomas Powell, not by Wordsworth himself, and Wordsworth had no opportunity to correct textual errors and had little control over accidentals such as punctuation and capitalization. In the case of the unpublished *The Manciple, (from the Prologue) And his Tale,* the reading text is taken from the only surviving fair copy of the poem, found in DC MS. 89 and probably copied in 1840. The reading text of the *Aeneid* presents more difficult problems. For Books I and II, the MS. 101B fair copy has been followed, incorporating all later revisions, including those in the autograph of Christopher Wordsworth, Jr. The rationale for this procedure can be found in the introduction to the *Aeneid* translation, page 171. Since the text of the extract published in *The Philological Museum* was never entered into the MS. 101B fair copy (the cleanest of the fair copies, which

Wordsworth circulated among friends), its readings are not incorporated into the reading text. The *Philological Museum* text, however, has been reproduced in Appendix III. Book III is an editorial construct. For the most part, the fair copy of MS. 101C has been followed, as it is the most complete and finished version, but the last lines of Book III, which appear only in MS. 89, have also been included. The texts of the extracts from Books IV and VIII have been taken from MS. 89, the only place they survive. The text of the brief extract from *Georgics*, Book IV, is taken from a letter of Mary Wordsworth to Edward Quillinan (November 12, 1823), rather than from MS. 89, where the text has been entered inaccurately.

The reading text of each poem is accompanied by an *apparatus criticus;* at the head of the apparatus is a list of authorized publications where the poem appears (if the poem was published) and its placement and classification by Wordsworth in collected editions of his poetry. The apparatus shows all verbal variations from the reading texts, except those recorded in manuscript transcriptions. Nonverbal variants are ordinarily listed separately, to avoid an overloaded apparatus. Manuscripts that are complex or particularly interesting are shown in full transcription with facing photographs, where possible. Because of the size of the folio pages in MS. 89, photographs of that manuscript are presented collectively, followed by full transcriptions.

Each poem with its apparatus is supplemented by the Manuscript Census at the beginning of the volume, describing the manuscripts in which it appears, published or manuscript notes to the poems by William Wordsworth, Samuel Taylor Coleridge, and Christopher Wordsworth, Jr., and the editor's notes, including a table of Wordsworth's possible borrowings from earlier translators of Virgil.

In the reading texts, care has been taken to follow the punctuation, spelling, and capitalization of the manuscripts and published versions exactly, except where the manuscripts are seriously deficient by modern standards. This is especially a problem with the MS. 89 copy of *The Manciple, (from the Prologue) And his Tale.* For this poem, punctuation from the draft in MS. 13 has been adopted when necessary; when the MS. 13 draft is also deficient, editorial punctuation has been sparingly introduced from the edition of Chaucer that Wordsworth was using, that found in Robert Anderson's *Works of the British Poets.* All editorial punctuation and spelling have been noted in the verbal apparatus at the foot of the page. Single-letter miswritings corrected by the copyist have not been recorded in the apparatus, nor have ampersand/and, thro'/through, and tho'/though variants.

In transcriptions, the aim is to show with reasonable typographic accuracy everything in the manuscript that can be helpful to a study of the poem's development. Even false starts and corrected letters can sometimes indicate the writer's intention, and normally they are recorded; simple reinforcement of letters, however, is not. Punctuation is shown as original or "base text" punctuation except where different punctuation marks are clearly distinguishable, or where one mark has clearly been converted to another, or where punctuation has been added together with verbal revision. Passages in Wordsworth's hand are in roman type; those in other hands are in italic, though identification of hands must sometimes be conjectural, especially for individual words or parts of words. Run-over lines are shown approximately as they appear in the manuscript. Revisions appear in reduced type—single words or parts of lines positioned as nearly as possible as they appear in the manuscript, entire lines emphasized by indentation. Material written over erasure and enclosed by a screen is not, however, reduced, since the screen itself signals a revision. Large X's and other deletion marks, such as horizontal cross-out lines and slashes that delete single letters, are regularly reproduced, as they are frequently helpful to the reader who is following the sequence of revisions. Texts of irrelevant material on the same page as the poem being reproduced are omitted, as are notations made by modern hands, such as those by Gordon Graham Wordsworth, the poet's grandson. In the numbering of leaves, stubs are counted. Pasteover revision slips are identified editorially by the suffix "P" added to the manuscript number. Editorial line numbers in the left margins correspond to those of the reading texts; lines of revision are normally not numbered. In both transcriptions and *apparatus criticus,* line numbers are occasionally assigned serially by page in the right margin to make possible reference to lines not in the reading text.

The following abbreviations are used in the *apparatus criticus:*

alt	Alternate reading; original not deleted.
apos	Apostrophe.
cap, caps	Capital, capitals.
ed	Editor's emendation.
del	Reading deleted.
eras	Erased, erasure.
exclam point	Exclamation point.
illeg	Illegible.
MS., MSS.	Manuscript, manuscripts. Followed by a number (not a date or number-letter combination), a shortened reference to a Dove Cottage manuscript or manuscripts.
om	Reading omitted.
orig	First reading; originally.
para	Indentation, usually beginning a prose or verse paragraph; or marking indicating indentation.
punct	Punctuation (excluding apostrophes and hyphens).
quot, quots	Quotation mark(s).
rev	Revised; revision; revised by (with initials). (The original may be canceled in any of various ways, including deletion, erasure, overwriting, or blotting, but will be given if legible.)

The following symbols are used in transcriptions and the *apparatus criticus*; the first four also appear in reading texts:

[ ]	Blank, defacement, tear, or trimmed-off word in the manuscript.
[?last]	Conjectural reading.

[? ?]	Illegible words; each question mark represents one word.
[~~? ? ?~~]	Deleted and illegible words; each question mark represents one word.
ha{d / ve	An overwriting: original reading, "have," converted to "had" by the writing of "d" on top of "ve."
s}	A short addition, sometimes only a mark of punctuation.
that more	Words written over a totally illegible erasure.
{that more / wh wa	Words written over a legible or partly legible erasure.

The following lifetime editions are cited:

A. Collective editions:

1820	*The Miscellaneous Poems of William Wordsworth* (4 vols.; London, 1820).
1827	*The Poetical Works of William Wordsworth* (5 vols.; London, 1827).
1832	*The Poetical Works of William Wordsworth* (4 vols.; London, 1832).
1836	*The Poetical Works of William Wordsworth* (6 vols.; London, 1836–1837).
1840	*The Poetical Works of William Wordsworth* (6 vols.; London, 1840). A stereotype reissue of the volumes of 1836 with various alterations, again reissued, with a few alterations, in 1841 and 1843.
1841	The revised stereotype issue of 1840.
1843	The revised stereotype issue of 1841.
1845	*The Poetical Works of William Wordsworth* (London, 1845). Reissued in stereotype, with minor alterations, 1847 and 1849.
1846	*The Poetical Works of William Wordsworth* (7 vols.; London, 1846). Another stereotyped reissue of the six volumes of 1836, incorporating further alterations, with an additional volume incorporating *PELY*, 1842; reissued, again with a few alterations, 1849.
1847	The revised stereotype reissue of 1845.
1849	The revised stereotype reissue of 1846.
1849P	The revised stereotype reissue of 1847.
1850	*The Poetical Works of William Wordsworth* (6 vols.; London, 1849–1850).

In the *apparatus criticus*, a citation of each volume in the list above implies its stereotyped reissues as well, unless otherwise noted, as follows:

1840 implies *1841, 1843*
1841 implies *1843*
1845 implies *1847, 1849P*
1846 implies *1849*
1847 implies *1849P*

B. Selective editions:

1820RD	*The River Duddon, A Series of Sonnets; Vaudracour and Julia: and Other Poems* (London, 1820).
PELY	*Poems, Chiefly of Early and Late Years* (London, 1842).

Part I: Selections from Chaucer, Modernized

Introduction

"When I began to give myself up to the profession of a poet for life," Wordsworth remarked, "I was impressed with the conviction, that there were four English poets whom I must have continually before me as examples — Chaucer, Shakespeare, Spenser, and Milton. These I must study, and equal if I could; and I need not think of the rest."[1]

Late in 1801, using the text found in Robert Anderson's *Works of the British Poets,* Wordsworth began his most important encounter with the poetry of Chaucer: his translation into modern English verse of the tales of the Prioress and Manciple, a selection from *Troilus and Cresida,* and *The Cuckoo and the Nightingale,* then believed to be Chaucer's.[2] It was the first extended composition that he had undertaken in almost a year, and it helped to generate the great outpouring of new poetry in the spring of 1802.[3] Yet much about the modernizations themselves remains obscure. Despite the information supplied by Dorothy Wordsworth's Grasmere journals, we know relatively little about their initial composition, in part because several of the earliest manuscripts were dismantled or lost. Nor has a full account been written of their publication and of Wordsworth's late revisions to them. And no one, since R. H. Horne's introduction to *The Poems of Geoffrey Chaucer, Modernized* (1841), has placed Wordsworth's efforts in context with earlier attempts to translate Chaucer, even though this ought to reveal much about his attitudes toward important predecessors such as Dryden and Pope. The result is a serious gap in Wordsworthian scholarship: about Wordsworth and Milton, or Wordsworth and Spenser, or Wordsworth and Shakespeare we know a great deal; about Wordsworth and Chaucer we know next to nothing, in spite of all that the poet said or wrote about the "morning

[1]Grosart, III, 459–460. This remark was recorded by CW, Jr., who notes that it was communicated to him by HCR.

[2]In 1897, Skeat was the first to show that the poem was not Chaucer's; he believed it to be by Thomas Clanvowe, although more recent scholarship suggests that John Clanvowe, the uncle or father of Thomas, was the author of the poem. See Scattergood, pp. 22–31.

[3]The relationship between the Chaucer modernizations and the poems of 1802 has been discussed by Conran, and less extensively by William Heath, *Wordsworth and Coleridge: A Study of Their Literary Relations in* 1801–1802 (Oxford, 1970), pp. 26–29, and Gene Ruoff, *Wordsworth and Coleridge: The Making of the Major Lyrics,* 1802–1804 (New Brunswick, 1989), pp. 42–44.

star" of English poetry.[4] It is the aim of the present work to fill this gap. I first trace briefly the history of the modernization of Chaucer's verse during the eighteenth century, concentrating on the methods of translation of John Dryden, the model for most modernizers of Chaucer, and contrasting his methods with those of Wordsworth. I then describe the early composition of Wordsworth's modernizations, comparing the well-known evidence in Dorothy Wordsworth's Grasmere journals with the manuscripts themselves. Finally, I discuss the later revisions to the modernizations and their publication, a part of the story that is particularly interesting because of Wordsworth's peculiar association with the literary adventurers Thomas Powell and R. H. Horne.

Earlier Modernizations

The effort to modernize Chaucer's poetry began just over a century before Wordsworth began his modernizations, with the publication of John Dryden's *Fables Ancient and Modern* (1700). Five Chaucerian works were included: *Palamon and Arcite* (a modernization of *The Knight's Tale*); *The Cock and the Fox* (a modernization of *The Nun's Priest's Tale*); *The Wife of Bath, her Tale; The Flower and the Leaf;* and an imitation of the portrait of the Parson from *The General Prologue.* In his preface to the volume, Dryden explains his reasons for modernizing Chaucer and his methods of doing so. Chaucer, he writes,

> is the Father of English Poetry, so I hold him in the same Degree of Veneration as the Grecians held Homer, or the Romans Virgil. He is a perpetual Fountain of good Sense; learn'd in all Sciences; and therefore speaks properly on all Subjects: As he knew what to say, so he knows also when to leave off; a Continence which is practis'd by few Writers, and scarcely any of the Ancients, excepting Virgil and Horace. (Preface to *Fables,* vii)

The problem is that his language has become so difficult for modern readers that his works are neglected.

> How few are there who can read Chaucer, so as to understand him perfectly? And if imperfectly, then with less Profit, and no Pleasure. . . . I think I have just Occasion to complain of them, who because they understand Chaucer, would deprive the greater part of their Countrymen of the same Advantage, and hoard him up, as Misers do their Grandam Gold, only to look on it themselves, and hinder others from making use of it. . . . I have translated some part of his Works, only that I might perpetuate his Memory, or at least refresh it, amongst my Countrymen. (Preface to *Fables,* xii–xiii)

Dryden's aim, then, is to restore Chaucer's place in the literary canon by making his works intelligible to readers unfamiliar with his archaic English.[5] To

[4]WW used the phrase "morning star" to describe Chaucer in both the *Reply to Mathetes* and the *Essay Supplementary to the Preface* (1815); see *Prose,* II, 12, 67.

[5]The editions of Chaucer themselves were partly responsible for the inaccessibility of his verse. Urry's edition (1721) was the first to use roman typeface and to include an annotated glossary.

do so, he admits to taking great liberties with the Middle English, dressing Chaucer's verse in modern English "habit": "Chaucer," he writes "is a rough Diamond, and must first be polish'd e'er he shines." Consequently,

> I have not ty'd myself to a Literal Translation; but have often omitted what I judg'd unnecessary, or not of Dignity enough to appear in the Company of better Thoughts. I have presumed farther in some Places, and added somewhat of my own where I thought my Author was deficient, and had not given his Thoughts their true Lustre, for want of Words in the Beginning of our Language. (Preface to *Fables*, xi–xii)

He is more specific about his procedure a bit later:

> When an ancient Word, for its Sound and Significancy, deserves to be reviv'd, I have that reasonable Veneration for Antiquity to restore it. All beyond this is Superstition. Words are not like Land-marks, so sacred as never to be remov'd: Customs are chang'd, and even Statutes are silently repealed, when the Reason ceases for which they were enacted. As for the other Part of the Argument, that his Thoughts will lose of their original Beauty by the innovation of Words; in the first place, not only their Beauty, but their Being is lost, where they are no longer understood, which is the present Case. (Preface to *Fables*, xii)

Dryden's method, then, is to preserve the broad outlines of Chaucer's plot, while paying little regard to his figures or diction, which were limited, he believed, by the rude age in which the poet lived. The modernizations are thus based on a progressive theory of the development of language; the English language, especially the language of its poetry, has become increasingly sophisticated since Chaucer's time, and it is the translator's role not to preserve the antique flavor of Chaucer's verse but to present it in such language and numbers as Chaucer would have written, had he lived in Dryden's England.

To illustrate Dryden's method, we need only set side by side his version of the opening lines of *The Wife of Bath's Tale* and Chaucer's original:

Dryden	Chaucer
In Days of Old, when Arthur fill'd the Throne,	In the old dayes of Kyng Artour
Whose Acts and Fame to Foreign Lands were blown;	(Of which the Bretons speaken great honour)
The King of Elfs and little Fairy Queen	
Gamboll'd on Heaths, and danc'd on ev'ry Green.	All was this land fulfilled of Fairie,
And where the jolly Troop had led the round	
The Grass unbidden rose, and mark'd the Ground:	The Elfe queene, with hir iolly companie
Nor darkling did they dance, the Silver Light	Daunced ful oft in many a greene mead:
Of Phœbe serv'd to guide their Steps aright,	
And, with their Tripping pleas'd, prolong'd the Night.	This was the olde opinion as I read.
Her Beams they follow'd, where at full she plaid,	I speake of many an hundred year ago,
Nor longer than she shed her Horns they staid,	
From thence with airy Flight to Foreign Lands convey'd.	But now can no man see none elfes mo,

Above the rest our Britain held they dear,
More solemnly they kept their Sabbaths here,
And made more spacious Rings, and revell'd half the Year.
I speak of ancient Times, for now the Swain
Returning late may pass the Woods in vain,
And never hope to see the nightly Train:
In vain the Dairy now with Mints is dress'd,
The Dairy-Maid expects no Fairy Guest,
To skim the Bowls and after pay the Feast.
She sighs and shakes her empty Shoes in vain,
No Silver Penny to reward her Pain:
For Priests with Pray'rs, and other godly Geer,
Have made the merry Goblins disappear;
And where they plaid their merry Pranks before,
Have sprinkled Holy Water on the Floor:
And Fry'rs that thro' the wealthy Regions run
Thick as the Motes, that twinkle in the Sun;
Resort to Farmers rich, and bless their Halls
And exorcise the Beds, and cross the Walls:
This makes the Fairy Quires forsake the Place,
When once 'tis hallow'd with the Rites of Grace:
But in the Walks where wicked Elves have been,
The Learning of the Parish now is seen,
The Midnight Parson, posting o'er the Green.
With Gown tuck'd up to Wakes; for Sunday next,
With humming Ale encouraging his Text;
Nor wants the holy Leer to Country-Girl betwixt.
From Fiends and Imps he sets the Village free,
There haunts not any Incubus, but He.
The Maids and Women need no Danger fear
To walk by Night, and Sanctity so near:
For by some Haycock or some shady Thorn
He bids his Beads both Even-song and Morn.
(*Fables*, ll. 1–41)

For now the great charity and prayeres
Of limitours and other holy Freres,
That searchen every land and every streame,
As thicke as motes in the Sunne beame,
Blissing hals, chambers, kitchens, & boures,
Cities, boroughes, castles, and hie toures,
Thropes, Bernes, Shepens, and Dairies,
This maketh that there been no Fairies:
For there as wont to walke was an Elfe,
There walketh now the limitour himselfe
In undermeles, and in mornings,
And saieth his Mattins and his holy things
As he goeth in his limitatioun:
Women may go safely up and doun
In every bush, and under every tree
There nis none other incubus but hee,
And he ne will doen hem no dishonour.[6]

In this translation, little in Chaucer has been omitted, nor has the order of ideas been significantly altered. But Dryden has elaborated on those ideas so extensively that his version, in its own way very charming, is virtually an independent poem. Whereas Chaucer's elves merely "Daunced . . . in many a greene mead," Dryden goes into great detail about fairy rings, which are not mentioned by Chaucer at all; a single word, "Dairies," becomes in Dryden a five-line vignette about the vain superstitions of milkmaids; and Dryden adds a portrait of a drunken Parson, riding about the parish at midnight, leering at "Country-

[6]I quote from the text published in *British Poets,* I, which was the text WW himself read.

Girl[s]." Rather than just polishing Chaucer, Dryden is going to great lengths to make the verse both more concrete and more discursive, adding portraits of persons and manners that are scarcely even implicit in the original. The result is a translation that is very free—much freer than his treatment of Virgil or Ovid—a translation closer to an imitation than to what he called paraphrase. Apparently, he felt extraordinary means were necessary to make Chaucer's poetry accessible to the reader of his day.

After the publication of Dryden's *Fables*, modernization and imitation of Chaucer became quite common: Alexander Pope, who modernized, and Matthew Prior and John Gay, who wrote Chaucerian imitations, were the most prominent poets to try their hands at Chaucer, and dozens of lesser ones did likewise.[7] Most modernizers followed Dryden's example by rendering the Middle English quite freely. Pope, for instance, condensed the *Wife of Bath's Prologue* to about half its original length, eliminating most of her bawdy language in the process, while an anonymous modernizer of *The Reeve's Tale* (1715) expanded Chaucer's 404 lines to 2602, far beyond the model of elaboration that Dryden provided.[8] Others were more scrupulous: Samuel Cobb's version of *The Miller's Tale,* though euphemistic where Chaucer is most blunt, is on the whole a faithful translation.[9] And it is important to note that, Dryden's *Palamon and Arcite* notwithstanding, the modernizers clearly favored the bawdy Chaucer. As a result, ordinary readers were much more likely to know the tales of the Miller, Reeve, and Shipman than any of Chaucer's more serious works.[10]

In 1741, the best of the modernizations were collected by George Ogle and published in three volumes as *The Canterbury Tales of Chaucer, modernis'd by several hands*; a Dublin edition, in two volumes, appeared the next year. Ogle's collection consists of something less than half of Chaucer's work: he included the relevant modernizations of Pope and Dryden (except *The Cock and the Fox,* Dryden's version of *The Nun's Priest's Tale*), *The Reeve's Tale* and *General Prologue* (supposedly by Thomas Betterton, although possibly by Pope, at least in part),[11] *The Miller's Tale* (by Cobb) and *The Summoner's Tale* (by Mr. Grosvenor—perhaps a pseudonym for Eustace Budgell).[12] Ogle himself contributed a translation of *The Clerk's Tale* (first published in 1739), parts of the *General Prologue,* and prologues to the individual tales, and he commissioned the luckless Samuel

---

[7]For a record of these imitations and modernizations, see Spurgeon, I, 271–504. For a more thorough discussion of them and texts of the modernizations, see Bowden, *passim.*

[8]Bowden, p. 31, remarks that the 1715 *Reeve's Tale* "holds the record for expansion." In the introduction to *CM,* Horne calls Pope's version of the *Wife's Prologue* "highly finished, . . . [but] suffice it to say that the licentious humour of the original being divested of its quaintness and obscurity becomes yet more licentious in proportion to the fine touches of skill with which it is brought into the light. Spontaneous coarseness is made revolting by meretricious artifice" (*CM,* pp. xv–xvi).

[9]When Nicholas accosts Alison, Cobb translates: "And privily he caught her by *That same.*"

[10]This point is stressed in Bowden's introduction, pp. ix–xx.

[11]As Bowden, p. 3, notes, "Samuel Johnson and other authorities matter-of-factly attribute [Betterton's modernizations] to Pope; during the eighteenth century only Pope himself, footnoting a letter for publication, claims that Betterton had anything to do with them. Internal and other external evidence, including [Bernard] Lintot's account book, also point to Pope." Nevertheless, "Pope scholars have evinced remarkably little interest" in solving this problem of attribution.

[12]Bowden, p. 73, following Spurgeon, presents the case that Mr. Grosvenor is Budgell's pseudonym.

Boyse to translate *The Squire's Tale* and the pseudo-Chaucerian *Tale of Gamelyn.*[13] In addition, Ogle republished John Dart's life of Chaucer, which first appeared in John Urry's 1721 edition of Chaucer's works, and included his own "Letter to a Friend," in which he praised Dryden's method of translation, especially his tendency "rather to add than diminish," and gave his own account, largely dependent on Dryden, of Chaucer's achievement. "I hold Mr. Dryden," wrote Ogle, "to have been the first, Who put the Merit of Chaucer into its full and true Light, by Turning Some of the Canterbury Tales into our Language, as it is now refin'd, or rather as He himself refin'd it"(Ogle, III, vii). He went on to praise Chaucer's skill at characterization— "You can name no Author even of Antiquity, whether in the Comic or in the Satiric Way, equal, at least superior, to Him"—and his mastery at "Introducing them properly on the Stage . . . and . . . Supporting them agreeably to the Part They were formed to personate" (Ogle, III, vii). It was Chaucer the master of character that Ogle attempted to present. His collection was a thoughtful effort to provide the modern reader with a wide variety of Chaucer's poems, and was the model for R. H. Horne's collection, in which Wordsworth published two of his modernizations. It may even be no accident that Horne's volume appeared exactly a century later: it was Ogle's work that he hoped to supersede.

Ogle's collection was not challenged until late in the century, when William Lipscomb, a Yorkshire clergyman, published his own collection of Chaucer modernizations, *The Canterbury Tales, complete in a Modern Version,* in three volumes (1795).[14] Lipscomb's aim was to update Ogle in light of the new knowledge available in Thomas Tyrwhitt's magnificent edition of *The Canterbury Tales,* and to present, for the first time, a virtually complete modern version of the work.[15] The modernizations in Ogle's collection were reprinted, except for those Tyrwhitt deemed spurious or Lipscomb too indelicate; to these Lipscomb added his own versions of all of the rest of the work, except *The Parson's Tale;* he then arranged the tales in the same order as in Tyrwhitt and reprinted many of his footnotes.[16] In addition, even though he reprinted the free adaptations of earlier writers, in his own work Lipscomb strove for more accurate translation. "[W]ith respect to translations in general," he wrote,

> I assent to the position that they should be rather free than servile, yet in that part of the present work, which has fallen to my share to execute, I have endeavoured to adhere to the

---

[13]According to Bowden, p. 136, Boyse was "a prime specimen of the Grub Street grub," who spent money faster than he earned it, pawned his clothing, drank excessively, and may have died "with pen still clutched in hand."

[14]Just before the appearance of Ogle's collection, Thomas Morell began to publish a dual-language edition of Chaucer, in which he reproduced Betterton's *General Prologue,* revised by himself, and Dryden's *Palamon and Arcite.* Morell published only *The General Prologue* and *The Knight's Tale.* For a discussion of his edition, see Alderson, p. 141. For the text of his corrections to Betterton, see Bowden, pp. 77–79.

[15]Tyrwhitt's edition appeared between 1775 and 1778; for its signficance, see Alderson, p. 160.

[16]For a fuller account of Lipscomb's procedures and a reprint of the text of his modernizations, see Bowden, p. 177. Bowden also discusses Lipscomb's procedures in *Chaucer Aloud* (Philadelphia, 1987), pp. 40–42, 103–109.

> great original the more faithfully, from the consideration that all those readers (a very numerous as well as a very respectable class) who have not given their time to the study of the old language, must either find a true likeness of Chaucer exhibited in this version, or they will find it no where else. . . . Hence I have imposed it on myself, as a duty somewhat sacred, to deviate from my original as little as possible in the sentiment, and have often in the language adopted his own expressions, the simplicity and effect of which have always forcibly struck me, whenever the terms he uses (and that happens not unfrequently) are intelligible to modern ears. (Lipscomb, I, vi–vii)

Thus, just as Tyrwhitt had attempted to produce a text of Chaucer as close as possible to what Chaucer actually wrote, so Lipscomb claimed to be attempting a modernized version as true to Chaucer's "likeness" as modern taste would allow.

In actual practice, however, Lipscomb's Chaucer was not all that close to the original. Little attempt was made to preserve Chaucer's verse form in stanzaic tales: *The Prioress's Tale,* for instance, was translated into pentameter couplets, and for the tail rhyme of *Sir Thopas* Lipscomb substituted a four-line ballad stanza. And even within the easier verse forms he took some liberties with Chaucer's language. The tales of the Miller and Reeve, so popular with earlier translators, were omitted altogether, and their portraits were excised from the *General Prologue*; for very different reasons he eliminated the "dry and uninteresting" *Parson's Tale.* Throughout, he admitted, "I have not thought myself tied down to the same fidelity," because of "the grossness and indelicacy" of the original. "In the following copy of him," he wrote, "it is hoped, as it is believed, that the pruning away of his indelicacies will not be found to have robbed him of any thing valuable, neither will the truth of the likeness appear to have been violated, since the exhibiting him free from stains has been effected scrupulously by the omission of the offensive passages, and not by the presumption to substitute fresh matter" (Lipscomb, I, viii). Thus in *The Manciple's Tale* Lipscomb renders the crow's nine-line report to Phoebus (which ends with "For on thy bedde thy wif I saw him swive") in a single couplet: "Nought, like a faithful friend, the crow conceal'd, / But all he heard, and all he saw reveal'd." In short, Lipscomb's was a bowdlerized Chaucer, "free from stains," perhaps—certainly very different from the bawdy Chaucer of earlier eighteenth-century modernizations.

It is in this context that Wordsworth's modernizations of Chaucer must be understood. They stand at the end of a full century of attempts to modernize Chaucer's verse, all of which aimed to recover for the modern English reader the acknowledged "Father" of the English poetic tradition. Simultaneous with these attempts were scholarly developments: the publication of John Urry's edition of Chaucer (1721) and Thomas Tyrwhitt's edition of *The Canterbury Tales* (1775–1778), the latter of which is one of the great scholarly achievements of the eighteenth century. Chaucer's meter, which was a bafflement to Dryden and earlier editors, could now be explained, and Chaucer's language was itself less mysterious, as reliable glossaries (such as those in Urry and Tyrwhitt) became available and the workings of Middle English grammar were described with greater accuracy.[17] These developments made possible Wordsworth's casual comment about Chaucer, buried in a footnote to the 1800 "Preface to *Lyrical Ballads*." "[T]he affecting parts of Chaucer," he wrote, "are almost always expressed in language pure and universally intelligible even to this day" (*Prose*, I, 124). John Dryden could not even have formulated this idea; that Wordsworth could is a testament to eighteenth-century philo-logy and editorial scholarship, especially to the monumental work of Tyrwhitt.

The *Lyrical Ballads* footnote also holds the key to understanding Wordsworth's methods of modernization. If Chaucer's language is, at its best, universally intelligible, then it follows that a translator should alter it as little as possible. That in fact is what Wordsworth sets out to do; the opening lines of *The Manciple's Tale* illustrate his methods very well.

Wordsworth

When Phœbus took delight on earth to dwell
Among mankind as ancient stories tell
He was the blithest Bachelor I trow
Of all this world, and the best Archer too:
He slew the serpent Python as he lay
Sleeping against the sun upon a day
And many another worthy noble deed
Wrought with his bow as men the same may read.
He played all music played on earthly ground
And 'twas a melody to hear the sound
Of his clear voice—so sweetly could he sing
Certes Amphion that old Theban King
Who wall'd a city with his minstrelsy
Was never heard to sing so sweet as he.
Therewith this Phœbus was the seemliest man
That is or hath been since the world began.
His features to describe I need not strive;
For in this world is none so fair alive;
He was moreover full of gentleness
Of honor and of perfect worthiness.

Chaucer

Whan Phebus dwelled here in erth adoun,
As olde bookes maken mentioun,
He was the moste lusty bacheler
Of all this world, and eke the best archer:
He slow Phiton the serpent as he lay
Sleping agains the sonne upon a day,
And many another noble worthy dede
He with his bow wrought, as men mowen rede.
Playen he coude on every minstrelcie,
And singen that it was a melodie
To heren of his clere voic the soun:
Certes the King of Thebes Amphioun,
That with his singing walled the citee,
Coud never singen half se wel as he.
Therto he was the semelieste man
That is or was sithen the world began.
What nedeth it his feture do descrive?
For in this world n'is non so faire on live;
He was therwith fulfilled of gentillesse,
Of honour, and of parfite worthinesse.

In this passage, Wordsworth has taken great pains to follow Chaucer line for line, even preserving the original rhymes more than half of the time, usually with the same rhyme words. Chaucer's sentence structure is generally followed, and when it is not, the cause is usually the exigencies of rhyme. Most interesting of all is Wordsworth's refusal to update Chaucer's language and idiom more than is absolutely necessary. For instance, Wordsworth merely changes the spelling of "Sleping agains the sonne," even though the idiom was virtually obsolete.

[17]For accounts of these developments, see Alderson, *passim,* and Paul Ruggiers, *Editing Chaucer: the Great Tradition* (Norman, Okla., 1984), p. 93.

"Certes" (l. 12) is used almost nowhere else in Wordsworth's poetry, except in his Chaucer modernizations, and the same is true of "I trow" in line 3 (here it is Wordsworth's addition for the sake of rhyme, probably in imitation of Chaucer's "iwis."). Elsewhere in the modernizations, medievalisms such as "eke," "Lemman," and "I wis" abound—words and phrases that Wordsworth uses nowhere else in his poetry.[18] Wordsworth's methods, then, are radically different from his predecessors': rather than letting Chaucer speak contemporary English, Wordsworth constructs a self-consciously archaic poetic idiom, one that never lets his readers forget that they are reading a medieval poem. He is experimenting with modern English, bending it out of its natural shape, to preserve as fully as possible the genuine language of Chaucer.

Composition

According to the Grasmere journals, Wordsworth began his Chaucer modernizations in early December 1801, as he, Dorothy, and Mary Hutchinson were rereading Chaucer's poems in Robert Anderson's multivolume anthology, *The Works of the British Poets.*[19] On December 2, Dorothy recorded, "I read the tale of Phoebus & the Crow [*The Manciple's Tale*] which he [William] afterwards attempted to translate & did translate a large part of it today" (*Grasmere Journals,* p. 44). Two days later, on December 4 and 5, William was at work on *The Prioress's Tale,* which he "finished . . . , and after tea Mary & he wrote it out" (*Grasmere Journals,* p. 45). The next day he again "worked a while at Chaucer," although we do not know which of the modernizations Dorothy was referring to, and from the 7th to the 9th he was translating the pseudo-Chaucerian *Cuckoo and the Nightingale* (*Grasmere Journals,* pp. 45–46). Two weeks later, on December 23, Dorothy recorded that "Mary wrote out the Tales from Chaucer for Coleridge," but it is unclear whether she referred to all the modernizations or just the selections from *The Canterbury Tales* (*Grasmere Journals,* p. 50). This copy, and perhaps another, apparently went with them to Keswick on December 28; it is uncertain when they returned. Two more entries mention the Chaucer modernizations. On February 5, 1802, Dorothy noted: "Sara's parcel came with waistcoat. The Chaucer not only misbound but a leaf or two wanting. I wrote about it to Mary & wrote to Soulby" (*Grasmere Journals,* pp. 62–63). And on April 28, 1802, Dorothy recorded that she "copied out the Prioress's tale" in the morning, "wrote out the Manciple's Tale" later in the day, and "corrected the Chaucers but I could not finish them" that night (*Grasmere Journals,* p. 92). This was the last time she mentioned the Chaucer translations in her journals. On the basis of her testimony, scholars have concluded, with varying degrees of certainty, that the three complete poems—the tales of the

[18] Other examples, such as "liever" and "liquorish," appear in manuscript drafts but not in the published versions. I depend here on Lane Cooper's *Concordance to the Poems of William Wordsworth* (London, 1911), which is of course badly outdated.

[19] In his introduction to Chaucer, Anderson explained that he used Tyrwhitt's edition for *The Canterbury Tales* and Urry's for the minor poems; he also reprinted Tyrwhitt's glossary and several of his notes.

Manciple and Prioress, and *The Cuckoo and the Nightingale*—were finished by April 1802 and possibly by December 23, 1801, and that the excerpt from *Troilus* is likely to have been composed about the same time.[20]

The surviving manuscripts, however, raise several questions about these conclusions. For *The Prioress's Tale* there are two early manuscripts, as well as marginalia in Wordsworth's hand found in the Folger Library copy of Anderson's *British Poets.*[21] The earlier manuscript, DC MS. 13, contains a fair copy in Dorothy Wordsworth's autograph of lines 149–end, and the later one, DC MS. 35, contains a nearly complete fair copy of the poem in the autograph of Mary Hutchinson.[22] The MS. 13 text has been considerably revised; MS. 35 has only a few corrections of copyist's errors. A comparison of the manuscripts reveals that Dorothy's fair copy in MS. 13 and the revisions there in her autograph predate MS. 35. MS. 13 revisions in William's and Mary's hands, however, clearly postdate MS. 35: there are ten places where their revisions move away from the MS. 35 text, and Mary revised or inserted the lines omitted from MS. 35. Considered together with the Grasmere journals, the manuscript evidence allows the following tentative reconstruction of the composition of the poem:

December 4–5, 1801, and perhaps earlier: initial drafts, in William's hand, in the margins of Anderson and on separate sheets that do not survive.

December 5, 1801: from the above, a fair copy, in Mary's hand, was drawn up. It does not seem to have survived.

December 5–23, 1801: from Mary's copy the MS. 13 fair copy, in Dorothy's hand, was made; she subsequently revised and corrected her copy.

December 23, 1801: from MS. 13 Mary drew up a new fair copy intended for Coleridge, probably MS. 35.

December 28, 1801: Mary, Dorothy and William walked to Keswick, where they probably left the new fair copy with the Coleridges. MS. 13 may also have been brought with them and may have remained in Mary Hutchinson's possession until February 5, 1802.

February 5, 1802: After mentioning a parcel received from Sara Hutchinson, Dorothy noted that "the Chaucer" (possibly MS. 13) was "misbound and a leaf or two [misplaced *del*] wanting." If she referred to MS. 13, the missing leaves are likely to be of *The Prioress's Tale.* Dorothy wrote to Mary (?about the manuscript) and to Anthony Soulby, a Penrith printer and bookseller.

April 28, 1802: Dorothy made another fair copy of *The Prioress's Tale,* which apparently does not survive.

---

[20]See, for instance, Reed's lengthy note in *Chronology: MY,* pp. 132–134. Working from manuscript evidence, Reed conjectures that *The Prioress's Tale* and *The Cuckoo and the Nightingale* were probably begun before *The Manciple's Tale.*

[21]*British Poets*—Folger is catalogued as Coffman A56. WW's marginalia to Chaucer are mentioned, but not published, in STC's *Marginalia,* I, ed. George Whalley (Princeton, 1980), p. 40.

[22]At some time in its history, MS. 13 was dismantled and its leaves were dispersed, and not all of the leaves seem to have survived. See Reed's discussion of the manuscript (*Chronology: MY,* p. 132). It is thus likely that the whole of *The Prioress's Tale* was originally copied there, but one leaf was subsequently lost. MS. 35 is complete except for l. 180, which is left blank, and ll. 138, 212, and 221, which were omitted.

This chronology does not account for William's and Mary's revisions in MS. 13. These revisions may have been entered at a later date, perhaps as late as 1819–1820, as the poem was being prepared for publication in *The River Duddon, A Series of Sonnets; Vaudracour and Julia: and Other Poems* (1820). But if MS. 13 accompanied the Wordsworths to Keswick in December 1801, the revisions could have been made on the trip. The reference to Soulby on February 5 is tantalizing in this regard. After visiting the Coleridges, William and Dorothy went on to Eusemere, where they stayed with the Clarksons from December 29 to January 23; Mary, in the meantime, went to Penrith to visit her aunt Elizabeth Monkhouse, and rejoined the company at Eusemere on January 17. It seems possible that William and Mary revised MS. 13 during or after the visit to the Coleridges, and she then took it with her to Penrith, intending to consult with Soulby about the possibility of his publishing it.[23] In any event, Soulby did not do so, but the journals suggest that the Wordsworths may have been thinking of publishing the modernizations locally, perhaps in pamphlet form.

The composition of *The Manciple's Tale* is more difficult to trace. We know that it was begun on December 2, 1801, and that Dorothy made a fair copy of it in April 1802, but exactly how much was copied and when the poem was completed are uncertain. As with *The Prioress,* two early manuscripts survive: a full draft, with many corrections, in DC MS. 13 and a fair copy of lines 1–86 in Mary Hutchinson's autograph, DC MS. 36. As these descriptions suggest, the manuscripts of *The Manciple's Tale* are in a rather different state from those of *The Prioress's Tale.* Like MS. 35, for instance, the MS. 36 fair copy was copied from MS. 13: its text corresponds exactly to the base text on 7^v of MS. 13. But it obviously is not complete. If it was copied with MS. 35 on December 23, 1801, it suggests that only lines 1–86 were completed, or (which is more likely) that Mary did not finish her copy work that day. The MS. 13 draft of *The Manciple's Tale* is also in a very different state from that of *The Prioress's Tale.* Whereas the MS. 13 base text of *The Prioress's Tale* is in a copyist's hand, most of the base text of MS. 13 is not: Mary copied lines 1–20, but the bulk of it is in William's hand, and after line 206 the text has been entered hastily, certainly not in his fair hand, and is not consecutive. These more hasty entries have been entered in a different ink from the rest of the base text, and its color matches revisions that William made elsewhere in the poem. Finally, although it is

[23]In *Grasmere Journals,* pp. 62, 176, 201, Pamela Woof does not attempt to solve the mystery of the reference to Soulby; Duncan Wu, in *Wordsworth's Reading,* 1770–1799 (Cambridge, 1993), notes that "Soulby also ran the Penrith Book Club used by [WW] in summer 1787" (p. 47), and speculates that Soulby "bound Wordsworth's Chaucer in February 1802" (p. 170n). By the latter, Wu seems to suggest that Wordsworth had bound an edition of Chaucer; that is, that he may have referred to a text other than Anderson's for his modernizations. Marginalia in *British Poets*—Folger, however, show that he used Anderson as the text for his modernizations. The Wordsworths' copy of Urry was not purchased until 1806 (*MY,* I, 4–5n), and WW himself attributed his mature knowledge of Chaucer's poetry solely to Anderson's anthology. Moreover, when he revised *Manciple* in 1840, he again used Anderson: there are several notations in the margins of *British Poets*—WL that are directly related to *Manciple* revisions and to corrections to Horne's versions of the *Prologue* and *Franklin's Tale.* I thus believe that the reference to Soulby probably has to do with manuscripts of the Chaucer translations, not with an edition of Chaucer's poems.

complete, the MS. 13 copy could not have been finished in 1801 or 1802: the only copy of lines 235–244 is in Dora Wordsworth's autograph, and a few revisions are in the autograph of John Carter, Wordsworth's clerk after 1813. This evidence all challenges the commonly held assumption that *The Manciple's Tale* was finished by Christmas 1801, or even by April 28, 1802, when Dorothy drew up her fair copy.[24] In fact, it is possible that as little as lines 1–86 of the poem was composed by Christmas, 1801, and only lines 1–206 by April, and that the ending of the poem and several of the MS. 13 revisions were written many years later. Thus, the following chronology of composition can be offered:

December 2, 1801: Work on *The Manciple's Tale* was begun, and "a large part" was translated—perhaps lines 1–86.

December 3–23, 1801: Further work on *The Manciple's Tale*, and at least lines 1–86 were copied into DC MS. 13 by Mary Hutchinson (lines 1–20) and William Wordsworth.

December 23, 1801: MS. 36 was probably copied on this date, from MS. 13; its text corresponds to the whole of the base text on 7^v of MS. 13, incorporating none of the revisions there.

December 28, 1801: A partial copy of *The Manciple's Tale* may have accompanied the Wordsworths to Keswick and Eusemere, perhaps MS. 36, and perhaps the MS. 13 copy also. It is possible that by this date the poem was finished through line 206.

April 28, 1802: Dorothy Wordsworth copied the poem, probably from MS. 13; her copy probably consisted of only lines 1–206.

The evidence is even scantier for *The Cuckoo and the Nightingale* and *Troilus and Cresida*. MS. 13 contains a fair copy, mainly in William's hand, of *Cuckoo*, lines 1–260 (less lines 201–205, 217–219, and 224–225 of the published text);[25] it contains nothing of the *Troilus* at all. Dorothy tells us that he worked on the former poem from December 7 to 9, 1801; about work on the *Troilus* she tells us nothing. In fact, evidence of the early version of the *Troilus* survives on just a single piece of paper from DC MS. 24, containing lines 47–98 of the poem. Another leaf of this manuscript contains epigraphs about Chaucer from Milton and Drayton. Wordsworth used the first of these as an epigraph to the published versions of *The Prioress's Tale;* both appear in DC MS. 89, immediately preceding fair copies of *The Cuckoo, Troilus,* and *The Manciple;* and the Drayton passage was used by Horne as an epigraph to *The Poems of Geoffrey Chaucer, Modernized*—and attributed to Wordsworth! This evidence suggests that perhaps MS. 24 once contained copies of all the Chaucer modernizations, perhaps Dorothy's lost fair

---

[24]In *Grasmere Journals*, p. 186, Woof writes that WW's "modern verse translations from Chaucer were finished in 1802." *Chronology: MY*, pp. 132–134, suggests that *Prioress, Cuckoo,* and *Manciple* were "probably composed" in December 1801, and that *Troilus* "perhaps" belongs to the same date.

[25]These lines were not in the text of the poem that Anderson published; they in fact incorporate readings from two manuscripts of the poem in the Bodleian Library. For a full discussion of this issue, see pp. 23–25, 71–72, below.

copies of *The Prioress* and *The Manciple;* but, like MS. 13, MS. 24 was dismantled and its leaves were dispersed, and the other copies of the Chaucer modernizations, if they ever existed, have been lost. One other bit of evidence helps to date *Troilus and Cresida.* Lines 104–105 of the poem, "All which he of himself conceited wholly / Out of his weakness and his melancholy," anticipate or echo lines 20–21 of *Resolution and Independence,* a poem written in the spring of 1802. Since it is likely that the translation was composed before the original work, we can conjecture that the *Troilus* may have been finished by that date. Thus work on it may have been more or less contemporary with the other Chaucer translations.

We can be only a bit more certain about *The Cuckoo and the Nightingale.* The evidence in Dorothy's journals suggest that the MS. 13 base text was entered by December 23, 1801; Mary Hutchinson may even have used it for her copy text as she prepared fair copies for Coleridge. But as no separate fair copy in her hand survives, we cannot be sure. Nor can we be sure of the date of the revisions to the poem in MS. 13. Most are by William, although a few are in Mary's hand, as is the base text for lines 103–120. Her few revisions may date from 1801, but his could have been entered years later, as late as 1819, when he gave Mary Calvert an autograph copy of the first stanza of the poem which incorporates revisions found in MS. 13. Finally, it seems that Wordsworth had reservations about Anderson's text of the poem, for he has written "Finis" underneath line 260, just after the nightingale takes his final leave of the narrator. This is a logical enough spot to leave off: the two birds have finished their debate and taken leave of each other. But in Anderson, a bird parliament follows, and the last lines of his text are an "Envoy" written in a different stanzaic form (and are in fact a wholly separate poem).[26] It seems likely that Wordsworth sensed these textual problems. They may have caused him to leave his translation incomplete.

Later Revisions

After the initial stage of composition, Wordsworth set his modernizations aside, turning to them again in 1819 and 1820 as he was preparing the *River Duddon* volume for press. In the interim, Chaucer and modernizations of his verse were not far from the poet's mind. When designing the Beaumonts' winter garden, for instance, he included "a small blind Path leading to a Bower, such as you will find described in the beginning of Chaucer's Poem of The Flower and the Leaf, and also in the begining of the Assembly of Ladies" (*MY,* I, 117–118), confidently translating one art into another for the delight of his noble patrons. More revealing are his remarks on Dryden's Chaucer, communicated to Walter Scott as Scott prepared his multivolume edition of Dryden's works. Dryden's language, wrote Wordsworth,

[26]Of the *Envoy,* Skeat, p. lxii, writes: "it is a very poor piece . . . unworthy . . . of Clanvowe, not to mention Chaucer."

> is not language that is in the high sense of the word poetical, being neither of the imagination or the passions; I mean of the amiable the ennobling or intense passions; I do not mean to say that there is nothing of this in Dryden, but as little, I think, as is possible, considering how much he has written. You will easily understand my meaning when I refer to his versification of Palamon and Arcite as contrasted with the language of Chaucer. Dryden has neither a tender heart nor a lofty sense of moral dignity: where his language is poetically impassioned it is mostly upon unpleasing subjects; such as the follies, vice, and crimes of classes of men or of individuals. (*EY*, p. 641)

In this letter Wordsworth repeats a common theme in his criticism of Dryden and Pope: their poetic achievement is limited by their failure to engage the loftier passions, and here Dryden's translation of *The Knight's Tale* is offered as convincing evidence. But it was not just Dryden's want of passion that concerned Wordsworth: he was just as troubled by his principles of translation. As the Dryden edition was in press, he wrote to Scott again: "Chaucer I think he has entirely spoiled, even wantonly deviating from his great original, and always for the worse" (*MY*, I, 191). Thus Dryden's infidelity to the Middle English was as damaging as lack of noble passion. By temperament and practice, thought Wordsworth, Dryden was unsuited to rendering Chaucer's poetry into modern English.

It would be another decade, however, before Wordsworth would be ready to challenge Dryden's translations in public, and then he did so in a very modest way: he published a revised version of *The Prioress's Tale* in *The River Duddon . . . and Other Poems* (1820). The poem was given some prominence in the volume: it had a separate fly-title, and on the verso a headnote explained his principles of translation. Neither Dryden nor Pope is mentioned in that headnote, but it is nevertheless clear that Wordsworth meant to distance himself from their methods: unlike them, he allowed himself "no farther deviations from the original than were necessary for the fluent reading, and instant understanding, of the Author." When deviations were necessary, he claimed to have made them "with as little incongruity as possible." And rather than bringing Chaucer's language up to date, Wordsworth admitted to writing in a deliberately archaic way: "the ancient accent has been retained in a few conjunctions . . . from a conviction that such sprinklings of antiquity would be admitted, by persons of taste, to have a graceful accordance with the subject." In short, he would give us no modern-dress Chaucer: Wordsworth instead attempted, as far as possible, to reproduce the experience of reading an ancient poem.

As Wordsworth was preparing *The Prioress* for publication, he apparently reviewed, and perhaps revised, his other Chaucer modernizations as well. *The Cuckoo and the Nightingale* was surely reviewed: two presentation manuscripts of its first stanza survive, one given to Mary Calvert and dated November 27, 1819, and another to an unknown recipient, dated London, 1820. The texts are virtually identical and incorporate revisions to the base text of MS. 13 in Wordsworth's own autograph. This evidence suggests, but does not confirm, that some of the MS. 13 revisions of the poem date to 1819–1820. In any case, we can be sure that Wordsworth had recently looked over the poem and committed parts of it to memory. Similarly, some of the MS. 13 revisions to *The*

Manciple's Tale may belong to 1819–1820, particularly those in the autographs of John Carter and Dora Wordsworth. In 1819, Carter had served as Wordsworth's amanuensis for the C-stage *Prelude*, so, about the same time, he may have assisted in minor revisions to the Chaucer pieces. Dora, too, was beginning to serve as her father's amanuensis, a role she would increasingly assume over the next two decades. That she entered lines 235–244 of *The Manciple* at this time cannot be proven, but it seems unlikely that the lines were entered in 1840, when we know the poem was revised, since she was in London at the time the revision most likely took place. So it seems possible that Wordsworth undertook a full review of his Chaucer materials in 1819–1820, ultimately deciding to publish just the one of them—*The Prioress's Tale*—as a sample of a faithful rendering of one of his favorite poets.

Wordsworth's attention to Chaucer in 1819–1820 was probably motivated by the revaluation of Chaucer's poetry then taking place in London literary circles. In 1818, William Hazlitt had discussed Chaucer at length in his *Lectures on the English Poets,* singling out the "simple and heroic" *Prioress's Tale* for special praise, and dismissing Dryden's modernizations as "show[ing] a greater knowledge of the taste of his readers and power of pleasing them, than acquaintance with the genius of his author."[27] But more important to Wordsworth was Leigh Hunt, who championed Chaucer as a model for modern poets and had himself proposed new methods of modernizing Chaucer's verse that were in direct opposition to those of Dryden and Pope. In an essay on Chaucer's unfinished *Squire's Tale,* initially appearing in *The Examiner* and republished in *The Round Table* in 1817, Hunt attacked Dryden in ways that sound very much like Wordsworth's letters to Scott:

> The writer who undertook to finish a story of Chaucer, should come to his task, not only with as much rhythmical vigour as Dryden, but with twenty times his nature and sentiment. . . . But modern versions, strictly so called, of an old poet, tend to divert attention from the illustrious original, and to foster an additional ignorance of him, in consequence of what one supposed to be the rudeness of his style, and the obscurities of his language.[28]

That is, not only was Dryden ill suited to modernize Chaucer, but his modernizations have actually hurt Chaucer's reputation: Dryden's attack on the rudeness and obscurity of Chaucer's language and his claim to have improved the elder poet have become a further excuse not to read him. Nevertheless, Hunt believes modernization is desirable, if conducted according to principles very different from Dryden's and remarkably like Wordsworth's own. According to Hunt, the modernizer should proceed by "altering only just as much as is necessary for comfortable intelligibility, and preserving all the rest, that which appears quaint as well as that which is more modern,—in short, as much of his author,—his nature,—his own mode of speaking and describing, as possible" (136). He then demonstrated his method by modernizing a few passages from *The Squire's Tale,* in which he altered little more than the spelling.

---

[27]Cited in Spurgeon, II, 102–103.

[28]*The Round Table,* I (Edinburgh, 1817), pp. 133, 135.

Whether Wordsworth knew Hunt's and Hazlitt's Chaucerian criticism is uncertain, but we can be sure they had created a climate in which a modernization of Chaucer according to Wordsworth's principles would be well received, and that Wordsworth knew it. He had been in and out of London repeatedly between 1815 and 1820, had always kept his eye upon Hunt and Hazlitt, and moved in circles where their writings were frequently, if often skeptically, discussed. Eighteen-twenty was an important year for Chaucerian criticism. Just before Wordsworth passed through London that summer, en route to a tour of the continent, Hunt was writing often about Chaucer in *The Indicator* (one of his essays included the first publication of Keats's *La Belle Dame Sans Merci*); in the May issue of *The London Magazine,* an essay on the "ancient state of the Jews in England" quoted from and praised "the beautiful" *Prioress's Tale*; in the same year Hunt's prose version of *The Pardoner's Tale* appeared in Ollier's *Literary Miscellany.*[29] And, as has already been mentioned, Wordsworth himself must have sensed the renewed popularity of Chaucer's verse, for he distributed to friends presentation copies of the first stanza of *The Cuckoo and the Nightingale.* In short, the time was ripe for newly wrought modernizations of Chaucer truer to the Middle English than past efforts; given Hazlitt's criticism in his 1818 *Lectures, The Prioress's Tale* may have seemed to Wordsworth an ideal example.

Unfortunately, reviewers of *The River Duddon* were not as pleased with *The Prioress's Tale* as Hazlitt had been. In general, *The River Duddon* was very well reviewed, and even gained grudging admiration from the most inveterate of Wordsworth's detractors. But *The Prioress's Tale* was either ignored or attacked. Only two reviews discuss it. "We should be glad," wrote the *British Review,* "that this tale should not be thrice told, but that this collection should, by leaving it out of future editions, be further improved in negative merit. It is horrible in its facts, disgusting in its narration, and odiously profane in its language."[30] *The Eclectic Review* was less disgusted with the tale than with Wordsworth's choice of it: "'The Prioress's Tale' from Chaucer is a very ill-chosen subject for the experiment of exhibiting the Father of English Poetry in a modern form. The legend is so exquisitely absurd that it must have been designed as a burlesque on the lying martyrological wonders of the Romish priesthood."
After summarizing the tale, the reviewer concludes: "To Mr. Wordsworth, indeed, we can conceive that such tales would recommend themselves by their puerility; that he would be even melted into tears by the affected solemnity of a sly old humorist like Chaucer; and that what was meant by him for satire might be mistaken by our Author for pathos."[31] *The Prioress's Tale,* then, like *Peter Bell* and *The Waggoner* (published the preceding year), shows Wordsworth at his sentimental worst, unable to distinguish genuine pathos from satire. As Wordsworth could not perceive the ridiculousness of his own poems, so he could not comprehend Chaucerian humor. It is surely this remark that led Wordsworth to add the following sentence to his headnote when *The Prioress* was republished in 1827: "The fierce bigotry of the Prioress forms a fine back ground for her

[29]Spurgeon, II, 121–129.
[30]*British Review* 16 (September 1820), 51.
[31]*Eclectic Review,* n.s. 14 (August 1820), 18.

tender-hearted sympathies with the Mother and Child; and the mode in which the story is told amply atones for the extravagance of the miracle."

The Poems of Geoffrey Chaucer, Modernized

In spite of the advice of *The British Review,* Wordsworth reprinted *The Prioress's Tale,* with minor revisions, in all collective lifetime editions of his poetry. The other modernizations, however, were set aside for another two decades, and were apparently little thought of. In 1825, for instance, Dorothy Wordsworth was surprised to find a fair-copy manuscript of *The Cuckoo and the Nightingale* stuffed in the family Bible. She sent it forthwith to Edward Quillinan, to become part of his collection of poetical extracts about nightingales.[32] But other than this single instance, the modernizations of Chaucer were virtually forgotten. Then, late in 1839, in a letter that is now lost, the literary adventurer and forger Thomas Powell wrote to Wordsworth, inviting him to contribute to a project he was about to embark upon: a collection of Chaucer's poems, modernized by various contemporary hands, and executed according to the principles of modernization exemplified in Wordsworth's *Prioress's Tale.* R. H. Horne, later famous for *Orion,* the farthing epic, was to edit the volume, and Leigh Hunt and Elizabeth Barrett were to be numbered among the contributors. Much to the chagrin of his family, Mary especially, Wordsworth accepted Powell's invitation, offering for publication all of the modernizations he had composed.

Of all Wordsworth's literary associates, Thomas Powell is surely the most ambiguous. A distinctly minor poet, playwright, and writer of miscellaneous prose, Powell worked in the offices of the London merchant Thomas Chapman, where, according to Robert Browning, "he obtained credit with Talfourd, who introduced him to various friends and myself."[33] His "credit" with Talfourd may have gained him access to Wordsworth as well, and since 1836 he had known the poet, writing some of the oiliest examples of epistolary flattery ever composed, wooing him with presents of rare books and Stilton cheese, sending Margaret Gillies to do portraits of Wordsworth and his family, and even naming his firstborn son Arthur Wordsworth Powell.[34] Sometime in 1839, he conceived of a

[32]EQ began this project in 1823 and a number of references to it occur in the Wordsworth family letters of this period. Among the extracts sent him was WW's translation of the nightingale simile from *Georgics,* Book IV; see p. 273 for further discussion.

[33]Browning's remark is quoted in Blainey, p. 114. For a full account of Powell's habits of embezzlement and forgery, see Wilfrid Partington, "Should a Biographer Tell?" *Atlantic Monthly,* August 1947, 56. His embezzlement having been discovered by his employer, Thomas Chapman, Powell employed Southwood Smith to help him fake insanity and then fled to New York City, where he became involved in a famous libel suit with Charles Dickens.

[34]In a letter to WW of October 10, 1836, for instance, Powell wrote: "The thought that the Author of 'Peter Bell' & the 'Excursion' had held communion with me awoke in me, like the morning Sunlight on the Memnon-Head, the music of Spring-Life when I lived in the world of Idea: a glow of first-delight came over my Spirit and I felt as I felt when a boy, and roaming among the lanes & green fields of [?] & Norwood; with 'The Excursion' or your Sonnets under my arm, ever and anon reading a few lines and then again looking at the fair scenery around me: O I never shall forget the mantle of sensation which shed over me the glorious Sabbath morn, when early I had wandered to the quiet green forest at Norwood. . . ." (TPP)

plan to modernize Chaucer's poems, persuaded Horne and Hunt to assist, and, as a finishing touch, lured Wordsworth into the project as well.

For his part, Wordsworth both encouraged Powell in his project, and endeavored to keep his distance from him. "For myself," he wrote late in 1839, "I cannot do more than I offered, to place at your disposal the Prioress's Tale, already published, the Cuckoo and the Nightingale, the Manciple's Tale, and I rather think, but I cannot just now find it, a small portion of the Troilus and Cresida" (*LY*, III, 756). When Powell attempted to enlist his aid in correcting his and Horne's translations, Wordsworth resisted. Of Powell's version of *The Flower and the Leaf*, for instance, he wrote:

I am much pleased with your attempt upon Chaucer—which I return submitting to y[r] judgment a few verbal alterations—insignificant as they are, they have cost me more trouble than I could well spare—which I mention because I cannot promise hereafter to bestow any pains upon the endeavours of yourself and y[r] Associates, in this very promising Work. (*LY*, IV, 4)

In another letter of the same month, he reiterated his reluctance more strongly:

You seem in too great a hurry to be in the press with Chaucer. He is a mighty Genius as you well know, and not lightly to be dealt with.— For my own part, I am not prepared to incur any responsibility in the execution of this project, which I much approve of, beyond furnishing my own little Quota. . . .

My approbation of the Endeavor to tempt people to read Chaucer by making a part of him intelligible to the unlettered, and tuneable to the modern ears, will be sufficiently apparent by my own little Contributions to the intended Volume. But beyond this I do not wish to do any thing; or rather it could not be right that I should. Little matters in Composition hang about and teaze me awkwardly, and at improper times when I ought to be taking my meals or asleep. On this account, however reluctantly, I must decline even looking over the Mss either of yourself or your Friends. . . .

—I hope I have now made myself sufficiently intelligible, and that Mr Horne etc will not be hurt that I decline, for the reasons given, the pleas[ure] which it would otherwise be, of perusing his Mss.— (*LY*, IV, 8)[35]

---

[35]In a letter of January 3, 1840, Powell had written: "Mr Horne is about the Knights Tale: he told me last night that he intended forwarding to me a specimen of his moderniz in order to receive your judgment on it: I will transmit it to you when I receive it" (TPP). Six days later, Horne sent two extracts from *The Knight's Tale* to Powell with the following note, now in the Beinecke Library:

Dear Mr Powell

Will you be so kind as over-look the foregoing fragments, and compare with your most truthful editions—oblige me with your comments, [?], and return this paper, as the copy I retain is in almost illegible pencil. You shall very soon have two more specimens of Chaucer's fresh and most rich-ripe descriptive poetry—attempted in modern. You can then move towards Mr Wordsworth with our project. [?I am dear Sir]

Very truly R. H. Horne.

P.S. There is a copy of Schlegel coming to you

This letter seems to imply not that Horne wanted WW to check over his translation but that he thought WW had not yet been approached about the project. Yet Powell had solicited WW's contributions at least a month earlier. Apparently, Powell was as duplicitous with Horne as he was with everyone else.

Horne's version of *The Knight's Tale* was not published in *CM*; besides the two extracts in the Beinecke (which consist of about 150 lines of verse), another manuscript draft of his translation survives in the collection of Paul F. Betz.

But Wordsworth's concerns were not simply to avoid the distractions associated with revising the contributions of Powell's "Coadjutors"; he was afraid that Powell in particular might be using him merely to promote his own sales and reputation. Consequently, a month later he wrote to Edward Moxon, his publisher:

Mr Powell, my Friend, has some thought of preparing for Publication some portions of Chaucer modernized so far and no farther than is done in my treatment of the Prioress's Tale. That will in fact be his model.—He will have Coadjutors, among whom I believe will be Mr Leigh Hunt, a man as capable of doing the work well as any living Author. I have placed at my Friend Mr Powell's disposal, in addition to the Prioress's Tale, three other pieces which I did long ago, but revised the other day. They are the Manciple's Tale, The Cuckoo and the Nightingale, and 24 Stanzas of Troilus and Cressida. This I have done mainly out of my love and reverence for Chaucer, in hopes that whatever may be the merits of Mr Powell's attempt, the attention of other Writers may be drawn to the subject; and a work hereafter be produced by different pens which will place the treasures of one of the greatest Poets within the reach of the multitude which now they are not. I mention all of this to you, because though I have not given Mr Powell the least encouragement to do so, he may sound you as to your disposition to undertake the Publication.—I have myself nothing further to do with it than I have stated. Had the thing been suggested to me by any number of competent Persons 20 years ago I would have undertaken the editorship, done much more myself, and endeavoured to improve the several Contributions where they seem to require it. But that is now out of the question. (*LY*, IV, 19–20)

Here Wordsworth's reservations are quietly voiced: having seen some of Powell's efforts and having been pressured rather more than he liked, he had begun to wonder if he ought to be associated with the project. Mary, writing to Isabella Fenwick, is more blunt:

It appears from a letter rec^{d} yesterday that the projectors of the intended publication have changed their purpose of modernizing all Chaucer, but first of all mean to give a Selection 'by way of feeling the pulse of the public'—and this sample is to consist of W^{ms} Prioresses Tale already published, the Cuckoo and Nightingale (now in Mr P$^{'s}$ hands) and those before you, while the other coadjutors give one piece each, a much larger quantity perhaps—but will this be a fair Specimen of what they mean to send out afterwards without aught from the Masters hand! To me it seems plain what the motive is—they are in haste to appear in connection with a name of influence.—I hope you do not think there will be any thing dishonorable in Mr W. changing his purpose at this late hour. (*LY*, IV, 35–36)

Wordsworth, of course, did not change his purpose, but Mary's fears proved to be well founded. On October 16, 1840, as *Chaucer Modernized* was about to go to press, he wrote Powell again, with evident displeasure.

Yesterday I received from a Lady from which I transcribe the following. 'I have read in a Newspaper that you are about to publish Chaucer's Tales modernized'—and a friend also tells me that he has seen an advertizement of your Publication in which my name stands first in large letters. Now dear Sir, you will remember that the condition upon which I placed these things at your disposal was, that for many reasons I should not be brought prominently forward in the Matter—but that my communications, given solely out of regard for you and reverence for Chaucer, should appear as unostentatiously as possible. I am therefore much concerned for what has been done, as it cannot be undone. (*LY*, IV, 129)

Powell's response came a week later. Pasted to the top of his letter is the following advertisement, clipped from a newspaper:

> CHAUCER'S POEMS MODERNIZED.
> By William Wordsworth, R. H. Horne, Miss E. B. Barrett,
> Richard Monckton Milnes, Thomas Powell, Leigh Hunt,
> Barry Cornwall, Lord Thurlow, Robert Bell, and others.
> The First Volume will contain various Poems and Tales, and an
> Introductory Preface by R.H. Horne, and a Life of Chaucer by
> Professor Leanhard Schmitz.Whittaker and Co., Ave Maria-lane.

Powell went on to protest:

I am inclined to think that your informant has led you to adopt a stronger impression than you would have done had you seen yourself the advertisement. . . . With regard to putting your name first you will I hope bear in mind the situation I was placed in.—to have put any name before yours would have been too much in the Cardinal Wolsay style of "Ego sim meus Rex", and the public would I am sure have very properly resented it: I trust this explanation will be satisfactory, for nothing would embitter my future life more than that you should imagine I had used your "honored and farfamed" name for my private purpose. . . . I need hardly add that every thing inclining to indelicacy of thought and expression will be expunged, for that is the worst part of the great poet, and a drawback to his fame. We might almost call the Book "The family Chaucer." (TPP)

Wordsworth was mollified, at least for the moment. "Now that I have seen it," he replied, "I find no fault with it. My age considered, no one can find fault with my name being placed first." Yet Powell was probably being disingenuous: I have not been able to discover other newspaper advertisements that might fit the description given by Wordsworth's informant, but there do survive several copies of *Chaucer Modernized,* in original boards, with Wordsworth's and Hunt's names on the spine as joint authors. Powell was lucky that none of those copies came into the poet's hands.

As one might expect, Wordsworth carefully revised his modernizations before sending them off to Thomas Powell for publication. We know from his February 1840 letter to Edward Moxon, quoted above, that most of the revisions were composed in January and February of that year, and that they were probably finished by March. We also know that the revised version of *The Cuckoo and the Nightingale* was in Powell's hands by February or March, the revised *Manciple's Tale* was seen by Isabella Fenwick about the same time, and the revised *Troilus* was sent to Powell by May.[36] But of the nature of these revisions we can be less certain. No manuscripts of the *Troilus* that reflect this stage of revision survive: all we have are stubs of a fair copy in MS. 89. There are

---

[36]The evidence can be found in letters from the period; see *LY*, IV, 19–20, 35–36, 69–71.

differences between the *Chaucer Modernized* text and DC MS. 24, but when the changes were made is impossible to determine.[37] Similarly, there are no manuscripts preserving revisions to *The Cuckoo and the Nightingale,* even though it was the most extensively revised of the three poems; once again, all that survives are stubs in MS. 89. But about the *Cuckoo* revisions we can be more precise. First, only lines 1–260 (less lines 201–205, 217–219, 224–225) survive in MS. 13, so it is fairly certain that the translation of lines 261–end was composed in 1840, as Wordsworth prepared the poem for publication. Second, on one of the stubs in MS. 89, the following fragment survives:

> Bodlean And as he flew, the Cuckoo ever & aye
> Bodlea Youth
> Kept crying farewell, farewell Pop

This is a preliminary version of the note to line 201 of the *Chaucer Modernized* text, which was reprinted and slightly expanded in all subsequent reprintings of the poem in Wordsworth's collected works. The note reads: "From a manuscript in the Bodleian, as are also stanzas 44 and 45, which are necessary to complete the sense."[38] This is a very curious footnote. Wordsworth was not in the habit of consulting ancient manuscripts, and even if he did, he probably was not skilled enough as a paleographer to be able to read them. He had been in Oxford in 1839 to receive an honorary degree, but it seems unlikely that he would have taken time out of a busy schedule to poke around in the Bodleian Library, looking at Chaucer manuscripts. Besides, he was in Oxford well before Powell approached him about the Chaucerian scheme, so he would have had no real cause to seek those manuscripts out. What, then, could the note be referring to?

As it happens, the answer is fairly straightforward; at the same time, it makes Wordsworth's publication of *The Cuckoo and the Nightingale* a more significant event than has been supposed. In January 1839 the following letter appeared in *The Gentleman's Magazine.*

MSS. of Chaucer in the Bodleian Library
Mr. Urban, Oct. 31

Understanding that your pages are open to receive stray facts of a literary nature, I venture to submit the following to you, in the hopes that you may consider it worth preserving for the use of students of Chaucer and lovers of our old poetry. Lately, in the Bodleian Library, I inquired into the manuscripts of Chaucer, with a view of seeing what possibility there was of materially correcting the text of his minor Poems—a work which has not as yet been attempted. There are three MSS. there; each containing a good many of Chaucer's smaller poems, with others of his successors, such as Lidgate. These are, Fairfax 16., Bodl. 638., and Arch. Seld. B. 24. Perhaps there may be others, which escaped my notice; but what I wish to call your attention to is not a general account of the value of these MSS. but some remarkable variæ lectiones.

---

[37]For these differences, see pp. 56–60, 146–149.
[38]For the shorter *CM* version of the note and *PELY* revisions, see p. 51.

Cuckoo and Nightingale

In both Fairf. 16. and Arch. Seld. B. 24, the following stanza is found inserted between the 40th and 41st of the present editions:

"With such a lorde wolde I never be,
For he is blynde and may not se,
And when he lyeth he not, ne when he fayleth,*
In this courte full selde trouthe avayleth,
So dyverse and so wilful is he."

Instead of the 43rd, which runs thus:

"Methought than that he stert up anone,
And glad was I that he was agone.
And evermore the Cuckow as he flay
Said, 'Farewell, farewell, Popingay;'
As though he had scorned me alone."

we find two stanzas supplying an idea, without which the story, such as it is, is defective. This, then, is valuable and worth noting:

"Methought then that I sterte out anone,
And to the broke I ran and gatte a stone,
And at the Cuckow hertily I cast,
And he for drede flyed away ful fast,
And glad was I when that he was gone.
And evermore the Cuckow as he fley,
He seyde, 'Farewel, farewel, Papyngay.'
As thogh he had scorned, thought me:
But ay I hunted him fro tre to tre,
Till he was fer al out of sight awey."

Both the MSS. which I have made notes of give this improvement, which must undoubtedly be the right reading; the third, I believe, agrees; but I have not made any memorandum.

. . . . Yours, &c. H.H.

*The MS. Seld. gives better:—

"Quhom he hurteth he not nie quhom he heleth."[39]

The information about the Bodleian manuscripts cited in this letter tallies exactly with several of the differences between MS. 13 and the text published in *Chaucer Modernized.* MS. 13 reflects Anderson's corrupt text, but *Chaucer Modernized* and all later reprintings of the poem incorporate the manuscript readings given by "H.H." in this letter. Rather than consulting the manuscripts themselves, then, Wordsworth consulted *The Gentleman's Magazine.* In fact, "H.H." is Herbert Hill, Robert Southey's nephew and, as of 1839, son-in-law. Hill lived in Rydal, just down the hill from Rydal Mount, and must have pointed out the piece in *The Gentleman's Magazine* himself.[40] What is more, Wordsworth's

---

[39] *Gentleman's Magazine,* n.s. 11 (January 1839), 50–51.

[40] For further discussion of Hill's authorship of the letter, see the Editor's Notes, pp. 71–72.

use of Hill's manuscript *lectiones* gives his *Cuckoo and the Nightingale* text some significance in the publishing history of the poem. The corrupt text that Wordsworth rejected was, to that time, the only published version of the poem: it first appeared in William Thynne's sixteenth-century edition of Chaucer's poems, and later editors had republished it, more or less following Thynne, in all subsequent editions of Chaucer's complete works. John Urry, as was his habit, had further corrupted the text in an effort to regularize Chaucer's meter, and it was Urry's text that Anderson reproduced. Wordsworth's *Cuckoo and the Nightingale* is the first published version of the poem, whether modernized or in the original Middle English, to incorporate the "better" manuscript readings. His modernization thus anticipates the textual scholarship of such Chaucerians as Frederick Furnivall and Walter Skeat by several decades.

The Manciple's Tale was also revised for publication at this time, but unlike *The Cuckoo* and *Troilus,* the manuscripts give us a clear record of what those revisions were. Mary Wordsworth, with William's occasional assistance, made a fair copy of the poem in MS. 89, apparently using MS. 13 as her copy text; in MS. 89 the fair copy immediately precedes the stubs of the fair copies of *The Cuckoo* and *Troilus,* and it follows the pair of quotations about Chaucer that can also be found in MS. 24. As the fair copy was drawn up, several corrections were made to the text, and a translation of the Manciple's portrait from Chaucer's *General Prologue* was added as a kind of introduction. The revisions themselves are fairly minor, but they do suggest that Wordsworth had become less comfortable with the abundance of archaisms in his earlier effort: in line 66, for instance, "Liever" was revised to "Rather," while "liquorish" in line 85 was revised to "wayward." But the revisions came to nought, for at the eleventh hour, Wordsworth decided not to publish the poem at all.

Wordsworth's decision came after considerable debate within the family circle. Mary in particular had disapproved of his contributing to Powell's project at all, as is indicated by her letter to Isabella Fenwick, quoted above, and she especially objected to William's contributing so much of his work. From her point of view, Powell and Horne were merely trying to profit from the Wordsworth name, and she was looking for ways for her husband either to back out of the project or to limit his involvement in it. In the case of *The Manciple's Tale,* she seems to have found a way. Apparently she persuaded him to send a copy of his modernization to Isabella Fenwick and her step-cousin, Henry Taylor, so that the latter would "say if he thinks the truth and beauty of the Manciple's Tale does not more than counterbalance any objection that might be made to the subject"(*LY,* IV, 35). As this is the same letter in which she complains of Powell's machinations, it does not take too much imagination to determine her aims: she wanted to limit William's contributions in any way possible, and if warnings about Powell and Horne would not work, then appeals to Victorian prudery might. "Mr. W," she wrote in a postscript to the letter, "begs you to keep the Mss till you hear from him again—after he hears your opinion about withdrawing his intention—I do trust it will be in accord with my own" (*LY,* IV, 36).

We do not know what response the Wordsworths received to this letter, but we do know that he consulted two others of his acquaintances—Edward Quillinan and Barron Field—about the propriety of *The Manciple's Tale.* Quillinan's response occasioned one of Wordsworth's most extended comments upon Chaucer. Writing to his daughter Dora, he protests:

Tell Mr Quillinan, I think he has taken rather a narrow view of the spirit of the Manciple's Tale, expecially as concerns morality. The formal prosing at the end, and the selfishness that pervades it flows from the genius of Chaucer, mainly as characteristic of the Narrator whom he describes in the Prologue as eminent for shrewdness and clever worldly Prudence. The main lesson, and the most important one, is inculcated as a Poet ought chiefly to inculcate his lessons, not formally, but by implication; as when Phoebus in a transport of passion slays a wife whom he loved so dearly. How could the mischief of telling truth, merely because it is truth, be more feelingly exemplified. The Manciple himself is not, in his understanding, conscious of this; but his heart dictates what was natural to be felt and the moral, without being intended, forces itself more or less upon every Reader.—Then how vividly is impressed the mischief of jealous vigilance and how truly and touchingly in contrast with the world's judgments are the transgressions of a woman in a low rank of life and one in high estate placed on the same level, treated. (*LY*, IV, 39)

These views were reiterated to Barron Field, who recorded them in his memoir of the poet and in an unpublished review of *Chaucer Modernized.* Field visited Rydal Mount in March 1840, about the same time as the letters to Dora and Miss Fenwick were written. During his visit, Field recalled that Wordsworth

read to me in manuscript his lines on hearing the Cuckow at the Monastery of San Francisco D'Assisi, and his modernization of Chaucer's Cuckow and Nightingale. The former is very long and happy. In illustration of the latter he [quoted *del*] referred to the part the [cuckow *del*] crow plays in the Manciple's Tale, and praised the father-poet's dramatic [skill and *inserted*] courage, in making the Manciple, whose only object in life was to be a trusty domestic draw this [only *del*] alone from the tale—

My sone, beware, and be non auctour newe
Of tidings, whether they ben false or trewe;
When so thou come, amonges high or lowe,
Kepe wel thy tonge, and thinke upon the crowe.

He wished that the delicacy of modern ears would allow him to translate the whole of this tale, and dwelt with rapture upon the remorse of Phoebus for having slain his adulterous wife—

For sorwe of which he brake his minstralsie,
Both harpe and lute, giterne and sautrie,
And eke he brake his arwes and his bowe.[41]

[41]Field later added the following: "In the year 1841 the poet threw his Cuckow and the Nightingale into a bad collection of pieces entitled 'Chaucer Modernized' by Mr Horne, in which Mr. Leigh Hunt attempted the Manciple's Tale, by softening the adultery into a kiss, and thus emasculating the whole moral. It is but justice however to that gentleman in early life my friend to say that his other modernizations of the old poet are very good." I quote directly from the manuscript of the Field memoir, BL Add. MS. 41325.

In the end, Mary got her way and William never sent Powell *The Manciple's Tale,* explaining to Henry Reed that "I could not place my version at the disposal of the Editor, as I deemed the subject somewhat too indelicate for pure taste to be offered to the world at this time of day" (*LY,* IV, 165). Leigh Hunt translated the tale instead, changing Chaucer's "swive" into a kiss (Field called this version "emasculat[ed]"),[42] and Powell had to be content with just *The Cuckoo and the Nightingale* and *Troilus and Cresida. An Extract* "from the Master's hand."

Chaucer Modernized appeared in December 1840, just in time for the Christmas book trade.[43] Powell and Horne had high hopes for its success, and even planned a second volume, if the first sold well enough. And apparently they hoped for further contributions from Wordsworth: Elizabeth Barrett, for instance, encouraged Powell to press Wordsworth for a new translation of the *Second Nun's Tale.*[44] But the reviews were mixed, sales were not so brisk as hoped, and the second volume never appeared. In *The Athenæum,* Henry Chorley had praise for the efforts of Hunt and Wordsworth but was brutal to Horne, calling his version of the *General Prologue* a "counterfeit presentment" and dismissing the whole volume as poorly conceived.[45] J. A. Grimes, writing for the *Monthly Magazine,* had praise for the project (he had modernized the tales of the Squire and Prioress himself) but less for its execution. Of Horne he wrote:

> Little knows he of the difficulty of translation,—and more particularly of that province of translation which consists in rendering the thoughts conceived in an obsolete dialect, into the same language, through the media of words and constructions, quaint without obscurity, perfectly intelligible, and yet not familiarized to the scale of modern conversation. . . . And little is he fitted for such an undertaking.[46]

For Wordsworth's efforts he had great respect: "The revered name that is attached to this specimen [*The Cuckoo and the Nightingale*], is a sure guarantee for an able execution of the task he has undertaken" (p. 81). Nevertheless, he chided the poet for changing the sex of the cuckoo from male to female and for translating the *Troilus* excerpt inaccurately (pp. 81, 83). Other reviews appeared in *The Church of England Quarterly Review* (which praised all the contributors), *The Court* (generally positive), and *The English Journal,* which went so far as to claim that the volume would "bring about a new era of poetry."[47] But the most damaging review of all was never published, although it found its way to Rydal Mount and is now in the Wordsworth Library, boxed with the Thomas Powell Papers. This review was by Barron Field; in it he blistered the efforts of Horne and Powell, whom he argued were incapable of understanding Middle English, and was only a bit kinder to Elizabeth Barrett. Of her modernization he was

---

[42]In his manuscript review of the volume, now in the TPP in the WL.

[43]In a letter to Mary Russell Mitford of December 10, 1840, Elizabeth Barrett announced that her copy of *CM* arrived "with a vernally green back" (*Browning Correspondence,* IV, 301).

[44]*Browning Correspondence,* IV, 309.

[45]*Athenæum,* no. 693 (February 6, 1841), 107–108.

[46]*Monthly Magazine,* 3rd ser., 5 (January 1841), 74.

[47]*Church of England Quarterly Review* 9 (April 1840), 26–49; *The Court, Lady's Magazine, Monthly Critic, and Museum,* January 1841, 58–60; *English Journal,* January 2, 1841, 7–9.

"happy to speak a little better, for the honour of the sex. The poetry is often true, but the learning does not seem to be greater than that of Messrs. Horne and Powell." And he pleaded with Wordsworth to reprint his own contributions in his next volume of poems, rather than leave it in such a "dung-hill." Horne's modernizations, wrote Field, are a cheap modern-dress imitation of Chaucer, to be compared with Thomas Stothard's famous print of the Canterbury pilgrims (which Field detested).[48] Wordsworth's are the genuine Chaucerian article: not like Stothard, but like the Canterbury Pilgrims of William Blake. "Poor William Blake!" Field concluded. "He was certainly a man of a genius kindred to that of Chaucer."[49]

Poems, Chiefly of Early and Late Years

The history of Wordsworth's work on his Chaucer modernizations comes to an end in 1842 with the publication of *Poems, Chiefly of Early and Late Years.* Partly an effort to control publication of his juvenilia and partly a collection of recent compositions, this volume was designed to form a supplementary seventh volume to the 1836 collective edition of Wordsworth's poetry, published by Edward Moxon and reissued in stereotype in 1840 and 1841. The volume was dominated by revised versions of two early unpublished works, *The Borderers* and *Guilt and Sorrow,* and two late poetic sequences, *Memorials of a Tour in Italy,* 1837, and *Sonnets upon the Punishment of Death.* Included as well were the translations from *Chaucer Modernized,* here published for the first time under Wordsworth's direct control. Just as Barron Field had advised, the poet included them in his next collection of verse. *The Cuckoo and the Nightingale* appears immediately after the *Memorials,* evidently to link it to the poem on St. Francis, *The Cuckoo at Laverna,* and the extract from the *Troilus* appears 57 pages later, just before a set of "Miscellaneous Sonnets." Because *Poems, Chiefly of Early and Late Years* contains the first versions of both works published by Wordsworth himself, it has been chosen as the basis for the reading texts in the present edition.

In preparing the two Chaucer modernizations for Moxon, Wordsworth slightly revised his work and took care to correct several typographical and textual errors that had found their way into *Chaucer Modernized.*[50] For the *Cuckoo,* he simply sent corrected proof sheets of Horne's volume, irregularly trimmed and bearing a note, in Mary Wordsworth's hand, directing the printer to place it after the *Memorials.* For the extract from *Troilus,* Mary drew up a new fair copy, DC MS. 151.2, which also follows the *Chaucer Modernized* text closely, correcting just a handful of errors. After this brief flurry of copying and correction,

[48]"Mr. Stothard's picture is Chaucer Modernized—the horses all barbs, from the Elgin Marbles, and the riders, refined and softened, in stage-dresses" (TPP).

[49]For the full text of Field's discussion of Blake, see Bruce Graver, "A New Voice on Blake," *Blake: An Illustrated Quarterly* 24, 3 (Winter 1990/1991), 91–94.

[50]Two of these errors are corrected in the errata to *CM.*

extensive work on the Chaucer modernizations was over. Eventually, in the collective edition of 1845, he grouped all three of the poems together under the heading "Selections from Chaucer Modernis'd,"[51] but all subsequent revisions were of the most trivial sort. Wordsworth had paid his tribute to Chaucer's genius, for which he never ceased to profess "love and reverence." As he wrote to Henry Reed in 1841:

> So great is my admiration of Chaucer's genius, and so profound my reverence for him as an instrument in the hands of Providence for spreading the light of literature thro' his native land that notwithstanding the defects and faults in this Publication [*Chaucer Modernized*], I am glad of it, as a mean for making many acquainted with the original, who would otherwise be ignorant of every thing about him, but his name. (*LY*, IV, 166)

[51]Interestingly enough, in the 1846 reissue of Moxon's multivolume *Poetical Works*, for which the poems in *PELY* were revised and incorporated into WW's classification system, only *The Cuckoo and the Nightingale* and *Troilus and Cresida* were grouped together, and they appeared without a subject heading.

Selections from Chaucer, Modernized Reading Texts

Reading Texts

The reading text for *The Prioress's Tale* is the one published in *The River Duddon . . . and Other Poems* (1820), the first published version of the poem, and the earliest complete version as well. Substantive revisions and variant readings in DC MS. 35 and subsequent lifetime editions of Wordsworth's poetry are recorded in the apparatus at the bottom of the page. Those in DC MS. 13 are not shown, since this manuscript is transcribed in full on pages 81–143.

The reading texts for *The Cuckoo and the Nightingale* and *Troilus and Cresida. Extract from Chaucer* are the texts published in *Poems, Chiefly of Early and Late Years*, the first authorized published version of both poems. The texts in *Poems, Chiefly of Early and Late Years* are chosen rather than *The Poems of Geoffrey Chaucer, Modernized* (1841) because Wordsworth had no direct hand in the printing of the latter volume, and the texts are inaccurate. Substantive revisions and variant readings in *The Poems of Geoffrey Chaucer, Modernized*, DC MS. 151, and subsequent lifetime editions of Wordsworth's poetry are recorded in the apparatus at the bottom of the page. Those in DC MS. 24 are not shown, since they are transcribed in full on pages 145–149.

The reading text for *The Manciple, (from the Prologue) And his Tale* is based on the fair copy, in the autographs of Mary and William Wordsworth, in DC MS. 89. Substantive revisions in MS. 89 are recorded in the apparatus at the bottom of the page, as are variant readings in DC MS. 36, as far as it goes. Substantive revisions and variant readings in DC MS. 13 are not shown, for the reason given above. Reading-text accidentals (punctuation, capitalization, spelling, accents) are based on MS. 89, except as follows:

1. Where MS. 89 accidentals are wrong or seriously deficient, accidentals are drawn sparingly from the other two manuscripts, which are usually more carefully punctuated than MS. 89. Here MS. 13 is cited when it helps to estab-lish reading-text accidentals.

2. Where all manuscripts are seriously deficient by modern standards, accidentals are sparingly introduced by emendation, and marked *ed.* Most such accidentals are drawn from the edition of Chaucer which Wordsworth used in translating, that found in Robert Anderson's *Works of the British Poets*, volume I. In each such case, readings of the manuscripts are shown in the Nonverbal Variants.

The Editor's Notes attempt to explain and illustrate Wordsworth's decisions in translating the Middle English. Anderson's text for the minor poems of Chaucer was reprinted, with a few variations in punctuation, from John Urry's edition of Chaucer's works (1721), and his text for *The Canterbury Tales* and his glossary were reprinted from Thomas Tyrwhitt's edition (1775–1778). Urry's edition is notoriously corrupt; Tyrwhitt's is one of the great editorial achievements of the eighteenth century. It is thus not surprising that several of Wordsworth's supposed "errors" in translating are traceable to errors in his text, nor should it be surprising that he managed to correct a few textual errors by referring to Tyrwhitt's glossary. Wordsworth was also skeptical of Anderson's text, at least of *The Cuckoo and the Nightingale*, and in a footnote first appearing on a stub in DC MS. 89, claims to be introducing a number of readings "from a Bodleian manuscript." These notes attempt in a very modest way to relate Wordsworth's modernizations to the editing history of Chaucer's poems, especially during the eighteenth century.

Nonverbal variants for *The Prioress's Tale* can be found on pages 75–76, for *The Cuckoo and the Nightingale* on page 76, for *Troilus and Cresida* on page 76, and for *The Manciple, (from the Prologue) And his Tale* on pages 77–78. The Editor's Notes can be found on pages 69–73.

THE PRIORESS'S TALE,

(FROM CHAUCER.)

published 1820RD, 173–186; *1820*, III, 113–126; *1827*, IV, 105–116; *1832*, I, 301–310; *1836*, I, 262–273; *1845*, 416–419, classed as *Selections from Chaucer, Modernised*. *1850*, V, 72–81, classed as *Selections from Chaucer, Modernised*.

fly-title omitted 1827–

title followed by (FROM CHAUCER) *1827–1843, 1846*

In the following Piece I have allowed myself no farther deviations from the original than were necessary for the fluent reading, and instant understanding, of the Author: so much however is the language altered since Chaucer's time, especially in pronunciation, that much was to be removed, and its place supplied with as little incongruity as possible. The ancient accent has been retained in a few conjunctions, such as alsō and alwāy, from a conviction that such sprinklings of antiquity would be admitted, by persons of taste, to have a graceful accordance with the subject.

---

headnote omitted MS. 35, placed below epigraph 1827–

1 Piece . . . farther] Poem . . . further *1820–*

1–2 I . . . original *rev to* no further deviation from the original has been made *MS. 1836/45, 1845–* deviations] deviation *1827–* were] was *1820–*

7–8 such as] as in *1820* as *1827–*

10 The fierce bigotry of the Prioress forms a fine back ground for her tender-hearted sympathies with the Mother and Child; and the mode in which the story is told amply atones for the extravagance of the miracle. *added 1827– but* back-ground *1832–*

THE PRIORESS'S TALE.

" Call up him who left half told
The story of Cambuscan bold."

O Lord, our Lord! how wonderously (quoth she)
Thy name in this large world is spread abroad!
For not alone by men of dignity
Thy worship is performed and precious laud;
But by the mouths of children, gracious God!
Thy goodness is set forth, they when they lie
Upon the breast thy name do glorify.

Wherefore in praise, the worthiest that I may,
Jesu! of thee, and the white Lily-flower
Which did thee bear, and is a maid for aye,
To tell a story I will use my power;
Not that I may increase her honour's dower,
For she herself is honour, and the root
Of goodness, next her Son our soul's best boot.

O Mother Maid! O Maid and Mother free!
O bush unburnt! burning in Moses' sight!
That down didst ravish from the Deity,
Through humbleness, the spirit that did alight
Upon thy heart, whence, through that glory's might,
Conceived was the Father's sapience,
Help me to tell it in thy reverence!

---

1 wonderously] marvellous *MS. 35*
2 large] huge *MS. 35*
6 goodness is set forth] bounty is performed *MS. 35*
7 glorify.] magnify *MS. 35*
10 for aye,] alway *MS. 35*
11 use] do *MS. 35*
14 goodness,] bounty *MS. 35*
18 did] didst *MS. 35*
19 thy] the *MS. 35*
20 was] is *MS. 35*

Lady, thy goodness, thy magnificence,
Thy virtue, and thy great humility,
Surpass all science and all utterance;
For sometimes, Lady! ere men pray to thee
Thou go'st before in thy benignity,
The light to us vouchsafing of thy prayer,
To be our guide unto thy Son so dear.

My knowledge is so weak, O blissful Queen!
To tell abroad thy mighty worthiness,
That I the weight of it may not sustain;
But as a child of twelvemonths old or less,
That laboureth his language to express,
Even so fare I; and therefore, I thee pray,
Guide thou my song which I of thee shall say.

There was in Asia, in a mighty town,
'Mong Christian folk, a street where Jews might be;
Assigned to them and given them for their own
By a great Lord, for gain and usury,
Hateful to Christ and to his company;
And through this street who list might ride and wend;
Free was it, and unbarr'd at either end.

A little school of Christian people stood
Down at the farther end, in which there were
A nest of children come of Christian blood,
That learned in that school from year to year
Such sort of doctrine as men used there,
That is to say, to sing and read alsō
As little children in their childhood do.

Among these children was a widow's son,
A little scholar, scarcely seven years old,
Who day by day unto this school hath gone,
And eke, when he the image did behold
Of Jesu's Mother, as he had been told,
This Child was wont to kneel adown and say
Ave Marie, as he goeth by the way.

---

24 Surpass] Passeth *MS. 35*
26 in] of *MS. 35*
27–28 And givest us the guidance of thy prayer
To be a light unto thy son so dear *MS. 35*
29 weak] great *MS. 35*
33 That laboureth] Laboureth *MS. 35*
35 thou] then *MS. 35*
42 Free . . . unbarr'd] For it was free and open *MS. 35*
43 people] folk there *MS. 35*
51 scarcely seven] that was sev'n *MS. 35*

This Widow thus her little Son hath taught
Our blissful Lady, Jesu's Mother dear,
To worship aye, and he forgat it not,
For simple infant hath a ready ear.
Sweet is the holiness of youth: and hence,
Calling to mind this matter when I may,
Saint Nicholas in my presence standeth aye,
For he so young to Christ did reverence.

This little Child, while in the school he sate
His primer conning with an earnest cheer,
The whilst the rest their anthem-book repeat
The Alma Redemptoris did he hear;
And as he durst he drew him near and near,
And hearkened to the words and to the note,
'Till the first verse he learn'd it all by rote.

This Latin knew he nothing what it said
For he too tender was of age to know;
But to his comrade he repaired, and prayed
That he the meaning of this song would show,
And unto him declare why men sing so;
This, oftentimes, that he might be at ease,
This child did him beseech, on his bare knees.

His Schoolfellow, who elder was than he,
Answered him thus;—"This song, I have heard say,
Was fashioned for our blissful Lady free;
Her to salute, and also her to pray
To be our help upon our dying day.
If there is more in this I know it not;
The song I learn,—small grammar I have got."

---

59 not,] nought *MS. 35* not; *1836–*
62 this] the *MS. 35*
65–67 This little Child learning his little book
As he sate at his primer in the school
Where children learn the anthem book by rule *MS. 35*
71 'Till] And *MS. 35* Till *1827–* learn'd] knew *MS. 35* learned *1820–*
72–78 This Latin wist he nought what it did say
For he so young and tender was of age
But on a day his fellow he 'gan pray
To expound to him this song that he might know
Its proper meaning and why men sing so
This oftentimes that he might have his ease
Prayed this Child to him on his bare knees *MS. 35*
79 than] then *MS. 35*
80 him] his *MS. 35*
83 To expound to him this song that *del and rev to text MS. 35*
85 The song] Song do *1820RD errata–*

"And is this song fashioned in reverence
Of Jesu's Mother?" said this Innocent,
"Now, certes, I will use my diligence
To con it all ere Christmas-tide be spent;
Although I for my Primer shall be shent,
And shall be beaten three times in an hour,
Our Lady I will praise with all my power."

His Schoolfellow, whom he had so besought,
As they went homeward taught him privily;
And then he sang it well and fearlessly,
From word to word according to the note:
Twice in a day it passed through his throat;
Homeward and schoolward whensoe'er he went,
On Jesu's Mother fixed was his intent.

Through all the Jewry (this before said I,)
This little child, as he came to and fro,
Full merrily then would he sing and cry,
O Alma Redemptoris! high and low:
The sweetness of Christ's Mother pierced so
His heart, that her to praise, to her to pray,
He cannot stop his singing by the way.

The Serpent, Satan, our first foe, that hath
His wasp's nest in Jew's heart, upswell'd—"O woe,
O Hebrew people!" said he in his wrath,
"Is it an honest thing? Shall this be so?
That such a Boy, where'er he list shall go
In your despite, and sing his hymns and saws,
Which is against the reverence of our laws!"

From that day forward have the Jews conspired
Out of the world this Innocent to chace;
And to this end a Homicide they hired,
That in an Alley had a privy place,
And, as the Child 'gan to the School to pace,
This cruel Jew him seized, and held him fast
And cut his throat, and in a pit him cast.

---

88 use] do *MS. 35*
97 Twice] Thrice *MS. 35*
107 that hath *over illeg eras MS. 35*
110 Is this an honest thing, can this be so? *MS. 35*
111 list] lists *1827–*
115 This Innocent out of this world to chase *MS. 35*
119 cruel] cursed *MS. 35*

I say that him into a pit they threw,
A loathsome pit whence noisome scents exhale;
O cursed folk! away ye Herods new!
What may your ill intentions you avail?
Murder will out; certes it will not fail;
Know, that the honour of high God may spread,
The blood cries out on your accursed deed.

O Martyr 'stablished in virginity!
Now may'st thou sing for aye before the throne,
Following the Lamb celestial," quoth she,
"Of which the great Evangelist, Saint John,
In Patmos wrote, who saith of them that go
Before the Lamb singing continually,
That never fleshly woman they did know.

Now this poor widow waiteth all that night
After her little Child, and he came not;
For which, by earliest glimpse of morning light,
With face all pale with dread and busy thought
She at the School and elsewhere him hath sought,
Until thus far she learned, that he had been
In the Jews' street, and there he last was seen.

With Mother's pity in her breast enclosed
She goeth, as she were half out of her mind,
To every place wherein she hath supposed
By likelihood her little Son to find;
And ever on Christ's Mother meek and kind
She cried, till to the Jewry she was brought,
And him among the accursed Jews she sought.

---

122 Where these Jews their things unclean did trail *MS. 35*
123 away . . . new!] o Herods Old and New! *MS. 35*
125 certes] certain *MS. 35* certès *1836–*
126–127 And know you that the honor of God may spread
The blood outcrieth on your cursed deed *MS. 35*
130 celestial *over illeg eras MS. 35*
134 woman] women *MS. 35*
137 For which at day-break, soon as it was light *MS. 35*
138 *line omitted MS. 35*
139 him hath] hath him *MS. 35*
140 far she learned,] much she had learn'd *MS. 35*
141 last was] was last *MS. 35*
144 To all and every place where she supposed *MS. 35*
148 accursed] cursed *MS. 35* accursèd *1827–*

She asketh, and she piteously doth pray
To every Jew that dwelleth in that place
To tell her if her Child had pass'd that way;
They all said Nay; but Jesu of his grace
Gave to her thought, that in a little space
She for her Son in that same spot did cry
Where he was cast into a pit hard by.

O thou great God that dost perform thy laud
By mouths of Innocents, lo! here thy might;
This gem of chastity, this emerald,
And eke of martyrdom this ruby bright,
There, where with mangled throat he lay upright,
The Alma Redemptoris 'gan to sing
So loud that with his voice the place did ring.

The Christian folk that through the Jewry went
Come to the spot in wonder at the thing;
And hastily they for the Provost sent;
Immediately he came not tarrying,
And praiseth Christ that is our heavenly King,
And eke his Mother, honour of Mankind:
Which done, he bade that they the Jews should bind.

This Child with piteous lamentation then
Was taken up, singing his song alway;
And with procession great and pomp of men
To the next Abbey him they bare away;
His Mother swooning by the Bier lay:
And scarcely could the people that were near
Remove this second Rachel from the Bier.

Torment and shameful death to every one
This Provost doth for those bad Jews prepare
That of this murder wist, and that anon:
Such wickedness his judgments cannot spare;

---

150 To every Jew that] Of every Jew who *MS. 35*
153–154 Gave it to her in thought that in that place
She to her little Son anon did cry *MS. 35*
155 a] the *MS. 35*
156 that] who *MS. 35*
157 Innocents, lo!] infants Lo! *MS. 35*
164 Come] Came *MS. 35*
166 he came not] *over illeg eras MS. 35*
174 Bier] bier *1836–1843* body *1845–*
177 shameful] shame and *MS. 35*
178 doth] does *MS. 35*
180 *left blank MS. 35*

Who will do evil, evil shall he bear;
Them therefore with wild horses did he draw,
And after that he hung them by the law.

Upon his Bier this Innocent doth lie
Before the Altar while the Mass doth last:
The Abbot with his Convent's company
Then sped themselves to bury him full fast;
And, when they holy water on him cast,
Yet spake this Child when sprinkled was the water,
And sang, O Alma Redemptoris Mater!

This Abbot who had been a holy man,
And was, as all Monks are, or ought to be,
In supplication to the Child began
Thus saying, "O dear Child! I summon thee
In virtue of the holy Trinity
Tell me the cause why thou dost sing this hymn,
Since that thy throat is cut, as it doth seem."

"My throat is cut unto the bone, I trow,"
Said this young Child, "and by the law of kind
I should have died, yea many hours ago;
But Jesus Christ, as in the books ye find,
Will that his glory last, and be in mind;
And, for the worship of his Mother dear,
Yet may I sing, O Alma! loud and clear.

This well of mercy Jesu's Mother sweet
After my knowledge I have loved alway,
And in the hour when I my death did meet
To me she came, and thus to me did say,
"Thou in thy dying sing this holy lay,"
As ye have heard; and soon as I had sung
Methought she laid a grain upon my tongue.

---

181 shall he bear;] he shall bear *MS. 35*
183 hung] hanged *MS. 35*
184 doth *rev from* does *MS. 35*
185 doth] does *MS. 35*
189 the] with *MS. 35*
190 And sang *inserted MS. 35*
191–192 This Abbot for he was a holy man
As all Monks are, or surely ought to be, *1820RD errata–, but* This] 'This *1827* "This *1832* Abbot, . . . man, *1827–*
194 Thus saying,] And said: *MS. 35*
195 In] By *MS. 35*
197 Since that] Seeing *MS. 35*
199 by the law of] in my natural *MS. 35*
202 his] this *MS. 35*

Wherefore I sing, nor can from song refrain,
In honour of that blissful Maiden free,
'Till from my tongue off-taken is the grain;
And after that thus said she unto me,
"My little Child, then will I come for thee
Soon as the grain from off thy tongue they take,
Be not dismay'd, I will not thee forsake!"

This holy Monk, this Abbot—him mean I,
Touched then his tongue, and took away the grain;
And he gave up the ghost full peacefully;
And, when the Abbot had this wonder seen,
His salt tears trickled down like showers of rain,
And on his face he dropped upon the ground,
And still he lay as if he had been bound.

Eke the whole Convent on the pavement lay,
Weeping and praising Jesu's Mother dear;
And after that they rose, and took their way
And lifted up this Martyr from the Bier,
And in a tomb of precious marble clear
Enclos'd his uncorrupted body sweet.—
Where'er he be, God grant us him to meet!

Young Hew of Lincoln! in like sort laid low
By cursed Jews—thing well and widely known,
For not long since was dealt the cruel blow,
Pray also thou for us, while here we tarry
Weak sinful folk, that God, with pitying eye,
In mercy would his mercy multiply
On us, for reverence of his Mother Mary!

---

212 *line omitted MS. 35*
215 said] saith *MS. 35*
217 they] thy *MS. 35*
222 *line omitted MS. 35*
224 dropped] fell *MS. 35*   upon the ground *over illeg eras MS.35*
228 rose] rise *MS. 35*
231–235 They did enclose his little body sweet
There he is now, God [give *rev to*] grant us him to meet

Young Hugh of Lincoln! that wert slain also
By cursed Jews a thing that is well known
For it was but a little while ago *MS. 35*
235 For it was done a little while ago— *1836–*
237 with pitying eye] ever the most high *MS. 35*

THE

CUCKOO AND THE NIGHTINGALE.

(FROM CHAUCER.)

I.

THE God of Love—*ah benedicite!*
How mighty and how great a Lord is he!
For he of low hearts can make high, of high
He can make low, and unto death bring nigh;
And hard hearts he can make them kind and free.

II.

Within a little time, as hath been found,
He can make sick folk whole and fresh and sound:
Them who are whole in body and in mind,
He can make sick,—bind can he and unbind
All that he will have bound, or have unbound.

III.

To tell his might my wit may not suffice;
Foolish men he can make them out of wise;—
For he may do all that he will devise;
Loose livers he can make abate their vice,
And proud hearts can make tremble in a trice.

IV.

In brief, the whole of what he will, he may;
Against him dare not any wight say nay;
To humble or afflict whome'er he will,
To gladden or to grieve, he hath like skill;
But most his might he sheds on the eve of May.

---

published *CM,* 35–52; *PELY,* 149–165; *1845,* 419–423, classed as *Selections from Chaucer* MODERNISED.; *1846,* VI, 100–115; 1850, V, 81–93, classed as *Selections from Chaucer. Modernised.*

subtitle (From Chaucer.)] (From Chaucer). *MS. 151.2 (MW)*

3–4 High can he make the heart that's low and poor,
And high hearts low, through pain that they endure, *Calvert and Cornell MSS. but*

3 heart] hearts *Calvert MS.* 4 low,] low— *Calvert MS.*

V.

For every true heart, gentle heart and free,
That with him is, or thinketh so to be,
Now against May shall have some stirring—whether
To joy, or be it to some mourning; never
At other time, methinks, in like degree.

VI.

For now when they may hear the small birds' song,
And see the budding leaves the branches throng,
This unto their rememberance doth bring
All kinds of pleasure mix'd with sorrowing;
And longing of sweet thoughts that ever long.

VII.

And of that longing heaviness doth come,
Whence oft great sickness grows of heart and home;
Sick are they all for lack of their desire;
And thus in May their hearts are set on fire,
So that they burn forth in great martyrdom.

VIII.

In sooth, I speak from feeling, what though now
Old am I, and to genial pleasure slow;
Yet have I felt of sickness through the May,
Both hot and cold, and heart-aches every day,—
How hard, alas! to bear, I only know.

IX.

Such shaking doth the fever in me keep
Through all this May that I have little sleep;
And also 'tis not likely unto me,
That any living heart should sleepy be
In which Love's dart its fiery point doth steep.

X.

But tossing lately on a sleepless bed,
I of a token thought which Lovers heed;
How among them it was a common tale,
That it was good to hear the Nightingale,
Ere the vile Cuckoo's note be utterèd.

XI.

And then I thought anon as it was day,
I gladly would go somewhere to essay
If I perchance a Nightingale might hear,
For yet had I heard none, of all that year,
And it was then the third night of the May.

XII.

And soon as I a glimpse of day espied,
No longer would I in my bed abide,
But straightway to a wood that was hard by,
Forth did I go, alone and fearlessly,
And held the pathway down by a brook-side;

XIII.

Till to a lawn I came all white and green,
I in so fair a one had never been.
The ground was green, with daisy powdered over;
Tall were the flowers, the grove a lofty cover,
All green and white; and nothing else was seen.

XIV.

There sate I down among the fair fresh flowers,
And saw the birds come tripping from their bowers,
Where they had rested them all night; and they,
Who were so joyful at the light of day,
Began to honour May with all their powers.

XV.

Well did they know that service all by rote,
And there was many and many a lovely note,
Some, singing loud, as if they had complained;
Some with their notes another manner feigned;
And some did sing all out with the full throat.

XVI.

They pruned themselves, and made themselves right gay,
Dancing and leaping light upon the spray;
And ever two and two together were,
The same as they had chosen for the year,
Upon Saint Valentine's returning day.

XVII.

Meanwhile the stream, whose bank I sate upon,
Was making such a noise as it ran on
Accordant to the sweet Birds' harmony;
Methought that it was the best melody
Which ever to man's ear a passage won.

XVIII.

And for delight, but how I never wot,
I in a slumber and a swoon was caught,
Not all asleep and yet not waking wholly;
And as I lay, the Cuckoo, bird unholy,
Broke silence, or I heard him in my thought.

XIX.

And that was right upon a tree fast by,
And who was then ill satisfied but I?
Now, God, quoth I, that died upon the rood,
From thee and thy base throat, keep all that's good,
For little joy have I now of thy cry.

XX.

And, as I with the Cuckoo thus 'gan chide,
In the next bush that was me fast beside,
I heard the lusty Nightingale so sing,
That her clear voice made a loud rioting,
Echoing thorough all the green wood wide.

XXI.

Ah! good sweet Nightingale! for my heart's cheer,
Hence hast thou stay'd a little while too long;
For we have had the sorry Cuckoo here,
And she hath been before thee with her song;
Evil light on her! she hath done me wrong.

XXII.

But hear you now a wondrous thing, I pray;
As long as in that swooning-fit I lay,
Methought I wist right well what these birds meant,
And had good knowing both of their intent,
And of their speech, and all that they would say.

XXIII.

The Nightingale thus in my hearing spake:—
Good Cuckoo, seek some other bush or brake,
And, prithee, let us that can sing dwell here;
For every wight eschews thy song to hear,
Such uncouth singing verily dost thou make.

XXIV.

What! quoth she then, what is 't that ails thee now?
It seems to me I sing as well as thou;
For mine 's a song that is both true and plain,—
Although I cannot quaver so in vain
As thou dost in thy throat, I wot not how.

XXV.

All men may understanding have of me,
But, Nightingale, so may they not of thee;
For thou hast many a foolish and quaint cry:—
Thou say'st OSEE, OSEE, then how may I
Have knowledge, I thee pray, what this may be?

XXVI.

Ah, fool! quoth she, wist thou not what it is?
Oft as I say Osee, Osee, I wis,
Then mean I, that I should be wonderous fain
That shamefully they one and all were slain,
Whoever against Love mean aught amiss.

XXVII.

And also would I that they all were dead,
Who do not think in love their life to lead;
For who is loth the God of Love to obey,
Is only fit to die, I dare well say,
And for that cause Osee I cry; take heed!

XXVIII.

Ay, quoth the Cuckoo, that is a quaint law,
That all must love or die; but I withdraw,
And take my leave of all such company,
For mine intent it neither is to die,
Nor ever while I live Love's yoke to draw.

XXIX.

For lovers of all folk that be alive,
The most disquiet have and least do thrive;
Most feeling have of sorrow woe and care,
And the least welfare cometh to their share;
What need is there against the truth to strive?

XXX.

What! quoth she, thou art all out of thy mind,
That in thy churlishness a cause canst find
To speak of Love's true Servants in this mood;
For in this world no service is so good
To every wight that gentle is of kind.

XXXI.

For thereof comes all goodness and all worth;
All gentiless and honour thence come forth;
Thence worship comes, content and true heart's pleasure,
And full-assured trust, joy without measure,
And jollity, fresh cheerfulness, and mirth;

---

143 sorrow] sorrow's *CM rev to* sorrow *CM errata*–
152 gentiless] gentleness *CM*

XXXII.

And bounty, lowliness, and courtesy,
And seemliness, and faithful company,
And dread of shame that will not do amiss;
For he that faithfully Love's servant is,
Rather than be disgraced, would chuse to die.

XXXIII.

And that the very truth it is which I
Now say—in such belief I'll live and die;
And Cuckoo, do thou so, by my advice.
Then, quoth she, let me never hope for bliss,
If with that counsel I do e'er comply.

XXXIV.

Good Nightingale! thou speakest wondrous fair,
Yet for all that, the truth is found elsewhere;
For Love in young folk is but rage, I wis;
And Love in old folk a great dotage is;
Who most it useth, him 'twill most impair.

XXXV.

For thereof come all contraries to gladness;
Thence sickness comes, and overwhelming sadness,
Mistrust and jealousy, despite, debate,
Dishonour, shame, envy importunate,
Pride, anger, mischief, poverty, and madness.

XXXVI.

Loving is aye an office of despair,
And one thing is therein which is not fair;
For whoso gets of love a little bliss,
Unless it alway stay with him, I wis
He may full soon go with an old man's hair.

XXXVII.

And, therefore, Nightingale! do thou keep nigh,
For trust me well, in spite of thy quaint cry,
If long time from thy mate thou be, or far,
Thou 'lt be as others that forsaken are;
Then shalt thou raise a clamour as do I.

XXXVIII.

Fie, quoth she, on thy name, Bird ill beseen!
The God of Love afflict thee with all teen,
For thou art worse than mad a thousand fold;
For many a one hath virtues manifold,
Who had been nought, if Love had never been.

XXXIX.

For evermore his servants Love amendeth,
And he from every blemish them defendeth;
And maketh them to burn, as in a fire,
In loyalty, and worshipful desire,
And when it likes him, joy enough them sendeth.

XL.

Thou Nightingale! the Cuckoo said, be still,
For Love no reason hath but his own will;—
For to th' untrue he oft gives ease and joy;
True lovers doth so bitterly annoy,
He lets them perish through that grievous ill.

XLI.

With such a master would I never be*;
For he, in sooth, is blind, and may not see,
And knows not when he hurts and when he heals;
Within this court full seldom Truth avails,
So diverse in his wilfulness is he.

XLII.

Then of the Nightingale did I take note,
How from her inmost heart a sigh she brought,
And said, Alas! that ever I was born,
Not one word have I now, I am so forlorn,—
And with that word, she into tears burst out.

XLIII.

Alas, alas! my very heart will break,
Quoth she, to hear this churlish bird thus speak
Of Love, and of his holy services;
Now, God of Love! thou help me in some wise,
That vengeance on this Cuckoo I may wreak.

XLIV.

And so methought I started up anon,
And to the brook I ran and got a stone,
Which at the Cuckoo hardlly I cast,
And he for dread did fly away full fast;
And glad, in sooth, was I when he was gone.

*From a manuscript in the Bodleian, as are also stanzas 44 and 45, which are necessary to complete the sense.

---

201 *footnote* From a manuscript in the Bodleian, as are also stanzas 44 and 45. *CM; rev to* . . . 44 and 45 [omitted *del*] not found in the common editions texts *rev to* *44 and 45 which are necessary to complete the sense *MS. 151.2 (WW)*

XLV.

And as he flew, the Cuckoo ever and aye,
Kept crying, "Farewell!—farewell, Popinjay!"
As if in scornful mockery of me;
And on I hunted him from tree to tree,
Till he was far, all out of sight, away.

XLVI.

Then straightway came the Nightingale to me,
And said, Forsooth, my friend, do I thank thee,
That thou wert near to rescue me; and now,
Unto the God of Love I make a vow,
That all this May I will thy songstress be.

XLVII.

Well satisfied, I thanked her, and she said,
By this mishap no longer be dismayed,
Though thou the Cuckoo heard, ere thou heard'st me;
Yet if I live it shall amended be,
When next May comes, if I am not afraid.

XLVIII.

And one thing will I counsel thee alsó,
The Cuckoo trust not thou, nor his Love's saw;
All that she said is an outrageous lie.
Nay, nothing shall me bring thereto, quoth I,
For Love, and it hath done me mighty woe.

XLIX.

Yea, hath it? use, quoth she, this medicine;
This May-time, every day before thou dine,
Go look on the fresh daisy; then say I,
Although for pain thou may'st be like to die,
Thou wilt be eased, and less wilt droop and pine.

L.

And mind always that thou be good and true,
And I will sing one song, of many new,
For love of thee, as loud as I may cry;
And then did she begin this song full high,
'Beshrew all them that are in love untrue.'

231–235 *printed twice in printer's proofs for PELY; WW notes:* This Stanza [observe is *del*] repeated by an oversight *JC adds:* See page 160 where this stanza appears *MS. 151.3*

LI.

And soon as she had sung it to the end,
Now farewell, quoth she, for I hence must wend;
And, God of Love, that can right well and may,
Send unto thee as mickle joy this day,
As ever he to Lover yet did send.

LII.

Thus takes the Nightingale her leave of me;
I pray to God with her always to be,
And joy of love to send her evermore;
And shield us from the Cuckoo and her lore,
For there is not so false a bird as she.

LIII.

Forth then she flew, the gentle Nightingale,
To all the Birds that lodged within that dale,
And gathered each and all into one place;
And them besought to hear her doleful case,
And thus it was that she began her tale.

LIV.

The Cuckoo—'tis not well that I should hide
How she and I did each the other chide,
And without ceasing, since it was daylight;
And now I pray you all to do me right
Of that false Bird whom Love can not abide.

LV.

Then spake one Bird, and full assent all gave;
This matter asketh counsel good as grave,
For birds we are—all here together brought;
And, in good sooth, the Cuckoo here is not;
And therefore we a Parliament will have.

LVI.

And thereat shall the Eagle be our Lord,
And other Peers whose names are on record;
A summons to the Cuckoo shall be sent,
And judgment there be given; or that intent
Failing, we finally shall make accord.

---

270 can not *rev from* cannot *MS. 151.3 (JC)*

LVII.

And all this shall be done, without a nay,
The morrow after Saint Valentine's day,
Under a maple that is well beseen,
Before the chamber-window of the Queen,
At Woodstock, on the meadow green and gay.

LVIII.

She thankèd them; and then her leave she took,
And flew into a hawthorn by that brook;
And there she sate and sung—upon that tree—
"For term of life Love shall have hold of me"—
So loudly, that I with that song awoke.

Unlearned Book and rude, as well I know,
For beauty thou hast none, nor eloquence,
Who did on thee the hardiness bestow
To appear before my Lady? but a sense
Thou surely hast of her benevolence,
Whereof her hourly bearing proof doth give;
For of all good she is the best alive.

Alas, poor Book! for thy unworthiness,
To show to her some pleasant meanings writ
In winning words, since through her gentiless,
Thee she accepts as for her service fit!
Oh! it repents me I have neither wit
Nor leisure unto thee more worth to give;
For of all good she is the best alive.

Beseech her meekly with all lowliness,
Though I be far from her I reverence,
To think upon my truth and stedfastness,
And to abridge my sorrow's violence,
Caused by the wish, as knows your sapience,
She of her liking proof to me would give;
For of all good she is the best alive.

---

290 *the line is cut away in MS. 151.2 and omitted by printer in MS. 151.3; added in MS. 151.3 (MW and WW)*

300 gentiless] gentleness *CM, MS. 151.2, rev from* gentleness *MS. 151.3 (WW)*

L'ENVOY

PLEASURE'S AURORA, Day of gladsomeness!
Luna by night, with heavenly influence
Illumined! root of beauty and goodnesse,
Write, and allay, by your beneficence,
My sighs breathed forth in silence,—comfort give!
Since of all good, you are the best alive.

EXPLICIT.

---

312 *In* British Poets—*WL, 1, 501, various ink and pencil marks, now erased, seem to be the beginnings of WW's initial draft of this stanza*
313 Luna] Land, *CM rev to* Luna *CM errata–*

TROILUS AND CRESIDA.

EXTRACT FROM CHAUCER.

Next morning Troilus began to clear
His eyes from sleep, at the first break of day,
And unto Pandarus, his own Brother dear,
For love of God, full piteously did say,
We must the Palace see of Cresida;
For since we yet may have no other feast,
Let us behold her Palace at the least!

And therewithal to cover his intent
A cause he found into the Town to go,
And they right forth to Cresid's Palace went;
But, Lord, this simple Troilus was woe,
Him thought his sorrowful heart would break in two;
For when he saw her doors fast bolted all,
Well nigh for sorrow down he 'gan to fall.

Therewith when this true Lover 'gan behold,
How shut was every window of the place,
Like frost he thought his heart was icy cold;
For which, with changèd, pale, and deadly face,
Without word uttered, forth he 'gan to pace;
And on his purpose bent so fast to ride,
That no wight his continuance espied.

Then said he thus,—O Palace desolate!
O house of houses, once so richly dight!
O Palace empty and disconsolate!
Thou lamp of which extinguished is the light;
O Palace whilom day that now art night,
Thou ought'st to fall and I to die; since she
Is gone who held us both in sovereignty.

---

published *CM*, 125–135; *PELY*, 206–214; *1845*, 423–424, *classed as Selections from Chaucer* MODERNISED.; *1846*, VI, 116–122; *1850*, V, 94–99, *classed as Selections from Chaucer. Modernised.*

title EXTRACT / from / TROILUS AND CRESIDA. *CM* Troilus & Cresida / Extract / from Chaucer *MS. 151.2; subtitle omitted 1845–*

12 break] burst *CM*

17 heart was icy *rev from* icy heart *MS. 151.2*

20 to *rev from* did *MS. 151.2*

O, of all houses once the crownèd boast!
Palace illumined with the sun of bliss;
O ring of which the ruby now is lost,
O cause of woe, that cause has been of bliss:
Yet, since I may no better, would I kiss
Thy cold doors; but I dare not for this rout;
Farewell, thou shrine of which the Saint is out!

Therewith he cast on Pandarus an eye,
With changèd face, and piteous to behold;
And when he might his time aright espy,
Aye as he rode, to Pandarus he told
Both his new sorrow and his joys of old,
So piteously, and with so dead a hue,
That every wight might on his sorrow rue.

Forth from the spot he rideth up and down,
And everything to his rememberànce
Came as he rode by places of the town
Where he had felt such perfect pleasure once.
Lo, yonder saw I mine own Lady dance,
And in that Temple she with her bright eyes,
My Lady dear, first bound me captive-wise.

And yonder with joy-smitten heart have I
Heard my own Cresid's laugh; and once at play
I yonder saw her eke full blissfully;
And yonder once she unto me 'gan say—
Now, my sweet Troilus, love me well, I pray!
And there so graciously did me behold,
That hers unto the death my heart I hold.

And at the corner of that self-same house
Heard I my most beloved Lady dear,
So womanly, with voice melodious
Singing so well, so goodly, and so clear,
That in my soul methinks I yet do hear
The blissful sound; and in that very place
My Lady first me took unto her grace.

---

32 has] hast *CM*
36 an] his *CM*
47 *in the copy of CM later presented to Fanny Wordsworth, there is a pencil mark to indicate the beginning of DC MS. 24*
61 in *rev from* yet in *MS. 151.2*

O blissful God of Love! then thus he cried,
When I the process have in memory,
How thou hast wearied me on every side,
Men thence a book might make, a history;
What need to seek a conquest over me,
Since I am wholly at thy will? what joy
Hast thou thy own liege subjects to destroy?

Dread Lord! so fearful when provoked thine ire,
Well hast thou wreaked on me by pain and grief;
Now mercy, Lord! thou know'st well I desire
Thy grace above all pleasures first and chief;
And live and die I will in thy belief;
For which I ask for guerdon but one boon,
That Cresida again thou send me soon.

Constrain her heart as quickly to return,
As thou dost mine with longing her to see,
Then know I well that she would not sojourn.
Now, blissful Lord, so cruel do not be
Unto the blood of Troy, I pray of thee,
As Juno was unto the Theban blood,
From whence to Thebes came griefs in multitude.

And after this he to the gate did go
Whence Cresid rode, as if in haste she was;
And up and down there went, and to and fro,
And to himself full oft he said, alas!
From hence my hope, and solace forth did pass.
O would the blissful God now for his joy,
I might her see again coming to Troy!

And up to yonder hill was I her guide;
Alas, and there I took of her my leave;
Yonder I saw her to her Father ride,
For very grief of which my heart shall cleave;—
And hither home I came when it was eve;
And here I dwell an outcast from all joy,
And shall, unless I see her soon in Troy.

---

73 desire *rev from* deem *MS. 151.2*
84 multitude] multitudes *MS. 151.2*
91 to *rev from* from *MS. 151.2*
95 of *rev from* [?for] *MS. 151.2*
98 *in the copy of CM later presented to Fanny Wordsworth, there is a pencil mark to indicate the end of DC MS. 24*

And of himself did he imagine oft,
That he was blighted, pale, and waxen less
Than he was wont; and that in whispers soft
Men said, what may it be, can no one guess
Why Troilus hath all this heaviness?
All which he of himself conceited wholly
Out of his weakness and his melancholy.

Another time he took into his head,
That every wight, who in the way passed by,
Had of him ruth, and fancied that they said,
I am right sorry Troilus will die:
And thus a day or two drove wearily;
As ye have heard; such life 'gan he to lead
As one that standeth betwixt hope and dread

For which it pleased him in his songs to show
The occasion of his woe, as best he might;
And made a fitting song, of words but few,
Somewhat his woeful heart to make more light;
And when he was removed from all men's sight,
With a soft night voice, he of his Lady dear,
That absent was, 'gan sing as ye may hear.

O star, of which I lost have all the light,
With a sore heart well ought I to bewail,
That ever dark in torment, night by night,
Toward my death with wind I steer and sail;
For which upon the tenth night if thou fail
With thy bright beams to guide me but one hour,
My ship and me Charybdis will devour.

As soon as he this song had thus sung through,
He fell again into his sorrows old;
And every night, as was his wont to do,
Troilus stood the bright moon to behold;
And all his trouble to the moon he told,
And said; I wis, when thou art horn'd anew,
I shall be glad if all the world be true.

---

111 ye *rev from* I *MS. 151.2*
114 best he might *rev from* best might *MS. 151.2*
115 of] whose *CM, MS. 151.2*
118 soft night] soft *CM*
127 thus sung through] had sung thorough *MS. 151.2*
132 art *rev from* are *MS. 151.2*

Thy horns were old as now upon that morrow,
When hence did journey my bright Lady dear,
That cause is of my torment and my sorrow;
For which, oh, gentle Luna, bright and clear,
For love of God, run fast above thy sphere;
For when thy horns begin once more to spring,
Then shall she come, that with her bliss may bring.

The day is more, and longer every night
Than they were wont to be—for he thought so;
And that the sun did take his course not right,
By longer way than he was wont to go;
And said, I am in constant dread I trow,
That Phäeton his son is yet alive,
His too fond father's car amiss to drive.

Upon the walls fast also would he walk,
To the end that he the Grecian host might see;
And ever thus he to himself would talk:—
Lo! yonder is my own bright Lady free;
Or yonder is it that the tents must be;
And thence does come this air which is so sweet,
That in my soul I feel the joy of it.

And certainly this wind, that more and more
By moments thus increaseth in my face
Is of my Lady's sighs heavy and sore;
I prove it thus; for in no other space
Of all this town, save only in this place,
Feel I a wind, that soundeth so like pain;
It saith, Alas, why severed are we twain?

A weary while in pain he tosseth thus,
Till fully past and gone was the ninth night;
And ever at his side stood Pandarus,
Who busily made use of all his might
To comfort him, and make his heart more light;
Giving him always hope, that she the morrow
Of the tenth day will come, and end his sorrow.

---

151 my] mine *CM*
163 night] hour *MS. 151.2*
164 ever] even *CM, MS. 151.2*
166 more] too *CM*
167 she *rev from* the *MS. 151.2*

The Manciple, (from the Prologue) And his Tale

A Manciple there was, one of a Temple
Of whom all Caterers might take example
Wisely to purchase stores, whate'er the amount,
Whether he paid or took them on account:
So well on every bargain did he wait,
He was beforehand aye in good estate:
Now is not that of God a full fair grace
That one Man's natural sense should so surpass
The wisdom of a heap of learned men.
Of masters he had more than three times ten
That were in law expert and curious,
Of which there was a dozen in that house
Fit to be stewards over land and rent
For any Lord in England, competent
Each one to make him live upon his own
In debtless honor, were his wits not flown;
Or sparely live even to his hearts desire;
Men who could give good help to a whole Shire
In any urgent case that might befal,
Yet could this Manciple outwit them all.

The Manciple's Tale

When Phœbus took delight on earth to dwell
Among mankind as ancient stories tell
He was the blithest Bachelor I trow
Of all this world, and the best Archer too:

Prologue missing MS. 36
5 So well on every *rev from* At all times for his *MS. 89 del to* So well for every *del to text MS. 89*
6 He was beforehand aye *rev from* And thus he kept himself *this revision was first canceled and "stet" written to retain the first reading, then it was reentered MS. 89*
8 natural sense *rev from* Mother-wit *MS. 89*
13–15 *rev from* All worthy to be Stewards of land and rent
Unto the wealthiest Lord, so [*rev to* men] provident
To [*rev to* And sage to] make him live out of his own *MS. 89*
14 England *rev from* Engl[?ish] *MS. 89*
16 debtless *rev from* deathless *MS. 89*
17 *rev from* Or live, if [*rev from* of] such were his desire *MS. 89* even *rev from* up *MS. 89*
18 could give *rev from* were able [?] *MS. 89*
title The Manciple's Tale *MS. 36*
1 took delight] here below *MS. 36* to] did *MS. 36*
2 As ancient histories to us do [*rev from* to] tell *MS. 36*
3 blithest] comeliest *MS. 36*
4 and the best] the bravest *MS. 36*

He slew the serpent Python as he lay
Sleeping against the sun upon a day
And many another worthy noble deed
Wrought with his bow as men the same may read.
He played all music played on earthly ground
And 'twas a melody to hear the sound
Of his clear voice—so sweetly could he sing
Certes Amphion that old Theban King
Who wall'd a city with his minstrelsy
Was never heard to sing so sweet as he.
Therewith this Phœbus was the seemliest man
That is or hath been since the world began.
His features to describe I need not strive;
For in this world is none so fair alive;
He was moreover full of gentleness
Of honor and of perfect worthiness.
    This Phœbus flower in forest and in court
This comely Bachelor, for his disport,
And eke in token of his victory earned
Of Python, as is from the story learned,
Was wont to carry in his hand a bow.
Now had this Phœbus in his house a Crow
Which in a cage he fostered many a day
And taught to speak as men will teach a jay.
White was this Crow as is a snow-white Swan;
And counterfeit the speech of every man
He could, when he had mind to tell a tale;
Besides, in all this world no Nightingale
Could ring out of his heart so blithe a peal;
No, not a hundred thousandth part as well.
    Now had this Phœbus in his House a Wife,
Whom he loved better than he loved his life,
And, night and day, he strove with diligence
To please her and to do her reverence;
Save only, for 'tis truth, the noble Elf
Was jealous and would keep her to himself:

---

15 Therewith] Thereto *MS. 36*
16 hath been] was even *MS. 36*
17 need] will *MS. 36*
22 comely *left blank MS. 36*
23 earned] earn'd *MS 36;* earned *rev from* won *MS. 89*
24 the *inserted MS. 89*
28 will] do *MS. 36* do *rev to* will *MS. 89*
30 every *rev from* any *MS. 36*
31 he had] he [ha *del*] had *MS. 89*
32 Besides *rev from* Therewith, *MS. 89*
33 heart] throat *MS. 36*
35 House *over illeg eras MS. 89*
36 And her he loved better than his life, *MS. 36*
39 for *over illeg eras MS. 89*   Elf [was jealous *del*] *MS. 89*

For he was loth a laughing stock to be
And so is every wight in like degree;
But all for nought,—for it availeth nought;
A good Wife that is pure in deed and thought
Should not be kept in watch and ward—and, do
The best you may, you cannot keep a Shrew.
It will not be,—vain labour is it wholly;
Lordings! this hold I for an arrant folly,
Labour to waste in custody of Wives;
And so old Clerks have written in their lives.
    But to my purpose as I first began.
This worthy Phœbus doeth all he can
To please her; weening that thro' such delight
And of his government and manhood's right
No man should ever put him from her grace;
But man's best pains, God knoweth, in no case
Shall compass to constrain a thing which nature
Hath naturally implanted in a Creature.
    Take any Bird and put it in a cage
And wait upon this Bird as nurse or page
To feed it tenderly with meat and drink
And every dainty whereof thou canst think,
And also keep it cleanly as thou may;
Altho' the cage of gold be never so gay,
Yet had this Bird by twenty thousand fold
Rather in forest that is wild and cold
Go feed on worms and such like wretchedness:
For ever will this Bird do more or less
To escape out of his cage whene'er he may:
His liberty the Bird desireth aye.
    Go take a Cat, and nourish her with milk
And tender flesh, and make her couch of silk
And let her see a mouse go by the wall,
Anon she waiveth milk and flesh and all,

---

42 in like degree;] as loth as he: *MS. 36*
46 may] can *MS. 36*
49 waste] *rev from* lose *MS. 89* lose *MS. 36*
53 weening *rev from* weeting *MS. 89* weening, *MS. 36* thro' *rev from* by *MS. 89* by *MS. 36*
54 of] for *MS. 36*
56 *rev from* But in good truth no man in any case *del to* But mortal man God *del MS. 89* But in God's truth there may no man take place *MS. 36*
57 Shall compass] Of Nature *MS. 36*
58 implanted] planted *MS. 36*
60 And to this little bird thyself engage *MS. 36*
63 also keep it] keep it also *MS. 36*
65 had *MS. 36* hath *MS. 89*
66 Rather] Liever *del to* Liefer *MS. 36*
67 such like] on such *MS. 36*
71 and *inserted MS. 89* nourish] foster *MS. 36*
74 waiveth] *left blank MS. 36*

And every dainty which is in that house
Such appetite has she to eat the mouse.
Behold the domination here of kind,
Appetite drives discretion from her mind.
  A she-wolf also in her kind is base;
Meets she the sorriest Wolf in field or chase
Him will she take—what matters his estate
In time when she hath liking to a Mate.
  Examples all for men that are untrue.
With women I have nothing now to do.
For men have still a wayward appetite
With lower thing to seek for their delight
Than with their wives, albeit women fair
Never so true, never so debonair.
All flesh is so newfangled, plague upon't,
That we are pleased with aught on whose clear front
Virtue is stampt, 'tis but for a brief while.
  This Phœbus, he that thought upon no guile
Deceived was for all his jollity,
For under him another one had she,
One of small note and little thought upon
Nought worth to Phœbus in comparison:
The more harm is, it happeneth often so
Of which there cometh mickle harm and woe.
  And so befel as soon as Phœbus went
From home, his Wife hath for her Lemman sent,
Her Lemman! certes that's a knavish speech;
Forgive it me, and that I you beseech.
  Plato the wise hath said, as ye may read
The word must needs be suited to the deed:
No doubtful meanings in a tale should lurk,
The word must aye be cousin to the work.

---

76 *line inserted MS. 89* has] hath *MS. 36*
77 Behold] Lo! here *MS. 36* here of] of her *MS. 36*
78 Appetite . . . discretion] And appetite drives judgement *MS. 36*
79 *rev from* A she wolf in her kind, also is [*rev from* is alsō] base *MS. 89*
79–80 *in* British Poets—*WL I, 172, there is a pencil line in the right margin, just underneath this couplet, probably related to revisions in both MS. 13 and MS. 89*
81 matters] matter *MS. 36*
82 a] her *MS. 36*
83 untrue. *MS. 13* untrue *MS. 89*
85 wayward] *rev from* froward *MS. 89* liquorish *MS. 36*
86 With] On *MS. 36* thing *rev from* things *MS. 89* seek for] accomplish *MS. 36, which ends here*
89 All *rev from* For *del back to* All *MS. 89*
92 that *rev from* thou
94 one *rev from* choice *MS. 89*
95 One *rev from* A *MS. 89*
98 Of *rev from* From *MS. 89*
100 his Wife *inserted MS. 89; in* British Poets—*WL I, 173, a pencil signal in the right margin indicates the omission in MS. 89*
106 cousin *rev from* cozen *MS. 89*

I am a bold blunt man, I speak out plain;
There is no difference truly, not a grain,
Between a wife that is of high degree
(If of her body she dishonest be)
And any low-born Wench no more than this
(If it so be that both have done amiss)
That, as the gentle is in state above,
She shall be called his Lady and his Love
And that the other a poor woman is
She should be called his harlot and his miss;
And yet in very truth mine own dear brother!
Men lay as low that one as lies this other.
Right so betwixt a haughty tyrant Chief
And a rough Outlaw or an errant thief,
The same I say, no difference I hold
(To Alexander was this sentence told)
But for the Tyrant is of greater might
By force of multitudes to slay downright
And burn both house and home, and make all plain,
Lo! therefore Captain is he called: again
Since the other heads a scanty company
And may not do so great a harm as he
Nor lay upon the land such heavy grief
Men christen him an outlaw or a thief.
    But I'm no man of texts and instances
Therefore I will not tell you much of these
But with my tale go on as I was bent—
    When Phœbus' wife had for her Lemman sent,
In their loose dalliance they anon engage:
This white Crow, that hung alway in the cage
Beheld the shame and did not say one word:
But soon as home was come, Phœbus, the Lord
The Crow sang Cuckow, Cuckow, Cuckow, "how

---

111 And *rev from* Than *MS. 89*
112 it so *rev from* so it *MS. 89*
113 as the *rev from* for that *MS. 89*
117 very *rev from* God's good *MS. 89* dear *inserted MS. 89*
118 that . . . this *rev from* this . . . that *MS. 89*
119 a haughty tyrant Chief *rev from* an outlaw, Robber chief *MS. 89*
120 And a rough Outlaw *rev from* Untitled Tyrant *MS. 89; in* British Poets—*WL I, 173, pencil signals in right margin are connected with this revision* rough *rev from* poor *del to* wild *del MS. 89*
126 again *rev from* but then *MS. 89*
127 Since *rev from* As *MS. 89*
129 Nor *rev from* Or *MS. 89*
130 outlaw or *rev from* tyrant and *MS. 89*
132 Therefore *rev from* And therefore *MS. 89*
135 In *rev from* Anon *MS. 89*
136 alway *rev from* always *MS. 89*

What, bird!" quoth Phœbus, "what song singst thou now,
Wert thou not wont to sing as did rejoice
My inmost heart so merrily thy voice
Greeted my ear, alas! what song is this?"
"So help me Gods, I do not sing amiss:
Phœbus" quoth he "for all thy worthiness
For all thy beauty and all thy gentleness
For all thy song and all thy minstrelsy
For all thy waiting, hood-winked is thine eye
By one we know not whom, we know not what,
A man to thee no better than a gnat,
For I full plainly as I hope for life
Saw him in guilty converse with thy wife."
What would you more, the Crow anon him told
By serious tokens and words stout and bold
How that his Wife had play'd a wanton game
To his abasement, and exceeding shame
And told him oft he saw it with his eyes.
Then Phœbus turned away in woeful guise:
Him thought his heart would burst in two with sorrow,
His bow he bent, and set therein an arrow
And in his anger he his wife did slay:
This is the effect, there is no more to say.
For grief of which he brake his minstrelsy
Both lute and harp, guitar, and psaltery
And also brake his arrows and his bow
And after that thus spake he to the Crow.
"Thou Traitor! with thy scorpion tongue" quoth he
"To my confusion am I brought by thee.
Why was I born, why have I yet a life?
O Wife, o gem of pleasure, o dear Wife
That wert to me so stedfast and so true
Now dead thou lièst with face pale of hue
Full innocent, that durst I swear, I wis.
O thou rash hand that wrought so far amiss!
O reckless outrage, O disordered wit
That unadvised didst the guiltless smite.

141–142 *in* British Poets—*WL, I, 173, there is a pencil mark, perhaps deleted, in the right margin next to this couplet*

150 A *rev from* By one, a *MS. 89*
157 his *inserted MS. 89*
159 heart would burst in two with sorrow *rev from* doleful heart would burst in two *MS. 89*
160 set . . . arrow *rev from* arrow forth he drew *MS. 89*
161 slay *ed.* stay *MS. 89*
163 grief *rev from* sorrow *MS. 89*
165 arrows *rev from* arrow *MS. 89*
166 that *rev from* this *MS. 89*
174 hand *rev from* head *MS. 89*
176 didst . . . guiltless *rev from* did . . . guilty *MS. 89*

What in my false suspicion have I done,
Why thro' mistrust was I thus wrought upon?"
   Let every man beware and keep aloof
From rashness and trust only to strong proof:
Smite not too soon before ye have learnt why
And be advised well and stedfastly
Ere ye to any execution bring
Yourselves from wrath on surmise of a thing.
Alas! a thousand folk hath ire laid low
Fully undone and brought to utter woe,
Alas, for sorrow I myself will slay."
   And to the Crow, "O vile wretch" did he say
"Now will I thee requite for thy false tale.
Whilom thou sung like any Nightingale
Henceforth, false thief, thy song from thee is gone
And vanished thy white feathers, every one,
In all thy life thou nevermore shalt speak.
Thus on a traitor I men's wrongs do wreak!
Thou and thy offspring ever shall be black,
ever again sweet noises shall ye make
But ever cry against the storm and rain
In token that through thee my Wife is slain."
   And to the Crow he sprang and that anon
And plucking his white feathers left not one
And made him black, and took from him his song
And eke his speech and out of doors him flung
Unto perdition, whither let him go;
And for this very reason, you must know,
Black is the colour now of every Crow.
   Lordings by this example you I pray
Beware and take good heed of what you say
Nor ever tell a Man in all your life
That he hath got a false and slippery Wife;
His deadly hatred till his life's last day
You will provoke. Dan Solomon, clerks say,
For keeping well the tongue—hath rules good store;
But I'm no Textman, as I said before.
Nathless this teaching had I from my Dame
"My Son think of the Crow in God's good name:
My Son full oftentimes hath mickle speech

---

178 thro' *over illeg eras MS. 89*

179 aloof *rev from* aloof from rashness *MS. 89*

180 *rev from* Trusting nought without strong proof *MS. 89; in* British Poets—*WL I, 173, erased pencil* [?only] *in right margin next to l. 180 is connected with this revision*

183 bring *rev from* bring yourselves *MS. 89*

184 from . . . on *rev from* in. . .for *MS. 89*

187 sorrow *rev from* anger *MS. 89*

192 vanished *rev from* also *MS. 89; in* British Poets—*WL I, 173, a pencil mark in right margin is probably connected to this revision*

Brought many a Man to ruin as Clerks teach,
But 'tis not often words bring harm to men
Spoken advisedly and now and then.
My Son be like the wise man who restrains
His tongue at all times, save when taking pains
To speak of God in honor, and in prayer.
Tis the first virtue, and the one most rare
My Son, to keep the tongue with proper care.
Wouldst thou be told what a rash tongue can do?
Right as a sword cutteth an arm in two
So can a tongue, my Child, a friendship sever
Parted in two to be disjoined for ever.
A babbler is to God abominable
Read Solomon so wise and honorable.
Read Seneca, the Psalms of David read.
Speak not dear Son, but beckon with thy head.
Make show that thou wert deaf if any Prater
Do in thy hearing touch a perilous matter.
The Fleming taught, and learn it if thou list
That little babbling causeth mickle rest.
My Son if thou no wicked word have said
Then need'st thou have no fear to be betrayed;
But who misspeaks, whatever may befal,
Cannot by any means his word recal.
Thing that is said, *is* said, goes forth anon
Howe'er we grieve repenting, it is gone.
The tale-bearer's his Slave to whom he said
The thing for which he now is fitly paid.
My Son beware, and be not Author new
Of tidings whether they be false or true.
Where'er thou travel, among high or low
Keep well thy tongue and think upon the Crow.

---

218 often *inserted MS. 89*
227 my *rev from* dear *MS. 89*
230 *line inserted MS. 89*
232 but *over illeg eras, del following* Son, *MS. 89*
233 Prater] Traitor *rev to* Prator *del to* Prater *MS. 89*
237 have *rev from* hath *MS. 89*
247 among *inserted MS. 89*

Editor's Notes

The Prioress's Tale

The motto is from Milton's *Il Penseroso,* ll. 109–110.

1 wonderously] Chaucer's word is "merveillous"; WW used "marvelous" in MS. 35. "Mervaille" is glossed "wonder, marvel" in Anderson, who reprinted Thomas Tyrwhitt's glossary from his highly regarded edition of *The Canterbury Tales* (1775–1778). This glossary is based on all the poems Tyrwhitt accepted as genuinely Chaucer's, including *The Cuckoo and the Nightingale.*

14 goodness] Chaucer's word is "bountee" here and in l. 22, and is preserved in Wordsworth's MS. 35 version. Anderson's glossary gives "goodness" as a translation for "bountee."

51 scholar] De Selincourt notes that Chaucer's "clergeon" should be translated "chorister," but Anderson's glossary has "young clerk." *OED* gives both meanings. Dowden, p. 21n, is helpful here: "Professor Skeat, in his Clarendon Press *Selections from Chaucer,* cites Du Cange: '*Clergonus,* junior vel puer choralis; jeune clerc, petit clerc ou enfant de choeur;' and Cotgrave, '*Clergeon,* a singing man, or Quirester in a Queer.'"

61 WW has added this line to the stanza, in violation of Chaucer's text and verse form. Apparently he was trying to preserve the full sense of "sely" in Chaucer's l. 60: "For sely childe wol away [Urry's error for "alway"] sonè lere." The line was apparently a favorite of WW's, for he quotes it as if it were Chaucer's in *Ecclesiastical Sonnets,* II, 31, l. 1.

65–66 Chaucer's lines are: "This litel child his litel book lerning, / As he sat in the scole at his primere. . . ." Dowden, p. 23, objects to WW's version of this line because it violates Chaucer's simplicity, and then remarks: "Besides, the pious boy cared not for the secular learning of his primer; his heart being set on Mary's praise, he by and by looked forward to being shent for his primer; even to being beaten for his neglect of it thrice in an hour." WW's earlier version of the lines, in DC MS. 35, is not open to this objection: "This little Child learning his little book / As he sat at his primer in the school. . . ."

113 our] "youre" is the now-accepted reading, but Anderson has "our."

122 Chaucer is more concrete: "Wher as thise Jewes purgen hir entraille." Hodder remarks that WW's translation "produces a stylistic 'toning down' of the Prioress's evident intention to arouse the disgusted indignation of her hearers by making a pointed contrast between the 'sweetness' of the 'litel clergeon' and his sordid fate." The version in MS. 35 is awkward and unmetrical, but closer to the riginal: "Where these Jews their things unclean did trail."

128 'stablished] Chaucer says "souded," glossed in Anderson as "consolidated, fastened together."

156–158 The rhyming of "laud" and "emerald" is from Chaucer, where the latter is spelled "emeraude."

174 Apparently WW intended "Bier" to be pronounced as if it had two syllables. This problem was eliminated in 1845, when "bier" was revised to "body."

187 "Then sped themselves" is written in WW's hand on p. 123 of vol. I of *British Poets*—Folger.

217 "Soon as" is written in WW's hand on p. 123 of vol. I of *British Poets*—Folger.

231 The manuscript versions of this line reflect Chaucer's text more nearly: "his litel body sweete." WW apparently felt that "sweet" implied something about the freshness of the body (as in *OED* definition 3), and thus the revision to "uncorrupted." Dowden's complaint (p. 22) that in this line "the simplicity and innocence of Chaucer are lost" is just.

235 The 1836 revision, which reinstated the original MS. 13 version of the line, is much closer to Chaucer's "For it n'is but a litel while ago." See Transcriptions, p. 129.

The Cuckoo and the Nightingale

Title Called *The boke of Cupid, god of love* in the manuscripts that give it a title, this poem was called *The Cuckoo and the Nightingale* in William Thynne's edition of Chaucer in 1532. It was thought to be Chaucer's from the publication of Thynne's edition until late in the nineteenth century, but manuscript Ff. I. 6, in the Cambridge University Library, clearly states "explicit Clanvowe" at the end. Skeat, who discovered Clanvowe's authorship, thought it by Thomas Clanvowe, but Scattergood, pp. 22–27, has argued more recently for the authorship of John Clanvowe, a friend of Chaucer and perhaps the uncle or father of Thomas.

1–2 These lines are a quotation from *The Knight's Tale*, ll. 1785–1786.

20 As de Selincourt notes, the best texts of the poem read "And most his myght he sheweth euer in May"—but Anderson, who reprinted John Urry's 1721 edition of the minor poems, has "And most his might he shedith er in May." Urry is following (and regularizing the meter of) the 1687 reprint of Speght, which has "And most his might he shedeth ever in May."

39 Anderson's text reads, incorrectly, "Bothe hot and cold, and axis every day": "and axis" should read "an accesse" (the error can be traced to Thynne's 1532 edition of Chaucer's works). In this case, WW's "heart-aches" is reasonably close to "accesse," defined in Anderson's glossary as "properly the approach of a fever, a fever." The glossary has no entry for "axis." Interestingly enough, Urry's glossary defines "axis" as "A Feaver. See Accesse," and "Accesse" is defined as in Tyrwhitt.

64 Anderson's text reads "The flouris and the grevis alike hie," reproducing an error ("grevis" for "gras") first appearing in Thynne's edition and reproduced in Speght and Urry. "Grevis" is glossed as "groves" in Anderson's glossary.

67 Dowden, p. 26, claimed that the original text reads "And saw the briddes crepe out of her boures," but in Anderson and all the printed editions up to WW's time, the "briddes trippe." Of the five surviving manuscripts, two have "crepe," two have "trippe," and one has "flee." And in Skeat, too, the "briddes trippe."

70 Again an error in Anderson's text has led WW astray. Anderson, following Urry, has "honouris," whereas all of the manuscripts and printed editions before Urry have "houres" or "hours." WW, following Anderson, thus has the birds doing honors to May, but the line actually means that they observe the equivalent of canonical hours in their worship of May.

72 This is an example of Urry's notorious attempts to correct a seemingly unmetrical line; his "And ther was many a full lovely note" reads "There was mony a lovely note" in all but one manuscript and in the earlier printed editions. WW's "many and many" attempts to reproduce this corruption of the text.

85 An awkward rendering of "That mightin ben yherde of any mon." In MS. 13, the line is translated more literally: "That ever might be heard of any man," revised to "by living man." See Transcriptions, p. 119.

89 WW's "unholy" is an attempt to render two adjectives in the Middle English: "sorry" and "leude." The version in MS. 13 again is closer to the original, where he retains "sorry" and translates "leude" as "unholy," but has not perfected the rhymes. See Transcriptions, p. 119. WW apparently felt uncomfortable in rendering "leude"; in l. 50 above, he translated it as "vile," revised from "sorry" in MS. 13. Hodder believes that this line is an example of WW's giving "priority to preserving the rhyme-scheme over other considerations."

100 WW follows Anderson's text word for word here, but the text is corrupt: "Echoing" (in Anderson "Ecchoing") has no manuscript authority. Speght has "Through all the greene wood wide." This is another instance in which Urry attempted to regularize the meter.

103 Anderson has "leude sory Cuckow," but "sory" has no manuscript authority and is Urry's addition. Speght has "For here hath ben the leaud cuckow."

105 A restrained rendering of "I pray to God that evil fire her bren!"

115 "Uncouth" is a translation of "elenge," glossed in Anderson as "strange. . . . It sometimes seems to signify dull, cheerless. . . ."

119 "Quaver" is a translation of "crakil," glossed in Anderson as "to quaver hoarsely in singing." Two manuscripts read "crakil," one reads "crake," and two read "breke hit".

171–172 According to Conran, p. 68, these lines anticipate ll. 48–49 of "Resolution and Independence": "We poets in our youth begin in gladness / But thereof come in the end despondency and madness."

180 WW has mistranslated, and the mistranslation is again owing to his use of Anderson.

In Anderson, as in Urry, the line reads: "He maie full sone of age yhave his haire" ("haire" is glossed as "haircloth"). Urry is following Speght. But no manuscript has "haire." Two have "crie" (an obvious error, since it does not rhyme), one has "aire," and two (as well as Thynne) have different spellings of "heyre," modern English "heir." The line actually means that "very soon his heir will come of age."

185 De Selincourt's note that "Wordsworth misses the point here" is misleading. In Anderson, the text is: "And then thou shalt yhotin as do I." (Skeat and Scattergood and all the manuscripts read "hoten." In fact, "yhotin" is yet another of Urry's attempts to regularize the meter.) *OED* cites this line as meaning "hoot," but there is a clear pun on "hoten," "to be called." If the nightingale does "raise a clamour" like a cuckoo, then it is crying "cuckoo," and the cuckoo-cuckold pun that de Selincourt says is lost is partly preserved.

200 Anderson's text reads: "That for defaute of courage he let 'hem spill." Urry's text reads: "That for defaute of courage he let' hem spill," indicating an elision which Anderson's reprint obscures. The manuscripts all read "grace" for "courage." The corrupt text originated in Thynne's 1532 edition and was subsequently reprinted; it may explain Wordsworth's rather free rendering of the line. In MS. 13 WW was closer to Anderson: "That for distress of mind themselves they kill," revised to "That in default of hearts. . . ." See Transcriptions, p. 105.

201n There are four manuscripts of *The Cuckoo and the Nightingale* in the Bodleian: Fairfax 16 (F), Bodley 638 (B), Arch. Selden B. 24 (S), and Tanner 346 (T). S has "hurtith" and "helith" in l. 203, readings unique to that manuscript. T, which is closely related to the manuscript source of Anderson's corrupt text, omits stanza 41 and ll. 217–219, 224–225, and thus cannot be the manuscript WW is referring to. F and B, two of the best manuscripts of the poem, have "lyeth" and "fayleth" where S has "hurtith" and "helith." On this basis we might conclude that it was S that WW consulted. But in ll. 202 and 225, WW's translation is closer to F and B: where S says "blynde alweye and," F and B say "blynde and," and where F and B say "fer al out of sight," S says "from sight out." Thus it is unclear which manuscript WW is referring to; he seems rather to be referring to a composite of the three. And in fact he is. A letter concerning the Bodleian manuscripts of *The Cuckoo and the Nightingale* appeared in *The Gentleman's Magazine* for January 1839 (this letter is quoted in full in the Introduction, pp. 24–25); it, and not the manuscripts themselves, is surely the source for WW's corrections—and they are corrections, for MS. 13 follows Anderson (see Transcriptions, p. 105). He has chosen to use the S reading of l. 203, suggested in a footnote to the letter (a reading that subsequent editors have rejected), and used F, as quoted in the letter, for ll. 202 and 225. And since the letter neglects to mention the variants in S in ll. 202 and 225, WW unwittingly has produced a modernization based on a conflation of F and S—two Bodleian manuscripts, not one. Nevertheless, WW's use of this letter gives his modernization a unique place in the history of the publication of *The Cuckoo and the Nightingale,* for it is the first publication of the complete text of the poem, whether modernized or in Middle English, to depart from the corrupt published texts and incorporate the manuscript readings of S, F, and B.

The letter to *The Gentleman's Magazine* is signed H. H.; its author is Herbert Hill, Jr., Southey's cousin and, after 1839, son-in-law. Hill was a fellow of New College, Oxford, from 1829 to 1839, and in 1837 accepted a position at the Bodleian, which he held at least until October 1838. Upon Hill's accepting the position, Southey wrote: "You will now in all likelihood apply yourself to serious literary pursuits, such as the place invites you to" (*New Letters of Robert Southey,* ed. Kenneth Curry, vol. 2 [New York, 1965], p. 463). Apparently, among those pursuits was an edition of Chaucer's minor poems, but the edition was never completed. It is likely that Hill himself supplied WW with the article from *The Gentleman's Magazine,* since he was then residing in Rydal, just down the hill from Rydal Mount. There thus remains the possibility that WW sought Hill's assistance when revising the poem.

212 Anderson, following Urry, has "leudè birdè," but all the manuscripts say "false" or "fals." Here Urry is following the earlier printed texts: Speght, for example, has "leaud bird." WW's "churlish" is yet another uneasy rendering of "leude."

232 All manuscripts but one read "amayed" for "dismaied"; Anderson's text has the latter reading, which WW has translated.

237 Anderson's text may account for the oddly inaccurate "his Love's saw." The best manuscripts simply read "the Cukkow, loves fo"; Anderson, following Urry, has "the Cuckow ne' his loves so" (with the elongated "s"). The same error is in Speght, who has: "y Cuckow, ne his loves so." WW clearly could make no sense of the line: MS. 13 has "the Cuckoo, no, no, no!"

See Transcriptions, p. 107.

243–245 WW's original version in MS. 13 is somewhat more literal. See Transcriptions, p. 107.

260 MS. 13 ends here; "Finis" is written underneath it.

291 In Urry, "*Explicit*" follows l. 290, indicating that the rest is a different poem. Anderson omitted the word, which is perhaps why WW treats ll. 291–317 as part of the same poem. But, as the note to l. 260 indicates, even in 1801 WW was uncertain about how much of the ending was genuine. Skeat, p. lxii, notes:

> This piece has always hitherto been printed *without any title*, and is made to follow The Cuckoo and the Nightingale, as if there were some sort of connection between them. This is probably because it happens to follow that poem in the Fairfax and Tanner MSS., and probably did so in the MS. used by Thynne, which has a striking resemblance to the Tanner MS. However, the poem is entirely absent from the Cambridge, Selden, and Bodley MSS., proving that there is no connection with the preceding poem, from which it differs very widely in style, in language, and in metre. . . . Briefly, it is a very poor piece; and my chief object in reprinting it is to shew how unworthy it is of Clanvowe, not to mention Chaucer. We have no right even to assign it to Lydgate. And its date may be later than 1450.

Skeat calls it an *Envoy to Alison.*

Troilus and Cresida. Extract from Chaucer.

The extract is from Book V, ll. 519–686.

8 to cover his intent] "his meinè for to blende," that is, to deceive his household. But Tyrwhitt does not gloss "meinè," and WW connects the word with "mene," glossed "to mean, to intend." Curiously, Urry glosses "meine" accurately: "A Company, a Retinue; All that live together in a House."

20 on his purpose] "as God would" in Anderson.

21 continuance] Chaucer's word is "countinaunce," modern English "countenance"; Dowden, pp. 21–22, first pointed out this error.

23 dight] "ydight" in Anderson and Urry, but Speght has "ihight," the now-accepted reading.

28 Anderson's text reads: "Sens she is went that wont was us to gie." "Gie" is glossed "to guide" in Anderson.

49 "Me captive caught first my right lady dere" in Anderson, which explains WW's awkward "captive-wise." But "captive" is one of Urry's attempts to smooth Chaucer's meter; Speght has "Me caught first my right Lady dere." WW's translation in MS. 24 is smoother: "[Fi]rst caught me captive my true Lady dear." See Transcriptions, p. 147.

50 joy-smitten heart] "ful lustily" in Anderson; "full lustily" in MS. 24. See Transcriptions, p. 147.

64 cried] "thought" in Anderson.

66 wearied] "weried" in Anderson, glossed as "to make war against." Hodder notes this error.

85–119 Quoted by Coleridge in *STCBL*, II, 92–93.

86 as if in haste she was] "a full gode paas" in Anderson.

104–105 Anderson's text reads: "And al this n'as but his melancholie, / That he had of him selfe suche fantasie." As Dowden, p. 25, was the first to note, the allusion to *Hamlet* is not Chaucerian. But perhaps more interesting is the echo or anticipation of *Resolution and Independence*, ll. 20–21, first noted by Conran, p. 68: "My old remembrances went from me wholly; / And all the ways of men, so vain and melancholy."

114 occasion] "encheson" in Anderson, glossed as "cause, occasion."

118 As Dowden, p. 25, rightly notes, "night" is not in the Middle English, nor is it in the *Chaucer Modernized* text of 1841. But it is not, as Dowden speculates, a printer's addition: it is the reading of MS. 151.2, the manuscript sent to the printer for *PELY.*

123 I steer and sail] "I stere and saile" in Anderson and the earlier printed editions, but modern texts have "in steere I saille." Dowden, p. 22, notes this error.

127–133 Quoted in *STCBL*, II, 93.

137 Luna] "Lucina" in Anderson and the earlier printed editions, glossed as "the moon."

155–156 more and more / By moments] "stoundemele" in Anderson, glossed as "momentarily, every moment."

The Manciple, (from the Prologue) And his Tale

Prologue

2 Caterers is Anderson's gloss for "achatours."

Tale

48 "Lordings" is not in Chaucer.

59–70 Hodder suggests that these lines are echoed in *Liberty*, ll. 60–70, as did BF, in his manuscript review of *CM*. De Selincourt, however, rightly states that *Liberty* echoes *The Squire's Tale*, ll. 603–609.

60 nurse or page] not in Chaucer.

66 Rather] Chaucer's word is "Lever"; MSS. 13 and 36 both have "Liever." See Transcriptions, p. 103.

85 wayward] "likerous" in Chaucer, originally rendered "liquorish" by Wordsworth in MS. 13. See Transcriptions, p. 103.

107 bold blunt] Chaucer's word is "boystous"; the original reading in MS. 13 is "boitrous" (for boistrous). See Transcriptions, p. 93.

116 harlot and his miss] "Wenche or his Lemman" in Chaucer; MS. 13 originally had "Lemman and his Miss." See Transcriptions, p. 95.

135 loose dalliance] for Chaucer's "lust volage"; originally "love and lover's rage" in MS. 13, revised to "love's delight." See Transcriptions, p. 95. Hodder singles out this line and l. 152 as examples of how Wordsworth softened the coarseness of Chaucer.

152 guilty converse] for Chaucer's "swive." MS. 13 originally had "For on thy bed I saw him with thy wife." See Transcriptions, p. 97. Hodder notes that "the expression 'criminal conversation' was still current in 1841 as a legal term meaning 'adultery.'" But she further notes that "it is a technical term quite at odds with the style of Chaucer's original poem and is hardly appropriate in the beak of a blunt-spoken crow." In *British Poets*—WL, I, 173, there is a broad line, in ink, through this passage and two ink blots near it.

155 play'd a wanton game] "doon hire lecherye."

203 Unto perdition] "Unto the devil" in Chaucer, and originally so in MS. 13. See Transcriptions, p. 111.

203–205 Wordsworth's triplet expands a couplet in Chaucer.

209 false and slippery Wife] for Chaucer's "How that another man hath dight his wif." This is another instance of Wordsworth's blunting the force of the original.

216–217 Wordsworth's translation here omits six lines of Chaucer:

> My sone, kepe wel thy tonge, and kepe thy frend;
> A wicked tonge is worse than a fend:
> My sone, from a fende men may hem blesse:
> My sone, God of his endeles goodnesse
> Walled a tonge with teeth, and lippes eke,
> For man shuld him avisen what he speke:

This is the text appearing in Anderson's *British Poets*.

229 babbler] "jangler" in Chaucer and in the original version in MS. 13. See Transcriptions, p. 113.

Nonverbal Variants

The nonverbal differences from reading texts listed here include variants in spelling, punctuation, and capitalization found in authorially influenced manuscripts and in lifetime editions, except for (1) those that appear in manuscripts presented in photographs and transcriptions, (2) those that are integral parts of verbal changes, and (3) those identified in a few special apparatuses as part of a distinctive phase of authorial or editorial revision of a complex manuscript. Also not recorded are ampersands, single-letter overwritings (corrected by the copyist), and reinforcements of punctuation marks when no change is made.

Abbreviations of lifetime printings cited are listed at the end of the Editorial Procedure. Manuscripts are identified in the Manuscript Census.

The Prioress's Tale

headnote

3 reading, . . . understanding,] reading . . . understanding *1827–* much] much, *1832–*

4 however] however, *1827–*

8 also] alsò *1836 rev to alsò MS. 1836/45 alsò 1845–* alway] alway *1820–1832* alwày *1836 rev to alwày 1836/45 alwày 1845–*

title PRIORESS'S] PRIORESS' *1836–*

epigraph "Call . . . bold." *rev to* Call . . . bold. *MS. 1836/45* 'Call . . . bold.' *1845–*

stanzas numbered I.–XXXIV. *1836–; stanzas begin with single quot 1827, double quot 1832*

1 O] 'O *1827* "O *1832–* Lord, our Lord!] Lord our lord *MS. 35* wonderously] wondrously *1820* wondrously' *1827* wondrously," *1832–*

2 Thy] 'Thy *1827* "Thy *1832–*

2, 4 *no punct MS. 35*

5 children,] Children *MS. 35*

6 forth,] forth; *1836–*

8 *no punct MS. 35*

9 thee, . . . Lily-flower] thee . . . lily flower *MS. 35*

10 thee] the *MS. 35* maid] Maid *MS. 35, 1832–*

11–14 *no punct MS. 35*

12–13 honour's . . . honour,] honor's . . . honor *MS. 35*

14 Son] Son, *1832–* soul's] souls *MS. 35*

15 O Maid] o Maid *MS. 35*

16 bush] Bush *MS. 35*

17–21 *no punct MS. 35*

20 Conceived] Conceivèd *1827–* Father's] father's *MS. 35*

22 Lady,] Lady! *MS. 35, 1845–* *no commas MS. 35*

23–24 *no punct MS. 35*

25–26 *no comma MS. 35*

26 go'st] goest *MS. 35, 1832–*

29 blissful] blisful *MS. 35*

29–60 *no punct MS. 35*

37 'Mong] Mong *MS. 35* be;] be, *1832–*

39 Lord] lord *MS. 35*

42 unbarr'd] unbarred *1820–*

43 school] School *MS. 35*

45 children] Children *MS. 35*

46 learned] learnèd *1827–*

47 used] usèd *1827–*

48 also] alsò *1827* alsò, *1832–*

50 widow's] Widow's *1832–*

61 hence,] hence *MS. 35*

62–79 *no punct MS. 35*

63 Saint] St *MS. 35*

66 primer] Primer *1845–*

68 Alma Redemptoris] *Alma Redemptoris 1820–*

72 said] said, *1827–*

77 This,] This *MS. 35, 1820–*

78 beseech,] beseech *1820–*

79 Schoolfellow] schoolfellow *MS. 35*

80 thus;—] thus; *MS. 35* thus:— *1820–* "This] This *MS. 35* 'This *1832–* *no commas MS. 35*

81–108 *no punct MS. 35*

83 day.] day: *1836–*

84 this] this, *1832–*

85 got.] got." *1827* got.' *1832–*

86 "And] '"And *1827* "'And *1832* 'And *1836–*
87 Mother?"] Mother?' *1832–* Innocent,] Inocent *rev to* Innocent *MS. 35* Innocent; *1832–*
88 "Now, certes,] "Now, certès, *1827* 'Now, certès, *1832–*
89 ere] 'ere *MS. 35*
90 Primer] primmer *MS. 35*
92 power."] power.' *1832–*
93 Schoolfellow] schoolfellow *MS. 35*
94 privily;] privily *1845–*
97 passed] passèd *1827–*
100 I,)] I) *1832–*
101 child,] Child, *1832–*
103 Alma Redemptoris!] Alma Redemptoris! *1820RD Alma Redemtoris! 1820–*
104 pierced] piercèd *1827–*
108 Jew's] Jews *MS. 35* upswell'd—] upswell'd *MS. 35* upswelled—*1820–* "O] O *MS. 35* 'O *1832–*
109 people!"] people! *MS. 35* people!' *1832–* *no comma MS. 35*
110 "Is] 'Is *1832–*
111 Boy,] Boy *MS. 35, 1820–*
112–122 *no punct MS. 35*
113 laws!"] laws!' *1832–1836, 1845–* laws! *1840–1843*
114 conspired] conspir'd *MS. 35*
115 chace] chase *MS. 35, 1827–*
117 Alley] alley *1836–*
118 School] school *1836–*
122 pit] pit, *1827–*
123 away] away, *1827–*
124 *no punct MS. 35*
125 fail;] fail *MS. 35*
127 accursed] accursèd *1827–*
128 'established in virginity!] stablished in Virginity *MS. 35*
128–131 *no punct MS. 35*
129 may'st] mayest *1820–1832*
130 celestial,"] celestial,' *1827–1832* quoth she,] (quoth she) *MS. 35*
131 "Of] 'Of *1827–1832*
132 Saint John,] St John *MS. 35*
133–136 *no punct MS. 35*
134 know.] know.' *1832*
135 widow] Widow *MS. 35*
138 thought] thought, *1832–*
139–146 *no punct MS. 35*
147 brought,] brought *MS. 35*
148–151 *no punct MS. 35*
151 Child] child *1820–* pass'd] passed *MS. 35, 1820–*
152 said Nay; but] said, Nay; But *MS. 35* said, Nay; but *1832* said—Nay; but *1836–*
155–156 *no punct MS. 35*
157 might;] might *MS. 35*
158 emerald] Emerald *MS. 35*
158–161 *no punct MS. 35*
159 ruby] Ruby *MS. 35*
161 Alma Redemptoris] *Alma Redemptoris 1820–*
162 loud] loud, *MS. 35, 1827–* ring.] ring *MS. 35* ring, *1820*
163 Through] Thro' *MS. 35*
164–179 *no punct MS. 35*
165 Provost] provost *MS. 35*
166 came] came, *1832–*
168 honour of Mankind:] honor of mankind *MS. 35*
169 bade] bad *MS. 35*
171 alway;] alwày *1832– rev to* al*wày* *MS. 1836/45*
174 Mother] mother *MS. 35*
176 Rachel] Rachiel *MS. 35* Bier] bier *MS. 35, 1836–*
182 draw,] draw *MS. 35* draw. *1850*
183–189 *no punct MS. 35*
184 Bier] bier *1836–*
185 Altar] altar *1836–*
186 Convent's] convent's *1836–*
190 Alma Redemptoris Mater!] *Alma Redemptoris Mater! 1820–*
191 man,] Man *MS. 35*
192–193 *no punct MS. 35*
194 "O] O *MS. 35* 'O *1832–* Child!] Child *MS. 35*
196–203 *no punct MS. 35*
197 seem."] seem.' *1832–1841, 1845, 1850* seem. *1843, 1846*
198 "My] '"My *1827* "'My *1832* 'My *1836–* trow,"] trow,' *1832–*
199 "and] 'and *1832–*
204 Alma!] *Alma! 1820–* *no comma, no period MS. 35*
205 This] 'This *MS. 35, 1836–* '"This *1827* "'This *1832* 'This *rev to* This *MS. 1836/45* well] Well *MS. 35* mercy . . . sweet] mercy, . . . sweet, *1836–*
206 alway,] alwày, *1832* alway; *1836–*
206–208 *no punct MS. 35*
209 Thou] 'Thou *1827, 1836–1843* lay,"] lay" *MS. 35* lay,' *1827, 1836–1843*
211–217 *no punct MS. 35*
212 Wherefore] "'Wherefore *1832* 'Wherefore *1836–* 'Wherefore *rev to* Wherefore *MS. 1836/45*
213 honour] honor *MS. 35*
214 'Till] Till *MS. 35, 1827–* *no hyphen MS. 35*

215 me,] me; *1836–*
216 "My] 'My *1827, 1836–1843*
217 take,] take: *1832–*
218 dismay'd] dismayed *1820–*
forsake!"] forsake *MS. 35*
forsake!' *1827, 1836–1843*
forsake!'" *1832, 1845, 1850*
219 This] 'This *1827*
219–229 *no punct MS. 1836*
220 Touched] Touch'd *MS. 35*
223 rain,] rain; *1836–*
228 way] way, *1832–*
229 Bier] bier *MS. 35, 1836–*
230 marble] Marble *MS. 35*
231 Enclos'd] Enclosed *1820–*
234 cursed] cursèd *1850*
236–239 *no punct MS. 35*
239 Mary!] Mary!' *1827* Mary!" *1832–*

The Cuckoo and the Nightingale

stanzas numbered in arabic numbers, CM

1 Love—*ah, benedicite!*] Love, ah benedicitè *Calvert MS.* Love, ah! benedicìte! *rev from* love, ah! benedicìte! *Cornell MS.*
5 hard *rev from* herd *Calvert MS.*
free.] free! *Calvert MS.*
6 time,] time *CM*
7 sound:] sound; *CM*
11 suffice;] suffice, *CM*
28 rememberance] remembrance *1845–*
29 sorrowing;] sorrowing, *CM*
35 martyrdom] Martyrdom *CM rev from* Martyrdom *MS. 151.2 (WW)*
41 keep] keep, *CM*
50 utterèd] utteréd *CM*
60 brook-side;] brook-side. *CM rev to* brookside; *MS. 151.2 (WW)*
68 they,] they *CM*
70 honour] *rev from* onour *MS. 151.2 (WW)*
83 Birds'] birds' *CM*
88 wholly;] wholly, *CM*
89 Cuckoo,] Cuckoo *CM*
103 had] heard *CM*
106 pray;] pray, *CM rev to* pray; *MS. 151.2 (WW)*
107 swooning-fit] swooning fit *CM*
155 mirth;] mirth: *CM*
175 poverty,] poverty *CM*
201 be*;] be*, *CM*
217 ran] ran, *CM*
222 —farewell, Popinjay!] —farewell Popinjay! *CM*
241 medicine;] medicine, *CM rev from* medicine *MS. 151.3*
260 bird] Bird *CM*
286 thankèd] thankéd *CM*
288 tree— *rev from* tree,— *MS. 151.3 (JC)* tree,— *CM*
289 "For] 'For *1850* me"— *rev from* me!" *MS. 151.3 (WW)*
301 fit!] fit; *CM*
307 stedfastness, *rev from* steadfastness, *MS. 151.3 (WW)*
310 liking] liking, *CM*
312 PLEASURE'S AURORA] Pleasure's Aurora *1845–*
314 *The concluding "e" of* goodnesse *underlined with an accompanying marginal check mark, apparently as a confirmation of the spelling MS. 151.3 (JC)*

Troilus and Cresida. Extract from Chaucer.

3 Pandarus *rev to* Pandrus *MS. 151.2* Brother] brother *CM*
9 Town] town *CM*
13 fast bolted] fast-bolted *CM, MS. 151.2*
15 behold,] behold *CM*
18 changèd, pale,] changéd pale *CM* changèd pale *MS. 151.2*
19 uttered] utter'd *CM* uttered *rev to* utter'd *MS. 151.2*
23 dight!] dight; *MS. 151.2, CM*
25 lamp] Lamp, *CM*
29 O,] O *MS. 151.2, CM*
crownèd] crowned *MS. 151.2, CM*
34 rout;] rout: *CM*
37 changèd] changéd *CM*
39 Aye] Aye, *CM*
44 everything] every thing *MS. 151.2, CM* rememberànce] rememberánce *CM*
47 Lady] lady *CM*
54 Now, . . . well,] Now . . . well *MS. 151.2, CM* pray!] pray; *CM, MS. 151.2*
58 beloved] belovèd *CM*
59 womanly,] womanly *MS. 151.2, CM*
60 clear,] clear *MS. 151.2*
67 me,] me *CM, MS. 151.2*
68 me,] me *CM*
71 provoked] provoked, *1845–*
73 know'st] knowest *MS. 151.2, CM*
80 sojourn.] sojourn, *MS. 151.2*
81 Now,] Now *MS. 151.2*
86 Cresid] Cresida *CM*
89 hope,] hope *CM*
91 Troy!] Troy. *CM, MS. 151.2*
94 Father] father *CM*
118 Lady] lady *CM, MS. 151.2*
120 star] Star *CM, MS. 151.2*

146 Phäeton] Phæton *MS. 151.2* Phaeton *CM*
147 father's] Father's *CM, MS. 151.2*
151 Lo!] Lo, *CM*
156 face] face, *CM, MS. 151.2*
161 Alas *rev from* alas *MS. 151.2* twain?] twain. *CM, MS. 151.2*
163 past] passed *1850*
164 Pandarus] Pindarus *MS. 151.2*

The Manciple, (from the Prologue) And his Tale

Prologue

4 account: *rev from* account,— *MS. 89*
11 curious, *ed* curious *MS. 89*

The Manciple's Tale

4 world,] world *MS. 36* too: *ed* too *MSS. 13, 36, 89*
8 read.] read *MS. 36*
9 played, *then comma deleted MS. 89* play'd . . . play'd *MS. 36*
11 voice—] voice *MS. 36*
14 he. *ed* he *MSS. 13, 36, 89*
16 began.] began *MS. 36*
17 describe] discribe *MS. 36* strive;] strive *MS. 36*
18 alive; *ed* alive *MSS. 13, 36, 89*
20 honor] honour *MS. 36* worthiness.] worthiness *MS. 36*
22 Bachelor, *ed* Bachelor *MS. 89* disport, *MSS. 13, 36* disport *MS. 89*
24 learned, *MS. 13* learn'd, *MS. 36* learned *MS. 89*
25 bow. *MS. 36* bow.— *rev from* bow,— *MS. 13* bow *followed by either period or dash MS. 89*
27 fostered] foster'd *MS. 36*
28 jay. *MS. 13* jay *MS. 89* Jay. *rev from* jay. *MS. 36*
29 swan;] swan *MS. 36*
30 counterfeit] countirfeit *MS. 36*
31 could, *MSS. 13, 36* could *MS. 89* tale;] tale: *MS. 36*
33 peal;] peal *MS. 36*
34 No,] No *MS. 36*
35 House . . . Wife,] house . . . Wife *MS. 36* a *MSS. 13, 36* a a *MS. 89*
37 And, . . . day,] And . . . day *MS. 36*
38 reverence; *MSS. 13, 36* reverence *MS. 89*
39 'tis *MS. 36* tis *MSS. 13, 89*
40 jealous] jealous, *MS. 36* himself: *MSS. 13, 36* himself *MS. 89*
41 laughing stock] Laughing-stock *MS. 36*
43 nought,— . . . nought;] nought, . . . nought. *MS. 36*
45 ward—and,] ward & *MS. 36*
46 Shrew.] Shrew; *MS. 36*
47 be,— . . . wholly;] be, . . . wholly: *MS. 36*
48 folly,] folly *MS. 36*
51 began. *ed* began *MS. 89*
53 her; *MSS. 13, 36* her *MS. 89* that] that, *MSS. 13, 36*
54 manhood's *ed* manhoods *MSS. 13, 36, 89*
55 grace; *MS. 13* grace *MS. 89* grace, *MS. 36*
56 man's *ed* mans *MS. 89*
57 nature] Nature *MS. 36*
58 Creature] creature *MS. 36*
59 Bird] bird *MS. 36*
62 think,] think *MS. 36*
64 Altho'] Although *MS. 36* gay, *MSS. 13, 36* gay *MS. 89*
65 Bird *MS. 36* Bird *rev from* bird *MS. 13* bird *MS. 89*
67 wretchedness: *MSS. 13, 36* wretchedness *MS. 89*
70 Bird . . . aye. *MSS. 13, 36* bird . . . aye *MS. 89*
72 flesh, *MSS. 13, 36* flesh *MS. 89* silk] silk, *MS. 36*
73 wall, *MSS. 13, 36* wall *MS. 89*
74 all, *MS. 36* all *MSS. 13, 89*
76 mouse. *MS. 36* mouse *MS. 89*
77 kind, *MSS. 13, 36* kind *MS. 89*
78 mind. *MSS. 13, 36* mind *MS. 89*
79 she-wolf] She-wolf *MS. 36* base; *ed* base *MSS.*
80 Wolf] wolf *MS. 36*
82 Mate. *MS. 36* Mate *MS. 89*
84 do.] do: *MS. 36*
86 delight] delight. *MS. 36, which ends here*
87 fair, *ed* fair *MSS.*
89 upon't, *rev from* upon't! *MS. 13* upon't *MS. 89*
91 while. *MS. 13* while *MS. 89*
93 jollity, *MS. 13* jollity *MS. 89*
94 she, *ed* She, *MS. 13* she *MS. 89*
96 comparison: *MS. 13* comparison *MS. 89*
100 sent: *ed* sent *MS. 89* Lemman *rev from* Lemon *MS. 89*
101 Lemman! *rev from* Lemon, *MS. 89* speech; *MS. 13* speech *MS. 89*
103 wise *MS. 13* wise, *MS. 89* said, *MS. 13* said *MS. 89*
104 deed: *ed* deed *MSS. 13, 89*
105 lurk, *ed* lurk *MSS. 13, 89*
106 work. *MS. 13* work *MS. 89*
107 man, *ed* Man, *MS. 13* man *MS. 89*

plain; *ed* plain *MSS. 13, 89*
108 grain, *MS. 13* grain *MS. 89*
117 brother! *MS. 13* brother *MS. 89*
118 other. *MS. 13* other *MS. 89*
120 thief, *MS. 13* thief *rev from* theif *MS. 89*
121 difference *rev from* difference, *MS. 89*
122 (To . . . told) *MS. 13* To . . . told *MS. 89*
125 plain, *MS. 13* plain *MS. 89*
126 called: *rev from* called, *MS. 89*
134 Lemman *rev from* Lemon *MS. 89*
135 engage: *MS. 13* engage *MS. 89*
137 word: *MS. 13* word *MS. 89*
143 alas! *ed* Alas! *MS. 13* alas *MS. 89*
150 gnat, *ed* gnat *MS. 89*
158 guise: *ed* guise *MS. 89*
168 thee. *MS. 13* thee *MS. 89*
169 life? *MS. 13* life *MS. 89*
173 wis. *MS. 13* wis *MS. 89*
174 amiss! *MS. 13* amiss *MS. 89*
176 smite. *MS. 13* smite *MS. 89*
177 done, *ed* done *MSS. 13, 89*
178 upon?"] upon"? *MS. 89*
180 proof: *MS. 13* proof *MS. 89*
184 thing. *MS. 13* thing *MS. 89*
186 woe, *MS. 13* woe *MS. 89*
191 Henceforth, . . . thief, *MS. 13* Henceforth . . . thief *MS. 89*
192 one, *MS. 13* one *MS. 89*
193 speak. *ed* speak *MS. 89*
195 black, *ed* black *MSS. 13, 89*
198 slain." *ed* slain *MS. 89* Slain *MS. 13*
203 perdition, *MS. 13* perdition *MS. 89* go; *MS. 13* go *MS. 89*
205 Crow. *MS. 13* Crow *MS. 89*
209 Wife; *ed* Wife *MSS. 13, 89*
212 store; *ed* store *MSS. 13, 89*
213 before. *MS. 13* before *MS. 89*
215 name: *ed* name *MSS. 13, 89*
217 teach, *MS. 13* teach *MS. 89*
219 then. *ed* then *MS. 89*
224 Son, *MS. 13* Son *MS. 89* care. *MS. 13* care *MS. 89*
225 do? *ed* do *MSS. 13, 89*
226 cutteth *rev from* cuttest *MS. 89*
227 tongue, . . . Child, *MS. 13* tongue . . . Child *MS. 89*
229 abominable. *ed* abominable *MSS. 13, 89*
230 honorable. *ed* honourable. *MS. 13* honorable *MS. 89*
231 read. *ed* read *MSS. 13, 89*
232 head. *MS. 13* head *MS. 89*
234 matter. *ed* matter *MSS. 13, 89*
236 rest. *ed* rest *MSS. 13, 89*
238 betrayed; *ed* betrayed *MSS. 13,89*
240 recal. *ed* recal *MS. 89* recall *MS. 13*
241 said, *ed* said *MSS. 13, 89*
242 Howe'er *rev from* However *MS. 89* gone. *ed* gone *MSS. 13, 89*
244 paid. *MS. 13* paid *MS. 89*
246 true. *ed* true *MSS. 13, 89*
247 travel, *ed* travel *MS.* 89

Selections from Chaucer, Modernized Transcriptions

DC MS. 13
(with Preceding and Facing Photographs)

DC MS. 13 is a handmade notebook, the sheets of which have been dispersed. Originally it contained at least six bifolia of laid paper folded to measure 25 by 39.1 cm., with chain lines running vertically at intervals of 2.7/8 cm., watermarked with a crowned shield containing a fleur-de-lys and countermarked W ELGAR over 1795. In the twelve-leaf notebook, as reconstructed, there are two stubs, and the third leaf is now at the Pierpont Morgan Library, New York. Wordsworth's work on modernizations of *The Prioress's Tale, The Cuckoo and the Nightingale,* and *The Manciple's Tale* survives on leaves 7^r–12^r and one of the stubs; 9^r is blank but for the title *The Manciple's Tale.* Except for 12^r, all surviving pages containing Chaucer material are divided horizontally into three columns each about 13 cm. wide; 12^r is divided horizontally into two columns each about 19.5 cm. wide.

Fair copy of *The Prioress's Tale,* lines 149–end, in the autograph of Dorothy Wordsworth (ll. 149–204) and William Wordsworth (ll. 205–end), with revisions by them and by Mary Hutchinson, can be found on 11^v (ll. 149–225) and 11^r, column 1 (ll. 226–end).

Fair copy of *The Cuckoo and the Nightingale,* lines 1–200, 206–216, 220–223, 226–260, in the autographs of William Wordsworth and Mary Hutchinson, with revisions by them, can be found on 8^v (ll. 196–200, 206–216, 220–223, 226–260), 10^r (ll. 41–120), 10^v (ll. 121–195), and 11^r, columns 2 and 3 (ll. 1–40); revision of lines 36–37 and 40, in William Wordsworth's autograph, can be found at the bottom of 11^r, column 1; revision of lines 242–243, in William Wordsworth's autograph, can be found among revisions to *The Manciple's Tale* on 12^r, column 2; on 8^v, column 3, after line 260, William has written and underlined "Finis."

Fair copy of *The Manciple's Tale,* in the autographs of Mary Hutchinson and William Wordsworth, with revisions by them and by Dora Wordsworth and John Carter, can be found on 7^r (ll. 90–176), 7^v (ll. 1–89), and 9^v (ll. 177–end); revision of lines 56–58, 87–91, 99–100, and 132–143 can be found on 12^r; revision of lines 156–158 in Mary Hutchinson's autograph and lines 186–187 can be found on one stub; much work on 7^v, columns 2 and 3, is not consecutive and is largely draft in William's autograph; 7^v, column 3, contains fair copy of lines 235–244 in Dora Wordsworth's autograph.

Full-page photographs of the manuscript pages are provided first, followed by photographs and facing transcriptions of the individual columns.

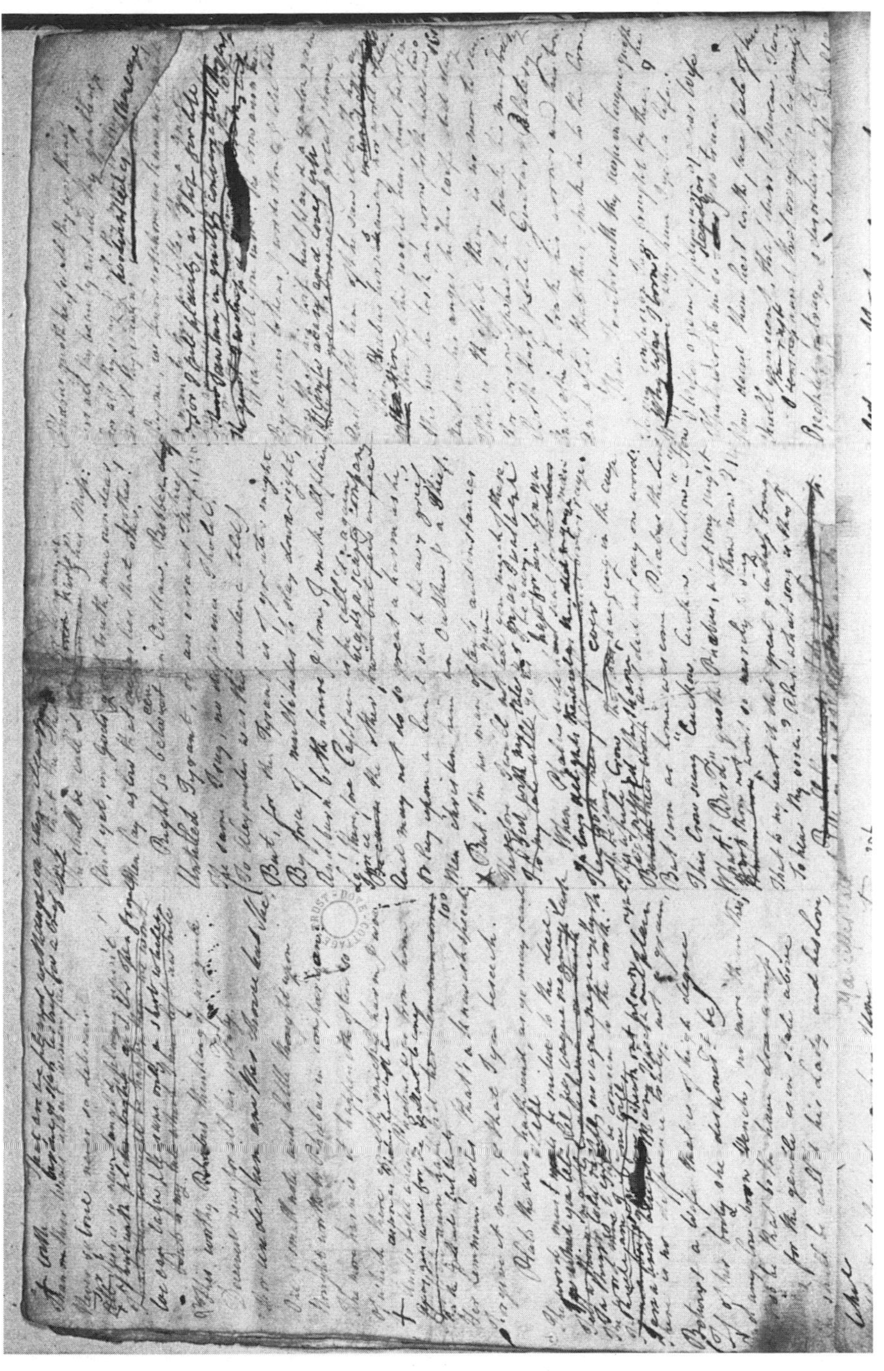

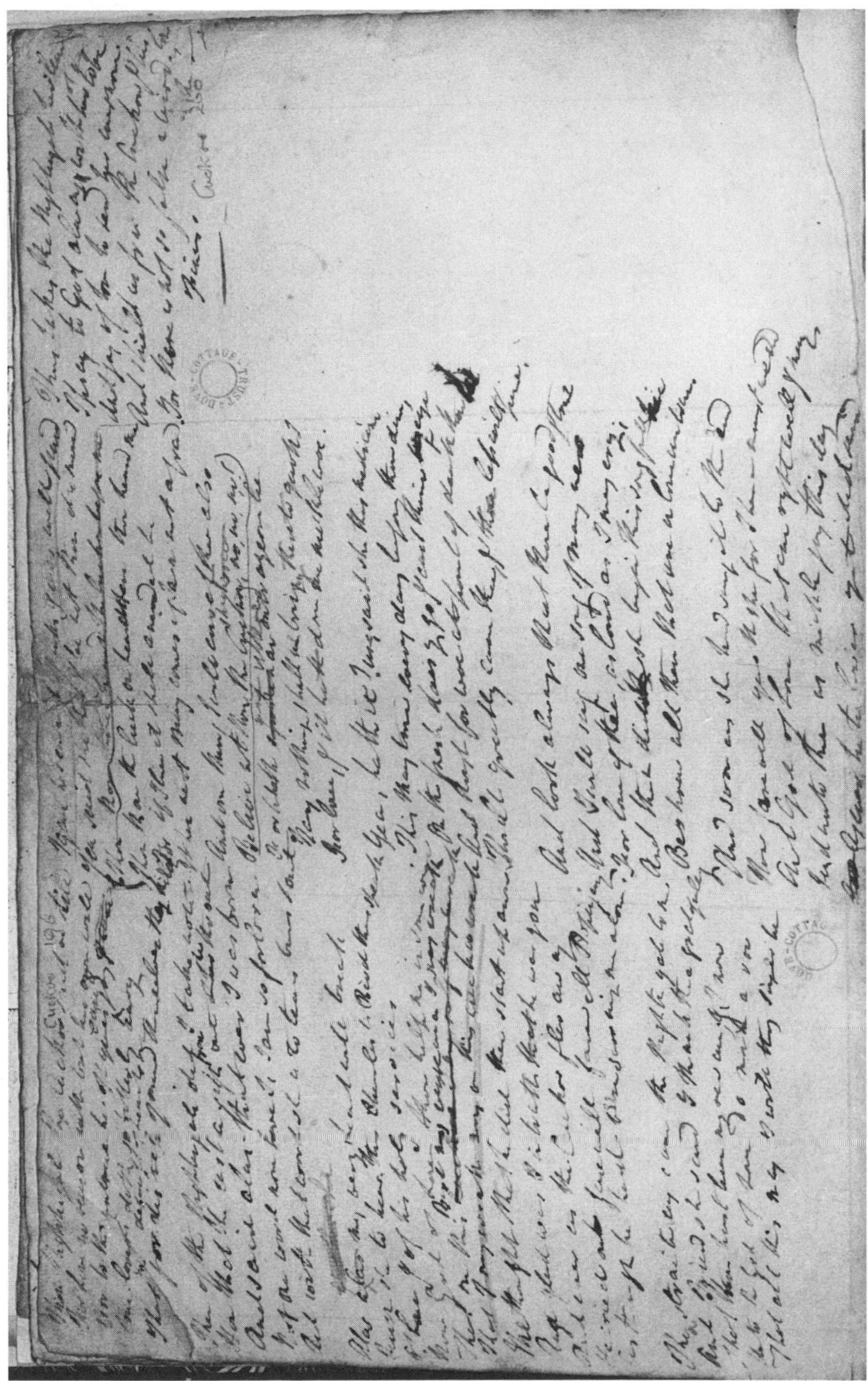

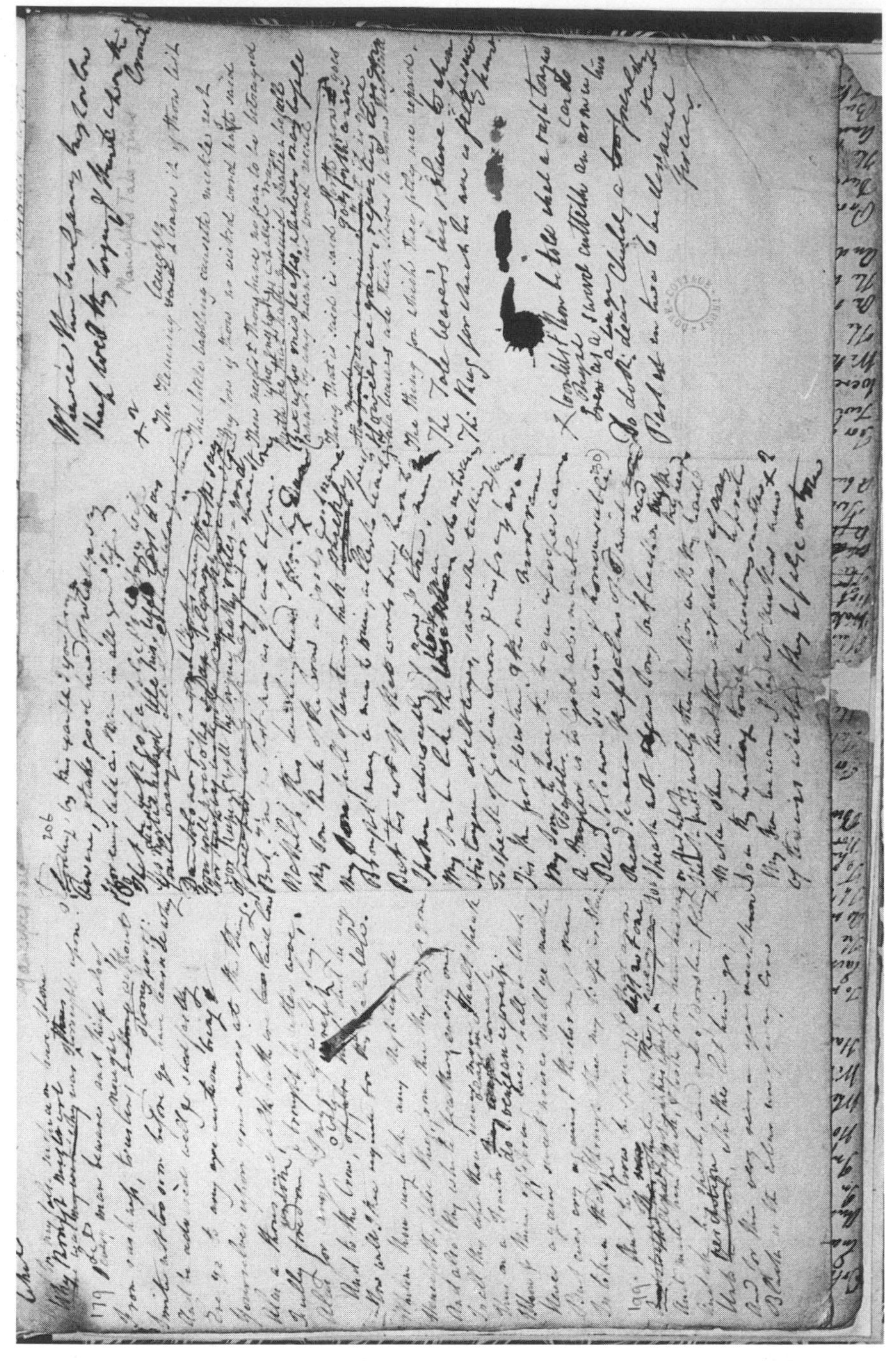

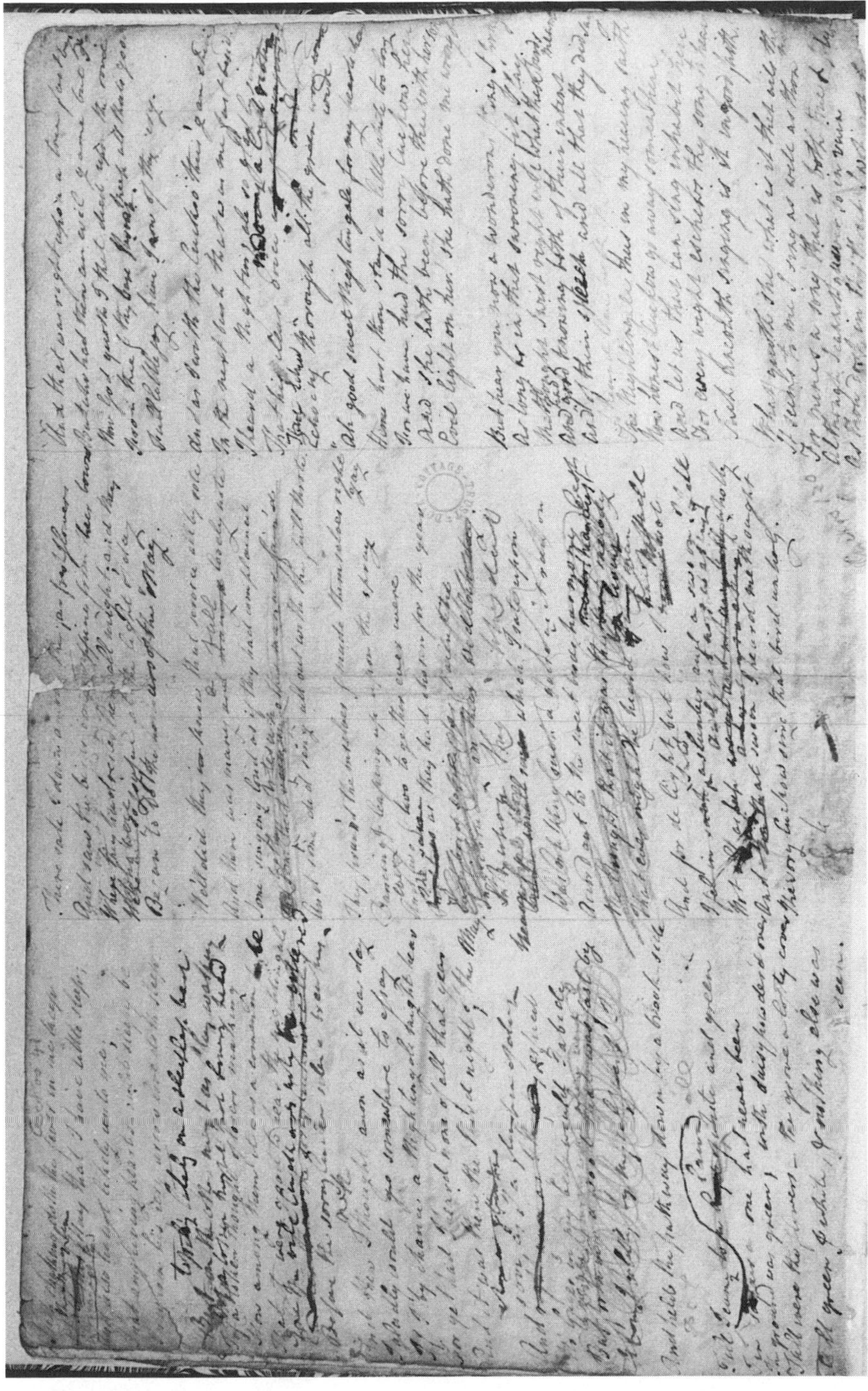

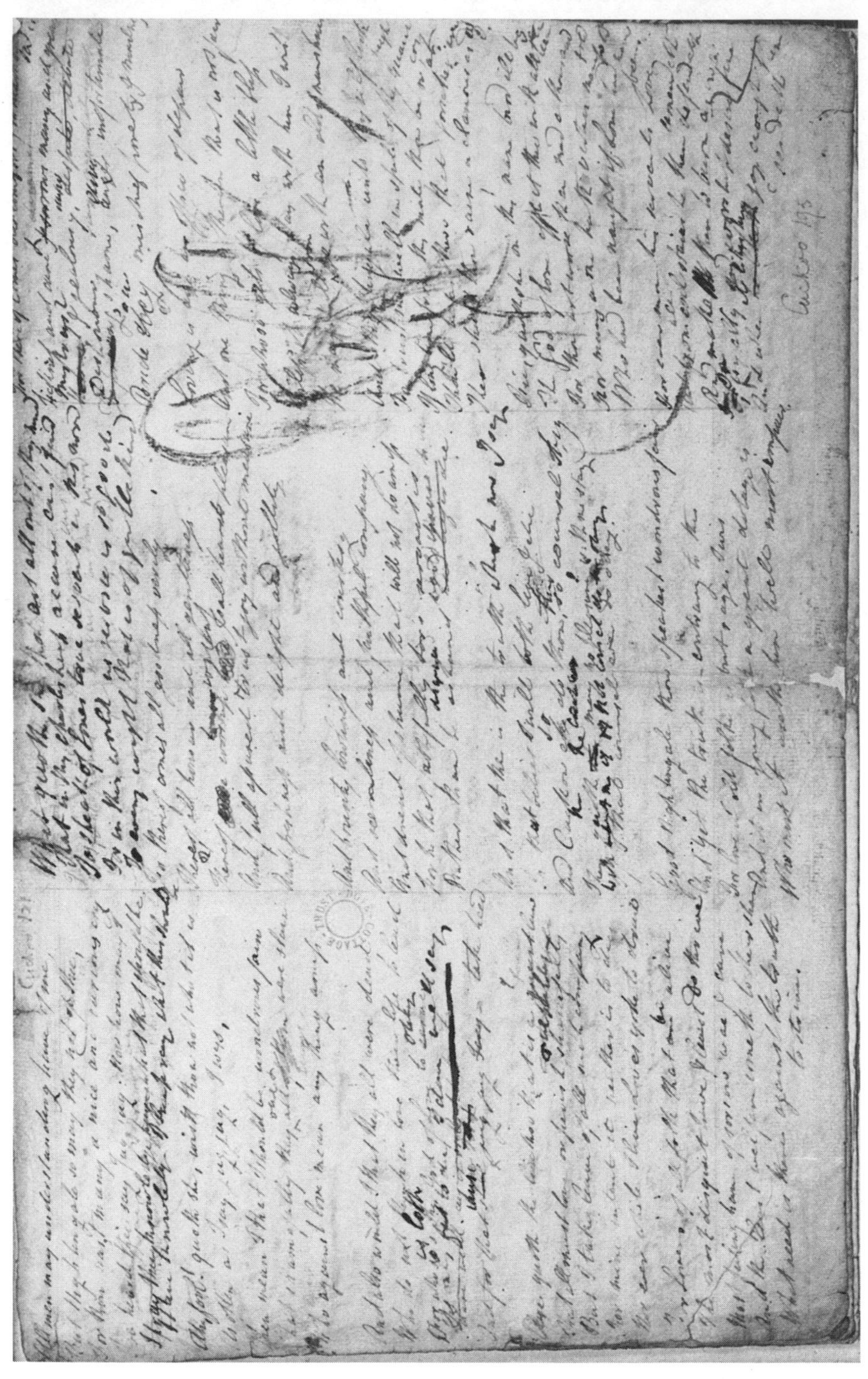

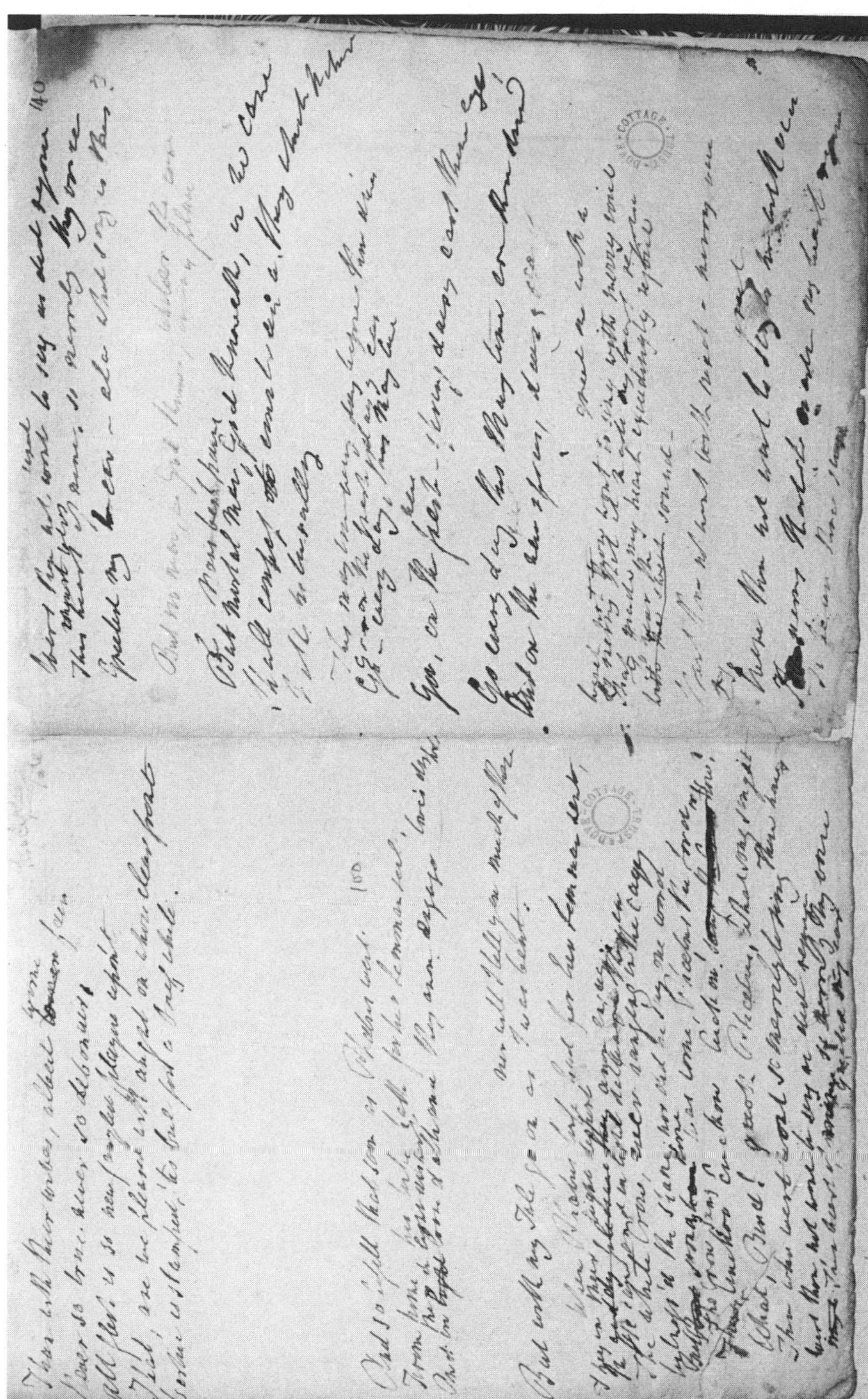

Than on their Wives albeit women fair

Never so true never so debonair

All such is so newfangled, plague upon't

We can take pleasure only a short while

This worthy Phoebus thinking of no guile

Deceived was for all his jollity

For under him another choice had she,

One of small note and little thought upon

Nought worth to Phœbus in comparison

The more harm is it happeneth often so

Of which there cometh mickle harm & woe

And so befell when Phœbus was from home

Her Lemman? certes that's a knavish speech;

Forgive it me, & that I you beseech.

Plato the wise hath said, as ye may read

The word must needs be suited to the deed.

There is no difference truly, not a grain,

Betwixt a Wife that is of high degree

(If of her body she dishonest be)

And any low-born Wench, no more than this,

(If so be that both have done amiss)

For the gentle is in state above

She shall be call'd his Lady and his Love,

She shall be call'd ...

And yet, in God's ...

Men lay as low that one ...

Right so betwixt ...

Untitled Tyrant, ...

The same I say, no ...

To Alexander was the ...

But, for the Tyrant ...

By force of multitude ...

And burn both house ...

Lo! therefore Captain ...

And may not do so ...

Or lay upon a land ...

Men christen him ...

But I'm no man of ...

Therefore I will not ...

When Phœbus wife ...

This white Crow that ...

But soon as home ...

This Crow sung "Cuckoo ...

What! Bird", quoth ...

That to my heart it did ...

To hear thy voice? Alas ...

[*The Manciple's Tale*]

[90] That are we pleased with aught on whose clear front
[91] + Virtue is stam tis but for a brief while
with
87 Than ~~on~~ their wives albeit women fair
88 Never so true never so debonaire
For [?]
89 ~~All~~ flesh is so new-fangl'd, plague upon't!
+ That with plain virtue and her open front
90 ~~That when we might be happy, then we won't~~
We can take pleasure only a short whiles—
91 ~~But to my tale which I have left awhile~~
92 This worthy Phœbus thinking of no guile
93 Deceived was for all his jollity,
94 For under him another choice had She,
95 One of small note and little thought upon
o }
96 Nought worth to Phœbus in comparis[?] } n:
97 The more harm is it happeneth often so
98 Of which there cometh mickle harm & woe.
as soon as Phœbus had left home
99 + And so befell when Phœbus was from home
Away goes word for the Gallant to come
100 ~~His Wife anon~~ hath bid ~~her Lemman come~~.
For the Gallant but thats 100
101 Her Lemman! certes that's a knavish speech;
102 Forgive it me, & that I you beseech.
103 Plato the wise hath said, as ye may read
still
104 The word must ~~needs~~ be suited to the deed
In what }
In wh } you tell let no vague meanings lurk
105 ~~Tell a thing rightly, Englishman or Turk~~
In things told rightly no vague meanings lurk
is ever
106 The word ~~must~~ still be cousin to the work.
~~Rude am I, if you will~~,
rous
107 ~~I am a boitrous man~~ I speak out plain right
I am a bold blunt Man, I speak out plain
108 There is no difference truly, not a grain,
109 Betwixt a Wife that is of high degree
110 (If of her body she dishonest be)
r } W }
111 And any low-bo[?] } n w } ench, no more than this,
112 (If it so be that both have done amiss)
113 That, for the gentle is in state above
114 She shall be call'd his Lady and his Love,

Signal at top of column corresponds with signal at left of revision to l. 90.

89 WW's revision of "For" for "All" is probably contemporary with *Manciple* work in MS. 89.

89–91 These lines were developed on 12[r], col. 1

94 Revision probably contemporary with *Manciple* work in MS. 89.

99 Signal in left margin corresponds with revision of ll. 119–120 on 12[r], col. 1.

104 "still" was originally written in pencil, and "ill" was reinforced in ink. This revision was not entered in MS. 89.

She shall be call'd his Wench & his Miss:
And yet, in God's good truth, mine own dear,
Men lay as low that one as lies that other!

Right so between an Outlaw, Robber, Chief
Untitled Tyrant, or an errant Thief,
The same I say, no difference I hold.
(To Alexander was this sentence told)
But, for the Tyrant is of greater might
By force of multitudes to slay down-right,
And burn both house & home, & make all plain,
Lo! therefore Captain is he call'd again
Since the other leads a scanty company
And may not do so great a harm as he,
Or lay upon a land such heavy grief,
Men christen him an Outlaw & a Thief.

* But I'm no man of texts and instances
Therefore I will not tell you much of these,
[illegible]

When Phœbus wife had sent for her lemman
[illegible]
The white Crow that ever hanging in the cage
Beheld their work, and did not say one word.
But soon as home was come Phœbus the Lord
This Crow sung "Cuckow, Cuckow, Cuckow!" "How
What! Bird," quoth Phœbus, what song sing'st thou now?
Wert thou not wont so merrily to sing
That to my heart it did great gladness bring
To hear thy voice? Alas! what song is this?"

And, that the other a poor Woman is
~~harlot~~ harlot
She shall be call'd his ~~Lemman~~ & his Miss:
And yet, in God's good truth, mine own dear brother!
Men lay as low that one as lies that other.
een
Right so betw~~ixt~~ an Outlaw, Bobber-~~cheff~~ chief
Untitled Tyrant, or an errant Thief,
The same I say, no difference I hold,
(To Alexander was this sentence told)
But, for the Tyrant is of greater might
By force of multitudes to slay down-right,
And burn both house & home, & make all plain,
C}
Lo! therefore c} aptain is he call'd:— again
Since heads a scanty company
~~Because~~ the other, ~~hath but few in fee~~
And may not do so great a harm as he,
Or lay upon the land such heavy grief
T}
Men christen him an Outlaw & a [?]} hief.
X But I'm no man of texts and instances
give
Therefore I will not ~~tell~~ you much of these,
But with my tale go on as I was bent
~~I to my tale will~~ go as I began
had for her Lemma
When Phœbus wife ~~had~~ sent for ~~her dear~~ man
In loves delights themselves they did engage
~~They took their fill of love and~~ lovers rage
is} He cam ever
The} white Crow ~~that was~~ ^ hanging in the cage
'}
Witness~~e~~} d the shame
~~Beheld their work~~, and did not say one word:
But soon as home was come Phœbus the Lord
C}
This c} row sung "Cuckow, Cuckow, Cuckow"—"How
What! Bird," quoth Phœbus, what song sing'st thou now?
Wert thou not
~~Whilom thou~~ ^ wont so merrily to sing
That to my heart it did great gladness bring,
To hear thy voice? Alas! what song is this?
~~By all the saints I do not sing amiss.~~
me Gods} I do not
So help me Gods} I d [?] sing amiss

119 WW wrote "Bobber" for "Robber."
131 Signal in left margin corresponds to revisions of ll. 132–143 on 12[r], cols. 1 and 2.
144 Revisions below the line were started in ink, then overwritten in pencil.

Phoebus quoth he, for all thy worthiness
For all thy beauty and all thy gentleness
For all thy song & all thy minstrelsy
For all thy watching hoodwinked is [illegible] thine eye
By one, we know not whom we know not what
A man to thee no better than a gnat
For I full plainly, as I hope for life
Saw him in quietly converse with thy wife
[illegible]
What will you more? the Crow anon him told
By serious tokens & words stout & bold
How that his wife had played a wanton game
[illegible] to his great shame,
And told him oft he saw it with his eyes
Then Phoebus turned away [illegible]
Him thought his woeful heart had burst in two
His bow he took, an arrow forth he drew 161
And in his anger he his wife did slay
This is the effect there is no more to say.
For sorrow of which he brake his minstrelsy
Both harp & lute, Guitar & Psaltery
And eke he brake his arrows and his bow.
And after that thus spake he to the Crow.
Thou Traitor with thy scorpion tongue quoth he
To my confusion hast brought by thee. 9
Why was I born? Why have I yet a life
O Wife, o gem of pleasure & dear wife
That wert to me so steadfast & so true
Now dead thou liest with face pale of hue
Full innocent, that durst I swear, [illegible]
O thou rash hand that wrought so far amiss!
Presumptuous outrage, o disordered wit
[illegible]

Phœbus, quoth he, for all thy worthiness
For all thy beauty and all thy gentleness
For all thy song & all thy minstrelsy
hoodwinked is thine eye
For all thy waiting, ~~ill is done to thee~~
By one, we know not whom we know not what
A man to thee no better than a gnat
For I full plainly, as I hope for life
G}
Thou ~~art dishonoured, so g}od give me lif~~e
~~There~~ Saw him in guilty converse with thy wife
For on ~~thy bed I saw him with thy Wife~~
~~The guilt I witnessd saw him with thy wife~~
What will you more. The Crow anon him told
By serious tokens & words stout & bold
How that his Wife had play'd a wanton game
Him to abase and cover with
~~Unto his great abasement &~~ great shame,
And told him oft he saw it with his eyes
s} ~~in wretched guise~~
Then Phœbus turn'd} away nor would replies.
~~the~~ Him
~~Him~~ thought his woeful heart had burst in two
His bow he took, an arrow forth he drew
160
And in his anger he his wife did slay
This is th'effect there is no more to say.
For sorrow of which he brake his minstrelsy
H} L} G} P}
Both h}arp & l}ute, g}uitar & p}slatery
And eke he brake his arrows and his bow.
And after that thus spake he to the Crow.
Thou Traitor with thy scorpion tongue quoth he
To my confusion I am brought by thee.
Why was I born?
~~Why was I [?bor]~~? why have I yet a life?
O Wife o gem of pleasure o dear Wife
steadfast
That wert to me so ~~sober~~ & so true
Now dead thou liest with face pale of hue
Full innocent, that durst I swear, I wis.
thou rash
O ~~senseless~~ hand that wrought so far amiss!
O reckless outrage o disorderd wit,
[?]
That [?~~thought~~] unadvisèd didst the guiltless smite.

156–158 Traces of a revision of these lines survive on a stub (1^v attached to leaf 12) in MS. 13; there "T / A / The /" appear in MW's hand. This revision appears to be toward MS. 89 and may be contemporary with *Manciple* work there.

The Manciples Tale

When Phœbus here below on earth did dwell
Among mankind as ancient stories tell
He was the lustiest Bachelor I trow
Of all this world and the best archer too
He slew the serpent Python as he lay
Sleeping against the sun upon a Day
And many another worthy noble deed
Wrought with his bow as men the same may read.

He played, all music played on earthly ground
And twas a melody to hear the sound
Of his clear voice, so sweetly could he sing
Certes Amphion that Old Theban King
Who wall'd a city with his minstrelsy
Was never heard to sing so sweet as he
Therewith this Phœbus was the seemliest man
That is or hath been since the world began
His features to describe I need not strive
For in this world is none so fair alive
He was moreover full of gentleness
Of honour and of perfect worthiness

This Phœbus flower in forest and in court
This comely Bachelor, for his disport,
And eke in token of his victory earn'd
Of Python, as is from the story learn'd,
Was wont to carry in his hand a bow, —
Now had this Phœbus in his house a Crow.

But no man in any case

The Manciple's Tale

~~took de~~light on *to*
1 *When Phœbus here below on earth did dwell*
Among mankind as antient stories tell
2 ~~*As ancient histories to us do tell*~~
blithest
3 *He was the ~~comeliest~~ Bachelor I trow*
and *b*
4 *Of all this world ~~and eke~~ the ~~brav~~^est Archer too*
5 *He slew the serpent Python as he lay*
6 *Sleeping against the sun upon a day*
7 *And many another worthy noble deed*
8 *Wrought with his bow as men the same may read.*
9 *He played, all music played on earthly ground*
10 *And twas a melody to hear the sound*
clear
11 *Of his ~~sweet~~ voice, so sweetly could he sing*
12 *Certes Amphion that Old Theban King*
e *s*
13 *Who wall'd a city with his minstra}l[?c]}y*
14 *Was never heard to sing so sweet as he*
with
15 *There~~to~~ this Phœbus was the seemliest man*
hath been
16 *That is ~~or was even~~ ^ since the world began*
e *need*
17 *His features to di}scribe I ~~will~~ not strive;*
18 *For in this world is none so fair alive*
moreover
19 *He was ~~therewith~~ full of ~~all~~ gentleness*
20 *Of honour and of perfect worthiness*
20
21 This Phœbus flower in forest and in court
22 This comely Bachelor, for his ~~her~~ disport,
23 And eke in token of his victory earn'd
24 Of Python, as is from the story learn'd,
.
25 Was wont to carry in his hand a bow,}—
26 Now had this Phœbus in his house a Crow.

---

1 Base text is in MH's autograph through l. 20, but "took delight on . . . to" is in JC's autograph; revision postdates MS. 36.

2 WW's revision postdates MS. 36.

3 "blithest" is in MH's autograph and postdates MS. 36.

4 "and" may be in JC's autograph; "b" is in an unidentifiable autograph. Both revisions postdate MS. 36.

11 "clear" is in MH's autograph and predates MS. 36.

15–16 WW's revision postdates MS. 36.

17 "need" is MH's; it was not entered in any other MS.

19 "moreover" is MH's and predates MS. 36.

22 Insertion of "comely" postdates MS. 36.

Which in a cage he [illegible] day
And taught to speak as men will teach a jay.
White was this Crow, as is a snow-white swan;
And counterfeit the speech of every man
He could, when he had mind to tell a tale:
Besides, in all this world no Nightingale
Could ring out of his throat so blithe a peal
No not a hundred thousand th part as well.

Now had this Phoebus in his house a Wife
And her he loved better than his life,
And night and day he strove with diligence
To please her, and to do her reverence;
Save only, for the truth, the noble Elf
Was jealous, and would keep her to himself;
For he was loth a laughing-stock to be
And so is every wight as loth as he;
But all for nought, for it availeth nought.
A good Wife that is pure in deed & thought
Should not be kept in watch & ward; & do
The best you can, you cannot keep a Shrew;
It will not be, vain labour is it wholly:
Lordlings, this hold I for an arrant folly
Labour to lose in custody of wives;
And so old Clerks have written in their lives.

But to my purpose as I first began
This worthy Phoebus doth all he can
To please her, weening that, by such delight
And for his government and manhood's right
No man should ever put him from her grace.
But in good truth there is nothing no man take place
shall constrain a thing which Nature
Hath naturally placed in a creature.

Which in a cage he [?fostered] many a day
will
And taught to speak as men ~~do~~ teach a jay.
;
White was this Crow, as is a snow-white swan,}
And countrefeit the speech of every man
:
He could, when he had mind to tell a tale,}
Besides, in all this world no Nightingale
Could ring out of his throat so blithe a peal
No not a hundred thousandth part as well.
    Now had this Phœbus in his house a Wife
And her he loved better than his life,
And night and day he strove with diligence
To please her, and to do her reverence;
Save only, for tis truth, the noble Elf
Was jealous, and would keep her to himself:
For he was loth a Laughing-stock to be
And so is every wight as loth as he;
But all for nought, for it availeth nought.
A good Wife that is pure in deed & thought
u
Sho^ld not be kept in watch & ward; &, do
The best you can, you cannot keep a Shrew;
It will not be, vain labour is it wholly:
Lordings, this hold I for an arrant folly
Labour to lose in custody of wives;
And so old Clerks have written in their lives.
    But to my purpose as I first began
This worthy Phœbus doeth all he can
To please her; weening, that, by such delight
And for his government and manhoods right
No man should ever put him from her grace;
no man
~~no man~~ in good truth^in any case
But ~~in Gods truth~~ there may no man take
place
Shall compass
~~Of Nature~~, to constrain a thing which Nature
Hath naturally planted in a creature.

in any case

But no man

28 WW's revision postdates MS. 36.
56–57 WW's revisions postdate MS. 36.

Take any bird & put it in a cage
And to this little bird thy self engage Go
To feed it tenderly with meat & drink
And every dainty whereof thou canst think,
And keep it also cleanly as thou may;
Although the cage of gold be never so gay,
Yet had this Bird by twenty thousand fold
Rather in forest that is wild and cold
Go feed on worms and on such wretchedness:
For ever will this Bird do more or less
To escape out of his cage whenever he may:
His liberty the Bird desireth aye.
Go take a Cat, & nourish her with milk
And tender flesh, and make her couch of silk,
And let her see a mouse go by the wall,
Anon she waiveth milk and flesh and all
And every dainty which is in that house
Such appetite hath she to eat the mouse.
Behold the domination here of kind,
And appetite drives discretion from her mind.
A She-wolf also in her kind is base
Meeteth she the sorriest wolf in field or chase
Him will she take what matter his estate
In time when she hath liking to a mate.
Examples all for men that are untrue
With women [illegible] thing [illegible] to do:
For men have still a [illegible] appetite
[illegible] lower thing to seek for their delight
their delight

Take any bird & put it in a cage
And to this little bird thy self engage
To feet it tenderly with meat & drink
And every dainty whereof thou canst think,
And keep it also cleanly as thou may;
Although the cage of gold be never so gay,
B}
Yet had this b}ird by twenty thousand fold
Rather
~~Leaver~~ in forest that is wild and cold
Go feed on worms and on such wretched
ness:
For ever will this Bird do more or less
To escape out of his cage whene'er he may:
His liberty the Bird desireth aye.
C} nourish
Ȼ Go take ~~thou~~ a c}at, & ~~foster~~ her with milk
And tender flesh, and make her couch of silk,
And let her see a mouse go by the wall,
Anon she waiveth milk and flesh and all
And every dainty which is in that house
Such appetite hath she to eat the mouse.
Behold here
Lo! ~~here~~ the domination ~~of her~~ kind,
discretion
~~And~~ appetite drives ~~judgement~~ from her
mind.
A She-wolf also in her kind is base
C}
Meets she the sorriest wolf in field or c}hase
Him will she take—what matter his
estate
a
In time when she hath liking to ~~her~~ mate
Examples all for men that are untrue.
With women I have nothing now to do:
froward ~~way~~-ward
For men have still a l~~iquorish~~ appetite
With seek for their delight
~~On~~ lower thing ~~to accomplish~~
their delight

---

61 WW wrote "feet" for "feed."
66, 71 WW's revisions postdate MS. 36.
74 Insertion of "waiveth" postdates MS. 36.
77 MH's revisions postdate MS. 36.
78, 82 WW's revisions postdate MS. 36.
85–86 WW's revisions postdate MS. 36. Here MS. 36 breaks off, suggesting that the rest of *Manciple* may have been completed after MS. 36 was copied.

[*The Cuckoo and the Nightingale*]

196 Thou Nightingale the Cuckow said be still
197 For Love no reason hath but his own will
r} ease &
198 For to the unt[?]}ue he oft gives^ joy ~~& ease~~
199 True lovers doth so bitterly anoy^
in default of hearts
200 That for distress of mind themselves they kill

206 Then of the Nightingale did I take note
from her
207 How that She cast a sigh out ~~of her~~ throat
208 And said alas—that ever I was born
209 Not one word have I, I am so forlorn
210 And with that word she into tears burst out.

~~quoth she~~
211 Alas ~~alas~~ my very heart will break
^
c}
212 Quoth she to hear this C}hurlish Bird thus speak
213 Of Love & of his holy services
214 Now God of Love thou help me in some wise
Bird my vengeance I may wreak
215 That on this ~~Cuckoo I myself may wreak~~
~~That I my wrath may on this cuckoo wreak~~
216 Methought that he did then start up anon
{d
220 An{g glad was I in truth ~~that~~ he was gone
221 And ever as the Cuckoo flew away
222 He cried out farewell farewell Popinjay
223 As though he had been scorning me alone.

n}
226 The } straitway came the Nightingale to me
227 And Friend she said I thank thee gratefully
th} &}
228 That [?]}ou hast been my rescue, } I now
229 Unto the God of Love do make a vow
230 That all this may I will thy singer be

211 Revisions and deletions are in pencil.
215 Revision below the line is deleted in pencil.
216–220 WW crossed "t's," reinforced "I," and deleted "that" in pencil.
223 "been" is reinforced in pencil.
226 Revision is in pencil.

Again he screamed [illegible] well paid
You said the [illegible] not then she said
Then Now [illegible]
Then than the Cuckoo or heard there then heard me
For if I live it shall amended be
If [illegible] not May comes if I am not afraid

And one thing I will ensure thee also
Believe not thou the Cuckoo, ~~[illegible]~~ she cried, no, no, no!
For he hath [illegible] as ever be
Nay nothing shall me bring thereto quoth I
For Love, & it hath done me mickle woe.

Yea, hath it? use said she this medicine
This May time every day before thou dine,
On the fresh daisy go & cast thine eye
And though for woe at point of death thou lie
Twill greatly ease thee, & thou less wilt pine.

And look always that thou be good & true
And I will sing one song of many new
For love of thee, as loud as I may cry;
And then did she begin this song full high
Beshrew all them that are of love untrue.

And soon as she had sung it to the end
Now farewell quoth she for I hence must wend
And God of love that can right well & may
Send unto thee as mickle joy this day
As ever he to Lover yet did send

Thus ta[...]
I pray to [...]
And joy of [...]
And this al[...]
For there [...]

231 I gave her earnest thanks & was well paid
232 Yea said she then & be not thou dismaied
~~Thou thou have heard the Cuckoo before me~~
dst
233 Thou thou the Cuckoo heard } ere thou heard me
234 For if I live it shall amended be
I
235 When next May comes if } am not afraid.

236 And one thing I will consel thee also
~~[?whatsoeer]~~
237 Believe not thou the Cuckoo, no, no, no! /
ha } [?] uttered
238 For h[?] } th ~~spoken~~ an outrageous lie
e } { ng
239 Nay nothing shall m[?] } bri { g thereto quoth I
240 For love, & it hath done me mickle woe.

241 Yea, hath it? use, said she this medicine
242 This May time every day before thou dine,
243 On the fresh daisy go & cast thine [~~?~~] eye
lie
244 And though for woe at point of death thou [?] }
, } ou
245 'Twill greatly ease thee } & thee } less wilt pine.

246 And look always that thou be good & true
247 And I will sing one song of many new
248 For love of thee, as loud as I may cry;
hie
249 And then did~~st~~ she begin this song full [?] }
250 Beshrew all them that are in love untrue.

251 And soon as she had sung it to the end
nd
252 Now farewell quoth she for I hence must wed }
253 And God of Love that can rght well & may
254 Send unto thee as mickle joy this day
255 ~~A [?And~~] As ever he to lover yet did send

231 The entire line is underscored in pencil.
233 The first version of the line is deleted in pencil.
237 Revisions and underlining are in pencil.
238 Revisions are in pencil.
239–240 "t's" are crossed and reinforcements are made in pencil.
245 Revisions are in pencil.

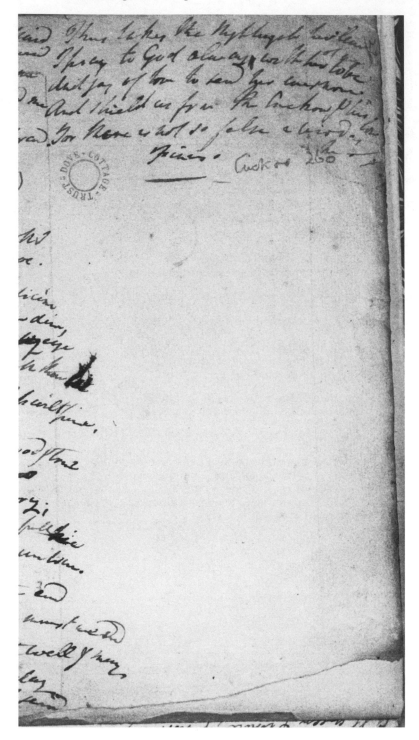

Thus listen the Nightingale [illegible]
I pray to God alway with [illegible]
And pray of [illegible] to send [illegible]
And shield us from the Cuckow [illegible]
For there is not so false a bird [illegible]
Spirits.
Cuckoo 260

256 Thus takes the Nightingale her leave
of me
257 I pray to God alway~~s~~ with her to be
258 And joy of love to send her evermore
259 And shield us from the Cuckow & his
lore
e }
260 For th[?] } re is not so false a bird as
he.

Finis.

---

257 "s" is deleted in pencil.

What
Why for my false suspicion have I done
Why brought mischief
The [illegible] why was thus brought upon.
179 Let every man beware and keep aloof
From rashness, trusting nought without
strong proof:
Smite not too soon before ye have learn'd why
And be advis'd well & steadfastly
Ere ye to any execution bring
Yourselves upon your anger at the thing.
Alas a thousand folk hath ire laid low
Fully undone & brought to utter woe.
Alas for anger I myself will slay!
And to the Crow, O false thief! did he say
Now will I thee requite for thy false tale.
Whilom thou sung like any nightingale
Henceforth, false thief, from thee thy song is gone
And also thy white feathers every one
In all thy life thou never more shalt speak
Thus on a Traitor do I vengeance wreak.
Thou & thine offspring ever shall be black
Never again sweet noises shall ye make
But ever cry against the storm & rain
In token that through thee my wife is slain.
199. And to the Crow he sprang & that anon
[illegible] white feathers left not one
And made him black, & took from him his song
And eke his speech, and out of doors him flung
Unto perdition, thither let him go;
And for this very reason ye must know
Black is the colour now of every Crow

[*The Manciple's Tale*]

What
~~What~~ In my false suspicion have I done
Why through mistrust ~~thus~~
~~Where was my wit?~~ why was I ^ wrought upon?
Let
O every man beware and keep aloof
nought
From rashness, trusting ~~nothing~~ without
strong proof:
Smite not too soon before ye have learn'd why
And be advisèd well & stedfastly
Ere ye to any execution bring ~~y~~
Yourselves upon your anger at the thing.
Alas a thousand folk hath ire ~~bro~~ laid low
undone
Fully ~~foredone~~ & brought to utter woe,
Alas for anger I myself will slay!
o vile wretch
And to the Crow ~~o f false thief!~~ did he say
Now will I thee requite for thy false tale.
Whilom thou sung like any Nightingale
Henceforth, false thief, from thee thy song is gone
And also thy white feathers, every one,
In all thy life thou never more shalt speak.
vengeance
Thus on a Traitor ~~I my anger~~ wreak.
Thou } do I vengeance wreak
Ne } & thine offspring ever shall be black
Never again sweet noises shall ye make
But ever cry against the storm & rain
In token that through thee my Wife is Slain.
the
And to Crow he sprung, & that anon
off ~~snow~~ left not one
~~And stripp'd his~~ ^ white feathers ^ ~~every one~~
And plucking his white
And made him black, & took from him his song
And eke his speech, and out of doors him flung
perdition
Unto ~~the devil~~, whither let him go;
And for this very reason you must know
Black is the colour now of every Crow.

186–187 Traces of what might be a revision of these lines, in MH's autograph, survive on the stub of leaf 1 in MS. 13: "/ e / ay"
200 Underlinings are part of the process of revision.

206
Lordlings, by this example I you pray
Beware, & take good heed of what you say
Nor ever tell a Man in all your life
That he hath got a foolish or [illegible] wife
His deadly hatred [illegible] his life's last day
You'll [illegible]
Dan Solomon [illegible] Clerks [illegible]
You will provoke [illegible] Dan Solomon, Clerks say
For [illegible]
For keeping well thy tongue [illegible] good
[illegible]
But, I'm no text-man as I said before.
Nevertheless this teaching learned I from my Dame
My son think of the Crow in God's good name
My son full often times hath muchspeaking
Brought many a man to ruin, as Clerks teach
But 'tis not oft that words bring harm to
Spoken advisedly & now & then.
My son be like the wise man who restrains
His tongue at all times, save when taking pains
To speak of God in honour & in prayer.
'Tis the first virtue & the most rare
My son, to have the tongue in proper care.
A Babbler is to God abominable.
Read Solomon so wise & honourable 230
Read Seneca the psalms of David read
Speak not dear son, but beckon with thy head
[illegible] unless [illegible] in the [illegible]
Make them that thou art deaf if any
Doth thy hearing touch a perilous matter
My son be ware & be not the author new
Of tidings whether they be false or true

206 Lordings by this example I you pray
207 Beware, & take good heed of what ye say
208 Nor ever tell a Man in all your life
209 That he hath got a false & slippery Wife
deadly
His mort~~al hatr~~ed till his lifes last day
210 ~~You'll bring his deadliest hate upon your head~~
211 ~~Dan Solomon, as learned Clerks have said~~
You will provoke. Dan Solomon, Clerks say
~~For keeping well the tongue hath given store~~
212 For keeping well the tongue hath rules—good
~~Of precepts, twenty ye may find or more~~ store
213 But I'm no Text-man as I said before.
Dame }
214 Nathless this teaching had I from my [?] }
215 My Son think of the Crow in goods good name
Son } mickle
216 My [?] } full oftentimes hath ~~too much~~ speech
r }
217 Brought many a man to s } uin, as Clerks teach,
218 But 'tis not oft that words bring harm to ~~men~~
men
219 Spoken advisedly, & now & then.
Wise }
[?] } Man
Wise Man }
220 My Son be like the [? ?] } who restrains
221 His tongue at all times, save when taking pains
222 To speak of God in honour & in pray'er.
223 Tis the first virtue & the one most rare
224 My Son, to have the tongue in proper care.
Babbler
229 A ~~Jangler~~ is to God abominable
230 Read Solomon so wise & honourable.
D }
231 Read Seneca the psalms of d } avid read
read
dear } wi }
232 Speak not my } Son, but beckon [?] } th
thy head.
or [?] to
[232] ~~Speak not~~ unless thou beckon with thy head
s } { any
233 Make S } hew that thou art deaf if { ever
a prater
234 Do in thy hearing touch a perilous matter
245 My Son beware & be not Author new X2
246 Of tidings whether they be false or true

---

206 Darker ink, similar to that of WW's revisions that postdate MS. 36, and less careful handwriting suggest that ll. 206–end may have been composed later than the rest of the poem. It is unclear what the signal at the top of the column refers to.

215 WW wrote "goods" for "gods."

224 Signal in 9v, col. 3, to right of line indicates that a passage in col. 3 is to be inserted.

234 Signal in right margin between ll. 234 and 245 corresponds to signal in 9v, col. 3, and indicates that a draft of ll. 235–244 in col. 3 is to be inserted.

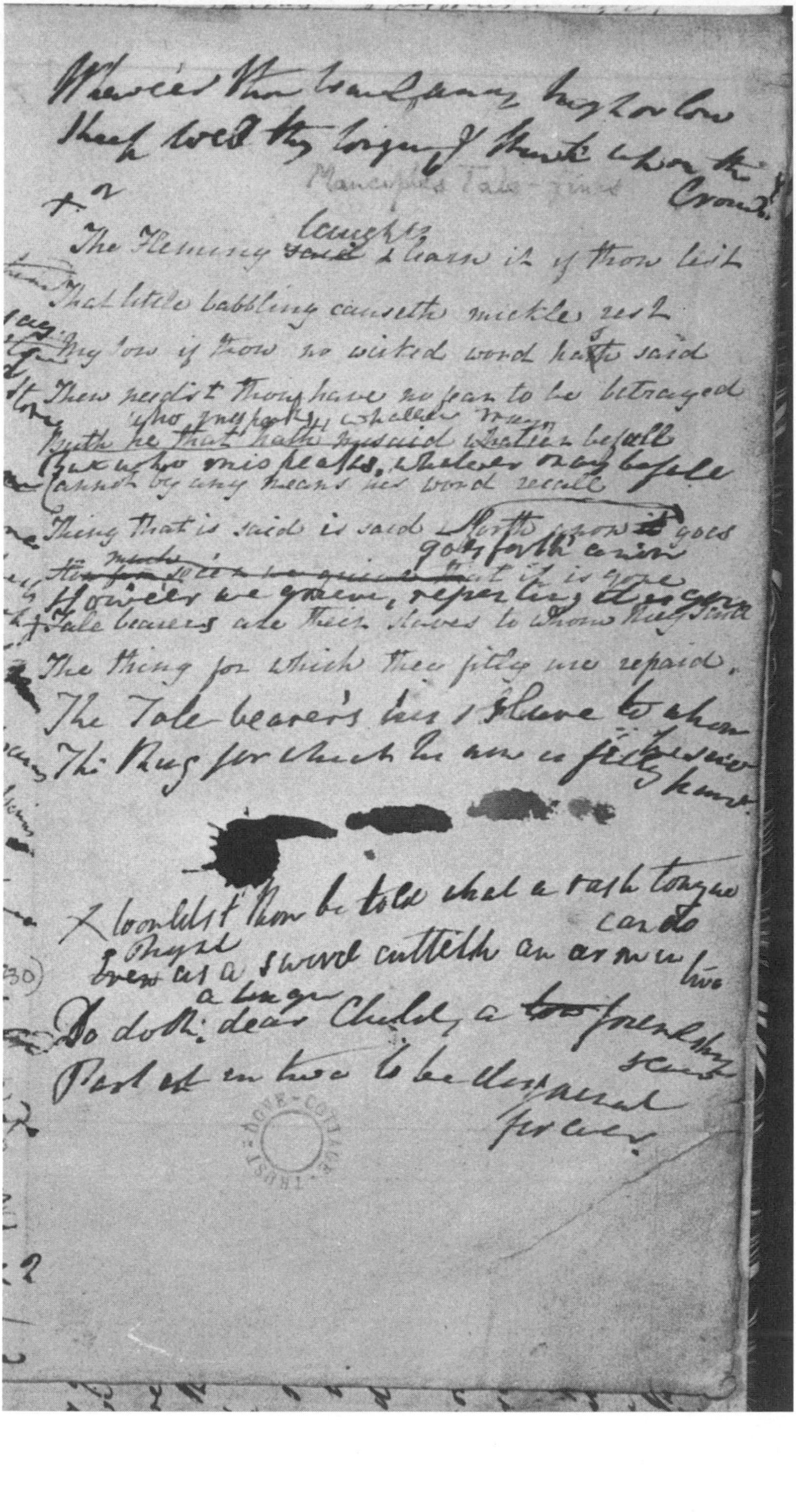

247 Where'er thou travel, among high or low
248 Keep well thy tongue & think upon the
Crow!

X 2 *taught*
235 *The Fleming ~~said~~ & learn it if thou list*
236 *That little babbling causeth mickle rest*
s
237 *My Son if thou no wicked word ha~~th~~ said*
238 *Then need'st thou have no fear to be betrayed*
who misspeaks, whateer may
239 *~~Buth he that hath misaid whate'er~~ befall*
But who mispeaks, whatever may befall
240 *Cannot by any means his word recall*
241 *Thing that is said is said &/forth anon ~~it~~ goes*
goes forth' anon
~~much~~
242 *~~How far soe'er~~ we ~~grieve that it~~ is gone*
Howeer we grieve, repenting it is gone
243 + *Tale bearers are their slaves to whom they said*
244 *The thing for which they fitly are repaid.*
s}
[243] The Tale bearer's his S} lave to whom
he said
[244] The thing for which he now is fitly paid.

225 X Wouldst thou be told what a rash tongue
can do
Right
226 ~~Even~~ as a sword cutteth an arm in two
S} a tongue
227 D} o doth, dear Child, a ~~ton~~ friendship
sever
n}
228 Part it} in two to be disjoined
forever.

235–244 The draft is in the autograph of Dora W, and hence belongs to a late stage of revision.
241 The curved mark between "said" and "goes" indicates the transposed version entered immediately below.
225–228 WW's revisions at page foot are for insertion in the adjoining column, following l. 224.

Cuckoo 41

[illegible] walking doth the fever in me keep
[illegible] May that I have little sleep;
[illegible] also it is not likely unto me,
That any living heart should sleepy be
In whom his fiery arrow Love doth keep.

[illegible] lately on a sleepless bed
But on the other night as they waking
[illegible] a lover [illegible] that [illegible]
Of a token thought of lovers making
How among them it was a common tale
That it were good to hear the nightingale
[illegible] the sorry Cuckoo [illegible] uttered
Before the sorry Cuckoo [illegible] breaking.

And then I thought anon as it was day
I gladly would go somewhere to essay
If I by chance a Nightingale might hear
For yet had I heard none of all that year
And it was then the third night of the May.

And soon as I a glimpse of day espied
No longer in my bed would I abide
But to a wood that was fast by
Alone I boldly [illegible]
And held the pathway down by a brook-side

Till I came to a lawn of white and green
So fair a one had never been
The ground was green, with daisy powder'd over
Tall were the flowers — the grove a lofty cover
All green & white, & nothing else was seen.

[*The Cuckoo and the Nightingale*]

41 Such shaking doth the fever in me keep
this May time
42 ~~Of all this~~ May that I have little sleep;
~~throughout this~~
43 And also tis not likely unto me;
44 That any living heart should sleepy be
45 In whom his fiery arrow love doth steep.
n}
tossil }g lately on a sleepless bed
46 But on the other night as I lay waking
I of a token thought that Lovers heed
47 I of a token thought of lovers making
lc}
48 How among them it was a common ta[?ke]}
49 That it were good to hear the nightingale
Ere the vile Cuckoos note be uttered
50 ~~Earlier than the sorry Cuckows call~~
Before the sorry Cuckow silence breaking
[?]
51 And then I thought anon as it was day
52 I gladly would go somewhere to essay
53 If I by chance a Nightingale might hear
54 For yet had I heard none of all that year
55 And it was then the third night of the May.
~~when a glimpse~~
soon as I a glimpse of day
56 And ~~right anon as I the day~~ ^ espied
3 4 5 1 2
57 No longer in my bed would I abide
to a neighbouring wood alone went I
To a
58 ~~But forth into a wood that was fast by~~
59 ~~Alone & boldly by myself went I~~
60 And held the pathway down by a brook-side
To a L lawn all
61 Till ^ I came ~~to a land~~ of ^ white and green
2 1
62 I in so fair a one had never been
63 The ground was green, with daisy powder'd over
64 Tall were the flowers—the grove a lofty cover
65 All green & white, & nothing else was
seen.

---

42 Revision below the line is in pencil.

46 "But . . . waking" was entered in pencil, then rewritten in ink across the pencil.

50 Traces of pencil remain beneath the ink; "uttered" was entered in pencil, then rewritten in ink across the pencil. The indecipherable word below the line is in pencil.

57 Penciled numbers indicate a revision in word order.

58–59 The revisions "to . . . I" and "to a" are in pencil, as are all deletions.

61 Numbers and curved line in ink, along with penciled carets, indicate a revision in word order; "land" was originally deleted to "lawn" in ink; "all" is in pencil, as are deletion strokes over "to . . . of."

There sate I down among the fair fresh flowers
And saw the birds come tripping from their bowers
Where they had rested them all night, and they
Who were so joyful at the light of day
Began to do the honours of the May.

Well did they know that service all by rote
And there was many and full lovely note
Some singing loud as if they had complained
Some with their notes in other manner fain'd
And some did sing all out with the full throte.

They prun'd themselves & made themselves right gay
Dancing & leaping upon the spray
And ever two & two together were
The same as they had chosen for the year
[illegible] upon [illegible] Valentine
[illegible] on their wedding day
[illegible] they did
[illegible] which I sate upon
Was making such a noise as it ran on
Accordant to the sweet birds harmony
Methought that it was the best melody
That ever might be heard by man
And for delight but how I know not well
I fell into a slumber and a swoon
Not all asleep and yet not wholly
And in that swoon I heard methought
The very Cuckow sing that bird unholy.

66 There sate I down among the fair fresh flowers
67 And saw the birds come tripping from their bowrs
There where they had rested
68 Where they had rested them all night; and they
Who were
69 ~~Were all~~^ so joyful at the light of day
70 Began to^ do the honours of the May.

71 Well did they ~~no~~ know that service all by rote
a full
72 And there was many ~~and many~~ a lovely note
73 Some singing loud as if they had complained
with notes an
74 ~~And some their voice another manner fain'd~~
75 And some^ did sing^ all out^ with the full throte.
,
76 They prun/ed themselves & made themselves right gay
77 Dancing & leaping up upon the spray
ever
78 And^ two & two together ~~ever~~ were
The same
79 ~~Right so~~ as they had chosen for the year
~~Each bird so fine her Valentine~~
80 ~~In February on their wedlock day.~~
St
In V. upon they [?] happy day
Meanwhile the
81 ~~And the small river~~ which I sate upon
82 ~~Was making such a noise as it ran on~~
83 Accordant to the sweet birds harmony
best
~~sweetest~~ heavnliest
84 ~~Methought that it was the best melody~~
by living
85 ~~That ever might be heard of any man~~
knew not well
not
86 And for delight, but how I ~~never~~ wot
Into
87 I ~~fel in such~~^ a slumber and a swoon I fell
l }^ and yet not waking { awaking
88 Not all asp } eep ~~nor yet and not~~ { ~~wholly~~ wholly
lying ~~and yet not waking~~
89 And ~~in~~ that swoon I heard methought
C } ~~the~~
90 The sory c } uckow sing that bird unholy.
[?holy ?C]

68–70 Revisions and caret are in pencil; traces of pencil remain above reinforced "urs" of "honours."

72 Deletions are in pencil and ink, revisions in pencil.

74–82 All revision, deletion, and carets are in pencil, except apostrophe in l. 76 and "The same" in l. 79.

84–85 "best" added above the line and all deletions except initial strokes through "best," "sweetest," and "of any" are in pencil.

86–89 "not" immediately above l. 86 is in pencil; "and yet not waking" above l. 88 was first entered in pencil, then reinforced in ink; deletion stroke in l. 89 is in pencil.

90 "the" in pencil is deleted by erasure, and revision below the line is in pencil.

And that was right upon a tree fast by
But who had then an evil game but I
Then God quoth I that died upon the rood
From thee & thy base throat keep all that's good
Full little joy have I now of thy cry.

And as I with the Cuckoo thus gan chide
In the next bush that was me fast beside
I heard a Nightingale so glad by [illegible]
That her clear voice made a loud rioting
Echoing thorough all the green wood wide

"Ah good sweet Nightingale for my heart's cheer
Hence hast thou stay'd a little while too long
For we have had the sorry Cuckow here
And she hath been before thee with her song
Evil light on her! she hath done me wrong.

But hear you now a wonderous thing I pray
As long as in that swooning-fit I lay
Methought I wist right well what these birds meant
And had good knowing both of their intent
And of their speech and all that they did say

The Nightingale thus in my hearing saith
Now honest Cuckow go away somewhere
And let us that can sing inhabit here
For every wight eschews thy song to hear
Such uncouth singing is it in good faith.

What quoth she what is it that ails thee
It seems to me I sing as well as thou
For mine's a song that is both true & plain
Although I cannot quaver so in vain
As thou dost in thy throat I wot not how

And that was right upon a tree fast by,
But who had then an evil game but I?
Now God quoth I that died upon the rood
From thee & thy base throat keep all that's good
For little joy have I now of thy cry

And as I with the Cuckoo thus 'gan chide
In the next bush that was me fast beside
I heard a Nightingale so gladly sing
made ~~ring~~ a loud rioting
That his clear voice ~~a mighty ringing~~
~~made~~
That Echoed
Echoing thörough all the green wood wide
wide
"Ah good sweet Nightingale for my hearts cheer
Hence hast thou stay'd a little while too long
For we have *had the sorry Cuckow here*
And she hath been before thee with her song,
Evil light on her! she hath done me wrong

But hear you now a wonderous thing I pray
As long as in that swooning-fit I lay
Methought I wist right well what these birds
meant
had
And ^ *good knowing both of their intent*
eech
And of their sp{each and all that they did say
~~I heard them both [?the] [?]~~
The Nightingale thus in my hearing saith
Now honest Cuckow go away somewhere
And let us that can sing inhabit here
v
For e{wery wight eschews thy song to hear
Such uncouth singing is it in good faith!

What (quoth she) what is it that ails thee
now
It seems to me I sing as well as thou
For mines a song that is both true & plain
i
Although I cannot qua}ver so in vain
As thou dost in thy throat I wot not how

103–120 MH picks up transcription in mid-line and carries on through l. 120.
110 Revision is written in pencil.

All men may understanding have of me,
But Nightingale so may they not of thee,
For thou hast many a nice and curious cry
I heard thee say Jug, jug: Now how may I
~~I pray thee knowledge give what that should be.~~
Have knowledge I thee pray what this should be

Ah, fool! quoth she, wist thou not what it is
As often as I say jug, jug, I wis,

Then mean I that I should be wondrous fain
That shamefully they all of them were slain
Who against love mean any thing amiss

And also would I that they all were dead
Who do not think in love their life to lead
For who is loth the God of Love to obey
[illegible]
And for that cause jug jug I say take heed

Eye, quoth the cuckoo that is a quaint law
That all must love or perish wretchedly
But I take leave of all such company
For mine intent it neither is to die
Nor ever while I live Loves yoke to draw

For Lovers of all folk that be alive
The most disquiet have & least do thrive
Most feeling have of sorrow woe & care
And the least welfare cometh to their share
What need is there against the truth to strive.

[*The Cuckoo and the Nightingale*]

All men may understanding have of me,
But Nightingale so may they not of thee,
For thou hast many a nice and curious cry
Ive heard thee say Jug jug: Now how may I
Have I thee pray
~~I pray thee~~ knowledge ~~have~~ what that should be
Have knowledge I thee pray what this should be
~~I pray thee~~
Ah, fool! quoth she, wisth thou not what it is
As often as I say jug, jug, I wys,
Then mean I that I should be wondrous fain
one &
That shamefully they ^ all ~~of them~~ were slain
~~ever~~ ~~aught~~
Who against love mean any thing amiss

And also would I that they all were dead
Who do not think in love their life to lead
is loth obey
For who ~~so's~~ the God of Love to ~~serve~~
Is only fit to die I dare well say
~~I dare well say is only fit to [?starve~~]
~~cause I cry~~
~~And for~~ that ~~still~~ ^ jug jug I ~~cry~~—take heed
fine
Aye quoth the Cuckoo that is a ~~queint~~ law
ruefully
That all must love or perish ~~shamefully~~
[~~?ruefully~~]
But I take leave of all such company
For mine intent it neither is to die
Nor ever while I live Love's yoke to draw
be
For Lovers of all folk that ~~are~~ alive
i}
The most disqu }et have & least do thrive
Most feeling have of sorrow woe & care
And the least welfare cometh to their share
What need is there against the truth
to strive.

125 Revision above the line and "I pray thee" below the line are in pencil; the latter is deleted by erasure. "Have . . . be" was originally written in pencil and rewritten in ink.

129 Revision is in pencil, in MH's autograph; deletion is in pencil.

130 Revisions are in pencil, apparently deleted by erasure.

133 "is" and deletion of "o" in "so's" are in pencil; "loth" was written in pencil, then reinforced in ink.

134 "Is" and the "f" of "fit" are in pencil.

135 "cause" was originally written in pencil, then reinforced in ink; the revision "I cry" is in pencil, as are the deletion strokes in "And for" and "I cry" and the dash after "I cry" in the base text.

136 Revision and deletion are in pencil.

137 Revisions and deletion are in pencil; that above the line is reinforced in ink, that below apparently erased.

What quoth she thou art all out of thy mind
That in thy churlishness a cause can'st find
To speak of Love's true servants in this mood
For in this world no service is so good
To every wight that is of gentle kind
For thereof comes all goodness verily
Thereof all honour and all gentleness
Thereof [illegible] worship [illegible] comfort [illegible] all hearts pleasure
And full assured trust joy without measure
And freshness and delight and jollity

And bounty lowliness and courtesy
And seemliness and faithful company
And dread of shame that will not do amiss
For he that faithfully Love's servant is
Rather than be disgraced [illegible] rather die.

And that this is the truth which now I say
In that belief I will both live & die
And Cuckoo so do thou, so counsel I
Then quoth he [illegible] may no pleasure with me stay
With [illegible] not [illegible]
[illegible] that counsel ever to obey.

Good Nightingale thou speakest wondrous fair
And yet the truth is contrary to this
For love in old folk is but rage, I wis
And it in young folk a great dotage is
Who most it useth him twill most impair.

146 What quoth she thou art all out of thy mind
147 That in thy churlishness a cause [?canst] find
148 To speak of Loves true servants in this mood
149 For in this world no service is so good
150 To every wight that is of gentle kind
151 For thereof comes all goodness verily
152 Thereof all honour and all gentleness
2 1[?] content
153 Thereof ~~come~~ worship^~~hope~~ & all heart's pleasure
154 And full assured trust joy without measure
155 And freshness and delight and jollity

156 And bounty lowliness and courtesy
m} i }
157 And see } le }ness and faithful company
158 And dread of shame that will not do amiss
[?honourubly]
159 For he that fathfully Lov's servant is
d }
disgrace } would chouse to die
160 Rather than be asham'd ~~had liefer~~ die.
[?]
161 And that then is the truth which now I say
162 In that belief I will both live & die
so ~~*this*~~ { *try*
163 And Cuckow ~~eke~~ do thou, ~~so~~ counsel {I
then he Cuckow
164 Then quoth ~~she~~^may no pleasure with me stay
With [?] me if I that counsel do [~~?~~] obey
165 If I that counsel ever do obey.

166 Good Nightingale thou speakest wondrous fair
167 And yet the truth is contrary to this
168 For love in old folk is but rage, I wis
169 And it in young folk a great dotage is.
i }
170 Who most it useth him 'twill most e}mpair.

146–150 This stanza was originally entered in pencil, then rewritten in ink across the pencil.

153 All revision and deletion are in pencil. The "2" and "1" in pencil are transposition signals.

159 Revision is in pencil, apparently deleted by erasure.

160 The added "d" in "disgraced" and the revision of "had liefer" are in pencil.

163 The revisions "so" and "try" appear to be in JC's autograph; "this," deleted in pencil, may be in Dora W's autograph.

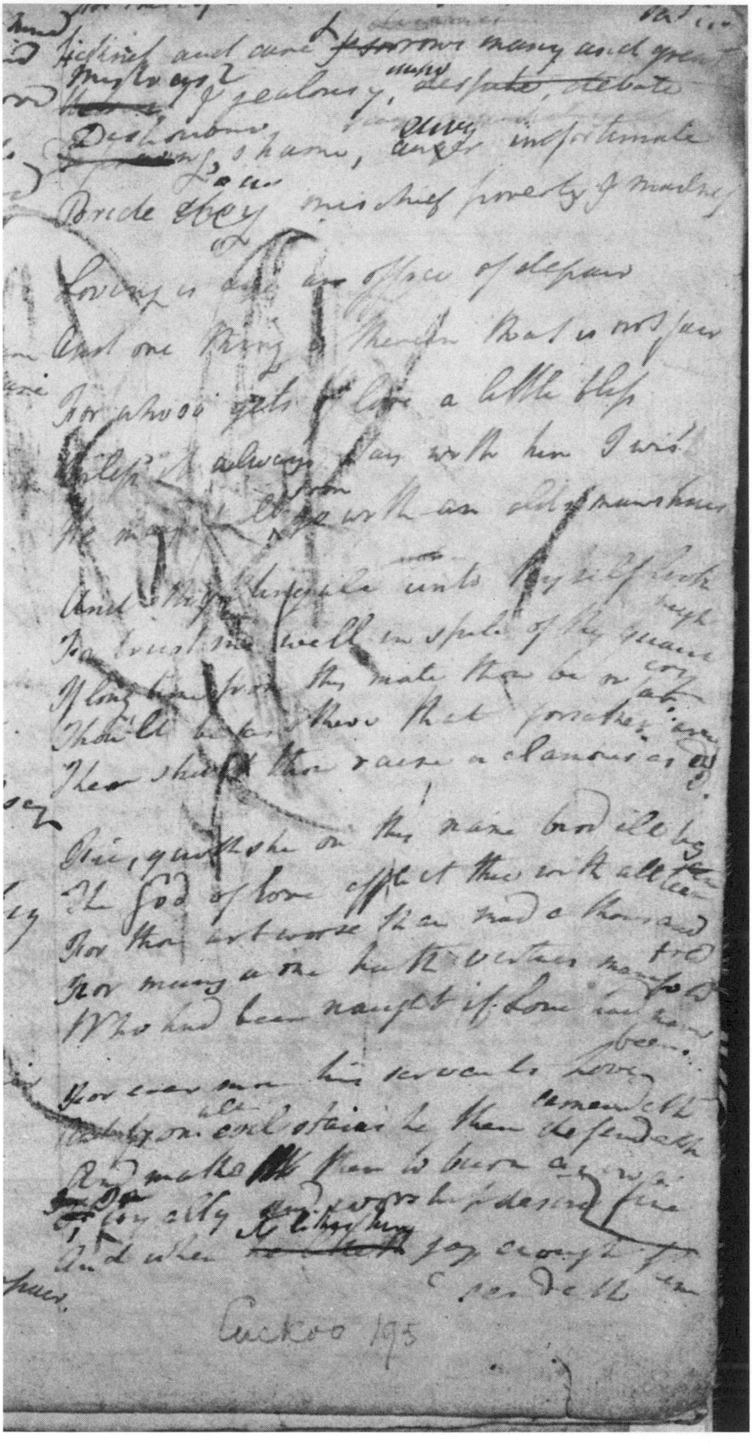

171 For thereof comes discomfort & ~~th~~ heart-sad
sadn[?]
~~& diseases~~
172 Sickness and care & sorrows many and great
Mistrust [?despi]
173 ~~Untrust~~, & jealousy, des~~pite, debate~~
[?rage anger] and [?dishonour] [?]
Dishonour *envy*
174 ~~Depraving~~, shame, anger importunate
and
175 Pride ~~envy~~ mischief poverty & madness

176 Loving is aye an office of depair
177 And one thing is therein that is not fair
178 For whoso gets of love a little bliss
179 Unless it always stay with him I wis?
soon
180 He may full ^ go with an old mans hair.

181 And Nightingale unto thyself look
nigh
182 For trust me well in spite of thy quaint
cry
183 If long time from thy mate thou be or far,
184 Thou'lt be as others that forsaken are
185 The {n / re} shalt thou raise a clamour as do
I.
186 Fie, quoth she on thy name bird ill be
seen
187 The God of Love afflict thee with all teen
188 For thou art worse than mad a thousand
fold
189 For many a one hath virtues manifold
190 Who had been naught if Love had never
been.
191 For ever more his servants Love
amendeth
all
192 And from evil stains he them defendeth
193 And maketh them to burn as in a
fire
~~In~~ In
194 ~~Of~~ ^ loyalty and worship desire
it likes him
195 And when ~~he liketh~~ joy enough them
sendeth

Ink smears in col. 3 seem unrelated to the process of composition.

172 "diseases" is in pencil, as is the deletion stroke; the added ampersand appears to be MH's.

174 "[?rage . . . ?dishonour]" is in pencil; "envy" may be in the autograph of JC.

Ere the whole Convent on the pavement lay
Weeping, and praising Jesus' Mother dear.
And after that they rose, and took their way
And lifted up this Martyr from his bier
And in a tomb of precious marble clear
They did enclose his little body sweet
Whereer he be
There he is now, God grant us him to meet.

in like sort laid low
Young Hugh of Lincoln! ~~that wert slain also~~
well & widely
By cursed Jews — then ~~that [illegible]~~ known
not long since was dealt the cruel blow
For ~~it was not a little~~ ~~[illegible]~~ ~~while ago~~
Pray also thou for us, while here we tarry
with pitying eye
Weak sinful folk, that God ~~[illegible] the most High~~
In mercy would his mercy multiply
On us — for reverence of his Mother Mary.

Prioress [illegible]

And there is [illegible] with feeling — What [illegible]
Your grey locks [illegible] a [illegible]
How hard alas to bear [illegible]

[*The Prioress's Tale*]

226 Eke the whole Convent on the pavement lay
r
227 Weeping, and p[?]} aising Jesu's Mother dear.
o i
228 And after that they ri } se, and took ther } r way
229 And lifted up this Martyr from his bier
230 And in a tomb of pretious marble clear
231 They did enclose his little body sweet
Whereer he be
232 There is he now ^ God grant us him to meet.

in like sort laid low
233 Young Hugh of Lincoln! ~~that wert slain also~~
well & widely
234 By cursed Jews a thing ~~that is well~~ known
not long since was dealt the cruel blow
235 For ~~it was but a little~~ ~~whill~~ ~~while ago~~
236 Pray also thou for us, while here we tarry
with pitying eye
237 Weak sinful folk, that God ~~even the most High~~
238 In mercy would his mercy multiply
239 On us for reverence of his Mother Mary.

[*The Cuckoo and the Nightingale*]

[36] And this is said with feeling—What though now
[37] I wear grey locks upon a worn black brow
[40] How hard alas to bear I only know

&c

232 Revision postdates MS. 35.
233–235 Revisions, in the autograph of MH, postdate MS. 35.
36–37, 40 These lines are in pencil.

The Cuckow & the Nightingale

The God of Love, ah benedicite!
How mightily and how great a Lord is he!
High can he make the heart that's low & poor,
The high heart low, and bring it to death's door;
And hard hearts he can make them kind & free.

Within a little time as hath been found
He can make sick folk whole & fresh & sound
Them who are whole in body and in mind
He can make sick - bind can he & unbind
All that he will have bound or have unbound

To tell his might my wit may not suffice
Foolish men he can make them out of wise

The Cuckow & the Nightingale

The God of Love, <u>ah benedičitè</u>!
How mighty and how great a Lord is he!
High can he make the heart that's low & poor,
And high hearts low through pains which they endure
~~The~~ high heart low, and bring it to death's door;
hard
And ~~proud~~ hearts he can make them kind & free.
hath
th}
Within a little time as ~~has~~ } been found
He can make sick follk whole & fresh & sound
Them who are whole in body and in mind
He can make sick—bind can he & unbind
All that he will have bound or have unbound.
might
To tell his might my wit may not suffice
Foolish me[ ] he can make them out of wise
For he may [ ] all that he will devise
Loose livers [?] [?can] make abate their vice
[?]can
And proud [ ]arts he'll make tremble in a trice.
In brief
~~Shortly~~, the [ ]hole of what he will he may
Against him dare not any wight say nay
To humb[ ]nd afflict whomeer he will
glanden grieve [? ? ? ? ? ? ? ?]
[?T] glad[ ] grieve he hath like skill
But most [ ]ight he sheds on th'eve of May,

---

4 The revision and deletion are in pencil.

11 The word "might" above the line is in pencil.

12–20 These lines are partly obliterated by the tear described in the note to *Prioress's Tale,* l. 177, below. The ink smudges here and in col. 3 are unrelated to the process of composition.

19 The revision above the line is in pencil, as is "glanden" in the left margin (a mistake for "gladden").

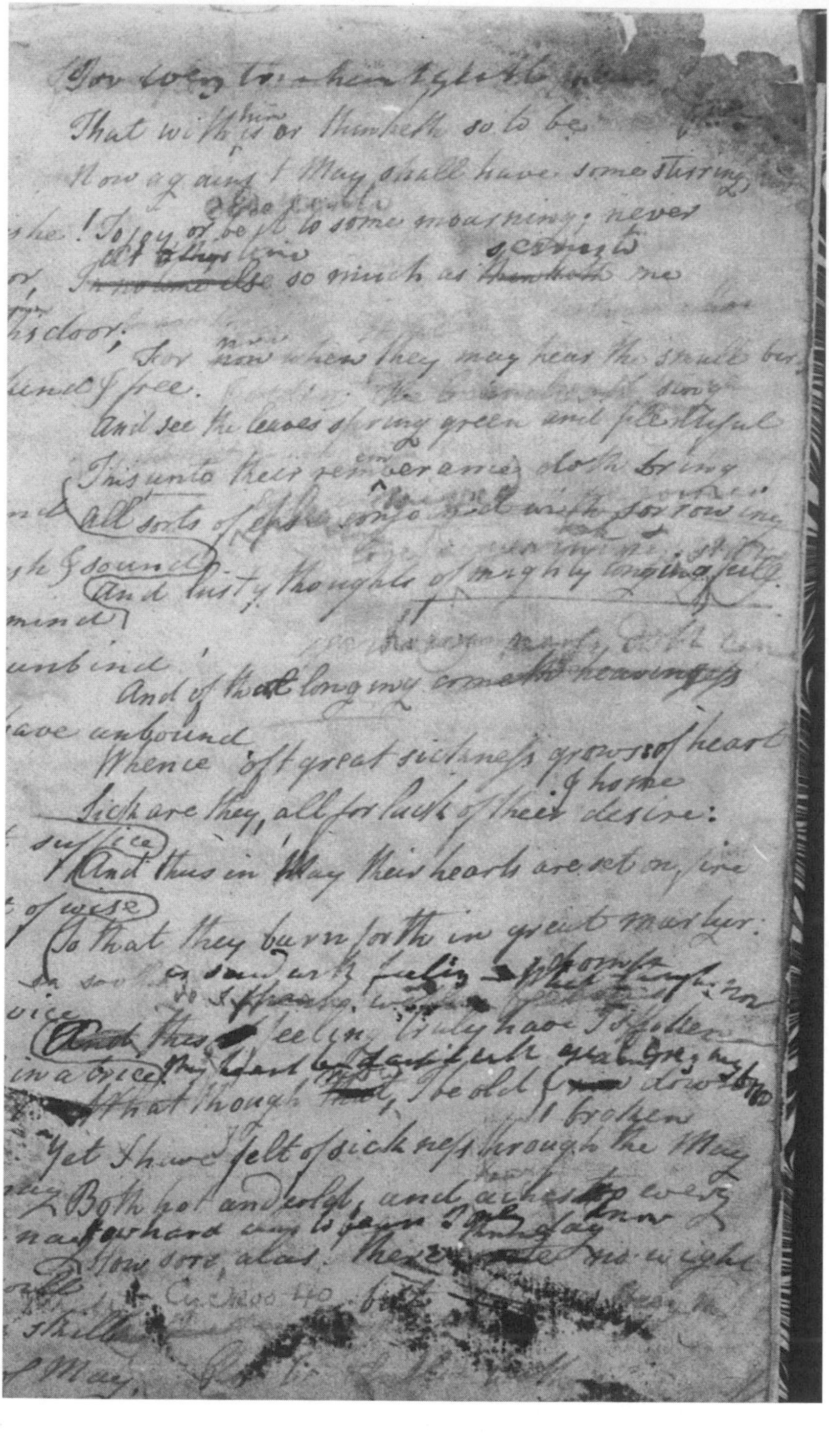

21 For every true heart gentle heart & free
him
22 That with^is or thinketh so to be
23 Now against May shall have some stirring,
else unto
24 To joy, or be it so some mourning; never
At {other / any time} seems to
25 ~~In no time else~~ so much as ~~thinketh~~ me
~~For now that they [? ?] the feathered choir~~
now
[?]
26 For ~~now~~ when they may hear the small birds
~~budding~~ ~~the branches throng~~ sing
27 And see the leaves spring green and plentiful
[?~~budding ?leaves ?the ?branches~~]
em b}
28 This ~~unto~~ their rem^berance doth s}ring
mixed}
~~bliss [?with} ?sorrowing] be joined~~
{pleasure
29 All sorts of^{~~ease conjoin'd~~ with sorrowing
deep &
~~love &~~ yearnings strong
30 And lusty thoughts of^might longing^full.
{heavy [?] doth come
{at {yearning
31 And of th{eir longing cometh heavinsess
32 Whence oft great sickness grows: of heart
& home
33 Sick are they, all for lack of their desire:
M}
34 And thus in m}ay their hearts are set on fire
35 So that they burn forth in great martyr:
is said with feeling—What though now dom
T} In soothe do I speak with feeling
36 ~~And t}his~~^of feeling truly have I spoken
My heart be damp'd with age and & Grey my brow
now
37 What though ~~that~~^I be old & ~~now~~ down-
I /broken
38 Yet ~~I~~ have felt of sickness through the May
heart
39 Both hot and cold, and^aches ~~too~~ every
How hard alas to bear I only know
,} knows day
40 How sore }alas! there ~~note~~ no wight
but I

[37] My blood be [?chilled] with age and Grey my [?brow]
blood be chilled with [?age]

---

21 In pencil, reinforced in ink.
24 Revision in pencil.
26 "For . . . choir" in pencil.
27–28 Revisions above and below line in pencil. Underlining in pencil.
29–31 All revision in pencil.
34 Revision entered in pencil, reinforced in ink.
36 Revision "In . . . feeling," "t," caret, and deletions are in pencil.
37–39 Revisions in pencil.

She asketh & she piteously doth pray
To every Jew that dwelleth in that place
To tell her if her Child had pass'd that way
They all said Nay; but Jesu of his grace
Gave it to her in thought that in a little space ~~this place~~
Her former ~~little~~ Son in that same spot did cry
Where he was cast into the pit hard by

O thou great God that dost perform thy laud
By mouths of Innocents, lo here thy might
This gem of chastity this emerald
And eke of martyrdom this ruby bright
There where with mangled throat he lay upright
The Alma Redemptoris gan to sing
~~So loud that all the place therewith did~~
So loud that with his voice the place did ring.

The Christian folk that thro' the Jewry went
Come to the spot in wonder at the thing
And hastily they for the Provost sent
Immediately he came not tarrying
And praiseth Christ that is our heavenly King
And eke his Mother, honour of Mankind
Which done, he bade that they the Jews should bind.

This Child with piteous lamentation then
Was taken up singing his song alway
And with procession great & pomp of men
To the next Abbey him they bare away;
His Mother swooning by the Bier lay:
And scarcely could the people that were near
Remove this second Rachael from the Bier.

[*The Prioress's Tale*]

She asketh & she piteously doth pray
Of every Jew that dwelleth in that place
To tell her if her Child had pass'd that way
J
They all said Nay; but j esu of his grace
a little space
Gave it to her in thought that in ~~that place~~
for   *in that same spot*
She to her ~~little~~ Son ~~anon~~ did cry
Where he was cast into the pit hard by

O thou great God that dost perform thy
laud
By mouths of Innocents, lo here thy might
This gem of chastity, this emerald
And eke of martyrdom this ruby bright
'
There where with mangle d throat he lay
upright
The Alma Redemptoris gan to sing
~~*So loud that all the place therewith did*~~
r
So loud that with his voice the place did
ring.
The Christian folk that thro' the Jewry went
Come to the spot in wonder at the thing
And hastily they for the Provost sent
h
Immediately c e came, not tarrying
And praiseth Christ that is our heavenly King
And eke his mother, honour of mankind
t
Which done, he bade that they J he Jews should
.
binds
This Child with piteous lamention then
Was taken up singing his song alway
And with procession great & pomp of men
To the next Abbey him they bare away;
B
His Mother swooning by the b ier lay:
And scarcely could the people that were near
Remove this second Rachael from the Bier.

---

149 Base text, through l. 204, is in the autograph of DW.
153–154 Revisions, in the autograph of MH, postdate MS. 35.
162 Revision, in the autograph of DW, predates MS. 35.

[illegible] to ~~all~~ every one
This [illegible] for those bad Jews prepare
That [illegible] wist, and that anon:
Such wickedness his judgments cannot spare
Who will [illegible] evil shall he bear
Them the[illegible] with wild horses did he draw
And after [illegible] hung them by the law.

[illegible] this Innocent doth lie
Upon his [illegible]
Before the [illegible] while the Mass did last
~~And after~~
The Abbot [illegible] his Convent's company
Then sped themselves to bury him full fast,
And when they holy water on him cast
Yet spake this Child when sprinkled was the water
And sang O Alma Redemptoris Mater!

This Abbot who had been a holy Man
And was as all Monks are or ought to be
In supplication to the Child began
Thus saying O dear Child I summon thee
In virtue of the holy Trinity
~~Tell me the cause~~ ~~why~~ ~~[illegible] cause~~ why
Tell me the cause why thou dost sing this hymne
~~Seeing~~ Since that thy throat is cut, as it doth seem

My throat is cut unto the bone I trow
Said this young Child, & ~~in my~~ by the law of [illegible] kind
I should have died, yea many hours ago
But Jesus Christ as in the books ye find
Will that his glory last & be in mind

Torment and
177 ~~*A*~~^ [? *shameful*] *death to* ~~*all &*~~ *every one*
178 *This Pro*[ ] *doth for those bad Jews prepare*
179 *That of this murder wist, and that anon:*
180 *Such wickedness his judgments cannot spare*
181 *Who will do evil evil shall he bear*
182 *Them ther*[ ]*fore with wild horses did he draw*
183 *And after* [ ]*t he hung them by the law.*

184 *Upon his* [ ]*er this Innocent doth lie*
185 *Before the* [ ] *while the Mass did last*
[183] ~~*And after* [ ] *the*~~
is
186 *The* } *Abbot with his Convent's Company*
187 *Then sped themselves to bury him full fast;*
188 *And when they holy water on him cast*
189 *Yet spake this Child when sprinkled was the water*
190 *And sang O Alma Redemptoris Mater!*

191 *This Abbot who had been a holy man*
192 *And was as all Monks are, or ought to be*
193 *In supplication to the child began*
Thus saying
194 *And said* } *o dear Child I summon thee*
195 *In virtue of the holy Trinity*
e
~~*Tell me the cause why thou*~~ } ~~*cause why*~~
196 *Tell me the cause why thou dost sing this hymn*
Since that
197 ~~*Seeing*~~^ *thy throat is cut, as it doth seem*
u
198 *My throat is cut i* }*nto the bone I trow*
by the law of
199 *Said this young Child, &* ~~*in my natural*~~ *kind*
200 *I should have died, yea many hours ago*
201 *But Jesu Christ, as in the books ye find*
202 *Will that this glory last, & be in mind*

---

177 MS. is torn, through l. 185, along a fold apparently made after the leaves had been dispersed.
180 Revision, in the autograph of MH, postdates MS. 35, where the line was left blank.
194 Overwriting, in the autograph of MH, posdates MS. 35.
196–197 Revision, in the autograph of MH, postdates MS. 35.
199 Revision, in the autograph of MH, postdates MS. 35.

And for the worship of his Lady [illegible]
Yet may I sing O Alma loud & cleer

This Well of mercy Jesu's Mother sweet
After my knowledge I have lov'd alway
And in the hour when I my death did meet
To me she came & thus to me did say
"Thou in thy dying sing this holy lay."
As ye have heard; and soon as I had sung
Methought she laid a grain upon my tongue.

Wherefore I sing nor can from song refrain
In honour of that blissful Maiden free
Till from my tongue off taken is the grain
And after that thus said she unto me
My little Child then will I come for thee
Soon as the grain from off thy tongue they take:
Be not dismay'd, I will not thee forsake.

This holy Monk, this Abbot him mean I
Touch'd then his tongue, and took away the grain;
And he gave up the Ghost full peacefully.
And when the Abbot had this wonder seen
His salt tears trickled down like showers of rain
And on his face he fell upon the ground
And still he lay as if he had been bound.

Prioress 225

203 *And for the worship of his mother dear*
204 *Yet may I sing O Alma loud & clear*

W}
205 This w }ell of mercy Jesu's Mother sweet
206 After my knowledge I have lov'd alway
207 And in the hour when I my death did
meet
208 To me she came & thus to me did say"
209 "Thou in thy dying sing this holy lay."
210 As ye have heard; and soon as I had sung
211 Methought she laid a grain upon my
tongue.

212 { *Wherefor I sing nor can from song refrain*
{ Blank here for one line
213 In honour of that blissful Maiden free
214 Till from my tongue off taken is the grain.
T}
215 And after t }hat thus said she unto me,
216 My little Child then will I come for thee:
217 Soon as the grain from off my tongue
they take:
218 Be not dismay'd, I will not thee forsake.

219 This holy Monk, this Abbot him mean
I,
220 Touch'd then his tongue, and took away
the grain;
221 And he gave up the Ghost full peacefully.
222 *And when the Abbot had this wonder seen*
223 His salt tears trickled down like showers
of rain.
The Abbots tears fell down
{ drop droppd o}
224 And on his face he { ~~fell~~ upon the gra }und
225 And still he lay as if he had been
bound

212 Revision, written in MH's autograph over WW's observation, postdates MS. 35, where the line is omitted.

222 Inserted in MH's autograph; this line is omitted in MS. 35.

224 Revisions postdate MS. 35.

Than with their wives, albeit worne seen
Never so true, never so debonair;
All flesh is so newfangled, plague upon't
That, are we pleased with aught on whose clear front
Virtue is stamped, 'tis but for a brief while.

And so it fell that soon as Phœbus went
From home his wife hath for her lemman sent,
Bent over [illegible]
And [illegible] they anon engage

nor will I tell you much of these
But with my Tale go on as I was bent.

When Phœbus' wife had for her lemman sent,
They in their sight deport
anon engage
[illegible]
The white Crow, ever hanging in the cage
Beheld the sport nor did he say one word
But when home was come, Phœbus the lord
The Crow sang Cuckoo Cuckoo! How!
What, Bird! quoth Phœbus, what song sing'st
Thou who wert wont so merrily to sing
Wert thou not wont to sing as did rejoice
This heart of [illegible] my voice
[illegible]

[*The Manciple's Tale*]

wome
[87] Than with their wives, albeit ~~Wmen~~ fair
[88] Never so true never so debonaire,
[89] All flesh is so new-fangled, plague upon't,
[90] That, are we pleased with aught on whose clear front
[91] Virtue is stamped, 'tis but for a brief while.

[99] And so befell that soon as Phœbus went
[100] From home, his Wife hath for her Lemman sent,
they in light disport love's disport
[135] And in ~~light~~ loose dalliance they anon engage

[132] nor will I tell you much of these
[133] But with my Tale go on as I was bent:
[134] When Phœbus Wife had for her Lemman sent,
They in their light disport
[135] In ~~giddy pleasure~~ they anon engage:
He came and in light dalliance they en
[136] The white Crow, ever hanging in the cage,
[137] Witness'd the shame; nor did he say one word
But Home
[138] ~~But~~ soon as ~~home~~ ^ was come, Phœbus the Lord,
The Crow sang
C H
[139] ~~Thus~~, Cuckoo c } uckow Cuckow! ~~sang the Crow~~ h } ow!
quoth
[140] What, Bird! { [?] Phœbus, what song sings't
Thou now,
[141] Thou who wert wont so merrily to sing
Wert thou not wont to sing or did rejoice
mine
[142] [?~~May~~] ~~[?~~] This heart of m } so merrily thy voice
[143] Greeted my my ear

These passages revise text on 7[r].

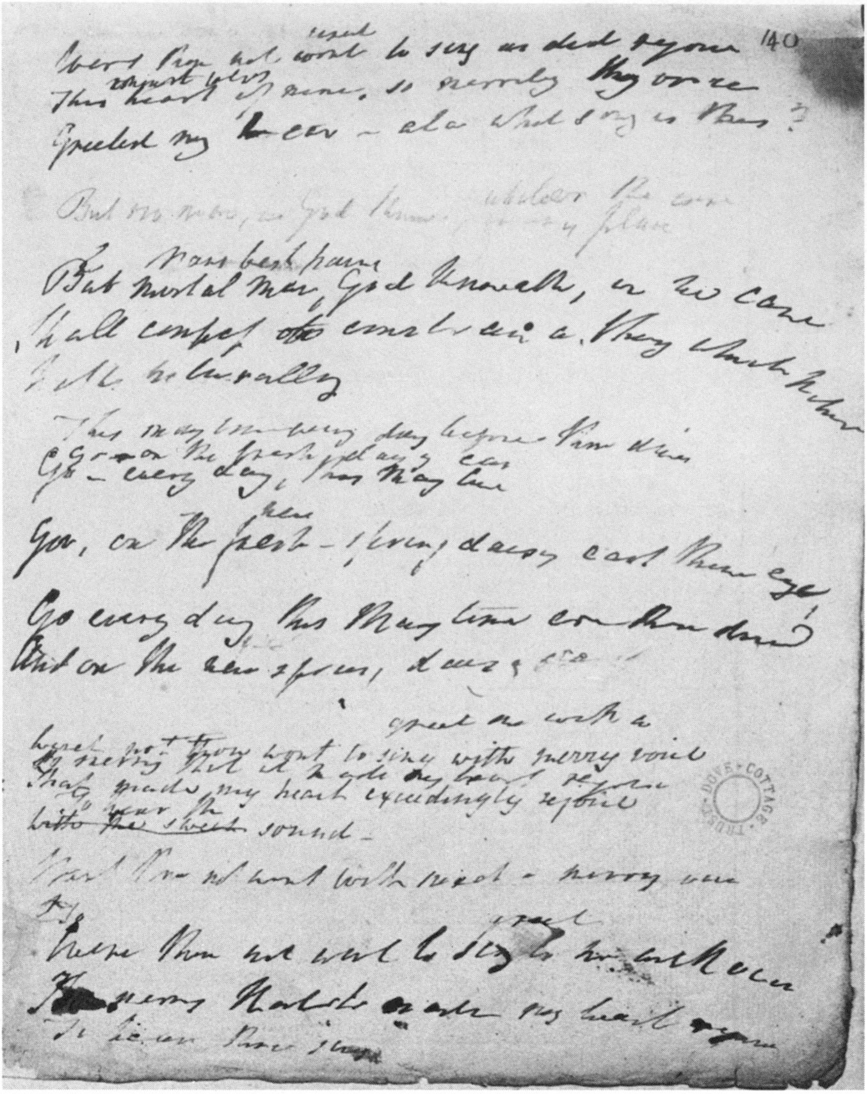

used
[141] Wert thou not wont to sing as did rejoice
~~inmost~~ very
[142] This heart of mine so merrily thy voice
[143] Greetd my ~~h~~ ear—alas what song is this?

whateer the case
[56] But no more, as God knows, in any place
[?] Mans best pains
[56] But mortal man, God knoweth, in no case
to }
[57] Shall compass or } constrain a thing which Nature
[58] hath naturally

[*The Cuckoo and the Nightingale*]

[242] This may time every day before thou dines
[243] Go—on the fresh daisy cas
[242] Go—every day, this May time
new
[243] Go, on the fresh-spring daisy cast thine eye,

[242] Go every day this May time ere thou dine
~~fresh~~
[243] And on the new spring daisy cast

[*The Manciple's Tale*]

greet me with a
[141] *Weret thou not wont to sing with merry voice*
So merry that it made my heart rejoice
[142] *That made my heart exceedingly rejoice*
To hear the
[143] *~~With the sweet~~ sound—*
[141] Wert thou not wont with such a merry voice
[142] ~~T~~ To
greet
[141] Were thou not wont to sing to me with voice
So }
[142] [?~~Too~~]} merry that it made my heart rejoice
[143] To hear thee sing

These three passages revise text on 7^{r}, 7^{v}, and 8^{v}.
56 The first full version of this line is in pencil.
141–143 The first version of these lines is in Dora W's autograph.

DC MS. 24 (with Facing Photographs)

DC MS. 24 consists of miscellaneous leaves from a notebook that Wordsworth used for drafts and copies of poems from 1801 to 1820; it is fully described in Jared Curtis's edition of *Poems, in Two Volumes, and Other Poems, 1800–1807* (Ithaca, 1983), page xix. Two leaves contain Chaucer material: the verso of leaf "e," which contains two quotations concerning Chaucer in William Wordsworth's autograph, and the recto and verso of leaf "f," which contain a draft, in the autographs of William Wordsworth and Mary Hutchinson, of *Troilus and Cresida. Extract from Chaucer*, lines 47–98. Both leaves are of laid paper, 14.5 by 22.3 cm., with chain lines running vertically at intervals of 2.7 cm. Leaf "e" has no watermark, and leaf "f" is watermarked with an emblem, partially visible. The recto of "e," containing a draft of the Prospectus to *The Recluse*, is transcribed in *Home at Grasmere*, edited by Beth Darlington (Ithaca, 1977), pages 265–267. On the verso is the quotation from Milton's *Il Penseroso* that Wordsworth used as an epigraph to *The Prioress's Tale* in all published versions of the poem and the quotation from Drayton's *Elegy to Henry Reynolds*, used as an epigraph on the title page of *The Poems of Geoffrey Chaucer, Modernized*, where it is attributed to Wordsworth. The text of the quotations in DC MS. 24 is as follows:

Call up him who left half told
The story of Cambuscan bold——

That noble Chaucer; in those former times
The first enrich'd our English with his rhimes;
And was the first of ours that ever broke
Into the Muse's treasure, and first spoke
In weighty numbers, delving in the mine
Of perfect knowledge.

The same quotations appear in DC MS. 89, 128v, with slight variations, preceding fair copies of *The Cuckoo and the Nightingale*, *Troilus and Cresida. Extract from Chaucer*, and *The Manciple, (from the Prologue) And his Tale* (the first two surviving only as stubs). It is probable, then, that the quotations in MS. 24 also preceded fair copies of the Chaucer translations, perhaps including *The Prioress's Tale*.

The partial draft of *Troilus and Cresida. Extract from Chaucer* is in Wordsworth's autograph through "the" of line 57; there the autograph changes to Mary Hutchinson's, in both the base text and the revisions. The title "Troilus and Cressida," written at the bottom of the recto, is in the modern autograph of Gordon Graham Wordsworth, and hence is not transcribed. In a copy of *The Poems of Geoffrey Chaucer, Modernized* in the Wordsworth Library, Grasmere, inscribed "William Wordsworth / Rydal Mount / to his dear Daughter / Fanny E. Wordsworth / 1848," there are pencil marks above line 47 of *Troilus* and after line 98, which are clearly related to the MS. 24 fragment of the translation.

So yonder saw I mine own Lady dance
And in that Temple she with her eyes
First caught me captive my true Lady dear,

And yonder have I heard full lustily
My dear heart Cressid laugh; and yonder play
I saw her also once full blissfully
And yonder once she unto ~~me~~ gan say
Now my sweet Troilus love me well I pray
And ~~thus~~ here so goodly did she me behold
That hers unto the death my heart I hold

And at the corner ~~there~~ of ~~yonder~~ that self same house
Heard I my ~~most~~ own beloved Lady dear
So womanly with voice melodious
Singing so well so goodly & so clear
That in my soul methinks, I yet do hear
The blissful sound ~~and~~ & in that ~~place~~ very place
My Lady first me took into her grace

Oh blissful God of Love then thus he cried
When I the process have in memory
How thou hast wearied me on every side
Men thence a book might make a history
What need ~~on me~~ to seek a ~~victory~~ conquest over me
Since I am wholly at thy will, what joy
Hast thou thy own liege subjects to destroy

Troilus and Cressida

47 Lo yonder saw I mine own Lady dance
48 And in that Temple She with her eyes
49 [ ]rst caught me captive my true Lady dear.

50 And yonder have I heard full lustily
51 My deart heart Cresseid laugh; and yonder play
52 I saw her also once full blissfully [?~~Of~~]
53 And yonder once She unto me gan say
54 Now my sweet Troilus love me well I pray
here
55 And ~~there~~ so goodly did she me behold
56 That hers unto the death my heart I hold
that self same
57 And at the *corner ~~there~~ of ~~yonder~~ house*
own
58 *Heard I my ~~most~~ belovéd Lady dear*
59 *So womanly with voice melodious*
60 *Singing so well so goodly & so clear*
61 *That in my soul methinks I yet do hear*
& ~~same~~
62 *The blissful sound ~~yonder~~ in that place*
very
63 *My Lady first me took into her grace*

64 *O blissful God of Love then thus he cried*
65 *When I the process have in memory*
66 *How thou hast wearied me on every side*
67 *Men thence a book might make—a history*
conquest
68 *What need ~~on me~~ to seek a ~~victory~~ over*
me
69 *Since I am wholly at thy will, what joy*
ie
70 *Hast thou thy own lei } ge subjects to destroy*

Will hast thou Lord! on me averted thine eyes
Thou mighty God in ...
Now mercy, Lord thou knowest it well I pray
Thy grace above all pleasures first & chief
And live & die I will in thy belief
For which I ask for guerdon but one boon
That Cresida again thou send me soon

Constrain her heart as quickly to return
As thou dost mine with longing her to see
Then know I well that she would not sojourn.
Now blissful Lord so cruel do not be
Unto the blood of Troy I pray of thee
As Juno was unto the Theban blood
From whence to Thebes came griefs in multitude

And after this he to the gate did go
Whence Cresid rode as if in haste she was
And up & down there went and to & fro
And to himself he said full oft alas
From hence my hope & solace forth did pass
Oh would the blissful God now for his joy
I might her see again coming to Troy.

And up to yonder hill was I her guide
Alas and there I took of her my leave
Yonder I saw her to her Father ride
For very grief of which my heart shall cleave
And hither home I came when it was eve
And here I dwell an outcast from all joy
And shall unless I see her soon in Troy

Well hast thou Lord! on me avenged thine ir[ ]
in ~~Lord of delight & grief~~
Thou mighty God ~~Sovereign of joy & grief~~
Now mercy, Lord thou, know{e}st well I desire
Thy grace above all pleasures first & chief
And live & die I will in thy belief
I ask
For which ^ for guerdon but one boon
a again
That Crese{da ^ thou send me ~~again but~~ soon
quickly
And train her heart as ~~strongly~~ to return
As thou dost mine with longing her to see
would
Then know I well that she ~~will~~ not sojourn.
Now
~~Then~~ blissful Lord so cruel do not be
~~Th~~ Unto the blood of Troy I pray of thee
~~this grant to me~~
As Juno was unto the Theban blood
From whence to Thebes came griefs in multitud{e / es}

And after this he to the gate did go
Whence Cresid rode as if in haste she was
re and
And up & down the{n went ~~un~~to & fro
And to himself he said/full oft ^ alas
From hence my hope & solace forth did pass
Oh would the blissful God now for his joy
ing
I might her see again com{eing to Troy
was [? ~~dear~~]
And up to yonder hill ^ I ~~was~~ her guide
Alas and there I took ^ of her my leave
Yonder I saw her to her Father ride
For very grief of which my heart shall cleave
And hither home I came when it was eve
And here I dwell an outcast from all joy
unless soon
And shall ~~till~~ I may see her ~~back~~ in Troy

Chaucer Modernizations in DC MS. 89

The Cuckoo and the Nightingale, Troilus and Cresida. Extract from Chaucer, and *The Manciple, (from the Prologue) And his Tale* originally appeared on 129^{r}–141^{r} of DC MS. 89, preceded on 128^{v} by the epigraphs from Milton and Drayton described in the headnote to DC MS. 24, page 145. *The Cuckoo and the Nightingale* and *Troilus and Cresida. Extract from Chaucer* appear only as stubs; *The Manciple, (from the Prologue) And his Tale* is complete, including the description of the Manciple from Chaucer's *General Prologue.* The autograph of the epigraph and what survives of *The Cuckoo and the Nightingale* and *Troilus and Cresida. Extract from Chaucer* is Mary Wordsworth's; hers is the principal autograph of *The Manciple, (from the Prologue) And his Tale* as well, although William has entered a few revisions; his is also the autograph of lines 30–51 of the base text. The following fragments survive on stubs:

129^{v} ide (*Cuckoo,* l. ?60)
130^{v} t / ow / [?be] (*Cuckoo,* ll. 108, 116, 125)
131^{v} fold / th / h / th (*Cuckoo,* ll. 188, 191, 192, 195)
132^{r} Bodlean And as he flew, the Cuckoo ever & aye
Bodlea Youth
Kept crying farewell, farewell Pop
As if in scornful (*Cuckoo,* ll. 221–223 and fragment in note to l. 201)
134^{v} n / ce / nce / e / eyes / s / fully / y / pray / hold (*Troilus,* ll. 43–44, 46–48, ?49, 52–54, 56)
135^{v} lead / dread (*Troilus,* ll. 111–112)
136^{v} et / space / n / t / ight / row / w (*Troilus,* ll. 153, 158, ?160, 163, 166–168)

A draft of *The Manciple, (from the Prologue)* appears on 137^{r}, followed by *The Manciple's Tale* on 137^{r}–141^{r}. The MS. 89 text of *The Manciple, (from the Prologue) And his Tale* is the base for the reading text, and all revisions and variant readings in MS. 89 are recorded in the *apparatus criticus.*

For a description of DC MS. 89, see *"The Tuft of Primroses" with Other Late Poems for "The Recluse,"* edited by Joseph F. Kishel (Ithaca, 1986), pages 73–79; see also the headnote to transcriptions of the *Aeneid* drafts in MS. 89, page 331.

Part II: Translation of Virgil's *Aeneid*

Introduction

Wordsworth's translation of Virgil's *Aeneid* is the longest poetic composition of his later years; it is also among his most neglected. It has suffered from the same neglect as all his later works, and this neglect has been compounded by the poet himself, who attempted to suppress the work. Although he completed nearly three books of it, just a brief excerpt, Book I, lines 901–end, was published during his lifetime, and that appeared only in the short-lived journal of classical studies *The Philological Museum.* Christopher Wordsworth, Jr., gave the translation prominence in his *Memoirs of William Wordsworth* (1851), publishing for the first time several letters by Wordsworth and Coleridge relating to it. But the poem itself remained in manuscript. Even the *Philological Museum* extract was rarely reprinted: never appearing in a Moxon edition, it was republished first in Henry Reed's 1851 American edition, and not again until 1884 by William Knight.[1] Only in 1947 did a complete text appear, in Ernest de Selincourt and Helen Darbishire's Clarendon edition of the *Poetical Works of William Wordsworth.* There it appeared inconspicuously in reduced type, as Appendix A to volume IV. It is not surprising that the work has been largely ignored.

Yet this was a major poetical project that absorbed Wordsworth during its six months of composition, and that he revised periodically for eight years. The manuscripts bear witness to his labors. The early drafts in DC MS. 89 are heavily corrected—eighty folio pages are crammed with text, revisions, and insertions, sometimes written between the lines, sometimes in the margins, and sometimes

---

[1]In a headnote to his reprint of the *PM* text, Knight wrote:

> This translation was first published in the *Philological Museum,* edited by Julius Charles Hare, and published at Cambridge in 1832, (Vol. I. p. 382, &c). Three Books were trans-lated, but the greater portion is still in MS. unpublished. Only what is now reproduced appeared in the Museum. It was never included by Wordsworth in any edition of his Works—a sign of his own estimate of its literary value. It was published by Professor Henry Reed in his American reprint of 1851. For an estimate of its value, and Coleridge's opinion of it, &c., see the Life of the Poet in the last volume.

Knight reprinted the letters as published in the *Memoir,* and mistakenly dated the translation to 1816. After Knight's edition, the *PM* extract was regularly reprinted.

with one part of the translation virtually superimposed on another. From these scarcely legible drafts, duplicate fair copies were drawn up, and the fair copies themselves were corrected and revised, in margins, on pasteovers, and on interleaves. Wordsworth consulted at least two Latin editions of the poem, and also had before him the translations of Dryden and Christopher Pitt, whom he acknowledged, and John Ogilby and Joseph Trapp, whom he did not. Moreover, a series of letters written to Lord Lonsdale reveals that Wordsworth had thought very carefully about his principles of translation, and may have been planning a theoretical introduction to the work on the same scale as one of Dryden's prefaces.

It is the aim of the present edition to present the full record of his careful, painstaking effort, and thereby to clarify the place of this translation in the Wordsworthian canon.

Initial Composition

Work on the *Aeneid* translation probably began in late summer, 1823. On July 19 of that year, William and Mary Wordsworth returned to Rydal Mount after several months of travel in England and abroad. It had been a year since the publication of *Ecclesiastical Sketches* and the *Memorials of a Tour on the Continent (1820)*, and the poet was looking for a new project. "[B]y accident," as he later wrote to Lord Lonsdale, he began "an experiment": a translation into heroic couplets of Virgil's *Aeneid*. It is highly unlikely that any composition took place while the Wordsworths were abroad, if only because of the number of books needed, nor is there any evidence that it was begun before their departure. But in August 1823 the translation was under way. First to be written were a few trial passages, such as the opening lines of Book III, and perhaps of Books I and II as well. By the end of the month, he had determined to work consecutively through the first book of the poem. We can be precise about the date because of the presence in MS. 89 of the autograph of Samuel Tillbrooke, bursar of Peterhouse College, Cambridge. Tillbrooke owned the Ivy Cottage (now the Glen Rothay Hotel) adjacent to Rydal Mount, and we know from Mary and Dorothy Wordsworth's letters that he visited the Wordsworths for several days in late August 1823.[2] Sometime during this visit, he copied lines 96–100 of Book I into MS. 89, probably at Wordsworth's dictation. Lines 1–95, mainly in Mary Wordsworth's hand, precede it, and subsequent work proceeds more or less consecutively until the end of Book I. Since the passage is so early in the poem, it seems likely that work on the translation began no more than a week or two before Tillbrooke's visit. And it is also likely that Tillbrooke, himself a classical scholar and friendly with some of the most accomplished classicists of his day,

[2]Tillbrooke is mentioned in DW and MW's letter to Thomas Monkhouse, dated August 20 [1823]; in her August 31 letter to Elizabeth Crump, DW notes that "Mr Tillbrooke has been with us for a few days" (*LY*, I, 210, 218).

encouraged Wordsworth to go forward with his attempt.[3] The challenge was to supplant John Dryden as the pre-eminent voice of Virgil in English. It was a challenge that Wordsworth was determined to meet.

Dryden's Virgil had long been one of the poet's bugbears: "in his translation from Vergil," wrote Wordsworth to Sir Walter Scott in 1805, "whenever Vergil can be fairly said to have had his eye upon his object, Dryden always spoils the passage" (*EY,* p. 641). To keep his own eye more fairly fixed, Wordsworth consulted at least two editions of Virgil: the Delphine edition (the edition that Dryden himself had employed) and the edition prepared by Jan Minel, the seventeenth-century Dutch scholar (Wordsworth's copy of the latter is now in the Cornell Wordsworth Collection). Both editions have extensive editorial notes, and the former also contains a paraphrase of Virgil's poems in Latin prose. Wordsworth paid very close attention to these editions, working into his translation passages from the commentary, and often choosing English derivatives of words used in the Delphine paraphrase. He also had before him four English translations of the *Aeneid*: those of Dryden and Pitt, found in volume 13 of Robert Anderson's *Works of the British Poets*; the 1650 edition of John Ogilby's translation, now in the Wordsworth Library; and probably Joseph Trapp's translation as well.[4] He borrowed freely from each of these translations, sometimes just for rhyme words, sometimes for significant phrases, and sometimes for whole lines and couplets. In a few places, Wordsworth's translation is a virtual pastiche of the translations of his predecessors. But he departed from them just as frequently, striving for an accuracy of translation and a fidelity to the physical properties of Virgil's language—its sounds and rhythms—that none of them had achieved. Whether he was borrowing or offering fresh poetic renderings, his aim is consistent: he was attempting to reproduce in English something he believed that his predecessors had lost—the genuine experience of reading Virgil's Latin.

After Tillbrooke's entry in MS. 89, it is likely that no further entries were made for over a month. The base text of lines 101–285 is in the hand of Dora Wordsworth, and she had left Rydal Mount on July 30, 1823, to work as an assistant at Miss Dowling's school in Ambleside. Despite her being nearby, family letters from August to October clearly speak of Dora as being away from home, and she did not return until the first week of October.[5] So it seems likely that, between late August and early October, Wordsworth either rested from

[3]In the summer of 1812, Tillbrooke visited the Wordsworths in the company of C. J. Blomfield, one of Richard Porson's students and a fellow of Trinity College, Cambridge. At that time, Blomfield had just edited, with J. H. Monk, Porson's *Adversaria;* he and Monk would then found the *Museum Criticum.*

[4]As the notes to the translation show, the case for his use of Ogilby is irrefutable: not only are there echoes of Ogilby's phrasing in WW's translation, but there are marks in the margins of Books I–III of Ogilby, and, at one point, a caricature of WW himself. The case for Trapp is not as clear: the Rydal Mount library catalogue, now in the Houghton Library at Harvard, lists among the translations owned by WW an *Æneis,* the relatively rare title that Trapp used. It seems possible, then, that Wordsworth owned a copy of Trapp; the location of that copy is now unknown.

[5]See, for instance, *LY,* I, 214, 217, 223.

translating, perhaps because of his chronic eye problems,[6] or prepared himself for his project by reading in the editions and translations just mentioned. If he translated at all, he did so sparingly in drafts that do not survive. But with Dora's return, composition proceeded rapidly: Mary, Dorothy, and Dora Wordsworth all took turns as amanuensis, and even John Carter, Wordsworth's clerk, entered a few lines. The bulk of Book I must have been completed by the beginning of the third week of October, for at that time William accompanied Mary and Dora to the Penrith races and "the Balls," a journey that lasted about a week. He spent three days at home, then went back to Penrith and Lowther Castle with Dorothy on October 28, and did not arrive at Rydal until November 3. In a letter of November 9, 1823, he announced to Lord Lonsdale that he had "just finished a Translation into English Rhyme of the first Æneid," and asked his lordship if he would be willing to look it over: "I should be much gratified if you would take the trouble of comparing some passages of it with the original. I have endeavoured to be much more literal than Dryden, or Pitt, who keeps much closer to the original than his Predecessor."[7] If this letter is accurate and Book I was indeed finished by that date, Wordsworth had composed nearly a thousand lines of verse in about three weeks.

Work on Book II did not proceed quite so quickly, as the heavily corrected drafts in MS. 89 attest. Yet rather than sending Book I to Lord Lonsdale as he had offered, Wordsworth decided to wait until Book II was finished. In a letter tentatively dated early December 1823, he explained to Lord Lonsdale his reasons for delay:

> I shall be much gratified if you happen to like my Translation, and thankful for any remarks with which you may honor me— I have made so much progress with the 2nd Book, that I defer sending the former 'till that is finished. It takes in many places a high tone of passion, which I would gladly succeed in rendering— When I read Virgil in the original I am moved, but not much so in the translations; and I cannot but think this owing to a defect in the diction; which I have endeavoured to supply, with what success you will erelong be enabled to judge.—

It is worthwhile to dwell upon this remark because of the clues it gives to Wordsworth's intentions. As in the *Lyrical Ballads* prefaces, he was concerned that the diction of his neoclassical predecessors was defective, mainly because it failed to move the reader. In *Lyrical Ballads,* he tried to reform poetic diction by a process of simplification; in his *Aeneid,* however, simplicity was not the aim. Being true to the language of rustics is appropriate when one treats rustic subjects, but when one works with the language of Virgil, a higher style is in order, a style as true to Virgil as possible. That higher style admits Latinate diction and syntax in ways that are unique in the corpus of Wordsworth's poetry.

Despite the hopeful tone of the December letter, Wordsworth's progress on

---

[6]In two letters of October 10, one to Elizabeth Crump and the other to Mary Laing, DW mentions that WW's eyes had been poorly of late (*LY,* I, 221–224).

[7]For the letters to Lord Lonsdale, here and elsewhere, I quote directly from the manuscripts, now part of the Lonsdale Archive in the Cumbria County Records Office, Carlisle. Partial texts of the letters may be found in Appendix I, pp. 561–567.

Book II was much slower than he anticipated. In the MS. 89 drafts of Book II, Mary was his principal amanuensis, and for a few hundred lines William entered the drafts himself. The middle third of the book, lines 329–664, is heavily revised—much more than any other part of the poem. Especially difficult were the appearance of Hector's ghost (ll. 361–405), Aeneas's encounter with Pantheus (ll. 432–453), and the battle sequences (ll. 552–661), passages that surely take the "high tone of passion" Wordsworth speaks of. We can date his progress more precisely by the presence of Dora Wordsworth's autograph. Dora served as amanuensis for about a third of Book I, but in Book II her presence is considerably reduced: only about a tenth of the manuscript is in her hand, and her hand disappears altogether after line 749. Dorothy Wordsworth tells us why, in a letter to Mary Laing of December 28, 1823. Dora, she writes,

> left us on Saturday the 19th, accompanied to London by Miss Jane Dowling. She will remain in Gloster Place till after New-year's-day, and then will go to Hendon (near Hampstead) to remain there till March or April when she will return to her Friends in Gloster place and will then have an opportunity of seeing London at leisure, and at the pleasantest season of the year.

Dorothy also relates that William's eyes have been "in their very best state," even though he has been "constantly busy," and that Dora has been "very useful" to him. At any rate, he had finished at least 749 lines of Book II by December 19, and, as the Christmas holidays approached, was compelled to be his own copyist for lines 750–835. Then, presumably after Christmas and perhaps from now-lost drafts, Mary entered the remainder of Book II, with relatively few corrections mainly in her own hand.

With Book II completed, the Wordsworths began the laborious task of preparing fair copies, while William pursued his translation of Book III. Duplicate fair copies were made: MS. 101A, in Mary Wordsworth's hand, and MS. 101B, in Dorothy's. Mary wrote out her manuscript first, copying directly from MS. 89, and Dorothy used Mary's fair copy as the basis for her text. Along the way, numerous small corrections were made (often in the spelling of classical names; William must have dictated much of MS. 89 because these spellings are often phonetic), punctuation was tinkered with, and a few lines were substantially revised, especially in MS. 101B. The process was finished by January 23, 1824, when the poet sent Lord Lonsdale the fair copy of Books I and II in Dorothy's hand, accompanied by an apologetic cover letter.

> I am quite ashamed of being so long in fulfilling my engagement. But the promises of Poets are like the Perjuries of Lovers, things at which Jove laughs.— At last, however, I have sent off the two first books of my Translations, to be forwarded by Mr Beckett. I hope they will be read by your Lordship with some pleasure, as they have cost me a good deal of pains. Translation is just as to labour what the person who makes the [effort *del*] attempt is inclined to. If he wishes to preserve as much of the original as possible, and that with as little addition of his own as may be, there is no species of composition that costs more pains.

Besides enumerating his pains, Wordsworth was also careful to distinguish his versification from that of Dryden and, especially, Pope:

> I ought to say a prefatory word about the versification, which will not be found much to the taste of those whose ear is exclusively accommodated to the regularity of Popes Homer. I have run the Couplets freely into each other, much more even than Dryden has done. This variety seems to me to be called for, if any thing of the movement of the Virgilian [metre *del*] versification be transferable to our rhyme Poetry. . . .

That is, not only was he making his diction more Latinate than usual; he was also making the cadences reflect those of the Latin hexameters. In so doing, he risked violating the expectations of an audience used to what he elsewhere called "the poison of Pope's Homer."[8]

Meanwhile, the pained poet moved forward with Book III, working against a tight deadline: an impending departure in mid-February to visit the Beaumonts at Coleorton.[9] He made rapid progress. By February 5, he had finished at least 770 lines,[10] and by his departure for Coleorton, some 832 lines of poetry had been finished, all of Book III except the Cyclops episode near its end.[11] The drafts in MS. 89 bear witness to Wordsworth's haste: there are not as many corrections as in earlier books, the entries of the individual copyists (Mary and Dorothy Wordsworth) are somewhat longer, and in places their handwriting, especially Mary's, becomes quite sloppy. From the drafts, Mary drew up a fair copy of lines 1–816—that is, all of Book III up to the untranslated Cyclops episode—and sewed it in a brown paper wrapper that could very well have come from Miss Dowling's school: on the front is an engraving of a mother reading to her child; on the back are three woodcuts of a bald-pated man stuck in the mud (in the middle one, he is beating an ass with a cudgel).[12] Whether this is Mary's

---

[8]"It will require yet half a century completely to carry off the poison of Pope's Homer," wrote WW to Walter Scott, January 17, 1808 (*MY*, I, 191).

[9]DW's December 28 letter is the first to mention this visit. She writes: "My Brother talks of setting off in the middle of February to spend a month with our Friends Sir George and Lady Beaumont; and I am to accompany him" (*LY*, I, 240). She speaks of the trip again on January 7, 1824, this time in a letter to EQ. After telling him she is "much hurried," she writes:

> My Brother and I are going to Coleorton next week, and as I shall set off on Monday I am now in the last bustle of preparation. He will join me at Kendal on Tuesday Evening, and on Wednesday we take the coach for Preston, where we shall halt one day at Mr Horrock's—another day at Liverpool with the Crumps, and hope to be with Sir George and Lady Beaumont on Saturday. (*LY*, I, 241)

The discrepancy about the dates of the visit is curious; it seems a deliberate evasion. She then goes on to say: "My Brother's eyes have been much better this winter, though he has worked very hard. It has not been Doro's fault that the transcript of the 'Nightingale' was not finished before she left home, and no doubt she has explained to you how it happened" (*LY*, I, 242). No doubt it was her duties as amanuensis for her father, as well as her unexpectedly abrupt departure for London, that prevented the transcript. About the 'Nightingale,' see p. 272.

[10]It should be noted that ll. 1–101 had been composed significantly earlier, probably contemporary with the opening lines of Book I. From its placement in MS. 89 (for which see Transcriptions, pp. 416–417), Book III, ll. 1–57, may even have been the first part of the translation composed.

[11]Space for it had been left on 186^v and 187^r of MS. 89.

[12]The three woodcuts are, in all probability, intended as illustrations to William Cowper's ballad *The Diverting History of John Gilpin.* I am indebted to Mark L. Reed for this suggestion.

sly comment on her husband's progress we will never know. But we do know that in the case of Book III duplicate fair copies were not drawn up. Apparently, there was not enough time.

In the middle of the composition of Book III, disaster struck: his lordship was not wholly impressed with the translation, and told Wordsworth so in a "friendly and frank communication." The poet was quick to respond, in the form of a six-page epistolary essay on his principles of translation. It seems that Lord Lonsdale objected to the diction of the translation, and so Wordsworth explained and defended himself: "My own notion of translation is, that it cannot be too literal, provided three faults be avoided, baldness, in which I include all that takes from dignity; and strangeness [and *del*] or uncouthness including harshness; and lastly, attempts to convey meanings which as they cannot be given but by languid circumlocutions cannot in fact be said to be given at all." Although he admitted that he might be guilty of these faults at times, he mainly cited passages from Dryden's translation, to show their flaws. The main passage he discussed is from Book II of the *Aeneid*, where Aeneas in a dream addresses Hector's ghost. Here is Dryden's version, as quoted by Wordsworth in the letter:

> O Light of Trojans and support of Troy
> Thy Father's Champion, and the Country's joy,
> O long expected by the friends, from whence
> Art thou returned so late for our defence
> Do we behold thee wearied as we are
> With length of labours, and with toils of war,
> After so many funerals of thy own
> Art thou restored to thy declining Town?

This I think not an unfavorable specimen of Dryden's way of treating the solemnly pathetic passages. Yet surely here nothing of the cadence of the original, and little of its spirit. . . .

What Wordsworth meant by "spirit" is not very clear, but what he meant by "cadence" is. Rather than imitate Virgil's enjambment, Dryden constructed a set of closed couplets, each with its own rise and fall. As a result, Virgil's cadences are utterly lost. Wordsworth's own version is quite different. This passage, by the way, was revised eight times between 1823 and 1827, when work on Book II ceased—on no passage did the poet work harder.

> O Light of Dardan Realms! Most faithful Stay
> To Trojan courage, why these lingerings of delay?
> Where hast thou tarried, Hector? From what coast
> Com'st thou long-wish'd for? That so many lost—
> Thy kindred or thy friends— such travail borne
> By this afflicted City—we outworn
> Behold thee![13]

[13]The text quoted here is that of the base text in MS. 101B, the manuscript sent to Lord Lonsdale, and differs from my reading text, which is based on the revised version of these lines, composed in 1827. For the reading text, see p. 226; for the original MS. 101B version, see Transcriptions, pp. 546–547.

Here the couplets are indeed run into one another, and something very like the movement of the Virgilian hexameter is preserved. Even so, the letter concludes with the following, rather weary, remark: "Had I begun the work 15 years ago I should have finished it with pleasure—at present, I fear, it will take more time than I either can or ought to spare. I do not think of going beyond the 4th Book.— " And in fact he did not proceed, from either fatigue or discouragement or an unwillingness to devote the time to it. But he had not wholly given up on what he had completed: instead, he packed the fair copy of Book III in his bags, asked Lord Lonsdale to forward Books I and II to Sir George Beaumont, and departed with Dorothy for Coleorton, London, and Cambridge, determined to obtain some second opinions.

It is necessary to consider why the opinions of Lord Lonsdale and, presumably, the Beaumonts were so important to Wordsworth.[14] The Lonsdale letters make clear that Wordsworth knew his exceedingly literal translation risked losing popular appeal. In the February 5 letter, he wrote:

> It was my wish & labour that my Translation should have far more of the genuine ornaments of Virgil than my predecessors. Dryden has been very careless of these, and profuse of his own, which seem to me very rarely to harmonize with those of virgil. . . . I feel it however to be too probable, that my Translation, [ma *del*] is deficient in ornament, because I must unavoidably have lost many of Virgil's, and have never without reluctance attempted a compensation of my own.

And in another letter to Lord Lonsdale, written February 17, 1824, from Coleorton, he cites two "harsh and bald" lines of his own translation, and remarks: "So true is Horace's remark 'in vitium ducit culpæ fuga &c.'"[15] His remarks about his versification, already discussed, have a similar tenor: readers accustomed "to the regularity of Popes Homer" will not find the couplets of his translation "to the[ir] taste." But couplets are necessary, because the "remote[ness]" of antique "religion, . . . warfare, their course of action and feeling" "require[s] every possible help and attraction of sound in our language." Apparently, Wordsworth considered Lord Lonsdale and the Beaumonts sympathetic, intelligent representatives of the class of readers he intended his translation for: sophisticated people of taste, whose ears were unspoiled by Pope's Homer, and who had enough of a classical education to appreciate the fidelity of his own efforts. Moreover, as Virgil translations were often published by subscription, he probably needed the approval of men such as Beaumont and Lord Lonsdale in order to promote his efforts and organize a subscription list.[16]

---

[14]No record survives of the Beaumonts' reaction to the translation, but WW certainly discussed it with them. On the back wrapper of Book II of MS. 101B a note, in WW's hand, indicates that the manuscript is to be sent to Lady Beaumont at her London address.

[15]Horace, *Ars Poetica,* l. 31. The full line reads: "in vitium ducit culpae fuga, si caret arte" (Avoidance of fault leads into error, if one lacks skill).

[16]I am indebted to R. A. Foakes for this suggestion. In 1794, James Beresford published his *Aeneid* by subscription (Joseph Johnson was the publisher), and in 1820, John Ring published by subscription a two-volume translation of Virgil. Ring published his work with Longman. Both works were prominently reviewed, and both were published by WW's own publishers, so it is likely that he knew of them. But there is no evidence that he used them in his own efforts.

And it is also possible that, in soliciting their opinions, he was looking for a dedicatee: as the Marquis of Normanby was to Dryden, so Lord Lonsdale or Sir George Beaumont might be to Wordsworth. In any case, his letter to Lord Lonsdale of February 17 sums up his view of the project: "I began my Translation by accident," he wrote;

> I continued it with a hope to produce a work which should be to a certain degree affecting, which Drydens is not to me in the least. Dr Johnson has justly remarked that Dryden had little talent for the Pathetic, and the tenderness of Virgil seems to me to escape him.—Virgil's style is an inimitable mixture of the elaborately ornate, and the majestically plain & touching. The former quality is much more difficult to reach [in our language *del*] than the latter, in which whoever fails must fail through want of ability, and not through the imperfections of our language.

Again, it is the pathos of Virgil—and Virgil's genuine style—that Wordsworth was hoping to capture, and hoping to do so without "a compensation of my own." The translation, then, was an experiment very much in keeping with the experiments of earlier years: with eye firmly fixed on his object, he was testing the extent to which the genuine language of Virgil's poetry might be reproduced in English, and still move and impart pleasure to his readers.

Coleridge

Wordsworth was already at Colcorton, en route to London, when he received his manuscripts back from Lord Lonsdale. While in London, in April 1824, he did something he had not done for many years: he lent a fair copy of the translation to Coleridge, so that he might correct the irregularities of diction that bothered his lordship so much. Not since the affair over *The White Doe of Rylstone* had Wordsworth entrusted Coleridge with a major poetical manuscript, and that he did so in this case is a testimony to the importance that Wordsworth attached to his translation. But Coleridge's reaction was, at best, lukewarm. His comments survive in a letter of April 12, 1824, and in detailed notes to Book I, which he drew up at Wordsworth's request and which the Wordsworths carefully preserved, pinned inside MS. 89. These notes are witty, cranky, incisive, and obtuse, sometimes all at once. They are also one of the most extensive records we have of Coleridge's attitude toward Virgil. Sometimes Coleridge praises Wordsworth's efforts—"From this line the Translation greatly & very markedly improves, the metre has bone & muscle"—sometimes he condemns—"I grow peevish with you for having wasted your time on a work so [very *del*] much below you, that you can not stoop & take."[17] Together with the *Aeneid* manuscripts, they constitute a significant final chapter in the literary relations of the two men.

---

[17]The first of these comments is from the notes, the second from STC's letter to WW of April 12. I quote from a photostat of the manuscript of the letter, which was formerly in the possession of Jonathan Wordsworth.

On April 3, 1824, Coleridge dined at Gloster Place, home of Thomas Monkhouse, where the Wordsworths were staying during their visit to London. On that evening, speculates E. L. Griggs, Wordsworth lent him the *Aeneid* manuscripts.[18] Five days later, Coleridge wrote to Mrs. Allsop: "There are three Rolls of Paper, Mr. W's translation of the 1. 2. and 3rd Books of Virgil, two in letter-paper, one in a little writing book, in the Drawer under the side board, in your dining Parlour—Be so good as to put them up & give them to the Bearer, should Mr. A. not be at home."[19] The letter clearly describes MS. 101B, the "two in letter-paper," and MS. 101C, the "little writing book." Throughout the MS. 101B fair copy of Book I are many traces of Coleridge's writing: marginal signals, line numbers, and two pencil notes, and there is a single pencil note in MS. 101C.[20] Coleridge worked hard for "three whole days" on the translation,[21] comparing it closely with the Latin and sometimes with Dryden, and frequently offering his own alternatives to passages he believed Wordsworth had "botch[ed]." At the same time, he was writing a delightfully irreverent commentary on Book I of the *Aeneid*, which he preserved on two folded sheets of letter paper, DC MS. 101D. For instance, of Neptune's chastisement of the unruly winds, he wrote: "The following speech is as good as the original—which for the life of me I could never read even at School but as a Tom Thumb Tragedy. The Quos ego, Sed motos . . . for exquisite vulgarity & boatswain matter is incomparable. . . ." Of Jupiter's prophecy to Venus of the greatness of Augustus Caesar, Coleridge remarked: "For myself, I wonder at your patience in wading thro' such a stiff Manes mortuum of Dullness! and that of the dullest sort, to wit, History in prosing narrative prophecy—with so ludicrously anachronical a familiarity of names and detail—old acquaintances of the last Platonic Sexmillenium!" In offering an alternative to a line describing the speed of a Spartan huntress, he wrote: "And leaves behind swift Hebrus in her flight. or course or speed (which, by the bye, with Virgil's pardon, she might have done on a Donky:)"

With this banter Coleridge mixed a number of less well tempered criticisms of Wordsworth's diction and syntax, which could not have amused the aspiring translator nearly so much. He was especially critical of the Latinity of Wordsworth's style—his tendency to bend English out of its natural shapes and patterns to reflect the Latin more exactly. "There are unenglishisms," Coleridge complained, "here & there in this translation of which I remember no instance in your own poems, one or two in the Descriptive Sketches excepted. Such as the Walter Scott abrupt nudity of the article. . . ." It is interesting that Coleridge singled out *Descriptive Sketches*. In reaching for a poetic style suitable for the sublimity of the Alps, Wordsworth adopted a Latinate diction and syntax that Coleridge had elsewhere called "knotty and contorted, as by its own impatient strength."[22] Émile Legouis, in enumerating the stylistic characteris-

---

[18] *STCL*, V, 347.

[19] *STCL*, V, 347.

[20] See Appendix II, pp. 569–577.

[21] Probably only April 9–10, as the letter to Mrs. Allsop is dated April 8, and the April 12 letter states that STC was ready to return the manuscripts on Saturday, April 10.

[22] *STCBL*, II, 77.

tics of *Descriptive Sketches*, noted its "irregular suppression of the article," the very fault Coleridge complained of in the translation, and also Wordsworth's "employment . . . of words used in an obsolete sense, at times with a somewhat pedantic regard to etymology, . . . the imitation of the Latin ablative absolute," and various kinds of Latinate inversions.[23] All of these are characteristics of the style of the *Aeneid* translation as well, and, as I have already suggested, are part of a consistent attempt to recreate the experience of reading a Latin poem.[24] But for Coleridge, these are defects of style which Wordsworth ought to have avoided.

As Coleridge read on, he grew increasingly irritated by Wordsworth's stylistic experiments. At line 424, he wrote: "I am sick of finding fault, the more discomfortably because my main feeling is that of faulting you for undertaking what compared with the original is scarcely a possibility, & your name is such that comparison with Dryden, Pitt, Beresford &c &c stands you in poor stead—nulla gloria præterire claudos."[25] And sixty lines later comes this note, the longest and most revealing of all. Wordsworth had written that Pygmalion's "arts . . . gave vain scope / In Dido's bosom to a trembling hope." Coleridge could hold back no longer.

> You have convinced me of the necessary injury which a Language must sustain by rhyme translations of great length. What would you have said at Allfoxdon or in Grasmere Cottage to giving vain scopes to trembling hopes in a bosom—Were it only for this reason, that it would interfere with your claim to a Regenerator & Jealous Guardian of our Language, I should dissuade the publication. For to you I dare not be insincere—tho' I conjecture, from some of your original Poems (of the more recent, I mean) that our tastes and judgements differ a shade or two more than formerly—& I am unfeignedly disposed to believe, that the long habits of minute discrimination have over-subtilized my perceptions. I have composed about 200 verses within the last 18 months—& from the dissatisfaction if they could be read in the most newspaper flat reading other than strongly distinguishable verse, I found them polished almost to sensual effeminacy . . . —You must therefore take my opinions for what they are—

The scars of all the old wounds show themselves here: memories of the happy days in Alfoxden and Grasmere, side by side with questions of insincerity and that sense of inferiority which irritated Coleridge so much, even as he nursed it. And underneath it all is the same question that lay beneath so much of *Biographia Literaria:* Why isn't Wordsworth getting on with *The Recluse*? Why is he wasting his time outhobbling the lame, when he could be seizing the fire? Coleridge's letter of April 12 summarizes his opinions pretty well:

> could I be persuaded, that if as well done as the nature of the thing (viz. a translation, Virgil in English) renders possible, it would not raise; but simply—sustain your well-merited fame, for pure diction, where what is not idiom is never other than logically correct; I doubt

---

[23]Legouis, pp. 133–134.

[24]This argument is more fully developed in Graver, *SP*.

[25]"To outrace the lame is nothing to brag about." I have been unable to locate a source for this phrase; it may be STC's invention. For information about Beresford and Hayley, see p. 195.

not, that the inequalities could be removed.— . . . Finally, my conviction is: that you undertook an impossibility: and that there is no medium between a prose Version, and one on the avowed principle of Compensation in the widest sense- / i.e. manner, Genius, total effect. I confine myself to Virgil when I say this.—

We can only guess how Wordsworth reacted to this missive. He had attempted to open the old channels of communication, and had seen too many signs of old, painful patterns of behavior—and he sent Coleridge no more poetical manuscripts. Nor did he take Coleridge's specific criticisms too seriously—only a couple of his suggestions were adopted, and those only temporarily.[26] Yet, near the end of his life, Wordsworth spoke with his nephew Charles Wordsworth about the *Aeneid* translation. "[H]e considered [it] a failure," wrote Charles, "as being attempted on an unprofitable plan (i.e. the plan of no compensation, not a word, or idea beyond what the original contains). . . ."[27] Here Wordsworth echoes Coleridge directly. Without a principle of compensation, he came to believe, too much poetic power is irretrievably lost. In the spring of 1824, however, he had other ideas.

Subsequent Revisions

After receiving the manuscripts back from Coleridge, Wordsworth continued to court advice from his friends: the Beaumonts, Charles Lamb, and perhaps Henry Crabb Robinson all were asked to look the translation over, and it was probably a matter of discussion at Trinity College, Cambridge, as well. The evidence is in the manuscripts, and in subsequent correspondence. On the back wrapper of one of the notebooks of MS. 101B Wordsworth wrote the following note: "To be sent to Lady Beaumont, Grosvenor Square—before or on Saturday Sennight. 20th April." The Wordsworths left London to visit Edward Quillinan at Lee Priory, Kent, on Friday, April 23, 1824. They stayed a week, and returned through London, en route to Cambridge, where they visited Christopher Wordsworth.[28] "Saturday Sennight" would have been May 1, exactly when they were back in London, and it is possible that they picked the manuscripts up at that time and took them to Cambridge, where they met or renewed acquaintance with several prominent scholars, including Julius Charles Hare.[29] But it is more likely that the manuscripts were passed on to someone else in London, probably to Charles Lamb. In December 13, 1824, Dorothy Wordsworth wrote Henry Crabb Robinson to ask Lamb "if my Brother's Translation of Virgil is in his

---

[26]They were entered in MS. 101A, perhaps just after the Wordsworths' return to Rydal Mount in 1824, but they were never entered into the clearner fair copy, MS. 101B. Thus in the reading text these revisions have been relegated to the apparatus.

[27]Mark L. Reed, "Wordsworth on Wordsworth and Much Else: New Conversational Memo-randa," *PBSA* 81, 4 (1987), 451–458.

[28]See *LY,* I, 264–267.

[29]Hare is included in CW's dinner list for May 5, 1824, as is WW's Hawkshead friend Robert Greenwood, William Whewell, and the geologist Adam Sedgwick. Sedgwick wrote the geological sections that were later published with WW's *Guide to the Lakes.* The dinner list is preserved in a manuscript notebook, O.12.52, in the Wren Library at Trinity College, Cambridge.

possession. Tell him, too, that if he would send us a letter either from his India House Desk or from Colebrook Cottage, we should all be well pleased,—and if addressed to my Brother I can insure him an answer from himself" (*LY,* I, 294).

Either Robinson was slow to ask or Lamb to respond, for not until May 1825 did Lamb write Wordsworth that he had "lost sight" of the *Aeneid,* and that he ought to check with Sir George Beaumont.[30] It seems, then, that the Wordsworths lost track of the fair copy manuscripts, 101B and 101C, for an extended period of time. When they got them back cannot be determined with certainty, but it is likely that Wordsworth received them directly from the Beaumonts when he, Mary, and Sara Hutchinson visited Coleorton in October and November 1825. If they did indeed receive the manuscripts at that time, it had been well over a year since he had seen them last.

We now enter a rather sketchy period in the history of the *Aeneid* translation. So far, an account has been given of the writing and copying of Books I and II and of one of the copies of Book III. It is with the partial copy of Book III, found in MS. 101A, that we now must contend. At some point Wordsworth decided to work once more on Book III, probably as a result of nearly losing his only fair copy of that book, perhaps intending to translate the Cyclops episode as he did so. The record of this work is a fair copy of Book III, lines 409–720, written almost entirely in Dorothy Wordsworth's autograph, and subsequently bound with Mary Wordsworth's fair copies of Books I and II. There are several reasons to think that this copy of Book III was made later, perhaps considerably later, than the other fair copies. First, the paper is different from the others in watermark and size, and the date of the countermark is later: 1823, rather than 1820–1822.[31] Second, the text of MS. 101C regularly reflects the latest revisions of MS. 89, whereas the MS. 101A text is revised away from MS. 89, and thus from MS. 101C, regularly. For instance, in 101C, lines 413–414 read: "And a Chaonian harbour won, we greet / Buthrotus perch'd upon her lofty seat." In 101A, these lines read: "And (a Chaonian Harbour [won we *del*] entering,) greet / Buthrotus perched upon his lofty seat." Unfortunately, it is impossible to determine from the revisions whether Dorothy was copying from 101C or from MS. 89, because the new readings in 101A are not found in either manuscript; thus we cannot determine definitively whether her copy of Book III was made before or after the return of 101C. But it seems probable that her copy was made after its return. Near the end of MS. 89 the following note appears in Dorothy's hand: "MSS. Virgil & Well Poem put in Mary's desk upstairs." The "Well Poem" is *Composed When a Probability Existed of our Being Obliged to Quit Rydal Mount as a Residence,* known in the Wordsworth circle as "Verses on Nab Well." MS. 89 contains a fair copy of this poem, and thus Dorothy's note may describe copies of both the Virgil and *Composed When a Probability* that were made contemporaneously. According to Joseph Kishel, the latter poem was finished by October 1826, when William read it to Henry Crabb Robinson.[32] Thus some work on the

---

[30]Lucas, III, 5.

[31]See Manuscript Census, pp. xx-xxi.

[32]*Tuft,* p. 10.

Virgil, in which MS. 89 was used, may have taken place about that time. Since all other revisions depend only on the fair copies and not on MS. 89, it is likely that Dorothy's note refers to when her partial fair copy of Book III was made. A date of late 1826 or early 1827 thus seems a reasonable conjecture for the partial fair copy of Book III in MS. 101A.[33] Perhaps Wordsworth was thinking of including the translation in the 1827 edition of his poems, and undertook the revision for that purpose; perhaps he wanted a back-up fair copy to MS. 101C. Whatever his purpose, this stage of revision must be considered abortive: the manuscript lacks the first 408 lines of Book III, it ends in a series of deletions, its punctuation is sparse and frequently inadequate, and none of its new readings was entered into the cleaner, more complete fair copy, MS. 101C. For these reasons, I have chosen MS. 101C as my copy text for Book III and relegated the variant readings of MS. 101A to the *apparatus criticus.*

The next stage of revision is easier to date: the revision of Book II, which Wordsworth undertook in conjunction with his nephew Christopher Wordsworth, Jr. In the summer of 1827, just having finished his first year at Trinity College, Cambridge, Christopher, Jr., spent the summer at Bowness in the Lake District, where a number of his Cambridge peers met for a course of summer study. According to his manuscript journal, Christopher arrived in the Lakes in early July, was back in Cambridge by early autumn, and regularly visited Rydal Mount on weekends.[34] Christopher, Jr., was an aspiring poet—he had just won university prizes for two of his poems—and an outstanding Latinist, who was reputed to have committed the *Georgics* to memory. So it was natural, and a little flattering, that his uncle might ask for his help on an *Aeneid* translation. That Wordsworth did so suggests that the translation had been a subject of discussion in Trinity College circles for some time. The Wordsworths spent two weeks in Cambridge in May 1824 and surely discussed the translation while they were there, at least with Samuel Tillbrooke, and probably with Christopher, Sr., and other Cambridge scholars whom they met. When William, Mary, and Sara Hutchinson visited Coleorton in 1825, Christopher, Sr., and one of his sons were also guests, and if the *Aeneid* manuscripts were returned at that time, they were probably discussed once again. Moreover, we know that literary subjects were very much on William's mind during his nephew's visits that summer: Christopher, Jr., records conversations about the revisions for *Poems,* 1827 ("his own Poems—new edit^{n} alterations—1000 lines"), his uncle's opinions on Moore, Byron, and Shelley,[35] and at least two discussions about the relationship between

---

[33]A scarcely legible entry in DW's journal (DC MS. 104) for January 10, 1827, may read "Wm at his Virgil."

[34]The journal is Trinity College, Cambridge, manuscript O.11.9. Although CW, Jr., records many of his uncle's literary opinions, he does not record his work on the *Aeneid* translation. There are, however, several gaps in the journal, especially during August. One of their subjects of conversation, incidentally, was CW, Jr.'s own verse, a Latin ode and an English poem on the Druids. CW, Jr.'s visits to Rydal are corroborated by entries in DW's journals, DC MS. 104.

[35]About Shelley, CW, Jr., records: "mad—greatest artist." About Moore: "smells of the perfumer and milliner—never contented with rings & a bracelet—must have rings in the ears—in the nose—rings everywhere—a man of considerable natural genius—" About Byron: "English Bards—I have not read it through, his prophecies generally have turned out false—" CW, Jr., supplied Alexander Grosart with a version of his journal, and several of these comments can be found in Grosart, III.

Homer and Virgil. The first took place in the course of a discussion of the recently deceased Canning: "My Uncle thought—he was a man who wd prefer Virgil to Homer—& wd not understand the grand tho simple poetry of the Holy Scriptures. . . ." The second is just a query—"Virgil how far Homeric?"—which seems to have followed from a discussion of Sophocles. Toward the end of the summer, perhaps in early September after Christopher had stopped making regular journal entries (his last concerned his walking tour of the Lakes, undertaken in August), William must have also asked his nephew to look over the *Aeneid* translation, probably with an eye to publishing it separately at Cambridge. If the revisions of Book III were part of the process of revision for the *Poems,* 1827, the revisions of Book II were not. Apparently, Wordsworth had given up the thought of publishing his work in a collection of his own poetry, and was considering instead a much narrower audience: the scholarly readers of a classical journal.

Christopher and his uncle worked together to revise about a hundred lines of Book II. They first drafted their revisions in MS. 101A, then Christopher deleted the corresponding passage in MS. 101B and entered the revision between the lines in his neatest hand. In some cases, it is clear that the two were working side by side on the same passage: both of their autographs are present in MS. 101A, sometimes revising each other's work. For instance, in both fair copy manuscripts Book II, lines 17–18, originally read: "I will attempt the theme, though in my breast / Memory recoils and shudders at the test." In MS. 101A, alternate versions appear in William's and Christopher's hands, and the finished revision entered between the lines is in Christopher's hand, slightly revised by his uncle. Christopher then entered this finished version in MS. 101B. But in other cases, Christopher seems to be working independently,[36] and in still others he has simply copied revisions into MS. 101B that are in his uncle's hand in MS. 101A.[37] When they had finished their revisions, Book II of MS. 101B was dismantled and interleaved, and Wordsworth apparently directed his nephew to copy the revisions onto facing interleaves. There is only one exception to this procedure: the revised version of Book II, lines 73–82. This passage was revised in Christopher's hand in MS. 101A; these revisions, and a few more, were entered by both Christopher and Dorothy Wordsworth in MS. 101B. Then a pasteover was made, and Dorothy Wordsworth copied out the revised text, with yet further revisions. Whether entered by Christopher, his uncle, his aunt, or a combination of the three, all the 1827 revisions to Book II ought to be considered authoritative. If Wordsworth did not personally compose them (and there is no definitive evidence that he did not), he certainly oversaw and approved their composition. Thus I have included them in my

[36]Book II, ll. 33–34, is a good example, where all revisions in both fair copy manuscripts are in CW, Jr.'s autograph.

[37]Book II, l. 99, is one of several passages where CW, Jr., either copied his uncle's revisions from MS. 101A or copied in ink revisions that his uncle had made in pencil.

reading text, whereas earlier editors of the translation did not.[38]

When Christopher Wordsworth, Jr., left the Lake District for Cambridge, he took with him Book II of MS. 101B, and probably Book I as well. Sometime that autumn, in a letter that does not survive, he wrote to his uncle with hopes of publishing it. In late November 1827 Wordsworth replied:

> As to the Virgil, I have no objections to its being printed if two or three good judges would previously take the trouble of looking it over, and they should think it worth while. Could Mr. Hare find time for that purpose, he or any others. On the other side I have given you a few corrections, and shall be glad of any of yours, or those of anybody else. . . .
>
> I find here Rose on the State of the Protestant Religion in Germany, which I never saw before. I have been very much interested in it. Did you learn whether Mr. Rose as Editor of Museum Crit: could afford me any pecuniary remuneration for the Virgil?[39]

Then, cross-hatched over the page, are revised versions of Book II, lines 55–56, 381–387, and 992–924,[40] and the following note: "Have the goodness to insert the above correction in your copy, if not for preference at least for choice. W.W."[41] Wordsworth speaks here with characteristic diffidence about his efforts: his experiences in 1824 with Lord Lonsdale and Coleridge have made him hesitant about publication. But if there is money to be had for it, and if an accomplished scholar like Julius Charles Hare can look it over, he will consent to publish the translation all the same. For the first time, he is ready to go to press. This stage of the poem, then, as it is presented in MS. 101B, must be considered the first finished state of Books I and II of the *Aeneid* translation. Thus the reading text of this edition reflects the 1827 state of the poem.

Publication

In turning to H. J. Rose or Julius Charles Hare for advice, Wordsworth could scarcely have named scholars of more divergent views. Both were fellows of Trinity College, Cambridge, and both had pursued their studies further in Germany. But there the similarities end. Rose, a former curate of Christopher Wordsworth, Sr., had recently spent a year in Germany, where he had encountered the new German rationalist criticism of the Bible. It seemed to him such a serious threat to Christian orthodoxy that he attacked it in a series of sermons, published in 1826 as *The State of the Protestant Religion in Germany*. This work

---

[38]In *PW*, IV, de Selincourt and Darbishire relegate almost all the MS. 101B revisions in CW, Jr.'s hand to their apparatus, without checking MS. 101A, and thus without determining whether CW, Jr., or WW composed the revision. And they accept the revision, almost all by CW, Jr., on the pasteover. Their handling of this stage of revision causes them to misrepresent WW's intentions in over 100 lines.

[39]I quote directly from the manuscript of the letter, Add. MSS. 46136, BL.

[40]These revisions reflect further drafting in MS. 101A, undertaken, apparently, after CW, Jr.'s departure. These drafts are recorded in the apparatus to the reading text or in the transcriptions of MS. 101.

[41]CW, Jr., never entered the revisions in his copy of Book II, MS. 101B.

drew the attention of Edward Pusey, who later drew Rose into the Tractarian movement.[42] In this context, the apparent interest in reviving the classical journal *Museum Criticum* is curious. Begun in 1813 by J. H. Monk and C. J. Blomfield, former students at Trinity College of the great Hellenist Richard Porson, the *Museum Criticum* was intended as a means of promoting Porson's methods of textual criticism and securing his place as the scholarly successor to Richard Bentley. The journal foundered in 1814 with the death of Blomfield's younger brother, Edward, was revived in the early 1820s, and then terminated after two more numbers, when both Monk and Blomfield were appointed to high clerical offices.[43] If Wordsworth is right about Rose's intentions—and his source is surely Christopher, Jr., or another member of the Bowness study group[44]—then Rose probably would have used the *Museum Criticum* to attack German scholarship, especially of the Bible, and promulgate instead a more insular and less threatening (at least to orthodox high churchmen) English tradition. In any case, Rose's plans, if he had any, fell through, and no further numbers of the journal appeared.

Julius Charles Hare, by contrast, was deeply read in German literature and scholarship, and embraced and championed the historical methodology of Barthold Georg Niebuhr. In 1827, he and his brother Augustus had just published the first edition of *Guesses at Truth,* itself something of a rationalist document, influential on the Broad Church movement.[45] In the next year, he and Connop Thirlwall would publish the first volume of their authorized translation of Niebuhr's monumental *Roman History,* another rationalist work, which discounted as poetic fictions the traditional accounts of early Rome in Livy and other Roman historians.[46] When Niebuhr was subsequently attacked by reviewers (especially in the *Quarterly*) because his methods promoted religious skepticism, Hare defended the historian, and German scholarship generally, in the first of a series of *Vindications* (1829).[47] Eventually, he founded a new periodical, *The Philological Museum,* a journal of classical studies published at Cambridge and intended as a successor to the *Museum Criticum.* But its aims were different. For rather than focusing on the English tradition, Hare used the

---

[42]See the *DNB* entry for H. J. Rose.

[43]Monk was named Dean of Peterborough, then Bishop of Gloucester; Blomfield was elevated to the see of Chester, and later translated to London. The whole run of the journal was published in 1826 by Cambridge University Press for John Murray.

[44]In his manuscript journal, 40^{v}, CW, Jr., mentions Rose's plans to edit the *Museum Criticum* and his problems in obtaining financial support.

[45]Hare was later to marry the daughter of one of the most prominent Broad Churchmen, F. D. Maurice. A later edition of *Guesses at Truth* was dedicated to WW.

[46]This book was in WW's library, and was one that the poet apparently attended to closely. In the *Memorials of a Tour in Italy, 1837,* WW included three sonnets concerned with Niebuhr's reinterpretation of Roman history, and, in a general way, that whole sequence of poems is concerned with the development of nineteenth-century historicism. See Manning, pp. 271–326.

[47]Besides Niebuhr, Hare was also a defender of F. A. Wolf, the controversial Homeric scholar. Of the two men, he wrote: "I know of no philological work, unless it be Wolf's *Prolegomena,* which has effected so much within the same space of time: it has flung an entirely new light over the whole region of ancient history; and hardly a treatise of any value on questions connected therewith has appeared during the last fifteen years in Germany, but we may trace the influence of Niebuhr upon it." This remark occurs in his *Vindication of Niebuhr's "History of Rome"* (1829), p. 15.

journal to import continental, especially German, scholarly methodology into Britain.[48] In the pages of the journal were included translations, discussions, and reviews of continental scholarship, and authors such as Niebuhr, Savigny, Voss, and Hermann are translated or referred to regularly. In its second number, published in 1832, next to reviews of Scholefield's *Aeschylus* (by Wordsworth's nephew John Wordsworth) and Kruse's *Hellas* and essays on Philip of Theangela and the accession of Darius, an excerpt from Book I of Wordsworth's *Aeneid* was published.[49] It was the only part of the poem Wordsworth ever allowed to appear in print.

Wordsworth first met Hare on May 5, 1824, at a dinner party at Trinity Lodge, where, in all probability, the newly composed translation was a subject of conversation: at least we know the two conversed, because Wordsworth asked Hare to send a message to Landor for him.[50] Hare subsequently encountered the Wordsworths at home and abroad on a fairly regular basis. He was in Rydal with Christopher, Jr., in early September 1827, when the revisions to Book II were made, and they surely discussed the translation, perhaps with an eye to publication.[51] Even if they did not, Hare may have seen the manuscripts that Christopher, Jr., brought back to Cambridge—if, that is, Christopher followed his uncle's directions. Hare breakfasted with Wordsworth in London in the spring of 1828, when he was introduced to Coleridge,[52] and the three men met by chance at Antwerp, in August of the same year.[53] But for the history of the *Aeneid* translation their most important meeting came in the summer of 1831. At that time, Hare was on a tour of the Lakes, and paid a call at Rydal Mount.[54] His intentions apparently were more than social. *The Philological Museum* project was under way, and he must have been looking for submissions from someone of Wordsworth's stature, if only

---

[48]In the Preface to the first number, Hare explicitly names Niebuhr, Muller, and Boeckh as scholars who ought to cause English philologists "to think and look about them" (*PM*, I, ii). A fuller account of Niebuhr, Hare, and the role of *PM* may be found in Manning, pp. 290–305.

[49]Manning, p. 301, writes: "That Wordsworth should have published his translation of the *Aeneid* in this context suggests that he thought there was no rigid opposition between his poetry and historicism as represented by Niebuhr." That may very well be, but I suspect that Hare had been badgering him to contribute, and that he was a little bit flattered to have his work appear in the midst of the erudition of his brother's world, even if by this time he had serious reservations about his principles of translation.

[50]In his own letter of thanks, dated December 11, 1824, WW writes: "I sent a message of thanks from Cambridge through Julius Hare, whom I saw at Cambridge in May last" (*LY*, I, 289–290).

[51]Of his visit SH recorded the following, in a letter to EQ of September 12, 1827: "We have had a Mr Hare—the most learned Man in Europe & the most entertaining—when you are learned enough for his conversation—but whose appearance & manners are truly remarkable." Later in the same letter, she wrote: "then followed Southey & Mr Hare—& on Sunday all the Boys from Bowness!" (*SHL*, p. 352). The last comment indicates that Hare was at Rydal Mount with CW, Jr., his brothers John and Charles, and perhaps the rest of the Bowness study group as well.

[52]The introduction to STC was one of Hare's most cherished experiences. In a letter of condolence written to MW after WW's death (in WL), he wrote of the profound influence STC and WW had on the young university men of his generation.

[53]Dora W, who thought Hare a pest, wrote to EQ that "Father would have written to you himself—but scarcely had we entered the Cathedral [in Antwerp] . . . when his Lover the Cambridge Hare rushed upon him" (*LY*, I, 620).

[54]Hare's 1831 visit is recorded in the Rydal Mount Visitors' Book.

to give variety and popular appeal to the new periodical.[55] He asked specifically for an extract from the *Aeneid* translation, and must have renewed his request formally in a letter written the following autumn. Wordsworth agreed, with reluctance, and the result was the publication of Book I, lines 901–end, on pages 382–386 of the second number of *The Philological Museum.* It finally appeared in print in February 1832, over eight years after its initial composition.

In the meantime, Wordsworth had largely set his translation aside. On October 31, 1830, Dorothy Wordsworth noted in her journal that she copied Virgil, and did so again on December 9, 1831. But other than these two notes, no record of work on the poem survives after the flurry of revisions in 1827. Exactly what revision or copying took place in 1830 is unclear. There is a chance, only a slight one, that Dorothy may have been referring to the partial fair copy of Book III, bound in MS. 101A. But it seems more likely that she was describing revisions to the end of Book I of MS. 101A, which anticipate the text of *The Philological Museum* extract. If that is the case, perhaps Hare had hopes of publishing the journal somewhat earlier than he actually did, and had solicited a contribution from Wordsworth at that time. But about the December 9, 1831, activity we can be more certain: that surely was the preparation of the copy text sent to Hare. Working with her brother from MS. 101A, Dorothy must have prepared a fair copy of *Aeneid,* Book I, lines 901–end, which was the basis for what appeared in *The Philological Museum.* But not without further revisions. *The Philological Museum* text differs from the 1824 fair copies in nearly thirty lines, and in three places even differs from the revisions in MS. 101A. Unfortunately, the fair copy sent to Hare does not seem to have survived.

When the extract appeared in *The Philological Museum,* it was accompanied by the following letter:

To the Editors of the PHILOLOGICAL MUSEUM.

Your letter reminding me of an expectation I some time since held out to you of allowing some specimens of my translation from the Æneid to be printed in the Philological Museum was not very acceptable: for I had abandoned the thought of ever sending into the world any part of that experiment,—for it was nothing more,—an experiment begun for amusement, and I now think a less fortunate one than when I first named it to you. Having been displeased in modern translations with the additions of incongruous matter, I began to translate with a resolve to keep clear of that fault, by adding nothing; but I became convinced that a spirited translation can scarcely be accomplished in the English language without admitting a principle of compensation. On this point however I do not wish to insist, and merely send the following passage, taken at random, from a wish to comply with your request. W. W.[56]

---

[55]He also solicited contributions from Landor: twelve Latin poems in the first number, and an imaginary conversation between Solon and Pisistratus in the third. The first number of the journal appeared in November 1831; in its preface, Hare writes that: "every subject that concerns antiquity, and can be treated philologically, comes within the compass of the plan which has been laid down for the Philological Museum" (*PM,* I, iv).

[56]The text of the letter is quoted from *PM,* I, 382. The letter itself does not seem to have survived.

This letter is Wordsworth's final verdict on the translation, a verdict he repeated a decade later to his nephew Charles. Only those who have the least need of a translation—the readers of journals like *The Philological Museum*—can appreciate efforts such as his, undertaken without a principle of compensation and hence sacrificing poetic beauties.[57] After nearly eight years, he had at last come to agree with Coleridge. For *The Recluse*, "fit audience . . . though few" may be acceptable, but not for a translation of Virgil.

---

[57]It is also significant that the passage WW chose was one for which STC offered unguarded praise. "[T]he latter part," he wrote in MS. 101D, "is done with great spirit." In addition, one of WW's revisions for *PM* was of a passage STC had criticized (Book I, ll. 984–993).

Translation of Virgil's *Aeneid*
Reading Text

Reading Text

The reading text for Books I and II of the *Aeneid* translation is drawn from DC MS. 101B, the fair-copy manuscript in the autograph of Dorothy Wordsworth dating from January 1824. This is the manuscript prepared for possible publication by Wordsworth and his nephew Christopher Wordsworth, Jr., in the summer of 1827. It is that stage of the translation that the reading text attempts to represent, incorporating revisions in the autographs of William Wordsworth, Dorothy Wordsworth, and Christopher Wordsworth, Jr. (See Introduction, pp. 169–170.) The version of Book I, lines 901–end, that Wordsworth published in *The Philological Museum* (1832) is also given in an appendix, pages 579–583. The *apparatus criticus* records all substantive revisions and variants found in MSS. 101A and 101B, those in Wordsworth's letters to Lord Lonsdale of February 5 and 17, 1824, and those in his letter to Christopher Wordsworth, Jr., of November 30, 1827. Where revisions are too complex to represent neatly in the apparatus, full transcriptions are given on pages 525–557. Samuel Taylor Coleridge's notes to Book I of the poem, both those found in MS. 101D and the notes in MS. 101B, are recorded in a separate band of footnotes, immediately underneath the reading text. Nonverbal variants from MSS. 101A and 101B are recorded in a separate apparatus on pages 317–328. Single-letter miswritings and ampersand/and, thro'/through, and tho'/though variants are not recorded. As a rule, Mary Wordsworth uses the ampersand, thro', and tho', while Dorothy Wordsworth does not. In a very few instances, readings in MS. 101A are preferred to those in MS. 101B: when Dorothy Wordsworth has made an obvious copying error that has escaped correction (as in Book I, l. 494—"fangs" for "thongs"; Book I, l. 512—"thrice" for "twice"; and Book I, l. 689—"such a" for "such"), when she has inadvertently omitted punctuation (as in Book I, ll. 82, 96, 372, 539, 810, 830), and when she has made obvious punctuation errors (as in Book I, ll. 96, 183). In the case of verbal errors, the MS. 101B reading has been recorded in the verbal apparatus at the foot of each page. Spellings of classical names, which sometimes vary even within the same manuscript, have been regularized, and manuscript spellings are recorded in the verbal apparatus.

The bulk of the reading text of *Aeneid*, Book III, is drawn from the most complete fair-copy manuscript, DC MS. 101C, in the autograph of Mary Wordsworth, with revisions by Mary, William, and Dorothy Wordsworth; this manuscript contains Book III, lines 1–816, and was copied in January or February 1824. The remainder of the reading text is drawn from DC MS. 89, the only manuscript in which Book III, lines 817–832, survive. The *apparatus criticus* records substantive revisions and variants in MS. 101C, Wordsworth's letter to Lord Lonsdale of February 5, 1824, and MS. 101A, which contains a fair copy of

Aeneid, Book III, lines 409–720, in the autograph of Dorothy Wordsworth, with revisions by Dorothy and William Wordsworth. For further discussion of MS. 101A and its dating, see the Introduction, pages 159–160, 167–168. MS. 89 variants are not represented, since that manuscript is transcribed in full on pages 331–524.

The passages from *Aeneid*, Books IV and VIII, are also from DC MS. 89, the only manuscript in which they survive. The translation of *Georgics*, Book IV, lines 570–575, survives in both MS. 89 and a letter from Mary Wordsworth to Edward Quillinan, dated November 12 [1823]. The text in the letter, in Mary Wordsworth's autograph, is more accurate than the MS. 89 text, in Dorothy Wordsworth's autograph, which contains an obvious misspelling. Hence the letter is used as the basis for the reading text. All revisions and variant readings can be found in the MS. 89 transcriptions, on pages 523–524.

The *apparatus criticus* for all three books can be found in a separate band underneath the reading text. In Book I, this band is usually the middle one, underneath the band containing Coleridge's notes. On pages where there are no such notes, the *apparatus criticus* can be found immediately under the reading text. In Books II and III, the *apparatus criticus* can be found in the top band underneath the reading text.

There are two sets of editorial notes. The first set, found in the bottom band underneath the reading text, records three notes in the fair-copy manuscripts of Books II and III (two by Christopher Wordsworth, Jr., in MS. 101B and one by Coleridge in MS. 101C)as well as notes and markings in the editions and translations of Virgil that Wordsworth owned and seems to have used. In addition, this set glosses Coleridge's notes to Book I, and attempts, in a limited way, to show the relationship between Wordsworth's translation and Virgil's Latin. I have recorded significant deviations from Virgil, a few typical or especially interesting ways in which Wordsworth has rendered the Latin, and instances in which Wordsworth's translation seems to depend on the commentaries in the two seventeenth-century editions of Virgil that he primarily used: the edition of Jan Minel (Minellius) and the Delphine edition of Charles de la Rue (Ruæus). I have also called attention to other places in Wordsworth's poetry where a passage of Virgil is either translated or clearly alluded to. This set of editorial notes appears in a separate band, underneath the verbal apparatus.

The second set of notes appears after the reading text. Here, I have recorded passages of earlier translations from which Wordsworth may have borrowed. Wordsworth admits to having consulted and borrowed from the translations of John Dryden and Christopher Pitt; there is also evidence that he consulted the translations of John Ogilby (1650) and Joseph Trapp (1718–1720). We know that he owned Ogilby's translation; his source for Trapp's translation is uncertain, although one of the entries in the Rydal Mount library catalogue (described in Shaver, p. 265, as MC.91)may refer to a copy of Trapp that Wordsworth owned. I have discovered no convincing evidence of his having consulted any other Virgil translations, and thus have confined my citations to these four versions. What constitutes a possible borrowing is, of course, debatable. I have adhered to three principles of selection.

1. Recorded passages are usually characterized by phrasing that is distinctively similar to Wordsworth's. Distinctively similar phrasing consists of several consecutive words that are almost exactly the same. It does not consist of single words, or words and phrases that can easily be accounted for by the translators' efforts to render the Latin closely.

2. Identical or very similar rhymes in equivalent passages are almost always recorded. The only exceptions are a very few instances in which only the rhyme sound is similar, and there is no distinctively similar phrasing in the lines themselves.

3. Phrases of equivalent meaning but dissimilar wording are sometimes recorded, if they are metrically similar and appear in identical or nearly identical places in the poetic line, or if they demonstrate ways in which the various translators have borrowed from one another.

It should be understood that no definitive claim is being made that Wordsworth did borrow a given phrase or line. Rather, the intention is to record possible or potential borrowings. A translator, especially one committed to both literal accuracy and iambic pentameter couplets as Wordsworth was, has a limited number of choices available, and hence many accidental similarities will exist between any two English translations of the same work. But Wordsworth tells us that his process of translation included consulting earlier translators, and it makes sense to record the extent to which he may have done so.

In the editorial notes, the following editions of Virgil have been cited: for Minellius, Wordsworth's own copy, *Publii Virgilii Maronis opera omnia cum annotationibus J. Minelli* (Hafnia, 1740), now in the Cornell Wordsworth Collection; for the Delphine Virgil, *Publii Virgilii Maronis opera interpretatione et notibus illustravit Carolus Ruæus ad usum Delphini* (London, 1725). It is unclear what edition of the Delphine Virgil Wordsworth possessed (despite the entry in Shaver, p. 264). The Latin text and line number references found in the editorial notes are from the Minellius edition.

Advertisement

It is proper to premise that the first Couplet of this Translation is adopted from Pitt— as are likewise two Couplets in the second Book; & three or four lines, in different parts, are taken from Dryden. A few expressions will also be found, which, following the Original closely are the same as the preceding Translators have unavoidably employed.

1st Book

Arms, and the Man I sing, the first who bore
His course to Latium from the Trojan shore,
A Fugitive of Fate:— long time was He
By Powers celestial toss'd on land and sea,
Through wrathful Juno's far-famed enmity;
Much, too, from war endured; till new abodes
He planted, and in Latium fix'd his Gods;
Whence flowed the Latin People; whence have come
The Alban Sires, and Walls of lofty Rome.
  Say, Muse, what Powers were wrong'd, what grievance drove
To such extremity the Spouse of Jove,
Labouring to wrap in perils, to astound
With woes, a Man for piety renown'd!
In heavenly breasts is such resentment found?

Before I commence this revision which had it but been an original poem of yours' most chearfully should I have done [done *over illeg deletion*], I must put you on your guard against the morbid hypercritical state of my taste—to my own grievance & Damage. [?] I can only put a mark + to the objections, that I feel confident are worth attending to: and —, where I am myself doubtful. S.T.C.
~~First Book~~

First Book
3 — A Fugitive of Fate, were it less dubious English, seems to give the sense of fato profugus, urged by propelling fate? [Propell'd by *del*] By destiny propelled? A fated Fugitive?—
4 By force supernal.
5 + might not "through" be omitted, & the lines put in Apposition? Stern Juno's unrelenting [unforgetting *alt*] enmity!
8–9 + came? any thing better than flow'd—have come might apply to the walls of l. R. but not to the Alban Sires.
10–14 This ff ph. should be retranslated-

---

the Advertisement, in MW's autograph, is unique to MS. 101B
Advertisement 5 which *rev from* in which
5 wrathful Juno's far-famed *rev to* Juno's unrelengting *MS. 101A (WW)*
8 flowed *rev from* flows *MS. 101B*

Right opposite the Italian Coast there stood
An ancient City, far from Tiber's flood,
Carthage its name; a Colony of Tyre,
Rich, strong, and bent on war with fierce desire.
No region, not even Samos, was so graced
By Juno's favour; here her Arms were placed,
Here lodged her Chariot; and unbounded scope,
Even then, the Goddess gave to partial hope;
Her aim (if Fate such triumph will allow)
That to this Nation all the world shall bow.
But Fame had told her that a Race, from Troy
Derived, the Tyrian ramparts would destroy;
That from this stock, a People, proud in war,
And train'd to spread dominion wide and far,
Should come, and through her favorite Lybian State
Spread utter ruin:— such the doom of Fate.
In fear of this, while busy thought recalls
The war she raised against the Trojan Walls
For her lov'd Argos (and, with these combined,
Work'd other causes rankling in her mind,
The judgement given by Paris, and the slight
Her beauty had receiv'd on Ida's height,
Th'undying hatred which the Race had bred,
And honours given to ravish'd Ganymed,)
Saturnian Juno far from Latium chaced
The Trojans, tossed upon the watery waste;

15–16 Dryden's seems preferable. longè applies to the whole, or rather the mouth of the Tiber completes the Italiam . . . Distant but lying opposite to the Italian Coast, where the Tiber disembogues itself.

18–28 + as neither translation or poetry. Pope; or Hayley, might [?balk] giving an unbounded scope (i.e. no scope at all) to partial hope; but not W.W.— much less in lieu of tenditque fovetque.— 28. wide & far. I fear a something ludicrous in the hystero-proterizing of a familiar idiom, so barefacedly for rhyme's sake.

---

32 The *rev from* That *MSS.* raised *rev from* waged *MS. 101A*

---

15 "Carthago, Italiam contra," l. 13. Ruæus paraphrases: "Carthago nomine, procul ex adverso Italia. . . . " The paraphrase seems to have influenced WW's translation.

17–18 In *British Poets*—WL, vol. XII, there is an ink blot next to Dryden's version of these lines.

18–28 STC's note to this passage mentions William Hayley (1745–1820), the poet and biographer who, like WW, had studied with Agostino Isola at Cambridge. Hayley was a friend of Blake and Southey; among his writings are several translations from French, Spanish, and Italian. WW owned the Dublin, 1785, edition of his poetry in three volumes. In a manuscript reminiscence now in the Berg Collection at the New York Public Library, Elizabeth Barrett records that in 1836 WW recited from memory Hayley's translation of a Dante sonnet.

21–24 "hic currus fuit: hoc regnum Dea gentibus esse, / Si quâ fata sinant, iam tum tenditque, fovetque," ll. 17–18. Ruæus paraphrases: "jam tunc Dea contendit ut illa imperet populis, protegitque eam in hanc spem, si fatum id quoquomodo permittat." His use of "spem" may have helped to suggest WW's hope/ scope rhyme.

28 In MS. 101B, "train'd" and "wide and far" are underlined in pencil.

29 *sic volvere Parcas,*" l. 22; glossed "Ita esset in fatis" by Minellius.

36 "Judicium Paridis, spretæque injuria formæ," l. 27. The reference to Mount Ida is not in the Latin.

Unhappy relics of the Grecian spear
And of the dire Achilles! Many a year
They roam'd ere Fate's decision was fulfill'd;
Such arduous toil it was the Roman State to build.
Sicilian headlands scarcely out of sight,
They spread the canvas with a fresh delight;
Then Juno, brooding o'er the eternal wound,
Thus inly;— "Must I vanquish'd quit the ground
"Of my attempt? Or impotently toil
"To bar the Trojans from the Italian soil?
"For the Fates thwart me;—yet could Pallas raise
"'Mid Argive vessels a destructive blaze,
"And in the Deep plunge all, for fault of one,
"The desperate frenzy of Oïleus' Son;
"*She* from the clouds the bolt of Jove might cast,
"And ships and sea deliver to the blast!
"Him, flames ejecting from a bosom fraught
"With sulphurous fire, she in a whirlwind caught,
"And on a sharp rock fix'd;— but I who move
"Heaven's Queen, the Sister and the Wife of Jove,
"Wage with one Race the war I waged of yore!
"Who then, henceforth, will Juno's name adore?
"Her altars grace with gifts, her aid implore?"
These things revolv'd in fiery discontent,
Her course the Goddess to Eolia bent,
Country of lowering clouds, where south-winds rave;
There Æolus, within a spacious cave
With sovereign power controuls the struggling Winds,
And the sonorous Storms in durance binds.
Loud, loud the mountain murmurs as they wreak
Their scorn upon the barriers. On a peak
High-seated, Æolus his sceptre sways,
Soothes their fierce temper, and their wrath allays.
This did he not,—sea, earth, and heaven's vast deep
Would follow them, entangled in the sweep;
But in black caves the Sire Omnipotent
The winds sequester'd, fearing such event;

---

46 + They set [sail *del*] their sails for the open sea, and met the [*illeg del*, the *del*] longer or bolder waves— [?This] is the sense— by a triplet it might be expressed.

---

63 aid implore *over illeg eras MS. 101B*
66 clouds *rev from* winds *MS. 101A*
67 There] Here *MS. 101A; rev from* Here *MS. 101B*
74 This *rev from* [?That] *MS. 101A*

---

41 "relliquias Danaûm," l. 30.

50–90 There is an ink blot on p. 107 of Ogilby (1650)—WL, where Ogilby's version of these lines appear.

59 In *British Poets*—WL "moves" is corrected in pencil to "move" in l. 64 of Pitt's translation.

76–77 "Sed pater omnipotens speluncis abdidit atris, / Hoc metuens," ll. 60–61. The translation preserves Virgil's placement of the participial phrase. Minellius glosses "abdidit" as "occlusit ventos."

Heap'd over them vast mountains, and assign'd
A Monarch that should rule the blustering kind;
By stedfast laws their violence restrain,
And give, on due command, a loosen'd rein.
    As she approach'd, thus spake the suppliant Queen;
"Æolus! (for the Sire of Gods and men
"On thee confers the power to tranquillise
"The troubl'd waves, or summon them to rise)
"A Race, my Foes, bears o'er the troubled Sea
"Troy and her conquer'd Gods to Italy.
"Throw power into the winds; the ships submerge,
"Or part,—and give their bodies to the surge.
"Twice seven fair Nymphs await on my command,
"All beautiful;— the fairest of the Band,
"Deïopeia, such desert to crown,
"Will I, by stedfast wedlock, make thine own;
"In everlasting fellowship with thee
"To dwell, and yield a beauteous progeny."
    To this the God. "O Queen, declare thy will
"And be it mine the mandate to fulfill.
"To thee I owe my sceptre, and the place
"Jove's favour hath assign'd me; through thy grace
"I at the banquets of the Gods recline;
"And my whole empire is a gift of thine."
    When Æolus had ceased, his spear he bent
Full on the quarter where the winds were pent,
And smote the mountain.—Forth, where way was made,
Rush his wild Ministers; the land pervade,
And fasten on the Deep. There Eurus, there
Notus, and Africus unused to spare
His tempests, work with congregated power,
To upturn the abyss, and roll the unwieldy waves ashore.
Clamour of Men ensues, and crash of shrouds;
Heaven and the day by instantaneous clouds

81–89 + obscure & reads uncouth. A Race my foes bears oer.—

89 —weak — age diversus, as more than part. or scatter: let the corses mount the surge! [or . . . surge! *inserted*] & at all events Theirs is unhappy—. Virgil avoids this confusion of antecedents. The Corses?

106 — And bear down on the Deep. + unused to spare his tempests. There Eurus, [Notus*del*] here Notus, and Africus (the Seaman's Fear!) Apt for the storm with esp. upturn &c— fasten] bear down *alt MS. 101B (STC's pencil)*

111 by] the *alt MS. 101B (STC's pencil)*

---

99 favour *rev from* favours *MS. 101B*

107 Africus *so MS. 89* Aficus *MS. 101A* Aficus *rev from* A[?b]icus, *MS. 101B*

110 shrouds *over illeg eras MS. 101A* shroud's *MS. 101B*

---

88 "submersasque obrue puppes," l. 69.

93 "Connubio . . . stabili," l. 73. Minellius glosses "stabili" as "firmo & indissolubili." Similarly, Ruæus paraphrases it as "firmo conjugio."

110 "venti, velut agmine facto," l. 82. WW's "wild Ministers" is an embellishment.

Are ravish'd from the Trojans; on the floods
Black night descends, and palpably, there broods.
The thundering Poles incessantly unsheath
Their fires, and all things threaten instant death.
    Appall'd, and with slack limbs, Æneas stands;
He groans, and heaven-ward lifting his clasp'd hands,
Exclaims; "Thrice happy they who chanced to fall
"In front of lofty Ilium's sacred Wall,
"Their parents witnessing their end;—Oh why,
"Bravest of Greeks, Tydides, could not I
"Pour out my willing spirit through a wound
"From thy right hand received, on Trojan ground?
"Where Hector lies, subjected to the spear
"Of the invincible Achilles; where
"The great Sarpedon sleeps; and o'er the plain
"Swift Simois whirls helmet, and shield, and men,
"Throngs of the Brave in fearless combat slain!"
    While thus he spake, the Aquilonian gale
Smote from the front upon his driving Sail,
And heaved the thwarted billows to the sky,
Round the Ship labouring in extremity.
Help from her shatter'd oars in vain she craves;
Then veers the prow, exposing to the waves
Her side; and lo! a surge, to mountain height
Gathering, prepares to burst with its whole weight.
Those hang aloft, as if in air; to these
Earth is disclosed between the boiling seas.
Whirl'd on by Notus, three encounter shocks
In the main sea receiv'd from latent rocks;

---

112 Are] Have *alt MS. 101B (STC's pencil)*

134 + Help from — craves. Is this a translation of Franguntur remi!— [but she *eras*] She renders the whole description obscure. is [remi *del*] Prow the Nom. or Accus. of veers— & is "veer" ever used of a part of a Ship. The Ship may veer; but can the Prow?— I but put the question.— Those & these occasion an [unnecessary *del*] additional perplexity. Item. The Voice may [give *del*] force a metrical effect on "prepares to burst with its whole weight."— I do not like the and lo! it produces a pause not intended—and removes the instantaneous in sequence—. Furet æstus avenis, you imply in "boiling"—but surely Virgil meant to show that the Storm had driven the fleet shoreward & into shallow water.

140 Encounter a shock received from? [In brevis et syrtis urget *del*] As to these lines, however, you construe them otherwise than I should & I doubt not, better, [from *del*] as having studied it, I should not give all the force to Virgils ab Alto that you have done. I should construe it. "from deep water" [?] But the "latentia" seems not a happy epithet in connection with Dorsum immane mari summo.—

---

113 palpably *rev in pencil from* palpable *MS. 101B* there *rev from* their *MS. 101A*
115 instant death. *rev in pencil and ink from* instant[?antaneous] death *MS. 101B*
121 Greeks *rev from* Grecians *MS. 101B*
127 helmet *rev in pencil to* his helmet *MS. 101A*
133 her . . . she *rev from* his . . . he *MS. 101B (DW following WW's pencil)* he *rev from* his *MS. 101A (MW following WW's pencil)*
136 whole *over illeg eras MS. 101A*
139 encounter *rev from* encounter'd *MS 101B*

---

124 subjected to the spear] "telo jacet Hector," l. 99.
140 latent rocks] "saxa latentia," l. 108.

Rocks stretched in dorsal ridge of rugged frame
On the Deep's surface; ALTARS is the name
By which the Italians mark them. Three the force
Of Eurus hurries from an open course
On straits and Shallows, dashes on the Strand,
And girds the wreck about with heaps of sand.
Another, in which Lycas and his Mate,
Faithful Orontes, share a common fate,
As his own eyes full plainly can discern,
By a huge wave is swept from prow to stern;
Headlong the Pilot falls;— thrice whirl'd around,
The Ship is buried in the gulph profound.
Amid the boundless eddy a lost Few,
Drowning or drown'd, emerge to casual view,
On waves which planks, and Arms, and Trojan Wealth bestrew.
Over the strong-ribb'd pinnace, in which sails
Ilioneus, the Hurricane prevails;
Now conquers Abas, then the Ships that hold
Valiant Achates, and Alethes old;
The joints all loosening in their sides, they drink
The hostile brine through many a greedy chink.
    Meanwhile, what strife disturb'd the roaring sea
And for what outrages the storm was free,
Troubling the Ocean to its inmost caves,
Neptune perceiv'd—incensed; and o'er the waves
Forth-looking with a stedfast brow and eye
Raised from the Deep in placid majesty,
He saw the Trojan Gallies scatter'd wide,
The men they bore oppress'd and terrified;
Waters and ruinous Heaven against their peace allied.
Nor from the Brother was conceal'd the heat
Of Juno's anger, and each dark deceit.
Eurus he call'd, and Zephyrus;—and the Pair,

163–170 And for what outrages—&c. Not translation. . and Neptune perc. incensed—I can scarcely read, as part of a sentence. It seems to my ear as if I were repeating single words—perceived, incensed, admired—&c.— "and terrified" a rhyme to "against their peace allied"!

171–172 + — . . . [A *del*] So simple in the original. Nor was Neptune any Stranger to his Sister's Tricks and Tempers—. The heat of anger is not the meaning of Iræ (plural)—nor does doli mean—["]dark deceit."

The following speech is as good as the original—which for the life of me I could never read even at School but as a Tom Thumb Tragedy. The Quos ego, Sed motos . . . for exquisite vulgarity & boatswain matter is incomparable.— Obiter dictum est: "Godhead" is far too theological & abstract a word.

---

147 Lycas *ed* Lyeus *MSS.*
151 thrice *over illeg eras MS. 101B*
164 inmost *over illeg eras MS. 101A*
165 and *over illeg eras MS. 101B*

160–161 "laxis laterum compagibus omnes / Accipiunt inimicum imbrem, rimisque fatiscunt," ll. 122–123. Minellius glosses "inimicum": "Incommodum & molestum, ita ut per rimas aqua influeret." Ruæus paraphrases: "omnes solutis juncturis laterum admittunt perniciosam aquam, & rimis dehiscunt."

Who at his bidding quit the fields of air,
He thus address'd. "Upon your Birth and Kind
"Have ye presumed with confidence so blind
"As, heedless of my Godhead, to perplex
"The Land with uproar, and the Sea to vex,
"Which by your act, O winds! thus fiercely heaves?
"Whom I—but better calm the troubled waves.
"Henceforth, atonement shall not prove so slight
"For such a trespass;— to your King take flight,
"And say that not to *Him*, but unto *Me*,
"Fate hath assign'd this watery sovereignty;
"Mine is the Trident—his a rocky Hold,
"Thy mansion, Eurus!— vaunting uncontroll'd,
"Let Æolus there occupy his hall,
"And in that prison-house the winds enthrall!"

He spake: and, quicker than the word, his will
Felt through the sea abates each tumid hill,
Quiets the deep, and silences the shores,
And to a cloudless heaven the sun restores.
Cymothoe shoves, with leaning Triton's aid,
The stranded ships—or Neptune from their bed
With his own Trident lifts them;—then divides
The sluggish heaps of sand; and gently glides,
Skimming, on light smooth wheels, the level tides.
Thus oft, when a sedition hath ensued,
Arouzing all the ignoble multitude,
Straight through the air do stones and torches fly,
With every missile frenzy can supply;
Then, if a venerable Man step forth,
Strong through acknowledged piety and worth,
Hush'd at the sight into mute peace, all stand
Listening, with eyes and ears at his command;
Their minds to him are subject; and the rage
That burns within their breasts his lenient words assuage.

---

192 Q[y] Unclouds the Heaven and the Sun restores
198 Ensued. "coorta est." This is a very remarkable instance of an inverted Simile. I imagine that Virgil's purpose was to prepare the reader's fancy for land and city imagery & interests.

---

176 ye *rev from* you *MS. 101B (DW following WW's pencil), MS. 101A (MW following WW's pencil)*
179 act, *rev from* [?acts] *MS. 101A*
185 the *rev from* this *MS. 101B*
194 or Neptune from their *rev from* and from their flinty *MS. 101B*
195 With his own *rev from* He with his *MS. 101B*
207 their breasts *rev from* his breast *MS. 101A (WW)*

175–176 "Tanta-ne vos generis tenuit fiducia vestri?" l. 132. Ruæus paraphrases: "Tantane vos cepit confidentia ex vestra origine?" WW's use of "confidence" for "fiducia" may thus derive from the Delphine paraphrase.
190 "tumida æquora," l. 142.
199 "ignobile vulgus," l. 149.

So fell the Sea's whole tumult, overawed
Then, when the Sire, casting his eyes abroad,
Turns under open Heaven his docile Steeds,
And with his flowing Chariot smoothly speeds.
  The worn-out Trojans, seeking land where'er
The nearest coast invites, for Lybia steer.
There is a Bay whose deep retirement hides
The place where Nature's self a Port provides,
Framed by a friendly island's jutting sides,
Bulwark from which the billows of the Main
Recoil upon themselves, spending their force in vain.
Vast rocks are here; and, safe beneath the brows
Of two heaven-threatening Cliffs, the Floods repose.
Glancing aloft in bright theatric show
Woods wave, and gloomily impend below;
Right opposite this pomp of sylvan shade,
Wild crags and lowering rocks a cave have made;
Within, sweet waters gush; and all bestrown
Is the cool floor with seats of living stone,
Cell of the Nymphs: no chains, no anchors, here
Bind the tired vessels, floating without fear:
Led by Æneas, in this shelter meet
Seven Ships, the scanty relics of his Fleet;
The Crews, athirst with longings for the land,
Here disembark; and range the wish'd-for strand;
Or on the sunny shore their limbs recline,
Heavy with dropping ooze, and drench'd with brine.
Achates, from a smitten flint, receives
The spark upon a bed of fostering leaves;
Dry fuel on the natural hearth he lays,
And speedily provokes a mounting blaze.
Then forth they bring, not utterly forlorn,

---

211 "Flowing" is very bold:— but I think it an improvement.

215 "Nature's self." not Virgilian. I wish, the 3 first lines of this passage, There is a Place, were equal to all the rest—me judice, they do not give the imagery of the original—if I understand the lines. the water splits itself into little coves or sinuses.

223 beautiful *in left margin in pencil, with pencil line down left margin, ll. 214–222, and pencil bracket in left margin, ll. 224–230, MS. 101B (STC)*

---

208 fell *rev from* felt *MSS.*

214 Bay *rev from* Boy *MS. 101B (following pencil signal)*

214–216 "Est in secessu longo locus: insula portum / Efficit objectu laterum," ll. 159–160. WW's "Nature's self" may depend on Ruæus's gloss: "Portum, à natura, non ab arte factum describit."

221 bright theatric show] "sylvis scena coruscis," l. 164.

225–226 "Intus aquæ dulces, vivoque sedilia saxo," l. 167.

228 "floating without fear" has no equivalent in the Latin.

231 There is a small pencil caricature of WW, perhaps by Dora W, in the right margin of Ogilby's translation, p. 111, where his version of these lines appears. WW is shown with his hand thoughtfully at his chin.

235 receives] "suscepitque," l. 175.

The needful implements, and injured corn,
Bruise it with stones, and by the aid of fire
Prepare the nutriment their frames require.
    Meanwhile Æneas mounts a cliff, to gain
An unobstructed prospect of the Main;
Happy if thence his wistful eyes may mark
The harrass'd Antheus, or some Phrygian Bark,
Or Capys, or the guardian Sign descry
Which, at the stern, Caïcus bears on high.
No Sail appears in sight, nor toiling oar;
Only he spies three Stags upon the shore;
Behind, whole herds are following where these lead,
And in long order through the vallies feed.
He stops—and, with the bow, he seiz'd the store
Of swift-wing'd arrows which Achates bore;
And first the Leaders to his shafts have bow'd
Their heads elate with branching horns; the Crowd
Are stricken next; and all the affrighted Drove
Fly in confusion to the leafy grove.
Nor from the weapons doth his hand refrain
Till Seven, a Stag for every Ship, are slain,
And with their bulky bodies press the Plain.
Thence to the port he hies; divides the spoil;
And deals out wine, which on Trinacria's soil,
Acestes stored for his departing Guest;
Then with these words he soothes each sorrowing breast.
    "O Friends, not unacquainted with your share
"Of misery, ere doom'd these ills to bear!
"O Ye, whom worse afflictions could not bend!
"Jove also hath for *these* prepared an end.
"The voices of dread Sylla ye have heard;
"Her belt of rabid mouths your prows have near'd;
"Ye shunn'd with peril the Cyclopian den:
"Cast off your fears, resume the hearts of men!
"Hereafter, this our present lot may be

---

242 nutriment.
253 Q?
he
He seized the bow; nor lack'd ~~then~~ ample store
feather'd shafts, Achates' quiver bore.
Of ~~swift-wing'd arrows: those Achates bore~~.

---

248 Caïcus *over illeg eras MS. 101B*
256 Their . . . horns *over illeg eras MS. 101B*
259 doth *rev from* does *MS. 101B* his *rev from* [?the] *(DW following WW's pencil) MS. 101B*
269 hath *rev from* has *MSS. (following pencil caret, MS. 101A)*
271 mouths *over illeg eras MS. 101A*
273 hearts *rev from* heart *MS. 101B*

---

245 "Happy" and "his wistful eyes" are WW's embellishments.
256 "elate" is WW's attempt to render "ferentes," l. 189, by using an English derivative of the past participle of *fero*.

"A cherish'd object for pleased memory.
"Through strange mishaps, through hazards manifold
"And various, we our course to Latium hold;
"There, Fate a settled habitation shews;—
"There, Trojan empire (this, too, Fate allows)
"Shall be revived.—Endure; with patience wait;
"Yourselves reserving for a happier state!"
    Æneas thus, though sick with weight of care,
Strives by apt words their spirits to repair;
The hope he does not feel his countenance feigns,
And deep within he smothers his own pains.
They seize the Quarry; for the feast prepare;
Part use their skill the carcase to lay bare,
Stripping from off the limbs the dappled hide;
And Part the palpitating flesh divide:
The portions some expose to naked fire,
Some steep in cauldrons where the flames aspire.
Not wanting utensils, they spread the board;
And soon their wasted vigour is restored;
While, o'er green turf diffused, in genial mood
They quaff the mellow wine, nor spare the forest food.
All hunger thus appeased, they ask in thought
For friends, with long discourses, vainly sought;
Hope, fear, and doubt contend if yet they live,
Or have endured the last; nor can receive
The obsequies a duteous voice might give.
Apart, for Lycas mourns the pious Chief;
For Amycus is touch'd with silent grief;
For Gyas, for Cloanthes; and the Crew
That with Orontes perish'd in his view.
    So finish'd their repast, while on the crown
Of Heaven stood Jupiter; whence looking down,

---

275 +—

279 + There are unenglishisms here & there in this translation of which I remember no instance in your own poems, one or two in the Descriptive Sketches excepted. Such as the Walter Scott abrupt nudity of the article— There, Trojan Empire (this too Fate allows)—

288–292 Not worth translating; but not well translated—in plain truth, slubbered over, as by ren-dering the original literally & disrhyming [the *del*] your lines would appear.

301 Why Apart? secum, below, means turned in on himself.
?All mourn; and more than all the pious Chief—
Him Amycus, him Lycus touch'd with grief—
Him Gyas & Cloanthes &c.—

---

277 we *over illeg eras MS. 101A*
280 Endure; *over illeg eras MS. 101B*
288 hide *over illeg eras MS. 101A*
291 steep in *over illeg eras MS. 101A*
296 thus *rev from* [?is] *MS. 101A*

280–281 "Durate, & vosmet rebus servate secundis," l. 207.

283–284 "Spem vultu simulat, premit altum corde dolorem," l. 209. This is a good example of WW's common practice of rendering a dense line of Virgil as a couplet.

He traced the sea where winged vessels glide,
Saw Lands, and shores, the Nations scatter'd wide;
And, lastly, from that all-commanding Height,
He view'd the Lybian realms with stedfast sight.
To him, revolving mortal hopes and fears,
Venus (her shining eyes suffused with tears)
Thus, sorrowing, spake: "O Sire! who rul'st the way
"Of Men and Gods with thy eternal sway,
"And aw'st with thunder, what offence, unfit
"For pardon, could my much-lov'd Son commit—
"The Trojans what—thine anger to awake?
"That, after such dire loss, they for the sake
"Of Italy see all the world denied
"To their tired hopes, and nowhere may abide!
"For, that the Romans hence should draw their birth
"As years roll round, even hence, and govern earth
"With power supreme, from Teucer's Line restor'd,
"Such was (O Father! why this change?) thy word.—
"From this, when Troy had perish'd, for my grief
"(Fates balancing with fates) I found relief;
"Like fortune follows:— When shall thy decree
"Close, mighty King, this long adversity?
"—Antenor, from amid the Grecian hosts
"Escaped, could thrid Illyria's sinuous coasts;
"Pierce the Lyburnian realms; o'erclimb the Fountain
"Of loud Timavus, whence the murmuring Mountain
"A nine-mouth'd channel to the torrent yields,
"That rolls its headlong sea, a terror to the fields.
"Yet to his Paduan seats he safely came;
"A City built, whose People bear his name;
"There hung his Trojan Arms, where now he knows
"The consummation of entire repose.
"But *we*, thy progeny, allow'd to boast
"Of future Heaven—betray'd—our Navy lost—
"Through wrath of One, are driven far from the Italian coast.
"Is piety thus honour'd? Doth thy grace

---

313 — Is there other authority for "the way" except the disputed reading in Shakespear & Massinger? We rule our ways.

---

316 much *rev from* [?son] *MS. 101B*
318 loss, they *rev from* losses borne, they *MS. 101B*
322 roll *rev from* role *MS. 101A*
324 thy *over illeg eras MS. 101B*
325 From *rev from* For *MS. 101B (DW following WW's pencil)* this *over illeg eras MS. 101B*
339 allow'd *over illeg eras MS. 101B*

---

307 the sea where winged vessels glide] "mare velivolum," l. 224. Ruæus glosses: "Ubi naves velis, quasi alis, volant. . . ."
315–316 "unfit for pardon" is WW's embellishment.
339 thy progeny] "tua progenies," l. 250.

"Thus in our hands the allotted sceptre place?"
On whom the Sire of Gods and human Kind,
Half-smiling, turn'd the look that stills the wind,
And clears the heavens; then, touching with light kiss
His Daughter's lip, he speaks;
"Thy griefs dismiss;
"And, Cytherea, these forebodings spare;
"No wavering fates deceive the objects of thy care.
"Lavinian Walls full surely wilt thou see,
"The promised City; and, upborne by thee,
"Magnanimous Æneas yet shall range
"The starry heavens; nor doth my purpose change.
"He (since thy soul is troubled I will raise
"Things from their depths, and open Fate's dark ways)
"Shall wage dread wars in Italy, abate
"Fierce Nations, build a Town, and rear a State;
"Till three revolving summers have beheld
"His Latian Kingdom, the Rutulians quell'd.
"But young Ascanius (Ilus heretofore,
"Name which he held till Ilium was no more,
"Now call'd Iülus) while the months repeat
"Their course, and thirty annual orbs complete,
"Shall reign, and quit Lavinium—to preside
"O'er Albalonga sternly fortified.
"Here, under Chiefs of this Hectorian Race,
"Three hundred years shall empire hold her place,
"Ere Ilia, royal Priestess, gives to earth,
"From the embrace of Mars, a double birth.
"Then Romulus, the elder, proudly drest

---

345 Why half-smiling.

365 It is plain that Virgil meant to avoid the trivial name, as one of our old Poets does in "the gate of ancient Lud"— by [an *del*] interposing [*inserted*] three words between longam and Alba. It seems likewise to require a more faithful translation.

367 Shall Empire hold her place = regnabitur? Border on the mock-heroic? For myself, I wonder at your patience in wading thro' such a stiff Manes mortuum of Dullness! and that of the dullest sort, to wit, History in prosing narrative prophecy—with so ludicrously anachronical a familiarity of names and detail—old acquaintances of the last Platonic Sexmillenium!—

---

349 No *rev from* A *MS. 101A* wavering *over illeg eras MS. 101A*

355 Fate's *over illeg eras MS. 101B*

361 till *rev from* in *MS. 101A*

362 Iülus *rev from* Ascanius *MS. 101B (DW following WW's pencil); so MS. 101A (MW following WW's pencil) but* Iülus] Iulus

363 complete *over illeg eras MS. 101A*

368 Ilia *over illeg eras MS. 101B*

---

347 More than a decade earlier, WW modeled the Wanderer's prophecy of the glories of universal, state-sponsored education (*Excursion* IX, 293–415) on this speech by Jupiter. In *The Excursion,* such phrases as "this Imperial Realm" (l. 295), "impious use" (l. 319), "genuine piety descend . . . from age to age" (ll. 361–362), and "as days roll on" (l. 385) recall the Virgilian model.

352 Magnanimous Æneas] "Magnanimum Æneam," l. 260

"In tawny wolf-skin, his memorial vest,
"Mavortian Walls, his Father's Seat, shall frame,
"And from himself, the People Romans name.
"To these I give dominion that shall climb,
"Uncheck'd by space, uncircumscrib'd by time;
"An empire without end. Even Juno, driven
"To agitate with fear earth, sea, and heaven,
"With better mind shall for the past atone;
"Prepar'd with me to cherish as her own
"The Romans, lords o'er earth, the Nation of the Gown.
"So 'tis decreed. As circling times roll on
"Phthia shall fall, Mycenæ shall be won;
"Descendants of Assaracus shall reign
"O'er Argos subject to the Victor's chain.
"From a fair Stem shall Trojan Cæsar rise;
"Ocean may terminate his power;—the skies
"Can be the only limit of his fame;
"A Julius he, inheriting the name
"From great Iülus. Fearless shalt thou greet
"The Ruler, when to his celestial Seat
"He shall ascend, spoil-laden from the East;
"He, too, a God to be with vows address'd.
"Then shall a rugged Age, full long defil'd
"With cruel wars, grow placable and mild;
"Then hoary Faith, and Vesta, shall delight
"To speak their laws; Quirinus will unite
"With his twin Brother to uphold the right.
"Fast shall be clos'd the iron-bolted Gates
"Upon whose dreadful issues Janus waits;

---

372 frame walls? — If you wish to strengthen the line, why not—Offspring of Mars Mavortian Walls shall frame.—

376 + — climb? by space? by time—[In *del*] Unmeasur'd in event [uncircumscrib'd in space *alt*] and without bound in time. In space unmeasur'd, without bound in time.

377 Even Juno, She That [Whose *alt*] wild alarms [are *del*] yet vex Heaven, Earth & Sea mad Alarum vexes Earth & Sea

380 — — I don't like, but can suggest nothing—Paraphrased is [spoilt *del*] crushed / else —
The Romans, Lords of all beneath the Sun
That in the Toga awe what clad in arms they won—

---

371 wolf-skin *rev from* wolfs-skin *MS. 101B; rev in pencil from* wolf's-skin *MS. 101A (WW)*
377 sea, *rev from* seas *MS. 101B*
383 Assaracus *rev from* the Assaracus *MS. 101A*
384 chain. *rev from* reign. *MS. 101A*
388 the *rev from* his *MS. 101A*
394 placable *rev from* peacable *MS. 101A*

"Within, on high-pil'd Arms, and from behind
"With countless links of brazen chains confin'd
"Shall Fury sit, breathing unholy threats
"From his ensanguin'd mouth that impotently frets."
This utter'd, Maia's Son he sends from high
To embolden Tyrian hospitality;
Lest haply Dido, ignorant of fate,
Should chase the Wanderers from her rising State.
He through the azure region works the oars
Of his swift wings, and lights on Lybian Shores:
Prompt is he there his mission to fulfil;
The Tyrians soften, yielding to Jove's will;—
And, above all, their Queen receives a mind
Fearless of harm, and to the Trojans kind.
Æneas, much revolving through the night,
Rose with the earliest break of friendly light;
Resolv'd to certify by instant quest
Who rul'd the uncultur'd region—man or beast.
Forthwith he hides, beneath a rocky cove,
His Fleet, o'ershadow'd by the pendant grove;
And, brandishing two javelins, quits the Bay,
Achates sole companion of his way.
While they were journeying thus, before him stood
His Mother, met within a shady wood.

419–420 Rightly translated? Surely, they were boar-spears not javelins:—lato ferro—and crispans, I imagined, means that play & give of [an *del*] a flexile weapon. Likewise, I would suggest that either concealed or some still better words should be put for hides, or that the whole sentence should be put in the participle absolute, as the English Reader can not quite free himself from the modern associations with the word Fleet. The Fleet, concealed beneath the r.c. And overshadowed by the p.g. Two quiv'ring Spears in hand, he quits the Bay—

---

401 chains *rev from* chain *MS. 101A*
406 haply *rev from* happy *MS. 101A*
414 through *over illeg eras MS. 101A*
418 rocky *over illeg eras MS. 101A*
422 While *over illeg eras MS. 101B*
423 wood. *rev from* woods— *MS. 101B*

400–403 "Furor impius intùs / Sæva sedens super arma, & centum vinctus ahenis / Post tergum nodis, fremet horridus ore cruento," ll. 294–296. Ruæus paraphrases: "intus sceleratus Furor sedens supra arma crudelia, & ligatus post terga centum æreis catenis, frendebit horrens ore sanguinolento." WW's rather awkward translation seems to depend on this paraphrase.

419 STC's objection to the word "fleet" is probably related to its association with sewers, as in *OED* 1b.

The habit of a Virgin did she wear;
Her aspect suitable, her gait, and air;—
Arm'd like a Spartan Virgin; or of mien
Such as in Thrace Harpalyce is seen,
Urging to weariness the fiery horse—
Outstripping Hebrus in his headlong course.
Light o'er her shoulders had she given the bow
To hang; her tresses on the wind to flow;
—A Huntress with bare knee;— a knot upbound
The folds of that loose vest, which else had swept the ground.
"Ho!" she exclaim'd, their words preventing, "say
"Have you not seen some Huntress here astray,
"One of my Sisters, with a quiver graced;
"Clothed by the spotted lynx, and o'er the waste
"Pressing the foaming boar, with outcry chased?"
    Thus Venus:—thus her Son forthwith replied;
"None of thy Sisters have we here espied,
"None have we heard;—O Virgin! in pure grace
"Teach me to name Thee; for no mortal face
"Is thine, nor bears thy voice a human sound:—
"A Goddess surely, worthy to be own'd
"By Phœbus as a Sister—or thy Line

424–429 &c. &cs.— I am sick of finding fault, the more discomfortably because my main feeling is that of faulting you for undertaking what compared with the original is scarcely a possibility, & your name is such that comparison with Dryden, Pitt, Beresford &c &c stands you in poor stead—nulla gloria præterire claudos— But I confess that I cannot read the compressed [dignified *del*] and sustained yet simple dignity of Virginis os habitusque (315—[?]320) & not find the English weak— "is seen"—suitable (aspect) gait, air;—mien—" —Arm'd like a Spartan Virgin—. . .

A Virgin [might she [? ?] & charms, *del*] she in Habit and (in Charms)
A Spartan Virgin [she *del*] seems—& such her arms . . . / merely to convey any sense of the climax,1 2 3 —

Urge to weariness is scarcely the dictionary meaning (me judice) of fatigat, at all events, not the poetic force — and the participles ing, ing, kill the rapidity of the movement—

And leaves behind swift Hebrus in her flight. or course or speed
(which, by the bye, with Virgil's pardon, she might have done on a Donky:)

437 — Clothed by?

438 . . . This is one of the sad necessities of rhyme in translation of continuous sentences. With shrill shouts pressing on the foamy Boar, is quite in the character if an animated inquiry; but to mortice on a supplementary description, "with outcry chased"—

444 + worthy to be own'd. does not even answer for a rhyme - botch— and does not give Virgil's sense, worthy to be owned by Phœbus as a Sister. The Question is simply— Are you Diana or at least one of [her *del*] Dian's Train?—

---

429 Hebrus *over illeg eras MS. 101A* his *over illeg eras MS. 101B*
431 on *rev from* in *MS. 101B*
437 waste *rev from* [?waist] *MS. 101B*
438 foaming *rev in pencil to* foamy *MS. 101A*

---

424 STC's note mentions James Beresford (1764–1840), whose blank-verse translation of the *Aeneid* was published by Joseph Johnson in 1794; Johnson had published *An Evening Walk* and *Descriptive Sketches* the previous year. Beresford was also the author of *The Miseries of Human Life; or The Last Groans of Timothy Testy and Samuel Sensitive, with a few supplementary sighs from Mrs. Testy,* which was admired by Scott. STC's line numbers refer to the Latin. "Nulla gloria . . .": "To outrun the lame is nothing to boast about." The phrase may be STC's own invention.

425 "her gait and air" is WW's embellishment.

"Is haply of the Nymphs; O Power divine
"Be thou propitious! and, whoe'er thou art,
"Lighten our labour; tell us in what part
"Of earth we roam, who these wild precincts trace,
"Ignorant alike of person and of place!
"Not as intruders come we; but were tost
"By winds and waters on this savage coast.
"Vouchsafe thy answer; victims oft shall fall
"By this right hand, while on thy name we call!"
Then Venus;—"Offerings these which I disclaim:
"The Tyrian Maids who chase the sylvan game
"Bear thus a quiver slung their necks behind,
"With purple buskins thus their ancles bind.
"Learn, Wanderers, that a Punic Realm you see;
"Tyrians the men, Agenor's progeny;
"But Lybian deem the soil: the natives are
"Haughty and fierce, intractable in war.
"Here Dido reigns; from Tyre compell'd to flee
"By an unnatural Brother's perfidy;
"Deep was the wrong; nor would it aught avail
"Should we do more than skim the doleful tale.
"Sichæus lov'd her as his wedded Mate,
"The richest Lord of the Phœnician State;
"A Virgin She, when from her Father's hands,
"By love induced, she pass'd to nuptial bands;
"Unhappy Union! for to evil prone,
"Worst of bad men, her Brother held the throne.
"Dire fury came among them, and, made bold
"By that blind appetite, the thirst of gold,
"He, feeling not, or scorning what was due
"To a Wife's tender love, Sichæus slew;

---

457 + +slung their necks behind . . . ! — V.T. mos [?] est gestare pharetram.
461 — does not give the force of Fines nor the personality of Libyis, which defines the genus intractabile bello.

451–452 *lines originally omitted, then inserted over erasure MS. 101B*
452 this *rev from* the *MS. 101B*
455 disclaim *rev from* disdaine *MS. 101A*
457 Bear *rev from* [Bear'st] *MS. 101A*
460 Agenor *over illeg eras MS. 101A*
464 perfidy *rev from* [?perjury] *MS. 101A*
469–492 *quotes as in MS. 101A; no open quotes MS. 101B*

---

447 Be thou propitious!] "Sis fœlix," l. 330, paraphrased by Ruæus, "Esto propitia," and glossed by Minellius "Propitia, auxiliatrix."
462 intractible in war] "intractabile bello," l. 339
469 "Cui pater intactam dederat," l. 345. Ruæus paraphrases: "huic Sichæo pater eam dederat adhuc virginem. . . ."
470 nuptial bands] Ominibus, l. 346, glossed by Ruæus "nuptiis" and by Minellius "Auspiciis, quæ cùmomni negotio, tum nuptiis maximè adhibita."
471 "Unhappy Union!" is WW's addition.

"Rush'd on him unawares, and laid him low
"Before the Altar, with an impious blow.
"His arts conceal'd the crime, and gave vain scope
"In Dido's bosom to a trembling hope.
    "But in a dream appear'd the unburied Man,
"Lifting a visage wond'rous pale and wan;
"Urged her to instant flight, and shew'd the ground
"Where hoards of ancient treasure might be found,
"Needful assistance. By the Vision sway'd,
"Dido looks out for fellowship and aid.
"They meet, who loathe the Tyrant, or who fear;
"And, as some well-trimm'd Ships were lying near,
"This help they seiz'd; and o'er the water fled
"With all Pygmalion's wealth;— a Woman at their head.
"The Exiles reach'd the Spot, where soon your eyes
"Shall see the Turrets of New Carthage rise:
"There purchas'd Barca; so they nam'd the Ground
"From the bull's hide whose thongs had girt it round.
"Now say,—Who are Ye? Whence? And whither bound?"
    He answer'd, deeply sighing, "To their springs
"Should I trace back the principles of things
"For you, at leisure listening to our woes,
"Vesper, 'mid gathering shadows, to repose
"Might lead the day, before the Tale would close.
"—From ancient Troy, if haply ye have heard
"The name of Troy, through various seas we steer'd,
"Until on Lybian Shores an adverse blast
"By chance not rare our shatter'd vessels cast.

---

480 You have convinced me of the necessary injury which a Language must sustain by rhyme translations of narrative poems of great length. What would you have said at Allfoxden or in Grasmere Cottage to giving vain scopes to trembling hopes in a bosom? —Were it only for this reason, that it would interfere with your claim to a Regenerator & Jealous Guardian of our Language, I should dissuade the publication. For to you I dare not be insincere—tho' I conjecture, from some of your original Poems (of [the *inserted*] more recent, I mean) that our tastes & judgements differ a shade or two more than formerly— & I am unfeignedly disposed to believe, that the long habits of minute discrimination have over-subtilized my perceptions. I have [?] composed [about *inserted*] 200 verses within the last 18 months— & from the dissatisfaction if they could be read [by *del*] in the most newspaper flat reading other than strongly distinguishable verse, I found them polished almost to sensual effeminacy . . . —You must therefore take my opinions for what they are—

107 + the principles of things, the technical phrase [for *del*] of the Orphic Poets— περι αρχων.

---

478 the *rev from* this *MS. 101B*
490 Pygmalion's *so MS. 101A* Pygmalian's *MS. 101B*
494 thongs *so MS. 101A* fangs *MS. 101B*
495 Ye *rev from* you *MS. 101B*
497 the principles of] these melancholy *MS. 101A*
500 Tale] tale *rev from* day *MS. 101A*

479–480 "Multa malus simulans, vanâ spe lusit amantem," l. 352.

482 WW has omitted two lines of Virgil which should follow this verse: "Crudeles aras, trajectaque pectora ferro, / Nudavit, cœcumque; domus scelus omne retexit," ll. 355–356.

499–500 "Ante diem clauso componet vesper Olympo," l. 374. WW may be following Ruæus's gloss: "Est, à morte ac tumulo: componere enim, est sepelire; & diem clauso Olympo componere, est, diem in coilo quasi in tumulo sepelire ac condere."

"Æneas am I, wheresoe'er I go
"Carrying the Gods I rescued from the Foe,
"When Troy was overthrown. A Man You see
"Fam'd above Earth for acts of piety;
"Italy is my wish'd-for resting-place;
"There doth my Country lie, among a Race
"Sprung from high Jove. The Phrygian Sea I tried
"With twice ten Ships (which Ida's grove supplied,)
"My Goddess Mother pointing out the way,
"Nor did unwilling Fates oppose their sway.
"Seven, scarcely, of that number now are left,
"By tempests torn;—Myself, unknown, bereft,
"And destitute, explore the Lybian Waste;
"Alike from Europe and from Asia chas'd."
He spake; nor haply at this point had clos'd
His mournful words; but Venus interpos'd.
"Whoe'er thou art, I trust, the heavenly Powers
"Disown thee not, so near the Punic Towers;
"But hasten to the Queen's imperial Court;
Thy Friends survive; their Ships are safe in port,
"Indebted for the shelter which they find
"To alter'd courses of the rough North-wind:
"Unless fond Parents taught my simple youth
"Deceitful auguries, I announce the truth.
"Behold yon twelve fair Swans, a joyous troop!
"Them did the Bird of Jove, with threatening swoop
"Rout, in mid Heaven dispers'd; but now again
"Have they assembled, and in order'd train
"These touch, while those look down upon, the plain,
"Hovering, and wheeling round with tuneful voice.
"—As in recover'd union all rejoice,

---

505 —Æneas I, who wheresoe'er I go Carry &c. . . super æthera = above Earth?— [not even to the Gods unknown. Renown'd of men nor to the gods unknown *del*] not the Gods confess my fame? —But the whole passage needs to be recomposed—you have so diluted [I *inserted*] the meaning. —I doubt your version of genus ab Jove summo—May it not be part of the answer to [vos *inserted*] Qui tandem? my [race *del*] kind from highest Jove—i.e. I am Jove's Grandson. —I 509,[— *del*] 512. .

534 These & those strike me as uncouth, there having been no previous division made — but dedere cantus is not with tuneful voice— send forth the shrill strain, chaunt.— My main objection is that the Imagery of this [(in the original *inserted*] rather obscurely expressed) passage is not distinctly made out in your lines.

---

512 twice *so MS. 101A* thrice *MS. 101B ("bis" in the original Latin)*
513–514 *rev from* Nor did unwilling Fates opppose their sway.
My Goddess-Mother pointing out the way! *MS. 101A*
515 of *rev from* now *MS. 101A*
517 explore *rev from* [?expose] *MS. 101A*
531 dispers'd . . . again *rev from* but now in ordered train *MS. 101A*
532 *omitted, then inserted over erasure MS. 101B (following WW's pencil at bottom of page)*
532–534 *squeezed into space for two lines MS. 101A (following WW's pencil in left margin and at bottom of page)*
535 all *rev from* these *MSS.*
535/536 And wheel on whizzing wings with tuneful voice, *MS. 101A del*

"So, with their Crews, thy Ships in harbour lie,
"Or to some haven's mouth are drawing nigh
"With every Sail full-spread; but Thou proceed;
"And fear no hindrance where thy path shall lead."
She spake; and, as she turn'd away, all bright
Appear'd her neck, imbued with roseate light;
And from the exalted region of her head
Ambrosial hair a sudden fragrance shed,
Odours divinely breathing;— her Vest flow'd
Down to her feet;— and gait and motion shew'd
The unquestionable Goddess. Whom his eyes
Had seen and whom his soul could recognize,
His filial voice pursueth as she flies.
"Why dost Thou, cruel as the rest, delude
"Thy Son with Phantoms evermore renew'd?
"Why not allow me hand with hand to join;
"To hear thy genuine voice, and to reply with mine?"
This chiding utter'd from a troubl'd breast,
He to the appointed walls his steps address'd.
But Venus round them threw, as on they fare,
Impenetrable veil of misty air;
That none might see, or touch them with rude hand,
Obstruct their journey, or its cause demand.
She, borne aloft, resumes the joyful road
That leads to Paphos—her belov'd abode;
There stands her Temple; garlands fresh and fair
Breathe round a hundred Altars hung, which there
Burn with Sabean incense, scenting all the air.
They who had measur'd a swift course were now
Climbing, as swift, a hill of lofty brow,
That overhangs wide compass of the Town,
And on the turrets, which it fronts, looks down.
Æneas views the City—pile on pile
Rising—a place of sordid Huts erewhile;
And, as he looks, the gates, the stretching ways,
The stir, the din, encreasing wonder raise.
The Tyrians work—one spirit in the whole;
These stretch the walls; these labour to uproll
Stones for the Citadel, with all their might;
These, for new Structures having mark'd a site,

542 Vertice = from the exalted region of her head?

536 Crews,] Crews *rev from* freight, *MS. 101A*
555 them *so MS. 101A* him *MS. 101B*
556 misty *over illeg eras MS. 101A*
561 her *rev from* a *MS. 101A*
572 whole *over illeg eras MS. 101B*
574 their *rev from* her *MS. 101A*

572 "one spirit in the whole" is WW's addition.

Intrench the circuit. Some on laws debate,
Or chuse a Senate for the infant State;
Some dig the haven out; some toil to place
A Theatre, on deep and solid base;
Some from the rock hew columns, to compose
A goodly ornament for future Shows.
—Fresh summer calls the Bees such tasks to ply
Through flowery grounds, beneath a summer sky;
When first they lead their progeny abroad,
Each fit to undertake his several load;
Or in a mass the liquid produce blend,
And with pure nectar every cell distend;
Or, fast as homeward Labourers arrive,
Receive the freight they bring; or, mustering, drive
The Drones, a sluggard people, from the hive.
Glows the vast work; while thyme-clad hills and plains
Scent the pure honey that rewards their pains.
"Oh fortunate!" the Chief, Æneas, cries
As on the aspiring Town he casts his eyes,
"Fortunate Ye, whose walls are free to rise!"
Then, strange to tell! with mist around him thrown,
In crowds he mingles, yet is seen by none.
    Within the Town, a central Grove display'd
Its ample texture of delightful shade.
The storm-vex'd Tyrians, newly-landed, found
A hopeful sign, while digging there the ground;
The head of a fierce horse from earth they drew,
By Juno's self presented to their view;

---

592 Is there authority for scent,? —[?] Except in Perfumers & Snuff Shops—? I retract that question; but is it not obscure in this place— & with a "while"?

598 — From this line the Translation greatly & very markedly improves [, *del*] the metre has bone & muscle.

---

576 the *rev from* a *MS. 101A (MW following WW's pencil)*
577 a *rev from* [?the] *MS. 101A*
580 hew *rev from* her *MS. 101A (MW following WW's pencil)*
582 Fresh *over illeg eras MS. 101A*
591 Glows *rev from* Grows *MSS.*
602 horse *over illeg eras MS. 101B*

582–592 These lines echo *Excursion* IX, 369–374, which is itself an allusion to Virgil:

—For, as the element of air affords
An easy passage to the industrious bees
Fraught with their burthens; and a way as smooth
For those ordained to take their sounding flight
From the thronged hive, and settle where they list
In fresh abodes—their labour to renew. . . .

585 WW's embellishment, although one true to Virgil's depiction of bees in *Georgics,* Book IV.

587 "dulci distendunt nectare cellas," l. 433. Minellius glosses: "Purissimo melle implent cavernas favorum."

592 "that rewards their pains" is WW's addition.

Presage of martial fame, and hardy toil
Bestow'd through ages on a generous soil.
Sidonian Dido here a Structure high
Rais'd to the tutelary Deity,
Rich with the Offerings through the Temple pour'd;
And bright with Juno's Image, there ador'd.
High rose, with steps, the brazen Porch; the Beams
With brass were fasten'd; and metallic Gleams
Flashed from the valves of brazen doors, forth-sent
While on resounding hinges to and fro they went.
Within this Grove Æneas first beheld
A novel sight, by which his fears were quell'd;
Here first gave way to hope, so long withstood,
And look'd through present ill to future good.
For while, expectant of the Queen, the stores
Of that far-spreading Temple he explores;
Admires the strife of labour; nor forbears
To ponder o'er the lot of noble cares
Which the young City for herself prepares;
He meets the Wars of Ilium; every Fight,
In due succession, offer'd to his sight.
There he beholds Atrides, Priam here,
And that stern Chief who was to both severe.
He stopp'd; and, not without a sigh, exclaim'd;
"By whom, Achates! hath not Troy been nam'd?
"What region of the earth but overflows
"With us, and the memorials of our woes?
"Lo Priamus! Here also do they raise
"To virtuous deeds fit monument of praise;

---

621 + *left margin and* the lot of *underlined in pencil MS. 101B; at page bottom is the following pencil note in STC's hand* + unfortunate, the provincial idiom of Lot for "a many"— If.instead of this line, [which breaks the already too slender transition, *inserted*] could you not improve on the original by [introducing *del*] marking the silent labor of the Artist, or something to break the crudeness of

621 —To ponder &c. Destroys the already too obscure copula of Artificium & miratur, & thus renders the He meets the wars of Ilium still cruder than Virgil's videt Iliacas— offer'd to his sight: seems likewise slovenly. In my Minelli Edition [is *del*] it is Atrides, not Atridem—

626 Achilles name is quite requisite, I think & to both severe? And fierce to both Achilles. As the Tear [Swell'd *del*] Bedimm'd his eyes, he stopped- . .

---

606 Sidonian *rev from* [?]donian *MS. 101A (MW following WW's pencil)* high *rev from* rais'd *MS. 101B*

631 Here *rev from* There *MS. 101B*

632 monument *rev from* monuments *MS. 101A*

620–622 "Artificumque manus inter se oprumque labores / Miratur," ll. 455–456. Ruæus has "laborem" for "labores." Ruæus paraphrases: "dum admiratur quæ sit felicitas illius urbis, & manus opificum invicem concordes, & difficultatem operum. . . ."

621 STC's note indicates that he, like WW himself, was using an edition of Virgil edited by Jan Minel, the seventeenth-century Dutch scholar.

"Tears for the frail estate of human kind
"Are shed; and mortal changes touch the mind."
He spake (nor might the gushing tears control;)
And with an empty Picture feeds his soul.
He saw the Greeks fast flying o'er the Plain,
The Trojan Youth—how in pursuit they strain!
There, o'er the Phrygians routed in the war,
Crested Achilles hanging from his Car.
Next, to near view the painted wall presents
The fate of Rhesus, and his snow-white tents,
In the first sleep of silent night, betray'd
To the wide-wasting sword of Diomed,
Who to the camp the fiery horses led;
Ere they from Trojan stalls had tasted food,
Or stoop'd their heads to drink Scamander's flood.
—The Stripling Troilus he next espied,
Flying, his Arms now lost, or flung aside;
Ill-match'd with fierce Achilles! From the fight
He, by his horses borne in desperate flight,
Cleaves to his empty Chariot, on the plain
Supinely stretch'd, yet grasping still the rein:
Along the earth are dragg'd his neck and hair;
The dust is mark'd by his inverted spear.
Meanwhile, with tresses long and loose, a train
Of Trojan Matrons seek Minerva's Fane;
As on they bear the dedicated Veil,
They beat their own sad breasts with suppliant wail,
The Goddess heeds not offerings, prayers, nor cries;
And on the ground are fix'd her sullen eyes.
—Thrice had incens'd Achilles whirl'd amain,
About Troy Wall, the Corse of Hector slain,
And barters now that Corse for proffer'd gold.
What grief, the spoils and Chariot to behold!

---

634 mortal *rev from* mortals *MS. 101B*
641 near *over illeg eras MS. 101B (DW following WW's pencil)*
642 snow-white tents, *rev from* snowy tent *MS. 101B*
651 flight] plight *MS. 101A*
660 nor *rev from* or *MS. 101B*
663 Corse *over illeg eras MS. 101B (DW following WW's pencil)*

633–634 cf. *Laodamìa,* 164–166: "—Yet tears to human suffering are due; / And mortal hopes defeated and o'erthrown / Are mourned by man. . . ." For some reason, WW omitted the next line of the poem from the translation: "Solve metus: feret hæc aliquam tibi fama salutem," l. 463. This line was translated as a couplet, much revised, in MS. 89 (see Transcriptions, p. 441), but was not entered into the fair copies.

653 "Supinely" reflects "resupinus," l. 476.

655 Here WW's translation ignores Ruæus's gloss of l. 478: "Non hasta Troili, quam adhuc manu retineret; nam amissis armis, id est, dilapsis, ferebatur; & sola lora manu implicata retinebat. Igitur hast Achillis. . . ." Minellius glosses: "Sulcatur & scalpitur hasta inversa, & per terram tracta."

And, suppliant, near his Friend's dead body, stands
Old Priam, stretching forth his unarm'd hands!
Himself, 'mid Grecian Chiefs, he can espy;
And saw the oriental blazonry
Of swarthy Memnon, and the Host he heads:
Her lunar shields Penthesilea leads;
A zone her mutilated breast hath bound;
And She, exulting on the embattled ground,
A Virgin Warrior, with a Virgin Train,
Dares in the peril to conflict with Men.
    While on these animated pictures gaz'd
The Dardan Chief, enrapt, disturb'd, amaz'd;
With a long retinue of Youth, the Queen
Ascends the Temple:—lovely was her mien;
And her form beautiful as Earth has seen.
Thus, where Eurotas flows, or on the heights
Of Cynthus, where Diana oft delights
To train her Nymphs, and lead the Choirs along,
Oreads, in thousands gathering, round her throng;
Where'er she moves, where'er the Goddess bears
Her pendant sheaf of arrows, she appears
Far, far above the immortal Company:
Latona's breast is thrill'd with silent ecstasy.
Even with such lofty bearing Dido pass'd
Among the busy crowd;— such looks she cast,
Urging the various works, with mind intent
On future empire. Through the Porch she went,
And, compass'd round with arm'd Attendants, sate
Beneath the Temple's dome, upon a Throne of State.
There, laws she gave; divided justly there
The labour; or by lot assign'd to each his share.
When, turning from the Throne a casual glance,

---

666 This & the following Lines should be altered— & the whole passage deserves it. By hurrying over what Virgil makes prominent (Eneas's height of Emotion, at this particular point) "his friend" becomes equivocal. [I *del*]

? And close beside his Friend's dead body stands
Priam, still suppliant with unweapon'd hands.

687 — Far, far above / too vague for supereminet— & tho' Virgil shows great want of Judgement in this outrè imitation of Homer, yet still I would give his meaning which your version submerges—

Where'er she winds her way[s *del*] [threads the dance *alt*] the Goddess bears
Her Quiver visible—still, still appears
The [Oread *del*] frontal Crescent far above the rest!
Mute Exultation thrills Latona's breast . . . .

seems more true to the intention.—

---

670 heads *rev from* leads *MS. 101A*
675 Dares *rev from* Dures *MS. 101A (MW following WW's pencil)*
687 Far *rev from* Th[?] *MS 101A*
696 share *over illeg eras MS. 101B*

---

669 oriental] "Eoas," l. 489. Both Ruæus and Minellius gloss "Eoas" as "orientales."

Æneas saw an eager Crowd advance
With various Leaders, whom the storms of Heaven
Had scatter'd, and to other shores had driven.
With Antheus and Sergestus there appear'd
The brave Cloanthes—followers long endear'd.
Joy smote his heart, joy temper'd with strange awe:
Achates, in like sort, by what he saw
Was smitten; and the hands of both were bent
On instant greeting; but they fear'd the event.
Stifling their wish, within that cloud involv'd,
They wait until the mystery shall be solv'd—
What has befallen their Friends; upon what shore
The Fleet is left; and what they would implore;
For Delegates from every Ship they were,
And sought the Temple with a clamorous prayer.
All entered;—and, leave given, with tranquil breast
Ilioneus preferr'd their joint request.
"O Queen! empower'd by Jupiter to found
"A hopeful City on this desart ground;
"To whom he gives the curb and guiding rein
"Of Justice, a proud People to restrain!—
"We, wretched Trojans, rescued from a Fleet
"Long toss'd through every Sea, thy aid entreat.
"Let, at thy voice, the unhallow'd fire forbear
"To touch our Ships; a righteous People spare;
"And on our fortunes look with nearer care!
"We neither seek as plunderers your abodes,
"Nor would our swords molest your houshold Gods:
"Our spirit tempts us not such course to try;
"Nor do the Vanquish'd lift their heads so high.
"There is a Country, call'd by Men of Greece
"Hesperia, strong in Arms, the soil of large increase,
"Œnotrians held it; Men of later fame
"Call it Italia, from their Leader's name.
"That Land we sought; when, wrapt in mist, arose
"Orion, help'd by every wind that blows;
"Dispers'd us utterly—on shallows cast;

---

704 by what he saw you would [not *del*] scarcely write this in a prose note.
712 clamore— with noise: Just when a parcel of Tars, made their way to the Temple with [*illeg del*] noisy Hail. Virgil wished to contrast the ship Crews & inferior officers with the stillness of Eneas & his Staff.

---

698 Crowd *rev from* Troop *MS. 101B, rev from* croud *MS. 101A*
701 us *in* Sergestus *over illeg eras MS. 101B*
703 heart *over illeg eras MS. 101A*
708 They wait] They *with penciled* wait *in margin and caret after* They *MS. 101A*
723 fortunes *ed* fortune's *MSS.*

---

730 Œnotrians] MS. 101A has Ænotrians, as did MS. 89 originally; this spelling is, to my knowledge, unique to Ogilby, and its occurrence here is further indication of WW's use of that translation.

"And we, *we* only, gain'd your shores at last.
"What race of man is here? Was ever yet
"The unnatural treatment known which we have met?
"What country bears with customs that deny,
"To shipwreck'd men, such hospitality
"As the sands offer on the naked beach,
"And the first quiet of the Land they reach?
"—Arms were *our* greeting; yet, if ye despise
"Man and *his* power, look onward, and be wise;—
"The Gods for right and wrong have awful memories.
"A man to no one second in the care
"Of justice, nor in piety and war,
"Ruled over us; if yet Æneas treads
"On earth, nor has been summon'd to the shades,
"Fear no repentance if, in acts of grace
"Striving with him, thou gain the foremost place.
"Nor want we, in Trinacria, towns and plains,
"Where, sprung from Trojan blood, Acestes reigns.
"Grant leave to draw our Ships upon your shores,
"Thence to refit their shatter'd hulks and oars.
"Were Friends and Chief restor'd, whom now we mourn,
"We to the Italian Coast with joy would turn,
"Should Italy lie open to our aim:
"But if our welfare be an empty name,
"And Thou, best Father of the Family
"Of Troy, hast perish'd in the Lybian Sea,
"And young Iülus sank, engulph'd with thee,
"—Then be it ours, at least, to cross the foam
"Of the Sicilian Deep; and seek the home
"Prepar'd by good Acestes, whence we come."
Thus spake Ilioneus: his Friends around
Declar'd their sanction by a murmuring sound.
With downcast looks, brief answer Dido made;
"Trojans, be griefs dismiss'd, anxieties allay'd.
"The pressure of occasion, and a reign
"Yet new, exact these rigours, and constrain
"The jealous vigilance my coasts maintain.
"The Ænean Race, with that heroic Town—
"And widely-blazing war—to whom are they unknown?

---

745 care, war, treads, shades— rather too confluent?—
768 — an odd line

---

735 your *rev from* our *MS. 101A*
742 ye *rev from* we MS. 101A *(MW following WW's pencil)*
751 Trinacria, *rev from* Trinacria's *MS. 101B*
766 by *rev from* with *MS. 101A, so MS. 101B (DW following WW'spencil)*
773 are they *over illeg eras MS. 101A*

"Not so obtuse the Punic breasts we bear;
"Nor does the Giver of the Day so far
"From this our Tyrian City yoke his Car.
"But if Hesperia be your wish'd-for bourne,
"Or to Trinacrian shores your prows would turn,
"Then, with all aids that may promote your weal,
"Ye shall depart;—but if desire ye feel,
"Fix'd in this growing Realm, to share my fate,
"*Yours* are the walls which now I elevate.
"Haste, and withdraw your Gallies from the sea;
"—Trojans and Tyrians shall be one to me.
"Would, too, that, storm-compell'd as ye have been,
"The Person of your Chief might here be seen!
"By trusty Servants shall my shores be traced
"To the last confines of the Lybian Waste,
"For He, the Cast-away of stormy floods,
"May roam through cities, or in savage woods."
Thus did the Queen administer relief
For their dejected hearts; and to the Chief,
While both were burning with desire to break
From out the darksome cloud, Achates spake.
"Son of a Goddess, what resolves ensue
"From this deliverance whose effects we view?
"All things are safe—thy Fleet and Friends restor'd,
"Save one, whom in our sight the Sea devour'd;
"All else respondent to thy Mother's word."
He spake: the circumambient cloud anon
Melts and dissolves, the murky veil is gone,
And left Æneas, as it pass'd away,
With god-like mien and shoulders, standing in full day.
For that same Parent of celestial race
Had shed upon his hair surpassing grace;
And, breathing o'er her Son the purple light
Of youth, had glorified his eyes, made bright,
Like those of Heaven, with joyance infinite.
So stood he forth, an unexpected Guest,
And, while all wonder'd, thus the Queen address'd.

---

789 —. Cast-away of <u>Floods</u> is this ever applied to the Sea—
803 — Here I think some substitute for humeros should be ventured—

---

776 our *inserted MS. 101B (DW following WW's pencil)*
779 weal *rev from* zeal *MS. 101A*
789 For *rev from* If *MS. 101B (DW following WW's pencil)*
790 May roam *over illeg eras, then del and reinserted MS. 101B (DW following WW's pencil)*
803 standing *over* in *eras MS. 101A*
806 And . . . o'er *over illeg eras MS. 101B*
807 Of . . . had *over illeg eras MS. 101B*

---

774 Not so obtuse] "Non obtusa," l. 567.

"He whom ye seek am I, Æneas—flung
"By storms the Lybian solitudes among.
"O Sole, who for the unutterable state
"Of Troy art humanly compassionate;
"Who not alone a shelter dost afford
"To the thin relics of the Grecian sword,
"Perpetually exhausted by pursuit
"Of dire mischance, of all things destitute,
"But in thy purposes with them hast shar'd
"City and home;—not we, who thus have far'd,
"Not we, nor all the Dardan Race that live,
"Scatter'd through Earth, sufficient thanks can give.
"The Gods (if they the Pious watch with love,
"If Justice dwell about us, or above)
"And a mind conscious to itself of right,
"Shall, in fit measure, thy deserts requite!
"What happy Age gave being to such worth?
"What blessed Parents, Dido! brought thee forth?
"While down their channels Rivers seaward flow,
"While shadowy groves sweep round the mountain's brow,
"While ether feeds the stars, where'er be cast
"My lot, whatever Land by me be traced,
"Thy name, thy honour, and thy praise, shall last!"
He spake; and turning tow'rds the Trojan Band,
Salutes Ilioneus with the better hand;
And grasps Serestus with the left—then gave
Like greeting to the rest, to Gyas brave,
And brave Cloanthes.
Inwardly amaz'd,
Sidonian Dido on the Chief had gaz'd
When first he met her view;—his words like wonder rais'd.
"What Force," said She, "pursues Thee—hath impell'd
"To these wild shores? In thee have I beheld
"That Trojan whom bright Venus, on the shore
"Of Phrygian Simois, to Anchises bore?
"And well do I recall to mind the day
"When to our Sidon Teucer found his way,
"An Outcast from his native Borders driven,
"With hope to win new Realms by aid from Belus given,

---

813 O *rev from* Oh *MS. 101B (following pencil signal)*
819 But *rev from* Not *MS. 101B*
820 home *over illeg eras MS. 101B*
825 to *rev from* of *MS. 101A*
826 fit measure *rev from* fitting [?] *then* measure *del, then added MS. 101A*
842 To . . . I *over illeg eras MS. 101B* In thee have I *rev from* Have I in thee *MS. 101A (MW following WW's pencil)*
845 to mind *inserted MS. 101A (MW following WW's pencil)*
846 our Sidon *over* [?our Te] *MS. 101B*

---

813 O Sole] "o sola," l. 597.

"Belus my Father, then the conquering Lord
"Of Cyprus newly-ravaged by his sword.
"Thenceforth I knew the fate of Troy that rings
"Earth round,—thy Name, and the Pelasgian King's.
"Teucer himself, with liberal tongue, would raise
"His Adversaries to just heights of praise,
"And vaunt a Trojan lineage with fair proof;
"Then welcome, noble Strangers, to our Roof!
"—Me, too, like Fortune after devious strife
"Stay'd in this Land, to breathe a calmer life;
"From no light ills which on myself have press'd,
"Pitying I learn to succour the distress'd."
These words pronounced; and mindful to ordain
Fit sacrifice, she issues from the Fane,
And tow'rds the Palace leads Æneas and his Train.
Nor less regardful of his distant Friends,
To the sea coast she hospitably sends
Twice ten selected steers, a hundred lambs
Swept from the plenteous herbage with their dams;
A hundred bristly ridges of huge swine,
And what the God bestows in sparkling wine.
But the interior Palace doth display
Its whole magnificence in set array;
And in the centre of a spacious Hall
Are preparations for high festival:
There, gorgeous vestments—skilfully enwrought
With Eastern purple; and huge tables—fraught
With massive argentry; there, carv'd in gold,
Through long, long series, the atchievements bold
Of Forefathers, each imaged in his place,
From the beginning of the ancient Race.
    Æneas, whose parental thoughts obey
Their natural impulse, brooking no delay,
Dispatch'd the prompt Achates, to report

---

850 ravaged *over illeg eras MS. 101A*
852 King's. *rev from* King, *MS. 101B (DW following WW's pencil)*
861 mindful *over illeg eras MS. 101A*
864 regardful *rev from* regardless *MS. 101A*
865 To the sea coast she hos *rev from* Nor less regardful of his *MS. 101B*
866 Twice *rev from* Thrice *MS. 101A (MW following WW's pencil)*
874 There *rev from* Here *MS. 101A*

---

864 In *British Poets*—WL, l. 895 of Dryden's translation has been corrected in pencil from "he" to "she."

867 "Swept from the plenteous herbage" is WW's embellishment.

869 "Munera, lætitiamque Dei," l. 636. Both Ruæus and Minellius gloss the phrase as "vinum."

875 Eastern purple] "ostroque superbo," l. 639. Ruæus paraphrases: "purpurâ illustri tincta." Minellius glosses: "Aulæa stragulaque purpurea artificiosè facta extenduntur."

The new events, and lead Ascanius to the Court;
Ascanius, for on him the Father's mind
Now rests, as if to that sole care confin'd;
And bids him bring, attendant on the Boy,
The richest Presents snatch'd from burning Troy;
A Robe of tissue stiff with shapes exprest
In threads of gleaming gold; an upper Vest
Round which acanthus twines its yellow flowers;
By Argive Helen worn in festal hours;
Her Mother Leda's wonderous gift—and brought
To Ilium from Mycenæ when she sought
Those unpermitted nuptials;—thickly set
With golden gems, a twofold coronet;
And sceptre which Ilione of yore,
Eldest of Priam's royal Daughters, wore
And orient Pearls, which on her neck she bore.
This to perform, Achates speeds his way
To the Ships anchor'd in that peaceful Bay.
    But Cytherea, studious to invent
Arts yet untried, upon new counsels bent,
Resolves that Cupid, changed in form and face
To young Ascanius, should assume his place;—
Present the maddening Gifts, and kindle heat
Of passion at the bosom's inmost seat.
She dreads the treacherous House and Punic tongue;
By Juno's rancour is her quiet stung:
The calm of night is powerless to remove
These cares, and thus she speaks to winged Love.
    "O Son, my strength, my power! who dost despise
"(What, save thyself, none dare through earth and skies)
"The giant-quelling bolts of Jove, I flee
"O Son, a Suppliant to thy Deity!
"What perils meet Æneas in his course;
"How Juno's hate with unrelenting force

---

883 events *inserted MS. 101A (MW over WW's pencil)*
884 now rests *eras at end of line MS. 101B*
892 Her Mother *rev from* By Argive *MS. 101B*
893 Mycenæ *ed* Mycæne *MSS.*
897 royal *inserted MS. 101A (MW following WW's pencil signal); added later MS. 101B (DW following WW's pencil)*
898 which *rev from* that *MS. 101A (MW following WW's pencil), MS. 101B (DW following WW's pencil)*
907 and Punic *del to* the double *MS. 101A (DW over WW's pencil)* Punic tongue; *over illeg eras MS. 101B*
908 By Juno's rancour is her quiet stung. *del to* She burns, she frets, by Juno's rancour stung; *MS. 101A (DW following WW's pencil; DW's punct)*

---

901 Here begins the passage published in *PM.*
907–908 In *British Poets*—WL, l. 933 of Dryden's translation has been corrected in pencil from "Tyrian's" to "Tyrians."
913 giant-quelling] "Typhoëa," l. 665. Ruæus: "Fulmina, quibus Gigant vicit, imprimisque Typhoëum...." Minellius: "Jovis fulmina ... Quibus Jupiter Typhoëum gigantem confecit...."

"Pursues thy Brother—this to thee is known;
"And oft-times hast thou made my griefs thine own.
"Him now Phœnician Dido in soft chains
"Of a seductive blandishment detains:
"Junonian hospitalities prepare
"Such apt occasion that I dread a snare.
"Hence, ere some hostile God can intervene,
"Would I by previous wiles inflame the Queen
"With passion for Æneas, such strong love
"That at my beck, mine only, She shall move.
"Hear, and assist;—the Father's mandate calls
"His young Ascanius to the Tyrian Walls;
"He comes, my dear delight, and costliest things,
"Preserv'd from fire and flood, for presents brings.
"Him will I take, and in close covert keep,
"'Mid Groves Idalian, lull'd to gentle sleep,
"Or on Cythera's far-sequester'd Steep;
"That he may neither know what hope is mine,
"Nor by his presence traverse the design.
"Do Thou but for a single night's brief space
"Dissemble, be that Boy in form and face!
"And when enraptur'd Dido shall receive
"Thee to her arms, and kisses interweave
"With many a fond embrace, while joy runs high,
"And goblets crown the proud festivity,
"Instil thy subtle poison, and inspire
"At every touch an unsuspected fire."
    Love, at the word, before his Mother's sight
Puts off his wings, and walks with proud delight
Like young Iülus; but the gentlest dews
Of slumber Venus sheds to circumfuse
The true Ascanius, steep'd in placid rest;
Then wafts him, cherish'd on her careful breast,
Through upper air to an Idalian glade;
Where he on soft *amaracus* is laid,
With breathing flowers embraced, and fragrant shade.

---

916 hate with unrelenting *rev from* unrelenting hate *MS. 101B*
919 Phœnician . . . in *del to* the generous . . . by *MS. 101A (DW following pencil signal)*
920 Of a seductive blandishment detains, *del to* Of kind entreaty at her Court detains *MS. 101A (DW)*
926 shall *over illeg eras MS. 101B*
927 mandate *rev from* summons *MS. 101A, MS. 101B (DW following WW's pencil)*
929 costliest *rev from* costlier *MS. 101A*

---

920 "blandisque moratur / Vocibus," ll. 670–671.
951 "mollis amaracus," l. 693. Ruæus: "Herba coronaria, suavissimi odoris, flosculos emittens perpusillos, candidos; marjolaine." "Amaracus" has proven a problem for translators. Pitt omits an English equivalent of the word. Trapp writes: "*Amaracus* sounds well in Latin: But *Sweet-Marjorum* would sound ill in English; and so I have changed it to *Jessamine.*" In his 1654 edition of Virgil, Ogilby has "sweet *Marjerom,*" so Trapp's remark is probably an implicit criticism of his predecessor. WW circumvents the problem altogether by using *amaracus.*

But Cupid, following cheerily his Guide
Achates, with the Gifts to Carthage hied;
He reach'd the Hall where now the Queen repos'd
Amid a golden couch, with awnings half enclos'd:
The Trojans, too (Æneas at their head)
On couches lie with purple overspread;
Meantime on cannisters is piled the bread;
Pellucid water for the hands is borne,
And napkins of smooth texture finely shorn.
Within, are fifty Handmaids who prepare,
As they in order stand, the dainty fare,
And fume the houshold Deities with store
Of odorous incense, while a hundred more,
Match'd with an equal number of like age,
But each of manly sex, a docile Page,
Marshal the banquet, giving with due grace
To cup or viand its appointed place.
The Tyrians rushing in, an eager Band,
Their painted couches seek, obedient to command.
They look with wonder on the Gifts—they gaze
Upon Iülus, dazzled with the rays
That from his ardent countenance are flung,
And charm'd to hear his simulating tongue;
Nor pass unprais'd the robe and veil divine,
Round which the yellow flowers and wandering foliage twine.
    But chiefly Dido, to the coming ill
Devoted, strives in vain her vast desires to fill;
She views the Gifts, upon the Boy then turns
Insatiable eyes, and gazing burns.
To ease a Father's cheated love he hung
Upon Æneas, and around him clung;
Then sought the Queen, who fix'd on him the whole
That she possess'd of look, mind, life, and soul;
And sometimes doth unhappy Dido plant
The Fondling in her bosom, ignorant

941 proud *over illeg eras MS. 101A*
954 to *rev from* of *MS. 101A*
955 He reached *del to* And when *MS. 101A (DW)* where now the Queen repos'd *del to* he entered there between *MS. 101A (DW)*
956 Amid *del to* Upon *MS. 101A (WW's pencil), then entire line del to*
The sharers of her golden couch was seen
Reclined in festal pomp the Tyrian Queen *MS. 101A (DW)*
959 in *rev to* on *MSS.* piled] heap'd *MS. 101A*
966 Match'd *over illeg eras MS. 101B*
973 Iülus *ed* Iulus *MSS.*
984–987 *del to* Then seeks the Queen with her his arts he tries
She fastens on the Boy enamoured eyes
Clasps in her arms nor weens o lot unblest *MS. 101A (DW)*
984–end *for revisions and variants in MS. 101A, see Transcriptions, pp. 527–531*

How great a God deceives her. He, to please
His Acidalian Mother, by degrees
Would sap Sichæus, studious to remove
The dead by influx of a living love,
Through a subsided spirit dispossess'd
Of amorous passion, through a torpid breast.
Now when the viands were remov'd, and ceas'd
The first division of the splendid Feast;
While round a vacant board the Chiefs recline
Huge goblets are brought forth;—they crown the wine.
Voices of gladness roll the walls around;
Those gladsome voices from the courts rebound;
From gilded rafters many a blazing light
Depends, and torches overcome the night.
The minutes fly—till, as the Queen commands,
A bowl of state is offer'd to her hands:
Then She, as Belus wont and all the Line
From Belus, fill'd it to the brim with wine:
Silence ensued. "O Jupiter! whose care
"Is hospitable Dealing, grant my prayer!
"Productive be this day of lasting joy
"To Tyrians, and these Exiles driven from Troy;—
"A day to future generations dear!
"Let Bacchus, donor of soul-gladdening chear,
"Be present! kindly Juno, be thou near!
"And Tyrians, may your choicest favours wait
"Upon this hour, the bond to celebrate!"
She spake; and shed an Offering on the board,
Then sipp'd the bowl whence she the wine had pour'd;
And gave to Bitias, bidding him take heart;
He rais'd—and, not unequal to his part,
Drank deep, self-drench'd from out the brimming gold:
Thereafter, a like course the encircling Nobles hold.
Graced with redundant hair Iopas sings
The lore of Atlas, to resounding strings—
The labours of the sun; the lunar wanderings:—
Whence human kind, and brute; what natural powers
Engender lightning; whence the falling showers.
He chaunts Arcturus, and that social Twain
The glittering Bears, and Pleiads charged with rain;

988–993 The six first lines of p. 43— Temtat prævertere jam resedes amore &c.. are obscure & run obstructedly. That through twice repeated.— Generally, however, the latter part is done with great spirit.

---

990 Sichæus *so MS. 101A* Sicheus *MS. 101B*
1017 Bitias *ed* Betus *MS. 101B* Belus *MS. 101A*

---

997 they crown the wine] "vina coronant," l. 724.

—Why Suns in winter, shunning Heaven's steep heights,
Post seaward; what impedes the tardy nights.
The learned Song from Tyrian hearers draws
Loud shouts,—the Trojans echo the applause.
—But, lengthening out the night with converse new,
Large draughts of love unhappy Dido drew;
Of Priam ask'd, of Hector, o'er and o'er—
What Arms the Son of bright Aurora wore;
What Coursers those of Diomed;—how great,
Achilles—"but O Guest! the whole relate;
"Retrace the Grecian cunning from its source,—
"Your own griefs—and your Friends'—your wandering course;
"—For now, till this seventh summer have ye ranged
"The sea, or trod the earth, to peace estranged!"

End of the First Book.

1029 seaward *rev from* onward *MS. 101B*
1030 Tyrian *over illeg eras MS. 101B*
1036 Coursers *rev from* Horses *MS. 101B*
1041 *close quots ed*

1034–1037 WW quotes these lines in a letter to Lord Lonsdale, dated February 17, 1824, but miswrites "Queen" for "Guest." See text of the letter in Appendix I, p. 567.

Second Book.

All breathed in silence, and intensely gaz'd,
When from the lofty couch his voice Æneas rais'd,
And thus began: "The task which you impose
O Queen, revives unutterable woes;
How by the Grecians Troy was overturn'd,
And her power fell—to be for ever mourn'd;
Calamities which with a pitying heart
I saw, of which I form'd no common part.
Oh! 'twas a miserable end! What One
Of all our Foes, Dolopian, Myrmidon,
Or Soldier bred in stern Ulysses' train,
Such things could utter, and from tears refrain?
And hastens now from Heaven the dewy night,
And the declining stars to sleep invite.
But since such strong desire prevails to know
Our wretched fate, and Troy's last overthrow,
I will begin with spirit resolute
To stifle pangs which well might keep me mute.
    The Grecian Chiefs, exhausted of their strength
By war protracted to such irksome length,
And, from the Siege repuls'd, new schemes devise;
A wooden Horse they build of mountain size.
—Assisted by Minerva's art divine,
They frame the work, and sheathe its ribs with pine,
An offering to the Gods—that they may gain

---

2 the *rev from* his *MS. 101A* his voice *inserted MS. 101A* rais'd *rev from* gaz'd *MS. 101A*

13 And . . . Heaven *over illeg eras MS. 101B*

17–18 I will attempt the theme, though in my breast
Memory recoils and shudders at the test. *MS. 101B, del to text; in MS. 101A,* 29^{r}*, revised thus by CW, Jr., and WW:*

begin with Spirit resolute
I will ~~attempt the theme, tho' in my breast~~
stifle pangs that
To ~~conquer thoughts~~ which well might keep
me
Memory recoils & shudders at the test. mute

Other versions appear on 28^{v}*:*

Altho' the suffering heart my breast within
Shudders, my mind recoils the tale I will begin *(CW, Jr.'s pencil)*
Stifling the pangs which well might keep me mute *(WW)*
{i
I will beg{an though wanting a strong chain
When thought looks back its horror to restrain. *(WW's pencil)*

21 devise; *rev from* devis'd *MSS.*

22 a wooden Horse they build *rev from* To build a wooden Horse *MSS. (CW, Jr.)*

23 *originally omitted, then inserted MS. 101B*

Their home in safety; this they boldly feign,
And spread the Tale abroad;—meanwhile they hide
By stealth, choice warriors in its gloomy side;
Throng the huge concave to its inmost den,
And fill that mighty womb with armed Men.
   In sight of Troy, an Island lies, by Fame
Amply distinguish'd, Tenedos its name;
Potent and rich, in time of Priam's sway:
A faithless Ship-road now, a lonely bay.
Here did the Greeks, when for their native land
We thought them sail'd, lurk on the desart strand.
From her long grief, at once, the Realm of Troy
Broke loose;—the gates are open'd, and with joy
We seek the Dorian Camp, and wander o'er
The spots forsaken, the abandon'd shore.
Here, the Dolopian ground its lines presents;
And here, the dread Achilles pitch'd his tents;
There, lay the Ships drawn up along the coast,
And here, we oft encounter'd, host with host.
Meanwhile, the rest an eye of wonder lift
Unwedded Pallas! on the fatal Gift
To thee devoted. First, Thymœtes calls
For its free ingress through disparted walls
To lodge within the Citadel:—thus He
Treacherous, or such the course of destiny.
Capys, with some of wiser mind, would sweep
The insidious Grecian Offering to the Deep,
Or to the flames subject it: or advise
To perforate and search the cavities;

---

28 By stealth, choice *rev from* Selected *MS. 101B (CW, Jr.); so MS. 101A in pencil but* stealth,] stealth

33–34 Potent & rich while Priam's sway endur'd,
Now a bare hold for Keels, unsafely moor'd. *MS. 101A del to*
Potent & rich but now, since Troy's decay
A faithless hold [*del to* road] for Ships, a lonely bay. *MS. 101A (CW, Jr.), then del to text (CW, Jr.) but* rich,] rich *and* sway;] sway,
Potent and rich while Priam's sway endur'd;
Now a bare hold for Keels, unsafely moor'd. *MS. 101B del to*
Potent and rich; but now since Troy's decay
A faithless road for Ships, a lonely bay. *MS. 101B (CW, Jr.) then* Potent and rich; *del to* Once rich and potent; . . . *MS. 101B del (CW, Jr.), rev to text on interleaf MS. 101B (CW, Jr.)*

36 strand *rev from* sand *MS. 101B*

42 the . . . tents; *over illeg eras MS. 101A*

46 Unwedded *rev from* Virgin *MS. 101B* on . . . Gift *over illeg eras MS. 101B* the *rev in pencil to* thy *MS. 101A*

47 To thee devoted *del in pencil to* The mighty horse. & . . . *MS. 101A (CW, Jr.)*

---

28 "?19" written in left margin, MS. 101B (CW, Jr.'s pencil), referring to the corresponding line in the Latin.

33–34 "dives opum, Priami dùm regna manebant: / Nunc tantùm sinus & statio malefida carinis," ll. 22–23. Ruæus paraphrases: "abundans opibus, dum regnum Priami stabat: nunc solum est sinus & statio parum tuta navibus."

This way and that the multitude divide,
And still unsettled veer from side to side.
Down from the Citadel a numerous Throng
Hastes with Laocoon; they sweep along,
And He, the foremost, crying from afar,
"What would ye? wretched Maniacs, as ye are!
"Think ye the Foe departed? Or that e'er
"A boon from Grecian hands can prove sincere?
"Thus do ye read Ulysses? Foes unseen
"Lurk in these chambers; or the huge Machine
"Against the ramparts brought, by pouring down
"Force from aloft, will seize upon the Town.
"Trojans! mistrust the Horse: whate'er it be,
"Though offering gifts, the Greeks are Greeks to me;"
This said, Laocoon hurl'd with mighty force
A ponderous spear against the monster Horse;
It smote the curved ribs, and quivering stood,
While groans made answer through the cavern'd wood.
We too, upon this impulse, had not Fate
Been adverse, and our minds infatuate,
We too, had rushed the den to penetrate,
Streams of Argolic blood our swords had stained,
Troy, thou might'st yet have stood, and Priam's Towers remained.
But lo! an unknown Youth with hand to hand
Bound fast behind him, whom a boisterous Band
Of Dardan Swains with clamour hurrying

55–56 Into conflicting judgments break and split
The crowd, as random thoughts the fancy hit. *MSS., then del in both by CW, Jr., to text, followed in MS. 101B by alt version marked Qy following WW's pencil draft on MS. 101A,* 28^{v}*:*
Rash in decision, constant to no side,
This way and that the multitude divide *MS. 101A,* 30^{r} *has alt version in WW's hand:*
This way and that the vulgar are inclined
Split into parties by the fickle mind. *WW sent this version to CW, Jr., in a letter dated November 30, 1827, but* vulgar] many *with* vulgar *alt*

59 He, *over illeg eras MS. 101B (following WW's pencil)*

62 can prove *rev from* could be *MS. 101A*

67–70 "Let not a fair pretence your minds enthrall;
"For me, I fear the Greeks, and most of all
"When they are offering gifts." With mighty force,
This said, he hurl'd a spear against the Horse; *MS. 101B del to text (CW, Jr.) on facing interleaf but* monster *rev from* towering *MS. 101A has same underlying text and revisions as MS. 101B, then l. 68 rev to* I fear the Greeks, nor fear them least of all *(CW, Jr.), then ll. 67–68 del in pencil to*
Trojans mistrust the gift, whateer it be,
Though offering gifts the Greeks are Greek to me *(CW, Jr.)*

69–95 *for revisions and variants in MS. 101A, see Transcriptions, pp. 532–533*

71 It smote *over illeg eras MS. 101B*

72 cavern'd *rev from* hollow *MS. 101B*

73–97 *for revisions and variants in MS. 101B, except on* 2^{v}*P, see Transcriptions, pp. 544–545*

79 boisterous *rev from* shouting *MS. 101B,* 2^{v}*P (CW, Jr.)*

80 clamour hurrying *rev from* boisterous hurry bring *MS. 101B,* 2^{v}*P (CW, Jr.)*

55–56 "Scinditur incertum studia in contraria vulgus," l. 39. Ruæus paraphrases: "Plebs ambigua distrahitur in opposita consilia."

Force with them to the shore, and place before the King.
Such his device when he those chains had sought,
A voluntary captive, fix'd in thought
Either the City to betray, or meet
Death, the sure penalty of foil'd deceit.
The curious Trojans, pouring in, deride
And taunt the Prisoner, with an emulous pride.
Now see the cunning of the Greeks exprest
By guilt of One, true image of the rest!
For, while with helpless looks, from side to side
Anxiously cast, the Phrygian throng he ey'd,
"Alas! what Land," he cries, "can now, what Sea
"Can offer refuge? What resource for me?
"Who 'mid the Greeks no breathing-place can find,
"And whom ye, Trojans, have to death consign'd!—"
Thus were we wrought upon; and now, with sense
Of pity touch'd that check'd all violence,
We cheer'd and urged him boldly to declare
His birth, his fortunes, what his tidings are;
And on what claims he ventures to confide;
Then somewhat eas'd of fear, he thus replied.
    "O King! a plain confession shall ensue
"On these commands, in all things plain and true.
"And first, the tongue that speaks shall not deny
"My origin; a Greek by birth am I:
"Fortune made Sinon wretched;—to do more,
"And make him false,—*that* lies not in her power.
"In converse, haply, ye have heard the name
"Of Palamedes, and his glorious fame;
"A guiltless Chief, for this condemn'd to die
"That he dissuaded war,—could that be treachery?

---

81 Force with them *rev from* Down to *MS. 101B, $2^{v}P$ (CW, Jr.)* before *rev from* behind *MS. 101B, $2^{v}P$*

97 pity *inserted MS. 101A*

99 His origin, what tidings he may bear, *MSS.; rev to text MS. 101B (CW, Jr.); rev to* His origin, and what his tidings are *(CW, Jr.'s pencil), then rev to text MS. 101A (CW, Jr., following WW's pencil), but no punct*

100 on *rev to* in *MS. 101A (following WW's pencil in margin)*

108 ye have *over illeg eras MS. 101B*

110–111 A Chief with treason falsely charged, and whom *MSS. rev to text MS. 101B (CW, Jr.); rev MS. 101A in margins of 30^{v} (WW's pencil)—see transcription—and to text (CW, Jr.) but* Chief,] Chief this condemn'd *rev to* this alone condemnd *(WW's pencil)* war,—] war: treachery?] treachery
A Guiltless Chieftain yet condemned to die
For having blamd the war, could that be treacher *alt MS. 101A (WW)*

110–114 "quia bella negabat a circumstance which wd prepossess the Trojans in favour of him and his associate (Sinon)," MS. 101A (CW, Jr.). The Latin text actually reads: "quem falsâ sub proditione Pelasgi / Insontem, infando indicio, quia bella vetabat, / Demisêre neci; nunc cassum lumine lugent," ll. 83–85. Ruæus paraphrases: "quem Græci sub falso prætextu proditionis innocentem morti addixerunt per crudelem calumniam, quia dissuadebat bellum; nunc deflent privatum luce."

"The Achaians crush'd him by nefarious doom,
"And now lament, when cover'd with the tomb.
"His Kinsman I; and hither by his side
"Me my poor Father sent, when first these fields were tried.
"While yet his voice the Grecian Chieftains sway'd
"And due respect was to his counsel paid,
"Ere that high influence was with life cut short,
"I did not walk ungraced by fair report.
"But when Ulysses (thousands can attest
"This truth) with envy rankling in his breast;
"Had compassed, what he blushed not to contrive,
"And hapless Palamedes ceas'd to live,
"I dragg'd my days in sorrow and in gloom,
"And mourn'd my guiltless Friend, indignant at his doom;
"This inwardly; and yet not always mute,
"Rashly I vow'd revenge—my sure pursuit,
"If e'er the shores of Argos I again
"Should see, victorious with my Countrymen.
"Nor fail'd these threats sharp hatred to excite;
"Hence the first breathings of a deadly blight:
"Hence, to appal me, accusations came,
"Which still Ulysses was at work to frame;
"Hence would he scatter daily 'mid the crowd
"Loose hints, at will sustain'd or disavow'd.
"Beyond himself for instruments he look'd,
"And in this search of means no respite brook'd
"Till Calchas his accomplice—but the chain
"Of foul devices why untwist in vain?
"Why should I linger?—If ye Trojans place
"On the same level all of Argive race,
"And 'tis enough to know that I am one,

---

112 him by *rev from* by a *MSS. (CW, Jr.)*
113 when *rev from* whom *MS. 101A*
116 Chieftains *over illeg eras MS. 101B*
117 due *rev from* dire *MS. 101B*
120–123 "Ulysses, envy rankling in his breast,
"(And these are things which thousands can attest)
"Thereafter turn'd his subtlety to give
"That fatal injury, and he ceas'd to live. *MS. 101B; so MS. 101A but* "Ulysses,] "—Ulysses breast,] breast he *inserted* ceas'd] ceased *rev to text MS. 101B (CW, Jr.) but* in *rev from* at *(CW, Jr.); so MS. 101A but* in] at breast;] breast, compassed,] compass'd live, *ed* live. *MS. 101B* live *MS. 101A*
130 *rev from* Sharp hatred did these open threats excite; *MSS. (CW, Jr.)*
133 at work] intent *alt MS. 101A*
142 *over illeg eras MS. 101B*

"Punish me promptly! Ithacus, that done,
"Would be rejoic'd, the brother Kings to buy
"That service, would esteem no price too high."
This stirr'd us more, whose judgments were asleep
To all suspicion of a crime so deep
And craft so fine. Our questions we renew'd;
And, trembling, thus the fiction he pursued.
"Oft did the Grecian Host the means prepare
"To flee from Troy, tired with so long a war;
"Would they had fled! but still the South-wind stopp'd
"Their going, and the hoisted sails were dropp'd;
"And when this pine-ribb'd Horse of monstrous size
"Stood forth, a finish'd Work, before their eyes,
"Then chiefly peal'd the storm through blacken'd skies.
"So, that the Oracle its aid might lend
"To fix our wavering minds, Eurypylus we send,
"Who brought the answer of the voice divine
"In these sad words giv'n from the Delian Shrine.
—"Blood flow'd, a Virgin perish'd to appease
"The winds, when first for Troy ye pass'd the seas;
"O Grecians! for return across the Flood,
"Life must be paid, a sacrifice of blood."
—"With this response an universal dread
"Among the shuddering multitude was spread;
"All quak'd in doubt at whom the Fates had aim'd
"This sentence, who the Victim Phœbus claim'd.

143–145 "Punish me;—would Ulysses might look on!
"And let the Atridæ hear, rejoiced with what is done!" *MS. 101B; so MS. 101A but* hear,] hear *rev to text MS. 101B (CW, Jr.) with* promptly *inserted and* that *rev from* if that were *in MS. 101A ll. 143–144 rev to* Punish me;—that woulud be a service done
To Ithacus, the Atridæ gladly would look on. *(WW) all then del to text (CW, Jr.) but* promptly *inserted following WW's pencil and* if that were *altered in same way as MS. 101B, no quots, no period, and* rejoic'd] rejoiced

146 whose *rev from* where *MS. 101A*

151 tired *rev from* tried *MS. 101A*

152 still the South-wind *rev from* winds as often *MSS. (CW, Jr.)*

158 fix our wavering minds *rev from* quell our doubts *MSS. (CW, Jr.) but MS. 101B* wavering thoughts *rev to* wavering minds *(CW, Jr.)*

160 Delian] Delphic *MS. 101A; rev from* Delphic *MS. 101B (CW, Jr.)*

162 for Troy ye *rev from* from Troy we *MS. 101A (MW following WW's pencil)*

164 of *rev from* or *MS. 101A*

167 in doubt *rev from* to think *MS. 101B (CW, Jr.); so MS. 101A but in pencil repeated in ink (CW, Jr.)*

143–145 "Hoc Ithacu velit, & magno mercentur Atridæ," l. 104. Ruæus paraphrases: "hoc optaverit Ulysses, & Atridæ magno pretio emerint." Trapp's note on this line is interesting: "It is, I think, impossible to make the literal English of magno mercentur, would *buy*, or *purchase with a vast Sum*, look graceful in this Place. And therefore I am forced to recede from the Original; and substitute a much lower Idea in the room of it." In *British Poets*—WL, l. 142 of Dryden's translation has been corrected in ink from "Ithaces" to "Ithacus."

149 thus the fiction he pursued] "ficto pectore fatur," l. 107.

"Then doth the Ithacan with tumult loud
"Bring forth the Prophet Calchas to the crowd;
"Asks what the Gods would have; and some, meanwhile,
"Discern what crime the Mover of the guile
"Is bent upon; and do not hide from me
"The issue, they in mute reserve foresee.
"Ten days refus'd he still with guarded breath
"To designate the Man, to fix the death,
"The Ithacan still urgent for the deed;
"At last the accomplice Seer announc'd that *I* must bleed.
"Assenting all with joyful transfer laid
"What each himself had fear'd upon one wretched head.
"Now came the accursed day;—the salted cates
"Are spread,—the Altar for the Victim waits;
"The fillets bind my temples—I took flight
"Bursting my chains, I own, and, through the night
"Lurk'd among oozy swamps, and there lay hid
"Till winds might cease their voyage to forbid.
"And now was I compell'd at once to part
"With all the dear old longings of the heart;
"Never to see my Country, Children, Sire,
"Whom they, perchance, will for this flight require;
"For this offence of mine of *them* will make
"An expiation, punish'd for my sake.
"But Thee, by all the Powers who hold their seat
"In Heaven, and know the truth, do I entreat.
"O King! and by whate'er may yet remain,
"Among mankind of faith without a stain,
"Have pity on my woes; commiserate
"A mind that ne'er deserv'd this wretched fate!"

---

172 crime *rev from* end *MSS. (CW, Jr.); in MS. 101B* the Mover of the guile *del and reinserted (CW, Jr.)*

173 bent upon *rev from* compassing *MSS. (CW, Jr.); in MS. 101A* and do not hide *del and reinserted (CW, Jr.)*

174 issue *rev from* crime which *MSS. (CW, Jr.)*

178 At last the unwilling voice *rev to* The accomplice Seer At last *MS. 101A (CW, Jr.)* accomplice Seer *rev from* unwilling voice *MS. 101B (CW, Jr.)* must bleed *over illeg eras MS. 101B*

179–180 All gave assent, each happy to be clear'd,
By one Man's fall, of what himself had fear'd. *MSS.; MS. 101A rev to*
The sentence all confirmed and gladly laid
The fate which each had feared on one poor wretched head *(CW, Jr.), then rev to*
Assenting all with joyful transfer laid
What each had fear'd himself, on one wretched head *(CW, Jr.), then rev to text; MS. 101B rev to*
Assenting all with joyful transfer laid
What each had feared himself upon one wretched head. *(CW, Jr.), rev to text (CW, Jr.)*

188 dear old *rev from* dearest *MS. 101A*

191 Of *them,* for this offence of mine, will make *MSS.; rev to text MS. 101B (CW, Jr. following WW's pencil, but without following WW's underlining of* them*)*

198 fate!"] fate" *rev from* [?hate] *MS. 101A*

---

179 Assenting all] "Assensere omnes," l. 130.

—We grant to tears, thus seconding his pray'r,
His life, and freely pity whom we spare:
Even Priam's self, He first of all, commands
To loose the galling cords and liberate his hands,
Then adds these friendly words; "Whoe'er thou be,
"Henceforth forget the Grecians, lost to thee;
"We claim thee now, and let me truly hear
"Why and by whom instructed did they rear
"This huge, unwieldy fabric? was the aim
"Relligion, or for war some engine did they frame?"
Straight were these artful words in answer given
While he uprais'd his hands, now free, to Heaven.
"Eternal Fires, on you I call; O Ye!
"And your inviolable Deity!
"Altars, and ruthless swords from which I fled!
"Ye fillets, worn round my devoted head!
"Be it no crime if Argive sanctions cease
"To awe me—none to hate the men of Greece!
"The law of Country forfeiting its hold,
"Mine be the voice their secrets to unfold!
"And ye, O Trojans! keep the word ye gave;
"Save me, if truth I speak, and Ilium save!
"The Grecian Host on Pallas still relied;
"Nor hope had they but what her aid supplied;
"But all things droop'd since that ill-omen'd time
"In which Ulysses, Author of the crime,
"Was leagu'd with impious Diomed, to seize
"That Image pregnant with your destinies;
"They, when the warders of the fort were slain
"Tore the Palladium from the holy Fane,
"And, fearing not the Goddess, touch'd the Bands

199–200 —His tears prevail, we spare the Suppliant's life,
Pitying the man we spare, without a strife; *MSS.*
Those tears prevail, and granting to his prayer
His life, we freely pity whom we spare: *alt MS. 101A (CW, Jr.), then* Those . . . his *del; rev to text MS. 101B (CW, Jr.), MS. 101A (CW, Jr., in pencil and ink following WW)*

202 galling cords and liberate *rev from* fetters, and unbind *MS. 101A (MW), MS. 101B (CW, Jr.)*

206–208 "Who mov'd them first this mons'trous Horse to rear?
"And why? Was some religious vow the aim?
"Or, for what use in war the Engine might they frame?" *MS. 101B; so MS. 101A but* frame?"] frame? *rev to text MS. 101B (CW, Jr.); so MS. 101A but* huge,] huge *and* some] Some

216 To awe me—,] To awe me, *MS. 101A; rev from* Cease to awe me, *MS. 101B*

219 gave *rev from* give *MS. 101B*

227–228 Tore the Palladium from the holy Fane,
The Guards who watch'd the Citadel first slain; *MSS.; rev to text MS. 101B (CW, Jr.); so MS. 101A (CW, Jr.) but* They,] They *and* the holy *rev to* its holy *(CW, Jr.)*

229 touch'd *over illeg eras MS. 101B*

---

209 WW has omitted the phrase "arte Pelasgâ," l. 152, from his translation.

"Wreathed round her virgin brow, with gory hands.
"Hope ebb'd, strength fail'd the Grecians since that day;
"Incens'd the Goddess turn'd her face away.
"This by no doubtful signs Tritonia shew'd;
"The uplifted eyes with flames coruscant glow'd,
"Soon as they placed her Image in the Camp,
"And trickl'd o'er its limbs a briny damp;
"And from the ground, the Goddess (strange to hear!)
"Leapt thrice, with buckler grasp'd, and quivering spear.
"—Then Calchas bade to stretch the homeward sail,
"And prophesied that Grecian Arms would fail
"Unless we for new omens should repair
"To Argos, thither the Palladium bear;
"And thence to Phrygian Shores recross the Sea,
"Fraught with a more propitious Deity.
"They went; but only to return in power
"With favouring Gods, at some unlook'd-for hour.
"—So Calchas read those signs; the Horse was built
"To soothe Minerva, and atone for guilt.
"Compact in strength you see the Fabric rise,
"A Pile stupendous, towering to the skies!
"This was ordain'd by Calchas,—with intent
"That the vast bulk its ingress might prevent,
"And Ilium ne'er within her Walls enfold
"Another Safeguard reverenced like the old.
"For if, unaw'd by Pallas, ye should lift
"A sacrilegious hand against the Gift,
"The Phrygian Realm shall perish. (May the Gods
"Turn on himself the mischief he forbodes!)
"But if your Town it enter—by your aid
"Ascending—Asia, then, in Arms array'd
"Shall storm the walls of Pelops, and a fate
"As dire on our Posterity await."

---

230 with *inserted over illeg eras MS. 101A*
231–234 *written in over two erased lines, probably ll. 233–234, MS. 101B*
232 Incens'd . . . face *rev from* From them . . . mind *MSS. (CW, Jr.)*
234 with *rev from* [?and] *MS. 101A* glow'd *over illeg eras MS. 101A*
238 grasp'd, and quivering spear *over illeg eras MS. 101B*
245 in *rev from* with *MS. 101B*
248 soothe *rev from* calm *MS. 101A; so MS. 101B (DW following WW's pencil)*
261 of *over illeg eras MS. 101B*

---

231 In the notes to his translation, Trapp writes of this line: "*Ex illo fluere, & retro sub lapsa referri,* is extremely elegant; but will not admit of close Translation."

233 "Nec dubiis ea signa dedit Tritonia monstris," l. 171.

234 "arsêre coruscæ / Luminibus flammæ arrectis," ll. 172–173. This is the only use of "coruscant" in WW's poetry.

248 and atone for guilt] "nefas quæ triste piaret," l. 184. Ruæus paraphrases: "quod expiaret funestum crimen." Minellius glosses "piaret" as "purgaret."

261–262 In *British Poets*—WL, there is a pencil mark beside ll. 257–258 of Dryden's translation, his version of these lines.

Even so the arts of perjur'd Sinon gain'd
Belief for this, and all that he had feign'd;
Thus were *they* won by wiles, by tears compell'd,
Whom not Tydides, not Achilles quell'd;
Who fronted ten years' war with safe disdain;
'Gainst whom a thousand Ships had tried their strength in vain.
To speed our fate, a thing did now appear
Yet more momentous, and of instant fear.
Laocoon, Priest by lot to Neptune, stood
Where to his hand a Bull pour'd forth its blood,
Before the Altar, in high offering slain;—
But lo! two Serpents, o'er the tranquil Main
Incumbent, roll from Tenedos, and seek
Our Coast together (shuddering do I speak.)
Between the waves, their elevated breasts,
Upheav'd in circling spires, and sanguine crests,
Tower o'er the flood: the parts that follow sweep,
In folds voluminous and vast, the Deep.
The agitated brine, with noisy roar,
Attends their coming 'till they touch the shore:
Sparkle their eyes suffus'd with blood, and quick
The tongues shot forth their hissing mouths to lick.
Dispers'd with fear we fly; in close array
These move, and tow'rds Laocoon point their way,
But first assault his Sons, their youthful prey.
—A several Snake in tortuous wreaths engrasps
Each slender frame; and fanging what it clasps
Feeds on the limbs; the Father rushes on,
Arms in his hand, for rescue; but anon
Himself they seize; and, coiling round his waist
Their scaly backs, they bind him, twice embrac'd
With monst'rous spires, as with a double zone;
And, twice around his neck in tangles thrown,
High o'er the Father's head each Serpent lifts its own.
Lo! while his priestly wreaths are sprinkled o'er
With sable venom, and distain'd with gore;
He strives with labouring hands the knots to rend,

275 and *rev from* to *MS. 101A*
284 The *rev from* Their *MSS.*
286 move *rev from* more *MS. 101A* tow'rds] tow'ards *MS. 101A, rev from* tow'rd *MS. 101B*
293 twice *rev from* thrice *MSS. (CW, Jr.)*
296 its *rev from* his *MS. 101B*
297 His priestly fillets thus are sprinkl'd o'er *rev to* Thus are His priestly fillets sprinkl'd o'er *MS. 101B (WW), then rev to text (CW, Jr.); so MS. 101A (WW), but* Lo! . . . wreaths are] Lo . . . wreath is
298 *del, then recopied on interleaf, all but concluding punct, MS. 101B (CW, Jr.)*
299 *rev from* And while his labouring hands the knots would rend *MS. 101A (WW's pencil and ink), MS. 101B (CW, Jr.)*

278 circling spires] "immensibus orbibus," l. 204. Ruæus paraphrases: "immensis spiris."

And utters cries that to the Heavens ascend;
Loud as a Bull—that, wounded by the axe
Shook off the uncertain steel, and from the altar breaks,
To fill with bellowing voice the depths of air!
—But tow'rd the Temple slid the Hydra Pair,
Their work accomplish'd, and there lie conceal'd
Couched at Minerva's feet, beneath her orbed Shield.
Nor was there *One* who trembled not with fear,
Or deem'd the expiation too severe
For him whose lance had pierc'd the votive Steed,
Which to the Temple they resolve to lead;
There to be lodg'd with pomp of service high
And supplication: such the general cry.
Shattering the Walls, a spacious breach we make;
We cleave the bulwarks—toil which all partake,
Some to the feet the rolling wheels apply;
Some round its lofty neck the cables tye:
The Engine, pregnant with our deadly foes,
Mounts to the breach; and ever, as it goes,
Boys, mix'd with Maidens, chaunt a holy song,
And press to touch the cords, a happy throng!
The Town it enters thus, and threatening moves along.
My Country, glorious Ilium! and ye Towers,
Lov'd habitation of celestial Powers!
Four times it halted mid the Gates—a din
Of armour four times warn'd us from within;
Yet tow'rds the sacred Dome with reckless mind
We still press on, and in the place assign'd
Lodge the portentous Gift, through frenzy blind.
Nor fail'd Cassandra now to scatter wide
Words that of instant ruin prophesied.
—But Phœbus will'd that none should heed her voice;
And we, we miserable men, rejoice;
And hang our Temples round with festal boughs,
Upon that day, the last which Fate allows.

---

300 And utters cries that *rev from* The cries he utters *MS. 101A (WW), MS. 101B (CW, Jr.)*
304 tow'rds *rev from* tow'rd *MS. 101A*
310 resolve *rev from* resolv'd *MS. 101A and from* resolv *MS. 101B*
313 make *rev from* made *MS. 101B*
324 mid *rev from* in *MS. 101A (CW, Jr.); so MS. 101B (CW, Jr., following WW's pencil)* Gates—a] Gates a *rev from* Gates 'mid *MS. 101B* gates—a *MS. 101A*
326 tow'rds *rev to* tow'rd *MS. 101A*
327 in the *over illeg eras MS. 101B*
331 heed *rev from* hear *MS. 101B (DW following WW's pencil)*
333 festal *rev from* festive *MS. 101A (MW following WW's pencil)*

322–323 In *British Poets*—WL, there is a pencil line beside ll. 316–317 of Dryden, the lines corresponding to these.

Meanwhile, had Heaven revolv'd with rapid flight,
And fast from Ocean climbs the punctual Night,
With boundless shade involving earth and sky
And Myrmidonian frauds:—the Trojans lie
Scatter'd throughout the weary Town, and keep
Unbroken quiet in the embrace of sleep.
This was the time when, furnish'd and array'd,
Nor wanting silent moonlight's friendly aid,
From Tenedos the Grecian Navy came,
Led by the royal Galley's signal flame:
And Sinon now, our hostile fates his guard,
By stealth the dungeon of the Greeks unbarr'd;
Straight, by a pendant rope adown the side
Of the steep Horse, the armed Warriors glide.
The Chiefs Thersander, Sthenelus, are there,
With joy deliver'd to the open air;
—Ulysses, Thoas, Achamas, the cord
Lets down to earth—and Helen's injur'd Lord;
—Pyrrhus, who from Pelides drew his birth;
And bold Machaon, first to issue forth,
Nor him forget, whose skill had fram'd the Pile,
Epèus, glorying in his prosperous wile.
—They rush upon the City that lay still,
Buried in sleep and wine; the Warders kill;
And at the wide-spread Gates in triumph greet
Expectant Helpers crowding from the Fleet.
It was the earliest hour when sweet repose,
Gift of the Gods, creeps softly on, to close
The eyes of weary mortals—Then arose
Hector, or to my dream appear'd to rise,
And stood before me with fast-streaming eyes:
Such as he was when horse had striven with horse,
Whirling along the plain his lifeless Corse,
The thongs that bound him to the Chariot thrust

339–340 *rev from* Throughout the City silent watch they keep
And with tired limbs receive the embrace of sleep *MS. 101B (DW following WW's pencil); so MS. 101A (MW) but* Scatter'd] Scattered *(MW following WW) and* keep] keep,
346 By stealth *over illeg eras MS. 101B*
349 Sthenelus, are *over illeg eras MS. 101B*
360 Helpers *rev from* helpers *MS. 101B* comrades *alt MS. 101B (WW's pencil)*
361–363 *rev from* It was as the earliest hour of slumberous rest
Gift of the Gods to Man [*rev from* man] with toil oppress;
When present to [*rev from* in *MS. 101B*] my dream, did Hector rise *MS. 101B (CW, Jr.)*
361–411 *for revisions and variants in MS. 101A, see Transcriptions, pp. 534–537*
364–389 *for revisions and variants in MS. 101B, see Transcriptions, pp. 546–547*

335–340 In *British Poets*—WL, there is a pencil mark beside l. 329 of Dryden's translation, the first of the lines equivalent to these; in l. 330 of Dryden, "centries" (for sentries) is underlined.

Through his swoln feet, and black with gory dust;—
A spectacle how pitiably sad!
How chang'd from that returning Hector, clad
In glorious spoils, Achilles' own attire!
From Hector hurling shipward the red Phrygian fire!
—A squalid beard, hair clotted thick with gore,
And that same throng of patriot wounds he bore,
In front of Troy receiv'd; and now, methought,
That I myself was to a passion wrought
Of tears, which to my voice this greeting brought.
"O Light of Dardan Realms! Most faithful Stay
"To Trojan courage, why these lingerings of delay?
"Where hast thou tarried, Hector? From what coast
"Coms't thou, long-look'd for? After thousands lost—
"Thy kinsmen or thy friends—such travail borne
"By desolated Troy, how tir'd and worn
"Are we, who thus behold thee! how forlorn!
"These gashes whence? this undeserv'd disgrace?
"Who thus defiled that calm majestic face?"
He nought to this—unwilling to detain
One, who had ask'd vain things, with answer vain;
But, groaning deep, "Flee, Goddess-born," he said,
"Snatch thyself from these flames around thee spread;
"Our Enemy is master of the Walls;
"Down from her elevation Ilium falls.
"Enough for Priam; the long strife is o'er,
"Nor doth our Country ask one effort more.
"Could Pergamus have been defended—hence,
"Even from this hand, had issued her defence:
"Troy her Penates doth to thee commend,
"Her sacred rites;—let these thy fates attend!
"Far sailing seek for these the fated Land
"Where mighty Walls at length shall rise at thy command!"

381–386 Where hast thou tarried Hector? From what coast
Coms't Thou long-wished for? After thousands lost,
Thy kindred and thy Friends, such travail borne
By all that [desolated *alt*] breathe in Troy, how tired and worn
We who behold thee! But why *thus* return?
These gashes whence? This undeserv'd disgrace
Who first defil'd that calm majestic face *alt WW to CW, Jr., November 30, 1827*

399 rites *rev from* stores *MS. 101B (CW, Jr.)*

400–401 *rev from* Sail, under their protection for the Land
Where mighty Realms shall grow at thy command!" *MS. 101B (CW, Jr., following WW, WW's punct)*

372–375 In *British Poets*—WL, there are pencil lines next to ll. 362–363 of Dryden's translation, the lines that correspond to these.

382 long-look'd for] "Exspectate," l. 283. Minellius glosses: "Diu desiderate."

388–389 "Ille nihil; nec me quærentem vana moratur," l. 287. Ruæus paraphrases: "Ille nihil ad hæc dixit, nec responsis detinet me petentem inutilia."

396–397 defended . . . defence] "defendi . . . defensa," l. 292.

—No more was utter'd; but his hand he stretch'd,
And from the inmost Sanctuary fetch'd
The consecrated wreaths, the potency
Of Vesta, and the fires that may not die.
Now wailings wild from street to street are pour'd,
And though apart, and 'mid thick trees embow'rd,
My Father's mansion stood, the loud alarms
Came pressing thither, and the clash of Arms.
Sleep fled: I climb the roof—and, where it rears
Its loftiest summit, stand with quicken'd ears.
So when a fire, by raging south winds borne,
Lights on a billowy sea of ripen'd corn,
Or rapid torrent sweeps with mountain flood
The fields, the harvest prostrates, headlong bears the wood;
High on a rock, the unweeting shepherd, bound
In blank amazement, listens to the sound.
Then was apparent to *whom* faith was due,
And Grecian plots lie bare to open view.
Above the spacious palace where abode
Deiphobus, the flames in triumph rode;
Ucalegon burns next; through lurid air
Sigean Friths reflect a widening glare.
Clamor and clangor to the heavens arise,
The blast of trumpets mix'd with vocal cries:
Arms do I snatch—weak reason scarcely knows
What aid they promise, but my spirit glows;
I burn to gather Friends, whose firm array
On to the Citadel shall force its way.
Precipitation works with desperate charms;
It seems a lovely thing to die in Arms.
Lo Pantheus! fugitive from Grecian spears,
Apollo's Priest;—his vanquish'd Gods he bears;
The other hand his little Grandson leads,
While from the Sovereign Fort, he tow'rd my threshold speeds.
—"Pantheus, what hope? which Fortress shall we try?

---

406 *rev from* Meantime, wild tumult through the streets is pour'd; *MS. 101B (CW, Jr.)* streets *rev from* street *MSS.*

410 roof— *rev from* [?wall,] *MS. 101B*

412 So *over* [?As] *eras MS. 101B* raging *over illeg eras MS. 101A*

426 Arms do I *rev from* Armour I *MS. 101B;* Armour I seize— *added in pencil and del on interleaf MS. 101B (CW, Jr.)*

435 And [*alt* while *(WW's pencil)*] from the Sovereign Fort, to reach my gate he speeds. *MS. 101A; MS. 101B reads:*
While [?reach ?my] gate
~~And~~ from the Sovereign Fort, he tow'rd my threshold speeds.
the words [?reach ?my] gate *are in WW's pencil*

404–405 the potency / Of Vesta] "Vestamque potentem," l. 296.

406–407 In *British Poets*—WL, there is a pencil line beside ll. 397–398 of Dryden's translation, the lines that correspond to these.

413 "billowy sea" is WW's embellishment.

"Where plant resistance?" He in prompt reply
Said, deeply mov'd,—"Tis come—the final hour;
"—The inevitable close of Dardan power
"Hath come:—we have been Trojans, Ilium was,
"And the great name of Troy; now all things pass
"To Argos; so wills angry Jupiter:
"Within the burning Town the Grecians domineer.
"Forth from its central stand the enormous Horse
"Pours in continual stream an armed Force;
"Sinon, insulting victor, aggravates
"The flames; and thousands hurry through the Gates,
"Throng'd, as might seem, with press of all the Hosts
"That e'er Mycenæ sent to Phrygian Coasts.
"Others with spears in serried files blockade
"The passes;—hangs, with quivering point, the blade
"Unsheath'd for slaughter,—scarcely to the foes
"A blind and baffled fight the Warders can oppose."
 Urged by these words, and as the Gods inspire
I rush into the battle and the fire,
Where sad Erinnys, where the shock of fight,
The roar, the tumult, and the groans invite;
Rypheus is with me, Iphitus, the pride
Of battles, joins his aid; and to my side
Flock Dymas, Hypanis, the moon their guide;
Nor last the young Corœbus, he who fed
A senseless passion, whom desire to wed
Cassandra, in those days to Troy had led.
He fought, the hopes of Priam to sustain,
His Son by wedlock; miserable Man
For whom a raving Spouse had prophesied in vain.

---

438 'Tis *ed.* T'is *rev from* t'is *MS. 101B* T'is *MS. 101A*
438–443 Tis come the final hour
The inevitable close of Dardan power
Hath come; we have been Trojans Ilium was
And the great name of Troy; now all things pass
To Argos—so wills angry Jupiter
Amid a burning Town the Grecians domineer. *WW to Lord Lonsdale, February 5, 1824*
445 in *rev from* [?its] *MS. 101A*
458 Iphitus *ed* Epytus *MSS.; see l. 583 below*
461–464 With young Corœbus, who had lately sought
Our walls, by passion for Cassandra brought;
He led to Priam an auxiliar train, *MSS. but* Corœbus *over illeg eras MS. 101B (DW following WW's pencil); rev to text MS. 101B (CW, Jr.); so MS. 101A but* desire *written over* the *see also Transcriptions, p. 543*

438–442 WW discusses this passage in a letter to Lord Lonsdale; see Appendix I, 565. Ruæus paraphrases ll. 324–325 of Virgil thus: "Venit suprema dies, et tempus inevitabile Trojanis. . . ." Minellius glosses: "venit ultima aut novissima dies regni Trojani & exitium irremediabile & inevitabile." Both may have influenced the translation.

446–448 In *British Poets*—WL, the words "throws" and "whom I fear" of ll. 443–445 of Dryden's translation are underlined; these are the corresponding lines of WW's translation.

464–466 *British Poets*—WL has a pencil line beside ll. 463–464 of Dryden's translation, the lines that correspond to these.

When these I saw collected, and intent
To face the strife with deeds of hardiment,
I thus began; "O Champions vainly brave
"If, like myself, to dare extremes ye crave,
"You see our lost condition;—not a God,
"Of all the Powers by whom this Empire stood,
"But hath renounc'd his Altar—fled from his abode.
"—Ye would uphold a City wrapp'd in fire;
"Die rather;—let us rush, in battle to expire!
"For safety hoping not, the vanquish'd have
"The best of safety, in a noble grave.—"
—Thus to their minds was fury added,—then,
Like wolves driven forth by hunger from the den,
To prowl amid blind vapours, whom the brood
Expect, their jaws all parch'd with thirst for blood,
Through flying darts, through pressure of the Foe,
To death, to not uncertain death, we go.
Right through the Town our midway course we bear,
Aided by hovering darkness, strengthen'd by despair.
Can words the havoc of that night express?
What power of tears may equal the distress?
An ancient City sinks to disappear;
SHE sinks who rul'd for ages.—Far and near
Multitudes, passive creatures, through streets, roads,
Houses of men, and thresholds of the Gods,
By reckless massacre are prostrated;
Nor are the Trojans only doom'd to bleed;
The Vanquish'd sometimes to their hearts recall
Old virtues, and the conquering Argives fall.
Fear, Anguish struggling to be rid of breath,
Are everywhere:—about, above, beneath
Is Death still crowding on the shape of Death.
Androgeus, whom a numerous Force attends,
Was the first Greek we met: he rashly deems us Friends.

---

475 Die *over illeg eras MS. 101B (DW following WW's pencil)* rush, *del to* run *MS. 101A (MW following WW's pencil)*

476–477 "At least one safety shall the vanquish'd have
"If they no safety seek but in the grave!" *MSS. but* Grave!" *MS. 101A; rev to text MS. 101B (CW, Jr.) with* not *inserted; so MS. 101A but* not,] not *and* grave.—"] Grave!"

479 Like *rev from* As *MS. 101A (MW over WW's pencil); MS. 101B (DW following WW's pencil)*

481 for] of *MS. 101A*

484 our *over illeg eras MS. 101B (DW following WW's pencil)*

485 strengthen'd by despair *rev from* and despair *MS. 101B (DW following WW's pencil)*

486–510 *for revisions and variants in MSS., see Transcriptions, pp. 538–539, 548–549*

---

485 "strengthen'd by despair" is WW's embellishment.

"What sloth," he cries, "retards you? Warriors haste!
"Troy blazes, sack'd by others, and laid waste;
"And Ye come lagging from your Ships the last!"
Thus he: and straight mistrusting our replies,
He felt himself begirt with enemies:
Voice fail'd—step faulter'd—at the dire mistake;
Like one, who through a deeply-tangl'd brake
Struggling, hath trod upon a lurking Snake,
And shrunk in terror from the unlook'd-for Pest,
Lifting his blue-swoln neck and wrathful crest.
Even so Androgeus, smit with sudden dread,
Recoils from what he saw, and would have fled.
Forward we rush; with arms the Troop surround;
The Men, surpriz'd and ignorant of the ground,
Subdued by terror fall an easy prey;
So are we favor'd in our first essay.
With exultation here Corœbus cries,
"Behold, O Friends, how bright our destinies!
"Advance;—the road which they point out is plain;
"Shields let us change, and bear the insignia of the Slain,
"Grecians in semblance; wiles are lawful—who
"To simple valour would restrict a foe?
"Themselves shall give us Arms." When this was said
The Leader's helmet nods upon his head,
The emblazon'd buckler on his arm is tied;
He fits an Argive falchion to his side.
The like doth Rypheus, Dymas,—all put on,
With eager haste, the spoils which they had won.
Then in the combat mingling, Heaven averse,
Amid the gloom a multitude we pierce,
And to the shades dismiss them. Others flee,
Appall'd by this imagin'd treachery;
Some to the Ships—some in the Horse would hide—
Ah! what reap they but sorrow who confide
In aught to which the Gods their sanction have denied?
Behold Cassandra, Priam's royal Child,
By sacrilegeous men, with hair all wild,
Dragg'd from Minerva's Temple! Tow'rd the skies
The Virgin lifts in vain her glowing eyes,
Her eyes, she could no more, for Grecian bands
Had rudely manacled her tender hands.
The intolerable sight to madness stung
Corœbus; and his desperate self he flung
For speedy death the ruthless Foe among!

---

511 so *over illeg eras MS. 101A*
515 terror fall *rev from* fear, become *MS. 101B (CW, Jr.); so MS. 101A but* terro *(WW)*
522 restrict *rev from* restrain *MS. 101B*
525 tied *rev from* tried *MS. 101B (DW's pencil);* tried *rev from* tied *MS. 101A*
527 doth *inserted MS. 101A*

We follow, and with general shock assail
The hostile Throng:—here first our efforts fail:
While, from the summit of the lofty Fane
Darts, by the People flung, descend amain;
In miserable heaps their Friends are laid,
By shew of Grecian Arms and Crests betray'd.
Wroth for the Virgin rescu'd, by defeat
Provok'd, the Grecians from all quarters meet.
The brother Kings and Ajax that way bend
Their efforts: the Dolopian squadron spend
Their fury there. Thus Winds break forth and fly
To conflict from all regions of the sky;
Notus and Zephyrus, while Eurus feeds
The strife, exulting on his orient steeds;
Woods roar, and foaming Nereus stirs the waves
Rouz'd by his Trident from their lowest caves.
They also, whomsoe'er through shades of night
Our stratagem had driven to scatter'd flight,
Now reappear—by them our Shields are known;
The simulating Javelins they disown,
And mark our utterance of discordant tone.
Numbers on numbers bear us down; and first
Falls bold Corœbus by Penelëus pierc'd
Before Minerva's Altar; next, in dust
Sinks Rypheus, one above all Trojans just
And righteous above all; but heavenly Powers
Judge by a light that ill agrees with ours.
Then Dymas, Hypanis are slain by Friends;
—Nor Thee abundant piety defends,

553–556 Combating there unite the Brother Kings;
And thither Ajax all his fierceness brings
By the Dolopians followed. As Winds fly
To charge from adverse quarters of the sky; *MS. 101B; so MS. 101A but* brings] brings, *and* followed] follow'd *rev to*
With Ajax combat there the Brother Kings;
And the Dolopian Squadron thither brings
Its utmost rage. Thus Winds break forth and fly
To conflict from all regions of the sky— *MS. 101B; so MS. 101A but* brings] brings, *and* sky—] sky; *rev to* sky,— *MS. 101B* sky— *rev to* sky; *rev to text MSS. (CW, Jr.) but* squadron] Squadron *MS. 101A*

557 feeds *over illeg* erus *MS. 101A*

559 and foaming Nereus stirs the waves *rev to* and Nereus stirs the foaming waves *MS. 101A (MW over WW's pencil)*

562 scatter'd *rev from* various *MS. 101A*

563 Now reappear; by them *rev from* Appear—the first by whom *MS. 101A*

567 Corœbus falls, him Peneleus hath pierc'd *MS. 101B; so MS. 101A but* pierc'd] pierced *rev to* Falls young Peneleus by Peneleus pierc'd *MS. 101A (CW, Jr.); rev to text MSS. (CW, Jr.)*

571 Ordain by lights that ill agree with ours. *MSS. but* our's *MS. 101A;* lights] laws *alt MS. 101A (WW's pencil); rev to text MS. 101B (CW, Jr.);* Ordain by lights *rev to text MS. 101A (WW)*

553ff. In WW's copy of Ogilby's translation, the upper left corner of the page with his version of these lines has been marked in ink with a box.

558 "lætus Eois / Eurus equis," ll. 417–418. Ruæus gives this paraphrase: "Eurus exultans equis orientalibus. . . ."

O Pantheus! falling with the garland wound,
As fits Apollo's Priest, thy brows around.
Ashes of Ilium! and ye duteous fires,
Lit for my Friends upon their funeral pyres;
In that sad fall, bear witness to my word!
I shunn'd no hazards of the Grecian sword,
No turns of war; with hand unsparing fought;
And earn'd, had Fate so will'd, the death I sought.
Thence am I hurried by the rolling tide,
With Iphitus and Pelias at my side;
One bow'd with years; and Pelias, from a wound
Aim'd by Ulysses, halts along the ground.
New clamours rise; the Abode of Priam calls,
Besieged by thousands swarming round the walls;
Concourse how thick! as if, throughout the space
Of the whole City, war in other place
Were hush'd, no death elsewhere. The Assailants wield
Above their heads shield shell-wise lock'd in shield;
Climb step by step the ladders, near the side
Of the strong portal daringly applied;
The weaker hand its guardian shield presents;
The right is stretch'd to grasp the battlements.
The Dardans tug at roof and turrets high,
Rend fragments off, and with these weapons try
Life to preserve in such extremity,
Roll down the massy rafters deck'd with gold,
Magnific splendours rais'd by Kings of old;
Others with naked weapons stand prepar'd
In thick array, the doors below to guard.
A bolder hope inspirits me to lend
My utmost aid the Palace to defend,
And succour there the vanquished. From behind,
A gateway open'd, whence, a passage blind
The various Mansions of the Palace join'd.

---

578 In that sad *rev from* Amid your *MSS. (CW, Jr.)* fall *inserted MS. 101B (DW following WW's pencil)*
580 turns] tide *alt in pencil MS. 101B (CW, Jr.)*
585 Aim'd *rev from* Given *MS. 101B (CW, Jr.); so MS. 101A (WW's pencil) but* Aimed *alt*
589 place. *rev from* place. The Assailants wield *MS. 101B*
591 heads shield *rev from* head shields, *MS. 101B*
603 hope *rev from* [?thought] *MS. 101B*
605 And succour there the vanquished *rev from* And strengthen those afflicted *MSS. (CW, Jr.) but* vanquish'd *rev in pencil from* vanish'd *MS. 101A;* those *over illeg eras MS. 101B*
606 blind *rev from* join'd *MS. 101A*
607 *line inserted later MS. 101A*

---

590 WW has omitted about a line of the Latin here: "Sic Martem indomitum, Danaosque ad tecta ruentes / Cernimus," ll. 440–441.

591 "Their Shields joined together, or locked in one another, in a convex Form, like the Shape of a Tortoise-Shell, (therefore called *Testudo*) making as it were a Roof, or Canopy, to cover a great Body of Men": Trapp's note.

598ff. In Ogilby (1650)—WL the upper right corner of the page with his version of these lines has been marked in ink with a box.

—Unblest Andromache, while Priam reign'd,
Oft by this way the royal presence gain'd,
All unattended oft this way would tread
With young Astyanax, to his Grandsire led.
Entering the gate, I reach'd the roof, where stand
The Trojans, hurling darts with ineffectual hand.
A Tower there was; precipitous the site,
And the Pile rose to an unrivall'd height;
Frequented Station, whence, in circuit wide
Troy might be seen, the Argive Fleet descried,
And all the Achaian Camp. This sovereign Tower,
With irons grappling where the loftiest floor
Press'd with its beams the wall, we shake, we rend,
And, in a mass of thundering ruin, send
To crush the Greeks beneath. But numbers press
To new assault with reckless eagerness:
Weapons and missiles from the ruins grow,
And what their hasty hands can seize they throw!
   In front stands Pyrrhus, glorying in the might
Of his own weapons, while his armour bright
Casts from the portal gleams of brazen light.
So shines a Snake, when, kindling, he hath crept
Forth from the winter bed in which he slept,
But swoln with glut of poisonous herbage now,
Fresh from the shedding of his annual slough,
Glittering in youth, warm with instinctive fires,
He, with rais'd breast, involves his back in gyres,
Darts out his forked tongue, and tow'rd the sun aspires.
Join'd with redoubted Periphas, comes on
To storm the Palace fierce Automedon,
Who drove the Achillean Car;—the Bands
Of Scyros follow, hurling fiery brands.
Pyrrhus himself hath seiz'd a halberd, cleaves
The ponderous doors, or from their hinges heaves;

---

610 All unattended oft *rev from* A lonely Visitant; *MS. 101A (WW), MS. 101B (CW, Jr.)*
612 stand *over illeg eras MS. 101A*
616 Frequented] Familiar *alt MS. 101A (WW's pencil)*
631 *rev from* Swoln with a glut of poisonous herbs;—but now, *MSS.; rev to text MS. 101B (CW, Jr.); so MS. 101A (WW) but* But *alt and* herbage] herbage, swoln *ed* Swoln *MSS.*
633 Glittering in *rev from* Glitters with *MS. 101B (DW following WW); rev from* Glittering with *MS. 101A*
635 out *rev from* with *MS. 101A, MS. 101B (CW, Jr.)* tow'rd *rev from* tow'rds *MS. 101A*
640 a halberd, cleaves] an axe, would cleave *MSS.;* axe, would *rev to* axe to *then rev to text MS. 101A (WW); rev to* an axe [?loud] cleaves *MS. 101B (CW, Jr.), then rev to text MS. 101B (CW, Jr.)*
641 heaves *rev from* heave *MSS.*

---

614 "Turrim in præcipiti stantem," l. 460.
640 "Ipse inter primos, correptâ dura bipenni / Limina perrumpit," ll. 479–480. Ruæus paraphrases: "Pyrrhus ipse inter primos correptâ securi durum limen perfringit."

And now, reiterating stroke on stroke
Hath hewn, through plates of brass and solid oak,
A broad-mouth'd entrance:—to their inmost seats
The long-drawn courts lie open: the retreats
Of Priam and ancestral Kings are bar'd
To instantaneous view; and Lo! the Guard
Stands at the threshold, for defense prepar'd.
  But tumult spreads through all the space within;
The vaulted roofs repeat the mournful din
Of female Ululation, a strange vent
Of agony, that strikes the starry firmament!
The Matrons range with wildering step the floors;
Embrace, and print their kisses on, the doors.
Pyrrhus, with all his Father's might, dispels
Barriers and bolts, and living obstacles;
Force shapes her own clear way—the doors have flown,
Off from their hinges; gates are overthrown,
By shock of horned engines batter'd down.
In rush the Grecian soldiery; they kill
Whom first they meet, and the broad area fill.
—Less irresistibly, o'er dams and mounds
Burst by its rage, a foaming River bounds,
Herds sweeping with their stalls along the ravag'd grounds.
Pyrrhus I saw with slaughter desperate;
The two Atridæ near the palace gate
Did I behold; and by these eyes were seen
The hundred Daughters with the Mother Queen;
And hoary-headed Priam, where he stood
Beside the Altar, staining with his blood
Fires which himself had hallow'd.—Hope had he,

---

643 hewn, *rev from* hewed, *MS. 101B*
644 their *rev from* its *MS. 101B*
651 Ululation, *rev from* Ululations, *MSS., then rev to* Ululations: *MS. 101A*
655 Pyrrhus *over illeg eras MS. 101A*
657–660 Force shapes her own clear way: the doors are thrown
Off from their hinges; gates are batter'd down
By the inrushing Soldiery, who kill *MS. 101B; so MS. 101A but* her *rev from* their *and* inrushing] in-rushing *rev to*
Force shapes her own clear way;—the doors have flown
Off from their hinges; gates are overthrown
By shock of horned engines batter'd down
In rush the Grecian Soldiery, they kill *MS. 101A (WW), MS. 101B (CW, Jr.); punct from version on interleaf MS. 101B (CW, Jr.)*
664 grounds. *so MS. 101A;* grounds *rev from* ground *MS. 101B*

650–651 "penitusque cavæ plangoribus ædes / Fœmineis ululant," ll. 487–488.
657 Above "have flown" in MS. 101B, CW, Jr., has written "495," the number of the corresponding line in the Latin.
668 "Vidi Hecubam, centumque nurus," l. 501.
669 The epithet "hoary-headed" is WW's embellishment.

Erewhile, none equal hope, of large posterity.
There, fifty bridal chambers might be told:—
Superb with trophies and barbaric gold!
Pillar and portal to the dust are brought;
And the Greeks lord it, where the fire is not.
Ask ye the fate of Priam? On that night
When captur'd Ilium blaz'd before his sight;
And the Foe, bursting through the Palace gate,
Spread through the privacies of royal state,
In vain to tremulous shoulders he restor'd
Arms which had long forgot their ancient Lord,
And girt upon his side a useless sword:
Then, thus accoutr'd, forward did he hie,
As if to meet the Enemy and die.
—Amid the Courts, an Altar stood in view
Of the wide heavens, near which a long-lived Laurel grew,
And, bending over this great Altar, made
For its Penates an embracing shade.
With all her Daughters, throng'd like Doves that lie
Cowering, when storms have driven them from the sky,
Hecuba shelters in that sacred place
Where they the Statues of the Gods embrace.
But when she saw in youthful Arms array'd
Priam himself; "What ominous thought," she said,
"Hangs, wretched Spouse, this weight on limbs decay'd?
"And whither would'st thou hasten? If we were
"More helpless still, this succour we might spare.
"Not such Defenders doth the time demand:
"Profitless here would be my Hector's hand.
"Retire; this Altar can protect us all,
"Or Thou wilt not survive when we must fall."
Then to herself she drew the aged Sire
And to the laurel shade together they retire.

---

672 none *ed* None *rev to* Erewhile, None *MS. 101A (WW), MS. 101B (CW, Jr.)*

675–676 All, in their pomp, lie level with the ground;
And where the fire is not, are Grecian Masters found. *MSS.; rev to text MSS. (CW, Jr.) but* dust are brought;] dust is brought *then rev to* ground are brought *MS. 101A (WW's pencil)*

684 hie *over illeg eras MS. 101A*

689 Penates an embracing *over illeg eras MS. 101A*

690 With all her *rev from* When with her *MS. 101A*

691 have *rev from* had *MS. 101B*

693 they *rev from* [?her] *MS. 101B*

697 thou *rev from* [?thee] *MS. 101A*

700 my *rev from* even *MS. 101A (WW), MS. 101B (CW, Jr.)* here would be *alt* now were even *MS. 101A (WW's pencil)*

703 This to herself: and to [?that] sacred spot *rev to* This to herself: and tow'rd the sacred spot *then to* Then to herself she drew the aged sire, *finally to text on interleaf (del) with* Sire] sire *and at bottom of page MS. 101B (CW, Jr.)* This to herself; and tow'rd the sacred spot *(with* tow'rd the sacred *over illeg eras) rev to text MS. 101A (WW)*

704 She drew the aged Man, to wait their common lot. *MSS. rev to text MS. 101B (CW, Jr.), MS. 101A (WW)*

But see Polites, one of Priam's Sons,
Charged with the death which he in terror shuns!
The wounded Youth, escap'd from Pyrrhus, flies
Through showers of darts, through thickening enemies,
Where the long Porticos invite: the space
Of widely-vacant Courts his footsteps trace.
Him, Pyrrhus, following near and still more near,
Hath caught at with his hand, and presses with his spear.
But when at length this unremitting flight
Had brought him full before his Father's sight,
He fell—and scarcely prostrate on the ground,
Pour'd forth his life from many a streaming wound.
Here Priam, scorning death and self-regard,
His voice restrain'd not, nor his anger spar'd;
"But shall the Gods," he cries, "if Gods there be
"Who note such crimes and care for piety,
"Requite this deed of thine with measure true,
"Nor one reward withhold that is thy due;
"Who thus a Father's presence hast defil'd,
"And forc'd upon his sight the murder of a Child!
"Not thus Achilles' self, from whom a tongue
"Vers'd in vain-glorious falsehood boasts thee sprung,
"Dealt with an enemy; my prayer he heard;
"A Suppliant's rights in Priam he rever'd;
"Gave Hector back to rest within the tomb,
"And me remitted to my royal home."
This said, the aged Man a javelin cast;
With weak arm—faltering to the shield it past;
Straight by the brass repell'd that feebly rung
Down from the boss the harmless weapon hung.
—Then Pyrrhus;—"To my Sire, Pelides, bear
"These feats of mine, ill relish'd as they are,
"Tidings of which I make thee messenger!
"To him a faithful history relate
"Of Neoptolemus degenerate;

---

708 thickening *rev from* press of *MS. 101A (WW), MS. 101B (CW, Jr.)*
712 his . . . his *rev from* the . . . the *MS. 101B*
716 *line inserted MS. 101B*
717 death and *over illeg eras MS. 101B*
718 anger *rev from* answer *MS. 101A (MW following WW's pencil)*
719 "Yet shall the Gods," he cries, "if Gods there be *MS. 101A with* But *as WW's pencil alt to* Yet *in MS. 101B* Yet *rev to* But *and alt* "But—he exclaims—the Gods if gods th *then* gods *rev to* Gods *then alt del leaving* Yet *rev to* But *MS. 101B (CW, Jr.)*
720 crimes *rev from* acts *MS. 101A (WW), MS. 101B (CW, Jr.)*
721 deed of thine *rev from* heinous crime *MS. 101A (WW), MS. 101B (CW, Jr.)*
724 a *rev to* his *MS. 101A (WW)*
726 falsehood *over illeg eras MS. 101B*
733–734 The tinkling shield the harmless point repell'd,
Which, to the boss it hung from, barely held. *MSS. alt as text MS. 101A (WW) but* Straight] Strait *so MS. 101B (CW, Jr.) but* Straight *rev from* Then *and* repell'd *alt* repelled

---

738–739 "Degeneremque Neoptolemum narrare memento," l. 549.

"Now die!"—So saying, towards the Altar, through
A stream of filial blood, the tottering Sire he drew;
His left hand lock'd within the tangled hair;
Rais'd, with the right, a brandish'd sword in air,
Then to the hilt impell'd it through his side;
Thus, 'mid a blazing City, Priam died.
Troy falling round him, thus he clos'd his fate,
Once the proud Lord of many an Asian State!
The abandon'd Corse lies stretched upon the shore
Head from the shoulders torn, its very name no more.
 Then first it was, that Horror girt me round,
Chill'd my frail heart, and all my senses bound;
The Image of my Father cross'd my mind;
Perchance in fate with slaughter'd Priam join'd;
Equal in age, thus may HE breathe out life;
Creusa also, my deserted Wife!
The Child Iülus left without defence,
And the whole House laid bare to violence!
Backward I look'd, and cast my eyes before;
My Friends had fail'd, and courage was no more;
All, wearied out, had follow'd desperate aims;
Self-dash'd to earth, or stifled in the flames.
 Thus was I left alone; such light my guide
As the conflagrant walls and roofs supplied;
When my far-wandering eyesight chanc'd to meet
Helen sequester'd on a lonely seat
Amid the Porch of Vesta. She, through dread
Of Trojan vengeance amply merited,
Of Grecian punishment, and what the ire
Of a forsaken Husband might require,
Thither had flown—there sate, the common bane
Of Troy and of her Country—to obtain
Protection from the Altar, or to try
What hope might spring from trembling secresy.
Methought my falling Country cried aloud,
And the revenge it seem'd to ask I vow'd;

---

740 saying towards *rev from* towards *MS. 101A*
741 filial *rev from* blood *MS. 101A*
744 his side *rev from* the air *MS. 101A*
748–749 Upon the shore lies stretch'd his mangled Frame,
 Head from the shoulders torn, a Body without name. *MS. 101B; so MS. 101A but* the shoulders *rev in pencil and ink from* his shoulders *rev to text MS. 101A (WW), MS. 101B (CW, Jr.) but* shore] Shore *and* its *rev from* is *MS. 101A*
756 Iülus *ed* Iulus *MSS.*
763 roofs *rev from* roof *MS. 101B (following WW's pencil); so MS. 101A*
768 punishment *rev from* punishments *MS. 101B*
769 forsaken *rev from* deserted *MS. 101A (WW), MS. 101B (CW, Jr.)* require *rev from* acquire *MS. 101A*

"What! shall she visit Sparta once again?
"In triumph enter with a loyal Train?
"Consort, and Home, and Sires and Children view
"By Trojan Females serv'd, a Phrygian retinue?
"For this was Priam slain? Troy burnt? The shore
"Of Dardan Seas so often drench'd in gore?
"Not so; for though such victory can claim
"In its own nature no reward of fame,
"The punishment that ends the guilty days
"Even of a Woman, shall find grateful praise;
"My soul, at least, shall of her weight be eas'd,
"The ashes of my Countrymen appeas'd."
  Such words broke forth; and in my own despite
Onward I bore, when through the dreary night
Appear'd my gracious Mother, vested in pure light;
Never till now before me did she shine
So much herself, of aspect so divine;
Goddess reveal'd in all her beauty, love,
And majesty, as she is wont to move,
A Shape familiar to the Courts of Jove!
The hand shc sciz'd her touch suffic'd to stay;
Then from her roseate lip these words found easy way.
  "O Son! what pain excites a wrath so blind?
"Or could all thought of me desert thy mind?
"Where now is left thy Parent worn with age?
"Wilt thou not rather in that quest engage?
"Learn with thine eyes if yet Creusa live,
"And if the Boy Ascanius still survive.
"Them do the Greeks environ:—that they spare,
"That swords so long abstain, and flames forbear,
"Is through the intervention of my care.
"Not Spartan Helen's beauty, so abhorr'd
"By thee, not Paris her upbraided Lord—
"The hostile Gods have laid this grandeur low,
"Troy from the Gods receives her overthrow.
"Look! for the impediment of misty shade
"With which thy mortal sight is overlaid
"I will disperse; nor thou refuse to hear

---

778 and . . . view *added later MSS.; in MS. 101B, addition signaled by pencil asterisk in left margin*
790 light *rev from* white *MS. 101B*
792 of aspect so *rev from* so thoroughly *MS. 101A (WW), MS. 101B (CW, Jr.)*
796 suffice'd *over illeg eras MS. 101B*
797 from . . . lip *rev from* through . . . mouth *MS. 101A (WW), MS. 101B (CW, Jr.)*
798 pain *entered late in space left blank MS. 101A (following WW's pencil)* so *over illeg eras MS. 101B*
801 quest *rev from* search *MS. 101A (WW), MS. 101B (CW, Jr.)*
802 thine *rev from* them *MS. 101A*
803 Ascanius *rev from* Iulus *MS. 101A (WW), MS. 101B (CW, Jr.)*
808 not *rev from* nor *MS. 101A (WW), MS. 101B (CW, Jr.)*

"Parental mandates, nor resist through fear!
"There, where thou see'st block rolling upon block,
"Mass rent from mass, and dust condens'd with smoke
"In billowy intermixture, Neptune smites
"The walls, with labouring Trident disunites
"From their foundation—tearing up, as suits
"His anger, Ilium from her deepest roots.
"Fiercest of all, before the Scæan Gate,
"Arm'd Juno stands, beckoning to animate
"The Bands she summons from the Argive Fleet.
"Tritonian Pallas holds *her* chosen seat
"High on the Citadel,—look back!—see there
"Her Ægis beaming forth a stormy glare!
"The very Father, Jove himself, supplies
"Strength to the Greeks, sends heaven-born enemies
"Against the Dardan Arms. My Son, take flight,
"And close the struggle of this dismal night!
"I will not quit thy steps whate'er betide,
"But to thy Father's House will safely guide."
—She ceas'd—and gathering shades her presence hide.
Dire faces are apparent, Deities
Adverse to Troy; the Gods, her mighty Enemies.
Now was all Ilium, far as sight could trace,
Settling and sinking in the Fire's embrace,
Neptunian Troy subverted from her base.
Even so, a Mountain-Ash, long tried by shock
Of storms endured upon the native rock,
When He is doom'd from rustic arms to feel
The rival blows of persevering steel,
Nods high with threatening forehead, till at length

---

815 There *rev from* Here *MS. 101B* where *rev from* when *MS. 101A*
817–820 Tower and Wall
Upheavd by Neptune's mighty Trident fall
To eart; his wrath their deep foundation bares
And the strong City from the roots uptears *alt MS. 101A (WW) with* from *rev from* by
826 stormy *rev from* stirring *MS. 101B*
830 struggle *rev from* [?strength] *MS. 101A*
833 She ceas'd *over illeg eras MS. 101B* gathering *rev from* did in *MS. 101A (WW), MS. 101B (CW, Jr.)*
834 Dire faces still are seen; and Deities *MS. 101A then* still are seen *rev to* appear *and* and *rev to* —[?the] *(WW's pencil), then rev to text; MS. 101B has* Dire faces still are seen, and Deities *over illeg eras (DW), then rev to text (CW, Jr.)*
835 Adverse to Troy appear,—her mighty Enemies. *MS. 101A, then* appear,— *rev to* the Gods— *(WW's pencil), then rev to text but* Troy;] Troy, *and* Gods,] Gods *MS. 101B has* Adverse to Troy appear, her mighty Enemies. *over illeg eras, rev to text (CW, Jr.)*
837 Fire's *rev from* fierce *MS. 101B*
841 When He is doom'd from *rev from* But now when doom'd from *MS. 101B (DW following WW's pencil); so MS. 101A but* He] he to feel *over illeg eras MS. 101B* *in MS. 101B at bottom of page the following version appears:* But now is doom'd from rustic arms to feel *(WW's pencil, eras)*
843 Nods high *rev from* It nods *MS. 101B (DW following WW's pencil)*

---

834 "Apparent diræ facies," l. 622.

Wounds unremitting have subdued his strength;
With groans the ancient Tree foretells his end;
He falls; and fragments of the mountain blend
With the precipitous ruin.—I descend,
And, as the Godhead leads, 'twixt foe and fire
Advance:—the darts withdraw, the flames retire.
 But when beneath her guidance I had come
Far as the Gates of the paternal Dome,
My Sire, whom first I sought and wish'd to bear
For safety to the Hills, disdains that care;
Nor will he now, since Troy hath fall'n, consent
Life to prolong, or suffer banishment.
"Think *Ye*," he says, "—the current of whose blood
"Is unimpair'd, whose vigour unsubdued,
"—Think *Ye* of flight;—that I should live, the Gods
"Wish not, or they had sav'd me these abodes.
"Not once, but twice, this City to survive,
"What need against such destiny to strive?
"While thus, even thus, compos'd my body lies,
"Depart! pronounce the funeral obsequies!
"Not long shall I have here to wait for death;
"A pitying Foe will rid me of my breath,
"Will seek my spoils; and should I lie forlorn
"Of sepulture, the thought may well be borne.
"Full long obnoxious to the Powers divine
"Life lingers out these barren years of mine;
"Even since the date when me the eternal Sire
"Swept with the thunderbolt, and scath'd with fire."
Thus he persists;—Creusa and her Son
Second the counter-prayer by me begun;
The whole House, weeping round him, deprecate
This weight of wilful impulse given to Fate;
He, all unmov'd by pleadings and by tears,
Guards his resolve, and to the spot adheres.

---

844 his *rev from* its *MS. 101A, MS. 101B (DW following WW's pencil)*
845 his *rev from* its *MS. 101A (MW following WW's pencil, MS. 101B (DW following WW's pencil)*
846 He *rev from* It *MS. 101A, MS. 101B (DW following WW's pencil)*
850 her *rev from* this *MS. 101A (WW), MS. 101B (CW, Jr.)*
851 the *rev from* my *MS. 101A*
856 he says, "the *rev from* says he *MS. 101A*
862 compos'd my *rev from* disposed the *MSS. (CW, Jr.)*
863 the *rev from* my *MS. 101A (MW?), MS. 101B (CW, Jr.)*
867 thought *rev from* loss *MS. 101A (MW?), MS. 101B (CW, Jr.)*
871 scath'd *rev from* [?touch'd] *MS. 101B* scathed *MS. 101A*
872 persists;— *rev from* persisted— *MS. 101A*
874 whole House, weeping round him, *rev from* total House with weeping *MS. 101B (CW, Jr.); so MS. 101A (WW) but no commas*
875 This *rev from* The *MS. 101B* impulse *over illeg eras MS. 101A*

---

873 DW has written "no more done" at page bottom, MS. 101B, 18v.

Arms once again attract me, hurried on
In misery, and craving death alone.
"And hast thou hop'd that I could move to find
"A place of rest, thee, Father, left behind?
"How could parental lips the guilty thought unbind?
"If in so great a City Heaven ordain
"Utter extinction; if thy soul retain
"With stedfast longing that abrupt design
"Which would to falling Troy add thee and thine;
"That way to death lies open;—soon will stand
"Pyrrhus before thee with the reeking brand
"That drank the blood of Priam; He whose hand
"The Son in presence of the Father slays,
"And at the Altar's base the slaughter'd Father lays
"For this, benignant Mother! didst thou lead
"My steps along a way from danger freed,
"That I might see remorseless Men invade
"The holiest places that these roofs o'ershade?
"See Father, Consort, Son, all tinged and dy'd
"Each in the other's life-blood, perish side by side?
"Arms bring me, Friends! bring Arms! our last hour speaks,
"It calls the Vanquish'd; cast me on the Greeks!
"In rallying combat let us join;—not all,
"This night, unsolac'd by revenge shall fall!"
The sword resumes its place; the shield I bear;
And hurry on to reach the open air;
When on the ground, before the threshold cast
Creusa check'd my course, my feet embrac'd,
And holding up Iülus, there cleaves fast!
"If thou, departing, be resolv'd to die,
"Let us be partners of thy destiny;
"But if on Arms, already tried, attend
"A single hope, then first this House defend;
"On whose protection Sire and Son are thrown;

878–879 Once more I turn to arms: death, death alone
My wish and purpose now, all others gone. *MS. 101A; so MS. 101B eras; rev to text MS. 101B (DW following WW's pencil, eras); so MS. 101A (MW) but* me,] me: *and* misery,] misery

880 hast *over illeg eras MS. 101A*

882 thought *rev from* thoughts *MS. 101A*

884 *in MS. 101A, at bottom of page, a variant, possibly of this line, was written and erased; it reads:* [? ? ?] my Soul [?contain]

897 Each in the other's life-blood *rev from* With mutual sprinklings *MS. 101B (CW, Jr.); so MS. 101A (WW) but* other's] others

903 on] now *MS. 101A; rev from* now *MS. 101B (CW, Jr.)* air; *over illeg eras, with pencil signal in left margin, MS. 101A*

905 Creusa check'd my course, *rev from* Lo! where Creusa hath *MS. 101A (WW), MS. 101B (CW, Jr.)*

906 Iülus *ed* Iulus *MSS.*

907 departing, be *rev in pencil and ink to* she cried, wilt go *MS. 101A (WW) at bottom of page* If thou cried she wilt go resolvd *MS. 101A (WW's pencil)*

908 *rev from* Take us through all that in thy road may lie; *MS. 101A (WW), MS. 101B (CW, Jr.)*

909 attend *over illeg eras MS. 101A*

"And I, the Wife that once was call'd thine own!"
  Such outcry fill'd the Mansion; when behold
A strange portent, and wonderous to be told!
All suddenly a luminous crest was seen;
Which, where the Boy Iülus hung between
The arms of each sad Parent, rose and shed,
Tapering aloft, a lustre from his head;
Along the hair the lambent flame proceeds
With harmless touch, and round his temples feeds!
In fear we haste, the burning tresses shake,
And from the fount the holy fire would slake;
But joyfully his hands Anchises rais'd,
His voice not silent as on Heaven he gaz'd;
  "Almighty Jupiter! if prayers have power
"To bend thee, look on us; I seek no more;
"If aught our piety deserve, Oh deign
"The hope this Omen proffers to sustain;
"Nor, Father, let us ask a second Sign in vain!"
  Thus spake the Sire, and scarcely ended, ere
A peal of sudden thunder, loud and clear,
Broke from the left; and shot through Heaven a Star
Trailing its torch that sparkl'd from afar;
Above the roof it ran, and in our sight
Set on the brow of Ida's sylvan height,
The long way marking with a train of light:
The furrowy track the distant sky illumes,
And far and wide are spread sulphureous fumes.
Uprisen from earth, my aged Sire implores
The Deities, the holy Star adores;
—"Now am I conquer'd—now is no delay;
"Gods of my Country! where Ye lead the way
"'Tis not in me to hesitate or swerve;
"Preserve my House, Ye Powers, this Little One preserve!
"Your's is this augury; and Troy hath still
"Life in the signs that manifest your will!
"I cannot chuse but yield; and now to Thee,
"O Son, a firm Associate will I be!"

---

913 outcry *over illeg eras MS. 101B*

914 *line inserted later MS. 101A* be told!] *rev from* behold! *MS. 101B (DW following WW's pencil)*

916 Iülus *ed* Iulus *MS. 101B* Iulus *rev from* Ilus *MS. 101A*

924 His *added later MS. 101A (MW following pencil signal, right margin), MS. 101B (DW following WW's pencil)*

934 Above the roof this star, conspicuous sight, *MS. 101B; so MS. 101A but* star] Star *then* conspicuous *rev to* pursued the *(WW), then all rev to text but* ran,] ran *MS. 101A (WW); in MS. 101B* this . . . sight *rev to illeg phrase (DW? eras), then to text (CW, Jr.)*

935 Set on the brow of *rev from* Ran to be hid on *MS. 101A (WW), MS. 101B (CW, Jr.)*

919–920 "tactuque innoxia molli / Lambere flamma comas," ll. 683–684.

937 furrowy track] "sulcus," l. 697.

He spake; and nearer through the City came,
Rolling more audibly, the sea of flame:
—"Now give, dear Father, to this neck the freight
"Of thy old age;—the burthen will be light
"For which my shoulders bend; henceforth one fate,
"Evil or good, shall we participate.
"The Boy shall journey, tripping at my side;
"Our steps, at distance mark'd, will be Creusa's guide.
"My Household! heed these words:—upon a Mound
"(To those who quit the City obvious ground)
"A Temple, once by Ceres honour'd, shews
"Its mouldering front; hard by a Cypress grows,
"Through ages guarded with religious care:
"Thither, by various roads, let all repair.
"Thou, Father! take these relics; let thy hand
"Bear the Penates of our native land;
"I may not touch them, fresh from deeds of blood,
"Till the stream cleanse me with its living flood."
Forthwith an ample vest my shoulders clad;
Above the vest a lion's skin was spread;
Next came the living Burthen; fast in mine
His little hand Iülus doth entwine,
Following his Father with unequal pace;
Creusa treads behind: the darkest ways we trace.
And me, erewhile insensible to harms,
Whom adverse Greeks agglomerate in Arms
Mov'd not, now every breath of air alarms;
All sounds have power to trouble me with fear,
Anxious for whom I lead, and whom I bear.
Thus, till the Gates were nigh, my course I shap'd,
And thought the hazards of the time escap'd;
When through the gloom a noise of feet we hear,
Quick sounds that seem'd to press upon the ear;
"Fly," cries my Father, looking forth, "Oh fly!
"They come—I see their shields, and dazzling panoply."
Here, in my trepidation, was I left,
Through some unfriendly Power, of mind bereft;
For, while I journey'd devious and forlorn,

---

949 City *over illeg eras MS. 101A*
955 tripping at *rev from* at my side *MS. 101B (DW following WW's pencil)*
961 *line inserted MS. 101A*
964 of *rev from* to *MSS.*
969 Burthen *rev from* Aurthen *MS. 101A*
970 Iülus *ed* Iulus *MSS.; rev from* Ilus *MS. 101A*
971 unequal *rev from* no equal *MS. 101A (WW), MS. 101B (CW, Jr.)*
975 of air *inserted MS. 101A*
986 while *rev from* whilst *MSS.*

---

974 "neque adverso, glomerati ex agmine Graji," l. 727.

From me, me wretched! was Creusa torn;
Whether stopp'd short by death, or from the road
She wander'd, or sank down beneath a load
Of weariness, no vestiges made plain:
She vanish'd, ne'er to meet these eyes again.
I sought her not; misgiving none had I
Until we reached the Sacred boundary
Of ancient Ceres. All, even all, save One
Were in that spot assembl'd; She alone,
As if her melancholy fate disown'd
Companion, Son, and Husband, nowhere could be found.
Who, man or God, from my reproach was free?
Had desolated Troy a heavier woe for me?
'Mid careful friends, my Sire and Son I place,
With the Penates of our Phrygian race,
Deep in a winding vale: my footsteps then retrace;

---

990 no vestiges made plain *rev from* [? ? ? ?vain] *MS. 101B (DW following WW's pencil, eras)*
992 had I *rev from* had we *MS. 101B (CW, Jr.)*
993 we *rev from* I *MS. 101B (CW, Jr.)*
992–994 My heart misgave me not; nor did mine eye
Look back till we had reached the boundary
Of antient Ares.— *alt WW to CW, Jr. November 30, 1827*
992–993 *rev from* Nor did I seek her lost, nor backward turn
My mind, until we reach'd the sacr'd bourne *MSS. (CW, Jr.); intermediate stages surviving in MS. 101A include the following: 48^{v}, at page foot (WW's pencil):*
Unconscious she was lost in thought
But not a backward-looking had I
thought had I
49^{r}, at page foot (CW, Jr., and WW's ink over pencil):
I sought her not I turnd not round
thought
~~Lost was she,~~ but misgiving none had I
[? ? ? ?] no thought had I
reach
Untill we reached the sacred
Until we reached the sacred bound
boundary,
ary
49^{r}, left margin running bottom to top (WW's pencil):
I sought her not—from all misgiving free
49^{v}, revising base text (WW and CW, Jr., revising MW):
fate
Her loss I knew not, nor to her did turn
Misgiving none was felt—nor did mine eye
Nor did I seek her lost, nor backward turn
A thought
My mind, until we reach'd the sacred bourne
Look back untill we reached the boundary
49^{v}, at bottom of page (WW's pencil):
That she was lost I knew not nor did turn
50^{v}, at top of page (WW's pencil):
But not a backward-looking thought
Even
Untill we reach'd the antient had I
1002 footsteps then *rev in pencil to* steps I then *MS. 101A (WW)*

Resolv'd the whole wide City to explore,
And face the perils of the night once more.
  So, with refulgent Arms begirt, I haste
Tow'rd the dark gates through which my feet had pass'd;
Remeasure, where I may, the beaten ground,
And turn at every step a searching eye around.
Horror prevails on all sides, while with dread
The very silence is impregnated.
Fast to my Father's Mansion I repair,
If haply, haply, she had harbour'd there.
Seiz'd by the Grecians was the entire Abode;
And now voracious fire its mastery shew'd.
Roll'd upward by the wind in flames that meet
High o'er the roof,—air rages with the heat;
Thence to the Towers I pass, where Priam held his Seat.
Already Phœnix and Ulysses kept,
As chosen Guards, the spoils of Ilium, heap'd
In Juno's Temple, and the wealth that rose
Pil'd on the floors of vacant porticos;
Prey torn through fire from many a secret Hold,
Vests, tables of the Gods, and cups of massy gold;
And, in long order, round these treasures stand
Matrons, and Boys, and Youths, a trembling Band!
  Nor did I spare with fearless voice to raise
Shouts in the gloom that fill'd the streets and ways;
And with reduplication sad and vain,
Creusa call'd, again and yet again.
While thus I prosecute an endless quest,
A Shape was seen, unwelcome and unblest;
Creusa's Shade appear'd before my eyes,
Her Image, but of more than mortal size;
Then I, as if the power of life had pass'd
Into my upright hair, stood speechless and aghast.
—She thus—to stop my troubles at their source;
"Dear Consort, why this fondly-desperate course?
"Supernal Powers, not doubtfully, prepare
"These issues: going hence thou wilt not bear
"Creusa with thee; know that Fate denies
"This fellowship; nor this permits the Ruler of the skies.
"Long wanderings will be thine, no home allow'd;
"Vast the extent of sea that must be plough'd

1007 remeasure *rev from* remeasur'd *MS. 101B*
1011 repair *rev from* repair'd *MS. 101B*
1041 nor this permits *rev from* and this *MS. 101A (WW), MS. 101B (CW, Jr.)*

"Ere, 'mid Hesperian fields where Tiber flows
"With gentle current, thy tired keels repose.
"Joy meets thee there, a Realm and royal Bride;
"—For lov'd Creusa let thy tears be dried:
"I go not where the Myrmidons abide.
"No proud Dolopian Mansion shall I see,
"Nor shall a Grecian Dame be serv'd by me;
"Deriv'd from Jove, and rais'd by thee so high,
"Spouse to the Offspring of a Deity,
"Such fate I dread not: on my native plains
"Me the great Mother of the Gods detains.
"Now, fare thee well! protect our Son, and prove,
"By tenderness for him, our common love."
  This having said—my trouble to subdue,
Into thin air she silently withdrew;
Left me, while tears were gushing from their springs,
And on my tongue a thousand hasty things;
Thrice with my arms I strove her neck to clasp,
Thrice had my hands succeeded in their grasp,
From which the Image slipp'd away, as light
As the swift winds, or sleep when taking flight.
  Such was the close; and now the night thus spent,
Back to my Friends an eager course I bent,
And here a crowd, with wonder I behold
Of new Associates, concourse manifold!
Matrons, and Men, and Youths that hither hied,
For exile gathering; and from every side
The wretched people throng'd and multiplied;
Prepared with mind and means their flight to speed
Across the seas, where I might chuse to lead.
  Now on the ridge of Ida's summit grey
Rose Lucifer, prevenient to the day:
—The Grecians held the Gates in close blockade,
Hope was there none of giving further aid;
I yielded, took my Father up once more;
And sought the Mountain with the Freight I bore.

End of the second Book

1046 thee] the *MS. 101A*

1047–1048 *marked for transposition with 1049–1050 or 1051–1052, then marks canceled MS. 101A*

1049 *inserted MS. 101A* Mansion shall I see *over illeg eras MS. 101A*

1049–1052 *orig 1051–1052 preceded 1049–1050 MSS.; rev to text MSS. (WW) after marks for transposition of 1053–1054 with 1049–1050 canceled*

1053 "Far otherwise; upon *MSS.; rev to* This fate I dread not: on *MS. 101B (CW, Jr.); so MS. 101A (WW) but* not:] not, *then rev to text MS. 101A (WW 's pencil), MS. 101B (CW, Jr.)*

1061 arms *rev from* hands *MS. 101A*

1067 crowd, with wonder *rev from* a marvellous number *MS. 101B (CW, Jr.); so MS. 101A (WW) but* crowd,] crowd behold *rev from* beheld *MS. 101B (following WW's pencil)*

Third Book

Now when the Gods had crush'd the Asian State,
And Priam's race, by too severe a fate;
When they were pleas'd proud Ilium to destroy,
And smokes upon the ground Neptunian Troy;
The sad Survivors, from their Country driven,
Seek distant shores, impell'd by signs from Heav'n.
Beneath Antandros we prepare a Fleet:—
There my Companions muster at the feet
Of Phrygian Ida, dubious in our quest,
And where the Fates may suffer us to rest.
Scarcely had breath'd the earliest summer gales
Before Anchises bid to spread the sails;
Weeping I quit the Port, my native coast,
And fields where Troy once was; and soon am tost,
An Exile on the bosom of the seas,
With Friends, Son, household Gods and the great Deities.
   Right opposite is spread a peopled Land,
Where once the fierce Lycurgus held command;
The martial Thracians plough its champain wide,
To Troy by hospitable rites allied,
While Fortune favour'd: to this coast we hied;
Where, entering with unfriendly Fates, I lay
My first foundations in a hollow bay;
And call the Men Æneades—to share
With the new Citizens the name I bear.
To Dionæan Venus we present,
And to the Gods who aid a fresh intent,
The sacred offerings:—and with honour due
Upon the shore a glossy Bull I slew
To the great King of Heaven.—A Mount was near
Upon whose summit cornel-trees uprear
Their boughs, and myrtles rough with many a spear.
Studious to deck the Altar with green shoots
Thither I turn'd; and, tugging at the roots
Strove to despoil the thicket; when behold
A dire portent, and wond'rous to be told!
No sooner was the shatter'd root laid bare

---

1 State *over illeg eras MS. 101C*
8 muster *rev from* master *MS. 101C*
21 to this coast we hied; *rev from* thither borne I lay *MS. 101C*
22 *line inserted over* And kindred Gods, while *MS. 101C*
24 And call the Men *rev from* The Men are called *MS. 101C*
26 Dionæan *so MS. 89* Dianæan *MS. 101C*

Of the first Tree I struggled to uptear,
Than from the fibres drops of blood distill'd,
Whose blackness stain'd the ground:—me horror thrill'd;
My frame all shudder'd, and my blood was chill'd.
Persisting in the attempt, I toil'd to free
The flexile body of another tree,
Anxious the latent causes to explore;
And from the bark blood trickled as before.
Revolving much in mind forthwith I paid
Vows to the sylvan Nymphs; and sought the aid
Of Father Mars, spear-shaking God, who yields
His stern protection to the Thracian fields;
That to a prosperous issue they would guide
The accident, the omen turn aside.
But, for a third endeavour, when with hands
Eagerly strain'd, knees press'd against the sands,
I strive the myrtle lances to uproot
With my whole strength (speak shall I, or be mute?)
From the deep tomb a mournful groan was sent,
And a voice follow'd, uttering this lament.
"Torment me not Æneas! Why this pain
"Given to a buried Man? O cease, refrain,
"And spare thy pious hands this guilty stain!
"Troy brought me forth, no alien to thy blood;
"Nor yields a senseless trunk this sable flood.
"Oh fly the cruel land; the greedy shore
'Forsake with speed, for I am Polydore.
"A flight of iron darts here pierced me through,
"Took life, and into this sharp thicket grew."
Then truly did I stand aghast, cold fear
Strangling my voice, and lifting up my hair.
Erewhile from Troy had Priam sent by stealth
This Polydore, and with him store of wealth;
Trusting the Thracian King his Son would rear:
For wretched Priam now gave way to fear,
Seeing the Town beleagured. These alarms

---

39 Than *rev from* Then *MS. 101C*
41 My frame all shudder'd, and *rev from* Quaked every limb, and all *MS. 101C*
44 latent *inserted MS. 101C (MW over WW's pencil)*
50 That to a prosperous issue *rev from* But, for a third endeavor *MS. 101C*
53 Eagerly *over illeg eras MS. 101C*
58 Æneas! *ed* Æneas? *MS. 101C*
65 pierced *rev from* perced *MS. 101C*
67 cold *rev from* with *MS. 101C*

---

44 "& causas penitus tentare latentes," l. 32.

49 Thracian fields] "Geticis . . . arvis," l. 35. Ruæus glosses: "populi Daciæ, Thraciæ tamen annumerati ob viciniam. . . ." Minellius: "Thraciæ arvis, cujus partem olim tenuerunt Getæ."

Spread to the Thracian King; and when the Arms
Of Troy were quell'd, to the victorious side
Of Agamemnon he his hopes allied;
Breaking through sacred laws without remorse
Slew Polydore, and seized the gold by force.
What mischief to poor Mortals has not thirst
Of gold created! appetite accurs'd!
Soon as a calmer mind I could recal
I seek the Chiefs, my Father above all;
Report the omen, and their thoughts demand.
One mind is theirs,—to quit the impious Land;
With the first breezes of the South to fly,
Sick of polluted hospitality.
Forthwith on Polydore our hands bestow
A second burial, and fresh mold upthrow;
And to his Manes raise beside the mound
Altars, which, as they stood in mournful round,
Cerulean fillets and black cypress bound:
And with loose hair a customary Band
Of Trojan Women in the circle stand.
From cups warm milk and sacred blood we pour,
Thus to the tomb the Spirit we restore,
And with a farewell cry its future rest implore.
    Then, when the sea grew calm, and gently creeps
The soft south-wind and calls us to the Deeps,
The Crew draw down our Ships; they crowd the Shore,
The Port we leave:—with Cities sprinkled o'er,
Slowly the Coast recedes, and then is seen no more.
    In the 'mid Deep there lies a spot of earth,
Sacred to her who gave the Nereids birth,
And to Ægean Neptune. Long was toss'd
This then unfruitful ground, and driven from coast to coast:
But, as it floated o'er the wide-spread Sea,
The Archer-God, in filial piety,
Between two Sister islands bound it fast,
For Man's Abode, and to defy the blast.
Thither we steer. At length the unruffled Place
Received our Vessels in her calm embrace.
We land—and, when the pleasant soil we trod,
Adored the City of the Delian God.

---

91 bound *rev from* found *MS 101C (MW following pencil signal)*
100 o'er *ed* oer *MS. 101C*

---

84 to quit the impious Land] "sceleratâ excedere terrâ," l. 60. Ruæus paraphrases: "abire ex impia regione . . . "
86 polluted hospitality] "pollutum hospitium," l. 61.
107 "pius Arcitenens," l. 75. Apollo is meant, of course, as both Ruæus and Minellius note.
108 two Sister islands] "Mycone celsâ Gyaroque," l. 76. WW omits their names in translating. The epithet "Sister" is WW's embellishment.

Anius, the King (whose brows were wreathed around
With laurel garlands and with fillets bound,
His sacred symbols, as Apollo's Priest)
Advanced to meet us, from our ships releas'd;
He recognized Anchises; and their hands
Gladly they join, renewing ancient Bands
Of hospitality; nor longer waits
The King, but leads us to his friendly gates.
 To seek the Temple was my early care;
To whose Divinity I bow'd in prayer
Within the reverend Pile of ancient stone:—
"Thymbreus! painful wanderings have we known;
"Grant, to the weary, dwellings of their own!
"A City yield, a Progeny ensure,
"A habitation destined to endure!—
"—To us, sad relics of the Grecian Sword,
"(All that is left of Troy) another Troy accord!
"What shall we seek? whom follow? where abide?
"Vouchsafe an augury our course to guide;
"Father, descend, and through our spirits glide!"
—Then shook, or seem'd to shake, the entire Abode;
A trembling seized the Laurels of the God;
The mountain rock'd; and sounds with murmuring swell
Roll'd from the Shrine:— upon the ground I fell,
And heard the guiding voice our fates foretell.
"Ye patient Dardans! that same Land which bore,
"From the first Stock, your Fathers heretofore;
"That ancient Mother will unfold her breast
"For your return;—seek *Her* with faithful quest;
"So shall the Ænean Line command the earth
"As long as future years to future years give birth."
 Thus Phœbus answer'd; and, forthwith, the Crowd
Burst into transport vehement and loud:
All ask what Phœbus wills; and where the bourne

---

118 Anchises *ed* Anchyses *MS. 101C*
125 known; *ed* known *MS. 101C*
127 ensure *rev from* insure *MS. 101C*
134 shake, *ed* shake *MS. 101C*
136 mountain *rev from* mountains *MS. 101C* and *over illeg eras MS. 101C*
140 *rev from* Your first Progenitors in days of yore *MS. 101C (MW following WW's pencil, MW's punct)*
144 birth." *quots ed* birth. *MS. 101C*
147 ask *over illeg eras MS. 101C*

---

125 Apollo is meant; Ruæus's gloss shows the importance of the name Thymbreus here: "Strabo 1. 13. ait campum esse Thymbram, in agro Trojano, quem Thymbrius fluvius interfluit, in Scamandrum influens, ubi templum est Apollinis Thymbræi; quibus loci ex Servio nomen est à copia thymbræ, herbæ condimentariæ. . . . Hîc Æneas Apollinem, non Delium vocat, sed Thymbræum: ut ostendat unum eundemque Deum esse, eumque sibi placabilem reddat, commemoratione Trojani cultûs et patrii templi."
129 WW has omitted the phrase "atque immitis Achilli," l. 87.

To which Troy's wandering Race are destin'd to return.
Then spake my aged Father, turning o'er
Traditions handed down from days of yore;
"Give ear," he said, "O Chieftains, while my words
"Unfold the hopes this Oracle affords!
"On the 'mid sea the Cretan Island lies,
"Dear to the sovereign Lord of earth and skies;
"There is the Idæan Mount, and there we trace
"The fountain-head, the cradle of our race.
"A hundred Cities, places of command,
"Rise in the circle of that fruitful Land;
"Thence to Rhœtean shores (if things oft heard
"I faithfully remember) Teucer steer'd,
"Our first progenitor; and chose a spot,
"His Seat of government when Troy was not;
"While yet the Natives housed in vallies deep;
"Ere Pergamus had risen, to crown the lofty steep.
"—From Crete came Cybele; from Crete we gained
"All that the Mother of the Gods ordain'd;
"The Corybantian Cymbals thence we drew;
"The Idæan Grove; and faithful Silence, due
"To rites mysterious; and the Lion Pair
"Ruled by the Goddess from her awful Car.
"Then haste—the Mandate of the Gods obey
"And to the Gnossian Realms direct our way;
"But first the Winds propitiate; and if Jove
"From his high Throne the enterprize approve,
"The third day's light shall bring our happy Fleet
"To a safe harbour on the shores of Crete."
He spake, appropriate Victims forth were led,
And by his hand upon the Altars bled;
A Bull to soothe the God who rules the Sea—
A Bull, O bright Apollo! fell to thee.
A sable Sheep for Hyems doth he smite
For the soft Zephyrs one of purest white.
Fame told that regions would in Crete be found
Bare of the foe, deserted tracts of ground;
Left by Idomeneus, to recent flight
Driven from those realms—his patrimonial right.

---

149 Father *rev from* Sire *MS. 101C*
155 There *rev from* Here *MS. 101C* Idæan *ed* Idean *MS. 101C*
156 fountain-head *rev from* fountains head *MS. 101C*
160 Teucer *ed* Tucer *MS. 101C*
173 Jove *rev from* force *MS. 101C*
181 for *rev from* to *MS. 101C (MW following WW's pencil)*
182 For *rev from* To *MS. 101C (MW following WW's pencil)* the *over illeg eras MS. 101C*

---

177 "The narrative on the whole eccellens but appropriate strikes me as a prosaic" written in STC's pencil, MS. 101C.

Chear'd by a hope those vacant seats to gain
We quit the Ortigian Shore, and scud along the Main;
Near ridgy Naxos, travers'd by a rout
Of madding Bacchanals with song and shout;
By green Donysa rising o'er the Deeps;
Olearos, and snow-white Parian steeps;
Flying with prosperous sail through sounds and seas
Starr'd with the thickly-clustering Cyclades.
Confused and various clamour rises high;
"To Crete and to our Ancestors," we cry
While Ships and Sailors each with other vie.
Still freshening from the stern the breezes blow,
And speed the Barks they chase, where'er we go;
Till rest is giv'n upon the ancient Shores
Of the Curetes to their Sails and Oars.—
So with keen hope I trace a circling Wall,
And the new City, by a name which all
Repeat with gladness, Pergamus I call.
The thankful Citizens I then exhort
To love their hearths, and raise a guardian Fort.
—The Fleet is drawn ashore; in eager Bands
The Settlers cultivate the allotted lands;
And some for Hymeneal rites prepare;
I plan our new Abodes, fit laws declare;
But pestilence now came, and tainted the wide air.
To piteous wasting were our limbs betrayed;
On trees and plants the deadly season preyed.
The men relinquished their dear lives,—or life
Remaining, dragged their frames in feeble strife.
Thereafter, Syrius clomb the sultry sky,
Parch'd every herb to bare sterility;
And forc'd the sickly corn its nurture to deny.
My anxious Sire exhorts to seek once more
The Delian shrine, and pardon thence implore;
Ask of the God to what these sorrows tend,
Whence we must look for aid, our voyage whither bend.

---

196 we *rev from* they *MS. 101C (MW following WW's pencil)*
197 vie. *ed* vie, *MS. 101C*
199 we *rev from* they *MS. 101C (MW following WW's pencil)*
209 rites *over illeg eras MS. 101C*
219 to seek *inserted MS. 101C*

189–194 These lines render three lines of Latin, and are a good example of what WW meant by his freer rendering of Book III. (See WW to Lord Lonsdale, February 5, 1824, Appendix I, p. 564.) The Latin reads: "Bacchatumque jugis Naxon, viridemque Donysam, / Olearon, niveamque Paron, sparsasque per æquor / Cycladas, & crebris legimus freta consita terris," ll. 125–127.

205 thankful Citizens] "lætam . . . gentem," l. 133. In *PW,* de Selincourt/Darbishire have "Citoyens" here and at Book III, l. 25; their error resulted from a misreading of MW's handwriting.

219–220 "Rursùs ad oraculum Ortygiæ, Phœbumque remenso / Hortatur pater ire mari," ll. 143–144. Ruæus paraphrases: "Pater meus hortatur me, ut remenso mari eam iterum ad oraculum Deli, et ad Phœbum. . . ."

'Twas night, and, couch'd upon the dewy ground,
The weary Animals in sleep were bound,
When those Penates which my hands had snatch'd
From burning Troy, while on my bed I watch'd,
Appear'd, and stood before me, to my sight
Made manifest by copious streams of light
Pour'd from the body of the full-orbed Moon,
That through the loop-holes of my chamber shone.
Thus did they speak; "we come, the Delegates
"Of Phœbus, to foretell thy future fates:
"Things which his Delian tripod to thine ear
"Would have announced, through us he utters here.
"When Troy was burnt we crost the billowy sea
"Faithful Attendants on thy arms, and *We*
"Shall raise to heaven thy proud Posterity.
"But thou thy destined wanderings stoutly bear,
"And for the Mighty, mighty Seats prepare;
"These thou must leave;—Apollo ne'er design'd
"That thou in Crete a resting-place shouldst find.
"There is a Country styled by Men of Greece
"Hesperia—strong in arms—the soil of large increase,
"Œnotrians held it; men of later fame
"Call it Italia, from their Leader's name:
"Our home is there; there lies the native place
"Of Dardanus, and Jasius—whence our race.
"Rise then; and to thy aged Father speak
"Indubitable tidings;—bid him seek
"The Ausonian Land, and Corithas; Jove yields
"No place to us among Dictean fields."
Upon the sacred spectacle I gaz'd,
And heard the utterance of the Gods, amazed.
Sleep in this visitation had no share;
Each face I saw—the fillets round their hair!
Chilled with damp fear I started from the bed,
And raised my hands and voice to heav'n,—then shed
On the recipient hearth untemper'd wine,
In prompt libation to the powers divine.

230/231 Known was each face I look'd on, seen each head
With fillets bound; while gelid damps oerspread
These trembling limbs. I started from my bed— *MS. 101C del*

244 Œnotrians *ed* Ænotrians *MS. 101C*

256 the *rev from* my *MS. 101C*

257 shed *rev from* said *MS. 101C*

258 On *rev from* Upon *MS. 101C* untemper'd *rev from* the untemper'd *MS. 101C*

259 In *rev from* A *MS. 101C*

---

230 loop-holes] "insertas . . . fenestras," l. 152. Minellius glosses: "Quæ ædibus interpositæ erant."

345 "Obscœnas pelagi ferro fœdare volucres," l. 241. Ruæus glosses: "Quia Harpyiæ Ponti aut Neptuni, et terræ dicuntur aliæ . . ." Hence, "aqueous and terrene."

This rite performed with joy, my Sire I sought,
Charged with the message which the Gods had brought;
When I had open'd all in order due
The truth found easy entrance; for he knew
The double Ancestors, the ambiguous race,
And own'd his new mistake in person and in place.
Then he exclaim'd, "O Son, severely tried
"In all that Troy is fated to abide,
"This course Cassandra's voice to me made known;
"She prophesied of this, and she alone;
"Italia oft she cried, and words outthrew
"Of realms Hesperian, to our Nation due:
"But how should Phrygians such a power erect?
"Whom did Cassandra's sayings *then* affect?
"Now, let us yield to Phœbus, and pursue
"The happier lot he offers to our view."
All heard with transport what my Father spake;
This habitation also we forsake;
And strait, a scanty remnant left behind,
Once more in hollow Ships we court the helpful wind.
  But when along the Deep our Gallies steer'd,
And the last speck of land had disappear'd,
And nought was visible, above, around,
Save the blank sky, and ocean without bound,
Then came a Tempest-laden Cloud that stood
Right over me, and rowz'd the blackening flood.
The fleet is scatter'd, while around us rise
Billows that every moment magnifies.
Day fled, and heaven enveloped in a night
Of stormy rains, is taken from our sight;
By instincts of their own the clouds are riven
And prodigal of fire—while we are driven
Far from the points we aim'd at, every bark
Errant upon the waters rough and dark.
Even Palinurus owns that night and day,
Thus in each other lost, confound his way.
Three sunless days we struggle with the gales,
And for three starless nights all guidance fails;
The fourth day came, and to our wistful eyes
The far-off Land then first began to rise,
Lifting itself in hills that gently broke
Upon our view, and rolling clouds of smoke:

---

262 When *rev from* Then *MS. 101C*
272 erect *rev from* effect *MS. 101C*
273 affect *rev from* effect *MS. 101C*
276 with *rev from* in [?the] *MS. 101C*
284 a *rev from* the *MS. 101C*
294 Palinurus *ed* Palenurus *MS. 101C*

Sails drop; the Mariners, with spring and stoop
Timed to their oars, the eddying waters scoop;
The Vessels skim the waves, alive from prow to poop.
Saved from the perils of the stormy seas,
We disembark upon the Strophades;
Amid the Ionian Waters lie this pair
Of Islands, and that Grecian name they bear.
The brood of Harpies when in fear they left
The doors of Phineus—of that home bereft
And of their former tables—thither fled,
There dwell with dire Celæno at their head.
No plague so hideous, for impure abuse
Of upper air, did ever Styx produce,
Stirr'd by the anger of the Gods to fling
From out her waves some new-born monst'rous Thing;
Birds they, with virgin faces, crooked claws;
Of filthy paunch and of insatiate maws,
And pallid mien—from hunger without pause!
Here safe in port we saw the fields o'erspread
With beeves and goats, untended as they fed.
Prompt slaughter follows; offerings thence we pay,
And call on Jove himself to share the prey.
Then, couch by couch, along the bay we rear,
And feast well pleased upon that goodly chear.
—But, clapping loud their wings, the Harpy brood
Rush from the mountain—pounce upon our food—
Pollute the morsels which they fail to seize—
And, screaming, load with noisome scents the breeze.
Again—but now within a long-drawn glade
O'erhung with rocks and boughs of roughest shade,
We deck our tables, and replace the fire
Upon the Altars; but, with noises dire,
From different points of Heaven, from blind retreats,
They flock—and hovering o'er defile the meats.
"War let them have," I cried, and gave command
To stem the next foul onset, arms in hand.
Forthwith the men withdraw from sight their shields,
And hide their swords where grass a covert yields.
But when the Harpies with loud clang once more
Gathered, and spread upon the curved shore,

---

302 stoop *rev from* scoop *MS. 101C*
305 seas, *rev from* sea, *MS. 101C*
312 Celæno *ed* Cælina *MS. 101C*
318 maws *rev from* claws *MS. 101C*
327 our *rev from* their *MS. 101C*
331 O'erhung *ed* Oerhung *MS. 101C*
339 a *rev from* in *MS. 101C*

---

397 "illustrating" is a Latinate attempt to render "Lustramur," l. 279.

From a tall eminence in open view
His trumpet sound of charge Misenus blew;
Then do our swords assault those Fowls obscene,
Of generation aqueous and terrene.
But what avails it?—oft-repeated blows
They with inviolable plumes oppose;
Baffle the steel; and, leaving stains behind
And spoil half-eaten, mount upon the wind;
Celæno only on a summit high
Perched—and there vented this sad prophesy.
"By war, Descendants of Laomedon!
"For our slain steers, by war would Ye atone?
"Why seek the blameless Harpies to expel
"From regions where by right of birth they dwell?
"But learn, and fast within your memories hold,
"Things which to Phœbus Jupiter foretold,
"Phœbus to me, and I to you unfold,
"I greatest of the Furies. Ye, who strive
"For Italy, in Italy shall arrive:
"Havens within that wished-for land, by leave
"Of favouring winds, your Navy shall receive;
"But do not hope to raise those promised Walls,
"E're on your head the curse of hunger falls;
"And, for the slaughter of our herds, your doom
"Hath been your very tables to consume,
"Gnaw'd and devour'd through utter want of food!"
She spake; and, borne on wings, sought refuge in the wood.
The haughty spirits of the Men were quail'd;
A shuddering fear through every heart prevail'd;
On force of arms no longer they rely
To daunt whom prayers and vows must pacify,
Whether to Goddesses the offence were given,
Or they with dire and obscene Birds had striven.
Due Rites ordain'd, as on the shore he stands
My Sire Anchises, with uplifted hands,
Invokes the greater Gods; "Ye Powers, disarm
"This threat, and from your Votaries turn the harm!"
Then bids to loose the Cables and unbind
The willing canvas, to the breeze resign'd.
Where guides the Steersman and the south-winds urge
Our rapid keels, we skim the foaming surge.
Before us opens midway in the flood

---

344 do *rev from* to *MS. 101C*
350 Celæno *ed* Celæna *MS. 101C*
353 Ye *rev from* you *MS. 101C*
361 Havens *rev from* Havens, *MS. 101C*
367 food!" *ed* food! *MS. 101C*
382 Our rapid *rev from* We skim *MS. 101C* the *rev from* upon the *MS. 101C*
383 in the *rev from* the deep *MS. 101C*

Zacinthus, shaded with luxuriant wood;
Dulichium now, and Samè next appears;
And Neritos a craggy summit rears:
We shun the rocks of Ithaca, ill Nurse
Of stern Ulysses! and her soil we curse:
Then Mount Lucate shews its vapoury head;
Where, from his temple, Phœbus strikes with dread
The passing Mariner; but no mischance
Now fear'd, to that small City we advance;
Gladly we haul the sterns ashore, and throw
The biting Anchor out from every prow.
    Unlooked-for land thus reach'd, to Jove we raise
The votive Altars which with incense blaze;
Our Youth, illustrating the Actian Strand
With Trojan Games, as in their native land
Imbue their naked limbs with slippery oil,
And pant for mastery in athletic toil;
Well pleas'd so fair a voyage to have shap'd,
'Mid Grecian Towns on every side escap'd.
—Sol through his annual round meanwhile had pass'd,
And the Sea roughened in the wintry blast;
High on the Temple Gate a brazen shield
I fixed, which mighty Abbas used to wield;
Inscriptive verse declar'd why this was done,
Arms from the Conquering Greeks and by Æneas won.
Then at my word the Ships their moorings leave,
And with contending oars the waters cleave;
Phæacian Peaks beheld in air and lost
As we proceed, Epirus now we coast;
And, a Chaonian harbour won, we greet
Buthrotus perch'd upon her lofty seat.
    Helenus, Son of Priam, here was Chief,
(So ran the tale ill-fitted for belief)
Govern'd where Grecian Pyrrhus once had reign'd,
Whose sceptre wielding, he, therewith, had gain'd
Andromache his Spouse—to nuptials led
Once more by one whom Troy had born and bred.

---

393 sterns *rev from* stern *MS. 101C*
395 to *ed* To *rev from* to *MS. 101C*
398 as on *rev from* us on *MS. 101C*
399 oil *over illeg eras MS. 101C*
409 Then at *del, then inserted MS. 101C (WW)* *MS. 101A begins here*
411 beheld] are seen *MS. 101A*
413 And (a Chaonian Harbour won) we greet *MS. 101A, then* won) we *del to* entering,)
414 her *rev from* its *MS. 101C* his *MS. 101A*
417 where . . . had *rev to* where once the Grecian Pyrrhus *MS. 101A*
418 And, with the sceptre of the Chief, had gained *MS. 101A*
420 born *so MS. 101A* borne *MS. 101C*

I long'd to greet him, wish'd to hear his fate
As his own voice the Story would relate.
So, from the Port in which our Gallies lay,
Right tow'rds the City I pursu'd my way.
A Grove there was, where by a streamlet's side
With the proud name of Simois dignified,
Andromache a solemn service paid,
(As chanc'd that day) invoking Hector's shade:
There did her hands the mournful gifts present
Before a Tomb—his empty Monument
Of living green-sward hallowed by her care;
And two funereal Altars, planted near,
Quicken'd the motion of each falling tear.
When my approach She witness'd, and could see
Our Phrygian Arms, she shrunk—as from a prodigy.
In blank astonishment and terror shook,
While the warm blood her tottering limbs forsook.
She swoon'd—and long lay senseless on the ground,
Before these broken words a passage found;
"Was that a real Shape which met my view?
"Son of a Goddess, is thy coming true?
"Liv'st thou? Or, if the light of life be fled,
"Hector—where is he?" This she spake,—then spread
A voice of weeping through the Grove, and I
Utter'd these few faint accents in disturb'd reply.
"Fear not to trust thine eyes; I live indeed,
"And fraught with trouble is the life I lead.
"Fallen from the height, where with thy glorious Mate
"Thou stood'st, Andromache, what change had Fate
"To offer worthy of thy former state?
"Say, did the Gods take pity on thy vows?
"Or have they given to Pyrrhus Hector's Spouse?"
  Then she with downcast look, and voice subdu'd;
"Thrice happy Virgin, thou of Priam's blood,
"Who, in the front of Troy by timely doom,
"Did'st pour out life before a hostile tomb;
"And, slaughter'd thus, wert guarded from the wrong
"Of being swept by lot amid a helpless throng!
"O happiest above all who ne'er didst press
"A conquering Master's bed, in captive wretchedness!

---

421 greet *del to* embrace *MS. 101A*
423 Port in which] Harbour [*del to* Haven] where *MS. 101A*
424 tow'rds] tow'rd *MS. 101A*
428 shade:] Shade. *over illeg eras MS. 101A*
440 which *rev from* that *MS. 101C*
445 disturb'd *inserted MS. 101C* disturbed *MS. 101A*
454 Thrice happy Virgin, thou *rev to* O Maiden happiest far *then rev to* O Thou sole happy Maid *MS. 101A (WW)*
457 slaughter'd . . . from] singly by this fate escape *alt MS. 101A (WW)*

"I, since our Ilium fell, have undergone
"(Wide waters cross'd) whate'er Achilles' Son
"Could in the arrogance of birth impose,
"And faced in servitude a Mother's throes.
"Thereafter, he at will the knot unty'd,
"To seek Hermione a Spartan Bride;
"And me to Trojan Helenus he gave—
"Captive to Captive—if not Slave to Slave.
"Whereat, Orestes with strong love inflam'd
"Of her now lost whom as a bride he claim'd,
"And by the Furies driv'n, in vengeful ire
"Smote Pyrrhus at the Altar of his Sire.
"He, by an unexpected blow, thus slain,
"On Helenus devolv'd a part of his Domain;
"Who call'd the neighbouring fields Chaonian ground,
"Chaonia nam'd the Region wide around,
"From Trojan Chaon—chusing for the site
"Of a new Pergamus yon rocky height.
"But thee a Stranger in a land unknown—
"What Fates have urged? What winds have hither blown?
"Or say what God upon our coasts hath thrown?
"Survives the Boy Ascanius? In his heart
"Doth his lost Mother still retain her part?
"What, Son of great Æneas, brings he forth
"In emulation of his Father's worth?
"In Priam's Grandchild doth not Hector raise
"High hopes to reach the virtue of past days?"
Then follow'd sobs and lamentations vain;
But from the City, with a numerous train,
Her living Consort Helenus descends;
He saw, and gave glad greeting to his Friends;
And tow'rds his hospitable palace leads,
While passion interrupts the speech it feeds.
As we advance I gratulate with joy
Their dwindling Xanthus, and their little Troy;
Their Pergamus aspiring in proud state,
As if it strove the old to emulate;—
And clasp the threshold of their Scæan Gate.

---

463 arrogance *over illeg eras MS. 101C*
465 Thereafter . . . knot *rev to* Erelong the knot of union he *then del to* Erelong my haughty Lord the knot *MS. 101A (WW)*
470 bride] wife *rev from* bride *MS. 101A (WW)*
473 When he by this unlook'd-for blow was slain, *MS. 101A*
476 Chaonia *rev from* Chaonian *MS. 101C*
482 Ascanius *MS. 101A* Ascanias *MS. 101C*
492 tow'rds] tow'rd *MS. 101A*
496–497 I see their Pergamus in princely state
Aspire, as if the old to emulate, *MS. 101A*
497 emulate *rev from* imitate *MS. 101C*

Nor fails this kindred City to excite
In my Associates unreserv'd delight;
And soon in ample Porticos the King
Receives the Band with earnest welcoming;
Amid the Hall high festival we hold,
Refresh'd with viands serv'd in massy gold;
And, from resplendent goblets, votive wine
Flows in libation to the Powers divine.
  Two joyful days thus past, the southern breeze
Once more invites my Fleet to trust the Seas;
To Helenus this suit I then prefer;
"Illustrious Trojan, Heaven's interpreter!
"By prescient Phœbus with his spirit fill'd;
"Skill'd in the tripod, in the laurel skill'd;
"Skill'd in the stars, and what by voice or wing
"Birds to the intelligence of mortals bring;
"Now mark:—to Italy my course I bend
"Urged by the Gods, who for this aim portend,
"By every sign they give, a happy end:
"The Harpy Queen, she only, doth presage
"A curse of famine in its utmost rage;
"Say Thou what perils I am first to shun,
"What course for safe deliverance must be run?"
  Then Helenus (the accustom'd Victims slain)
Invoked the Gods their favour to obtain.
This done, he loos'd the fillets from his head,
And took my hand; and, while a holy dread
Possessed me, onward to the Temple led,

---

501 And soon in ample portico *rev to* Soon in a spacious portico *MS. 101A*
502 welcoming; *rev from* welcomings *MS. 101C*
506 Powers *rev from* Power *MS. 101A*
508 Once *rev from* one *MS. 101C*
515 *rev from* Hear and advise: to Italy I bend *MS. 101C (MW over WW's pencil)*
515–516 Hear and advise. To Italy [my course *del*] I bend,
Urged by the Gods, my way; and they portend, *MS. 101A*
519 A] The *MS. 101A*
520 Say Thou] Now say *MSS rev to* O say *MS. 101C (MW following WW's pencil) rev to text MS. 101C (WW)*
521 safe *rev to* sure *MS. 101A* must be run *rev from* I must run *MS. 101C*
522–523 Then he [Whereat *alt*] the victims previously slain
Invok'd the [He prays the *alt*] Gods their ordonnance to gain *MS. 101C (WW's pencil drafts)*
522 Then *ed* "Then *MS 101C* Then Helenus] The royal Seer *MS. 101A*
523 Invoked *ed* "Invoked *MS 101C* Adored *MS. 101A*
524 *rev from* And loos'd the fillets from his sacred head *MS. 101C (MW over WW's pencil); MS. 101A as unrevised MS. 101C but* "And] And *and* loos'd] loosed *and* head,] head;
525 And *ed* "And *MS 101C* Then *MS. 101A*
526 Possessed *so MS. 101A* Possessed *MS 101C*

---

501 ample Porticos] "porticibus . . . amplis," l. 353.

Thy Temple, Phœbus!—from his lip then flow'd
Communications of the inspiring God.—
"No common auspices (this truth is plain)
"Conduct thee, Son of Venus! o'er the Main;
"The high behests of Jove this course ordain.
"But, that with safer voyage thou may'st reach
"The Ausonian harbour, I will clothe in speech
"Some portion of the future; Fate hath hung
"Clouds o'er the rest; or Juno binds my tongue.
"And first, *that* Italy, whose coasts appear,
"To thy too confident belief, so near,
"With havens open for thy sails, a wide
"And weary distance doth from thee divide.
"Trinacrian waves shall bend the pliant oar;
"Thou, through Ausonian gulphs, a passage must explore,
"Trace the Circean Isle, the infernal Pool,
"Before thy City rise for stedfast rule.
"Now mark these Signs,—and store them in thy mind;
"When, anxiously reflecting, thou shalt find
"A bulky Female of the bristly Kind
"On a sequester'd river's margin laid,
"Where Ilex branches do the ground oershade;
"With thirty Young-ones couch'd in that Recess,
"White as the pure white Dam whose teats they press,
"*There* found thy City;—on *that* soil shall close
"All thy solicitudes, in fixed repose.
"Nor dread Celæno's threat; the Fates shall clear
"The way, and at thy call Apollo interfere.
"But shun those Lands where our Ionian sea
"Washes the nearest shores of Italy.
"On all the coasts malignant Greeks abide;
"Narycian Locrians there a Town have fortified;

---

527 Thy *so MS. 101A* "Thy *MS 101C*
528 Communications *so MS. 101A* "Communications *MS 101C*
529 this] the *rev from* this *MS. 101A*
531 behests *rev from* behest *MS. 101C (ink over pencil)*
542 Trace the Circean Isle] Circean Isles and *rev to* Tread Circe's Island, and *MS. 101A*
543 Cross, ere thy City rise for stedfast [*del to* settled *(WW)*] rule. *MS. 101A*
544–545 —Now mark these tokens: soon as thou shalt find *MS. 101A*
546 *repeated, then del MS. 101C*
547 On] By *MS. 101A*
548 On ground which ilex branches overshade, *MS. 101A*
552 All . . . fixed] Thy cares and labours in assured *alt MS. 101A (WW)*
553 threat; *rev from* threats; *MS. 101A* threat *MS 101C* shall clear *del MS. 101A*
554 The] Thy *MS. 101A* and . . . interfere] and Phœbus at thy call appear *alt MS. 101A (WW)* interfere. *so MS. 101A* interfere *MS 101C*
555 sea *rev from* shore *MS. 101C*
557 abide *over illeg eras MS. 101A*
558 Narycian *over illeg eras MS. 101A*

"Idomeneus of Crete hath compass'd round
"With soldiery the Salentinian ground;
"There, when Thessalian Phyloctetes chose
"His resting-place, the small Petilia rose.
"And, when that sea past over, thou shalt stand
"Before the Altars kindled on the strand,
"While to the Gods are offer'd up thy vows,
"Then in a purple veil enwrap thy brows,
"And sacrifice thus cover'd, lest the sight
"Of any hostile face disturb the rite.
"Be this observance kept by thee and thine,
"And this to late posterity consign!
"But when by favouring breezes wafted o'er,
"Thy Fleet approaches the Sicilian shore,
"And dense Pelorus gradually throws
"Its barriers open—to invite thy prows,
"That passage shunn'd, thy course in safety keep
"By steering to the left, with ample sweep.
"'Tis said, when heaving Earth of yore was rent,
"This ground forsook the Hesperian Continent:
"Nor doubt, that power to work such change might lie
"Within the grasp of dark Antiquity.
"Then flow'd the sea between, and, where the force
"Of roaring waves establish'd the divorce,
"Still, through the Straits, the narrow waters boil,
"Dissevering Town from Town, and soil from soil.
"Upon the right the dogs of Scylla fret;
"The left by fell Charybdis is beset;
"Thrice tow'rds the bottom of a vast abyss

---

561 when *rev from* where *MS. 101C* where *MS. 101A*
563 And, *rev from* But *MS. 101C* But *MS. 101A* stand *rev from* find *MS. 101C*
564 kindled *rev from* kneeling *MS. 101C (MW over WW's pencil)* kindling *MS. 101A*
566 in . . . enwrap] cast a purple amice o'er *MS. 101A*
574 Its *rev to* Her *MS. 101A (WW)*
575 shunn'd, *rev from* shun *MS. 101C* shun; *MS. 101A*
587 tow'rds] tow'rd *MS. 101A*

---

561 Thessalian Phyloctetes] "Melibœi / . . . Philoctetæ," ll. 401–402. Ruæus glosses: "Philoctetes, Pæantis filius, Melibœæ rex, urbis in Thessaliâ . . . "

566 purple veil] "Purpureo . . . amictu," l. 405. Ruæus paraphrases: "purpureo velo." In l. 757, below, WW uses the Latinate "amice" to translate "amictus."

569–570 "Hunc socii morem sacrorum, hunc ipse teneto; / Hac casti maneant in relligione nepotes," ll. 408–409. Ruæus paraphrases: "Socii servent hanc consuetudinem sacrificiorum, tu ipse hanc serva: posteri pii persistant in hâc ceremoniâ."

585 Virgil makes no mention of Scylla's dogs here, but Ruæus glosses: "Phorci filiam, à Circe commutatam dicunt in monstrum. cujus suprema pars fœmineam speciem retinuerit, infima in canes abierit: quorum latratu fluctuum strepitum exprimere voluerunt; ipsumque monstrum in scopula latere, eòque naves attrahere ac lacerare fabulati sunt." Scylla's dogs are described in Ovid's *Metamorphoses,* Book XIII, 730, and Milton draws on Ovid's description in his depiction of Sin in *Paradise Lost,* Book II, a passage that WW may also have had in mind.

"Down, headlong down, the liquid precipice
"She sucks the whirling billows, and, as oft
"Ejecting, sends them into air aloft.
"But Scylla, pent within her Cavern blind,
"Thrusts forth a visage of our human kind,
"And draws the Ship on rocks: She, fair in show,
"A Woman to the waist, is foul below;
"A huge Sea-Beast—with Dolphin tails, and bound
"With Water Wolves and Dogs her middle round!
"But Thou against this jeopardy provide
"Doubling Pachynus with a circuit wide;
"Thus shapeless Scylla may be left unseen,
"Unheard the yelling of her brood marine.
"But, above all, if Phœbus I revere
"Not unenlighten'd, an authentic Seer,
"Then, Goddess-born, (on this could I enlarge
"Repeating oft and oft the solemn charge)
"Adore imperial Juno, freely wait
"With gifts on Juno's Altar, supplicate
"Her potent favour, and subdue her hate;
"So shalt thou seek, a Conqueror at last,
"The Italian Shore, Trinacrian dangers past!
"Arrived at Cumæ and the sacred floods
"Of black Avernus resonant with woods,
"Thou shalt behold the Sybil where She sits
"Within her Cave, rapt in extatic fits,
"And words and characters to leaves commits.

---

593 Ship *rev from* Ships *MS. 101C* ships *MS. 101A*
595 tails] tail *MS. 101A*
597 this] the *MS. 101A*
599 may *rev from* shall *MS. 101C (MW over WW's pencil)*
601 if] of *MS. 101A*
603 could] would *MS. 101A*
606 Altar] Altars *MS. 101A*
608 So *rev from* Thust *MS. 101C*
608–609 So shalt thou reach (Sicilian limits past)
The Italian shore, a conqueror at last. *MS. 101A*
610 at *inserted MS. 101C*
614 words *rev from* signs *MS. 101C (MW over WW's pencil)* signs *MS. 101A*

594–596 Virgil is a bit more graphic: "pulchro pectore virgo / Pube tenùs: postrema, immani corpore Pistrix, / Delphinum caudas utero commissa luporum," ll. 426–427.

600 A loose rendering of "& cæruleis canibus resonantia saxa," l. 432.

610 WW alluded to this passage many years earlier in *The Ruined Cottage*, MS. B, ll. 443–448:
The windows they were dim, and her few books,
Which one upon the other heretofore
Had been piled up against the corner panes
In seemly order, now with straggling leaves
Lay scattered here and there, open or shut,
As they had chanced to fall.

613 rapt in extatic fits] "Insanam," l. 443. WW seems to follow Minellius's gloss here: "afflatum numine & furore divino. . . ."

614 "foliisque notas & nomina mandat," l. 444. Minellius glosses "notas" as "litteras" and "nomina" as "res notis descriptas". Ruæus paraphrases "mandat" as "committet."

"The prophesies which on those leaves the Maid
"Inscribes, are by her hands in order laid
"Mid the secluded Cavern, where they fill
"Their several places, undisturb'd and still.
"But if a light wind entering through the door
"Scatter the thin Leaves on the rocky floor,
"She to replace her prophesies will use
"No diligence; all flutter, where they chuse,
"In hopeless disconnection loose and wild;
"And they, who sought for knowledge, thus beguil'd
"Of her predictions, from the Cave depart,
"And quit the Sybil with a murmuring heart.
"But thou, albeit ill-dispos'd to wait,
"And prizing moments at their highest rate,
"Though Followers chide, and ever and anon
"The flattering winds invite thee to be gone,
Beg of the moody Prophetess to break
"The silent air, and for thy guidance speak.
"She will disclose the features of thy doom,
"The Italian Nations, and the Wars to come;
"How to escape from hardships, or endure,
"And make a happy termination sure;
"Enough—chains bind the rest, or clouds obscure.
"Go then, nor in thy glorious progress halt,
"But to the stars the Trojan name exalt!"
So spake the friendly Seer, from hallowed lips;
Then orders sumptuous presents to our Ships;
Smooth ivory, massy gold, with pond'rous store
Of vases fashion'd from the paler ore,
And Dodonæan Cauldrons;—nor with-holds
The golden halberk, knit in triple folds,
That Neoptolemus erewhile had worn;
Nor his resplendent crest which waving plumes adorn.
Rich offerings also grace my Father's hands;
Horses he adds with Equerries; and Bands
Of Rowers, and supply of Arms commands.

---

627 But *rev from* And *MS. 101C (MW following WW's pencil)*

631 Prophetess] Soothsayer *alt MS. 101C (WW)*

638–639 *rev from* "Go then, and high as heaven's ethereal vault
"The Trojan name by glorious deeds exalt!" *MS. 101C (MW following WW's pencil, MW's punct); MS. 101A same as unrevised MS. 101C but* then,] then: *and* exalt!"] exalt.

641 *rev from* Then orders presents to our parting Ships; *MS. 101C (MW over WW's pencil) but* our *erroneously del; MS. 101A same as unrevised MS. 101C but* Ships;] Ships,

644 Dodonæan *over illeg eras MSS.*

646 worn *rev from* won *MS. 101A* Neoptolemus *rev from* Neoptolimus *MS. 101A* Neoptolomus *MS. 101C*

621–626 Expanding "Nunquam deinde cavo volitantia prendere saxo, / Nec revocare situs, aut jungere carmina curat: / Inconsulti abeunt, sedemque odêre Sibyllæ," ll. 450–452.

—Meanwhile Anchises bids the Fleet unbind
Its sails for instant seizure of the wind.
The Interpreter of Phœbus then address'd
This gracious farewell to his ancient Guest;
"Anchises! to celestial honors led,
"Beloved of Venus, whom she deign'd to wed,
"Care of the Gods, twice snatch'd from Ilium lost,
"Now for Ausonia be these waters cross'd!
"Yet must thou only glide along the shores
"To which I point; far lies the Land from ours
"Whither Apollo's voice directs your powers:
"Go, happy Parent of a pious Son;
"No more—I baulk the winds that press thee on."
Nor less Andromache, disturb'd in heart
That parting now we must for ever part,
Embroider'd Vests of golden thread bestows;
A Phrygian Tunic o'er Ascanius throws;
And studious that her bounty may become
The occasion, adds rich labours of the loom;
"Dear Child," she said, "these also, to be kept
"As the memorials of my hand, accept!
"Last Gifts of Hector's Consort, let them prove
"To thee the symbols of enduring love;
"Take what Andromache at parting gives
"Fair Boy!—sole Image that for me survives
"Of my Astyanax—in whom his face,
"His eyes are seen, his very hands I trace;
"And now, but for obstruction from the tomb,
"His years had open'd into kindred bloom."
To these, while gushing tears bedew'd my cheek,
Thus in the farewell moment did I speak;
"Live happy Ye, whose race of fortune run

---

651 unbind *over illeg eras MS. 101C*
652 seizure *over illeg eras MS. 101A*
654 ancient *rev from* parting *MS. 101C (MW over WW's pencil)* parting *MS. 101A*
659 must thou only] only hope to *MS. 101A*
664 disturb'd *so MS. 101A* disturbd *rev from* disturb *MS. 101C (MW following WW's pencil)*
667 o'er *so MS. 101A* oer *MS 101C*
668 may *rev from* [?can] *rev from* might *MS. 101C (MW over WW's pencil)*
669 adds rich *rev from* added *MS. 101C (MW following WW's pencil)*
670–671 *rev to* Take also, said she what my own hands wove *del, then reinserted but* wove] wove; *MS. 101A (WW)*
671 memorials *rev from* memorial *MS. 101C*
673 To thee the symbols] To thee the tokens *rev to* Treasur'd memorials *MS. 101A (WW)* enduring] her steadfast *MS. 101A* Her steadfast *alt MS. 101C (WW's eras pencil)*
675/676 When *MS. 101A (WW's pencil, page bottom)*
676–707 *for revisions and variants in MS. 101C, see Transcriptions, pp. 554–557*
678 from the tomb] of the tomb *MS. 101A del* And his unfolding youth with thine [would *del*] had [now have *del*] kept pace." *alt MS. 101A (WW)*

---

678 There is no mention of Astyanax's tomb in Virgil.
682 Page bottom of MS. 101A, 58v, underneath this line, WW has written "When" in pencil.

"Permits such life; from trials undergone
"We to the like are call'd; by you is quiet won.
"No seas have Ye to measure; nor on you
"Is it impos'd Ausonia to pursue,
"And search for fields still flying from the view.
"Lo Xanthus here in miniature!—*there* stands
"A second Troy, the labour of your hands,
"With happier auspices—in less degree
"Exposed, I trust, to Grecian enmity.
"If Tiber e'er receive me, and the sod
"Of Tiber's meadows by these feet be trod,
"If e'er I see our promis'd City rise,
"The neighbouring Nations, bound by ancient ties,
"Hesperian and Epirian, whose blood came
"From Dardanus, whose lot hath been the same,
"Shall make one Troy in spirit. May that care
"To our Descendants pass from heir to heir!"
We coast the high Ceraunia, whence is found
The shortest transit to Italian ground;
Meanwhile the sun went down, and shadows spread
O'er every mountain dark'ned to its head.
Tired of their oars the Men no sooner reach
Earth's wish'd-for bosom than their limbs they stretch
On the dry margin of the murmuring Deep,
Where weariness is lost in timely sleep.
Ere Night, whose Car the Hours had yok'd and rein'd,
Black Night, the middle of her orbit gain'd,

---

683 from trials undergone] *one* peril if we shun, *MS. 101A*
684 We . . . call'd;] "Tis but to meet a worse: *MS. 101A*
687 the] your *MS. 101A*
688–691 Before your sight a mimic Xanthus flows;
By your own hands the Troy that guards you rose
With happier auspices — to stand more free,
ould wish of mine avail, from Grecian enmity. *MS. 101A*
692 e'er *so MS. 101A* e're *MS. 101C*
694 e'er *so MS. 101A* e're *MS. 101C* I . . . rise,] our destined City I behold, *MS. 101A*
695 The *rev to* Then *MS. 101A* Nations . . . ties] Towns, and Tribes akin of old *MS. 101A*
699 To our *rev from* May the *MS. 101A* heir!" *so MS. 101A* heir! *MS. 101C*
700 coast the] sail near *MS. 101A*
701 transit to Italian] passage to Hesperian *MS. 101A*
704 Eased of the oar, upon earth's wished-for breast *rev to* Each oar allotted, on . . . *MS. 101A (WW)*
705 We seek refreshment, and prepare for rest, *MS. 101A, then* seek refreshment *del to* chear the body *(WW)*
706–707 Nor did indulgent Nature fail to steep
On the dry margin of the murmuring Deep *MS. 101A, then*
Dispers'd on the dry margin of the deep; *inserted between ll. 705 and 706 (WW); for further revisions of ll. 704–720 in MS. 101A, see Transcriptions, pp. 550–553*

708–709 "Nec dum orbem medium nox horis acta subibat," l. 512. The references to "Black Night" and its "Car" are WW's embellishments.

Up from his couch doth Palinurus rise,
Looks to the wind for what it signifies,
And to each breath of air a watchful ear applies;
Next all the Stars gliding through silent Heaven
The Bears, Arcturus, and the cluster'd Seven,
Are noted,—and his ranging eyes behold
Magnificent Orion arm'd in gold.
When he perceives that all things low and high
Unite to promise fix'd serenity,
He sends the summons forth; our Camp we raise—
Are gone—and every Ship her broadest wings displays.
    Now, when Aurora redden'd in a sky
From which the Stars had vanish'd, we descry
The low faint hills of distant Italy.
"Italia!" shouts Achates: round and round
Italia flies with gratulant rebound,
From all who see the coast, or hear the happy sound.
Not slow is Sire Anchises to entwine
With wreaths a goblet, which he fill'd with wine;
Then, on the Stern he took his lofty stand,
And cried, "Ye Deities of sea and land
"Through whom the Storms are govern'd, speed our way
"By breezes docile to your kindliest sway!"
—With freshening impulse breathe the wish'd-for gales;
And, as the Ships press on with greedy sails,
Opens the Port; and, peering into sight,
Minerva's Temple tops a craggy height.
The Sails are furl'd by many a busy hand;
The veering prows are pointed to the Strand.
Carved into semblance of a bow the Haven
Looks to the East; but not a wave thence driven
Disturbs its peacefulness; their foamy spray
Breaks upon jutting rocks that fence the Bay.
Two towering cliffs extend with gradual fall
Their arms into the Sea, and frame a wall
In whose embrace the harbour hidden lies;
And, as its shelter deepens on our eyes,
Back from the shore Minerva's Temple flies,

---

714 cluster'd *rev from* clustering *MS. 101C*
721 Now, when *del, then inserted MS. 101C (WW)*
728 he *rev from* is *MS. 101C (MW following WW's pencil)*
733 wish'd-for gales; *apos ed* wished-for gales *MS. 101A*
735 Opens the Port;] The Port unfolds *alt MS. 101A (WW)*
742 upon] on the *MS. 101A* fence *rev from* guard *MS. 101C (WW)*
747 *MS. 101A ends here*

---

725 gratulant rebound] "læto . . . clamore," l. 524.
739–740 the Haven / Looks to the East] "Portus ab Eoo fluctu," l. 533. Ruæus glosses: "ad orientem obvertitur. . . ."

Four snow-white Horses, grazing the wide fields,
Are the first omen which our landing yields;
Then Sire Anchises—"War thy tokens bear
O hospitable land! the Horse is arm'd for war;
War do these menace; but as Steed with Steed
Oft join in friendly yoke, the sight may breed
Fair hope that peace and concord will succeed."
To Pallas then in clanking armour mail'd,
Who hail'd us first, exulting to be hail'd,
Prayers we address—with Phrygian amice veil'd;
And, as by Helenus enjoin'd, the fire
On Juno's altar fumes—to Juno vows aspire.
When we had ceas'd this service to present,
That instant, seaward are our Sail-yards bent,
And we forsake the Shore—with cautious dread
Of ground by Native Grecians tenanted.
The Bay is quickly reach'd that draws its name
From proud Tarentum, proud to share the fame
Of Hercules though by a dubious claim:
Right opposite we ken the Structure holy
Of the Lacinian Goddess rising slowly;
Next the Caulonian Citadel appear'd,
And the Scylacian bay for Shipwrecks fear'd;
Lo, as along the open Main we float,
Mount Etna, yet far off! and far remote.
Groans of the Sea we hear;—deep groans and strokes
Of angry billows beating upon rocks,—
And hoarse surf-clamours,—while the flood throws up
Sands from the depths of its unsettled cup.
My Sire exclaim'd, "Companions, we are caught
"By fell Charybdis; flee as ye were taught!
"These, doubtless, are the rocks, the dangerous shores,
"Which Helenus denounc'd—away—with straining oars!"

---

751 the Horse is *rev from* horses are *MS. 101C (WW)*
753 Oft *rev from* Off *MS. 101C*
754 will *rev from* may *MS. 101C*
761 are *rev from* were *MS. 101C*
764–766 Hence we behold the bay that bears the name
Of proud Tarentum, proud to share the fame
Of Hercules, though by a dubious claim; *WW to Lord Lonsdale, February 5, 1824*
768 slowly *rev from* lowly *MS. 101C*
769 *caret after* appear'd *MS 101C*
777 Companions, *rev from* Conquerors *MS. 101C (WW)*
780 oars!" *ed* oars! *MS. 101C*

---

757 Phrygian amice] "Phrygio . . . amictu," l. 545.

764–766 WW comments on this passage in a letter to Lord Lonsdale of February 5, 1824; see Appendix I, p. 564. Ruæus glosses ll. 551–552 thus: "*Herculeum Tarentum* cur appelletur non liquet: videturque Virgilius de nominis veritate ipse dubitare, cum addit *si vera est fama.*" In WW's copy of Minellius, ll. 551–552 through "Cernitur" are underlined, and an unknown hand has written WW's version of these lines, as published in the *Memoirs*, where the letter to Lord Lonsdale was first published.

Quick, to the left the Master Galley veers
With roaring prow, as Palinurus steers;
And for the left the bands of Rowers strive,
While every help is caught that winds can give.
The whirlpool's dizzy altitudes we scale,
For ghastly sinking when the waters fail.
The hollow rocks thrice gave a fearful cry;
Three times we saw the clashing waves fling high
Their foam, dispers'd along a drizzling sky.
The flagging wind forsook us with the sun,
And to Cyclopian shores a darkling course we run.
   The Port, which now we chance to enter, lies
By winds unruffled though of ample size;
But all too near is Etna, thundering loud;
And ofttimes casting up a pitchy cloud
Of smoke—in whirling convolutions driven,
With weight of hoary Ashes, high as heaven,
And globes of flame; and sometimes he gives vent
To rocky fragments, from his entrails rent;
And hurls out melting substances—that fly
In thick assemblage, and confound the sky;
While groans and lamentations burthensome
Tell to the air from what a depth they come.
The enormous Mass of Etna, so 'tis said,
On lightening-scorch'd Enceladus was laid;
And, ever pressing on the Giant's frame,
Breathes out, from fractured chimneys, fitful flame,
And, often as he turns his weary side
Murmuring Trinacria trembles far and wide,
While wreaths of smoke ascend and all the welkin hide.
We through the night enwrapp'd in woods obscure
The shock of those dire prodigies endure
Nor could distinguish whence might come the sound,
For all the stars to ether's utmost bound
Were hidden or bedimm'd, and Night withheld
The Moon, in mist and lowering fogs conceal'd.

---

783 bands *rev from* banks *MS. 101C*
787 *omitted, then added MS. 101C*
788 clashing waves fling *over illeg eras MS. 101C*
789 *rev from* Three times to heaven we saw the waters spout
And the sky moistened with a briny spout. *MS. 101C*
796 driven, *over illeg eras MS. 101C*
811–812 We through [*rev from* Cover'd through] all that night by woods obscure
Do we those fearful prodigies endure *del MS. 101C*
811–816 We thro the / The shock / Nor cou / For all / Were h / The [*rev from* In] lig *stub MS 101C, which ends here; remainder of reading text based on MS. 89; punct ed*

---

816 L. 638 in Virgil. There is a paragraph break at this point in Ruæus, and a new page in Minellius. WW has omitted the Cyclops episode, perhaps intending to compose it later (space for it had been left in MS. 89).

These left, we harboured on the joyless coast
Of Drepanum; here, harassd long and tossd,
And here my Sire Anchises did I lose
Help in my cares and solace of my woes
Here O best Father best beloved and best
Didst thou desert me when I needed rest.
Thou from so many perils snatch'd in vain;
Not Helenus though much in doleful strain
He prophesied, this sorrow did unfold.
Not dire Celæno this distress foretold.
This trouble, was my last; Celestial Powers
O Queen, have brought me to your friendly shores.
    Sole speaker, thus Æneas did relate
To a hush'd audience the decrees of Fate,
His wandering course remeasured, 'till the close
Now reach'd, in silence here he found repose.

Book IV, Lines 688–692

She who to lift her heavy eyes had tried
Faints while the deep wound gurgles at her side
Thrice on her elbow propp'd she strove to uphold
Her frame—thrice back on the couch it roll'd
Then with a wandering eye in heaven's blue round
She sought the light and groaned when she had found.

Book VIII, Lines 337–366

This scarcely uttered they advance and straight
He shews the Altar and Carmental gate
Which yet by virtue of its Roman name
Preserves the nymph Carmenta's ancient fame
Who first the glories of the Trojan line
Predicted, and the noble Pallantine.
Next points he out an ample sylvan shade
Which Romulus a fit Assylum made
Turns thence and bids Æneas fix his eyes
Where under a chill rock Lupercal lies
Named from Lycean Pan, in old Arcadian guise.

---

817 L. 707 in Virgil.

---

11 "Parrhasio dictum Panos de more Lycæi," l. 344. Ruæus paraphrases: "appelatum ex cultu Arcadico Panos Lycæi." Thus WW's "old Arcadian guise."

Nor left he unobserved the neighbouring wood
Of sacred Argolatum stained with blood.
Where Argus fell, his Guest—the story told
To the Tarpeian Rock their way they hold,
And seek the Capitol now bright with gold,
In those far-distant times a spot forlorn
With brambles choked and rough with savage thorn.
Even then an influence of religious awe
The rustics felt subdued by what they saw
The local spirit creeping through their blood
Even then they feared the rock, they trembled at the wood.
This grove (said he) this leaf-crowned hill—some God
How named we know not, takes for his abode,
The Arcadians verily believe that oft
They have beheld great Jove himself—aloft
Shaking his lurid Ægis in their sight
And covering with dence clouds the stormy height.
Here also sees two mouldering towns that lie
Mournful remains of buried Ancestry;
Yon crumbling fortress father Janus framed,
And Saturn this, each from the Founder named.
    Conversing thus their onward course they bent
To poor Evander's humble tenement;
Herds range the Roman forum—in the Street
Of proud Carinæ, bellowing herds they meet
When they had reached the house he said, this Gate
Conquering Alcides entered; his plain state
This palace lodged; O guest like him forbear
To frown on scanty means and homely fare
Dare riches to despise; with aim as high
Mount thou, and train thyself for Deity.
    This said through that low door he leads his guest
The great Æneas to a couch of rest
There propped he lay on withered leaves, oerspread
With a bear's skin in Lybian desarts bred.

---

15 WW's fascination with this passage helps to explain his disappointment with the Capitoline Hill and Tarpeian Rock when he finally visited Rome in 1837:

Is this, ye Gods, the Capitolian Hill?
Yon petty Steep in truth the fearful Rock,
Tarpeian named of yore, and keeping still
That name, a local Phantom proud to mock
The Traveller's expectation? *At Rome*, ll. 1–5 (*Memorials of a Tour in Italy, 1837*, III).

Georgics, Book IV, Lines 511-515

Even so bewails, the poplar groves among,
Sad Philomela her evanished Young;
Whom the harsh Rustic from the nest hath torn,
An unfledged brood; but on the bough forlorn
She sits, in mournful darkness, all night long;
Renews and still renews, her doleful song,
And fills the leafy grove, complaining of her wrong.

1ff. This passage is part of the Orpheus epyllion of *Georgics*, Book IV; Orpheus, lamenting the death of Eurydice, is compared to a mother nightingale lamenting the death of her young. WW first translated the passage in 1788, as part of an attempt, apparently abortive, to translate the entire epyllion. In a letter of May 27, 1823, now in WL, EQ asked SH to "mark for me" any passages about nightingales that she or others of the Wordsworth circle might find; over the next year or so, they sent him several such passages, referring frequently to a project called "The Nightingale." Whether this project was intended to be an original poem or just a collection of extracts is not clear, but in a letter of November 12, 1823, MW included WW's new translation of Virgil's nightingale simile, to be added to EQ's collection. By May 1824, EQ had composed "To the Poet," in which he compared WW to a nightingale.

Editor's Notes

The following set of notes records Wordsworth's possible borrowings from four earlier translators: John Ogilby, John Dryden, Joseph Trapp, and Christopher Pitt. Wordsworth admitted to borrowing from Dryden and Pitt, and annotations in his personal copy of the 1650 edition of Ogilby's translation indicate that he consulted it as well. It seems likely that he also used Trapp's translation, just as he did when translating the *Georgics* in 1788–1789. For further discussion of what constitutes a potential borrowing, see the headnote to the reading text on pages 178–179.

For Dryden's translation, I quote from the text published in Robert Anderson's *Works of the British Poets* (13 vols.; Edinburgh, 1792–1795), the text Wordsworth consulted, but for ease of reference I have supplied line numbers from *The Works of Virgil in English, 1697*, edited by William Frost and Vinton Dearing (2 vols.; Berkeley, 1987). For Pitt, I also quote from Anderson's text, and supply line numbers from the Joseph Warton–Christopher Pitt translation of Virgil, *The Works of Virgil. In English Verse* (4 vols.; London, 1752). For Trapp, I quote from *Virgil's Aeneis*, translated by Joseph Trapp (2 vols.; London, 1718–1720), and for Ogilby I quote directly from the edition of his Virgil translation that Wordsworth owned, *The Works of Virgil*, translated by John Ogilby (London, 1650), now in the Wordsworth Library, Grasmere. Ogilby's translation lacks line numeration, so references are to page numbers.

Book I

1–2 Arms, and the Man I sing, the first who bore
His course to Latium from the Trojan shore; Pitt, ll. 1–2

4–5 . . . Much toss'd by land and sea
By wrath of Gods, and lasting enmity
Of cruell Juno. . . . Ogilby, pp. 105–106

. . . toss'd on Land, and Sea, Trapp, l. 3

And haughty Juno's unrelenting hate; Dryden, l. 2

And urg'd by Juno's unrelenting rage; Pitt, l. 5

6–7 Much too in War he suffer'd; Trapp, l. 5

abodes / gods Pitt, ll. 7–8

8–9 . . . whence Latine Originals,
The Alban fathers, and Romes lofty walls. Ogilby, p. 106

From whence the race of Alban fathers come,
And the long glories of majestic Rome. Dryden, ll. 9–10

Whence sprung the Latin Progeny, the Kings
Of Alba, and the walls of Tow'ring Rome. Trapp, ll. 7–8

come / Rome Pitt, ll. 9–10

10–13 Say Muse, what Power was injur'd? on what ground
Heavens Queen, a Prince for Piety renown'd, Ogilby, p. 166

14 Can rage so fierce inflame a heavenly breast? Pitt, l. 16

15–18 Carthage the name, belov'd by Juno more
Than her own Argos, or the Samian shore. Dryden, ll. 23–24

Fronting th'Italian Coast, and Tyber's Mouth,
But far remote, an ancient City stood,
Carthage its Name, a Colony of Tyre, Trapp, ll. 14–16

19–20 By Tyrians held; rich, fierce in War, which place
Juno was said more than all Lands to grace; Ogilby, p. 106

21 Here stood her chariot, . . . Dryden, l. 25; Pitt, l. 23

25–26 But of a race she heard, that should destroy
The Tyrian tow'rs, a race deriv'd from Troy, Pitt, ll. 26–27

27–28 A People ruling wide, and proud in War, Trapp, l. 24

29–30 She ponder'd this, and fear'd it was in fate;
Nor could forget the war she wag'd of late,
For conqering Greece against the Trojan state. Dryden, ll. 33–35

33–34 Besides, long causes working in her mind,
And secret seeds of envy, lay behind. Dryden, ll. 36–37

The late long War, which first she wag'd at Troy,
For her own Argos, . . . Trapp, ll. 27–28

resign'd, / But every cause hung heavy on her mind; Pitt, ll. 34–35

35 The Judgment giv'n by Paris, and th'Affront Trapp, l. 32

37–38 The grace bestow'd on ravish'd Ganimed,
Electra's glories, and her injur'd bed. Dryden, ll. 40–41

41 Reliques of Greeks and sterne Æacides Ogilby, p. 106

She drove the relics of the Grecian war: Pitt, l. 41

44 So vast the Work to raise the Roman State! Trapp, l. 40

53–54 She, for the fault of one offending foe, Dryden, l. 62

For Ajax' Frenzy? For the Guilt of One? Trapp, l. 49

57–63 Him breathing flame, his brest quite thorow struck,
With whirl-winds snatch'd, and on a sharp rock stuck.
But I, Heaven's Queen, Sister and Wife to Jove,
So many years war with one Nation move: Ogilby, p. 107

. . . But I, the Queen
Of Gods, the Sister, and the Wife of Jove,
With This one Race so many Years make War:
And who will Juno's Deity adore
Henceforth? Trapp, ll. 53–58

But I, who move . . . Pitt, l. 64

64–65 Such things revolving, fir'd with discontent,
Shee to the Land of Storms (Æolia) went, Ogilby, p. 107

Such Thoughts revolving in her fiery Breast
Alone, the Goddess to Æolia comes, Trapp, ll. 59–60

67 Where, in a spacious cave of living stone, Dryden, l. 78

. . . Here, in his capacious Cave, Trapp, l. 62

68–69 confines / windes Ogilby, p. 107

With power imperial curbs the struggling winds,
And sounding tempests in dark prisons binds, Dryden, ll. 80–81

binds/ winds Pitt, ll. 72–73

72–73 In a high towr, here sceptred Æolus swayes,
Softens their furie, and their rage allayes; Ogilby, p. 107

74 Which did he not, . . . Dryden, l. 86; Trapp, l. 70

80–81 Then did a King by firm decree ordain,
Who knows to check, or when to give the rein: Ogilby, p. 107

restrain / to loose the rein Pitt, ll. 86–87

86–88 appease / A Race, my foe, now sail the Tyrrhen Seas,
Bearing to Latium conquer'd Gods and Troy: Ogilby, p. 107

A race of wandering slaves abhorr'd by me,
With prosperous passage cut the Thuscan sea: Dryden, ll. 101–102

A Race my Foe steers o'er the Tuscan Sea,
Transporting Ilium, and their vanquish'd Gods
To Italy: Add Fury to thy Winds; Trapp, ll. 81–83

90 Twice seven most beauteous Nymphs on us attend, Ogilby, p. 107

96–97 To this the god—'Tis yours, O queen! to will
The work, which duty binds me to fulfil. Dryden, ll. 112–113

100 You raise me to the Banquets of the Gods; Trapp, l. 95

108–110 Th'whole Ocean vext tumbling vast waves to shore,
Cryes of men follow, shrowds and tackling rore: Ogilby, p. 108

roar / shore Dryden, ll. 126–127; Pitt, ll. 115–116

111–112 Heaven and the day, black night broods on the maine; Ogilby, p. 108

And heaven itself is ravish'd from their eyes! Dryden, l. 130

. . . By sudden Clouds the Heav'ns and Day
Are ravish'd from the Trojans' Eyes; Dun Night Trapp, ll. 105–106

115 And all things menace quick destruction. Ogilby, p. 108

And ev'ry Object threatens present Death. Trapp, l. 109

116–120 Then said, Most happy you, whose funerals
Your Parents saw under the Trojan walls. Ogilby, p. 108

Who chanc'd to die beneath Troy's lofty Walls,
Before their Parents' Eyes! O Diomede, Trapp, ll. 113–114

. . . the Trojan hero stands,
He groans, and spreads to heaven his lifted hands.
Thrice happy those! whose fate it was to fall
(Exclaims the chief) beneath the Trojan wall. Pitt, ll. 124–127

124–128 Why lost I not this life by that hand, where
Hector the stout fell by Achilles Spear?
Where great Sarpedon, where so many bold
Heroes, Shields, Helmets in Symois Streams are roll'd. Ogilby, p. 108

Where Hector fell by fierce Achilles' spear,
And great Sarpedon, the renown'd in war;
. . . slain / . . . main Pitt, ll. 134–137

129–132 rise / skies Ogilby, p. 108

Thus while the pious prince his fate bewails,
Fierce Boreas drove against his flying sails,
And rent the sheets: the raging billows rise,
And mount the tossing vessel to the skies: Dryden, ll. 146–149

prevails / sails Pitt, ll. 138–139

139–143 By South-winds drove on hidden Rocks three came,
Rocks far from shore Italians altars name, Ogilby, p. 109

145–146 Bilg'd them in Banks, and stuck in Beds of Sand.
One, true Orontes bore, and Lycian bands, Ogilby, p. 109

Dash'd on the shallows of the moving sand,
And in mid ocean left them moor'd a-land. Dryden, ll. 160–161

. . . inclos'd with Banks of Sand. Trapp, l. 134

land / sand Pitt, ll. 152–153

151–152 Pitch'd on his head: but she thrice hurried round,
With a swift eddie in the Ocean drown'd. Ogilby, p. 109

round / Sunk, in the whirling gulf devour'd and drown'd. Pitt, ll. 159–160

155 With arms of men, oars, planks, and Trojan goods. Ogilby, p. 109

Men, Arms, and Planks, and Trojan Wealth appear. Trapp, l. 141

160–161 At gaping Chinks admit the hostile Flood. Trapp, l. 146

166–169 Serene in majesty, then roll'd his eyes
Around this space of earth, and seas, and skies.
He saw the Trojan fleet dispers'd, distress'd
By stormy winds and wintry heaven oppress'd. Dryden, ll. 180–183

180 Whom I—but first 'tis fit we should compose
The trouble Ocean: Trapp, ll. 160–161

Whom I—but first I'll calm the waves again. Pitt, l. 185

183–184 Are mine, not his; by fatal lot to me
The liquid empire fell, and trident of the sea. Dryden, ll. 197–198

187–188 With hoarse commands his breathing subjects call,
And boast and bluster in his empty hall. Dryden, ll. 201–202

195–197 Opening vast Syrts, he calms the raging tides,
And with light wheels over the surface glides. Ogilby, p. 110

Then heaves them off the shoals: where e're he guides
His finny coursers, and in triumph rides,
The waves unruffle, and the sea subsides. Dryden, ll. 210–212

And with light Wheels o'er the smooth Surface rides. Trapp, l. 176

Then mounted on his radiant car he rides,
And wheels along the level of the tides. Pitt, ll. 200–201

200–205 mutinie / flye . . . / All silent listning stand; . . . Ogilby, p. 110

And stones and brands in rattling vollies fly,
And all the rustic arms that fury can supply; Dryden, ll. 215–216

Now Stones and Firebrands fly; Rage Arms supplys:
If chance they then espy a Sage, rever'd
For Piety, and Worth; All silent stand,
List'ning with Ears attentive: . . . Trapp, ll. 179–182

Of stones and brands, a mingled tempest flies,
With all the sudden arms that rage supplies: Pitt, ll. 204–205

214–216 glide. / There was a place, far in, an Isle whose side Ogilby, p. 110

And forms a port secure for ships to ride,
Broke by the jutting land on either side:
In double streams the briny waters glide. Dryden, ll. 230–232

Far in a deep recess, her jutting sides
An isle projects, to break the rolling tides, Pitt, ll. 216–217

223–226 . . . a trembling wood displaid
Above, and darke groves gave a horrid shade.
A cave was opposite with rocks o're-growne,
Within sweet springs, and seats of living stone, Ogilby, p. 110

Within, fresh Springs, and Seats of living Stone, Trapp, l. 199

Where polish'd seats appear of living stone, Pitt, ll. 227–228

229–230 The Dardan hero brings to this retreat
Sev'n shatter'd ships, the relics of his fleet. Pitt, ll. 231–232

231–232 land / sand Ogilby, p. 111

With fierce desire to gain the friendly strand,
The Trojans leap in rapture to the land,
And, drench'd in brine, lie stretch'd along the sand. Pitt, ll. 233–235

235–236 Short flame succeeds a bed of wither'd leaves
The dying sparkles in their fall receives: Dryden, ll. 247–248

237–238 preys/ mounts into a blaze Pitt, ll. 238–239

243–244 Mean-while Æneas climbs a Rock, and all
The Prospect o'er the spacious Main commands; Trapp, ll. 213–214

249–250 No sail in view; Three Stags upon the Shore Trapp, l. 218

253–258 He stands, but snatch'd the Bow and Shafts before,
Which for his Prince faithfull Achates bore;
And first, their Leaders, as they nearer drew;
Their tall Heads crown'd with branching Crests, he slew;
Then picks the Vulgar out, untill he drove
The rest, for safety, to the shelt'ring Grove; Ogilby, p. 173

And Bow, the Weapons which Achates bore;
And first the Leaders, bearing high their Heads
With branching Horns, upon the Ground extends.
The Vulgar next . . . Trapp, ll. 222–225

264–265 In Sicily, and gave his parting guests;
The Prince divides, and cheers their troubled brests. Ogilby, p. 111

feast, / Which kind Acestes gave his parting guest, Pitt, ll. 262–263

280–281 Endure the hardships of your present state,
Live, and reserve your selves for better fate. Dryden, ll. 289–290

Endure; reserve yourselves for better Fate. Trapp, l. 245

With manly patience bear your present state,
And with firm courage wait a better fate. Pitt, ll. 278–279

284–286 This said, with weighty cares opprest, he feigns
Hope in his face, within deep griefe restraines.
They take the quarrie and prepare the feast; Ogilby, p. 112

287 Flea off the Skins, and lay the Entrails bare: Trapp, l. 250

288–291 Some from the body strip the smoking hide,
Some cut in morsels, and the parts divide;
These bid, with busy care, the flames aspire;
Those roast the limbs, yet quiv'ring, o'er the fire. Pitt, ll. 284–287

295–299 Their Hunger now appeas'd, with long Discourse
Next for their lost Companions they enquire;

Doubtful 'twixt Hope and Fear, if yet they liv'd,
Or bore the last Extremes, . . . Trapp, ll. 256–259

. . . and quaff the gen'rous wine. Pitt, l. 291

311–312 To him, revolving in his breast such cares,
Sad, having drown'd her sparkling eyes in tears Ogilby, p. 112

To Him, such Cares revolving in his Breast,
Sad Venus, her bright Eyes all drown'd in Tears, Trapp, ll. 270–271

. . . the mournful queen of love appears;
Her starry eyes were dimm'd with streaming tears; Pitt, ll. 304–305

313–315 Spake Venus; Thou, who by eternal Law
Rul'st men and Gods, and dost with thunder awe, Ogilby, p. 112

eternal sway / obey Pitt, ll. 308–309

319–320 Still, for the sake of Italy, deny'd
All other regions, all the world beside? Pitt, ll. 312–313

323 From Teucer's Blood restor'd; . . . Trapp, l. 281

326 . . . and ballanc'd Fates with Fates. Trapp, l. 285

329–330 Pierce the Illyrick Straights, . . . Ogilby, p. 113

Antenor, from the midst of Grecian hosts,
Could pass secure, and pierce the Illyrian coasts: Dryden, ll. 332–333

335–337 Yet here at length he did Patavium frame,
Built Trojan seats, and gave to them a name; Ogilby, p. 113

name / fame Dryden, ll. 338–339

Yet with his colonies, secure he came,
Rais'd Padua's walls, and gave the realms a name,
Then fix'd his Trojan arms; . . . Pitt, ll. 329–331

339 But we, your progeny, . . . Pitt, l. 333

340–341 Are banish'd earth, and for the wrath of one, Dryden, l. 342

. . . for the Spight of One,
(Unworthy Treatment!) are betray'd and driv'n
Far from th'Italian Coasts. Trapp, ll. 299–301

our vessels lost / the promis'd coast Pitt, ll. 335–336

347–353 Fear not, my Cytherea, Fates Decree
For thine stand fix'd; thou promis'd walls shalt see
Of strong Lavinium, and with high Stars range
Great soul'd Æneas; my Decrees not change. Ogilby, p. 113

Thou shalt behold thy wish'd Lavinian walls, Dryden, l. 352

. . . Nor is my Purpose chang'd. Trapp, l. 310

Your eyes Lavinium's promis'd walls shall see,

And here we ratify our first decree. Pitt, ll. 345–346

356–357 He shall great wars in Latium wage, subject
Proud Nations, Laws impose, and walls erect; Ogilby, p. 113

In Italy shall wage successful war;
Shall tame fierce nations . . . Dryden, ll. 359–360

360–364 But young Ascanius, now Iulus, late
Call'd Ilus, whil'st great Ilium held her State,
Shall reign full thirty yeers, with months complete,
And from Lavinium shall transfer his seat; Ogilby, p. 113

Now called Iulus, shall begin his reign. Dryden, l. 365

But young Ascanius, now Iülus call'd,
(Ilus he was, when Ilium's Empire stood) Trapp, ll. 318–319

(Now call'd Iülus, . . .
While thirty rolling years their orbs complete, / . . . seat Pitt, ll. 359–361

366–367 Here full three hundred Years th'Hectorean Race Trapp, l. 323

368–369 Till Ilia, Queen and Priests shall bring forth,
Pregnant by Mars, at once a double birth. Ogilby, p. 114

373–376 And, from Himself, the Name of Romans give.
To These I fix no Bounds of Place, or Time,
But endless Empire grant: Ev'n She, who now Trapp, ll. 330–332

378–381 The Romans, Lords of all, and the gown'd Race. Ogilby, p. 114

At length aton'd, her friendly power shall join,
To cherish and advance the Trojan line.
The subject world shall Rome's dominion own,
And, prostrate, shall adore the nation of the gown. Dryden, ll. 382–385

Rome's lordly Sons, the Nation of the Gown.
So 'tis decreed: An Age in circling Months Trapp, ll. 336–337

own / crown / The world's majestic lords, the nation of the gown.
Pitt, ll. 375–377

382–384 Assaracus House shall make the high Micene
And Phthia tame, and o're proud Argos reign. Ogilby, p. 114

In Greece, Assaracus, his sons shall reign,
And vanquish'd Argos wear the victor's chain. Pitt, ll. 380–381

385–389 Then Trojan Cæsar springs of a fair Strain,
With Seas to bound his power, with Stars his fame,
Julius, from great Julus comes that name. Ogilby, p. 114

Then Cæsar from the Julian stock shall rise,
Whose empire ocean, and whose fame the skies,
Alone shall bound; . . . Dryden, ll. 390–392

Cæsar from Troy's illustrious Blood shall rise;
The Sea shall bound his Empire, Heav'n his Fame:
Julius! a name from great Iülus sprung! Trapp, ll. 341–343

406–407 To Trojan guests; lest, ignorant of fate,
The queen might force them from her town and state: Dryden, ll. 410–411

408–409 On fanning wings, and straight touch'd Lybia's shores; /. . . Moors
Ogilby, p. 114

412–413 inclin'd / mind Pitt, ll. 408–409

414–417 But many cares that night the Prince revolves,
And with the dawn to search strange coasts resolves,
On what shores driven by winds, by whom possest,
(For lands he saw untill'd) if man, or beast Ogilby, p. 115

422–423 Lo, in the deep recesses of the wood,
Before his eyes his goddess mother stood: Dryden, ll. 433–434

pursu'd / wood Pitt, ll. 420–421

430–431 out-go / bow Ogilby, p. 115

437–438 With quivers girt, they spotted Linx-skins wear,
Or chasing of the foaming Boar did hear: Ogilby, p. 115

And urging in loud Chace a foaming Boar. Trapp, l. 388

pace / Urge with full cries the foaming boar in chase? Pitt, ll. 434–435

439–440 Thus Venus said. Then Venus son reply'd,
None of thy Sisters we nor heard, or spy'd: Ogilby, p. 115

None of your sisters have we heard or seen, Dryden, l. 450;

None of your Sisters has been seen, or heard Trapp, l. 390

451–456 . . by this hand shall
Before thy altars many offerings fall. Ogilby, p. 115

But tell a stranger, long in tempests toss'd,
What earth we tread, and who commands the coast?
Then on your name shall wretched mortals call,
And offer'd victims at your altars fall.
I dare not, she reply'd, assume the name
Of goddess, or celestial honours claim: Dryden, ll. 457–462

Our Victims shall before your Altars fall. Trapp, l. 399

461–462 appear / terrible in war Pitt, ll. 453–454
463 Dido reigns here, . . . Ogilby, p. 116

465 Great were her wrongs, . . . Dryden, l. 471

471–472 fill'd the throne / alone Pitt, ll. 463–464

474–476 He blinde with love of gold, Sychæus too
Secure, in secret at the Altar slew: Ogilby, p. 116

481–482 But in a Dream, with Visage wondr'ous pale, Trapp, l. 423

487 Those who did hate or fear the Tyrant, meet, Ogilby, p. 116

They meet, and all combine to leave the state,
Who hate the tyrant, or who fear his hate. Dryden, l. 497–498

490 . . . a woman leads the way. Dryden, l. 502

491–492 At last they landed, where from far your eyes
May view the turrets of new Carthage rise: Dryden, ll. 505–506

. . . At last they hither came,
Where now Those strong and stately Walls you'll see,
And the high Turrets of new Carthage rise. Trapp, ll. 436–438

They came, where now you see new Carthage rise,
And yon proud citadel invade the skies. Pitt, ll. 488–489

493–495 Call'd Byrsa from the bargain, so much ground
Bought as a Buls hide might encompasse't round.
But who are you? whence come? or whither go? Ogilby, p. 116

The wand'ring exiles bought a space of ground
Which one bull-hide enclos'd and compass'd round; Pitt, ll. 490–491

At length inform me, Who, and Whence you are,
And Whither bound. Trapp, ll. 442–443

498–500 And would you hear the annals of our woes,
Vesper would first day in Olympus close. Ogilby, p. 117

The golden sun would sink, and ev'ning close,
Before my tongue could tell you half our woes. Pitt, ll. 498–499

501–502 We from old Troy (by chance if to your eare
Troys name hath come) through divers Seas did steer; Ogilby, p. 117

From ancient Troy, by force expell'd, we came,
If you by chance have heard the Trojan name:
On various seas, by various tempests tost, Dryden, ll. 517–519

We from old Troy, if haply such a Name
Has reach'd your Ears, thro' various Seas are toss'd, Trapp, ll. 449–450

From ancient Troy (if e'er you heard the name)
Through various seas; . . . Pitt, ll. 501–502

505–506 My household gods, companions of my woes,
With pious care I rescued from our foes; Dryden, ll. 523–524
I am the good Æneas, known by Fame
Above the Heav'ns; who rescu'd from the Foe, Trapp, ll. 452–453

511–512 I twice ten ships launch'd to the Phrygian Sea: Ogilby, p. 117

517–518 At once from Europe, and from Asia barr'd. Trapp, l. 461

Myself, from Europe and from Asia cast,
A helpless stranger, rove the Libyan waste. Pitt, ll. 514–515

531–533 . . . now earth in a long train
They seem to take, or taken to disdain; Ogilby, p. 117

538–544 . . . But proceed,
And, as That Path directs, pursue your Way.
She said; And, as she turn'd, her rosy Neck
Shone bright; Her Hair a Fragrancy divine
Ambrosial breath'd; . . . Trapp, ll. 480–484

And breath'd ambrosial scents around her head. Pitt, l. 537

547–548 The prince pursu'd the parting deity,
With words like these: Ah! whither dost thou fly? Dryden, ll. 562–563

Pursu'd her, as she fled: . . . Trapp, l. 487

coy disguise, / He thus pursues his mother as she flies. Pitt, ll. 540–541

551–552 Ah! cruel? Why is it deny'd to join / Our Hands, . . . Trapp, ll. 489–490

555 But Venus, as they went, around them threw Trapp, l. 492

561–563 Where garlands ever green, and ever fair,
With vows are offer'd, and with solemn prayer, Dryden, ll. 576–577

564–565 brow / below Pitt, ll. 556–567

565–567 Now they ascend a hill, which much the town
Oretops, and looks on adverse Bulwarks down. Ogilby, p. 118

down / town Dryden, ll. 580–581

581 High Ornaments to grace the future Scene. Ogilby, p. 183

The stately Ornaments of future Scenes. Trapp, l. 513

587–590 And with the purest Nectar stretch the Hive,
Or ease the laden, or imbattld drive
The Drones, a slothful cattel, from the Cels. Ogilby, p. 118

All, with united force, combine to drive
The lazy drones from the laborious hive; Dryden, ll. 606–607

Warm at the fragrant work, in bands they drive
The drone, a lazy robber, from the hive. Pitt, ll. 582–583

593–595 Blest men whose wals now rise, Æneas said, Ogilby, p. 118

Thrice happy you, whose walls already rise:
Æneas said; and view'd, with lifted eyes, Dryden, ll. 610–611

The prince surveys the lofty tow'rs, and cries,
Blest, blest are you, whose walls already rise: Pitt, ll. 584–585

596–597 Then, strange to tell, he mingled with the crowds, Pitt, l. 586

And mingling with the Croud is seen by None. Trapp, l. 526

598–599 Amid the town, a stately grove display'd
A cooling shelter, and delightful shade. Pitt, ll. 588–589

600–601 ground / found Dryden, ll. 618–619

found / ground   Pitt, ll. 590–591

602–603 drew / foreshew   Dryden, ll. 620–621

610–613 Brasse Portal mount, with steps, and beams of brasse,
And the joyn'd hunges rung with brazen Gates.   Ogilby, p. 119

614–615 What first Æneas in this place beheld,
Reviv'd his courage, and his fear expell'd.   Dryden, ll. 632–633

618 For whil'st, attending on the Queen, he staid   Ogilby, p. 183

For while, expecting there the queen, he rais'd   Dryden, l. 634

620–622 The artists emulous hand, and works so rare,   Ogilby, p. 119

While he the town admires, and wond'ring stands
At the rich labours of the artist's hands;   Pitt, ll. 606–607

625–626 Atrides, Priam, and severe to Both / Achilles.   Trapp, ll. 547–548

There Priam stood, and Agamemnon here,
And Pelus' wrathful son, to both severe.   Pitt, ll. 612–613

629–630 What Region now abounds not with our Woes?   Trapp, l. 550

636 And with an empty Picture fed his mind.   Dryden, l. 652

And with an empty Picture fed his Soul,   Trapp, l. 555

642–644 Neere this he Rhesus snowie tents survaid
Weeping, his men in their first sleep betraid,   Ogilby, p. 119

Which, in the first Repose by Night betray'd,   Trapp, l. 563

645–647 And to his campe the fiery horses hasts,   Ogilby, p. 119

Then took the fiery steeds, ere yet the food
Of Troy they taste, or drink the Xanthian flood.   Dryden, ll. 661–662

Who drove his coursers from the scene of blood,
E'er the fierce steeds had tasted Trojan food,
Or drank divine Scamander's fatal flood.   Pitt, ll. 634–636

648–649 defy'd / try'd   Dryden, ll. 663–664

650–657 Holding the reins, earth soyls his neck and hair,
Scribling the dust with his inverted spear.   Ogilby, p. 120

Unequally with great Achilles match'd:
He to the empty Chariot clings supine,
Yet holds the Reins; His Head along the Ground
Is dragg'd: The Spear inverted scrawls the Dust.
Mean-while to unappeas'd Minerva's Fane . . .   Trapp, ll. 569–573

Still, though in death, he grasps the flowing reins,
His startled coursers whirl him o'er the plains: Pitt, ll. 641–642

660–661 Beating their breasts, sad in the humblest guise:

But th'angry Goddesse fix'd on earth her eyes. Ogilby, p. 120

664–665 gold / sold Dryden, ll. 678–679

sold / gold Pitt, ll. 653–654

667 And Priam stretching out his suppliant Hands. Trapp, l. 581

671 . . . moony Shields / Penthesilea leads, . . . Trapp, ll. 584–585

674–675 Amidst the thickest bands she chargeth then,
And the bold virgin dares encounter men. Ogilby, p. 120

And, tho' a Virgin, dares engage with Men. Trapp, l. 588

676–677 Thus, while the Trojan hero stood amaz'd,
And, fix'd in wonder, on the picture gaz'd, Pitt, ll. 669–670

681–682 height / sight Dryden, ll. 699–700

693–694 gate / sate Pitt, ll. 681–682

709–710 With cries, the royal favour to implore,
They came, a train selected, from the shore: Pitt, ll. 697–698

713–714 request / rest Dryden, ll. 729–730

715 . . . O Queen, whom Jove impow'rs to build Trapp, l. 622

717–718 restrain / reign Dryden, ll. 737–738

730–731 B'Ænotrians til'd; Posteritie they fame
Since call'd it Italie, from their Princes name. Ogilby, p. 121

Th' Oenotrians held it once, by common fame,
Now call'd Italia, from the leader's name. Dryden, ll. 750–751

(For martial deeds and fruits, renown'd by fame)
But since Italia, from the leader's name; Pitt, ll. 717–718

736 What Race of Men / Is This? Trapp, ll. 644–645

751–757 strain / reign Pitt, ll. 742–743

753–754 Permit our ships a shelter on your shores,
Refitted from your woods with planks and oars; Dryden, ll. 776–777

Permit us, from your woods, new planks and oars
To fell, and bring our vessels on your shores; Pitt, ll. 744–745

760 . . . and swallow'd in the Lybian sea, Pitt, l. 749

767–768 Dido with downcast looks in brief replies,
Trojans, dismiss your Doubts, seclude your Cares: Trapp, ll. 672–673

774 Not so obtuse are our Phoenician Breasts; Trapp, l. 679

784 Trojan, and Tyrian shall from me receive Trapp, l. 687

789–790 abodes, / He roams the towns, or wanders thro' the woods. Pitt, ll. 779–780

797–799 All safe you see; your friends and fleet restor'd;
On (whom we saw) the whirling gulf devour'd. Pitt, ll. 785–786

799–803 Scarce had he spoken, when the cloud gave way,
The mists flew upward, and dissolv'd in day. Dryden, ll. 822–823

. . . The rest confirms your Mother's Words.
He scarce had spoke; When strait the ambient Cloud
Dissolves itself, . . . Trapp, ll. 700–702

811 He whom you seek am I: by tempests tost, Dryden, l. 834

816 Her sons, the relics of the Grecian war; Pitt, l. 806

823–824 The Gods (if there by any Providence
Or Justice will the pious recompence) Ogilby, p. 123

825 And your own Mind self-conscious of the Right, Trapp, l. 724

827–828 . . . O! what age of worth,
What so great Parents, such as thee brought forth? Ogilby, p. 124

In you this age is happy, and this earth:
And parents more than mortal gave you birth. Dryden, ll. 852–853

831–833 Your honour, name, and praise, shall never die. Dryden, l. 857

. . . while Ether feeds the Stars;
Your Honour, Name, and Praise shall ever live; Trapp, ll. 729–730

While ether shines, with golden planets grac'd,
So long your honour, name, and praise shall last: Pitt, ll. 819–820

833–835 Thy honour, name, and fame, shall last, what Land
So-ever me invites. Then his right hand
Ilioneus takes, . . . Ogilby, p. 124

843–844 The same Æneas, whom fair Venus bore
To fam'd Anchises on th'Idean shore? Dryden, ll. 874–875

849–850 restor'd / sword Dryden, ll. 878–879

851–852 Already from That Time I know the Fate
Of Troy, your Name, and all the Grecian Kings. Trapp, ll. 746–747

859–860 At last compell'd me on these Shores to rest,
Taught by my Woes, to succour the distrest. Ogilby, p. 189

For I my self, like you, have been distress'd;
Till heaven afforded me this place of rest. Dryden, ll. 888–889

To pity and to succour the Distress'd. Trapp, l. 755

864–871 Next, to the shores twenty fat Beeves she sends,
With them a hundred Swine to feast his friends;
And with the Ews as many fatned Lambs, Ogilby, p. 124

Nor yet less careful for her absent friends,
Twice ten fat oxen to the ships she sends: Dryden, ll. 894–895

. . . twenty Bulls she sends;
An hundred bristly Boars with spacious Chines;
An hundred fatted Lambs; with Ewes; and Wine,
Gift of the jolly God. Trapp, ll. 759–762

Twice fifty bleating lambs and ewes she sends,
And twice ten brawny oxen to his friends:
A hundred bristly boars, and monstrous swine;
With Bacchus' gifts, a store of generous wine.
The inner rooms in regal pomp display'd,
The splendid feasts in ample halls are made; Pitt, ll. 853–858

875–877 infold / Huge silver tables, where ingrave'd in gold Ogilby, p. 125

mould / old / gold. Pitt, ll. 861–863

879 From the first Founder of the Royal Race. Trapp, l. 770

886–889 And, fraught with precious gifts, to bring the boy
Snatch'd from the ruins of unhappy Troy:
A robe of tissue, stiff with golden wire;
An upper vest, . . . Dryden, ll. 913–916

892–898 The Scepter too which once Ilion bore,
Priam's first Daughter, the Pearl-chain she wore, Ogilby, p. 125

And unpermitted Hymenéal Rites,
She brought, her Mother Leda's wond'rous Gift:
A Sceptre too, which once Ilione,
The eldest Daughter of King Priam, bore: Trapp, ll. 781–784

899–900 To bring the splendid gifts, without delay,
Swift to the fleet, Achates bends his way. Pitt, ll. 882–883

903–904 That Cupid should assume the shape and face
Of sweet Ascanius, and the sprightly grace: Dryden, ll. 929–930

907–908 For much she fear'd the Tyrians, double tongued,
And knew the town to Juno's care belong'd. Dryden, ll. 933–934

911 My Son, my strength, whose mighty power alone Dryden, ll. 936
My Son, my Strength, my mighty Pow'r alone; Trapp, l. 796

919–920 Him Dido courts, and stayes with blandishments. Ogilby, p. 125

And often hast thou mourn'd with me his pains;
Him Dido now with blandishment detains: Dryden, ll. 943–944

Him now Phoenician Dido entertains,
And soothes with Speeches bland; Trapp, ll. 802–803

detains / plains Pitt, ll. 902–903

921 Junonian entertainments Ogilby, p. 126

929–933 Brings gifts preserv'd from Troyes flame and the deep.

In high Cytherum him I'll cast asleep, Ogilby, p. 126

I mean to plunge the boy in pleasing sleep,
And, ravish'd, in Idalian bowers to keep? Dryden, ll. 954–955

steep / sleep Pitt, ll. 916–917

936–937 Assume his form only one nights short space;
Use art, a boy put on a boyes known face, Ogilby, p. 126

Take thou his form and shape. I beg the grace
But only for a night's revolving space;
Thy self a boy, assume a boy's dissembled face. Dryden, ll. 958–960

942–943 inspire / fire Pitt, ll. 924–925

944–945 He walks Iülus in his mother's sight;
And in the sweet resemblance takes delight. Dryden, ll. 967–968

950–952 And in soft Marjerom the boy she layd,
Whose flowres imbrac'd him with a pleasant shade. Ogilby, p. 126

Where blooming Jessamine around him breathes
With Flow'rs, in fragrant Shade. Trapp, ll. 829–830

There on a flow'ry bed her charge she laid,
And, breathing round him, rose the fragrant shade. Pitt, ll. 934–935

958–963 The servants water bring and serv'd up bread
In chargers; some neat-fringed towels spread,
And fifty Dames to serve the bill of fare,
Had charge within, and Incense to prepare, Ogilby, p. 126

They wash; the menial train the tables spread;
And heap in glitt'ring canisters the bread. Pitt, ll. 944–945

972–973 All on the Trojan gifts with wonder gaze;
But view the beauteous boy with more amaze! Dryden, ll. 990–991

976–977 Nor pass unprais'd the vest and veil divine,
Which wandering foliage and rich flowers entwine. Dryden, ll. 994–995

978–979 Chiefly th'unhappy Queen, to future Rage / Devoted, Trapp, ll. 852–853

982–983 When he about Æneas Neck had hung,
And serv'd great love of a feign'd Father long, Ogilby, p. 193

The guileful god, about the hero long,
With children's play, and false embraces, hung;
Then sought the queen: . . . Dryden, ll. 1000–1002

984–989 Goes to the Queen: She fixes all her Sight,
And Soul upon him; sometimes on her Lap
Fonds him; nor thinks how great a God she bears.
He, mindful of his Mother, by Degrees Trapp, ll. 858–861

988–995 but Cupid is / Mindfull of Venus, blotting by degrees
Sychæus out, and tries with lively love
Fixed thoughts, and resolutions to remove. Ogilby, p. 127

994–1001 Now, when the rage of hunger was appeas'd,
The meat remov'd, and every guest was pleas'd,
The golden bowls with sparkling wine are crown'd,
And through the palace cheerful cries resound,
From gilded roofs depending lamps display Dryden, ll. 1011–1015

Large massy Bowls they place, and crown the Wine. Trapp, l. 866

bounds / resounds Pitt, ll. 973–974

1004–1005 A Golden Bowl, whose sparkling Jems did shine,
The Queen commands to fill with richest Wine, Ogilby, p. 194

Now Dido crowns the bowl of state with wine,
The bowl of Belus, and the regal line. Pitt, ll. 977–978

1008–1009 joy / Troy Pitt, ll. 985–986

1010–1012 Thou, Bacchus, god of joys and friendly cheer,
And gracious Juno, both be present here: Dryden, ll. 1026–1027

1023 The wand'ring Moon, the Labours of the Sun; Trapp, l. 889

1028 Why Suns, in Winter, . . . Trapp, l. 893

1033–1035 And drank large draughts of love with vast delight.
Of Priam much inquir'd, of Hector more;
Then ask'd what arms the swarthy Memnon wore; Dryden, ll. 1050–1052

Of Priam much, of Hector much enquires: Trapp, l. 899

1037–1038 My guest from first original relate
Greeks trecheries (she said) and your own fate, Ogilby, p. 128

my godlike guest, relate / Ilion's fate Pitt, ll. 1021–1022

Book II

1 All gaz'd in silence, . . . Pitt, l. 1
2 When, from his lofty couch, he thus began: Dryden, l. 2

3–4 . . . is to renew / Unutterrable woes; Trapp, ll. 3–4

Ah mighty queen! you urge me to disclose,
And feel, once more, unutterable woes; Pitt, ll. 3–4

9–16 Which of the Dolops, Myrmidons, or fierce
Ulysses souldier, such things to rehearse
Could tears refrain? And now the dewie night
Is almost spent; rest setting Stars invite;
But if that you desire our chance to know,
And brief would hear Troys finall overthrow: Ogilby, pp. 129–130

And now the latter watch of wasting night,
And setting stars, to kindly rest invite.
But, since you take such interest in our woe,
And Troy's disastrous end desire to know, Dryden, ll. 11–14

Of dire Ulysses, could refrain from Tears?
And now the dewy Night is hast'ning swift
From Heaven; and setting Stars persuade to Sleep.
But if you have such strong Desire to learn Trapp, ll. 9–12

. . . but since you long to know,
And curious listen to the story'd woe; Pitt, ll. 13–16

22–24 A horse frame like a mountain, by divine
Minerva's art, the sides with wrought firre joyne. Ogilby, p. 130

. . . an Horse erect
Of Mountain-Bulk, by Pallas' Art divine, Trapp, ll. 18–19

25–26 gain / main Pitt, ll. 21–22

27–28 Thus they pretend; but in the hollow side,
Selected numbers of their soldiers hide; Dryden, ll. 23–24

hides / sides Pitt, ll. 23–24

31–34 In sight lay Tenedos, the Ile well knowne
By fame, and rich whilst Priam held the Crowne,
Now but a bay, to Ships a faithlesse rode. Ogilby, p. 130

Renown'd for wealth; but since a faithless bay,
Where ships expos'd to wind and weather lay. Dryden, ll. 29–30

In Sight lies Tenedos, an Isle renown'd
By Fame, and rich, while Priam's Kingdom stood;
Now but a Bay, and faithless Port for Ships. Trapp, ll. 25–27

An isle, in antient times renown'd by fame,
Lies in full view, and Tenedos the name?
Once blest with wealth, while Priam held the sway,
But now a broken, rough, and dang'rous bay: Pitt, ll. 27–30

37–38 . . . transported Troy
Forgot her woes, and gave a loose to joy; Pitt, ll. 33–34

40 The Posts abandon'd, and forsaken Shore. Trapp, l. 34

55–56 The giddy vulgar, as their fancies guide,
With noise say nothing, and in parts divide. Dryden, ll. 50–51

. . . The fickle Multitude
Vote Contradictions, and in Parts divide. Trapp, ll. 46–47

65–66 town / down Dryden, ll. 60–61

67 . . . Whate'er it be, I dread the Greeks, Trapp, l. 58

71–72 He whirl'd the mighty Spear: That quiv'ring stood; Trapp, l. 62

76–77 He had Argolick dens with steele constrain'd:
Now Troy had stood, and Priams high Towers remain'd. Ogilby, p. 131

. . . Thou, Troy, hadst Now
Been standing; and great Priam's Tow'rs entire. Trapp, ll. 67—68

78–81 Behold! mean while the Dardan Shepherds bring
One bound with mighty clamours to the King. Ogilby, p. 131

Mean time, with shouts, the Trojan shepherds bring
A captive Greek in bands, before the king: Dryden, ll. 76–77

92–93 Woe's me, he said, what Land or Sea is free?
What Refuge now remains for wretched me? Ogilby, p. 200

Then said, Alas! what earth remains, what sea
Is open to receive unhappy me! Dryden, ll. 87–88

98 All Fury ceas'd: We urge him to declare Trapp, l. 88

102–105 All truths what ere, to thee great King will I
Confesse, nor that I am a Greeke deny; Ogilby, p. 132

108–109 If you have heard of Palamedes name,
From Belus sprung, his glory great by fame, Ogilby, p. 132

If any chance has hither brought the name
Of Palamedes, not unknown to fame, Dryden, ll. 103–104

You know, perchance, great Palamedes' name,
Through many a distant realm renown'd by fame; Pitt, ll. 104–105

110–113 Condemn'd, tho' guiltless, when he mov'd for peace,
Condemn'd for treason by the voice of Greece.
Though false the charge, the glorious hero bled,
But now the Greeks deplore the warrior dead. Pitt, ll. 106–109

124 I drag'd my days in darkness and despair, Pitt, l. 119

134–135 Scatters ambiguous Rumours thro' the Croud, Trapp, l. 117

For conscious of his guilt, my death he vow'd,

And with dark hints amus'd the list'ning crowd. Pitt, ll. 128–129

138–141 Why triviall things recount I thus in vain?
Wherefore delay? if all the Grecian strain
You in one list esteem, . . . Ogilby, p. 132

144–146 . . . this Ulysses would,
This with much treasure would Atrides buy. / . . . why Ogilby, p. 132

148–151 His former trembling once again renew'd,
With acted fear, the villian thus pursu'd;
Long had the Grecians (tir'd with fruitless care,
And weary'd with an unsuccessful war) Dryden, ll. 146–149

159–160 We sent Eurypilus to Phoebus' shrine,
Who brought the sentence from the voice divine; Pitt, ll. 148–149

163–164 flood / blood Pitt, ll. 152–153

169–170 Ulysses then, importunate and loud,
Produc'd sage Calchas to the trembling crowd, Pitt, ll. 158–159

173–174 The artists dire plot many did to me
Foretell, and wisely did th'event foresee. Ogilby, p. 133

175–176 . . . Ten days reserv'd,
And mute he stands; refusing with his Voice
To sentence any, or expose to Death: Trapp, ll. 149–151

179–180 And what Each fear'd would light upon himself,
All on the Ruin of one Wretch devolve. Trapp, ll. 155–156

laid / head Pitt, ll. 168–169

183–184 I grant, I broke my bonds, scap'd death by flight,
And hid with reeds, in a foul lake all night Ogilby, p. 133

189–190 My tender infants, or my careful sire,
Whom they returning will to death require? Dryden, ll. 189–190

199–200 We grant both life, and pity to his tears. Ogilby, p. 134

201–204 False tears true pity move: the king commands
To loose his fetters, and unbind his hands:
Then adds these friendly words; Dismiss thy fears,
Forget the Greeks, . . . Dryden, ll. 197–200

Then Thus in friendly Words; Whoe'er Thou art,
Forget th'abandon'd Greeks; . . . Trapp, ll. 179–180

And, melting first, the good old king commands
To free the captive, and to loose his hands. Pitt, ll. 194–195

211–214 Eternall fires, you powers from violence free,
Altars dire swords I scap'd, my witnesse be, Ogilby, p. 134

You, Ye Eternal Fires, I hear attest,
And your inviolable Deity; Trapp, ll. 188–189
And you divine inviolable flames,

Ye fatal swords and altars, which I fled,
Ye wreaths that circled this devoted head; Pitt, ll. 207–209

219–220 gave / save Dryden, ll. 214–215

223–228 Fatal Palladium from the sacred face
(Ent'ring) they snatch'd, the high tow'rs warders slain, Ogilby, p. 134

But from that execrable point of time,
When Ithacus, the first in ev'ry crime,
With Tydeus' impious son, the guards had slain,
And brought her image from the Phrygian fane, Pitt, ll. 218–221

229–230 Took the bless'd image, and with bloody hand
Rudely the virgin fillets then profan'd; Ogilby, p. 134

hands/ bands Dryden, ll. 222–223; Pitt, ll. 222–223

231 Our ebbing Hopes ran back, our Strength decay'd; Trapp, l. 206

237–238 trembling speare / repaire Ogilby, p. 134

241–242 repair / war Pitt, ll. 242–243

249–250 high / skie Ogilby, p. 135

size / skies Pitt, ll. 248–249

271 Laocoon, Neptune's priest by lot that year Dryden, l. 267

Laocoon, Neptune's Priest by Lot assign'd, Trapp, l. 246

274–275 With Orbs immense, incumbent on the Main Trapp, l. 251

. . . two serpents glide / And roll incumbent . . . Pitt, ll. 276–277

281–282 roar / shore Pitt, ll. 284–285

283–286 (Their glaring Eyes distain'd with Blood, and Fire)
And lick'd their hissing Mouths with quiv'ring Tongues.
Pale at the sight we fly: Trapp, ll. 258–260

. . . we fled in dire dismay;
Strait to Laocoon they direct their way; Pitt, ll. 288–289

292–293 Their scaly Backs twice round his Neck convolv'd: Trapp, l. 268

haste / embrac'd Pitt, ll. 294–295

309–310 All judge Laocoon justly doom'd to bleed,
Whose guilty spear profan'd the sacred steed. Pitt, ll. 309–310

335–340 Mean time the rapid Heavens roll'd down the Light,
And on the shaded ocean rush'd the night: Dryden, ll. 328–329

Mean-while the Hemisphere rolls round, and Night
Swift rushes from the Sea; in dusky Shade
Involving Earth, and Heav'n, and Grecian Frauds.
The Trojans, scatter'd o'er the Walls, lie hush'd

In Silence; . . . Trapp, ll. 306–310

Now had the sun roll'd down the beamy light,
And from the caves of ocean rush'd the night; Pitt, ll. 335–336

357–358 Th'invade the town, buried in sleep and wine; Ogilby, p. 137

T'invade th' town, oppress'd with sleep and wine. Dryden, l. 347

They seize the Town, immers'd in Sleep, and Wine; Trapp, l. 325

361–387 Twas now the Season, when the first Repose,
Sweet Gift of Gods, on weary Mortals creeps:
Lo! in a Dream, before my slumb'ring Eyes
The much afflicted Hector seem'd to stand,
Profuse of Tears; drag'd with the Chariot Wheels,
As heretofore; besmear'd with bloody Dust;
And thro' his swelling Feet transfix'd with Thongs.
Ah me! How was he from That Hector chang'd,
Who once return'd Triumphant in the Spoils
Of great Achilles; or who flung his Fire
Amidst the Grecian Vessels! Foul his Beard;
His Hair all clung, and clotted with his Blood:
And in his Body all the Wounds receiv'd
Before his Native Walls. I first began,
And weeping in These mournful Accents spoke.
O Thou, the Light, and certain Hope of Troy;
How, Hector, hast thou been detain'd? From whence
Com'st thou so long expected? How fatigu'd,
After such various Labours of the State,
And so much Slaughter of thy Countrymen,
Do we behold thee? What unworthy Hand
Has soil'd thy Face serene? Or why Those Wounds? Trapp, ll. 328–349

'Twas now the time when first kind heaven bestows
On wretched man the blessings of repose;
When, in my slumbers, Hector seem'd to rise
A mournful vision! to my closing eyes.
Such he appear'd, as when Achilles' car
And fiery coursers whirl'd him through the war;
Drawn thro' his swelling feet the thongs I view'd,
His beauteous body black with dust and blood.
Ye gods! how chang'd from Hector, who with joy
Return'd in proud Achilles' spoils to Troy;
Flung at the ships, like heav'ns almighty sire,
Flames after flames, and wrapt a fleet in fire.
Now gash'd with wounds that for his Troy he bore,
His beard and locks stood stiffen'd with his gore.
With tears and mournful accents I began,
And thus bespoke the visionary man! Pitt, ll. 359–374

366–369 Drag'd at a chariot, black with bloody dust,
As e'rst, and through his swoln feet reines were thrust, Ogilby, p. 137

Swoln were his feet, as when the thongs were thrust
Thro' the bor'd holes, his body black with dust. Dryden, ll. 356–357

372–375 Squalid his beard, his haire with blood concrete, Ogilby, p. 137

Or him, who made the fainting Greeks retire,
and lanch'd against their navy Phrygian fire.
His head and beard stood stiffen'd with his gore;
And all the wounds, he for his country bore, Dryden, ll. 360–363

379–387 O Dardan light! O Troys chief confidence!
Why such delay? O Hector, from what coast
Com'st thou desir'd? that thee, so many lost,
After such labours, of the town, and men,
Weary we view: what sad chance thy serene
Looks hath defil'd? or why those wounds view I? Ogilby, p. 138

386–387 Why stream these wounds? or who could thus disgrace
The manly charms of that majestic face? Pitt, ll. 381–382

390–395 The foes, already, have possess'd the wall,
Troy nods from high, and totters to her fall. Dryden, ll. 383–384

Fly, Goddess-born, and save thee from These Flames.
The Enemy has gain'd our Walls; and Troy
Is tumbling from it's Height. Enough is done
For Priam and our Country: . . . Trapp, ll. 352–355

the walls / Are won by Greece, and glorious Ilium falls;
Enough to Priam . . . Pitt, ll. 385–387

408–409 Louder, and yet more loud, I hear th' alarms
Of human cries distinct, and clashing arms! Dryden, ll. 401–402

Near, and more near, approach the dire alarms;
The voice of woe, the dreadful din of arms. Pitt, ll. 401–402

412–413 As when rough winds, fire, in standing corn,
Or mountain floods, with a rapt torrent born, Ogilby, p. 138

born / corn Dryden, ll. 406–407

416–419 . . . amaz'd, on lofty rocks,
The shepherd ingorant, receives the sound:
Then truth appear'd, and Grecian treason found. Ogilby, p. 138

And Grecian Faith / Lay plain to View: Trapp, ll. 377–378

Now Hector's warning prov'd too clear and true,
The wiles of Greece appear'd in open view; Pitt, ll. 413–414

422 Ucalegon burns next, the seas are bright Dryden, l. 419

424–425 New clamours, and new clangors now arise,
The sound of trumpets mix'd with fighting cries! Dryden, ll. 421–422

426 Arms with mad Haste I snatch; Trapp, l. 384

430–431 My bosome burns: rage, fury, judgement charms;
And we conceive it brave to die in arms. Ogilby, p. 139

With frenzy seiz'd, I run to meet th' alarms,
Resolv'd on death, resolv'd to die in arms! Dryden, ll. 423–424

Anger and Rage precipitate my Soul,
And glorious 'twas, I thought, to die in Arms. Trapp, 388–389

432–434 Lo! Pantheus, from the Grecian Darts escap'd
Pantheus Otriades, Apollo's Priest,
Bears in his Hands the holy Utensils,
His little Grandson, and his vanquish'd Gods. Trapp, ll. 390–393

432–433 appears / fears Pitt, ll. 427–428

439–441 Trojans we were, Troy was, and the high state
Of Troy hath been: . . . Ogilby, p. 139

And Troy's inevitable Hour is come;
We Trojans have been, Ilium once has been,
And the long Glory of the Dardan Race: Trapp, ll. 398–400

443–447 . . . bold Sinon stirs the flame / Insulting; Ogilby, p. 139

And armed hosts, an unexpected force,
Break from the bowels of the fatal horse! Dryden, ll. 441–442

And Greece now domineers in flaming Troy.
The lofty Steed in the mid City pours
Arm'd Troops; and Sinon Conqu'ror scatters Fire,
Insulting: Others thro' the open'd Gates Trapp, ll. 402–405

454–455 inspires / fires Dryden, ll. 453–454; Pitt, ll. 449–450

456 Where sad Erynnis . . . Ogilby, p. 209

461–466 With young Choroebus, who by love was led
To win renown, and fair Cassandra's bed;
And lately brought his troops to Priam's aid:
Forewarn'd in vain by the prophetic maid. Dryden, ll. 461–464

471–473 . . . those kept this Realms, our Gods
Their altars have forsook, and blest abodes: Ogilby, p. 140

You see our hopeless state; how every god,
Who guarded Troy, has left his old abode; Pitt, ll. 469–470

474–475 conspire / involv'd in fire Dryden, ll. 473–474

You aid a town already sunk in fire;
Fly, fly to arms, and gloriously expire; Pitt, ll. 471–472

480–481 food / blood Dryden, ll. 481–482

. . . while the savage brood,
Stretch'd in the cavern, pant and thirst for blood; Pitt, ll. 479–480

482–483 So we through weapons and th'opposing Foe
To certain Death on resolutely goe; Ogilby, p. 210

484–485 dare / square / despair Dryden, ll. 485–487

486 . . . Who the Horror of That Night,
The Ruins and Confusion can express? Trapp, ll. 442–443

488–489 yeers / appears Ogilby, p. 140

490–491 abodes / the temples of her gods Pitt, ll. 489–490

493–495 The vanquished their courages recall,
And now the Grecian Conquerors do fall: Ogilby, p. 140

. . . Nor do the Trojans bleed
Alone; The Vanquish'd in their Turn resume
Their Courage; and the conqu'ring Grecians fall. Trapp, ll. 448–450

499–500 And first Androgeus whom a train attends,
With style familiar hail'd us as his friends; Pitt, ll. 495–496

502–503 In flames your friends have laid all Ilion waste,
And you come lagging from your ships the last. Pitt, ll. 499–500

506–508 As when some peasant in a bushy brake,
Has, with unwary footing, press'd a snake, Dryden, ll. 510–511

So the pale swain, who treads upon a snake
Unseen, and lurking in the gloomy brake, Pitt, ll. 505–506

510–511 head / fled Ogilby, p. 141

513–515 In vain; for him and his we compass'd round,
Possess'd with fear, unknowing of the ground;
And of their lives an easy conquest found. Dryden, ll. 515–517

Fierce we rush in, the heedless foes surround,
And lay the wretches breathless on the ground: Pitt, ll. 509–510

521–522 Let us change shields, in Grecian armour go;
Who fraud or valour questions in a foe? Ogilby, p. 141

523 Themselves shall give us Arms. Thus having said, Trapp, l. 478

526 And claps an Argive Sword unto his side. Ogilby, p. 211

pride / side Pitt, l. 524

533–535 Some fly to th'Ships, and swift to safe shores bend,
Others with base fear struck, again ascend
The mighty horse, and in the known bulk hide.
Ah, who may hope if by the Gods deni'd! Ogilby, p. 141

538–541 To heaven her bright eyes raising then in vain;
Her yes, for cords her tender hands restrain. Ogilby, p. 141

Whom not Minerva's shrine, nor sacred bands,
In safety could protect from sacrilegious hands: Dryden, ll. 545–546

Throwing in vain her glaring Eyes to Heav'n;
Her Eyes; for Bonds confin'd her tender Hands. Trapp, ll. 496–497

Dragg'd by the shouting victors;—to the skies
She rais'd, but rais'd in vain, her glowing eyes;
Her eyes—she could no more—the Grecian bands
Had rudely manacled her tender hands; Pitt, ll. 539–542

553 The brother-kings with Ajax join their force, Dryden, l. 563

555–556 Thus, when the rival winds their quarrel try,
Contending for the kingdom of the sky, Dryden, ll. 565–566

rise / skies Pitt, ll. 555–556

557–559 Notus, and Zephyrus, and Eurus swift
Exulting with his Eastern Steeds: The Woods
Roar loud; Trapp, ll. 511–513

559–560 The woods resound, and fomie Nereus raves,
And with his Trident stirs up dreadful waves. Ogilby, p. 142

563–565 To them our Argive helms and arms are known,
Our voice and language diff'ring from their own. Pitt, ll. 565–566

568–569 Next Ripheus fell, most faithful to his trust;
Nor in all Troy was known a man more just, Ogilby, p. 142

572–573 attends / friends Dryden, ll. 579–580; Pitt, ll. 571–572

580–583 Witness, ye heavens! I live not by my fault
I strove to have deserv'd the death I sought.
But when I could not fight, and would have dy'd,
Borne off to distance by the growing tide, Dryden, ll. 587–590

Midst flames and foes a glorious death I sought,
And well deserv'd the death for which I fought. Pitt, ll. 577–578

584–585 And Pelias halting by Ulysses' Wound. Trapp, l. 534

ground / wound Pitt, ll. 581–582

588–589 race / space Dryden, ll. 597–598

591 Shield lock'd in shield, . . . Pitt, l. 589

594–595 Shields their left hands protect, oppose defence
'Gainst darts, their right hand seise the battlements. Ogilby, p. 142

ascent / battlement Dryden, ll. 605–606

605–607 A secret portico contriv'd behind,
Great Hector's mansion to the palace join'd, Pitt, ll. 605–606

616–617 descry'd / ride Dryden, ll. 627–628

636–639 With him was Periphas and Automedon,
Achilles Squire and Charioteer comes on;
These seconded by all the Scyrian bands,
Who on the roofes cast fire, and flaming brands. Ogilby, pp. 143–144

642–644 Then hews huge pillars, cleaving knotty oke,
And a large breach with a wide passage broke; Ogilby, p. 144

647–648 guard / heard Ogilby, p. 144

657–661 Gates with his battering Ram are overthrown,

And from their hinges Jaums are tumbled down.
They force their way: the first they meet they kill,
And royall Courts the basest souldiers fill. Ogilby, p. 144

In rush the Greeks, and all th' apartments fill;
Those few defendants whom they find they kill. Dryden, ll. 675–676

. . . The thronging Greeks break in; then kill
The first they meet; Trapp, ll. 608–609

662–663 Not half so fierce the foamy deluge bounds,
And bursts resistless o'er the levell'd mounds; Pitt, ll. 660–661

667–668 Sad they beheld, amid the mournful scene,
The hundred daughters with the mother queen, Pitt, ll. 666–667

669–672 The hundred wives, and where old Priam stood,
To stain his hallow'd altar with his blood.
The fifty nuptial beds (such hopes had he,
So large a promise of a progeny). Dryden, ll. 683–686

And Priam on the Altars, with his Blood . . . Trapp, l. 617

674 The Posts with Trophies, and Barbarick Gold
Magnificent, Trapp, ll. 621–622

684 . . . to his Side / Girds an unprofitable Sword; Trapp, ll. 629–630

686–687 Uncover'd but by heaven, there stood in view
An altar; near the hearth a laurel grew, Dryden, ll. 700–701

688–689 shade / fled Ogilby, p. 145

. . . cov'ring with it's Shade / The Household-Gods. Trapp, ll. 635–636

display'd / shade Pitt, ll. 687–688

690–694 Driven like a flock of doves along the sky,
Their images they hugg, and to their altars fly. Dryden, ll. 706–707

. . . embrac'd the Statues of the Gods.
But when in youthful Arms she saw the King; Trapp, ll. 639–640

Hither, like doves, who close-embody'd fly
From some dark tempest black'ning in the sky, Pitt, ll. 689–690

699–700 . . . no such defenders . . . Ogilby, p. 145

Nor such Defenders does the Time require; Trapp, l. 644

demands / hands Pitt, ll. 697–698

701–702 Draw neer; this altar may protect us all,
Or here in death we will together fall. Ogilby, p. 145

But come; This Altar shall protect us All: Trapp, l. 646

705–708 Behold! Polytes one of Priams sons
Having escap'd from slaughtering Pyrrhus, runs

Wounded to seek some sheltring place, he flyes
Through arms, through foes, courts, and long galleries; Ogilby, p. 145

Behold Polites, one of Priam's sons,
Pursu'd by Pyrrhus, there for safety runs. Dryden, ll. 718–719

When lo! Polites, one of Priam's Sons, Trapp, l. 650

When lo! Polites, one of Priam's sons,
Through darts and foes, from slaught'ring Pyrrhus runs, Pitt, ll. 705–706

723–725 Guilt, that a father's sacred eyes defil'd
With blood, the blood of his dear murder'd child! Pitt, ll. 721–722

729–730 Hectors pale corps should have a native tombe,
And me again sent with a convoy home. Ogilby, p. 146

731 This said, his feeble hand a javelin threw, Dryden, l. 742

733–734 along / rung Pitt, ll. 731–732

734–739 But on the bosse did hang the harmlesse speare.
Then Pyrrhus said: this newes my father beare,
My cruell deeds remember to relate;
And how that I his sonne degenerate. Ogilby, p. 146

Then Pyrrhus thus: Go thou from me to fate;
And to my Father my foul deeds relate.
Now die: . . . Dryden, ll. 746–748

. . . his degen'rate Boy:/ Now die. Trapp, ll. 680–681

. . . his degenerate boy. Pitt, l. 736

742–743 His right hand held his bloody faulchion bare;
His left he twisted in his hoary hair: Dryden, ll. 753–754

744–745 Which to the hilts he buries in his side.
So finish'd Priams fates, and thus he dy'd, Ogilby, p. 146

Deep to the Hilt he plunges in his Side. Trapp, l. 685

Then to the hilt with all his force apply'd,
He plung'd the ruthless fau'chion in his side. Pitt, ll. 743–744

748–749 . . . the Head from off the Shoulders torn;
A Trunk dishonour'd, and without a Name. Trapp, ll. 692–693

Now lies a headless carcase on the shore,
The man, the monarch, and the name no more! Pitt, ll. 749–750

752–753 My Father's image fill'd my pious mind,
Lest equal years might equal fortune find. Dryden, ll. 766–767

. . . My Father's Image to my Mind Trapp, l. 695

behind / mind Pitt, ll. 755–756

754–755 The equall aged King give up his life

With a sad wound, and my neglected wife, Ogilby, p. 146

Again I thought on my forsaken wife,
And trembled for my son's abandon'd life. Dryden, ll. 768–769

761 . . . flung themselves into the Flames. Trapp, l. 704

762–763 Thus, wandering in my way, without a guide,
The graceless Helen in the porch I spy'd Dryden, ll. 774–775

770–771 That common bane of Greece and Troy, I found. Dryden, l. 779

776–777 train / again Pitt, ll. 774–775

780–781 shore / gore Pitt, ll. 778–779

782–783 Not so. Although no memorable name
Have female punishments, or such conquests fame; Ogilby, p. 147

786–790 please / these Ogilby, p. 147

The punish'd crime shall set my soul at ease:
And murmuring manes of my friends appease.
Thus while I rave, a gleam of pleasing light
Spread o'er the place, and shining heavenly bright,
My mother stood reveal'd before my sight. Dryden, ll. 797–801

The Manes of my Country to appease. Trapp, l. 731

bright / night Pitt, ll. 788–789

793–795 above / love Dryden, ll. 804–805

800–801 age / rage Pitt, ll. 796–797

802–806 Look if your helpless father yet survive;
Or if Ascanius, or Creüsa, live.
Around your house the greedy Grecians err;
And these had perish'd in the nightly war,
But for my presence and protecting care. Dryden, ll. 812–816

Think if thy dear Creüsa yet survive,
Think if thy child, the young Iülus live; Pitt, ll. 798–799

821–822 seats / Scæan gates Ogilby, p. 148
Heav'ns awful queen, to urge the Trojan fate,
Here storms tremendous at the Scæan gate; Pitt, ll. 817–818

827–829 supplies / Deities Ogilby, p. 148

See, Jove new courage to the foe supplies,
And arms against the town the partial deities. Dryden, ll. 835–836

. . . Jove himself the Grecian Troops
With Courage, and new Strength supplies; Himself
Excites the Gods against the Dardan Arms. Trapp, ll. 768–770

834–835 . . . great Deities reveal'd / Themselves averse to Troy. Ogilby, p. 148

847–849 Thence led by her, I passe through foes and fire;
Weapons give place, and horrid flames retire. Ogilby, p. 148

Descending thence, I 'scape through foes, and fire:
Before the goddess, foes and flames retire. Dryden, ll. 856–857

Conducted by the Godhead I descend; Trapp, l. 787

849 And Foes: The Darts give way, the Flames retire. Trapp, l. 789

850–851 Soon as, these various dangers past, I come
Within my rev'rend father's ancient dome, Pitt, ll. 849–850

856–858 . . . You, he said, whose Blood
Runs in clear Channels with Youth's spritely Flood, Ogilby, p. 221

. . . You, he cry'd whose Blood
Runs vigorous in youthful Veins, do You
Secure yourselves by Flight. Trapp, ll. 794–796

864–865 These weak old hands suffice to stop my breath:
At least the pitying foes will aid my death, Dryden, ll. 872–873

870–871 expire / fire Dryden, ll. 878–879

Since, in his wrath, high heaven's almighty sire
Blasted these limbs with his avenging fire. Pitt, ll. 869–70

874–875 Fate / sate Ogilby, p. 149

880–882 Think you (deer Sir) I'll stir, you left behinde?
Can such strange words fall from a Fathers minde? Ogilby, p. 149

883–884 ordain / remain / slain Dryden, ll. 893–895

888–891 . . . Reeking fresh with Priam's Blood,
Pyrrhus will soon be here; who slew the Son
Before his Father's eyes, the Father's self
Before his Altars. Trapp, ll. 825–828

898–901 Arm, arm, the last hour calls the vanquished. Ogilby, p. 149

I hear thee, fate, and I obey thy call:
Not unreveng'd the foe shall see my fall. Dryden, ll. 909–910

Arms, Arms, my Friends; Tho' vanquish'd, This last Day
Calls us to Arms: Give me the Greeks again; Trapp, ll. 834–835

'Tis well—we will not tamely perish all,
But die reveng'd, and triumph in our fall. Pitt, ll. 904–905

907–908 If death be your design, at least, said she,
Take us along to share your destiny. Dryden, ll. 920–921

919–920 With a soft touch, and round his temples fed. Ogilby, p. 150

Harmless with gentle Touch it glided o'er
His Hair, and lambent round his Temples fed. Trapp, ll. 854–855

Then on his locks the lambent glory preys,
And harmless fires around his temples blaze. Pitt, ll. 924–925

927 . . . and if aught / Our Piety deserves, Trapp, ll. 861–862

939–942 The good old man with suppliant hands implor'd
The gods protection, and their star ador'd.
Now, now, said he, my son, no more delay,
I yield, I follow where heaven shews the way. Dryden, ll. 948–951

Proceed, my friends, no longer I delay,
But instant follow where you lead the way. Pitt, ll. 946–947

949–950 flame / came Ogilby, p. 150

951–952 Dear Father, get upon my Shoulders streight,
Nor shall your burthen be to me a Weight. Ogilby, p. 224

Haste, my dear father ('tis no time to wait),
And load my shoulders with a willing freight. Dryden, ll. 962–963

965–966 For me unfit to touch, return'd from blood
And so great battels, till the living flood
Cleanse me again. Ogilby, p. 151

975–977 . . . now feare
Each breath of wind, the smallest noise I heare;
Alike both for my sonne and burthen dread. Ogilby, p. 151

At every shadow now am seiz'd with fear:
Not for myself, but for the charge I bear. Dryden, ll. 990–991

Now ev'ry breath of Air, each ruffling Sound
Alarms, sollicitous for Him I led,
And Him I bore. Trapp, ll. 908–910

980–983 A frightful noise of trampling feet we hear;
My father, looking through the shades with fear,
Cry'd out, Haste, haste, my son, the foes are nigh;
Their swords and shining armour I descry. Dryden, ll. 994–997

near / hear Pitt, ll. 984–985

990–991 Or sunk fatigu'd; or straggled from the train;
But ah! she never blest these eyes again! Pitt, ll. 996–997

992–994 Nor lookt behind, nor mist her till we come
To sacred seats, and ancient Ceres tomb. Ogilby, p. 151

1005–1006 Now to the gate I run with furious haste,
Whence first from Ilion to the plain I past; Pitt, ll. 1011–1012

1009–1012 Then, to my father's house I make repair,
With some small glimpse of hope to find her there: Dryden, ll. 1026–1027

. . . Thence Home I go, to see
If haply she had thither back repair'd: Trapp, ll. 943–944

1022–1023 roll'd / bowls of massy gold Pitt, ll. 1027–1028

1028–1029 in vain / again Pitt, ll. 1035–1036

1040–1041 My fates permit me not from hence to fly;
Nor he, the great comptroller of the sky. Dryden, ll. 1056–1057

1046–1047 glide / Bride Ogilby, p. 153

There end your toils: And there your fates provide
A quiet kingdom, and a royal bride: Dryden, ll. 1064–1065

There shall thy fates a happier lot provide,
A glorious empire, and a royal bride. Pitt, ll. 1051–1052

1054–1056 But the Majestick Mother of the Gods
Detains me in these Coasts: Farewell; and love
Your Son, our common Care. Trapp, l. 985–987

Farewell; and to our son thy care approve,
Our son, the pledge of our commutual love. Pitt, ll. 1061–1062

1063–1064 Swift as the wind, with momentary flight,
Swift as a fleeting vision of the night. Pitt, ll. 1067–1068

1066–1068 Then I my Friends re-visit, night grown old,
Where numbers I admiring did behold
Of new Associates . . . Ogilby, p. 228

1069–1071 Eager the wretches pour from ev'ry side,
To share my fortunes on the foamy tide; Pitt, ll. 1075–1076

1074–1075 And now, o'er Ida with an early ray
Flames the bright star, that leads the golden day. Pitt, ll. 1079–1080

Book III

1–2 After the Gods had the Asian State,
And Priam's guiltless Line t'exterminate, Ogilby, p. 154

When heaven had overturn'd the Trojan state,
And Priam's throne, by too severe a fate: Dryden, ll. 1–2

When heav'n destroy'd, by too severe a fate,
The throne of Priam, and the Phrygian state, Pitt, ll. 1–2

4 . . . and all Neptunian Troy / Smoking in Ruins: Trapp, ll. 3–4

The pride of Asia, smok'd upon the ground; Pitt, l. 4

13–14 Weeping I leave the Port, and native strands, Ogilby, p. 155

Weeping I leave my Country-Shores, the Ports,
And Fields where Troy had stood; and exil'd launch Trapp, ll. 12–13

15–18 Fields where Troy was, exil'd am born through seas
With friends, my son, Lars and great Deities.
Far off the Thracians plow a warlike Land
And vast, which once Lycurgus did command: Ogilby, p. 155

Against our coast appears a spacious land,
Which once the fierce Lycurgus did command: Dryden, ll. 19–20

26 To Dionæan Venus vows are paid, Dryden, l. 29

28–29 Upon those shores a snowy Bull I slew. /. . . grew Ogilby, p. 155

32 . . . horrid with thick-pointed Spears. Trapp, l. 31

39–41 With broken Roots, Drops of fresh Blood distill'd,
And trickling Gore in blushes stain'd the Field. Ogilby, p. 232

. . . black Drops of Blood distill'd,
And stain'd the Ground with Gore; Me Horror chills
Shudd'ring, and Fear congeals my curdling Blood. Trapp, ll. 37–39

44–45 Curious the latent causes to explore,
With trembling hands a second plant I tore; Pitt, ll. 40–41

46 . . . Much in my Thoughts / Revolving, Trapp, ll. 42–43

48–49 And powerfull Mars, who rules the Getick field
To blesse the signs, the Omen prosperous yeild. Ogilby, p. 155

53–54 But when once more we tug'd with toiling hands,
And eager bent my knees against the sands; Pitt, ll. 48–49

59–64 gore / Fly cruell coasts, ah fly this treacherous shore. Ogilby, p. 156

Spare to pollute thy pious hands with blood:
The tears distil not from the wounded wood;
But every drop this living tree contains
Is kindred blood, and ran in Trojan veins:
O fly from this unhospitable shore,
Warn'd by my fate; for I am Polydore! Dryden, ll. 60–65

. . . Troy gave me Birth,
No Foreigner to Thee; Nor doth this Blood
Flow from the Roots, and senseless Fibres: Fly,
Ah! fly These cruel Coasts, This greedy Shore.
For I am Polydore; an Iron Crop
Of Darts o'erwhelms me here transfix'd, Trapp, ll. 53–58

Ah! fly this barbarous land, this guilty shore,
Fly, fly the fate of murder'd Polydore. Pitt, ll. 56–57

67–68 Then was my mind perplex'd with doubtfull fear,
Amaz'd struck dumb, erected was my haire. Ogilby, p. 156

declare / hair Dryden, ll. 68–69

73 . . . and Troy beleaguer'd round, Ogilby, p. 156

85–86 And with full sails from tainted friendship fly. /. . . high Ogilby, p. 156

Polluted with inhospitable Crimes, Trapp, l. 79

89–91 . . . And Altars to his Manes built, Trapp, l. 83

upbound / around Pitt, ll. 84–85

94–96 Then bowls of tepid milk and blood we pour,
And thrice invoke the soul of Polydore. Dryden, ll. 93–94

97–98 ships/ deeps Pitt, ll. 92–93

114–115 Anius the priest, and king, with laurel crown'd,
His hoary locks with purple fillets bound, Dryden, ll. 106–107

122–123 repair / pray'r Pitt, ll. 112–113

124–126 own / town Dryden, ll. 116–117

131–133 what way / Now must we seek? whom follow? or where lay Ogilby, p. 157

guide / tide Pitt, ll. 122–123

139–140 Ye hardy Trojans, The same Land which first
Gave Birth to your Forefathers, Trapp, ll. 127–128

Ye valiant sons of Troy, the land that bore
Your mighty ancestors to light before, Pitt, ll. 130–131

148 Our wand'ring Course, and whither to return. Trapp, l. 136

149–150 revolving o'er / before Pitt, ll. 140–141

155–156 There is th'Idæan Mountain, Trapp, l. 141

There antient Ida stands, and thence we trace
The first memorials of the Trojan race; Pitt, ll. 146–147

175–176 fleet / Crete Dryden, ll. 158–159

179–182 A bull to Neptune, such was Phoebus right,

To storms a black sheep, to faire winds a white. Ogilby, p. 158

193–194 Olearus, Chalkie Parus, pass through Seas
Sow'd thick with Isles, and scatter'd Cyclades; Ogilby, p. 237

Cyclades / seas Dryden, ll. 174–175

195–197 cry / fly Dryden, 178–179; fly / cry Pitt, ll. 180–181

200–201 bore / shore Dryden, ll. 180–181

202–204 Where I did build our long'-for Citie's wall,
And our new Town did Pergamea call; Ogilby, p. 237

With eager speed I frame a town, and call
From antient Pergamus the rising wall. Pitt, ll. 184–185

205–208 sands / lands Ogilby, p. 158

The name itself was grateful; I exhort
To found their houses, and erect a fort.
Our ships are haul'd upon the yellow strand.
The youth begin to till the labour'd land. Dryden, ll. 184–187

210–211 air / year Dryden, ll. 190–191

cares / shares Pitt, ll. 192–193

216–220 Nor scape the beasts: for Syrius from on high
With pestilential heat infects the sky:
My men, some fall, the rest in fevers fry.
Again my Father bids me seek the shore
Of sacred Delos and the god implore: Dryden, ll. 194–198

Their wonted food the blasted fields deny,
And the red dog-star fires the sultry sky. Pitt, ll. 200–201

227–230 A clear full-orbed Moon gave me the sight,
Which through the windows showr'd a stream of light; Ogilby, p. 237

Before me stood; majestically bright,
Full in the beams of Phoebe's entering light. Dryden, ll. 205–206

bright / light Pitt, ll. 210–211

231–232 Gates / Fates Ogilby, p. 237

relate / fate Dryden, ll. 209–210

235–236 By us, companions of thy arms and thee,
From flaming Ilion o'er the swelling sea. Pitt, ll. 216–217

237 . . . we to Heav'n will raise / Your future Progeny, Trapp, ll. 211–212

242–245 By Œnotrians till'd; Posterity, they fame,
Since call'd it Italy, from their Princes name, Ogilby, p. 238

Th' Oenotrians held it once; by later fame,
Now call'd Italia from the leader's name. Dryden, ll. 223–224

There is a Place, by Greeks Hesperia call'd,
An ancient Land, renown'd in Arms, and rich
In fertile Glebe: The Oenotrians once possess'd,
And till'd the Soil; The Moderns now, 'tis said,
Have from their Chief the Land Italia nam'd. Trapp, ll. 217–221

For martial deeds and fruits renown'd by fame;
But since, Italia, from the leader's name. Pitt, ll. 226–227

248–251 . . . Rise, and to your aged Sire
With Joy relate These certain Tidings; Seek
The Realms of Coritus, Ausonian Realms;
Great Jove denies you the Dictæan Fields. Trapp, ll. 224–227

254–255 Nor did I sleep, I knew what Pow'rs they were,
By their Celestial looks and veiled hair. Ogilby, p. 238

Their Looks, their Forms, and Fillets of their Hair; Trapp, l. 230

264–265 He knew the double Stock, and doubtfull Race,
And his new error of the antient place. Ogilby, p. 238

The double Parents, and ambiguous Race, Trapp, l. 237

He owns his error of each ancient place,
Our two great founders, and the double race. Pitt, ll. 244–245

278–279 leaving few behind / . . . wind Dryden, ll. 252–253

286–287 eyes / flies Dryden, ll. 260–261

294–295 Not skilful Palinure in such a sea,
So black with storms, distinguish'd night from day;
Nor knew to turn the helm, or point the way. Pitt, ll. 273–275

296–297 Three starless nights the doubtful navy strays
Without distinction, and three sunless days. Dryden, ll. 266–267

298–299 spy / sky / eye Pitt, ll. 278–280

305–306 Iles standing in the great Ionian Seas,
And by the Grecians called Strophades; Ogilby, p. 239

At length I land upon the Strophades,
Safe from the danger of the stormy seas: Dryden, ll. 274–275

309–312 Where dire Celæno other Harpies led,
When frighted they from Phineas Table fled. Ogilby, p. 239

317–319 The Fowls have virgin face, and hook'd Claws,
Still purging Bellies, alwaies greedy Maws
With Hunger pale. Ogilby, p. 239

323 . . . invite / The Gods, and Jove himself to share the Prey; Trapp, ll. 289–290

330–331 Again—but now within a long-drawn glade,
O'erhung with rocks and boughs of roughest shade, Ogilby, p. 241

shade / made Dryden, ll. 299–300

334–335 Meat / eat Ogilby, p. 241

repeat / meat Dryden, ll. 305–306

338–339 Fields / Shields Ogilby, p. 241

340–341 Then, as the Harpies from the hills once more
Pour'd shrieking down, and crowded round the shore, Pitt, ll. 320–321

346–347 dis-compose / Blows Ogilby, p. 241

352 War too, ye Offspring of Laomedon, Trapp, l. 321

354–355 Innocent Harpies form their Realms t'expell?
If so, what I shall say, remember well: Ogilby, p. 241

356–360 What Jove to Phoebus, Phoebus me forefold,
I greatest of the Furies now unfold. Ogilby, p. 242

The eldest Fury, I to You unfold.
For Italy you sail, and court the Winds;
At Italy you shall arrive, Trapp, ll. 326–328

367–368 wood / stood / blood Pitt, ll. 346–348

373–374 Whether dire Goddesses, or Birds obscene. Trapp, l. 338

375–376 Anchises then, raising to Heav'n his hands,
Implores the Gods, and Sacrifice commands. Ogilby, p. 242

396 And with the promis'd Fires his Altars blaze. Trapp, l. 359

397–400 Naked our Youth practise on th'Actrian Soyl
Their Ilian Games, and wrestle, steep'd in Oil. Ogilby, p. 242

Our youth their naked limbs besmear with oil,
And exercise the wrestlers noble toil. Dryden, ll. 364–365

Naked, in slipp'ry Oil: Trapp, l. 363

411–412 The sight of high Phæacia soon we lost,
And skim'd along Epirus' rocky coast. Dryden, ll. 376–377

413–414 To the Chaonian Port our Course we bend,
And high Buthrotus lofty Walls ascend. Ogilby, p. 243

Enter Chaonia's Harbour; and ascend
Buthrotus, lofty City. Trapp, ll. 377–378

423–424 And left the Fleet, where they in safety lay.
By chance, sad Gifts, and Annual Rites that day Ogilby, p. 243

427–430 Andromache the mournful Off'rings paid,
And solemn Sacrifice at Hector's Tomb,
His empty Tomb; Trapp, ll. 389–391

By chance, Andromache that moment paid
The mournful offerings to her Hector's shade. Pitt, ll. 402–403

436–437 Her beauteous frame the vital warmth forsook,
And, scarce recover'd, thus at length she spoke: Pitt, ll. 412–413

444–445 cry / reply Dryden, ll. 403–404

456 . . . before an hostile Tomb, Trapp, l. 414

460 . . . to touch the Conquering Masters Bed. Ogilby, p. 245

466 Grecian Hermione, a Spartan Bride, Trapp, l. 422

467–468 And me to Helenus his Servant gave.
But him Orestes, who did strangely rave Ogilby, p. 245

Then me to Trojan Helenus resign'd Dryden, l. 426

473–474 regain'd / remain'd Dryden, ll. 431–432

On Helenus devolv'd (the tyrant slain,)
A portion of the realm, a large domain: Pitt, ll. 446–447

481–483 What God has brought you to our Coasts unknown?
How fares the young Ascanius? Does he live? . . .
Does yet the Boy with Grief remember aught
Of his lost Mother? Trapp, ll. 433–434, 437–438

488–491 Weeping, she said, and spent much Tears in vain,
When from the City, with a stately Train,
The Heroe Helenus, Priam's Off-spring, bends
His Course to us, acknowledging his Friends, Ogilby, pp. 245–246

At length her lord descends upon the plain,
In pomp attended with a numerous train: Dryden, ll. 444–445

When lo! in royal pomp the king descends
With a long train, and owns his ancient friends. Pitt, ll. 458–459

498 And hug the Lintels of the Scæan Gate. Trapp, l. 450

501–502 Them in large stately Rooms the King receives; Trapp, l. 452

503–504 Crown'd with rich wine the foamy goblets hold;
And the vast feast was serv'd in massy gold. Pitt, ll. 470–471

507 Two days were past, and now the southern gales Pitt, l. 472

509–510 When to the Prophet I my Sute preferr.
Inspired Trojan, Heavens Interpreter, Ogilby, p. 246

515–517 O say; for all religious rites portend
A happy voyage and a prosperous end; Dryden, ll. 465–466

518–519 Yet dire Celæno Iudgement doth presage,
Denouncing Famine, and Celestial Rage Ogilby, p. 246

520–521 O say what dangers I am first to shun,
What toils to vanquish, and what course to run. Dryden, ll. 471–472

522–526 Then takes his Fillet from his scared Head,

And to thy Thresholds, me, great Phoebus, led, Ogilby, p. 246

Unbinds the fillet from his holy head;
To Phoebus next my trembling steps he led,
Full of religious doubts and awful dread. Dryden, ll. 475–477

Here Helenus, performing first the Rite
Accustom'd, sacrificing Oxen slain,
Implores the Favour of the Gods, unbinds
The Fillets of his consecrated Head; Trapp, ll. 471–474

Unbinds the fillets from his sacred head,
Then, by the hand, in solemn state he led Pitt, ll. 494–495

529–531 explain / the main / gain Dryden, ll. 484–486

536–542 shores / oars Dryden, ll. 492–493

First, from th'Italian Ports, which you so near
Imagine, ignorant, a long Extent
Of Ocean, and a Voyage difficult
Divide you: First Trinacrian Waves must bend
Your Oars; Ausonian Seas must be explor'd,
Th'Infernal Lakes, Ææan Circe's Isle; Trapp, ll. 488–493

First then, that Italy, that promis'd land
Though thy fond hopes already grasp the strand,
(Though now she seems so near,) a mighty tide,
And long, long regions from your reach divide.
Sicilian seas must bend your plunging oars;
Your fleet must coast the fair Ausonian shores, Pitt, ll. 510–515

544–546 When, lost in contemplation deep, you find
A large white mother of the bristly kind, Pitt, ll. 520–521

559–560 Has fixt his armies on Salentine ground,
And awes the wide Calabrian realms around. Pitt, ll. 536–537

562–564 stands / commands Dryden, ll. 515–516

566–568 . . . with a purple Veil
Cover your Head: lest any hostile Face
Appearing, should disturb the solemn Rites, Trapp, ll. 517–519

Lest hostile faces should appear in sight,
To blast and discompose the hallow'd rite. Pitt, ll. 544–545

569–570 This pious use thou must impose on thine,
In this thy cast Posterity instruct. Ogilby, p. 247

shrine / line Pitt, ll. 546–547

575–578 Far to thy left thy course in safety keep,
And fetch a mighty circle round the deep.
That realm of old, a ruin huge! was rent
In length of ages from the continent; Pitt, ll. 552–555

608–609 With humble Presents win, Conqueror at last;
Then steer Italian Shores, Sicilia past.

When thou shalt reach to Cuma's sacred Floods,
And hear'st Avernus thundring through the Woods, Ogilby, pp. 248–249

610–618 Arriv'd at Cumæ, when you view the flood,
Of black Avernus, and the sounding wood,
The mad prophetic sibyl you shall find,
Dark in a cave, and on a rock reclin'd.
She sings the fates, and in her frantic fits,
The notes and names inscrib'd, to leaves commits.
What she commits to leaves, in order laid,
Before the cavern's entrance are display'd: Dryden, ll. 561–568

Discloses Fate; and Characters, and Verse
Commits to Leaves. Whatever Lines on Leaves
The Virgin writes, she into Order just
Ranges, and lays them in her Grot secluse;
They in their Places rest unmov'd: Trapp, ll. 567–571

The mystic numbers, in the cavern laid,
Are rang'd in order by the sacred maid; Pitt, ll. 594–595

619–625 . . . But when,
The Door turn'd on it's Hinge, a Blast of Wind
Disturbs their Scite; she never is concern'd
To catch them flying in her hollow Rock;
Never recalls them to their former Cells,
And marshals them no more: The Votaries
Depart untaught, and curse the Sibyl's Cave. Trapp, ll. 571–577

641–644 He gives Command to carry to our Ships
Presents of polish'd Iv'ry, pond'rous Gold,
And Dodonæan Cauldrons, Trapp, ll. 592–594

651–652 Mean-while Anchises bids refit our Ships
With Sails, and not delay the willing Winds. Trapp, ll. 601–602

And now my sire gave orders to unbind
The gather'd sails, and catch the rising wind; Pitt, ll. 631–632

655–656 led / bed Pitt, ll. 635–636

657–658 lost / coast Dryden, ll. 612–613

664 Nor less Andromache, Trapp, l. 613

672–673 Take these Remembrances my own hand wove,
To testifie Andromache's long Love; Ogilby, p. 251

Accept, she said, these monuments of love;
Which in my youth with happier hands I wove: Dryden, ll. 628–629

675–676 O Thou! the sole, surviving Image left
Of my Astyanax! Trapp, ll. 622–623

676–677 Such were his motions! such a sprightly grace
Charm'd from his eyes, and open'd in his face! Pitt, ll. 661–662

686–696 If e're on Tyber's pleasant Banks I land,

And Walls shall see, given me by Fates command: Ogilby, p. 251

The labour of your hands, another Troy;
With better auspice than her ancient towers Dryden, ll. 646–647

No Italy, still flying, to pursue.
Xanthus in Imag'ry you see, and Troy
Which your own Hands have made; with more Success,
I hope, and less obnoxious to the Greeks.
If ever Tyber, and it's neighb'ring Fields
I see, and Walls allotted us by Fate;
Epirus, and Hesperia, Trapp, ll. 631–637

Nor seek for Latium, that deludes the view,
A coast that flies as fast as we pursue.
Here you anew Scamander can enjoy;
Here your own hands erect a second Troy; . . .
If e'er the long-expected shore I gain,
Where Tyber's streams enrich the flow'ry plain;
Or if I live to raise our fated town;
Our Latian Troy and yours shall join in one; Pitt, ll. 671–674, 677–680

700–701 We pass Ceraunian Mountains through the Sound,
And a short Passage to Ausonia found. Ogilby, p. 251

(The shortest passage to th' Italian shore). Dryden, l. 661

706–707 keep / sleep Dryden, ll. 666–667

There, by the murmurs of the heaving deep
Rock'd to repose, they sunk in pleasing sleep. Pitt, ll. 691–692

710–712 skies / Then careful Palinurus did arise, Ogilby, p. 252

Then wakeful Palinurus rose, to spy
The face of heaven, and the nocturnal sky;
And listen'd every breath of air to try: Dryden, ll. 671–673

713–720 He did Arcturus, and the kids behold,
Triones, and Orion arm'd with Gold. Ogilby, p. 252

And both the bears is careful to behold;
And bright Orion arm'd with burnish'd gold.
Then, when he saw no threatening tempest nigh,
But a sure promise of a settled sky; Dryden, ll. 676–679

The Stars all sliding in the silent Sky,
The rainy Hyades, and either Bear,
Arcturus, and Orion arm'd with Gold.
When all the Face of Heav'n he sees serene;
He gives the sounding Signal from his Ship;
We strike our Tents, and spread the Canvas Winds. Trapp, ll. 653–658

In the blue vault his piercing eyes behold,
And huge Orion flame in arms of gold. Pitt, ll. 701–702

721–730 A joyfull hail to Italy goes round. Ogilby, p. 252

When we from far, like bluish mists, descry

The hills, and then the plains of Italy.
Achates first pronounc'd the joyful sound;
Then Italy the cheerful crew rebound;
My sire Anchises crown'd a cup with wine,
And offering, thus implor'd the powers divine: Dryden, ll. 684–689

Italia, first Achates cries aloud;
Italia all our Crew with joyful Shouts
Salute. Anchises then a Goblet crowns,
Fills with Wine, and standing on the Deck
Aloft, invokes the Gods. Trapp, ll. 662–666

Now every star before Aurora flies,
Whose glowing blushes streak the purple skies:
When the dim hills of Italy we view'd,
That peep'd by turns, and div'd beneath the flood.
Lo! Italy appears, Achates cries,
And Italy with shouts, the crowd replies.
My sire, transported, crowns a bowl with wine,
Stands on the deck, and calls the pow'rs divine: Pitt, ll. 707–714

733 . . . Strait the wish'd-for Gales / Swell fresh: Trapp, ll. 669–770

735–736 Minerva's temple then salutes our sight;
Plac'd as a land-mark, on the mountain's height Dryden, ll. 696–697

745–747 'Mongst towrie Rocks it double grounded lyes
Against all Storms; from Shore the Temple flyes. Ogilby, p. 252

. . . And from the Shore the Temple flies. Trapp, l. 678

lie / fly Pitt, ll. 728–729

748–749 beheld / field Dryden, ll. 708–709

Here first, a dubious omen I beheld;
Four milk-white coursers graz'd the verdant field. Pitt, ll. 730–731

750–751 My Father said, Fair Soyl, thou War dost bear;
Horse are in battle arm'd, and threaten War: Ogilby, p. 252

. . . These Steeds are arm'd for War. Trapp, l. 682

War, cry'd my sire, these hostile realms prepare;
Train'd to the fight, these steeds denounce the war. Pitt, ll. 732–733

770 And Scylacæan strands / For shipwrecks fear'd: . . . Dryden, l. 727

781–782 veer'd / steer'd Dryden, ll. 737–738

790–791 Mean while the Winds forsake us with the Sun,
And to unknown Cyclopian Coasts we run. Ogilby, p. 253

The flagging winds forsook us, with the sun;
And weary'd, on Cyclopean shores we run. Dryden, ll. 744–745

805 Above him was the mighty Ætna laid, / . . . convey'd Ogilby, p. 254

808–810 As often as he turns his weary sides,

He shakes the solid isle, and smoke the heavens hides. Dryden, ll. 759–760

. . . And whene'er
He shifts his weary Side, Trinacria all
Groans trembling, and with Smoke obscures the Sky. Trapp, ll. 731–733

817–820 Here, after endless labours, often tost
By raging storms, and driven on every coast,
My dear, dear father, spent with age, I lost.
Ease of my cares and solace of my pain, Dryden, ll. 931–934

The Port of Drepanum, a joyless Coast, Trapp, l. 888

Wretch as I was, on this detested coast,
The chief support of all my woes, I lost;
My dear, dear father—sav'd, but sav'd in vain
From all the tempests of the raging main. Pitt, ll. 966–969

826–827 Not Helenus, who did sad Fates unfold,
This Loss declar'd, nor dire Celæno told; Ogilby, p. 259

Nor dire Celæno, That hard Fate foretel. Trapp, l. 895

829–832 Æneas thus, whil'st all attentive sate,
Declar'd Heavens pleasure, and the work of Fate.
His Voyage thus describ'd. then made a close,
And having done, he went to take repose. Ogilby, p. 259

Thus, while the room was hush'd, the prince relates
The wondrous series of his various fates;
His long, long wand'rings, and unnumber'd woes:
Then ceas'd; and sought the blessings of repose. Pitt, ll. 976–979

Book IV

1–2 To raise her heavy Eyes in vain she try'd,
The Crimson Fountain bubbling in her side. Ogilby, p. 287

6 Heaven's glorious Light, and at the finding groan'd. Ogilby, p. 287

Book VIII

1–4 Scarce said, he shews an Altar as they came,
And the Carmental Gate, a Roman name,
Which antient honour Nymphs did dedicate,
To Carmens, skilfull of ensuing Fate; Ogilby, p. 413

gate / state name / dame Dryden, ll. 445–448

He said; and, moving on, the Altar shew'd,
And the Carmental Gate, (a Roman Name) Trapp, ll. 427–428

15–16 Next to the Capitol their course they hold,
Then roof'd with reeds, but blazing now with gold. Pitt, ll. 458–459

18 . . . now rich with Gold, then rough with Thorns. Trapp, l. 441

23 This Grove, he said, This Hill with leafy Top Trapp, l. 445

25–28 . . . Th'Arcadians think that Jove
Himself they oft have seen, when Storms he rous'd,

And shook his dreadful Ægis from the Clouds. Trapp, ll. 447–449

31–32 This, Father Janus, that, King Saturn fram'd;
Janiculum this, that was Saturnia nam'd. Ogilby, p. 414

37–41 When to the Seat they came, These Gates, he said,
Alcides enter'd; Him This Court receiv'd:
Dare to scorn Wealth, Trapp, ll. 458–460

43–44 prest / guest Pitt, ll. 482–483

45–46 bed / o'erspread Dryden, ll. 482–483

Nonverbal Variants

The presentation of nonverbal variants is described on page 74.

Advertisement

6 Translators *rev from* translators

Book I

3 Fugitive . . . He *rev from* fugitive . . . he *MS. 101B* Fate:—] Fate— *MS. 101A*

5 enmity;] enmity *MS. 101A*

8 flowed] flow'd *MS. 101A*

10 Say,] Say *MS. 101A*

15 Coast] coast *MS. 101A*

19 even *rev to* e'en *MS. 101A*

20 favour; *rev in pencil and ink from* favour *MS. 101A*

21 lodged] lodg'd *MS. 101A*

27 stock] Stock *MS. 101A*

33 and,] and *MS. 101A* combined,] combin'd *rev in pencil to* combin'd,) *then rev del MS. 101A*

34 Work'd] Worked *MS. 101A* mind, *rev from* mind) *MS. 101B* mind *followed by pencil caret MS. 101A*

35 judgement] judgment *MS. 101A* given] giv'n *MS. 101A*

36 Ida's] Idas *MS. 101A* height, *rev from* height; *MS. 101B* height; *MS. 101A*

37–39 *brace, signifying a triplet, del by erasure, MSS.*

38 Ganymed,) *rev from* Ganymed; *MS. 101B, rev from* Ganymed;) *MS. 101A*

39 chaced] chased *MS. 101A*

40 tossed] toss'd *MS. 101A*

43 fulfill'd] fulfilled *MS. 101A*

49–63 *no open quotes MS. 101A*

49 Or] or *MS. 101A*

54 Oïleus] Oïleu's *MS. 101A, rev from* [?]leus *MS. 101B* Son;] Son. *rev from* Son, *MS. 101A*

59 I] I, *MS. 101A*

61 wag'd] waged *MS. 101A*

62 Who *rev from* Who, *MS. 101B*

63 implore?"] implore? *MS. 101A*

64 revolv'd] revolved *MS. 101A*

65 bent, so *MS. 101A* bent *MS. 101B*

66 south *rev from* South *MS. 101B* rave;] rave;— *MS. 101A*

67 cave] cave, *MS. 101A*

70 murmurs] murmurs— *MS. 101A*

73 their *rev from* thier *MS. 101A*

74 not,—] not— *rev from* not,— *MS. 101A* earth,] earth *MS. 101A*

77 winds] Winds *rev from* winds *MS. 101A*

83 Æolus!] Æolus *MS. 101A* men] Men *MS. 101A*

84 tranquillise] tranquillize *MS. 101A*

85 troubl'd] troubled *MS. 101A*

86 Sea] sea *MS. 101A*

87 conquer'd] conquered *MS. 101A*

92 Deïopeia] Deiopeia *rev from* Deiopiea *MS. 101A*

96 To *so MS. 101A* "To *MS. 101B* God. *rev in pencil to* God; *MS. 101B* God; *MS. 101A*

97 mine *rev from* mine, *MS. 101B*

104 mountain.—] mountain. *MS. 101A*

105 Ministers *rev from* ministers *MS. 101B*

106 Deep. *rev from* Deep, *MS. 101A*

109 abyss,] abyss *rev from* abyss, *MS. 101A* unwieldy *rev from* unwield *MS. 101B*

115 death. *so MS. 101A* death *MS. 101B*

117 groans, *rev from* groans; *MS. 101B* heaven-ward] heav'n-ward *MS. 101A*

118 Exclaims; *rev from* Exclaims, *MS. 101B*

119 Wall, *rev from* Wall— *MS. 101B*

120 end;—Oh] end; oh *MS. 101A*

124 received,] receiv'd, *MS. 101A*

126 o'er *rev from* over *MS. 101B*

126–128 *brace in pencil, MS. 101A*

133 shatter'd] shattered *MS. 101A* craves; *rev from* craves: *MS. 101B*

137 air; *rev in pencil and ink from* air, *MS. 101B*, air, *MS. 101A*

140 sea *rev from* sea, *MS. 101B*

143 Three *rev in pencil to* Three, *MS. 101A*

145 straits] Straits *MS. 101A*

147 Mate, *rev in pencil to* Mate *MS. 101A*

154 Drowning] Drowning, *MS. 101A*

155 Arms] arms *MS. 101A*

157 Hurricane *rev from* hurricane *MS. 101B*

162 sea] sea, *MS. 101A*

164 Ocean *rev from* ocean *MS. 101B*

165 perceiv'd—] perceived— *MS 101A, rev from* perceiv'd *MS. 101B*

168 Gallies *rev from* gallies *MS. 101B*

169 bore] bore, *MS. 101A* terrified *so MS. 101A*, terrified;, *MS. 101B*

170 their *rev from* there *MS. 101A*

171 conceal'd] concealed *MS. 101A*
173 call'd] called *MS. 101A*
176 presumed] presum'd *MS. 101A*
185 Trident—] Trident,— *MS. 101A*
186 Eurus!—] Eurus! *MS. 101A*
188 prison-house] Prison-house *MS. 101A*
189 and,] and *MS. 101A*
190 sea] sea, *rev from* see *MS. 101A* hill,] hill; *MS. 101A*
193 Cymothoe] Cymothoë *MS. 101A, rev from* Cymothoë *MS. 101B (DW following pencil signal)* Triton's] Tritons *MS. 101A*
194 ships—] Ships, *MS. 101A*
200 Straight] Strait *MS. 101A*
201 missile] Missile *rev from* Missle *MS. 101A*
202 Then,] Then *MS. 101A*
203 acknowledged] acknowledg'd *MS. 101A*
204 peace, *rev in pencil and ink from* peace *MS. 101A*
208 Sea's] Seas *MS. 101A* tumult,] tumult *rev from* tumult, *MS. 101A*
209 Then,] Then *rev from* Then, *MS. 101A*
214 Bay] bay *MS. 101A*
218 themselves,] themselves *MS. 101A*
220 Floods *rev from* [?floods] *MS. 101B*
225 Within, *rev from* Withing *MS. 101A*
227 Nymphs:] Nymphs; *MS. 101A*
248 Which,] Which *MS. 101A*
250 Stags] stags *MS. 101A*
253 stops— *rev from* stops, *MS. 101B* seiz'd] seized *MS. 101A, rev from* seize *MS. 101B*
256 heads] heads, *MS. 101A* Crowd] crowd *MS. 101A*
260 Seven *rev from* seven *MSS*
263 Trinacria's *rev from* [?Tricanria's] *MS. 101A*
264 guest] Guest *rev from* guest *MS. 101B*
266 Friends, *rev from* Friends! *MS. 101B*
267 ere] e're *MS. 101A rev in pencil to* ere
268 Ye,] Ye *MS. 101A* bend! *rev from* bend, *MS. 101B*
269 end. *rev from* end! *MS. 101B*
272 shunn'd] shunned *MS. 101A* den:] den; *MS. 101A*
274 Hereafter,] Hereafter *MS. 101A*
279 empire *rev from* empire, *MSS.*
280 patience *rev from* patience, *MS. 101B*
282 thus, *rev from* thus; *MS. 101B*
286 seize *rev from* sieze *MS. 101A* Quarry *rev from* quarry *MS. 101A*
296 appeased] appeas'd *MS. 101A*
297 discourses, *rev from* discourse[?] *MSS.*
302 Amycus] Amicus *MS. 101A, rev from* Amicus *MS. 101B*
306 Heaven *rev from* Heaven, *MS. 101B*
307 sea *rev from* sea, *MSS.*
308 Lands *rev from* lands *MS. 101B*
312 Venus (her . . . tears) *rev from* Venus, her . . . tears, *MS. 101B*
314 Men] men *MS. 101A*
315 thunder, *rev from* thunder! *MS. 101B*
316 commit— *rev from* commit, *MS. 101B*
317 What—thine *rev from* what!—Thine *MS. 101B*
324 (O . . . change?) *rev from* —O . . . change?— *MS. 101B* was (O] was—O *rev to* was—(O *MS. 101A* change?)] change?) *rev to* change?—) *MS. 101A* word.— *rev from* word. *MS. 101B* word, *MS. 101A*
326 *paren added, ink over pencil MS. 101B*
331 o'erclimb] *so MS. 101A* o'er climb *MS. 101B*
339 But] But, *MS. 101A* allow'd] allowed *MS. 101A*
340 Navy *rev from* navy *MS. 101B* lost— *rev from* lost.— *MS. 101B*
341 One *rev from* one *MSS.*
350 Walls *rev from* walls *MS. 101A*
351 promised] promis'd *MS. 101A*
354 He *rev from* He, *MS. 101B*
364 reign,] reign,— *rev from* reign, *MS. 101A* Lavinium— *rev from* Lavinium, *MS. 101B*
365 Albalonga *rev from* Albalonga, *MSS.*
372 Mavortian]Marvotian *MS. 101A* Father's] *so MS. 101A* Fathers *MS. 101B* frame,] frame; *MS. 101A*
373 And] And, *MS. 101A*
376 Juno, *so MS. 101A* Juno *MS. 101B*
377 sea, *rev from* seas *MS. 101B*
379 Prepar'd] Prepared *MS. 101A*
381 'tis] tis *MS. 101A*
382 Phthia *rev from* [?Phia] *MS. 101A*
384 Argos *rev from* Argos, *MS. 101A*
390 Seat] seat *MS. 101A*
392 address'd.] addressed, *MS. 101A*
393 Age *rev from* age *MS. 101A* defil'd *rev from* defil'd, *MS. 101A*
396 laws,] laws; *MS. 101A*
397 Brother] Brother, *MS. 101A*
399 waits;] waits: *MS. 101A*
400 high-pil'd] high-piled *MS. 101A*
401 confin'd] confined *MS. 101A*
404 utter'd] uttered *MS. 101A*
409 Shores] shores *MS. 101A*
410 fulfill; *rev in pencil from* fulfill, *MS. 101A*
411 soften,] soften— *MS. 101A*
412 And,] And *MS. 101A*
415 Rose] 'Rose *MS. 101A*
417 beast.] beast,— *MS. 101A*
419 Fleet,] Fleet *MS. 101A*
421 way.] way; *MS. 101A*
424 Virgin *so MS. 101A* virgin *MS. 101B*

428 horse— *rev from* horse *following pencil signal, MS. 101A*
430 given] giv'n *MS. 101A*
439 Venus:—] Venus;— *MS. 101A*
442 Thee; *rev from* thee; *101B;* Thee, *rev from* thee, *MS. 101A*
445 Sister— *rev from* Sister; *MS. 101B*
457 Bear *rev from* Bears *MS. 101A*
458 bind. *rev from* bind— *MS. 101B* bind, *MS. 101A*
461 soil:] soil; *MS. 101A, rev from* soil, *MS. 101B*
462 intractable] intractible *rev from* intractable *MS. 101A*
464 perfidy; *rev from* perfidy[?] *MSS.*
465 wrong; *rev from* wrong, *MS. 101B*
466 skim *underlined in pencil, MS. 101A* tale.] tale: *MS. 101A*
467 Sichæus *rev from* Tichæus *MSS.* Mate *rev from* mate *MS. 101B*
468 State;] State, *MS. 101A*
470 induced,] induced *MS. 101A*
471 Union] union *MS. 101A*
473 them,] them; *MS. 101A*
474 gold,] gold. *MS. 101A*
475 He,] He *MS. 101A* scorning] scorning, *MS. 101A*
476 Wife's *rev from* wife's *MS. 101A* Sichæus] Sychæus *MS. 101A*
477 unawares,] unawares *MS. 101A*
479 conceal'd] concealed *MS. 101A*
488 And,] And *MS. 101A* Ships] ships *MS. 101A*
489 seiz'd] seized *MS. 101A* fled *rev from* fled, *MS. 101A*
493 BARCA;] *Barca, MS 101A*
495 say,—] say, *MS. 101A* Who] who *MS. 101A*
496 springs] springs, *MS. 101A*
498 you,] you *MS. 101A*
502 steered,] steered; *MS. 101A*
503 Shores] shores *MS. 101A*
505 go] go, *MS. 101A*
506 Foe] foe *MS. 101A*
507 You] you *MS. 101A*
508 Fam'd] Famed *MS. 101A* Earth *rev from* earth *MS. 101B* piety;] piety *MS. 101A*
509 *hyphens supplied in ink following pencil instruction MS. 101A*
510 Race] race *MS. 101A*
512 Ships (which . . . supplied,)] ships which . . . supplied, *MS. 101A, rev from* Ships, which . . . supplied, *MS. 101B*
513 Goddess Mother] Goddess-mother *MS. 101A* way,] way; *MS. 101A*
516 Myself] myself *MS. 101A*
518 chas'd] chased *MS. 101A*
524 port,] port; *MS. 101A*
526 alter'd] altered *MS. 101A*
530 swoop] swoop, *MS. 101A*
535 —As *rev from* As *MS. 101A* rejoice,] rejoice *MS. 101A*
536 So,] So *MS. 101A* lie,] lie; *MS. 101A*
537 haven's] Haven's *MS. 101A*
538 full-spread] full spread *MS. 101A*
539 hindrance] hind'rance, *MS. 101A* lead. *so MS. 101A* lead *MS. 101B*
540 and,] and *MS. 101A*
548 pursueth] pursueth, *MS. 101A*
551 me] me, *MS. 101A*
553 chiding] Chiding *rev from* chiding *MS. 101A* troubl'd] troubled *MS. 101A*
559 *commas inserted following WW's pencil MS. 101A*
560 Paphos—] Paphos, *MS. 101A*
564 course] course, *MS. 101A*
566 Town *rev from* town *MS. 101B*
568 City— *rev from* City,— *MS. 101B*
569 Huts *rev from* huts *MS. 101B*
574 Citadel *rev from* citadel *MS. 101B*
575 Structures *rev from* structures *MS. 101B*
576 Intrench *rev from* Entrench *MS. 101B*
578 haven] Haven *MS. 101A* out;] out, *MS. 101A*
582 —Fresh *rev from* Fresh *MS. 101B* Bees *rev from* bees *MS. 101B*
588 Or,] Or *MS. 101A* Labourers *rev from* labourers *MS. 101B*
589 mustering,] mustering *MS. 101A*
590 *orig written at top of MS. 101B, 18v, then del and added at bottom of 18r, to complete the triplet* hive.] hive; *MS. 101A*
593 fortunate!"] fortunate"! *MS. 101A* cries] cries, *MS. 101A*
601 sign] [?Tign] *rev to* Sign *MS. 101A* ground;] ground: *rev from* ground; *MS. 101A*
611 Gleams] gleams *MS. 101A*
612 Flashed] Flash'd *MS. 101A*
623 Ilium *rev from* Illium *MS. 101B*
625 Atrides, *rev from* Atrides,— *MS. 101B*
627 exclaim'd;] exclaim'd,— *MS. 101A*
631 Here *rev from* here *MS. 101B*
633 kind] Kind *MS. 101A*
634 mind."] mind!" *MS. 101A*
635 spake (nor *rev from* spake; nor *MS. 101B* controul] control *MS. 101A*
638 Youth *rev from* youth *MS. 101B*
639 war] War *MS. 101A*
640 Achilles *rev from* Achilles, *MSS.* Car.] Car! *MS. 101A*
646 Ere] 'Ere *MS. 101A*
648 Troilus *rev from* Troilus, *MSS.* espied] espi'd *rev from* espied, *MS. 101A*

649 Flying, *rev to* Flying,— *MS. 101A*
653 rein: *rev from* rein *MSS.*
659 wail,] wail. *MS. 101A*
662 —Thrice *rev from* Thrice *MS. 101B* incens'd] incenced *MS. 101A*
663 Wall *rev from* wall *MS. 101A*
664 Corse *rev from* corse *MS. 101B (DW following WW's pencil)* corse *MS. 101A*
665 grief, *rev from* grief! *MS. 101A* Chariot *rev from* chariot *MS. 101A*
666 body,] body *MS. 101A*
670 heads:] heads. *rev from* heads; *MS. 101A*
673 She *rev from* she *MSS.*
674 A Virgin Warrior *so MS. 101A* A virgin Warrior *MS. 101B* Train] train *MS. 101A*
675 peril *rev from* peril, *MS. 101B*
676 gaz'd] gazed *MS. 101A*
677 enrapt] enwrapt *MS. 101A, rev in pencil from* enwrapt *MS. 101B* amaz'd] amazed *MS. 101A*
678 Youth *rev from* youth *MS. 101B*
679 Temple:— *rev from* Temple, *MS. 101B*
681 Eurotas *rev from* Eurotus *MS. 101B* Eurotus *MS. 101A*
684 throng;] throng: *MS. 101A*
688 ecstasy] extacy *rev from* estasy *MS 101A*
690 crowd;—] crowd:— *MS. 101A*
693 And,] And *MS. 101A*
695 There, *rev from* There *(following WW's pencil) MS. 101B*
697 When,] When *MS. 101A*
702 Cloanthes— *rev from* Cloanthes, *MS. 101B* Cloanthes, *MS. 101A*
703 awe:] awe *MS. 101A*
708 solv'd— *rev from* solv'd *MS. 101B, rev from* solv'd, *MS. 101A*
714 preferr'd] preferred *MS. 101A*
717 curb] curb, *MS. 101A*
718 restrain!—] restrain! *MS. 101A*
719 We,] We *MS 101A*
720 entreat. *rev from* entreat[?;] *MS. 101B*
721 unhallow'd] unhallowed *MS. 101A*
725 houshold] household *MS. 101A*
727 Vanquish'd *rev from* vanquish'd *MS. 101A*
730 Œnotrians] Ænotrians *MS. 101A* Men *rev from* men *MS. 101B*
738 country] Country *MS. 101A*
743 *his*] his *MS. 101A* wise;—] wise; *MS. 101A*
745 man] Man *MS. 101A*
754 shatter'd] shattered *MS. 101A*
760 Troy, *rev from* Troy! *MS. 101B*
761 Iülus *rev from* Iulus *MS. 101A* engulph'd] engulphed *MS. 101A*
764 Prepar'd] Prepared *MS. 101A*
765 his *rev from* His *MS. 101A*
766 Declar'd] Declared *MS. 101A*
770 rigours *rev from* regours *MS. 101B*
771 vigilance *rev from* vigilence *MS. 101A (WW's pencil)*
783 sea] Sea *MS. 101A*
788 Waste *rev from* waste *MS. 101A*
789 Cast-away *rev from* cast-away *MS. 101B*
792 Chief *rev from* Cheif *MS. 101A*
796 deliverance *rev from* deliverence *MS. 101A*
798 sight *rev from* sight, *MS. 101B*
800 anon *rev from* inon *MS. 101A*
801 dissolves, *rev from* dissolves; *MS. 101B*
803 shoulders,] shoulders *MS. 101A*
806 And,] And *MS. 101A* purple] *purple MS. 101A (underlined in pencil)*
809 Guest *rev from* guest *MS. 101B*
810 And,] And *MS. 101A*
812 among. *rev from* among, *MS. 101B*
816 sword,] sword. *MS. 101A*
823–824 Gods (if . . . above) *rev from* Gods, if . . . above, *MS. 101B*
825 right,] right *MS. 101A*
827 Age *rev from* age *MS. 101B*
828 thee *rev from* the *MS. 101A*
829 seaward] sea-ward *MS. 101A*
830 groves *rev from* Groves *MSS.*
833 praise,] praise *MS. 101A*
834 tow'rds] towards *MS. 101A*
835 Ilioneus *rev from* Ilioneus, *MS. 101B* Ilioneus, *MS. 101A* hand,] hand, *rev in pencil from* hand; *MS. 101A, rev from*hand; *MS. 101B*
837 Gyas *rev from* Cyas *MS. 101B*
838 amaz'd] amazed *MS. 101A*
839 Sidonian *rev from* Sido[?]ian *MS. 101A (MW following pencil signal)* gaz'd] gazed *MS. 101A*
840 rais'd] raised *MS. 101A*
841 Force . . . She *rev from* force . . . she *MSS.* She, "pursues] She pursues *MS. 101A* impell'd] impelled *MS. 101A*
845 recall] recal *MS. 101A*
847 Outcast *rev from* Outcast, *MS. 101B*
852 King's] Kings *MS. 101A*
853 himself,] himself *MS. 101A*
854 Adversaries *rev from* adversaries *MS. 101B*
856 welcome,] welcome *MS. 101A*
857 Fortune *rev from* fortune *MS. 101B*
858 Stay'd *rev from* Staid *MS. 101B* Land *rev from* land *MS. 101B*
861 pronounced] pronounc'd *MS. 101A*
863 Palace] palace *MS. 101A*
875 Eastern] eastern *MS. 101A* tables—] tables *MS. 101A*
876 there, carv'd] there carved *MS. 101A*
878 Forefathers, *rev from* Forefathers—

MS. 101B
882 Dispatch'd] Dispatched *MS. 101A*
887 Presents *rev from* presents *MSS.*
888 Robe *rev from* robe *MS. 101A* exprest *rev from* expressed *MS. 101B (DW following WW's pencil)*
894 nuptials] Nuptials *MS. 101A*
895 coronet; *rev to* coronet, *MS. 101A*
897 Daughters,] *so MS. 101A* Daughters *MS. 101B* wore *rev from* wore, *MS. 101B* wore; *rev in pencil to* [?wore,] *MS. 101A*
898 bore. *rev in pencil to* bore! *MS. 101A*
905 Gifts *rev from* gifts *MS. 101A*
908 stung:] stung. *MS. 101A*
911 strength . . . power *rev in pencil to* Strength . . . Power *MS. 101A*
912 *parens added MS. 101B*
913 Jove! *rev to* Jove, *MS. 101B* Jove, . . . flee] Jove . . . flee *with pencil carets to indicate insertion of commas after* Jove *and* flee *MS. 101A*
914 Son,] Son *with pencil caret to indicate insertion of comma MS. 101A*
915 Æneas *rev from* Aneas *MS. 101A*
917 Brother— . . . known *rev from* Brother (. . . known) *MS. 101B*
920 detains: *rev from* detains; *MS. 101B* detains *MS. 101A*
922 snare, *rev from* snare; *MS. 101B*
924 I, . . . wiles,] I . . . wiles *MS. 101A*
926 She *rev from* she *MS. 101B*
927 assist;— *rev from* assist; *MS. 101B*
930 Preserv'd] Preserved *MS. 101A* flood,] flood *MS. 101A*
933 a's *in* Cythera's *over illeg eras MS. 101A*
935 "Nor] Nor *MS. 101A*
936 Thou *rev from* thou, *MS. 101B and from* thou *MS. 101A*
938 enraptur'd *rev from* inraptur'd *MS. 101B* enraptured *rev from* enwraptured *MS. 101A*
942 Instil] Instill *MS. 101A* subtle] subtile *MS. 101A*
946 Iülus] Iulus *MS. 101A*
952 embraced] embrac'd *MS. 101A*
953 Guide *rev from* guide *MS. 101B*
954 Gifts *rev from* gifts *MS. 101B*
963 fare,] fare; *MS. 101A*
964 houshold] household *MS. 101A*
967 Page *rev from* page *MS. 101B*
972 Gifts *rev from* gifts *MS. 101B*
983 clung;] clung— *MS. 101A*
989 Acidalian *rev from* A[?]dalian *MS. 101B (DW following WW's pencil)*
1004–1005 Belus *rev from* Belas *MS. 101B*

Book II

title Second] 2nd *MS. 101A*
1 gaz'd] gazed *MS. 101A*
9 Oh!] Oh, *MS. 101A*
11 Soldier *rev from* soldier *MS. 101B*
21 And,] And *MS. 101A* devise; *rev from* devis'd; *MS. 101A*
23 —Assisted] Assisted *MS. 101A*
49 He *rev from* he *MS. 101B*
50 Treacherous, *rev from* Treacherous; *MS. 101B*
57 Citadel] Citadel, MS. 101A
59 He *rev from* he MS. 101B
60 are! *rev from* are? *MS. 101A*
74 infatuate, *ed* infatuate *MSS.*
97 touch'd] touch'd, *MS. 101A*
98 cheer'd] chear'd, *MS. 101A*
101 Then *rev from para indent MS. 101B; pencil dash added to indicate no para indent MS. 101A*
102 *no para indent MS. 101A; so MS. 101B, then* O King! *del and rewritten indented*
107 *that*] that *MS. 101A*
108 haply,] haply *MS. 101A*
119 ungraced], ungrac'd *MS. 101A*
125 Friend,] Friend *MS. 101A*
135 disavow'd] disavowed *MS. 101A*
140 —If] If *MS. 101A*
143–145 *quots ed*
146–149 *quots commencing lines del eras MS. 101B*
146 judgments *rev from* judgment *MS. 101A*
148 renew'd;] renew'd, *MS. 101A*
153 dropp'd;] dropp'd: *MS. 101A*
155 eyes,] eyes *MS. 101A*
156 peal'd *rev from* pealed *MS. 101B;* pealed *MS. 101A* skies.] skies: *MS. 101A*
160 giv'n *rev from* given *MS. 101B* given *MS. 101A*
162 winds,] winds *MS. 101A*
174 issue,] issue *MS. 101A*
176 death, *rev from* death; *MS. 101B*
182 waits;] waits. *MS. 101A*
187 compell'd] compelled *MS. 101A*
196 mankind *rev to* mankind, *MS. 101A*
200 spare: *so MS. 101A* spare *MS. 101B*
201 He *rev from* he *MS. 101B (DW following WW's pencil)*
206 Why . . . instructed *rev from* Why? . . . instructed? *MS. 101B (CW, Jr.)*
209 Straight] Strait *MS. 101A* given] giv'n *MS. 101A*
224 Author *rev from* author *MS. 101B (DW following WW's pencil)*
230 Wreathed] Wreath'd *MS. 101A*
232 away.] away; *MS. 101A*
235 placed] plac'd *MS. 101A*
236 trickl'd] trickled *MS. 101A*
242 bear;] bear, *MS. 101A*

247 —So *rev from* So *with no para indent MS. 101B* signs;] signs: *MS. 101A*
248 guilt.] guilt; *MS. 101A*
254 Safeguard *rev from* safeguard *MS. 101B*
257 perish. *so MS. 101A* perish *MS. 101B*
262 Posterity *rev from* posterity *MS. 101B*
263 perjur'd] perjured *MS. 101A*
264 feign'd;] feign'd *MS. 101A*
272 blood,] blood *MS. 101A*
275 Tenedos,] Tenedos *MS. 101A*
279 follow *so MS. 101A* follow— *MS. 101B*
282 coming 'till] coming till *MS. 101A; rev from* coming, till *MS. 101B*
283 suffus'd] suffused *MS. 101A*
296 own. *so MS. 101A* own *MS. 101B*
305 accomplish'd,] accomplish'd; *MS. 101A*
306 Couched] Couch'd *MS. 101A*
308 severe *rev from* severe, *MS. 101B*
309 Steed *rev from* steed *MS. 101B*
316 tye:] tye; *MS. 101A*
318 ever,] ever *MS. 101A*
319 Boys,] Boys *MS. 101A*
320 throng!] throng. *MS. 101A*
324 Gates,] gates— *MS. 101A*
326 reckless *underlined in pencil MSS.* mind *underlined in pencil MS. 101B*
328 portentous] portentious *MS. 101A*
332 rejoice;]rejoice: *MS. 101A*
336 Night *rev from* night *MS. 101B (DW following WW)*
341 array'd] arrayed *MS. 101A*
345 fates] Fates *MS. 101A*
347 Straight,] Strait *MS. 101A*
349 Thersander, Sthenelus, *rev from* Thersander—Stenelus— *MS. 101B;* Thersander—Sthenelus *rev from* The-sander—Sthenelus, *MS. 101A*
351 s *in* Achamas *over illeg eras MS. 101B*
352 injur'd] injured *MS. 101A*
354 forth, *rev from* forth— *MS. 101B* forth; *MS. 101A*
356 Epèus] Ephèus *MS. 101A*
359 Gates *rev from* Gates, *MS. 101B*
361 repose, *rev in pencil from* repose *MS. 101B*
390 Flee *so MS. 101A* flee *MS. 101B*
392 Enemy *rev from* enemy *MS. 101B*
400–401 Land . . . Walls] land . . . walls *MS. 101B (CW, Jr.)*
403 Sanctuary *rev from* sanctuary *MS. 101B*
410 fled:] fled; *MS. 101A*
411 ears.] ears: *MS. 101A*
424 Clamor] Clamour *MS. 101A*
427 promise, *rev from* promise— *MS. 101B*
432 Lo Pantheus! *rev from no para indent MS. 101B*
438 Said,] Said *MS. 101A*
441 Troy; *rev from* Troy— *MS. 101B*
442 Argos; *rev from* Argos— *MS. 101B*
445 stream] stream, *MS. 101A*
446 victor] Victor *MS. 101A*
449 e'er *rev from* ere *MS. 101A* Coasts *rev from* coasts *MS. 101A*
454 Urged *so MS. 101A* Urge'd *MS. 101B* inspire] inspire, *MS. 101A*
456 Erinnys,] *so MS. 101A but underlined;* Erinnnys *left blank and added later MS. 101B (DW over WW's pencil)*
458 Rypheus *rev from* Ripheus *MS. 101A (MW following WW's pencil), MS. 101B (DW following WW's pencil)*
460 Hypanis] Hypamus *MS. 101A, with WW's pencil correction* nis *above and below the line; rev from* Hypanus *MS. 101B (DW following WW's pencil)*
463 led.] led; *MS. 101A*
464 sustain, *ed* sustain *MSS.*
471 condition;—] condition,—*MS. 101A*
473 renounc'd *rev from* renounced *MS. 101B*
474 "—Ye] —"Ye *MS. 101A*
479 hunger *rev from* hunger, *MSS.* den,] den *MS. 101A*
485 strenghten'd] strength'ned *MS. 101A*
511 so] so, *MS. 101A, rev from* so, *MS. 101B*
512 would] *would MS. 101A* fled.] fled; *MS. 101A, rev from* fled; *MS. 101B*
513 surround; *rev from* surround, *MS. 101B* surround: *MS. 101A*
515 Subdued] Subdu'd *MS. 101A*
521 semblance; *rev from* semblance— *MS. 101B*
526 falchion *rev from* falcheon *MSS.*
533 hide— *rev from* hide. *MS. 101B* hide— *MS. 101A*
538 Tow'rd *rev from* Toward *MS. 101A*
548 amain;] amain, *MS. 101A*
552 meet.] meet; *MS. 101A*
557 Notus] Notus, *MS. 101A*
563 known; known. *MS. 101A*
564 disown,] disown; *MS. 101A*
566 down;] down, *MS. 101A*
567 Penelëus *rev in pencil from* Peneleus *MS. 101A*
569 just] just, *MS. 101A*
570 all;] all, *MS. 101A*
572 Hypanis *rev from* Hypanus *MS. 101B (DW following WW's pencil); rev from* Hypamus *MS. 101A*
573 Thee *rev from* thee *MS. 101A*
574 Pantheus!] Pantheus, *MS. 101A*
575 around.] around! *MS. 101A*
578 bear. . .word! *rev in ink over pencil to* (bear . . . word!) *MS. 101A*
584 and] and, *MS. 101A*
588 if,] if *MS. 101A*

590 hush'd,] hush'd— *MS. 101A, rev from* hush'd *MS. 101B*
601 prepar'd] prepared *MS. 101A*
606 blind] blind, *MS. 101A*
607 Mansions *rev from* mansions *MS. 101B (DW following WW's pencil)* mansions *MS. 101A*
608 reign'd,] reign'd *MS. 101A*
612 gate, *rev from* gate *MS. 101A (WW's pencil)*
615 unrivall'd] unrivalled *MS. 101A*
616 Station *rev from* station *MS. 101B*
620 rend,] rend,— *MS. 101A*
625 seize] seize, *MS. 101A*
628 light.] light; *rev from* light, *MS. 101A*
635 sun] Sun *MS. 101A*
636 Periphas *rev from* Periphus *MS. 101B rev from* Perephus *MS. 101A* on] on, *MS. 101A*
637 Palace] Palace, *MS. 101A*
638 Car;— *rev from* Car, *MS. 101B* Car; *MS. 101A*
639 brands. *so MS. 101A* brands *MS. 101B*
643 hewn, *rev in pencil and ink from* hewn *MS. 101A* brass *rev from* brass, *MS. 101B*
644 entrance:— *rev from* entrance *MSS.* seats] seats. *MS. 101A*
645 open:] open:— *MS. 101A*
647 Lo *rev from* lo *MS. 101B* lo *MS. 101A*
648 prepar'd.] prepar'd! *rev from* prepar'd, *MS. 101A*
662 mounds *rev from* mounds, *MS. 101B*
666 palace] Palace *MS. 101A*
671 he, *rev from* he *MS. 101B*
673 There,] There *MS. 101A* told:—] told; *MS. 101A, rev from* told; *MS. 101B*
674 gold! *so MS. 101A* gold *rev from* gold, *MS. 101B*
680 state,] State, *MS. 101A, rev from* state *MS. 101B*
684 hie,] hie *MS. 101A*
685 Enemy *rev from* enemy *MS. 101A*
687 lived] liv'd *MS. 101A*
691 sky,] sky. *MS. 101A*
692 place] place, *MS. 101A*
696 decay'd] decayd *MS. 101A*
702 Thou *rev from* thou *MS. 101A*
706 charged] charg'd *MS. 101A, apos added above* "e" *MS. 101B*
715 ground,] ground *MS. 101A*
716 wound. *so MS. 101A* wound, *MS. 101B*
717 Priam,] Priam *MS. 101A* death] death, *MS. 101A* self-regard,] *so MS. 101A* self-regard *MS. 101B*
719 be *rev from* be, *MS. 101B*
725 self,] self *MS. 101A*
726 falsehood *rev from* falshood *MS. 101B*
728 rever'd] revered *rev from* rever'd *MS. 101A*
731 said,] *so MS. 101A* said; *MS. 101B*
732 faltering] faultering *MS. 101A*
737 messenger *rev from* mesinger *MS. 101B*
740 —So] So *MS. 101A*
744 side; *rev from* side — *MS. 101B*
754 HE] He *MS. 101A*
758 look'd, and *rev from* look'd, a *MS. 101B*
764 eyesight] eye-sight *MS. 101A*
766 Vesta.] Vesta *MS. 101B* Vesta. *rev from* Vesta, *MS. 101A*
767 vengeance *rev from* vengeance, *MSS.*
770 flown— *rev from* flown, *MS. 101B*
771 Country— *rev from* Country, *MS. 101B*
773 secresy *rev from* secrecy *MS. 101A*
775 ask] ask, *MS. 101A*
776 What!] What *MS. 101A*
777 Train?] Train, *MS. 101A*
778 Sires] Sires, *MS. 101A*
790 Appear'd] Appeard *MS. 101A*
796 seiz'd] seized *MS. 101A* suffic'd] sufficed *MS. 101A*
804 environ:—] environ,— *MS. 101A*
808 Lord— *rev from* Lord.— *MS. 101B* Lord, *MS. 101A*
819 foundation—] foundation, *rev to* foundation,— *MS. 101A*
821 Scæan] Siæan *MS. 101A*
822 beckoning] beck'ning *rev from* beconing *MS. 101A*
833 ceas'd— *rev from* ceas'd, *MS. 101B*
835 Enemies *rev from* enemies *MS. 101B*
839 Even so,] Even so; *MS. 101A* Mountain-Ash *rev from* mountain-Ash *MS. 101B* mountain-Ash *MS. 101A*
840 storms *rev from* storms, *MS. 101B* endured] endur'd *MS. 101A*
843 threatening] threat'ning *MS. 101A* forehead,] forehead *MS. 101A*
848 'twixt] twixt *MS. 101A*
849 Advance:—] Advane:— *MS. 101A*
850 But] —But *no para indent MS. 101A*
852 sought *rev from* sought, *MS. 101B* sought, *MS. 101A* bear] bear, *MS. 101A*
853 safety *rev from* safety, *MS. 101B*
856 *Ye*] Ye *rev from Ye rev from* Ye *MS. 101A*
859 abodes *rev to* Abodes *MS. 101A*
863 Depart! *rev from* Depart, *MS. 101B*
864 death; *rev from* death, *MS. 101A*
866 and] and, *MS. 101A*
879 alone. *so MS. 101A;* alone *MS. 101B*
881 thee, Father] thee Father *MS. 101A*
882 unbind? *rev from* unbind *MS. 101B* unbind! *rev from* unbind *MS. 101A*
885 stedfast *rev from* steadfast *MS. 101A*
896 tinged] ting'd *MS. 101A*

898 me, *rev in pencil from* me *MS. 101A*
904 cast *rev from* cast, *MS. 101B*
914 portent, and wonderous] portent and wond'rous *MS. 101A* told! *rev from* told, *MS. 101A*
924 Heaven] heaven *MS. 101A* gaz'd;] gaz'd. *MS. 101A*
926 us;] us, *MS 101A*
932 Star] Star, *MS. 101A*
933 sparkl'd] sparkled *MS. 101A*
936 light: *rev from* light. *MS. 101B* light; *MS. 101A*
940 adores;] adores. *MS. 101A*
942 Ye *rev from* ye *MS. 101B*
943 'Tis] Tis *MS. 101A*
944 Little *rev from* little *MSS*
954 participate] participitate *rev from* parcipitate *MS. 101A*
955 Boy *rev from* boy *MS. 101B* journey,] journey *MS. 101A*
957 Mound *rev from* mound *MS. 101A*
959 honour'd] honor'd *MS. 101A*
967 clad; *rev from* clad: *MS. 101B*
974 Greeks *rev in pencil to* Greeks, *MS. 101A* Arms *rev from* arms *MS. 101A*
979 thought *over illeg eras MS. 101B (DW following WW's pencil)*
989 wander'd] wandered *MS. 101A*
990 plain:] plain; *MS. 101A*
991 vanish'd, *rev from* vanish'd *MS. 101B* again. *so MSS. but rev to* again, *MS. 101B*
994 One *rev from* one*MS. 101B*
995 assembl'd;] assembled: *MS. 101A*
997 Companion, Son, and Husband *rev from* Companion—Son and Husband—*MS. 101B*
1000 friends] Friends *MS. 101A*
1002 retrace;] retrace, *MS. 101A*
1003 explore,] explore *MS. 101A*
1007 Remeasure,] Remeasure *MS. 101A*
1011 repair,] repair *MS. 101A; rev from* repair'd, *MS. 101B*
1012 If haply, *rev from* If haply— *MS. 101B* haply, she] haply She *MS. 101A; rev from* haply, She *MS. 101B*
1013 Seiz'd] Seized *MS. 101A* Abode *rev from* abode *MS. 101A*
1014 now] now, *MSS. rev to* now *MS. 101B* shew'd,] shewd. *MS. 101A*
1028 reduplication] re-duplication *MS. 101A*
1029 again. *rev from* again; *MS. 101B*
1036 source;] source, *MS. 101A*
1040 know] know, *MS. 101A*
1044 'mid] mid *MS. 101A*
1046 royal] Royal *MS. 101A* Bride; *rev from* Bride? *MSS.*
1049 see,] see *MS. 101A*
1051 Deriv'd] Derived *MS. 101A*
1065 now] now, *MS. 101A*
1066 bent,] bent; *MS. 101A*
1076 blockade,] blockade; *MS. 101A*
subscript the Second] 2^{d} *MS. 101A*

Book III

7 Fleet:— *rev from* Fleet,— *MS. 101C*
16 Friends . . . Son *rev from* friends . . . son *MS. 101C*
24 Æneades— *rev from* Æneades; *MS. 101C*
28 offerings:— *rev from* offerings, *MS. 101C*
30 Heaven— *rev from* Heaven. *MS.101C* Mount *rev from* mount *MS. 101C*
36 told! *rev from* told. *MS. 101C*
38 Tree *rev from* tree *MS. 101C*
40 ground:— *rev from* ground,— *MS. 101C*
45 before *rev from* before, *MS. 101C*
47 Nymphs; *rev from* nymphs, *MS. 101C*
59 Man *rev from* man *MS. 101C*
63 shore *rev from* shore, *MS. 101C*
78 seized *rev from* siezed *MS. 101C*
84 Land *rev from* land *MS. 101C*
89 mound *rev from* mound, *MS. 101C*
93 Women *rev from* women *MS. 101C*
95 Spirit *rev from* spirit *MS. 101C*
99 Crew *rev from* crew *MS. 101C*
100 leave:— *rev from* leave, *MS. 101C*
102 spot *rev from* Spot *MS. 101C*
106 Sea *rev from* sea *MS. 101C*
110 Place *rev from* place *MS. 101C*
124 stone:— *rev from* stone;— *MS. 101C*
130 accord! *rev from* accord. *MS. 101C*
131 seek? . . . follow? *rev from* seek, . . . follow, *MS. 101C*
134 Abode *rev from* abode *MS. 101C*
136 rock'd; *rev from* rock'd, *MS. 101C*
142 *Her rev from* her *MS. 101C*
152 affords! *rev from* affords. *MS. 101C*
158 Land *rev from* land *MS. 101C*
159 Rhœtean *rev from* Rhœtæn *MS. 101C*
160 remember) *rev from* remember *MS. 101C*
161 progenitor; *rev from* progenitor) *MS. 101C*
162 Seat *rev from* seat *MS. 101C*
166 ordain'd; *rev from* ordain'd. *MS. 101C*
168 Idæan *rev from* Idean *MS. 101C*
170 Car. *rev from* Car: *MS. 101C*
171 haste— *rev from* haste, *MS. 101C*
180 thee. *rev from* thee; *MS. 101C*
182 Zephyrs *rev from* Zyphers *MS. 101C* white. *rev from* white, *MS. 101C*
184 ground; *rev from* ground, *MS. 101C*
185 Idomeneus *rev from* Idomemus *MS. 101C*

192 Olearos *rev from* Olearius *MS. 101C*
202 *para indent orig omitted MS. 101C; rev to text (WW)*
204 call. *rev from* call: *MS. 101C*
216 Syrius *rev from* Syrias *MS. 101C*
231 we *rev from* We *MS. 101C*
236 We *rev from* we *MS. 101C*
239 prepare; *rev from* prepare: *MS. 101C*
240 design'd *ed* designd *MS. 101C*
243 increase, *ed* increase *MS. 101C*
247 Jasius— *rev from* Jaseus, *MS. 101C*
250 yields *rev from* yeilds *MS. 101C*
251 Dictean *rev from* Dictæan *MS. 101C*
257 heav'n,—*rev from* heav'n: *MS. 101C*
258 recipient *rev from* recipiant *MS. 101C*
263 entrance; *rev from* entrance, *MS. 101C*
270 outthrew *rev from* outhrew *MS. 101C*
271 Nation *rev from* nation *MS. 101C*
280 Gallies *rev from* gallies *MS. 101C*
284 Tempest-laden Cloud *rev from* tempest-laden cloud *MS. 101C*
291 fire— *rev from* fire; *MS. 101C*
301 smoke: *rev from* smoke; *MS. 101C*
306 Strophades *rev from* Strophedes *MS. 101C*
314 Styx *rev from* Sty[?k] *MS. 101C*
316 Thing *rev from* thing *MS. 101C*
319 pause! *rev from* pause, *MS. 101C*
322 follows; *rev from* follows, *MS. 101C*
327 mountain— *rev from* mountain, *MS. 101C*
335 o'er *rev from* o'er, *MS. 101C*
343 Misenus *rev from* Musanus *MS. 101C*
344 Fowls *rev from* fowls *MS. 101C*
345 aqueous *rev from* aqueus *MS. 101C*
346 it? *rev from* it, *MS. 101C*
352 Descendants *rev from* descendants *MS. 101C*
355 dwell? *rev from* dwell. *MS. 101C*
365 "E're *rev from* E're *MS. 101C*
374 Birds *rev from* birds *MS. 101C*
375 Rites *rev from* rites *MS. 101C*
378 harm! *rev from* harm. *MS. 101C*
384 Zacinthus *rev from* zacinthus *MS. 101C*
387 Ithaca . . . Nurse *rev from* Ithica . . . nurse *MS. 101C*
388 Ulysses! *rev from* Ulysses, *MS. 101C*
396 blaze; *rev from* blaze, *MS. 101C*
400 toil; *rev from* toil, *MS. 101C*
403 —Sol *rev from* Sol *MS. 101C* pass'd *ed* passd *MS. 101C*
409 *MS. 101A begins here*
410 cleave;] cleave: *MS. 101A*
411 Phæacian *rev from* Phærecian *MS. 101C* Peaks] peaks *MS. 101A* air] air, *MS. 101A*
412 proceed,] proceed:— *MS. 101A*
413 And,] And, *rev to* And *MS. 101A*
414 Buthrotus perch'd] Buthrotus, perched *MS. 101A* seat.] seat *MS. 101A*
415 Chief *rev from* chief *MS. 101A*
416 tale ill-fitted] tale, ill fitted *MS. 101A*
417 Govern'd] Governed *MS. 101A* reign'd,] reigned; *MS. 101A*
419 Andromache] Andromoche *MS. 101A* Spouse—] *rev from* Spouse, *MS. 101C* spouse, *MS. 101A*
421 long'd] longed *MS. 101A* wish'd] wished *MS. 101A*
422 Story] story *MS. 101A*
423 So, . . . Gallies] So . . . gallies *MS. 101A* lay,] lay *MS. 101A*
424 pursu'd] pursued *MS. 101A*
426 dignified,] dignified *MS. 101A*
427 Andromache *rev from* Andromache, *MS. 101C, rev from* Andromoche *MS. 101A* paid,] paid *MS. 101A*
428 chanc'd] chanced *MS. 101A* shade: *rev from* shade, *MS. 101C* Shade. *rev from* shade. *MS. 101A*
430 Tomb—his . . . Monument] Tomb (his . . . monument) *MS. 101A*
431 green-sward] green-sward, *MS. 101A* care; *rev from* care, *MS. 101A*
432 funereal *rev from* funerial *MS. 101C* Altars] altars *MS. 101A*
433 Quicken'd] Quickened *MS. 101A*
434 She *rev from* she *MS. 101C* she *MS. 101A* witness'd,] witnessed *rev from* witnessed, *MS. 101A*
435 shrunk—] shrunk *MS. 101A* prodigy.] prodigy; *rev from* prodigy, *MS. 101A*
436 astonishment *so MS. 101A* astonisment *MS. 101C*
438 swoon'd— *rev from* swoon'd *MS. 101C* swooned *MS. 101A* ground,] ground *MS. 101A*
439 found;] found, *MS. 101A, rev from* found, *MS. 101C*
440 Shape] shape *MS. 101A* view?] view, *MS. 101A*
441–443 *no open quots MS. 101A*
441 Goddess, is *rev from* Goddess! Is *MS. 101C*
443 spake,—] spake; *MS. 101A*
445 Utter'd] Uttered *MS. 101A* disturb'd] disturbed *MS. 101A*
446–452 *no open quots MS. 101A*
448 height,] height *MS. 101A* Mate] mate *MS. 101A*
450 offer] offer, *MS. 101A*
452 Spouse?"] spouse? *MS. 101A*
453 she] she— *MS. 101A* subdu'd;] subdued, *MS. 101A*
454 Virgin,] Virgin *rev from* virgin *MS. 101A*

blood,] blood *MS. 101A*
455–487 *no open quots MS. 101A*
455 Who,] Who *MS. 101A* Troy] Troy, *MS. 101A*
456 Did'st] Didst *MS. 101A*
457 slaughter'd] slaughtered MS. 101A
458 throng!] Throng! *MS. 101A*
459 O] O, *MS. 101A* all] all, *MS. 101A* ne'er *so MS. 101A* neer *MS. 101C*
460 bed,] bed *MS. 101A*
462 cross'd] crossed *MS. 101A*
464 Mother's] mother's *MS. 101A*
465 unty'd,] untyed *MS. 101A*
466 Hermione] Hermione, *MS. 101A*
468 "Captive to Captive *rev from* "Captive to captive *MS. 101C; so MS. 101A, but* "Captive] —Capitive Slave to Slave *rev from* slave to slave *MS. 101A*
469 "Whereat, Orestes] Whereat Orestes, *MS. 101A* inflam'd] inflamed *MS. 101A*
470 her now lost *rev from* her now lost, *MS. 101C* her, now lost, *MS. 101A* claim'd] claimed *MS. 101A*
471 And] And, *MS. 101A* driv'n] driven *MS. 101A*
474 devolv'd] devolved *MS. 101A* Domain;] domain, *MS. 101A*
475 call'd] called *MS. 101A*
476 nam'd] named *MS. 101A* Region *rev from* region *MS. 101C* region *MS. 101A*
477 Chaon— *rev from* Chaon: *MS.101C* site] *so MS. 101A* site— *rev from* site: *MS. 101C*
479 thee] thee, *MS. 101A* Stranger] Stranger— *MS. 101A* unknown—] unknown *MS. 101A*
480 Fates] fates *MS. 101A* blown?] *so MS. 101A* blown *MS. 101C*
481 say] say, *MS. 101A* coasts] Coasts *MS. 101A*
482 Ascanius *rev from* Ascanias *MS. 101C*
484 Æneas] Æneus *MS. 101A*
487 days?] *rev from* days. *MS. 101C* days. *MS. 101A*
488 follow'd] followed *MS. 101A* vain;] vain: *MS. 101A*
489 City,] City *MS. 101A* train,] train *MS. 101A*
490 Consort Helenus] consort, Helenus, *MS. 101A*
491 saw, *rev to* saw; *MS. 101A*
495 Xanthus, *del to* Xanthus *MS. 101A*
499 excite *rev from* exite *MS. 101C*
500 unreserv'd delight;] unreserved delight *MS. 101A*
502 welcòming;] welcoming. *MS. 101A*
504 Refresh'd] Refreshed *MS. 101A* serv'd] served *MS.101A*
505 And,] And *MS. 101A* resplendent *rev from* resplendant *MSS.* goblets,] goblets *MS. 101A*
507 past *rev from* pass'd *MS. 101C* passed *MS. 101A*
508 Seas;] seas. *MS. 101A*
509 prefer;] prefer, *MS. 101A*
510 interpreter *rev from* interpretor *MS. 101C*
511–521 *no open quots MS. 101A*
511 fill'd;] filled *MS. 101A*
512 Skill'd . . . skill'd;] Skilled . . . skilled, *MS. 101A*
513 Skill'd] Skilled *MS. 101A*
514 bring; *rev from* bring, *MS. 101C* bring, *MS. 101A*
517 end: *rev from* end; *MS. 101C* end. *MS. 101A*
518 Harpy Queen] harpy queen *rev to* harpy Queen *MS. 101A*
519 rage;] rage. *MS. 101A*
521 course] course, *MS. 101A* deliverance] deliverance, MS. 101A run?"] run *MS. 101A*
522 *parens added over commas MS. 101C* accustom'd Victims] accustomed victims *MS. 101A, rev from* accustom'd victims *MS. 101C*
523 Gods] gods *MS. 101A* obtain.] obtain, *MS. 101A*
525 hand; *rev from* hand, *MS. 101C*
526 led,] led— *MS. 101A*
527 flow'd] flowed *MS. 101A*
528 God.—] God, *MS. 101A*
530–639 *no open quots MS. 101A*
530 Venus!] Venus, *MS. 101A* Main] main *MS. 101A*
532 But,] But *MS. 101A*
534 future; *rev from* future, *MS. 101C* future: *MS. 101A*
535 rest; *rev from* rest, *MS. 101C*
536 Italy,] Italy *MS. 101A*
540 oar;] oar *MS. 101A*
541 Thou,] Thou *MS. 101A* gulphs,] gulphs *MS. 101A* explore,] explore *MS. 101A*
542 Circean *rev from* Cercean *MS. 101C* Pool, *rev from* pool, *MS. 101C* pool *MS. 101A*
544 Signs— *rev from* signs, *MS. 101C*
546 Female] female *MS. 101A* Kind] kind, *MS. 101A*
547 sequester'd river's margin laid,] sequestered River's margin, laid *MS. 101A*
549 Young-ones couch'd . . . Recess,] young ones couched . . . recess, *MS. 101A*

550 Dam] dam *MS. 101A*
551 City;—] City— *MS. 101A* *that*] that *MS. 101A*
552 solicitudes,] solicitudes *MS. 101A* repose.] repose; *MS. 101A*
553 Celæno's *rev from* Cælæna's *MS. 101C*
555 Lands *rev from* lands *MS. 101C* lands *MS. 101A* sea] Sea *MS. 101A*
556 Italy.] Italy; *MS. 101A*
557 abide;] abide, *MS. 101A*
558 there *rev from* there, *MS. 101C* Town] town *MS. 101A*
559 Idomeneus *rev from* Idomoneus *MS. 101C* Idomenus *MS. 101A* compass'd] compassed *MS. 101A*
560 ground;] ground, *MS. 101A*
561 Thessalian Phyloctetes *rev from* Thesalian Phylectetus *MS. 101C* Thessalian Philoctetes *MS. 101A*
563 when] when (*rev from* when, *MS. 101A* past over,] pass'd over) *MS. 101A*
564 Altars] altars *MS. 101A*
565 offer'd] offered *MS. 101A*
567 sacrifice]sacrifice, *MS. 101A* cover'd] covered *MS. 101A*
570 consign!] consign. *MS. 101A*
571 when] when, *MS. 101A* o'er, *so MS. 101A* o'er *MS. 101C*
573 Pelorus *rev from* Peloris *MS. 101C*
574 open—] open *MS. 101A*
576 left,] left *MS. 101A*
577 *no para indent MS. 101A* Tis] 'Tis *MS. 101A* Earth *rev from* earth *MS. 101C*
578 Continent:] Continent; *rev from* Continent, *MS. 101A*
579 doubt,] doubt *MS. 101A* power *rev from* Power *MS. 101C*
580 Antiquity] antiquity *MS. 101A*
581 flow'd] flowed *MS. 101A* between, *rev from* between; *MS. 101C*
582 establish'd] established *MS. 101A*
583 Still,] Still *MS. 101A* Straits,] straits *MS. 101A*
584 Town . . . Town] town . . . town *MS. 101A*
585 Scylla *rev from* Sylla *MS. 101C* fret;] fret, *MS. 101A*
586 beset;] beset. *MS. 101A* Charybdis *rev from* charybdis *MS. 101A*
587 Thrice] Thrice, *MS. 101A*
588 down,] down *MS. 101A* precipice] precipice, *MS. 101A*
589 billows, and,] billows; and *MS. 101A*
591 Cavern] cavern *MS. 101A*
593 She *rev from* she *MS 101C* she *MS. 101A*
595 Sea-Beast— *rev from* sea Beast *MS. 101C* sea beast *MS. 101A* Dolphin] dolphin *MS. 101A*
596 Water Wolves] water-wolves *MS. 101A* Dogs] dogs *MS. 101A* round!] round, *MS. 101A*
597 Thou *rev from* thou *MS. 101C* thou *MS. 101A* provide] provide, *MS. 101A*
598 Pachynus *rev from* Pachymus *MS. 101C* Pacchynus *MS. 101A* wide;] wide, *MS. 101A*
600 marine. *rev from* marine, *MS. 101A*
602 unenlighten'd] unenlightened *MS. 101A*
603 Goddess-born,] Goddess-born! *MS. 101A* (on] on *MS. 101A* enlarge *rev from* enlarge) *MS. 101C* enlarge, *MS. 101A*
604 charge)] charge, *MS. 101A*
605 Juno,] Juno; *MS. 101A*
607 hate;] hate: *MS. 101A*
610 P *indicating para indent in left margin MS. 101A*
612 She *rev from* she *MS. 101C* she *MS. 101A*
613 extatic] ecstatic *MS. 101A*
615 prophesies] prophesies, *MS. 101A*
617 Mid] 'Mid *MS. 101A*
618 undisturb'd] undisturbed *MS. 101A*
619 But] But, *MS. 101A*
620 Leaves] leaves *MS. 101A*
622 diligence;] diligence: *MS. 101A* flutter,] flutter *MS. 101A* chuse,] chuse *MS. 101A*
623 disconnection *rev from* disconnection, *MS. 101A*
624 they,] they *rev from* they, *MS. 101A* beguil'd] beguiled *rev from* beguiled, *MS. 101A*
625 depart,] depart *MS. 101A*
627 ill-dispos'd] ill-disposed *MS. 101A*
629 Followers] followers *MS. 101A*
630 winds] Winds *MS. 101A* gone,] gone *MS. 101A*
633 doom,] doom *MS. 101A*
634 Wars] wars *MS. 101A*
637 Enough—] Enough;— *MS. 101A*
640 Seer,] Seer *MS. 101A* hallowed] hallow'd *MS. 101A*
641 Ships;] Ships, *MS. 101A*
642 pond'rous] ponderous *MS. 101A*
643 fashion'd] fashined *MS. 101A* ore,] ore; *MS. 101A*
644 Cauldrons;—] Cauldrons; *MS. 101A* with-holds] withholds *MS. 101A*
645 halberk] hauberk *MS. 101A* triple *so MS. 101A* treple *MS. 101C*
647 resplendent *rev from* resplendant *MSS.* crest] crest, *MS. 101A*
649 adds] adds, *MS. 101A* Bands] bands *MS. 101A*

650 Rowers] rowers *MS. 101A* Arms] arms *MS. 101A* commands. *rev from* commands: *MS. 101C*
651 —Meanwhile] Meanwhile *with para indent MS. 101A*
652 sails] Sails *MS. 101A*
653 address'd *rev from* addrest *MSS*
654 Guest;] Guest, *MS. 101A*
655 Anchises! *rev from* Anchises, *MS. 101C* Anchises, *MS. 101A* honors] honours *MS. 101A*
656–663 *no open quots MS. 101A*
656 deign'd] deigned *MS. 101A*
657 snatch'd] snatched *MS. 101A* lost,] lost *MS. 101A*
658 Now] Now, *MS. 101A* cross'd *rev from* crost *MS. 101A*
660 point;] point: *MS. 101A* Land *rev from* land *MS. 101C*
661 powers:] powers. *MS. 101A*
662 Son;] Son! *MS. 101A*
664 disturb'd] disturbed *MS. 101A*
665 That parting now] That, parting now, *MS. 101A* now *rev from* now, *MS. 101C*
666 Embroider'd Vests] Embroidered vests *MS. 101A* bestows;] bestows, *MS. 101A*
667 Tunic] tunic *MS. 101A* o'er *so MS. 101A* oer *MS. 101C*
668 And] And, *MS. 101A*
669 loom;] loom. *MS. 101A*
670 also,] also *MS. 101A del*
671–689 *no open quots MS. 101A*
671 memorials *rev from* memorial *MS. 101C* hand, accept!] hand accept, *MS. 101A then line del,* accept! *rev from* accept *MS. 101C*
672 Consort, *rev from* Consort— *MS. 101C* consort, *MS. 101A*
673 love;] love. *MS. 101A*
674 Andromache *rev from* Andromeche *MS. 101C* Andromoche *MS. 101A* gives] gives, *MS. 101A*
675 Boy!—] Boy, *MS. 101A* Image *rev from* image *MS. 101C* image *MS. 101A*
676 Astyanax—] Astyanax, *MS. 101A*
677 seen,] seen; *MS. 101A*
678 tomb,] tomb *MS. 101A*
679 open'd] opened *MS. 101A* bloom."] bloom. *MS. 101A*
680 bedew'd] bedewed *MS. 101A* cheek,] cheek *MS. 101A*
681 speak;] speak, *MS. 101A*
682 happy Ye,] happy, ye *MS. 101A*
683 life;] life—*MS. 101A*
684 quiet] Quiet *rev from* quiet *MS. 101A* won.] won, *MS. 101A*
685 Ye to measure;] ye to measure, *MS. 101A*
686 impos'd] imposed *MS. 101A* Ausonia] Ausania *MS. 101A*
696 Epirian *rev from* Eperian *MS. 101A* came] came, *MS. 101A*
701 ground;] ground. *MS. 101A*
703 mountain dark'ned] mountain, darkened *MS. 101A* head.] head: *MS. 101A*
710 Palinurus *rev from* Palenurus *MS. 101C*
721 redden'd] reddened *MS. 101A*
722 vanish'd,] vanished *MS. 101A*
723 Italy.] Italy *MS. 101A*
724 "Italia!" *so MS. 101A* Italia! *MS. 101C* Achates:] Achates!" *MS. 101A*
725 gratulant *rev from* gratulent *MS. 101C (MW following WW's pencil)* rebound,] rebound *MS. 101A*
728 fill'd] filled *MS. 101A* wine.] wine: *MS. 101A*
729 Then,] Then *MS. 101A* Stern] stern *MS. 101A* stand,] stand *MS. 101A*
731–732 *no open quots MS. 101A*
731 Storms] storms *MS. 101A* govern'd,] governed *MS. 101A*
732 sway!"] sway." *MS. 101A*
733 —With] With *MS. 101A* wish'd-for gales;] wished-for gales, *MS. 101A*
734 And,] And *MS. 101A* Ships] ships *MS. 101A* sails,]sails *MS. 101A*
735 Port;] Port, *MS. 101A* sight,] sight *MS. 101A*
736 height. *rev from* height, *MS. 101C*
737 furl'd] furled *MS. 101A* hand; *rev from* hand, *MS. 101C* hand, *MS. 101A*
738 Strand] strand *MS. 101A*
739 bow] bow, *MS. 101A* Haven] haven *MS. 101A*
740 East; *rev from* East, *MS. 101C*
741 peacefulness; *rev from* peacefulness, *MS. 101C* peacefulness: *MS. 101A*
744 Sea, *rev from* Sea *rev from* Sea, *MS. 101C* sea, *MS. 101A*
745 lies; *rev from* lies, *MS. 101C* lies, *MS. 101A*
746 eyes,] eyes *MS. 101A*
747 *MS. 101A ends here*
751 war; *rev from* war, *MS. 101C*
752 menace; *rev from* menace, *MS. 101C*
762 Shore— *rev from* shore, *MS. 101C*
770 fear'd; *rev from* fear'd, *MS. 101C*
778 Charybdis; *rev from* Charybdis *MS. 101C*
794 loud; *rev from* loud, *MS. 101C*

Translation of Virgil's *Aeneid* Transcriptions

Aeneid Drafts in DC MS. 89 (Preceded by Photographs)

DC MS. 89 is a leather-bound folio used by the Wordsworths at Rydal Mount from about 1820 onward. It contains miscellaneous late poetry and prose, in various hands, and is alphabetically thumb-indexed. Not all entries, however, accord with the index. The book appears to have contained a total of 238 leaves, in 21 gatherings (4 sixteens, 8 twelves, 7 eights, one six, and one more probably of sixteen, now reduced to four); 201 of these leaves survive, 2 of them partially cut away, and there are 25 stubs. The book as originally bound contains two kinds of paper, one watermarked with a fleur-de-lis over a large, diagonally striped medallion and countermarked PR, the other with a fleur-de lis over a similar but smaller medallion, countermarked RC. The leaves measure approximately 28 by 43.8 cm.; chain lines run vertically at intervals of 2.7 cm. There are three pasteovers, one of blue-tinted wove stock and two of cream wove stock.

MS. 89 contains full drafts of the *Aeneid* translation, in the autographs of John Carter, Dorothy, Dora, Mary, and William Wordsworth, and Samuel Tillbrooke. Several notations in the manuscript, usually having to do with line numbers in the original Latin, are in the autograph of Gordon Graham Wordsworth, the poet's grandson, and hence are not transcribed. The page numbers, which likewise are in Gordon Graham Wordsworth's autograph, are not transcribed. In addition to drafts of the translation, the following note, in Dorothy Wordsworth's autograph, is found on 226^{r}: "MSS. Virgil & Well Poem put in Mary's desk upstairs." For the "Well Poem," *Composed when a probability existed of our being obliged to quit Rydal Mount as a Residence,* see *"The Tuft of Primroses," with Other Late Poems for "The Recluse,"* edited by Joseph F. Kishel (Ithaca, 1986).

Because of the size of the pages in MS. 89, it is not possible to present photographs with facing-page transcriptions. Consequently, photographs of the manuscript pages are presented first, followed on page 416 by transcriptions.

3d Book

Now when the Gods had crushed the Asian states,
And Priam's race not meriting such fates,
When they were pleased proud Ilium to destroy,
And smokes upon the ground Neptunian Troy;
The sad survivors from their Country driven
Seek distant shores, impelled by sighs from heaven.
Beneath Antandros we prepare a Fleet,
And there my companions muster at the feet
Of Phrygian Ida, dubious in our quest
Where the fates may suffer us to rest.
Scarcely had breathed the earliest summer gales
Before Anchises bids to spread the sails.
Weeping I quit the port, my native coast,
And fields where Troy once was; & borne an host,
An exile on the bosom of the seas,
With friends, son, household Gods, & the great deities.
While Fortune favoured; thither borne I lay

And kindred Gods, while Troy maintained her sway;
There, galled with unfriendly fates, I lay
My first foundations in a hollow Bay.
Aeneadae the men I needed, to share
With the new citizens the name I bear.
To Dionean Venus I present,
And to the Gods who aid a fresh intent,
The sacred offerings; & with honor due
Upon the shore a glossy Bull I slew
To the great King of Heavens. A mount was near
Upon whose summit cornel was upreared
Their boughs & myrtles rough with many a spear.
Studious to deck the altar with green shoots
Thither I turned, & tugging at the roots,
When, behold,
A dire portent & wonderous to be told!
No sooner was the sheltered root laid bare
Of the first tree I struggled to uptear,
Than from the fibres drops of blood distilled
Whose blackness stained the ground. Pale horror thrilled
Awaked every limb & all my blood was chilled
Persisting in the attempt I toiled to free
The flexile body of another tree,
Anxious the latent causes to explore,
And from the bark blood trickled as before.
Revolving much in mind forthwith I paid
Vows to the sylvan nymphs, & sought the aid
Of father Mars, spear-shaking God who yields
His stern protection to the Thracian fields.
But for a third endeavour when with hands
Eagerly strain'd, knees pressed against the sands,
I strove the myrtle lances to uproot
With my whole strength, (speak shall I or be mute)
From the deep tomb a mournful groan is heard
And a voice followed, uttering this lament.
That to a prosperous issue they would guide
The accident, the omen turn aside

1 Book

255

Arms & the Man I sing, the first who bore
His course to Latium from the Trojan shore
A Fugitive of Fate:— long time was he
By Powers celestial tossed by land & sea
Thro wrathful Juno's far-famed enmity;
Much, too, from war endured; till new abodes
He planted, & in Latium fixed his gods; —
Whence flows the Latin people; whence have come
The Alban Sires, & walls of lofty Rome.
Say Muse what Power was wrong'd; what grievance drove
To such extremity the Spouse of Jove,
Labouring to wrap in perils, to astound
With woes, a Man for piety renowned!
In heavenly breasts is such resentment found?
* Right opposite the Italian coast there stood
An ancient City, far from Tiber's flood;
Carthage its name, a colony of Tyre,
Rich, strong, & bold in war with fierce desire.
No region, not even Samos, was so graced
By Juno's favour; here her arms were placed
Here lodged her chariot; & unbounded scope
(Even then the Goddess gave to fond hope
Her [illegible] Fate such triumph will
That to this Nation all the world shall bow.
But Juno had told her that a race, from Troy
Derived, the Tyrian ramparts would destroy;
That, from this stock, a people, proud in war
And trained to spread dominion wide & far,
Should come, & thro' her favorite Lybian state
Spread utter ruin— such the doom of Fate.
In fear of this, while busy thought recalls
That war, she raised against the Trojan walls
For her loved Argos (&, with these combined,
Worked other causes rankling in her mind;
The judgement given by Paris, the slight
Her beauty had received on Ida's height;
Th'undying hatred which the race had bred,
And honours given to ravished Ganymed;)
Saturnian Juno far from Latium chased
The Trojans, tossed upon the watery waste;
Unhappy relics of the Grecian spear
And of the dire Achilles. Many a year

1st Book

They roamed, ere Fate's decision was fulfilled;
Such arduous toil it was, the Roman State to build.
Sicilian headlands scarcely out of sight,
They spread the canvas with a fresh delight.
When Juno, brooding o'er the eternal wound,
Thus inly: Must I vanquished quit the ground
Of my attempt, or impotently toil
To bar these Trojans from the Italian soil?
For the Fates thwart me; yet could Pallas raise
'Mid Argive vessels a destructive blaze,
And in the deep plunge all, for fault of one,
The desperate frenzy of Oileus' son.
She from the clouds the bolts of Jove might cast,
And ships & sea deliver to the blast:
Him, flames expiring from a bosom fraught
With sulphurous fire, she in a whirlwind caught,
And on a sharp rock fixed; but I, who move
Heaven's Queen, the Sister & the Wife of Jove,
Wage with one race the war I waged of yore!
Who then, henceforth, will Juno's name adore?
Her altars grace with gifts, her aid implore?
These things revolved in fiery discontent,
Her course the Goddess to Eolia bent,
Country of lowering clouds, where South winds rave;
Here Eolus within a spacious cave, controuls the struggling winds,
[illegible] sovereign power [illegible]
And the sonorous storms in durance bind.
Loud, loud the mountain murmurs as they seek
Their way upon the barriers. On a peak,
High-seated, Eolus his sceptre sways,
Soothes their fierce temper, & their wrath allays.
This did he not, sea, earth, & heaven's vast deep,
Would follow them, entangled in the sweep;
But in black caves the Sire Omnipotent
The winds sequestered, fearing such event;
Heaped over them vast mountains, and assigned
A monarch that should rule the blustering kind;
[illegible]
And give at his command a loosened rein.
As thus approached thus spake the suppliant Queen
Eolus! for the Sire of Gods & men
On thee confers the power to tranquillize
The troubled waves, or summon them to rise,
A race, my foes, [illegible] on the Tyrrhene sea
[illegible]
Troy & her conquered Gods, to Italy.

1st Book

Throw power into the winds; the ships submerge,
Or part give the bodies to the surge.
Thrice seven fair nymphs await on my command,
All beautiful, the fairest of the band,
Deiopeia, [illegible] by crown
will I [illegible] [illegible] to yours,
[illegible]
In everlasting fellowship with thee,
To dwell, & yield a beauteous progeny.
[illegible] God [illegible] declare [illegible] thy will
[illegible] O queen, thy will
And be it mine the mandate to fulfill.
To thee I owe my sceptre, and the place
Jove's favour hath assigned me; through thy grace
I at the banquets of the Gods recline;
And my whole empire is a gift of thine.
When Aeolus had ceased, his spear he bent
Full on the quarter where the winds were pent,
And smote the mountain. Forth, where way is made,
Rush his wild ministers, the land pervade,
And fasten on the deep. There Eurus, there
Notus, & Africus unused to spare
His tempests, work with congregated power,
To upturn the abyss, & roll the unwieldy waves ashore.
Clamour of men ensues, & crash of shrouds;
Heaven & the day, by instantaneous clouds,
Are ravished from the Trojans; on the floods
Black night descends, & palpable there broods.
The thundering Poles incessantly unsheath
Their fires, & all things threaten instant death.
Appall'd, & with slack limbs, Aeneas stands;
He groans, & heaven-ward lifting his clasp'd hands,
Exclaims; "Thrice happy they who chanced to fall
In front of lofty Ilium's sacred wall,
Their parents witnessing their end.—O why,
Bravest of Greeks, Tydides, could not I
Pour out my willing spirit thro' a wound
From thy right hand received, on Trojan ground
Where Hector lies subjected to the spear

Of the invincible Achilles, where
The great Sarpedon sleeps; o'er the plain,
Swift Simois whirls helmets, & shields, & men,
Throngs of the brave in fearless combat slain!

B While thus he spake the Aquilonian gale
Smote, from the front, upon his driving sail,
And heaved the billows ~~mass~~ to the sky,
Round the Ship, labouring in extremity,
Help from her shattered oars in vain she craves;
Then veers the prow, exposing to the waves
Her side; & lo! a surge, to mountain height
Gathering, prepares to burst with its whole weight.
Those hang aloft as if in air, to these
Earth is disclosed between the boiling seas;
Whirled on by Notus three encountered shocks
In the main sea, received from latent Rocks;
Rocks stretched, in dorsal ridge of rugged frame
On the deep's surface; Altars is the name
By which the Italians mark them. Three the force
Of Eurus hurries, from an open course,
On straits & shallows, dashes on the strand,
And girds the wreck about with heaps of sand.
Another, in which Lycus & his mate
Faithful Orontes share a common fate,
As his own eyes full plainly can discern,
By a huge wave is swept from prow to stern;
Headlong the pilot falls; thrice whirl'd around,
The Ship is swallowed in the gulf profound.
Amid the boundless eddies a lost few,
Drowning or drowned, emerge to casual view,
On waves which planks, & arms, & Trojan wealth bestrew.
Over the stony-ribb'd pinnace in which sails
Ilioneus, the hurricane prevails;
Now conquers Abas, then the ships that hold
Valiant Achates, & Aletes old;
The joints all loosening in their sides, they drink
The hostile brine thro' many a greedy chink.

What strife disturb'd the roaring sea
Meanwhile [illegible] the murmur of the Main,
And for what outrage the storm was free,
[illegible] the tempests without check or rein
Troubling the Ocean to its inmost caves
Neptune perceived incensed; & o'er the waves
Forth looking with a steadfast front & Eye
Raised from the deep in placid majesty,
He saw the Trojan Gallies scattered wide,
They then they lodge oppressed & terrified
[illegible] Waters and ruinous Heaven
[illegible] against their peace allied.
Nor from the Brother was concealed the heat
Of Juno's anger, & each dark deceit.
Eurus he called & Zephyrus & the pair
Who at his bidding, quit the fields of Air
He thus addressed. Upon your birth & kind
Have ye presumed with confidence so blind
As heedless of my Godhead to perplex
The land with uproar & the Sea to vex,
Which by your act O kings thus fiercely heaves?
Whom I — but better calm the troubled waves.
Henceforth atonement shall not prove so slight
For such a trespass; to your King take flight,
And say, that not to Him but unto me
Fate hath assigned this watery sovereignty;
Mine is this trident — his a rocky hold,
Thy mansion, Eurus! — vaunting uncontroll'd
Let Eolus there occupy his hall,
And in that prison-house the winds enthrall."
He spake & quicker than the word his will,
Fell thro' the Sea, abates each tumid hill,
Quiets the deep, & silences the shores,
And to a cloudless Heaven the Sun restores.
Cymothoë shoving, with leaning Triton's aid,
The stranded Ships; & from their flinty bed
He with his Trident lifts them; then divides

1st Book

The sluggish heaps of sand, & gently glides,
Skimming on {light} smooth wheels the level tides.
~~Next~~ Thus oft, when a sedition hath ensued
Arousing all the ignoble multitude,
Straight thro' the air do stones & torches fly,
With every missile frenzy can supply;
Then, if a venerable Man step forth,
Strong thro' acknowledged piety & worth,
Hushed at the sight into mute peace all stand
Listening, with eyes & ears at his command;
Their ~~minds~~ minds to him are subject, & the rage
That burns within their breasts his lenient words asswage.
~~Hence~~ {So} fell the Sea's whole tumult, ~~overawed~~
Then, when the Sire, casting his eyes abroad,
Turns, under open Heaven, his docile Steeds,
And with his flowing Chariot smoothly speeds.

C The worn-out Trojans, seeking land where'er
The nearest coast invites, for Lybia steer.
~~Within a long withdrawing bay there lies~~
There is a bay where deep retirement hides
~~Concealed from all but searching eyes~~
The place where Nature's self a port
~~Where Nature's self a friendly~~ ~~port~~ provides,
Formed by ~~an~~ {friendly} Islands' ~~far projecting~~ {jutting} sides;
Bulwark from which the billows of the Main
Recoil upon themselves, spending their force in vain.
Vast rocks are here; & safe beneath the brows
Of two heaven-threatening cliffs, the floods repose.
Glancing aloft, in bright theatric show
Woods wave, & gloomily impend below;
Right opposite this pomp of sylvan shade,
Wild crags & lowering rocks a cave have made;
Within, sweet waters gush; & all bestrown
Is the cool floor with seats of living Stone;
Cell of the Nymphs: no chains, no anchors here
Bind the tired vessels, floating without fear.

1st Book

Lodged by Aeneas, in this shelter meet
Seven Ships, the scanty relics of his fleet;
The crews, athirst with longings for the land,
Here disembark, & range the wished for strand;
Or on the sunny shore their limbs reclining,
Heavy with dropping ooze & drenched with brine
Lie drench'd, & wasted with the feverish brine.
Achates, from a smitten flint, receives
The spark upon a bed of fostering leaves;
Dry fuel on the natural hearth he lays,
And speedily provokes a mounting blaze.
Then forth they bring, not utterly forlorn,
The needful implements, & injured corn;
Bruise it with stones, & by the aid of fire
Prepare the nutriment their frames require.

Meanwhile Aeneas mounts a cliff, to gain
An unobstructed prospect of the main;
Happy if thence his wistful eyes may mark
The harass'd Antheus, or some Phrygian bark,
Or Capys, or the guardian sign descry
Which, at their stern, Caicus bears on high.
No sail appears in sight, nor toiling oar;
Only he spies three stags upon the shore;
Behind, while following upon these
Whole herds are seen to follow where they lead,
And in disorder long troop through the vallies feed.
He stops, & with the bow he seized & store
Of swift winged arrows, which Achates bore;
And first the Leaders, his shafts have bowed
Their heads elate with branching horns; the crowd
Are stricken next, and all the scattered droves
Till seven a stag for every Ship, are slain.
Fly in confusion to the leafy grove.
Nor from the weapons does his Hand refrain
Till seven, a stag for every Ship, are slain,
And with their bulky bodies press the plain.
Hence seeks the harbour
Thence to the port he hies divides the spoil;

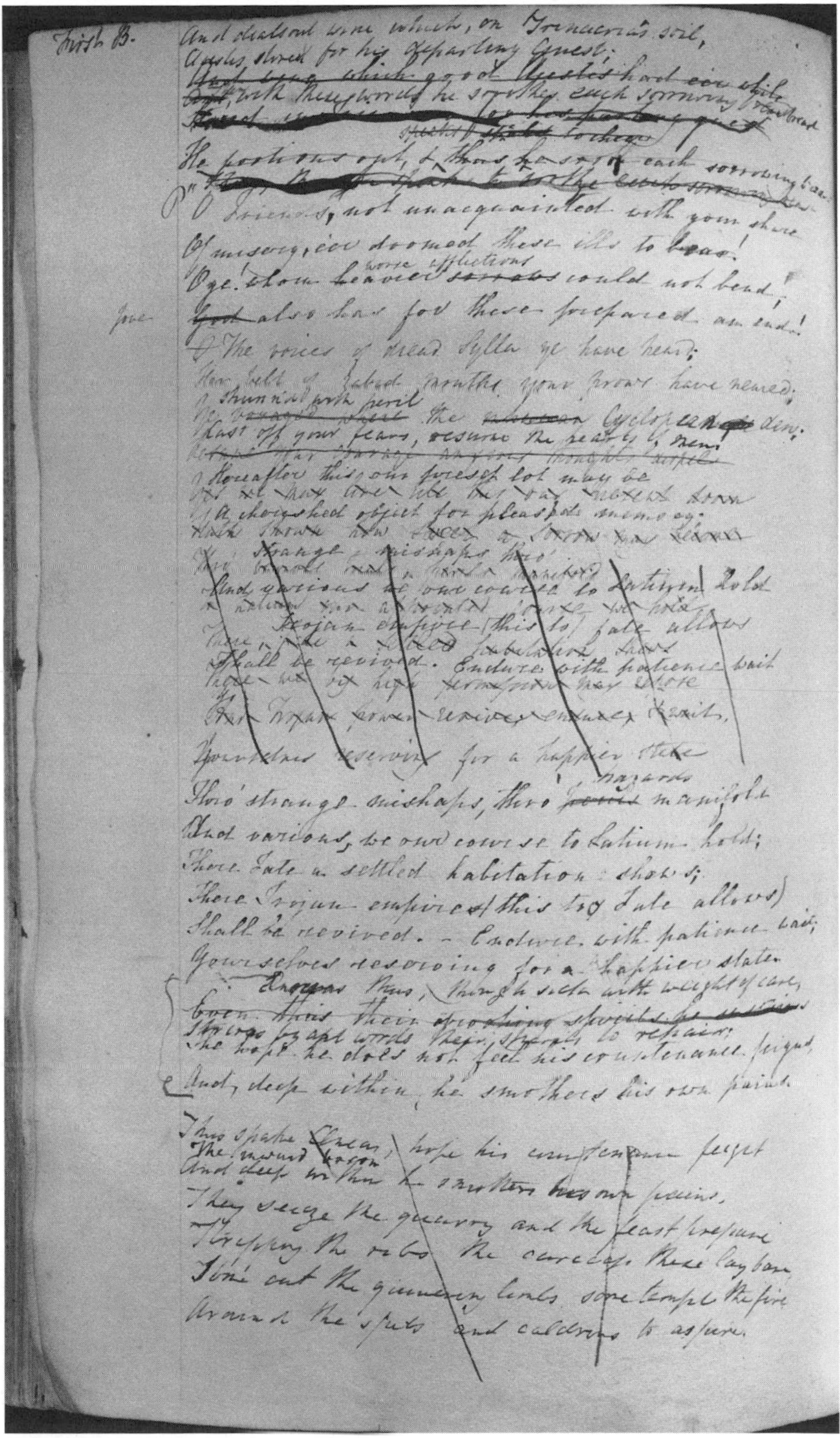

Virgil B. And chalsond wine which, on Trinacria's soil,
Acestes stored for his departing Guest;
And ... which good Acestes had ere while
... with these words he soothes each sorrowing breast
[illegible]
He portions out, & thus he soothes each sorrowing breast
[illegible]
O friends, not unacquainted with your share
Of misery, ere doomed these ills to bear!
O ye, whom heavier worse afflictions could not bend,
Jove God also has for these prepared an end!
The voices of dread Scylla ye have heard;
How belt of jabed mouths your prows have neared;
Ye shunn'd with peril the Cyclopean den;
Cast off your fears, resume the hearts of men;
[illegible]
Hereafter this our present lot may be
[illegible]
A cherished object for pleased memory.
[illegible]
Thro' strange mishaps thro'
[illegible]
And various we our course to Latium hold
[illegible]
Trojan empire (this to) fate allows
[illegible]
Shall be revived. Endure with patience wait
[illegible]
[illegible]
Yourselves reserving for a happier state
Thro' strange mishaps, thro' hazards manifold
And various, we our course to Latium hold;
There fate a settled habitation shows;
There Trojan empire (this too fate allows)
Shall be revived. — Endure with patience wait;
Yourselves reserving for a happier state.
Aeneas thus, though sick with weight of care,
Even thus their drooping spirits he ...
Strives by apt words their spirits to repair;
The hope he does not feel his countenance feigns,
And, deep within, he smothers his own pains.

Thus spake Aeneas; hope his countenance feigns
The wounded Trojan
And deep within he smothers his own pains.
They seize the quarry and the feast prepare
Stripping the ribs the carcass these lay bare
Some cut the quivering limbs some tempt the fire
Around the spits and caldrons to aspire.

1st Book

Thus spake Aeneas hope his countenance feigns
The inward bosom smothers her own pains
They seize the game, for the feast prepare;
Not use their skill the carcass to lay bare
Stripping from off the ribs the dappled hide;
And part the palpitating flesh divide:
The portions some expose to naked fire
Some steep in cauldrons where the flames aspire.
Not wanting utensils they spread the board
And soon their wasted vigour is restored;
While, o'er the green turf diffused, in genial mood
They quaff the mellow wine, nor spare the forest food.
All hunger thus appeased, they ask in thought
For friends, with long discourse now vainly sought;
Hope, fear, & doubt, contend if yet they live,
Or have endured the last; nor can receive
The obsequies a duteous voice might give.
Apart, for Lycus mourns the pious chief;
For Amicus is touched with bitter grief;
For Gyas, for Cloanthus; & the crew
That with Orontes perished in his view.
So finished their repast, while on the crown
Of heaven stood Jupiter, whence looking down,
He traced the sea where winged vessels glide,
Saw lands, & shores, the Nations scattered wide;
And [in] castle, from that all-commanding height
He viewed the Lybian realms, with [steadfast] sight.
To him revolving mortal hopes & fears,
Venus, her shining eyes suffused with tears,
Thus sorrowing spake. O Sire! who rul'st the way
Of Men & Gods with thy eternal sway,
[illegible] with murder; what offence, unfit
For pardon, could my much-loved Son commit?
The Trojans what? [illegible] thine anger to awake
That [illegible] such dire losses for the sake
Of Italy [illegible] denied
For, that the Romans hence should draw their birth
As years rolled round, even hence & govern the earth
With [illegible] from Teucer's line restored
Such was — O Father why this change? thy word.

First Book

From this, when Troy ~~was withered~~ had perish'd for my grief
Fates balancing with fates, I found relief;
Like fortune follows: when shall thy decree
Close, mighty King, this long adversity?
Antenor, from amid the Grecian hosts
Escaped, could thread Illyria's sinuous coasts,
Pierce the Liburnian realms, o'er-climb the fountain
Of loud Timavus, whence the murmuring mountain
Its nine-mouthed channel to the torrent yields,
~~[illegible]~~ That rolls its headlong sea, a terror to the fields.
Yet to his Paduan seats he safely came,
The city built, ~~whose~~ People ~~bore~~ bear his name;
There hung his Trojan arms, where now he knows
The consummation of entire repose.
But we thy progeny, allowed to boast
Of future heaven, betrayed—our navy lost;
Thro' wrath of one, are driven far from the Italian coast.
Is piety thus honoured? doth thy grace
Thus in our hands the allotted sceptre place?
On whom the Sire of Gods & human kind,
Half-smiling, turned the look that stills the wind,
And clears the heavens; then, touching with light kiss
His daughter's lip, he speaks; Thy ~~fears~~ griefs dismiss,
And Cytherea these forebodings spare;
No wavering fates deceive the objects of thy care.
Lavinian walls full surely wilt thou see,
The promised city; & upborne by thee,
Magnanimous Aeneas yet shall range
The starry heavens; nor doth my purpose change.
He, (since thy soul is troubled, I will raise
Things from their depths & open fate's dark ways)
Shall wage dread wars in Italy, abate
Fierce Nations, build a town, & rear a State;
Till three revolving summers have beheld
His Latian ~~rule~~ kingdom, the ~~[illegible]~~ Rutulians quelled.
But young Ascanius (Ilus heretofore,
Name which he held till Ilium was no more,
Now called Iulus) while the months repeat
Their course, & thirty annual orbs complete,
Shall reign, & quit Lavinium ~~to abide~~ preside
O'er Albalonga, strongly fortified.
Here, under Chiefs of this Hectorean race,
Three hundred years shall empire hold her place;
Ere Ilia, royal Priestess, gives to earth
From the embrace of Mars a double birth.
Then Romulus, the elder, proudly drest
In tawny wolf-skin, his memorial vest, & in
Mavortian walls (so styled from Mars) shall [illegible]
The people Romans call from his own name.
To these I give dominion that shall climb,
Unchecked by space, uncircumscribed by time,
An empire without end. Even Juno, driven
To agitate with fear earth, sea, & heaven,
~~[illegible]~~
~~[illegible]~~ hast [illegible]
Prepared with me to cherish as her own
The Romans, lords o'er earth, the nation of the gown.
So 'tis decreed. As circling times roll on
Phthia shall fall, Mycenae shall be won;
Descendants of Assaracus shall reign
O'er Argos, subject to the victor's chains
From a fair stem shall Trojan Caesar rise;
Ocean may terminate his power — the skies
Can be the only limits of his fame;
A Julius he, inheriting the name
From great Iulus. Fearless shalt thou greet
The Ruler, when to his celestial seat
He shall ascend, spoil-laden from the east;
He, too, a God to be with vows addressed.
Then shall a rugged age full long defiled
With cruel wars, grow placable & mild;

First Bk 245

This uttered Maia's son he sends from high
To embolden Tyrian hospitality;
Lest haply Dido ignorant of fate
Should chase the Wanderers from her rising state;
He thro the azure region works the oars
Of his swift wings, & lights on Lybian shores:
Prompt is he there his mission to fulfil;
The Tyrians soften, yielding to Jove's will;
And, above all, their Queen receives a mind
Fearless of harm, & to the Trojans kind.
Aeneas much revolving thro' the night
Rose with the earliest break of friendly light
Resolved to certify by instant quest
Who ruled the uncultured region, man or beast
Forthwith he hides beneath a rocky cove
His fleet ~~[illegible]~~ overshadowed by the ~~[illegible]~~ pendant grove
And brandishing two javelins quits the bay
Achates sole Companion of his way
While they ~~had reached the centre of a wood~~ were journeying thus, before him stood
His Mother, ~~suddenly before him stood~~ met within a shady wood
The habit of a virgin did she wear
Her aspect suitable her gait & air;—
Armed like a Spartan virgin, or of mien
Such as in Thrace Harpalyce ~~in Thrace~~ is seen
~~Her~~ Urging to weariness the fiery horse—
~~And~~ Outstripping Hebrus in his headlong course.
Light oer her shoulders had she given the bow
To hang, her tresses on the wind to flow,
A huntress with bare knee—a knot upbound
~~[illegible]~~
The folds of that loose vest which else had swept the ground
"Ho" she exclaimed, "their words preventing," say,
Have you not seen some Huntress here astray
~~With a quiver graced clothed by the spotted~~
One of my sisters with a quiver graced;
Clothed by the spotted lynx, & o'er the waste
Pressing the foamy boar with outcry chased?
Thus Venus—~~thus~~ her son forthwith replied,
"None of thy Sisters have we here espied,
None have we ~~Or~~ heard, O virgin, ~~tell me by what name~~ in pure grace
Teach me ~~[illegible]~~ thy name ~~thou wouldst be styled~~, for not a mortal ~~[illegible]~~ face
Is thine, ~~[illegible]~~, nor bears thy voice a human sound;—
A goddess surely, worthy to be owned
By Phoebus as a Sister; or thy line
Is haply ~~[illegible]~~ of the nymphs. O Power divine
Be thou propitious and ~~[illegible]~~ whoe'er thou art,

First Book

Our [illegible] in what [illegible] pretext [illegible]
Of earth, we roam, who these [illegible] walls,
Ignorant alike of person & of place!
Not as intruders come, but [illegible] lost
By winds & waters on the savage coast.
Vouchsafe thy answer; victims oft shall fall
By this right hand, while on thy name we call!

The Tyrian Maids with quivers chase the game
Wont thus to bear them slung [illegible] behind
And wrap their ancles [illegible] purple buskins bound.

The Tyrian Maids who chase the forest game
Bear thus a quiver slung their necks behind
Learn purple buskins round their ancles bind,
Wanderers that a Punic realm you see,
Tyrians the men Agenor's progeny;
But Lybian deem the soil; the natives are
Haughty & fierce intractable in war.
Here Dido reigns, from Tyre compelled to flee
By an unnatural Brother's perfidy.
Sichaeus loved her as the noblest Mate,
The richest Lord of the Phoenician State.
A virgin she when from her Father's hands
By love induced she past to nuptial bands;
Unhappy union! for to evil prone,
Worst of bad men, her Brother held the throne.
Dire fury came among them; and made bold
By that blind appetite the thirst of gold,
[illegible] with an impious blow.
His arts concealed the crime, & gave vain scope
In Dido's bosom to a trembling hope.
But in a dream appeared the unburied Man,
Lifting a visage wonderous pale and wan;
Urged her to instant flight, & shewed the ground
Where hoards of ancient treasure might be found,
Needful assistance; by the Vision sway'd,
Dido looks out for fellowship & aid,
They meet who loathe the Tyrant, or who fear;
And, as some welltrimmed Ships were lying near,

Turn over

Second book

2d Book

All breathed in silence and

When from the lofty couch his voice Æneas raised,

O Queen! unutterable woes;

How by the Grecians Troy was overturned,

And her power fell to be for ever mourned;

245

And the declining stars to sleep invite

Memory recoils, & shudders at the test.

The Grecian chiefs, exhausted of their strength

And, from the siege repulsed, new schemes devised

To build a wooden horse of mountain size

Assisted by Minerva's art

They frame the work, & sheathe its ribs with pine;

An offering to the Gods—that they may gain

Their home in safety; thus they boldly feign;

In sight of Troy an island lies by fame

Amply distinguished Tenedos its name

While Priam reigned a place of throng'd resort

And spread the tale abroad,—meanwhile, they hide

Selected warriors in its gloomy side;

Throng the huge concave to its inmost den,

And fill that mighty womb with armed Men.

In sight of Troy an Island lies, by fame

Amply distinguished, Tenedos its name;

Potent long in the time of Priam's sway

Now merely for chance keels an unsafe bay.

turn over 8 leaves for continuation

1st Book

Lying near

This help they seized, and o'er the water fled,
With all Pygmalion's wealth, a Woman at their head.
The Exiles reached the spot where soon your eyes
Shall see the Turrets of New Carthage rise.
There purchased Barca so they named the ground,
Forget the bull's hide whose thongs had girt it round;
Now say who are ye, whence & whither bound?

He answered, deeply sighing: To their springs
Should I trace back these melancholy things
For you at leisure listening to our woes,
Vesper, mid gathering shadows, to repose
Might lead the day, before the Tale could close.
From ancient Troy if haply ye have heard
our Ships through divers seas
by a sudden tempest tossed,
Aeneas am I: where'er I go
The Gods I rescued from the foe,
When Troy was overthrown. A man you see
Famed above Earth for acts of piety.
Italy is my wished-for resting place;
There doth my country lie among a Race
Sprung from high Jove; the Phrygian Sea I tried
With twice ten Ships which Ida's Grove supplied,
My Goddess Mother pointing out the way
Seven scarcely of that number now are left
By tempests torn: unknown, bereft
And destitute, explore the Lybian waste;
Alike from Asia and from Europe chased.
He spoke, nor haply at this point had closed
His mournful words; but Venus interposed.
Whoe'er thou art, I trust, the heavenly Powers
Disown thee not, so near the Punic Towers;
But hasten to the Queen's imperial Court
Thy Friends survive, their Ships are safe in Port.

9th Book

Indebted for the shelter which they found
To altered courses of the rough north wind:
Unless [illegible] fond Parents taught my simple youth
Deceitful auguries, [illegible] Sanctioned the truth.
Behold yon native fair Swans, a joyous troop!
Them did the Bird of Jove with threatening swoop
Rout in mid heaven; but now in order'd train
They touch, or scarcely fail to touch the Plain.
As in recovered union these rejoice
And [illegible] whizzing wings with tuneful voice
So with their freight the ships in harbour lie
Or to some haven's mouth, air drawing high
With every sail full spread, but thou proceed
And fear no hindrance, where thy truth shall lead.
She spake; and as she turned away, all bright
Appeared her neck imbued with roseate light;
And, from the exalted region of her head,
Ambrosial hair with sudden vital fragrance shed,
Odours divinely breathing;—her Vest flowed
Down to her feet, in gait & motion shewed
The unquestionable Goddess. Whom his eyes
Had seen and whom his soul could recognise
His filial voice pursueth, as she flies.
Why dost thou cruel as the rest delude
Thy Son with phantoms [illegible] & oft renewed?
Why not allowed me hand with hand to join,
To hear thy genuine voice, & to reply with mine
This chiding uttered from a troubled breast
He to the appointed walls his steps addressed
For Paphos [illegible] the Goddess; joyful road
Followed, that leads to her beloved abode,
There stands her temple, garlands fresh & fair
Wreath round a hundred altars [illegible] which there
Burn with Sabean incense scenting all the air.
They who had measured a swift course were now
Climbing [illegible] hill [illegible] lofty brow
That overhangs wide compass of the Town,
And on the turrets which it fronts looks down.

1st Book

with the city pile on pile [illegible]

Æneas [illegible] [illegible] [illegible] the [illegible]
[illegible] a place of sordid huts erewhile
[illegible] [illegible] [illegible] [illegible]
The gates [illegible] pavements & the stretching ways,
The stir, the din, unceasing wonder raise
The Tyrians work one spirit in the whole;
These [illegible] the walls, these labour to uprole
Stones for the citadel with all their might
These for new structures having marked a site
Entrench the circuit. Some on laws debate
[illegible] choose a Senate for the infant State
[illegible] [illegible] [illegible] [illegible]
[illegible] [illegible] [illegible] [illegible] [illegible]
Some dig the haven out, some toil to place
A Theatre on deep & solid base;
[illegible] some from the rock hew columns to compose
A goodly ornament for future shows.
[illegible] [illegible] [illegible] [illegible] [illegible] Fresh Summer
[illegible] [illegible] [illegible] [illegible] [illegible] [illegible]
When first they lead their progeny abroad,
Each fit to undertake his several load;
Or in a mass the fiery produce blend
And with nectar every cell distend;
Or, post as home-bound labourers arrive,
Receive the freight they bring; or, mustering, drive
The drones a [illegible] people from the hive;
Glows the work [illegible] while time-clad hills & plains
Scent the pure honey that rewards their pains.
Oh fortunate! the Chief Æneas cries"
[illegible] on the aspiring town he casts his eyes
Fortunate ye whose walls are already free to rise,
Then strange to tell with mist around him thrown
[illegible] [illegible] [illegible] [illegible] [illegible] [illegible] him thrown
In crowds he mingles, yet is seen by none.

Within the town a central grove displayed
Its ample texture of delightful shade;
The storm-vexed Tyrians, newly landed, found
A hopeful sign while digging there the ground;
The head of a fierce horse from Earth they drew,
By Juno's self presented to their view;
Presage of martial fame & hardy toil
Bestowed thro' ages on a generous soil

1st Book

Sidonian Dido here a Structure high
Raised to the tutelary Deity,
Which with the offerings thro' the temple poured
And bright with Juno's image there adored;
High rose, the brazen porch on steps; the beams
With bosses were fastened, & metallic gleams
Flashed from the valves of brazen doors forth sent
While resounding hinges to & fro they went.
Within this grove Aeneas first beheld
A novel sight by which his fears were quelled;—
Here first gave way to hope so long withstood
And looked thro' present ill, to future good.
For while, expectant of the Queen, the stores
Of that far-spreading temple he explores;
Admires the strife of labour; nor forbears
To ponder over the lot of noble cares
Which the young city for herself prepares;
He meets the wars of Ilium, every fight
In due succession offered to his sight.
There he beholds Atrides—Priam here—
And that stern Chief who was to both severe.
He stopped, & not without a sigh exclaimed,
By whom Achates hath not Troy been named?
What region of the earth but overflows
With us & the memorials of our woes?
Lo Priamus! here also do they raise
To virtuous deeds fit monuments of praise;
Tears for the frail estate of human kind
Are shed & mortal changes touch the mind
Dispel thy fear
Nor doubt that we shall prosper by
The shape, & while the plenteous tear-drops roll,
With an empty picture feeds his soul
For he beheld the youth of Ilium's train
After the Greeks fast flying thro' the plain
There the Phrygians routed fled the war
Crested Achilles hanging from his car

striving labourers

Then banish fear
Dispel thy fears

1st Book

Then to his view the painted walls present
The fate of Rhesus & his snow-white tents,
In the first sleep of silent night betrayed
To the wide-wasting sword of Diomed,
Who to the camp the fiery horses led,
Ere they from Trojan stalls had tasted food
Or stooped their heads to drink Scamander's flood.
Troilus next espied [illegible]
[illegible] flung his arms aside;
Unmatched with fierce Achilles, from the fight
[illegible] in desperate flight
Cleaves to his empty Chariot, on the plain
Supinely stretched, yet grasping still the rein;
Along the earth are dragg'd his neck & hair;
The dust is mark'd by his inverted spear.
Meanwhile, with tresses long & loose, a train
Of Trojan matrons seek Minerva's fane;
[illegible] bear the veil
[illegible] breasts with suppliant wail
They beat their own sad breasts [illegible]
The Goddess heeds not offerings prayers or cries;
And on the ground are fixed her sullen eyes
Thrice had Achilles whirled amain
[illegible] Hector slain,
[illegible] now that corse [illegible] for gold
[illegible] the spoils
[illegible] the chariot to behold!
And suppliant [illegible] near his friend's dead body stands
Old Priam stretching forth his unarmed hands!
Himself 'mid Grecian Chiefs he can espy,
And saw the Oriental blazonry
Of swarthy Memnon, & the Host he leads;
Her Lunar Shields Penthesilea leads;
Her zone her mutilated breast hath bound;
And she, exulting on the embattled ground,
A Virgin Warrior with a Virgin train,
Dares in the field to conflict with men.
While on these animated pictures gazed
The Dardan Chief, enwrapt, disturb'd, amazed;
With a long retinue of youth, the Queen
Ascends the Temple; lovely was her mien,
And her Form beautiful as Earth has seen.

1st Book ~~And her form beautiful at each [illegible]~~

251

Thus, where Eurotas flows, or on the heights
Of Cynthus, where Diana oft delights
To train her Nymphs, and lead the Choirs along,
Oreads, in thousands, gathering round her throng:
Where'er she moves, where'er the Goddess bears
Her pendant sheaf of arrows, she appears
Far, far above the immortal Company:
Latona's breast is thrill'd with silent ecstasy.
Even with such lofty bearing Dido pass'd
Among the busy crowd;– such looks she cast
Urging the various works, with mind intent ~~intent~~ ~~thereon~~
To future empire.– Thro' the Porch she went ~~came~~
And compass'd round with ~~armed~~ attendants, sate
2d to ~~And girt with armed attendants, took her seat~~
Beneath the Temple's dome, upon a throne of State.
There, laws ~~ordained~~ she gave, divided justly there
The labour, or by lot to each assigned his share.
When, ~~and~~ turning from the throne a casual glance ~~with a [illegible] at a glance~~
Aeneas saw an ~~[illegible] band~~ ~~troop of~~ eager crowd advance,
In With ~~many Trojans~~ many Trojans ~~various leaders~~, whom the storms of heaven
Had scattered, & ~~to various~~ on other shores had driven.
With Antheus & Sergestus there appeared
The Brave Cloanthus, following long endeared ~~[illegible]~~
Joy smote his heart ~~But the~~ joy tempered with ~~a fearful~~ strange awe;
^ ~~[illegible] he beheld~~
~~That which he looked upon~~ ~~Achates saw~~
Achates, in like sort, by what he saw ~~[illegible]~~
~~Both trembled~~ Was smitten; and the hands of both were bent
On instant greeting; but they feared the event.
Stifling their wish, ~~within~~ & within that cloud involved
They wait, until the mystery shall be solved,
What has befallen their Friends, upon what shore
The Fleet is left; & what they would implore:
For delegates from every ship they were,
And sought the Temple with a clamorous prayer.
All entered– & leave given, with tranquil breast
Ilioneus preferred their joint request.

1st Book

O Queen empowered by Jupiter to found
A hopeful city on this desert ground
Whom he commissioned also with the rein
Of justice a proud people to restrain
We wretched Trojans rescued from a [illegible] fleet,
Long tossed thro every sea, thy aid entreat;
Let at thy voice the unhallowed fire forbear
To touch our ships; a righteous people spare,
And on our fortunes look with nearer care.
We neither seek as plunderers your abodes,
Nor would our swords molest your Household Gods;
Our spirits tempt us not such course to try,
Nor do the vanquished lift their crests so high.
There is a country called by men of Greece
Hesperia strong in arms & of large increase
The Oenotrians held it; [illegible]
Call it Italia from their leader's name.
That land we sought; when wrapped in hail-wrack
Orion, helped by every wind that blows,
Dispersed us utterly on shallows cast;
And we, we only gained your shores at last.
What race of man is here! was ever yet
The unnatural treatment known that we have met?
What country bears with customs that deny,
To shipwrecked men such hospitality
As the sands offer on the naked beach,
And the first quiet of the land they reach.
Arms were our greeting; yet if ye despise
Man and his power look onward & be wise;
The Gods for right & wrong have memory.
A man to no one second in the care
Of justice, nor in piety and war,
Ruled over us; if yet Aeneas treads
On earth, nor has been summon'd to the shades,
Then no repentance fear if thou take place
Of him, O Queen, foremost in acts of grace!

1st Book

Thou hast we in Trinacria towns & plains
For our support [illegible]
Where, sprung from Trojan [illegible] Acestes reigns?
[illegible] Acestes [illegible]
Grant leave to draw our ships upon your shore,
And thence to refit their shattered hulks & oars
If Fate our [illegible] were restored & Chief
[illegible] to the Italian coast [illegible] Italian shore,
Should Italy lie open to our aim:
But if our Welfare should be an empty name,
And thou, best Father of the Family
Of Troy, hast perish'd in the Libyan sea,
And young Iulus sank engulphed with thee,
Then be it ours at least to seek the home
Then be it ours at least to cross the foam
Of the Sicilian Deep, & seek the home
Prepared by good Acestes, whence we come
Thus spake Ilioneus; his Friends around
Declared their sanction with a murmuring sound
No more — done
With down-cast looks brief answer Dido made
Trojans be fears dismissed anxieties allayed
The [illegible] of occasion & a reign
Yet new, exact these rigors, and constrain;
And force the jealous vigilance my wastes maintain.
The Aenean race, with that heroic Town
And widely-blazing war, to whom are they unknown?
Not so obtuse the Punic breasts we bear;
Not so averse is Phoebus, not so far
From Tyrian ramparts does he yoke his Car.
But if Hesperia be your wished for bourne
Or to Trinacrian Shores your prows would turn,
Then, with all aids that may promote your weal,
Ye shall depart; but if desire ye feel
Joined in this growing realm to share my State,
Yours are the walls which now I elevate.
Haste, and withdraw your gallies from the seas
Trojans & Tyrians shall be one to me.
Would too, that, Storm-compelled as ye have been,
The person of your Chief might here be seen!

1st Book

By trusty servants shall my shores be traced
Even to the confines of the Lybian waste,
If he the coast surveys or tempestuous floods,
Sojourns [illegible] or [illegible] the woods
Ponder thro' cities, or in savage woods.
Thus did the Queen administer relief
For their dejected hearts; & to the Chief,
While both were burning with desire to break
From out the darksome cloud, Achates spake:
"Son of a Goddess what resolves ensue
From this deliverance whose effects we view?
All things are safe,—thy fleet & friends restored;
Save one whom in our sight the Sea devoured
All else respondent to thy Mother's word."
He spake; the circumambient cloud anon
Melts & dissolves, the murky veil is gone,
And left Æneas as it passed away
With godlike mien & shoulders standing in full day;
For that same Parent of celestial race
Had breathed upon her Son surpassing grace
Of youth, & glorified his eyes made bright
Like those of heaven with joyance infinite.
That [illegible] the [illegible], an unexpected guest,
And while all wondered thus the Queen addressed,
He whom you seek am I, Æneas, flung
By storms the Libyan solitudes among.
O sole who for the unalterable state of Troy
Art humanely compassionate;
Who not alone a shelter dost afford
To these the relics of the Grecian sword,
Perpetually exhausted by pursuit
Of dire mischance, of all things destitute;
But in thy purposes with them hast shared
City & home,—not we, who thus have fared,
Not we, nor all the Dardan race that live
Scattered through earth, sufficient thanks can give

1st Book

The Gods (if ... which with love
Of justice dwell about us, or above)
Watching the Righteous, do their course approve)
And a mind conscious to itself of right,
Shall in fit measure, thy deserts requite.
What happy joyful age gave being to such worth?
What blessed parents, Dido, brought thee forth?
While down their channels rivers seaward flow,
Long as the Rivers to the sea shall ...
While shadowy groves sweep round the mountains brow,
Or mountain shadows ... with the sea
While ether feeds the stars, wherever be cast
Long as ... my lot is cast
... and the stars, wherever my lot be cast
My lot whatever land by me be traced,
Thy name, thy honour, and thy praises, shall last!
He spake, and turning towards the Trojan band
Salutes Ilioneus with the better hand,
And grasps Serestus with the left—then gave
The greetings to the rest, to Gyas brave,
And to brave Cloanthus.

Inwardly amazed
Sidonian Dido on the Chief had gazed,
When first he met her view;—his woes like wonder raised
What force, said she, pursues thee? hath impelled
To these wild shores? I ... have I beheld
That Trojan whom bright Venus, on the shore
Of Phrygian Simois, to Anchises bore?
Well do I recall to mind
And ... forgotten is the day
When to our Sidon Teucer found his way,
An Outcast from his native borders driven,
With hope new realms to win, by aid from Belus given,
Belus my father, then the conqueror lord
Of Cyprus newly ravaged by his sword.—
Thenceforth I knew the fate of Troy that rings
Earth round—thy name, and the Pelasgian Kings.
Teucer himself with liberal tongue would raise
His adversaries to just heights of praise,
And paint a Trojan lineage with fair proof;
Then welcome, noble Strangers, to our Roof!

Long as the Rivers to the sea shall go
By shadowy groves sweep round the mountains brow

When first ... strangely ...
tale

1st Book

~~[illegible] I was [illegible] [illegible] pupil~~
~~[illegible]~~
~~[illegible] after devious strife~~
~~Hence [illegible] to [illegible]~~
Stay'd in this Land, to breathe a calmer life
She too, like fortune after devious strife
Stay'd in this land to breathe a calmer life.
From no light ills which on myself have press'd
Pitying I learn to succour the distress'd.
These words pronounced & mindful to ordain
Fit sacrifice she issues from the Fane
And towards the palace leads Aeneas his train,
Nor less regardful of his distant friends,
To the sea coast she hospitably sends
Twice ten selected Steers, a hundred Lambs
Swept from the plenteous herbage with their Dams;
A hundred bristly ridges of huge swine,
And what the God bestows in sparkling wine.
But the interior palace doth display
Its whole magnificence in set array;
And in the centre of a spacious hall
The preparations for high festival:
There gorgeous vestments skillfully enwrought
With eastern purple; & huge tables fraught
With massive argentry; there, carved in gold,
Thro' long long series, the achievements bold
Of forefathers each imaged in his place
From the beginning of the ancient race.
Aeneas, whose parental thoughts obey
Their natural impulse, brooking no delay,
Dispatched the prompt Achates to report
The new events, & lead Ascanius to the Court;
Ascanius, for on him the Father's mind
Now rests, as if to that sole care confined;
And bids him bring, attendant on the boy,
The richest presents snatched from burning Troy;
A robe of tissue stiff with shapes express'd
In threads of glittering gold; an upper vest
Round which acanthus twines its yellow flowers,
By Argive Helen worn in festal hours;
Her Mother Leda's wondrous gift, & brought
To Ilium from Mycenae when she sought
Those unpermitted nuptials; thickly set
With gold & gems, a twofold coronet;
And sceptre which Ilione of yore
Eldest of Priam's royal Daughters, bore;
And orient pearls that on her neck she bore.
This to perform Achates speeds his way
To the ships anchored in that peaceful Bay.

1st Book P

257

But Cytherea, studious to invent
Arts yet untried, upon new counsels bent,
Resolves that Cupid, changed in form & face
To young Ascanius, should assume his place;
Present the maddening gifts, & kindle heat
Of passion at the bosom's inmost seat.
She dreads the treacherous Hayse and Punic tongue;
By Juno's rancor is her quiet stung:
The calm of night is powerless to remove
These cares, & thus she speaks to winged Love.
"O Son, my strength, my power! who dost despise
(What, save thyself none dare thro' earth & skies)
The Gyant-quelling bolts of Jove, I flee
O Son, a suppliant to thy Deity!
What perils meet Aeneas in his course,
How Juno's hate with unrelenting force
Pursues thy Brother—this to thee is known;
And oft-times hast thou made my griefs thy own.
Him now Phoenician Dido in soft chains
Of a seductive blandishment detains;
Junonian hospitalities prepare
Such apt occasion that I dread a snare.
Hence, ere some hostile God can intervene,
Would I by previous wiles inflame the Queen
With passion for Aeneas, such strong love
That at my beck, mine only, she shall move.
Hear & assist; the Father's summons calls
His young Ascanius to the Tyrian walls;
He comes, my dear delight,—& costliest things,
Preserved from fire & flood, for presents brings.
Him will I take & in close covert keep,
Mid Groves Idalian lulled to gentle sleep,
Or on Cythera's far sequestered steep,
That he may neither know what hope is mine
Nor by his presence traverse the design
Do thou, but for a single night's brief space
Dissemble be that Boy in form & face!
And when enraptured Dido shall receive
Thee to her Arms, & kisses interweave
With many a fond embrace, while joy runs high,
And Goblets crown the social festivity,
Instill thy subtle poison, & inspire
At every touch an unsuspected fire.

1st Book

Love, at the word, before his Mother's sight
Puts off his wings & walks with proud delight
the gentlest dews
Like young Iulus; but a ~~deep sleep,~~
Of slumber, Venus sheds to circumfuse
~~[illegible] Venus [illegible] to sleep,~~
steeped
The true Ascanius ~~in~~ placid rest;
Then wafts him, cherished on her careful breast
~~[illegible] to her fostering breast~~
Through upper air,
~~[illegible]~~ to an Idalian grove glade,
Where he on soft Amaracus is laid,
With breathing flowers & embraced & fragrant shade.
But Cupid, following cheerily his guide
Achates, with the gifts to Carthage hied,
~~To~~ reached the Hall where now the Queen upon
Amid a golden couch, with awnings half enclosed;
The Trojans
~~[illegible]~~ too (Æneas at their head)
On couches lie with purple overspread,
~~Each [illegible] occupies [illegible] festal bed,~~
time piled
Mean~~while~~ in cannisters is ~~heaped~~ the bread,
~~And~~ for Pellucid water for the hands is born,
~~To [illegible] the hands & [illegible] attendants [illegible]~~
~~With smooth Pellucid water [illegible] the hands is [illegible]~~
~~With napkins of fine thread, [illegible]~~
And ~~with~~ napkins of smooth texture finely shorn.
Within, are fifty handmaids who prepare,
As
~~While~~ they in order stand, the dainty fare;
fume the household Deities with store
~~And lighted [illegible] incense breathing [illegible]~~ before
Of odorous incense; the while
~~The household Gods, the [illegible]~~ a hundred more,
Matched with an equal number of like age
But each of manly sex, a docile page,
Marshal
~~Arrange~~ the banquet, giving ~~its~~ with due grace
To cup or viand its appointed place.
The Tyrians rushing in, an eager band,
Their painted couches seek, obedient to command.
wonder
They ~~gaze on~~ look with on ~~the~~ Gifts — they gaze
Upon Iulus, dazzled with the rays
That from his ardent countenance are flung,
charmed to hear his simulating tongue
And, ~~cheated by the speech of his dissembling tongue~~
Nor pass unpraised the robe, & veil divine
Round which the yellow flowers & wandering foliage twine.
But chiefly Dido, to the coming ill
Devoted, strives in vain her vast desires to fill;
She views the gifts, upon the boy then turns
Insatiate eyes & gazing burns
cheated
To ease a Father's cheated love he hung
Upon Æneas, & around him clung;

1st Book Then sought the Queen, who fixed ~~upon~~ him the whole
That she possessed of look, mind, life, & soul; 259
And sometimes doth unhappy Dido clasp
The Fondling in her bosom, ignorant
How great a God deceives her. He—to please
His Acidalian Mother, by degrees
Would sap ~~Sichæus~~ Sichæus, studious to remove
The dead by influence of a living love,
Thro' a subsided spirit, dispossessed
Of amorous passion, thro' a torpid breast.
Now when the viands were removed, withdrawn & ceased
The first division of the splendid feast;
While round a vacant board the Chiefs recline,
Huge goblets are brought ~~they bring forth &~~ they crown the wine;
Voices of gladness roll the walls around;
Those gladsome voices from the courts rebound;
From gilded rafters many a blazing light n
Depends, & torches overcome the night.
The minutes fly—till, as the Queen commands,
A bowl of state is offered to her hands:
Then she, as Belus wont, & all the line
From Belus, filled it to the brim with wine;
Silence ensued.—"O Jupiter! whose care
Is hospitable dealing, grant my prayer!
Productive be this day of lasting joy
To Tyrians, & these Exiles driven from Troy;
~~May~~ And days to future generations ~~hold it~~ dear!
Let Bacchus, donor of ~~exulting~~ soul-gladdening cheer
Be present; kindly Juno, be thou near!
And, Tyrians, may your choicest favor wait
Upon this hour, the bond to celebrate!"
She spake, & shed an offering on the board,
Then sipped the bowl, whence the wine had poured;
~~He took~~ And gave to Bitias, bidding him take heart;
He raised it, not unequal to his part,
Drank deep, self-drenched from out the brimming gold;
Thereafter a like course the encircling Nobles hold.

1st Book

Graced with redundant hair, Iopas sings
The lore of Atlas, to resounding strings—
The labours of the sun, the lunar wanderings;—
Whence human kind, and brute, what natural powers
Engender lightning; whence the falling showers,
He chaunts Arcturus and that social Twain
The Bears, and Pleiads bedimmed with rain
Why winter suns, in winter, plunging[?] Heaven steep,
Post seaward; what impedes the tardy nights—
The learned Song from Tyrian hearers draws
Loud shouts,— the Trojans echo the applause.
But lengthening out the night with converse new,
Large draughts of love unhappy Dido drew;
Of Priam asked, of Hector oer & oer—
What arms the Son of bright Aurora wore;
What steeds of Diomede;— how great
Achilles— but O Guest! the whole relate,
Betray the Grecian cunning from its source—
Your own Griefs— and your Friends— your wander-
-ing course;
For now, till this seventh summer, have you ranged
The sea, or trod the earth, to peace estranged!

End of the first Book.

× The glittering Bears, and Pleiads deject with rain

Second Book

Potent & rich while Priam's sway endured

Now a bare hold for keels unsafely moored.

There did the Greeks, when for their native land

Bound to their native harbours as we thought.

From long grief at once the Realm of Troy

Broke loose — the gates are opened & with joy

We seek the Dorian camp, & wander o'er

The spots forsaken, the abandoned shore.

Here the Dolopian ground its lines presents;

And here the dread Achilles pitched his tents;

There lay the ships drawn up along the coast;

And here we oft encountered, host with host.

Meanwhile the rest an eye of wonder lift

To Pallas! First, Thymoetes calls

For its free ingress, thro' desparted walls,

And lodged within the citadel; — thus he

Treacherous, or such the course of destiny.

Capys with some of wiser mind would sweep

The insidious Grecian offering to the deep,

Or to the flames subject it; or advise

To perforate and search the cavities;

Into conflicting judgements break & split

The crowd, at random thoughts the fancy hit.

Down from the citadel a numerous throng

Hastes with Laocoon, they sweep along,

And he the foremost — crying from afar,

"What would ye, wretched madmen as ye are!

Think ye the foe departed? or that e'er

A boon from Grecian hands can prove sincere?

Thus do ye read Ulysses? Foes unseen

Lurk in these chambers; or the huge Machine

Against the ramparts brought, by pouring down

Force from aloft, will seize upon the town.

Let not a fair pretence your minds enthrall;

For me, I fear the Greeks, & most of all

Second Book

When they are offering gifts." With mighty force,
This said, he hurled a spear against the horse;
It smote the curved ribs, & quivering stood
While groans made answer from the hollow wood;
Then, but for loss of mind & adverse fate,
We too, had rushed the den to ~~violate~~ penetrate;
Streams of Argolic blood our swords had stained,
Troy, thou mightst yet & Priam's towers remained!
But lo! an unknown Youth with hand to hand
Behind him fastened, whom a clamorous band
Of Dardan shepherds to the King hath brought.
Using thus his scheme when the Greek chiefs had sought [?],
A voluntary captive fixed in thought
Either the City to betray, or meet
Death, the sure penalty of foiled deceit.
The curious Trojans pouring in deride
And taunt the Prisoner with an emulous pride.
~~Now would you know the Greeks~~
Now see the cunning of the Greeks express
By guile of one an image of the rest.
Forlorn [?] with helpless looks from side to side
Anxiously cast, the Phrygian throng he eyed.
"Alas what lands he cries can now, what seas
Can offer refuge? What resource for me?
Who mid the Greeks no breathing place can find,
And whom ye Trojans have to death consigned!"
Thus were we wrought upon & now with sense
Of pity touched that checked all violence,
We cheered & urged him boldly to declare
His origin; what tidings he may bear;
And in what claims he ventures to confide.

3d Book line 41

Torment me not Aeneas
Aeneas, why torment me? Why this pain
Given to a buried man? [illegible] Cease
[illegible] thy pious hands [illegible]
Troy brought me forth, no alien to thy blood
Nor [illegible] a senseless trunk this sable flood
Oh fly the cruel land; the greedy shore,
Forsake with speed for I am Polydore
A flight of iron darts here pierced me through
Took life, and into this sharp thicket grew.
Then truly did I stand aghast, cold fear
Strangling my voice & lifting up my hair.—

3d Book

Erewhile had ... from Troy had Priam sent by stealth
This Polydore, and with him store of wealth
Trusting the Thracian King his Son would rear
For wretched Priam now gave way to fear,
Seeing the Town beleaguered. These alarms
Spread to the Thracian King, and when the Arms
Of Troy were quelled he took the conqueror's side
And the just anger of the Gods
Of Troy were quelled, to the victorious side
Of Agamemnon he his hopes allied
Breaking through sacred laws without remorse
Slew Polydore, & seized the gold by force
What mischief to, poor mortals, has not thirst
Of gold created! & appetite accursed!
Soon as a calmer mind I could recal
I seek the Chiefs, my Father above all
Report the omen, and their thoughts demand
One mind is theirs, to quit the impious Land,
With the first breezes of the South to fly
Sick of polluted hospitality.
Forthwith on Polydore our hands bestow
A second burial & fresh mould up throw
Raise ... beside the mound
Altars, which as they stood in mournful round,
Cerulean fillets and black cypress bound;
And with loose hair a customary Band
Of Trojan women in the circle stand.
From cups warm milk and sacred blood we pour
Thus to the tomb the Spirit we restore
And with a farewell cry its future rest implore

Then, when the sea grew calm, & gently creeps
The soft South wind & calls us to the Deeps
The crew draw down our ships; they crowd the shore
The Port — We leave the Port; with cities sprinkled o'er,
Slowly the coast recedes, & then is seen no more.

3d Book

Then somewhat ... of fear he thus replied.
"O King a plain confession shall ensue
On these commands, in all things plain & true.
And first the tongue that speaks shall not deny
My origin; a Greek by birth am I.
Fortune made Sinon wretched; to do more
And make him false—this lies not in her power.

2d Book

In converse, readily ye have heard the name
Perchance in course of common speech the name
Of Palamedes & his glorious fame;
A Chief with treason falsely charged, & whom
The Achaians crushed, by a nefarious doom,
And unalarmed when covertly with the tomb
[illegible]
His kinsman I, & hither by his side
Me my poor father sent, where first these fields were tried
While yet his voice the Grecian Chieftains swayed,
And I also his best way to his counsels [illegible]
[illegible] but with his life cut short,
I did not walk ungraced with fair report.
Ulysses with envy rankling in his breast
(And these are things which thousands can attest)
Thereafter turned his subtilty to give
That fatal injury, & he ceased to live;
I dragged my days in sorrow & in gloom,
And mourned my guiltless friend, indignant at his doom;
This inwardly; & yet, not always mute,
I rashly vowed revenge, my sure pursuit,
If again the shores of Argos I again
Should see, victorious with my Countrymen.
Sharp hatred did these open threats excite;
Hence the first breathings of a deadly blight;
Hence, to appall me, accusations came,
Which still Ulysses was at work to frame;
Hence would he scatter slily with the crowd
Loose hints, with wile sustained or disavowed;
Beyond himself for instruments he looked
[illegible] this search of means no respite brooked,
Till Chalcas his accomplice — but the chain
Of foul devices why rehearse in vain?
[illegible] of ye, alike
On the same level all of Argive race, ..

2d Book And 'tis enough to know that I am one, 268
Punish me,— would Ulysses might look on!
And let the Atridæ hear, rejoiced with what is done!"
~~That~~ This stirred us more whose judgements were asleep
To all suspicion of ~~their~~ a crime so deep
And craft so fine. Our questions we renewed;
And, trembling, thus the fiction he pursued.
~~Long~~ Oft did the Grecian Host the means prepare
To flee from Troy, tired with so long a war;
Would they had fled! ~~the~~ but winds as often stopped
Their going, & the hoisted sails were dropped;
~~So that the~~
And when this pine-ribbed horse of monstrous size
Stood forth, a finished work, before their eyes,
Then chiefly pealed the storm ~~from~~ thro' blackened skies;
So, that the Oracle its aid might lend
To quell our doubts, Eurypylus we send,
Who brought the answer of the voice divine
In these sad words, given from the Delphic shrine.
"Blood flowed, a virgin perished to appease ~~the~~
The winds when first for Troy ye passed the seas;
O Grecians! for return across the flood,
Life must be paid, a sacrifice of blood.
With this response a universal dread
Among the shuddering multitude was spread;
All quaked to think at whom the Fates had aimed
This sentence, who the victim Phœbus claimed.
Then doth the Ithacan, with tumult loud,
Bring forth the prophet Calchas to the crowd,
Asks what the Gods would have; & some meanwhile
Discern [illegible] and the Schemer of the
~~Presaging the [illegible]~~ the author of the guile
Of [illegible], and do not [illegible] from men
~~With [illegible] foresee~~
Of the crime which they in [illegible] foresee.
~~But do not hide what they [illegible]~~
Ten days, refused he still with guarded breath
To designate ~~the~~ the man, to fix the death;

Second Book

The Ithacan still urgent for the deed;
At last the unwilling voice announced that I must bleed;
All gave assent, each happy to be cleared,
By one thief's fall, of what himself had feared.
Now came the accursed day,— the salted cates
Are spread, the altar for the victim waits;
The ~~temple~~ fillets bind my temples, I took flight
Burst thro' my chains, I own it, thro' the night,
Lurked among oozy swamps, & there lay hid
Till winds might cease their voyage to forbid.
And now was I compelled at once to part
With all the dear old longings of the heart;
Never to see my Country, Children, ~~friends~~ Sire,
Whom they perchance will for thy flight require;
Of them for this offence of mine will make
An expiation, punished for my sake.
But thee, by all the Powers who hold their seat
In heaven, & know the truth, do I entreat
O King, & by whatever may yet remain
Among mankind of faith without a stain,
Have pity on my woes; commiserate
A mind that ne'er deserved this wretched fate!
~~Moved by~~ Their tears prevail; ~~Moved by these tears~~ we spared the suppliant's life,
Pitying the Man we spare
~~And kind compassion~~ yield without a strife;
~~Now~~ Even Priam's self, unasked of all, ~~first affable the~~ commands
To loose his fetters, & unbind his hands;
D. Then adds these friendly words; "Whoe'er thou be,
"Henceforth forget the Grecians, lost to thee;"
We claim thee now — let me truly hear
Who moved them first this monstrous horse to rear,
And why? Was some religious vow the aim?
Or for what use in ~~the~~ war this engine ~~did~~ might they frame?
Straight were these artful words in answer given,
While he upraised his hands, now free, to heaven.
Eternal fires on you I call, O ye
And your inviolable Deity!

2d Book Altars & ruthless swords from which I fled!
Ye fillets, worn round my devoted head!
Be it no crime if Argive sanctions cease
To awe me, none to hate the men of Greece!
The law of Country forfeiting its hold,
Mine be the voice their secrets to unfold!
And ye O Trojans! keep the word ye gave,
Save me, if truth I speak, & Ilium save!
"The Grecian host on Pallas still relied,
Nor hope had they but what her aid supplied;
But all things drooped since that ill omened time
In which Ulysses author of the crimes
Leagued with impious Diomede to seize
That Image pregnant with your destinies;
Tore the Palladium from the holy Fane,
The guards who watched the citadel first slain,
And, fearing not the Goddess, touched the bands
Wreathed round her virgin brows with gory hands;
Hence ebbed the strength from that day.
From them the Goddess turned her mind away.
By what dire sign
Soon as that image to the Camp was brought
And from the ground the Goddess, (strange to hear!)
Leapt thrice, her Buckler grasp'd & and quivering spear.
Then Calchas bade to stretch the homeward sail;
And prophesied that Grecian Arms would fail
Unless new omens they for repair
To Argos, thither the Palladium bear
And hence to Phrygian shores recross the sea
Bring back a more propitious Deity.
They went; but only to return in power
With favouring Gods, at some unlooked for hour.
So Calchas read those signs; the Horse was built
To calm Minerva, & atone for guilt.
You see the Fabric rise
Compact in strength towering to the sky!
A pile stupendous

2d Book This was ordained by Calchas with intent
That the vast bulk its ingress might prevent,
~~Through gates or walls and Ilium reinforced~~
And Ilium ne'er with in her walls enfold
Another Safeguard reverenced like the old.
For if unawed by Pallas, ye should lift
~~Your~~ A sacrilegious hand against the Gift,
The Phrygian realm shall perish. (May the Gods
Turn on himself the mischief he forebodes!)
But if it enter your town ~~assisted~~ by your aid,
~~The City~~ Ascending, Asia, then, in arms arrayed
Shall storm the walls of Pelops, & a fate
As dire on our Posterity await.
Even so the arts of perjured Sinon gained
Belief for this, & for all that he had feigned;
Thus ~~And~~ were they ~~were~~ won by wiles, by tears compelled,
Whom not Tydides, not Achilles quelled;
Who fronted ten years' war with safe disdain,
'Gainst whom a thousand Ships had tried their strength in vain.
To speed our fate a thing did now appear,
~~Yet~~ more momentous, & of direr import fear.
Laocoon, priest by Lot to Neptune, stood
Where to his hand a Bull poured forth its blood
Before the Altar, in high offering, slain —
~~When~~ But lo! two Serpents, o'er the tranquil Main
Incumbent, roll from Tenedos, & seek
Our Coast together (shuddering do I speak)
Between the waves, their elevated ~~crests~~ breasts
Upheaved In circling spires, and sanguine crests
Tower o'er the ~~wave~~ flood; the parts that follow sweep,
In folds voluminous & vast, the Deep.
The agitated brine, with noisy roar
Attends their coming, till they touched the shore.
Sparkle their eyes suffused with blood and quick
The tongues shot forth their hissing mouths to lick.
Dispersed with fear, we fly; in close array
These move, & towards Laocoon point their way;
But first assault his sons, their youthful prey.
~~Each~~ A several Snake in tortuous wreaths engrasps
Each slender frame; and fanging what its clasps,

2 Book Feeds on the limbs; the Father rushes on,
Arms in his hand, for rescue, but anon
Himself they seize; and, writhing round his waist
Their scaly backs, they bind him, thrice embraced
With monsterous spires, as with a double zone;
And, twice around his neck in tangles thrown
High o'er the Father's head each serpent lifts its own.
The fillets round his brows, are sprinkled o'er
With sable venom and distained with gore.
And while his hands labouring the knotted spires would rend,
The cries he uttered to the Heavens ascend;
Loud as a Bull — that, wounded by the axe,
Shook off the uncertain steel, and from the altar breaks,
To fill with bellowing voice the depth of air!
But towards the Temple slid the hydra pair
[illegible] lie concealed
Their wrath succumbs [illegible] Couched at Minerva's feet, beneath her orbed shield.
Nor was there One who trembled not with fear
Or deemed the expiation too severe
For him who hurled that sacrilegious spear
For him whose hand the guilty weapon sped.
But to the Temple let the [illegible] be led;
[illegible] the people [illegible] the general cry
And prayers [illegible] Deity

Or deemed the expiation too severe

For him whose lance had pierced the votive steed;
Which to the Temple they resolved to lead;
There to be lodged with pomp of service high
And supplication: such the general cry.
Shattering the walls a spacious breach we make;
We cleave the bulwarks — toil which all partake.
Some to the feet the rolling wheels apply;
Some round its lofty neck the cables tie;
The Engine pregnant with our deadly foes
Mounts the breach; & ever, as it goes,

Second Book

Boys mixed with maidens chaunt a holy song,
And press to touch the cords, a happy throng!
The Town it enters thus, & threatening moves along.
My country, glorious Ilium, & ye towers
Loved habitation of celestial powers!
Four times it stopped before the gates — a din
Of armour four times warned us from within;
Yet towards the sacred Dome with reckless mind
We still press on, & in the place assigned
Lodge the portentous Gift, thro' frenzy blind.
Nor failed Cassandra now to scatter wide
Words that of [illegible] instead of when
[illegible] prophesied
But Phoebus willd that none should heed her voice;
And we, [illegible] miserable men, rejoice
And hang our temples round with festal boughs,
Upon that day the last which fate allows.
Meanwhile had Heaven revolved with rapid flight,
And fast from Ocean climbs the [illegible] Night,
With boundless shade involving earth and sky
And Myrmidonian frauds; The Trojans lie
Throughout the town dispersed, in silence deep
And with tired limbs receive the embrace of Sleep
This was the time when all the powers arrayed,
And now from Tenedos, by friendly aid
Nor wanting silent moonlight's friendly aid,
[illegible] the Grecian Navy came,
Led by the royal Galley's [illegible] signal flame:
Sinon, now safe, only [illegible] Fates his guard,
[illegible] the dungeon of the Greeks unbarred;
Straight by a pendant rope adown the side
Of the steep Horse, the armed warriors glide
The Chiefs Thessander, Sthenelus are there,
With joy deliver'd to the open air
Ulysses, Thoas, Acamas the Lord
[illegible] slides down to earth, and Helen's injured Lord —
Pyrrhus who from Pelides drew his birth,
And bold Machaon [illegible]
Nor him forget whose skill the [illegible] framed
Epeus, glorying in his prosperous wile
They rush upon the City that lay still,
Buried in sleep & wine — the warders kill. See side

And at the wide-spread gates in triumph fill
Expectant helpers crowding from the Fleet.

This was the time when furnished & arrayed

Second Book

Sleep fled, I climb the roof, & where it rears
Its loftiest summit, stand with quickened ears;
As when a fire by raging south winds borne,
Lights on a billowy sea of ripened corn,
Or rapid torrent sweeps with mountain flood
The fields, the harvest prostrates, headlong bears the wood.
High on a rock the unweeting shepherd, bound
In blank amazement, listens to the sound:

Above the spacious palace where abode
Deiphobus, the flames in triumph rode,
Ucalegon burns next; through lurid air
Sigean Friths reflect a widening glare;
Clamour & clangor to the heavens arise,
The blast of trumpets mixed with vocal cries.

The other hand his little Grandson leads

Panthus what hope? Which fortress shall we try?

Within the burning town the Grecians domineer.
Forth from its central stand the enormous horse
Pours its continual stream of armed force;
Sinon, insulting Victor aggravates
The flames,

The passage hangs, with quivering point, the blade,
Unsheathed for slaughter; scarcely to the foes
A blind & baffled fight the Warders can oppose.

I rush into the battle & the fire
Where sad Erinnys, where the shock of fight,

2d Book

The roar, the tumult, & the groans, invite; — 273
Ripheus is with me, Epytus the pride
Of battles joins his aid, and to my side
Flock Dymas, Hypanis, the moon their guide;
With young Chorœbus who had lately sought
Our walls by passion for Cassandra brought;
He led to Priam an auxiliar train,
His son by wedlock; miserable man
For whom a raving spouse had prophesied in vain.
When I saw them collected & content
To face the strife with deeds of hardiment,
I thus began; "O Champions vainly brave
If like myself to dare extremes ye crave
~~You see our last condition to before your sight~~
~~...~~
~~...~~
~~... all the guardian Gods their altars have left~~
To uphold a city wrapped in fire;
Die rather, let us rush in battle to expire;
At least one safety shall the vanquished have
If they no safety seek but in the grave!"
Thus to their minds was fury added; then,
As wolves driven forth by hunger from the den,
To prowl amid blind vapours, whom the brood
Expect, their jaws all parched with thirst for blood,
Thro' flying darts, thro' pressure of the foe,
To death, to not uncertain death, we go;
Right thro' the town the midway course we bear,
Added by hovering darkness, & despair
Can words the havoc of that night express?
What power of tears may equal the distress?
An ancient City sinks & disappears
~~A city dominant this length of years~~
~~Her streets are filled with carnage, & the abodes~~
~~Of men, the hallowed thresholds of the Gods,~~
~~With lifeless trunks ... defiled;~~
~~Nor ... the sufferers Trojans bleed alone.~~
The vanquished sometimes to their hearts recall
Old virtues, & the conquering Argives fall.

Second Book

Sorrow is every where, & fiery scath
Fear Anguish struggling to be rid of breath,
And Death still crowding on the shape of Death.
Was the first Greek we met; he rashly deems us friends
[illegible]
Haste friends [illegible]
Troy blazes, sacked by others & laid waste;
And ye come lagging from your ships the last!
Thus he & straight mistrusting our replies
He felt himself begirt with enemies.
Voice failed, step faltered—at the dire mistake;
Like One who, thro' a deeply-tangled brake
Struggling, hath trod upon a lurking Snake;
And shrunk in terror from the unlooked-for pest
Lifting his blue-swoln neck & wrathful crest;
Even so Androgeos, smit with sudden dread,
Recoils from what he saw, & would have fled;
Forward we rush, — with arms the troop surround;
The Them surprized, & ignorant of the ground,
Subdued by fear, become an easy prey;
Thus are we favoured in our first essay.
With exultation here Coraebus cries;
Behold O friends how bright our destinies!
Advance—the road which they point out is plain;
Shields let us change, & bear the insignia of the slain,
Grecians in semblance—
wiles, are lawful—who
to simple valour would restrict a foe
Themselves shall give us arms; when this was said,
The leader's helmet nods upon his head,
The emblazoned buckler on his arm is tied;
He fits An Argive falchion to his side!
The like doth Rhypheus, Dymas, all put on,
Withe eager haste, the spoils which they had won.
Then in the [illegible] mingling Heaven averse
Amid the gloom a multitude we pierce,
[illegible] some shipward flee,
Appalled by this imagined treachery;
Some to the ships [illegible] some [illegible] the horse would hide
Ah what reap they but a sorrow [illegible]
In aught to which the gods their sanction have denied.
Behold Cassandra Priam's royal child
By sacrilegious [illegible] with hair all wild,
Dragged from Minerva's temple; towards the skies

2d Book

The Virgin [illegible] in vain her glowing eyes
[illegible] Her eyes, for she could no more, for Grecian bands
Had rudely manacled her tender hands.
The intolerable sight to madness stung
Coroebus; & his desperate self he flung
On speedy death the ruthless foe among!
We follow, & with general shock assail
The hostile throng: here first
Our efforts fail;
[illegible] from the summit of the lofty Fane
Darts by their people flung, [illegible] remain,
In miserable heaps their friends are laid,
By shew of Grecian arms & crests betrayed.
Wroth for the Virgin rescued, by defeat
Provoked the Grecians from all quarters meet;
Combating here unite the brother Kings,
And thither Ajax all his fierceness brings,
By the Dolopians followed. As winds fly
To charge from adverse quarters of the sky,
Notus & Zephyrus, & [illegible]
[illegible] while Eurus feeds
The strife, exulting on his orient steeds;
Woods roar, and foamy Nereus stirs the waves,
Rouzed by his trident from their lowest caves,
They also, whomsoe'er thro' shades of night
Our stratagem had driven to various flight,
Appear, & the first by whom our shields are known,
The simulating javelins they disown
And mark our utterance of discordant tone.
[illegible] our numbers bear us down;
Coroebus falls first, whom Peneleus hath pierced
Before Minerva's altar; next in dust
Sinks Ripheus, one above all Trojans just
And careful of the right, but heavenly Powers
Ordering by lights that ill agree with ours.
Then Dymas, Hypanis by friends are slain by friends;
Nor thee abundant piety defends
O Pantheus, falling with the [illegible] wound,
[illegible] Apollo [illegible]
As fits Apollo's Priest, thy brows around.
Ashes of Ilium! & ye, dire in fires
Lit for my friends upon their funeral pyres,
Amid your fall, bear witness to my word
I shunned no hazards of the Grecian sword,

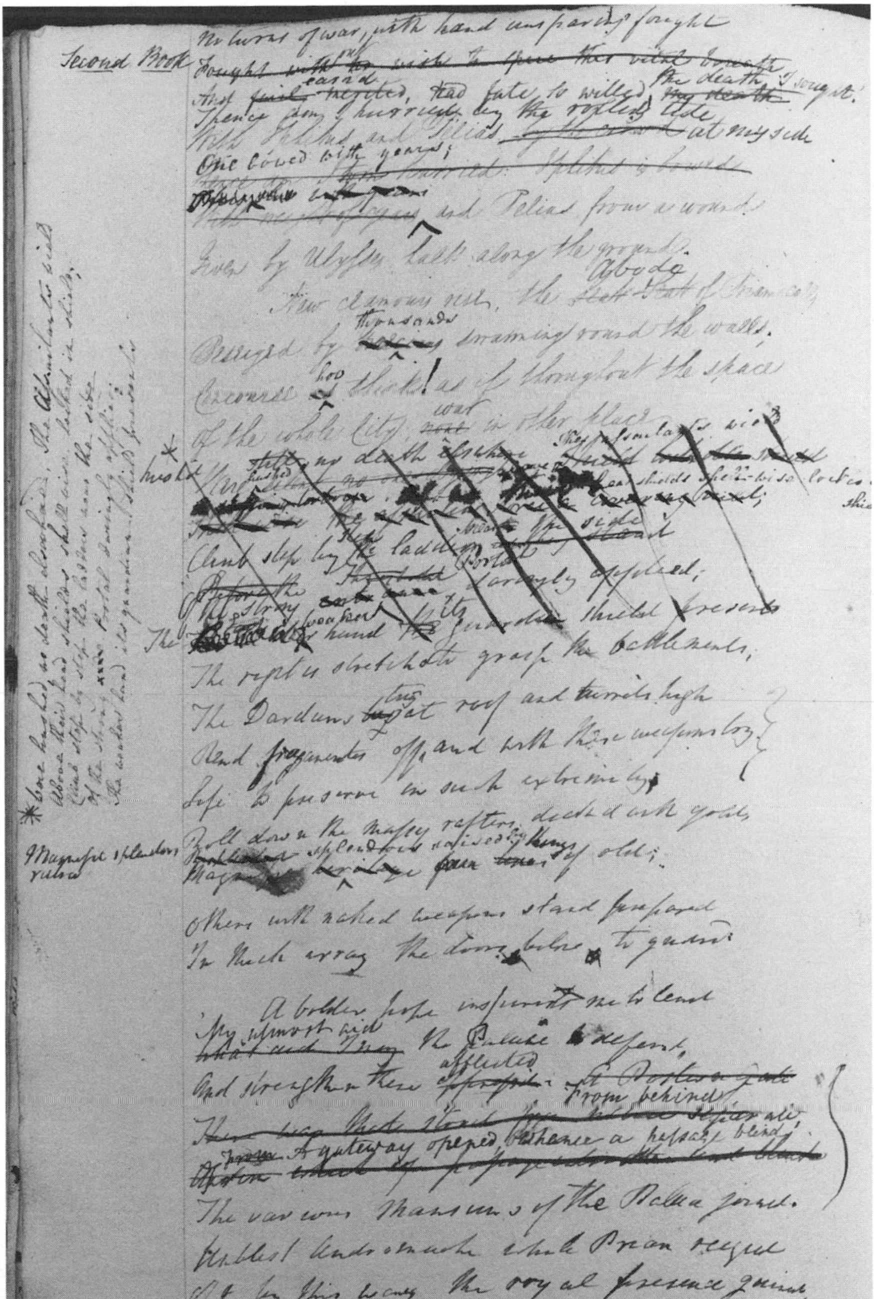

2d Book

2 Book
277

[illegible deleted draft lines, struck through]
Entering the gate I reached the roof where stand
The Trojans, hurling darts with ineffectual hand
A Tower there was precipitous the scite
And the Pile rose to an unrivalled height
Frequented station whence in circuit wide
Troy might be seen the Argive fleet descried
And all the Achaian camp [illegible] this sovereign Tower
With irons grappling where the loftiest floor
Pressed with its beams the wall we shake we rend
And in a mass of thundering ruin send
To crush the Greeks beneath. But numbers press
To new assault with reckless eagerness
Weapons & missiles from the ruins grow
And what their hasty hands can seize, they throw!

Entering the gate I reached the roof where stand
The Trojans, hurling darts with ineffectual hand.
A Tower there was, precipitous the scite,
And the Pile rose to an unrivalled height;
Frequented Station whence in circuit wide
Troy might be seen, the Argive fleet descried,
And all the Achaian camp. This sovereign Tower
With irons, grappling where the loftiest floor
Pressed with its beams the wall, we shake, we rend
And in a mass of thundering ruin send
To crush the Greeks beneath. But numbers press
To new assault with reckless eagerness:
Weapons & missiles from the ruins grow;
And what their hasty hands can seize, they throw!

In front stands Pyrrhus glorying in the might
Of his own weapons, while his armor bright
Casts from the portal gleams of brazen light.
So shines a Snake when threading he hath crept
Forth from the winter bed on which he slept,
Swoln with a glut of poisonous herbs, but now
Fresh from the shedding of his ancient slough

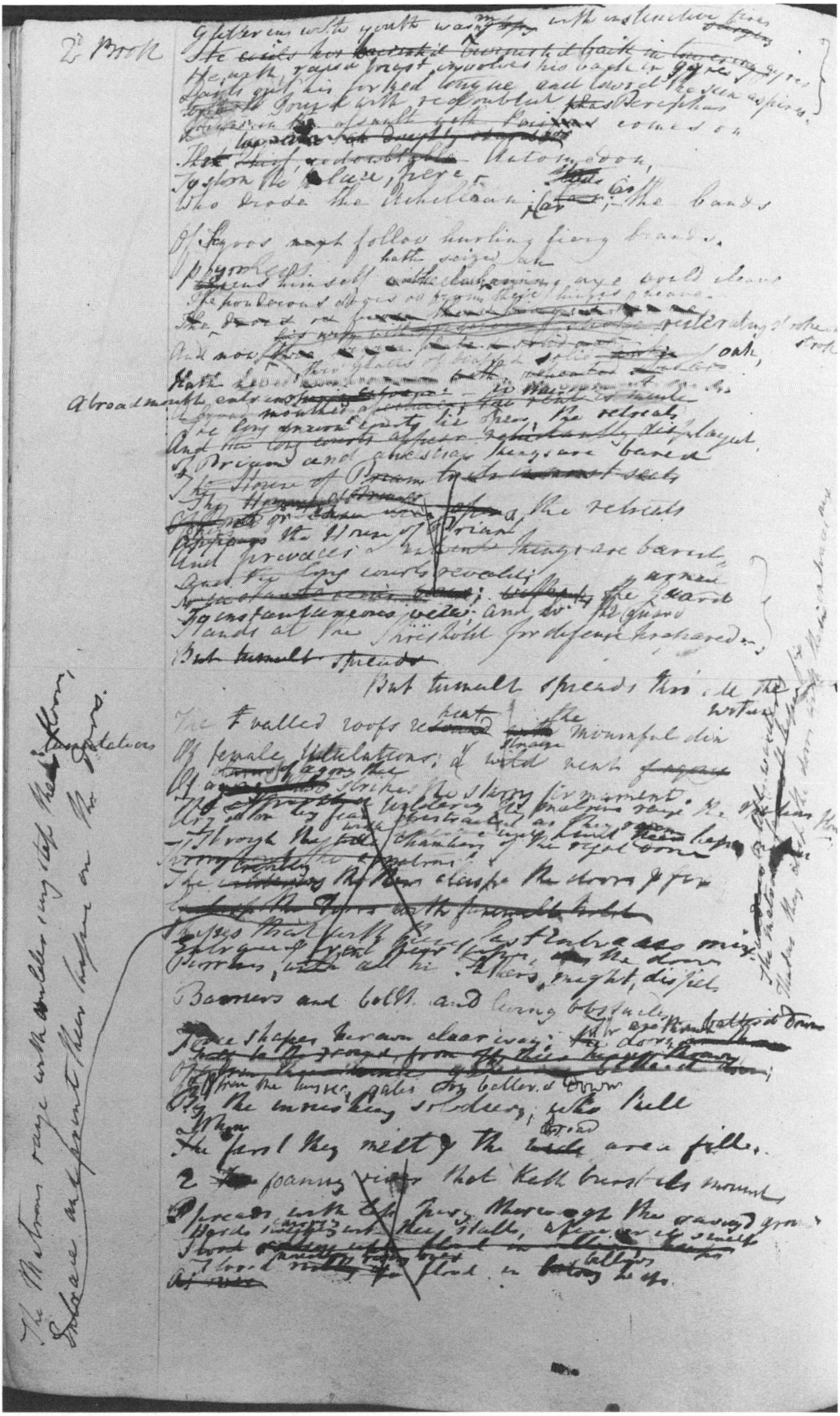

2 Book

Less irresistibly over dams and mounds
Burst by its rage a foaming River bounds,
Herds sweeping with their stalls along the ravaged ground.
Pyrrhus I saw with slaughter desperate;—
The two Atridae near the palace gate
And I beheld, and by these eyes were seen
The hundred Daughters with the Mother Queen;
And hoary headed Priam where he stood
Beside the altar, staining with his blood
Fires which himself had hallowed. Hope had he,
Now equal hope, of large posterity;
Of stately fifty bridal chambers might be told,
Superb with trophies and barbaric gold;
All, in their pomp, lie levelled with the ground,
And where the fire is not, are Grecian masters found.

Ask ye the fate of Priam? On that night
When captured Ilium blazed before his sight;
And the foe, bursting through the palace gate,
Spread through the privacies of royal state,
To arm his tremulous shoulders he restored
Arms which had long forgot their ancient lord,
And girt upon his side a useless sword;
Then thus accoutred forward did he hie,
As if to meet the enemy and die.
Amid the court an altar stood in view
Of the wide heavens, near which a long-lived laurel grew,
And, bending over this great altar, made
For its Penates an embracing shade

Hecuba and the statues of the Gods embrace.
But when she saw, in youthful arms arrayed
Priam himself, what ominous thought she said
Hath weighed thee weapons on limbs decayed?
And whither wouldst thou hasten? if we be
There [illegible] shall this succour we might spare
Not such aid nor defenders doth the time demand
Profitless were would be'en Hector's hand

2d Book

Return, this altar can protect us all,
Or thou wilt not survive when we must fall."
Thus to her self; and to the sacred spot
She drew the aged Man to wait their common lot.

But see Polites one of Priam's sons
Chased with the death which he in terror shuns!
Thro' showers of darts, thro' press of enemies, the wounded youth escaped from Pyrrhus, flies
Where the long Porticos invite; the space
Of widest vacant courts his footsteps trace,
Fierce Pyrrhus following near & still more near
Doth seem caught with the hand, & presses with the spear.
But when at length this unremitting flight
Had brought him full before his Father's sight,
He fell, & scarcely prostrate on the ground,
Poured forth his life from many a streaming wound.
Then Priam [illegible] respect
[illegible] loose in words the [illegible] of his soul
[illegible] anger [illegible] from a soul unchecked by fear
Ye shall the Gods he cries if Gods there be
Who note such acts & care for piety,
Requite this heinous crime with measure true
Nor one reward withhold that is thy due
Who thus a Father's presence hast defiled
And forced upon his sight the murder of a Child.
Not thus Achilles self from whom thy tongue
[illegible] boasts that thou art sprung,
[illegible] his prayer he heard
A suppliant's rights in Priam he revered
Gave Hector back to rest within the tomb
And me remitted to my royal home.
This said, the aged Man a javelin cast
With weak arm — faltering to the shield it past
The tinkling shield the harmless point repelled,
Which, to the boss it hung from, barely held.
Then Pyrrhus, "To my Sire Pelides bear
These feats of mine ill relished as they are
Tidings of which I make thee messenger.

Here Priam, scorning death & self regard
Nor once restraining [illegible] his angry [illegible]

2d Book To him a faithful history relate 2 Book 281
Of Neoptolemus degenerate;
Now die!" So saying towards the Altar, thro'
A Stream of filial blood the tottering Sire he drew,
His left hand locked within the tangled hair
Raised with ~~his~~ [the] right a brandished sword in air
[sword coruscant in mid air]
Then to the hilt impelled it thro' his side;—
Thus mid a blazing city Priam died:
Troy falling round him thus he closed his fate,
Once the proud Lord of many an Asian state.
Upon the shore lies stretched his mangled Frame,
Head from the shoulders torn, a Body without name.

Now Then first it was that Horror gathered round
Chill'd ~~thy~~ [my] frail heart and all ~~thy~~ [my] senses bound;
[The image of my Father crept]
~~My Father's image flash'd across~~ my mind;
Perchance in fate with slaughter'd Priam join'd;
Equal in age thus may He breathe out life,
Creusa else, my deserted Wife!
The Child Iulus left without defence
And the Whole House laid bare to violence!
Backward I look'd I cast my eyes before,
My Friends ~~were gone~~ [had fainted] and courage was no more
All, wearied out had follow'd desperate aims,
Itself dash'd to earth or ~~[illegible]~~ [stifled] in the flames
Thus was I left alone, ~~those~~ [such] light my guide
As the conflagrant walls and roofs supplied;
When my far-wandering eyesight chanced to meet [falsehood]
Helen sequestered on a lonely seat
Amid the Porch of Vestal. She, through dread
Of Trojan vengeance amply merited,

2d Book

Of Grecian punishments and what the ire
Of a deserted husband might require,
Thither had flown, there sate,—the common bane
Of Troy and of her country, to obtain
Protection from the altar, or to try
What hope might spring from trembling secrecy.
Methought my falling Country cried aloud,
And the revenge it seemed to ask, I vowed;
"What shall she visit Sparta once again?
In triumph enter with a royal Queen?
Consort and home and sires and children view,
By Trojan females served a Phrygian retinue?
For this was Priam slain? Troy burnt? the shore
Of Dardan seas so often drenched in gore?
Not so; for though such victory can claim
In its own nature no reward of fame,
The punishment that ends the guilty days
Even of a Woman, shall find grateful praise;
My Soul at least shall of her weight be eased
The ashes of my Countrymen appeased.—

These words burst forth and in my mind despite
Onward I bore it, when through the dreary night
Appeared my Mother, graceful in pure light;
Never till now before me did she shine
To meet herself so thoroughly divine,
Goddess [illegible]
And [illegible] to the [illegible] above.
[illegible] to stay
[illegible]
Then through her roseate mouth [illegible]
These words found way

O Son what power excites a wrath so blind
Or how could all thought of me desert thy mind?
Where, says is left, thy Parent worn with age
[illegible]
Wilt thou not rather in that [illegible] engage

Lives with thine eyes of yet Creusa live?— 2 Book 283

And if thy boy Ascanius still survive?

Them do the Greeks environ; that they spare

That swords so long abstain and flames forbear

Is through the intervention of my care.

Not Spartan Helen's beauty so abhorred

By thee, nor Paris her unbounded Lord

The hostile Gods have laid this grandeur low

Troy from the Gods receives her overthrow.

Look! for the impediment of misty shade

With which thy mortal sight is overlaid

I will disperse; nor thou refuse to hear

Parental mandates, nor resist through fear.

Here, where thou seest block off rolled upon block

Mass rent from mass, and dust commixed with smoke

In billowy intermixture, Neptune smites

The walls, with Trident dislocates

From their foundation, tearing up as roots

[illegible] Ilium from her deepest depth

Fiercest of all before the Scaean gate

Armed Juno stands beckoning to incite

[illegible]

[illegible] her confederate bands [illegible]

Tritonian Pallas holds her chosen seat

High on the Citadel, look backward there—

Her Aegis, beaming forth a stormy glare:—

The very Father, Jove himself, supplies

Strength to the Greeks, sends heaven-born enemies

Against the Dardan arms. My Son! take flight,

And close the struggle of this dismal night!

I will not quit thy steps whatever betide

But to thy Father's home will safely guide.

She ceased and sunk in shade her presence hid.

Now as I looked, all Ilium seemed sinking in the fires,
Neptunian Troy subverted from her base.
Even so, a Mountain-Ash, long tried by shock
Of storms endured upon the native rock,
The rustic blows of persevering steel,
It nods with threatening forehead, till at length
Wounds ... have subdued its strength,
With groans the ancient tree foretells its end,
It falls & fragments of the mountain blend
With the precipitous ruin.—I descend,
And as the Godhead leads, 'twixt foe & fire
Advance,—flit the darts withdrawn, the flames retire:
But when beneath this guidance I had come
Far as the gates of the paternal Home,
My Sire whom first I sought & wished to bear
Into the lofty hills, disdaining that care,
Shuns a protracted life, nor will consent
... banishment. X
"Think ye" he says "the current of whose blood
"Is unimpaired, whose vigour is unsubdued,
"Think ye of flight;—that I should live the Gods
"Wish not, or they had saved me these abodes.
"Not once but twice this City to survive!
"What need against such destiny to strive?
"While thus even thus disposed the body lies
"Depart, pronouncing farewell obsequies.
"Not long shall I have here to wait for death;
"A pitying foe will rid me of my breath;
"Will seek my spoils, & should I lie forlorn
"Of sepulture the loss may well be borne.
"Till long obnoxious to the Powers divine
"Life lingers out these barren years of mine,
"Ever since the date when me the eternal Sire
"Smote with the thunderblast, & touched with fire."
Thus he persists—Creusa & her Son
Second the counter-prayer by me begun,
The total house with weeping deprecate
This weight of wilful impulse given to Fate;
He all unmoved by pleadings & by tears
Guards his resolve & to the spot adheres.

Once more to arms, to battle, death alone
My wish & all purpose, now ... 385
Remaining hope, all others gone!"
"And trust'st thou hoped that I could move to find
A place of rest, thee Father left behind,
How could parental lips the guilty thought unbind?
"If in so great a City Heaven ordain
Utter extinction; if thy soul retain
With stedfast longing that abrupt design
Which would to falling Troy add thee & thine,
That way to death lies open,—soon will stand
Pyrrhus before thee with the reeking brand
That drank the blood of Priam; he whose hand
The son in presence of the Father slays,
And at the Altar's base the slaughtered Father lays.
For this, benignant Mother! didst thou lead
My steps along a way from danger freed?
That I might see remorseless foemen invade
The holiest places that these roofs overshade?
See Father, Consort, Son all tinged & dyed
With mutual sprinklings, perish side by side?
Arms bring me, Friends! bring Arms! our last hour speaks,—
It calls the vanquished; cast me on the Greeks!
In rallying combat let us join—not all
This night, unsolaced by revenge will fall.'
The sword resumes its place, the shield I bear
And hurry now to reach the open air;
When on the ground, before the threshold cast,
prone Creusa hath my feet embraced,
And holding up Iulus, there cleaves fast!
'If thou departing be resolved to die,
Take us thro' all that in thy road may lie;
But if on arms already tried attend
A single hope, then first this House defend,
In whose protection Sire & Son are thrown,
And I, the Wife that once was called thine own!'
Such outcry filled the Mansion; when, behold
A strange portent, & wonderous to be told!
All suddenly a luminous crest was seen;
Which, where the Boy Iulus hung between
The arms of each sad parent, rose & shed,
Tapering aloft, its lustre from his head!
Along the hair the lambent flame proceeds
With harmless touch, & round his temples feeds!

2 Book

In fear we haste, the burning tresses shake
And from the fount the holy fires would slake;
But joyfully his hands Anchises raised,
The voice not silent as on heaven he gazed.
Almighty ~~Almighty~~ Jupiter if prayers have power
To bend thee, look on us, I seek no more;
If aught our piety deserve O deign
The hope this omen proffers to sustain.
~~Thy help ... ... in vain~~
~~Nor Father let ... ... in vain,~~
~~... this omen ... the hope ...~~
Nor Father let us ask a second sign in vain
Thus spake the Sire & scarcely ended, ~~ere~~
A peal of sudden thunder
~~Upon the left it thundered~~ loud & clear
Broke from the left, & shot
~~Crash of the thunder! Then~~ thro' heaven a star
~~Shot like torch~~ Trailing its torch that sparkled from afar,
Above the roof ~~their~~ star conspicuous sight
Ran to be hid on Ida's silvan height
~~Of Ida seeking then the silvan ...~~
The long
~~And its~~ way marking with a train of light;
The furrowy track the distant sky illumes;
And far & wide are spread sulphureous fumes.
Uprisen from earth my aged Sire implores
The Deities, the holy star adores;
"Now, am I conquered ~~— now is~~ no delay;
"Gods of my country, where ye lead the way,
'Tis not in me to hesitate or swerve!
~~... ... ... nor swerve~~
"Preserve my house, ye Powers, this little one preserve!
"Yours is this augury: & Troy hath still
Life in the signs that manifest your will;
~~I yield nor ... refuse my ... to be~~
~~A willing Partner of thy way with thee~~
I cannot chuse but yield; & now to thee
O Son, a firm associate will I be!

He spake; & nearer thro' the City came,
Rolling more audibly, the sea of flame:
"Now give, dear Father, to this neck the freight
Of thy old age; the burthen will be light
For which my shoulders bend; henceforth our fate,
~~Henceforth our~~ Evil or good, shall we participate:

Second Book 287

The Child shall journey tripping at my side;
Our steps, at distance marked, will be Creusa's guide.
My Household! heed these words;—Upon a mound
(To those who quit the City obvious ground)
A temple, once by Ceres honoured, shows
Its mouldering front; hard by a cypress grows,
Thro' ages guarded with religious care:
Thither, by various roads, let all repair.
Thou, Father! take these relics; let thy hand
Bear the Penates of our native land;
I may not touch them, fresh from deeds of blood,
Till the stream cleanse me with its living flood.
Forthwith an ample vest my shoulders ~~with a vest were~~ clad;
Above the vest a lion's skin was spread;
Next came the living Burthen; fast in mine
His little hand Iulus doth entwine,
~~Ere~~ Following his father with no equal pace;
Creusa treads behind; the darkest ways we trace:
And me, erewhile insensible to harms,
Whom adverse Greeks agglomerate in arms
Moved not, now every breath of air alarms;
All sounds have power to trouble me with fear,
Anxious for whom I lead, & whom I bear.
Thus, till the Gates were nigh, my course I shaped,
And thought the hazards of the time escaped;
When thro' the gloom a noise of feet we hear,
Quick sounds that seemed to press upon the ear;
"Fly," cries my Father looking forth, "O fly!"
They come,—I see their shields & dazzling panoply.
Here in my trepidation was I left,
Through ~~By~~ some unfriendly Power, of mind bereft;
For, whilst I journeyed devious & forlorn,
From me, me wretched was Creusa torn;
Whether stopped short by death, or from the road
She wandered, or sunk down beneath a load
Of weariness, might proof be sought in vain;
She vanished—never to meet these eyes again.

Second Book

Nor did I seek her lost, nor backward turn
My mind, untill we reached the sacred bourne
Of ancient Ceres. All even all, save One
Were in the spot assembled; she alone,
As if her melancholy fate disowned
Companion, son, & husband, no where could be found.
Who man or God from my reproach was free?
Had desolated Troy a heavier woe for me?
Mid careful friends my Sire & son I place,
With the Penates of our Phrygian race,
Deep in a winding vale; my footsteps then retrace.
Resolved the whole wide city to explore,
And face the perils of the night once more.
So girt with arms I seek the walls I haste
Toward the dark gates thro which my feet had past;
Remeasured where I may the beaten ground
And turned at every step a searching eye around.
Horror prevails on all sides, while with dread
The very silence is impregnated.
Fast to my Father's Mansion I repaired
If haply, haply she had harboured there.
Seized by the Grecians was the entire Abode,
And now voracious fire its mastery showed
Is rolled upward by the wind
High o'er the roof air rages with the heat;
Thence to the Towers I pass, where Priam held his seat;
Already Phœnix & Ulysses kept,
As chosen Guards, the spoils of Ilium, heaped
In Juno's temple; & the wealth that rose
Piled on the floors of vacant porticos;
Prey torn thro' fire from many a secret Hold,
Vests, tables of the Gods, & cups of massy gold;
And in long order round these treasures stand
Matrons, & Boys, & Youths, a trembling band!
Nor did I spare with fearless voice to raise
Shouts in the gloom, that filled the streets & ways;
And, with re-duplication sad & vain,
Creusa called, again & yet again;
While thus I prosecute an endless quest,
A Shape was seen, unwelcome & unblest;
Creusa's Shade appeared before my eyes,
Her Image, but of more than mortal size;
Then I, as if the power of life had passed
Into my upright hair, stood speechless & aghast.

[illegible]

289

2d Book
She thus — to stop my troubles at their source
Dear consort why thy fondly ... course?
~~Thus she began, my trouble to subdue~~
Superior Powers, not doubtfully prepare
These issues; forgoing hence, thou wilt [illegible] not leave
Creusa with thee; know that fate denies
This fellowship, & this the Ruler of the skies.
Long wanderings will be thine, no home allowed;
And vast the extent of sea that must be ploughed,
E'er thou on Hesperian fields where Tiber flows
With gentle current, thy tired keels repose.
Joy meets thee there, a Realm & royal Bride;
For loved Creusa let thy tears be dried;
I go not where the Myrmidons abide;
Derived from Jove, & raised by thee so high,
Spouse to the Offspring of the Deity,
No proud Dolopian Mansion shall I see
Nor shall a Grecian Dame be served by me;
Far otherwise; upon my native plains
Me the great Mother of the Gods detains.
Now, fare thee well! protect our son, & prove
By tenderness for him, our common love.
This having said my trouble to subdue,
Into thin air she silently withdrew;
Left me while tears were gushing from their springs,
And on my tongue a thousand hasty things;
Thrice with my arms I strove her neck to clasp;
~~Thrice had my hands succeeded in their grasp~~
From my weak hands the image slipped away, as lightly
As the swift winds or Sleep when taking flight;
Such was the close & now the night thus spent
~~Back to my friends [illegible]~~
Back to my friends all eager course I bent;
And here a marvellous number I behold
Of new associates, concourse manifold!
Matrons, & men, & youth that hither hied,
For exile gathering, & from every side,
The wretched people thronged & multiplied,
Prepared with mind & means their flight to speed
Across the seas, where I might chuse to lead.
Now on the ridge of Ida's summit grey
Rose Lucifer, prevenient to the day;
The Grecians held the gates in close blockade;
Hope was there none of giving farther aid;
I yielded, took my Father up once more,
And sought the mountain with the Freight I bore. End 2d Book

3rd Book

3rd Book ~~Amid the sea there lies~~ Mid the mid sea, there lies a   continued from 15 leaves back
line 72 ~~There is an Isle, a pleasant~~ spot of earth   291
Sacred to her who gave the Nereids birth
And to Aegean Neptune. Long was toss'd
This then unfruitful ground, & driven from coast to coast
But as it floated o'er the wide-spread sea
The Archer God in filial piety
Between two Sister Islands bound it fast
For man's abode, and to defy the blast.
Thither we steer. At length the unruffled place
Receiv'd our Vessels in her calm embrace
We land—and ~~shout~~ when the pleasant soil we trod
Adored the City of the Delian God.
Chief Anius, the King (~~his temples~~ whose brows were wreathed around
With ~~sacred~~ laurel garland & with fillets bound
~~The sovereign who served~~ His sacred symbols as Apollo's ~~..~~ priest)
Advanced to meet us, from our ships released;
He recognised Anchises; & their hands
Gladly they join, renewing antient Bands
Of hospitality; nor longer waits
The King, but leads us to his friendly gates.
To seek the Temple was my early care,
To whose Divinity I bowed in prayer
Within the reverend Pile of ancient stone;—
"Thymbraeus! painful wanderings have we known
Grant to ~~us~~ the weary, dwellings of their own!
A City yield, a progeny insure,
A habitation destined to endure!—
To us, sad relics of the Grecian Sword,
(All that is left of Troy) another Troy ~~afford~~ accord.
What shall we seek? Whom follow? where abide?
Vouchsafe an augury our course to guide / some trusty omen for our guide
Father, descend & through our spirits glide!—
Then shook, or seemed to shake, the ~~whole~~ entire abode
A trembling seized the laurels of the God
The mountain rock'd—& sounds with murmuring sound
Roll'd from the Shrine;—upon the ground I fell
And heard the guiding voice our fates foretell

3 Book

"Ye patient Dardans! seek the same Land that bore
Your first progenitors in days of yore
That ancient Mother will unfold her breast
For your return — seek her with faithful quest
So shall the Aenean Line command the earth
As long as future years to future years give birth
Thus Phoebus answered and, forthwith, the Crowd
Burst into transport vehement & loud;
All ask what Phoebus wills; and where the bourne
To which Troy's wandering Race are destined to return.
Then spake my aged Father, turning o'er
Traditions handed down from days of yore ×
"In the mid sea the Cretan Island lies
Dear to the sovereign Lord of earth & skies
There is the Idaean Mount, & there we trace
The fountain-head, the cradle of our race.
A hundred Cities, places of command,
Rise in the circle of that fruitful Land;
Thence to Rhaetean shores, if things oft heard
I faithfully remember, Teucer steered,
Our first progenitor, and chose a spot,
His seat of government when Troy was not;
While yet the Natives housed in valleys deep
Ere Pergamus had risen to crown the lofty steep
From Crete came Cybele, all that the Mother of the Gods ordain'd
The Corybantian Cymbals thence we drew;
The Idaean Grove; & faithful silence, due
To rites mysterious; and the Lion Pair
Ruled by the Goddess from her awful Car. —
Then haste the Mandate of the Gods obey
And to the Gnossian Realms direct our way;
But first the Winds propitiate; & if Jove
From his high throne the enterprize approve,
The third day's light shall bring our happy fleet
To safe harbour on the shores of Crete
He spake; appropriate Victims forth were led
And by his hand upon the Altars bled:
A Bull to soothe the God who rules the Sea —
A Bull, O bright Apollo! fell to thee;
A sable Sheep to Hyems next he slew
To the soft Zephyrs, one of purest white

X "Give ear," he said, "O Chieftains! ... the hopes this Oracle affords"

Fame tells that regions may in Crete be found
Bare of the foe deserted tracts of ground,
Left by Idomeneus to recent flight
Driven from those realms his patrimonial right
Cheered by a hope those vacant seats to gain
We quit the Ortygian shore & scud along the main;
Near Naxos, traversed by a rout
Of maddening Bacchanals, with song & shout
By green Donysa rising o'er the deeps
Olearos & snow-white Parian steeps
Flying with prosperous sail thro' sounds & seas
Starred with the thickly-clustering Cyclades.
Confused & various clamour rises high;
To Crete & to our Ancestors they cry
While ships & sailors still each other vie,
Still freshening from the stern the breezes blow,
And speed the barks, they haste where'er we go
Till rest is given, upon the ancient shores
Of the Curetes, to their sails & oars.—
So with keen hope I trace a circling wall
[illegible] new city by a name which all
Repeat with gladness Pergamus I call
[illegible]
The thankful citizens I then exhort
To love their hearths, and raise a guardian Fort: see Margin
The ships are drawn ashore; with eager hands
The settlers occupy the allotted lands
[illegible]
On trees and plants the deadly season preyed
[illegible]
The men surrendered their dear lives; or, life
Remaining, dragg'd their limbs in feeble strife
[illegible]
Parched every herb to bare sterility
[illegible] corn its nurture to deny.
And forced the sick [illegible] to seek once more
[illegible]
The Delian shrine & pardon thence implore
Ask of the God to what these sorrows tend
Whence we must look for aid, our voyage whither tend.

'Twas night, & couch'd upon the dear ground
The weary animals in sleep were bound
When those Penates which my hands had snatched
From burning Troy, while on my bed I watch'd
Appeared & stood before me in vision to my sight
Made manifest by copious streams of light.

[illegible]

3d Book

Thus did they speak "we come the Delegates
Of Phoebus to foretell thy future fates

Pour'd from the body of the full-orb'd Moon
That thro' the loop-holes of my chamber shone
Thus they appeared & spake "Thy future fates
Phoebus [illegible] his Delegates - to thine ear
Uttering the words which [illegible]
The world infant should'st thou to Delos steer
When Troy was burnt we cross'd the billowy sea
Faithful attendants on thy arms, & we
Shall raise to Heaven thy proud Posterity
But thou thy destined wanderings stoutly bear
And for the mighty, mighty Seats prepare
These Abodes most fair. Apollo never designed
That thou in Crete a resting place shouldst find
There is a country styled by men of Greece
Hesperia - strong in arms - the soil of large increase
Œnotrians held it; men of later fame
Call it Italia from their Leader's name
Thy home is there; there lies the native place
Of Dardanus & Jasius, whence our race
Rise then, & to thy aged Father speak
These indubitable tidings;- bid him seek
The Ausonian land, & Corythus; Jove yields
No place to us among Dictaean fields
Upon the sacred spectacle I gazed
And heard the utterance of the Gods, amazed
[illegible]
Upon my hearth the pure untempered wine
A prompt libation to the powers divine.
This rite performed with joy, my Sire I sought,
Charged with the message which the Gods had brought:
When I had opened all in order due,
The truth found easy entrance; for he knew
The double ancestors, the ambiguous race;
And owned his new mistake, in person & in place.
Then he exclaimed "O Son! severely tried
In all that Troy is fated to abide,
This course Cassandra's voice to me made known
She prophesied of this, & she alone"
Italia oft she cried, & words outthrew
Of realms Hesperian to our Nation due.

295

[illegible]
A fixt abode upon the [illegible]
But who would Phrygians [illegible] such a power erect
Heard the Prophetess but faith was checked
Whom did Cassandra's sayings then affect?
Now let us yield to Phoebus, & pursue
The happier lot he offers to our view.
All heard with transport what my Father spake;
This habitation also we forsake;
And straight, a scanty remnant left behind,
Once more in hollow Ships we court the helpful wind.
P But when along the Deep our galleys steer'd
And the last speck of land had disappear'd
And nought was visible above around
But The black sky, & ocean without bound
Then came a tempest-laden cloud that stood
Right over me, and bronzed the blackening flood
The fleet is scattered while around us rise
Billows that every moment magnifies
Day fled & heaven enveloped in a night
Of stormy rains, is taken from our sight.
By instincts of their own the clouds are riven
And prodigal of fire; while we are driven
Far from the points we aimed at, every bark
Errant upon the waters rough & dark
Even Palinurus owns that night & day
Thus in each other lost confound his way
Three sunless days we struggle with the gales
And for three starless nights all guidance fails
On the fourth day came & to our wistful eyes
The far off land, then first began to rise
[illegible]
Lifting itself in hills, that rapidly broke
[illegible]
Upon our view, & rolling clouds of smoke
[illegible]
Sails drop; & the Mariners with spring & stoop
[illegible]
Inclined to their oars, the eddying waters scoop
The Vessels skim the waves, drive from prow to poop
Saved from the perils of the stormy seas
We disembark upon the Strophades.
Named the Ionian waters lie this pair
Of islands & that Grecian name they bear
[illegible]
[illegible]
[illegible]
[illegible]
The brood of harpies which in fear they left
The doors of Phineus, of that home bereft
And of their former tables, hither fled

3 Book

There dwell with dire, Celena at their head
No plague so hideous for impure abuse
Of upper air did ever Styx produce
Stirred ~~with~~ by the anger ~~of~~ of the Gods to fling
~~Out of the~~ Out her waves some ~~execrable~~ new born monstrous thing
Birds they, with virgin faces, crooked claws
Of filthy paunch & of ~~insatiate~~ insatiate maws
And pallid mien from hunger without pause

~~Here lodged in tranquil harbour we espied~~
~~Lot of one ground the Port the fields overspread~~
~~With herds & goats unwatched as they fed~~
~~And ... over ... meadow bed~~
~~... through ...~~
~~Roaming at large unwatched as they fled fed~~
~~Large~~ Prompt Slaughter made, we for the Gods purvey
And call on Jove himself to share the prey
Then couch by couch ~~upon~~ along the Strand we rear
And feast well pleased upon that ~~goodly~~ dainty chear.

Here safe in Port we saw the fields overspread
With ~~herds~~ beeves & ~~goats~~ goats untended as they fed
Prompt slaughter follows, offerings thence we pay
And call on Jove himself to share the prey
Then couch by couch along the bay we rear
And feast well-pleased upon that goodly cheer
But clapping loud their wings the harpy brood
Rush from the mountain, pounce upon our food
Pollute the morsels which they fail to seize
And screaming load with noisome scents the breeze
Again—but now within a long drawn glade
Overhung with rocks & boughs of roughest shade
We deck our tables & replace the fire
Upon the altars; but with noises dire
From different points of heaven from or blind retreats
They ~~flock~~ & hovering over defile the meats
"War let them have" I cried & gave command,
To stem the next foul onset arms in hand
Forthwith the men withdraw from sight their shields
And hide their swords where grass a covert yields
But when the harpies with loud clang once more
Gathered & spread upon the curved shore
From a tall eminence in open view
His trumpet sound of charge Mycenus blew
Then ~~to~~ our swords assault those fowls obscene
Of generation aqueous & terrene

+ Here lodged in Port we saw the fields overspread
with goodly herds untended as they fed
With Beeves & shaggy goats not told [illegible]
~~Large~~ Prompt

3 Book

297

But what avails it, oft repeated blows
They with inviolable plumes oppose
Baffle the steel & leaving stains behind
And spoil half eaten mount upon the wind
Celaeno only from on a summit high
Perched & these once vented this sad prophesy.
By war descendants of Laomedon
For our slain steers by war would you atone
Why seek the blameless Harpies to expel
From regions where by right of birth they dwell
But learn & fast within your memories hold
Things which to Phœbus Jupiter foretold
Phœbus to me & I to you unfold,
I greatest of the Furies. Ye who strive
For Italy, that ye Italy shall arrive
Havens within that wished for lands by leave Of the favouring winds your Navy shall receive
But do not hope to raise those promised walls
Ere on your head the curse of hunger falls
And for the slaughter of our herds your doom
Hath been your very tables to consume
This uttered back she flew to the forest's gloom
Gnaw'd and devour'd thro' utter want of food.
She spake; and, borne on wings, sought refuge in the wood
The haughty spirits of the men were quailed quail'd
A shuddering fear thro' every heart prevail'd
On force of arms no longer they rely
To daunt whom prayers and vows must pacify,
Whether to Goddesses the offence were given
Or they with dire and obscene birds had striven:
Fit offering made as on the shore he stands
My sire Anchises, with uplifted hands
Invokes the greater Gods ye powers disarm
Upon making at the ... demands ... the harm
This threat & from your votaries ... on the shore he stands
Invokes the greater Gods while on the shore ... fears,
" Ye Powers! annul a threat that ... "
Avert the ill, and guard your worshippers
Then bids to loose the cables, & unbind
The willing canvas, to the breeze resign'd
Southward, we ... the south winds urge
... the Steersman & the ... along the ... tides
Our rapid keels ... the foaming surge
At the wind ... of the steersman guides

Bymbrr by fear appalled
The haughty spirits of the men grew quailed

Due rites ordain'd

Where guides
we skim

3d. B

Before us opens, midway in the flood,s
Zacynthus, shaded with luxuriant wood[s]
Dulichium rose & Same next appears
And Neritos a craggy summit rears
We shun the rocks of Ithaca, ill nurse
Of stern Ulysses & her soil we curse
Then Mount Leucate shews its vapoury head
Where from his temple Phœbus strikes with dread
The passing mariner, but no mischance
Now feared, to that small city we advance
Gladly we haul the sterns ashore & throw
The bitter anchor out from every prow
Unlook'd-for land thus reach'd, to Jove we raise
The votive altars which with incense blaze
Our Youth illustrating the Actian strand
With Trojan games as in their native land
Besmear their naked limbs with slippery oil
And pant for mastery in athletic toil;
Well pleased so fair a voyage to have shaped
Mid Grecian towns, on every side escaped.
Sol through his annual round meanwhile had pass'd
And the sea roughened in the wintry blast;
A brazen shield [illegible]
Fix'd on the temple gate a brazen shield
[illegible] which mighty Abas bore
Inscription verse declared why this was done
"Arms from the conquering Greeks by Æneas won."

The signal given this friendly port to leave
Contending oars the sparkling waters cleave
Phœacia's peaks [illegible] seen & lost
As we proceed, Epirus now we coast
And Chaonium won we greet
Buthrotum perched upon its lofty seat
Helenus, son of Priam, here was Chief
So ran the tale ill-fitted for belief

Began here Did
Then, at my word, the ships unmooring leave
And with contending oars the waters cleave.

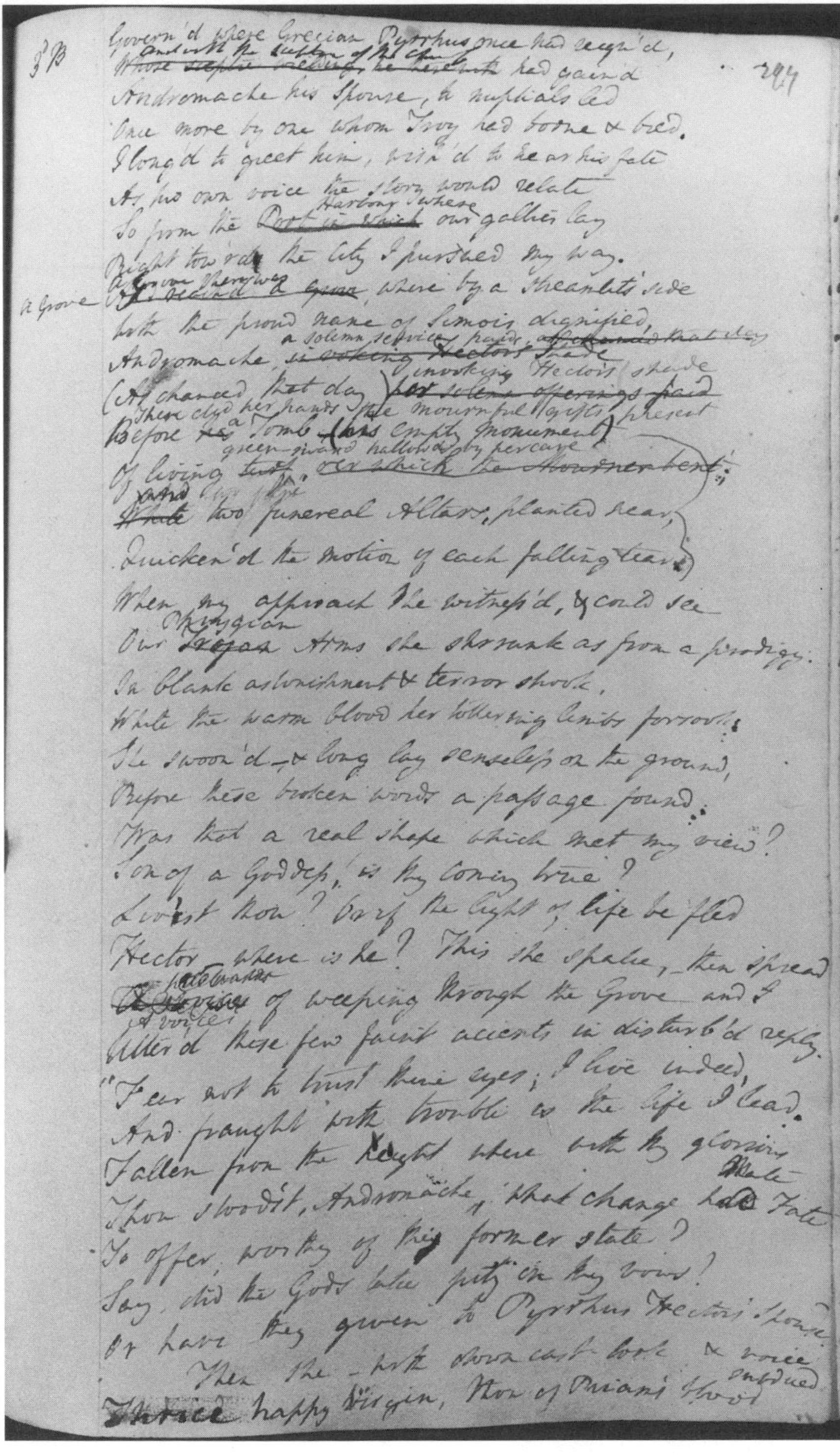

3 B

Govern'd where Grecian Pyrrhus once had reign'd,
And with the sceptre of the Cha
Whose sceptre wielding, he herewith had gain'd
Andromache his Spouse, to nuptials led
Once more by one whom Troy had borne & bred.
I long'd to greet him, wish'd to hear his fate
As his own voice the story would relate
Harbour where
So from the Port in which our gallies lay
Right towards the City I pursued my way.
A Grove thereby was
A Grove Of a sacred A Grove, where by a Streamlet's side
With the proud name of Simois dignified,
a solemn service paid, as chanced that day
Andromache, invoking Hector's shade
invoking Hector's shade
(As chanced that day) her solemn offerings paid
There clasp'd her hands the mournful Widow; present
Before his a Tomb (an empty monument)
green-sward hallow'd by her care
Of living turf, o'er which the Mourner bent;
And two pious Altars
While two funereal Altars, planted near,
Quicken'd the motion of each falling tear.
When my approach she witness'd, & could see
Phrygian
Our Trojan Arms she shrunk as from a prodigy;
In blank astonishment & terror shook,
While the warm blood her tottering limbs forsook;
She swoon'd, & long lay senseless on the ground,
Before these broken words a passage found:
Was that a real shape which met my view?
Son of a Goddess, is thy coming true?
Livest thou? Or if the light of life be fled
Hector where is he? This she spake, then spread
A voice of weeping through the Grove and I
Utter'd these few faint accents in disturb'd reply.
"Fear not to trust thine eyes; I live indeed,
And fraught with trouble is the life I lead.
Fallen from the height where with thy glorious
Mate
Thou stood'st, Andromache, what change hath Fate
To offer worthy of thy former state?
Say, did the Gods take pity on thy vows!
Or have they given to Pyrrhus Hector's Spouse?
Then she with downcast look & voice subdued
Thrice happy Virgin, thou of Priam's blood

244

3d. B. Who in the front of Troy by timely doom
Didst pour out life before a hostile tomb;
And, slaughter'd thus, wert guarded from the wrong
Of being swept by lot amid a ~~[illegible]~~ helpless [illegible] throng
O happiest above all who ne'er didst press
A conquering Master's bed in captive wretchedness!
I since our Ilium fell, have undergone
(Wide waters cross'd) what e'er Achilles' Son
Could in the arrogance of birth impose
And faced in servitude a mother's throes.
Thereafter, he at will the knot unty'd
To seek Hermione a Spartan Bride;
And me to Trojan Helenus he gave—
Captive to captive—if not slave to slave.
Whereat, Orestes with strong love inflamed
Of her, now lost, whom as a bride he claim'd,
And by the Furies driven, in vengeful ire
~~Slew~~ Smote Pyrrhus at the Altar of his Sire. + Lede
He, by an ~~unsuspected blow~~ unexpected blow thus slain
On Helenus devolv'd a part of his domain;
Who call'd the neighbouring fields Chaonian ground,
~~And gave [illegible] so he nam'd the region wide~~ around,
~~Chaonia~~ ! Chaonia named the Region wide around,
From Trojan Chaon; chusing for the site
Of a new Pergamus yon ~~[illegible]~~ rocky height
But thee, a stranger in a land unknown
What fates have urged? What winds have hither blown?
Or say what God ~~hath~~ upon our Coasts hath thrown.
Survives the Boy Ascanius? In his heart
Doth his lost Mother still retain her part?
What, Son of great Aeneas, brings ~~[illegible]~~ forth
In emulation of his Father's worth?
In Priam's Grand child doth not Hector's name rouse
High hopes to reach the virtue of past days
~~These words Then follow'd lamentations long~~
~~To this succeeded~~
Then follow'd sobs & lamentations vain
But from the City with a numerous train
Her living consort Helenus descends
He saw, & ~~glad~~ gave glad greeting to his Friends

[Left margin, written vertically:] When he by this [illegible] for the [illegible] slain / To Helenus devolv'd a part of his domain / Who called

And tow'rds his hospitable palace leads
While passion interrupts the speech it feeds.
As we advance I gratulate with joy
Their shrivelled Xanthus & their little Troy
Their Pergamus,
As if the Old to emulate;
And clasp the threshold of their Scaean Gate;
Meanwhile my Followers share the fresh delight
Which in my breast these kindred walls excite
Nor fails this kindred City to excite
In my Associates unreserv'd delight,
And soon in ample Porticoes the King
Receives the Band with earnest welcoming;
Amid the Hall high festival we hold
Refresh'd with viands serv'd in massy gold
And from resplendent goblets votive wine
Flows in libation to the Powers divine.
Two joyful days thus passed; the southern breeze
Once more invites my sails to trust the seas
To Helenus this suit I then prefer;
Illustrious Trojan, Heaven's interpreter,
By prescient Phoebus with his spirit fill'd;
Skill'd in the tripod, in the laurel skill'd;
Skill'd in the stars, and what by voice or wing
Birds to the intelligence of mortals bring;
Hear and advise. To Italy I bend
Urg'd by the Gods who for this aim portend
By every sign they give a happy end;
The Harpy Queen the only doth presage
The curse of famine in its utmost rage
Now say, what perils first I am to shun
What course for safe deliverance
The royal Seer Helenus (accustom'd victims slain
In prayer, Address the Gods, their favour to obtain
Unbound the fillets from his sacred head
Then took my hand & while a holy dread
Oppress'd me, onward to the Temple led,
Thy Temple, Phoebus! from his lips then flow'd
Communications of the inspiring God.—

To common sense ... (this truth is plain)
... conducts thee, Son of Venus, o'er the main
... this course ordain.

That with safer voyage thou mayst reach
The Ausonian harbours, I will clothe in speech
Some portion of the future; Fate hath
Clouds o'er the rest; or Juno binds my tongue.
And first that Italy, whose coasts appear,
To thy too confident belief, so near,
With havens open for thy sails, a wide
And weary distance doth from thee divide.
Trinacrean waves thy pliant oar
... thou Ausonian gulphs a passage must explore;
... of Circe and the infernal pool,
... City rise for stedfast rule.
Now mark these tokens — soon as thou shalt find
A bulky female of the bristly kind:
By a sequestered river's margin laid
On ... branches overshade;
With thirty young-ones couch'd in that recess
White as the pure white dam whose teats they press.
There found thy City — on that soil shall close
All thy solicitudes, in fixed repose.
Nor dread Celæno's threat; the Fates shall clear
The way, and oh thy call Apollo interfere
But shun those lands where our Ionian sea
Washes the nearest shores of Italy
On all the coasts malignant Greeks abide
Narycian Locrians there, a town hath fortified
Idomeneus of Crete hath compassed round
With soldiery, the Salentinian ground.
There where Thessalian Phyloctetes chose
His resting place, there small Petilia rose
But when that sea is past over,
Before the Altars kindling on the Strand
While to the Gods are offered up thy vows
Then cast a purple amice o'er thy brows
And sacrifice thus cover'd lest the sight
Of any hostile face disturb the rites
Be this observance kept by thee and thine
And this to late posterity consign!

But when by favoring breezes wafted o'er
Thy Fleet approaches the Sicilian shore
Pelorus' straits unfolding by degrees
Steering that shore along
Erewhile when Earth by violence was rent
This ground forsook the Hesperian Continent
Nor doubt that power to work such change might lie
Within the grasp of dark antiquity
Then flow'd the Sea between & by the force
Of roaring waves established the Divorce
Still thro' the straits the narrow waters boil
Dissevering Town from Town & soil from soil
The Dogs of Scylla fret
The Left by fell Charybdis is beset
Thrice towards the bottom of a vast abyss
Down, headlong down the liquid precipice
She sucks the whirling billows and as oft
Ejecting, sends them into air aloft
But Scylla, pent within her cavern blind
Thrusts forth a visage of our human kind
A woman to the waist is foul below
A huge Sea Beast with Dolphin tail
With water wolves & Dogs her middle
But thou against this jeopardy provide
Doubling Pachynus with a circuit wide
Thus shall Scylla be left unseen
Unheard the yelling of her brood marine
But above all if Phoebus I revere
Nor unenlightened an authentic seer
Then Goddess born (on this would I enlarge
Repeating oft & oft the solemn charge)
Adore imperial Juno freely wait
With gifts on Juno's altars supplicate
Her potent favour & subdue her hate
To Italy (thus conqueror at last)
Shalt thou proceed Sicilian dangers past
Thus shalt thou seek (a conqueror at last)
The Italian Shore, Trinacrian limits past

Book Arriv'd at Cumae & the sacred floods
Of black Avernus resonant with woods
Thou shalt behold the Sybil where she sits
Within her Cave, rapt in ecstatic fits
And signs & Characters to leaves commits.
The prophecies which on those Leaves the Maid
Inscribes are by her hands in order laid
And in the secluded cavern there they fill
Their several places undisturb'd & still
But if a light wind entering thro the door
Scatter the thin Leaves on the Rocky floor
She to replace her prophecies with care
No diligence employs flutter where they chuse
In hopeless disconnection loose & wild
And they who sought for knowledge thus beguil'd
Without her predictions from the Cave depart
And quit the Sybil with a murmuring heart
But thou albeit ill disposed to wait
And prizing moments at their highest rate
Tho' followers chide & ever & anon
The flattering winds invite thee to be gone
Beg of the moody Prophetess to break
The silent air & for thy guidance speak
She will disclose the features of thy doom
The Italian Nations & the wars to come
How to escape from hardships or endure
And make a happy termination sure
Enough chains bind the rest or clouds obscure
Go then & high as heaven's ethereal vault
The Trojan name by glorious deeds exalt.
So spake the friendly Seer from hallow'd lips
Then orders presents to our parting ships
Smooth ivory massy gold & weighty ponderous store
Of vases fashioned from the paler ore.
And Dodonaean Cauldrons; nor withholds
The golden hauberk knit in triple folds
Which that Neoptolemus erewhile had worn
Nor his resplendant crest which waving flames adorn
High offerings also grace my Father's hands
Horses he adds, with Equerries, & bands
Of Rowers & supply of arms commands

The ministrants from the Cave drew
Found sought the Sybil with a murmuring heart

3d Book

Meanwhile Anchises bids the Fleet unbend
Its sails for instant seizure of the wind
The interpreter of Phoebus then had addrest
This gracious farewell to his parting guest
Anchises! to celestial honours led
Beloved of Venus, whom she deigned to wed;
Care of the Gods, twice snatch'd from Ilium lost,
Now for Ausonia be these waters cross'd!
Yet only hope to glide along the shores
To which I point; far lies the land from ours
To whither Apollo's voice directs your powers.
Go happy Parent of a pious Son!
No more I baulk the winds that press thee on.
Nor less Andromache disturb'd in heart
That parting now we must for ever part,
Embroider'd Vests of golden thread bestows,
A Phrygian Tunic o'er Ascanius throws,
And studious that her bounty may become
The occasion, adds rich labours of the loom.
Dear Child! she said, these also, to be kept
As the memorials of my hand, accept.
[illegible]
Last gifts of kindred Concord, let them prove
To thee the tokens of her lasting love:
Take what Andromache at parting gives,
Thy Boy, sole image that for me survives
Of my Astyanax; in whom his face,
His eyes are seen, his very hands I trace.
And now but for obstruction of the tomb
His years had open'd into kindred bloom.
To these, while gushing tears bedew'd my cheek,
Thus in the farewell moment did I speak
"Live happy ye whose race of fortune run
Permits, with life, from hard fate undergone
Permits you to live, from labour done
[illegible] by you is quiet won
No seas have ye to measure now on you
Is it impos'd Ausonia to pursue
And search for fields still flying from the view.
Before your sight a [illegible]
[illegible]
[illegible] Troy [illegible] you, by your labour rose
[illegible]
With happier auspices in less degree,
[illegible] to Grecian enmity.
[illegible]

If Tiber e'er receive me & the sod
Of Tiber's meadows by these feet be trod
If e'er our destined city I behold
Then neighbouring towns & tribes akin of old
Hesperian & Epirian whose blood came
From Dardanus whose lot hath been the same
Shall make one Troy in spirit. May that care
To our Descendants pass from heir to heir.—

Beneath Ceraunian Rocks our Gallies steer
(No other course finds Italy so near.)
Meanwhile the Sun descends, & o'er the head
Of every mountain blackening shadows spread.
Tired of the oar, the men rejoice & then each
Hath spread his limbs in ease along the beach.
On the dry margin of the murmuring Deep
They lie not wanting long the embrace of sleep
along the shore our ease together bound
Near the Ceraunian the [illegible] whence is found
The shortest passage to Italian ground
Meanwhile the Sun went down & shadows spread
O'er every mountain darkned to its head
Tired of their oars the men no sooner reach
Earth's wish'd for bosom than along the beach
They spread their limbs beside the murmuring Deep
Where weariness is lost in timely sleep.
Ere the whose car the Hours had yoked & reined
Black Night, the middle of her orbit gain'd,
Up from his couch doth Palinurus rise
Looks to the winds for what ill signifies
And to each breath of air a watchful ear applies.
Next all the Stars gliding thro' silent heaven
The Bears, Arcturus & the watery seven
He notices and ranging wide his eyes behold
Magnificent Orion arm'd in gold.
Assured that all presages
When he perceives all things low & high
Unite to promise fix'd serenity
He sends the summons forth our Camp we raise
Are gone & every Ship her broadest wings displays.

Earth's wishd for bosom then along their beach
They spread their limbs beside the murmuring
Their weary limbs beside the murmuring Deep
They spread and in the [illegible] of slumber

Book

They stretched
They spread their limbs beside

And in the [illegible]

The End

We sail near high Ceraunia, whence is found
The shortest passage to Hesperian ground.
Meanwhile the sun went down & shadows spread
O'er every mountain darken'd to its head
Ensu'd of the oar [illegible] this wish'd for beach
We seek refreshment & prepare for rest:
Nor did indulgent Nature fail to steep
On the dry margin of the murmuring deep
Our weary limbs in the soft dew of sleep.
Risen from couch ere Night with slow ascent
Had measured half the vaulted firmament
Prompt Palinurus looks with cautious eyes
To every cloud for what it signifies
And to

3d Book line 521

Now, when Aurora reddened in a sky
From which the stars had vanish'd, we descry
The low faint hills of distant Italy
"Italia" shouts Achates; round & round, gratulant
Italia flies with gratulant rebound,
From all who see the coast, or hear the happy sound.
Not slow is our Anchises to entwine
With wreaths a goblet, which he fill'd with wine;
Then cried "Ye on the stern he took his lofty stand,
And cried "Ye Deities of Sea & Land
[illegible] to speed our way
[illegible]
All breezes docile to your kindliest sway
[illegible] wish'd for goal
[illegible]
[illegible] speedy sails
[illegible]
The Port [illegible] on sight
Opens the Port [illegible] into sight
Minerva's temple upon a craggy height crowns
crowns

[illegible]

3.d Book

The Sails are furled by many a busy hand,
The veering prows are pointed to the strand.
Curved into [Scythian] the fashion of a bow the haven
Looks towards the east, but not a wave that from the east all drove,
Waves that disturbs its [peacefulness] rest; their foamy spray
Breaks upon jutting rocks that [fence] guard the bay.
Two towering cliffs extend with gradual fall
Their arms into the sea, & frame a wall.
In whose embrace the harbour hidden lies;
And, as its shelter deepens on our eyes,
Back from the shore, Minerva's temple flies.

Endo

Four snow-white Horses grazing the wide field [Pascua]
Are the first omen which our landing yields
Then Sire Anchises—"War thy tokens bear
O hospitable Land, the Horse is arm'd for war;
War do these menace, but as, steed with steed
Oft joins in friendly yoke the sight may breed
Fair hope that peace & concord will succeed.
To Pallas then in clanking armour, would
Who hail'd us first exulting to be hail'd
Prayers we address with Phrygian amice veil'd,
And as by Helenus enjoin'd the fire
On Juno's altar fumes—to Juno vows aspire.
When we had clos'd this service to present,
That instant Seaward are our sail-yards bent,
And we forsake the shore, with cautious dread
Of ground by native Grecians tenanted.
The Bay is quickly reached that draws its name
From proud Tarentum, proud to share the fame
Of Hercules tho' by a dubious claim;
Right opposite we ken the Structure holy
Of the Lacinian Goddess rising slowly,
Next the Caulonian Citadel appears
And the Scylacian bay for Shipwrecks fear'd.
Lo, as along the open Main we float,
Mount Etna, yet far off! & far remote
Groans of the sea we hear,—deep groans & strokes
Of angry billows beating upon rocks,
And hoarse surf clamours; while the flood throws up
Sands from the depths of its unsettled cup.

3d Book 309

~~My [illegible]~~ ~~[illegible]~~
Twixt two dire [illegible]; Dreadfully we are caught
By fell Charybdis; [illegible] flee, as ye were taught!
Doubtless
These are the rocks, and these the dangerous shores
Which Helenus denounced — away with straining oars!
Straight, to the left the [illegible] galley veers
With roaring prow as Palinurus steers.
And for the left the bands of Rowers strive
While every help is caught that winds ~~that~~ can give
The whirlpool's dizzy altitudes we scale
For ghastly sinking when the waters fail
Thrice did the craggy and hollow rocks cry out
Thrice [illegible] we saw the dash the [illegible]
Thrice to heaven we saw the waters spurt
[illegible] the sky [illegible] with a briny spout
The flagging wind forsook us with the sun
And to Cyclopean shores a darkling course we ran.

~~The Port we entered is of ample size~~
~~Fearless of winds but Etna thunders nigh~~
~~[illegible]~~
~~Large [illegible], and its waters lie~~
~~Fearless of winds~~
~~Untouched by winds in still security~~
And unmolested by the winds it lies
But all too near is Etna thundering loud
And ofttimes casting forth a pitchy cloud
Of smoke in whirling convolutions driven
With weight of fiery hoary embers, high as heaven.

The Port which now we chance to enter, lies
By winds unruffled tho' of ample size
But all too near is Etna thundering loud
And ofttimes casting up a pitchy cloud
Of smoke in whirling convolution driven
With weight of hoary ashes high as heaven
And globes of flame & sometimes he gives vent
To rocky fragments from his entrails rent
And hurls out melting substances that fly
In thick assemblage & confound the sky
While groans & lamentations burthensome
Tell to the air from what a depth they come.
The enormous mass of Etna, so 'tis said,
On lightning-scorched Enceladus was laid
And ever pressing on the Giant's frame
Breathes out from fractured chimneys fitful flame

The hollow rocks three times a fearful cry
Three times we saw the dashing waves fling high
Their foam. [illegible] a dizzy [illegible]

3.d Book

And often as he turns his weary side
Murmuring Trinacria trembles far & wide
While wreaths of smoke ascend & all the welkin hide.
We, through the
Cover'd thus all that night enwrapp'd in woods obscure
The shock of the storm alone
Do we those fearful prodigies endure
Nor could we distinguish whence the sound might come &
For all the stars in ether's utmost bound
Proceeded for the stars of heaven were drowned
Were hidden or bedimm'd
In widely spreading clouds & Night withheld the moon
In f The Moon, in mist & showery fogs conceal'd 587

3.707 These left, we harboured in the joyless coast
Of Drepanum; here, long by tempests tost,
[illegible] did I lose
And here my [illegible] [illegible] lose
Help in my cares and solace of my woes
Here, O best Father best beloved and best
Didst thou desert me when I needed rest,
Thou from so many perils saved in vain
Not Helenus 'mid many things of dread [illegible] the doleful strain
[illegible] of prophecy foretold this
Foretold thy bitter pain;
[illegible]
This trouble was my last; by heavenly Powers
O Queen, thence brought am I to your friendly shores;
Sole Speaker, thus Aeneas did relate
To a hushed audience the decrees of Fate,
His wandering course recounted, & the close
Thus reached, in silence here found repose
718. end

709 And here my [illegible] did I lose
Help in my cares and solace of my woes
Here O best Father best beloved and best
Didst thou desert me when I needed rest.
[illegible] rest;
Thou from so many perils snatched in vain;
Not Helenus [illegible] in doleful strain
Of prophecy, this sorrow did unfold.
Not [illegible] foretold.

Sole Speaker thus Aeneas did relate
To a mystic audience the decrees of Fate
His wandering course pursued; and when the close
[illegible] reached, in silence here he found repose
His wandering course recounted and [illegible] the close
Was reached, [illegible] in silence found repose

This scarcely uttered they advance & straight
He shews the Altar & Carmental gate
Which (as the record says) by its Roman name
Preserves the nymph Carmentis' ancient fame
[illegible] the glories of the Trojan line
Predicted [illegible] the noble Palatine.
[illegible] points out an ample sylvan shade
[illegible]
Where under a chill rock, Lupercal lies
Named from Lycaean Pan in old Arcadian guise.
Nor left he unobserved the neighbouring wood
Of sacred Argiletum stained with blood.
Where Argus fell, his Guest — the story told
To the Tarpeian rock their way they hold,
And to the Capitol now bright with gold.
In those far-distant times a spot forlorn
With brambles choked & rough with savage thorn;
Even then an influence of religious awe
The rustics felt subdued by what they saw
The local spirit creeping thro' their blood
[illegible] at the wood
This grove (said he) this leaf-crown'd hill — some God
How named we know not, takes for his abode;
The Arcadians think that Jove himself aloft
Hath here declared his presence oft & oft
Shaken [illegible]
[illegible]
Here also see two mouldering towns that lie
Mournful remains of buried ancestry.
[illegible] father Janus framed,
And Saturn this, each from its founder named.
Conversing thus their onward course they bent
To poor Evander's humble tenement;
[illegible]
[illegible] Roman forum [illegible]
And bellowing [illegible]
[illegible]
When they had reached the house he said, This Gate

Thro' gate conquering Alcides entered ~~passed~~; his plain ~~simple~~ state 367
This palace lodged; O guest like him forbear
To frown on scanty means & homely ~~scanty~~ fare
Dare riches to despise; with aim as high
Mould thou, & train thyself for Deity.
This said thro' that low door he leads his guest
The great Aeneas to a couch of rest
There propped he lay on withered leaves, overspread
With a bear's skin in Lybian deserts bred. VIII. 366
There lay the Chief on withe [illegible]

360-1 Herds range the Roman Forum, through the barriers
Of proud Carinae bellowers resound —
Herds range the Roman forum nature gray
And proud Carinae bellow as they pass
Herds range the Roman forum, in the streets
Of proud Carinae bellowing herds they [illegible]

craves thy soul
Just vengeance dost thou crave for rigid Harmodius,
To whom before Minerva's altar [illegible]
The conscious Tyrant [illegible] glittering [illegible]
For the [illegible] the [illegible] [illegible] with myrtles [illegible],
[illegible] fancy [illegible]
The [illegible] [illegible] of Brutus [illegible]
To [illegible] with [illegible] [illegible] the [illegible]
[illegible] from [illegible] rocks, [illegible] with [illegible]
The [illegible] [illegible] his deadly [illegible]
[illegible] shall [illegible] forego;
[illegible] [illegible]
Of liberty that [illegible] [illegible] fountain
[illegible] [illegible] [illegible]
[illegible] the [illegible] the hollow [illegible]
[illegible] [illegible] his [illegible] of [illegible]

Or place in your [illegible]
The [illegible] the [illegible]

Could but the vanquished beat out of their mind
All hope of safety—safety they might find

She who to raise lift her heavy eyes had tried
Faints while the deep wound gurgles at her side
Thrice on her elbow propp'd she strove to uphold
Her frame—thrice back upon the couch [illegible] roll'd
Then with a wandering eye in heaven's blue round
She sought the light & groaned when she had found
What, son of great Aeneas [illegible] forth
In emulation of his father's worth
[illegible] recall the [illegible] of [illegible] days
[illegible] named we know not takes for his abode
The Arcadians think that Jove himself, aloft,
Hath here declared his presence oft & oft
[illegible]
Shaking his [illegible] Egis in their sight
And gathering round the hill tempestuous night

Even so bewails, the poplar groves among,
Sad Philomela her evanish'd young;
Whom the harsh rustic from the nest hath torn,
An unfledg'd brood; but on the bough forlorn
She sits, in mournful darkness, all night long;
Renews, & still renews, her doleful song,
And fills the leafy grove, complaining of her wrong.

[DC MS. 89, 101ᵛ]

3ᵈ Book

1 *Now when the Gods had crushed the Asian State,*
by too severe a
2 *And Priam's race ~~not~~ ~~meriting~~ such fate,*
3 *When they were pleased proud Ilium to destroy,*
4 *And smokes upon the ground Neptunian Troy;*
5 *The sad Survivors from their Country driven*
distant
6 *Seeks/ ~~various~~ shores, impelled by signs from heaven,*
7 *Beneath Antandros we prepare a Fleet;*
There
8 *~~And~~ my Companions muster at the feet*
9 *Of Phrygian Ida, dubious in our quest*
10 *And where the fates may suffer us to rest.*
11 *Scarcely had breathed the earliest summer gales/*
bid bids to spread
12 *Before Anchises ~~bids~~ ~~to~~ ~~stretch~~ the sails/;*
13 *Weeping I quit the port, my native coast,*
14 *And fields where Troy once was; & soon am tost,*
15 *An exile on the bosom of the Seas,*
16 *With friends, son, household Gods & the great Deities.*
line new P ~~is spread~~
17 *~~Not distant~~ ~~Far off there lies a violent~~ ~~martial~~ land*
To a vast distance spreads a peopld Land
18 *Where once the fierce Lycurgus held command;*
The ~~martial~~ hardy Thracians till the champain wide
19 *~~Its ample fields are tilled by men of Thrace~~*
To Troy by hospitable rites allied
20 *~~Long time to Troy a hospitable place~~*
21 *While Fortune favoured; thither borne I lay*

Right opposite is
~~To a vast distance~~ spreads/ a peopled land
Where once the fierce Lycurgus held command
plough
The martial Thracians ~~till~~ its champain wide
To Troy by hospitable rites allied
~~While Fortune favourd thither borne I lay~~

[DC MS. 89, 102ʳ]

W
21 And kindred Gods, w} hile Troy maintain'd her sway;
22 There, entering with unfriendly fates, I lay
23 *My first foundations in a hollow Bay.* ?
22 *~~Entering with unpropitious Fates, & there,~~*
~~And~~ ~~I call~~ *are called* Æ
24 *~~Calling~~ ~~the~~The Men E} neades; to share*
new ~~glad~~
25 *With the ~~new~~ citizens the name I bear.*
o *we*
26 *To Dia} nean Venus ~~I~~ present,*
fresh
~~fresh~~
27 *And to the Gods who aid a new} intent*

1–57 Autograph not WW's is MW's, except where noted. Material at top of 101ᵛ is part of *Pelayo*; see *Poems, 1807–1820*, pp. 49–51, 498, for the text and further discussion of that poem.

sacred
28 *The ~~needful~~ offerings; & with honor due*
29 *Upon the shore a glossy Bull I slew,*
A } Mount
30 *To the great King of heaven. a* } ~~*tomb*~~ *was near*
~~*A tomb wa*~~ *trees* *uprear*
31 *Upon whose summit, cornel ~~plants~~ ~~uprear~~*
d *ly* }
32 ~~*And myrtle, rough with many bristing*~~ } ~~*spear*~~ }
Their boughs, & myrtles rough with many a spear.
33 *Studious to deck the Altar with green shoots*
tugging at
34 *Thither I turned, & ~~labored, by~~ the roots,*
[?~~Pressd~~] Strove to despoil the thicket
35 ~~*To tear up the leafy thicket*~~*; when, behold/;*
36 *A dire portent, & wonderous to be told!*
{ *as*
37 *No sooner w* { *ere the shattered roots laid bare*
38 *Of the first tree I struggled to uptear,*
an }
39 *Then* } *from the fibres drops of blood distill'd* ?
d } — } thrilled } ?
40 *Whose blackness stains* } *the ground,* } *me horror* [?*chilled*] } ?
Quaked every limb, & all my blood was chilled
~~*Me horror thrilled*~~ *a*
41 ~~*And my blood curdles with the deadly chills*~~
toild
42 *Persisting in the attempt I ~~strove~~ to free*
43 *The flexile body of another tree,*
44 *Anxious the latent causes to explore;*
45 *And from the bark blood trickled as before.*
46 *Revolving much in mind forthwith I paid*
47 *Vows to the sylvan nymphs, & sought the aid*
48 *Of father Mars, spear-shaking God, who yields*
Thracian
His } *Thr* }
49 *A* } *stern protection to the D* } *acian fields.* ⧣
52 *But for a third endeavour when with hands*
53 *Eagerly strain'd, kness pressed against the sands,*
~~*With my whole str*~~
54 *I strive the myrtle lances to uproot*
55 *With my whole—strength, (speak shall I or be mute?)*
was sent
56 *From the deep tomb a mournful groan ~~is heard~~.*
57 ~~*And with this voice the silent air is stirred*~~.
the ~~mute air there~~
And a voice followed, uttering this lament.
50 ⧣ *That to a prosperous issue they would guide*
51 *The accident, the omen turn aside*

[Left margin, vertical:]
Searching the latent
~~Anxious to~~ search the cause, when as before
The violated mirtle ran with gore

50–51 Autograph is DW's.
56–57 Revision is in DW's autograph.

[DC MS. 89, 149r]

1st Book

✶Right against Italy & from the flood
Of Tyber's mouth not far remote a city stood

1 *Arms & the Man I sing, the first who bore*
to Latium from the Trojan
2 *His course ~~from Ilium to the Italian~~ shore*
Fugitive of fate:—Long time was he,
3 *An ~~Exile forced by fate~~, ~~on land & sea~~*
P
By p } owers celestial, tossed on land & sea
4 *~~Much was the Chieftain toss'd by heaven's decree~~*
Thro' ;
5 *~~And~~ wrathful Juno's far-famed enmity,* }
:
6 *Much, too, from war endured { , till new abodes*
in *fixed*
7 *He planted, & ~~to~~ Latium ~~brought~~ his Gods;*
8 *Whence flows the Latin people; whence have come*
Rome
9 *The Alban Sires, & walls of lofty* [?] }.
wrong'd;
P *~~hurt~~, what grievance drove*
10 *Say Muse what p } ower was ~~wrath what injury drove~~*
spouse.
11 *To such extremity the ~~Wife~~ of Jove,*
12 *Labouring to wrap in perils, to astound*[?]
13 *With woes, a Man for piety renowned!*
14 *In heavenly breasts is such resentment found?*
Italian coast there stood
15 ✶ *Right opposite the ~~mouth of Tiber's flood~~*
An ancient City, far from Tiber's flood;
16 *~~In distant Africa, a city stood~~*
a Colony of Tyre,
17 *Carthage its name, ~~by Tyrians occupied:~~*
strong, & bent on war with fierce desire.
18 *Rich, ~~powerful were its study & its pride~~*
No region, not even Samos, was so graced
19 [?~~E'en~~] ~~*more than Samos was the region graced*~~
20 *By Juno's favour; here her Arms were placed*
unbounded scope
21 *Here lodged her chariot; & ~~the Goddess now~~*
~~if the Fates allow~~
24 *~~Fosters a hope that to this state shall bow~~*
~~to this state shall bow~~
realm
23 *~~Nations & Kingdoms, if the Fates allow~~*

{ *Even then the Goddess gave to partial hope*
Her aim (if Fate such triumph will allow)
That to this Nation all the world shall bow.

me
25 *But fa { t had told her that a race, from Troy*
26 *Derived, the Tyrian ramparts would destroy;*
27 *That, from this stock, a people, proud in war*
28 *And trained to spread dominion wide & far,*
29 *Should come, & thro' her favorite Lybian state*
30 *Spread utter ruin—such the doom of Fate.*

1–95 Autograph not WW's is MW's, except where noted.
15 Revision, written vertically in left margin, is in Dora W's autograph.

In fear of this, while ~~Memory~~ recalls busy thought recalls
~~This fearing, & remembering how of Yore~~
she ~~first~~ raised ~~before~~ against the Trojan walls
Th{at/e war, ~~She raised to the Trojan Shore~~
For her {loved/dear Argos (&, with these con{bined,/fined
Worked other causes rankling in her mind;)
Paris,
~~Paris~~
The judgement given by {[?] & the slight
Her beauty had received on Ida's height;
Th'undying hatred which the race had bred,
And honours given to ravished Ganemed;)
~~With these inflamed She~~ far from Latium chased
Saturnian Juno
Trojans
The ~~wanderers~~ tossed upon the watery waste;
unhappy Grecian
~~Trojans the~~ relics of the ~~Achaian~~ spear,
And } of the dire
Of } ~~pitiless~~ Achilles. Many a year

[DC MS. 89, 149v]

1st Book

They roamed, ere Fate's decision was fulfilled;
uch } arduous toil
So v } ~~ast a work~~ it was, the Romans State to build.
Sicilian headlands scarcely out of sight,
y }
The } spread the canvas with a fresh delight.
{en
Th{ere brooding oer
~~When~~ Juno, ~~smarting with~~ the eternal wound,
inly; ,vanquishd, quit the ground
Thus ~~to herself~~—Must I ~~desist uncrowned~~
Of my attempt? or impotently toil
~~By victory unable from the bound~~
To bar this Trojan from the Italian soil?
Of Italy ~~the Trojan King to turn~~
For thy Fates thwart me;—
~~Me fate opposes~~ yet could Pallas raise
'Mid ~~For~~ Argive vessels a destructive blaze,
And in the deep plunge all, for fault of one;
The desperate frenzy
{frenzy
~~And for the~~ {~~fury~~ of Oileus' Son.
She from the clouds the bolt of Jove might cast,
And ships & sea deliver to the blast!
Him, flames ejecting from a bosom fraught
{ind
With sulphurous fire, she in a whirlw{ing caught,

{ ;
59 *And on a sharp rock fixed* { ,*—but I, who move*
60 *Heav'ns Queen, the Sister & the wife of Jove,*
61 *Wage with one race the war I waged of yore!*
62 *Who then, henceforth, will Juno's name adore?*
63 *Her Altars grace with gifts, her aid implore?*

{ *v*
64 *These things re* { *solved in fiery discontent,*
65 *Her course the Goddess to Eolia bent,,*
{ *south* { :—
66 *Country of lowering clouds, where* { *fierce -winds rave* { ,
Æ } *spacious*
67 *Here E* } *olus within a* ~~*mighty*~~ *cave,*
~~Under his scepter~~ *With* *controuls* the struggling winds,
68 ~~*Dark prison of his*~~ ^ *sovereign pow'r* ^ ~~*fast binds*~~
And the sonorous storms in durance binds.
69 ~~*Sonorous tempests & the struggling winds*~~
as they wreak
70 *Loud, loud the mountain murmurs* ~~*as they reak*~~
. } *O* }
71 *Their scorn upon the barriers;* } *o* } *n a peak,*
s, }
72 *High-seated, Æolus his scepter sway* }
wrath ~~*all*~~
73 *Soothes their fierce temper, & their* ~~*wrath*~~ *allays.*
{ ,
74 *This did he not* { *—sea, earth, & heaven's vast deep,*
follow
75 *Would* ~~*rush with*~~ *them, entangled in their* ~~*sleep*~~ *sweep;*
76 *But in black caves the Sire Omnipotent*
77 *The winds sequestered, fearing such event:*
Heap'd over them vast mountains, and assign'd
78 ~~*Heaped hills above them & a king he sent*~~
~~A Monarch to controul~~ the blustering Kind,
80 ~~*Who by fixed laws their fury might restrain*~~
fit
79 A monarch ~~who~~ should rule the blustering Kind
By stedfast laws their violence restrain
81 *And give* ~~*when*~~ *on due command a loosened rein.*
{ *he*
As s { *o* ~~*him*~~ *approached thus spake the suppliant Queen*
82 ~~*Æolus*~~ *(* ^ ~~*in these words the suppliant Queen*~~
Æolus,
83 ~~*Address'd him*~~ ^ *) for the Sire of Gods & men*
84 *On thee confers the power to tranquilize*
troubled { *or*
85 *The* ~~*obedient*~~ *waves,* { *& summon them to rise,*
A race, my foes, bears oer the Tyrrhene sea
86 ~~*A race in constant enmity with me*~~
~~*oer the*~~
~~*Is now transporting* ^ *Tyrrhene sea*~~
87 *Troy & her conquered Gods, to Italy.*

[DC MS. 89, 150r]

1st Book

88 *Throw power into the winds; the ships submerge,*

{ —
89 *Or part* { *& give the bodies to the surge.*
90 *Twice seven fair nymphs await on my command,*
91 *All beautiful;—the fairest of the band,*
such desert to crown
92 *Deiopeia,* ~~*shall be made thy wife*~~
stedfast make thine
Will I ~~I will~~ by by^wedlock ~~rites[?]~~ ~~it thy~~ own,
93 ~~*Who, for such high deserts, shall pass her life*~~*;*
94 *In everlasting fellowship with thee/*
To dwell, ~~shall~~ [?]
95 P ~~*Conjoined*~~*, & yield a beauteous progeny*
To this the God— *declare* ~~*make known*~~
96 ~~*He answered:*~~ ~~*Fix O*~~ *queen*^ ~~*upon*~~ *thy will*
And be it mine
97 ~~*My duty is,*~~ *the mandate to fulfill.*
98 *To thee I owe my sceptre, and the place*
th
99 *Jove's favour ha*~~*d*~~ *assigned me; through thy grace*
100 *I at the banquets of* the Gods recline;
101 And my whole empire is a gift of thine.

In everlasting fellowship with thee
To live & yield a beauteous progeny

P
e
102 *When Æolus had ceased, his spear h*~~*ad*~~ *bent*
103 *Full on the quarter where the winds were pent,*
F
104 *And smote the Mountain/—f* } *orth, where way is made,*
105 *Rush his wild ministers, the land pervade,*
106 *And fasten on the deep. There Eurus, there*
107 *Notus, & Africus unused to spare*
108 *His tempests, work with congregated power,*
109 *To upturn the abyss, & roll the unwieldy waves ashore.*
110 *Clamor of Men ensues & crash of shrouds;*
111 *Heaven & the day, by instantaneous clouds,*
:
112 *Are ravished from the Trojans,* } *on the floods*
113 *Black night descends, & palpably three broods.*
114 *The thundering Poles incessantly unsheath*
115 *Their fires, & all things threaten instant death.*
116 P *Appall'd, & with slack limbs, Æneas stands;*
117 *He groans, & heavenward lifting his clasp'd hands,*
{ ; { "T
118 *Exclaims* { { *thrice happy they who chanc'd to fall*
I
119 *In front of lofty A* } *lium's sacred wall,*

---

95 "P" in left margin, here and elsewhere, is WW's paragraph signal.

96–100 Base text, through "of" in l. 100, is probably in the autograph of the Rev. Samuel Tillbrooke. Revisions "declare" in l. 96 and "And be it mine" in l. 97 are in the autograph of DW; "He answered" in l. 96 is in the autograph of MW.

102–260 Base autograph and revisions not WW's are Dora W's, except where noted.

Their parents witnessing their end.—O why,
Bravest of Greeks, Tydides, could not I
Pour out my willing spirit thro' a wound
From thy right hand received, on Trojan ground
Where Hector lies subjected to the spear

[DC MS. 89, 150ᵛ]

Of the invincible Achilles; where
The great Sarpedon sleeps; &, oer the plain,
Swift Simois whirls helmets, & shields, & men,
Throngs of the brave in fearless combat slain!"
A
P *While thus he spake the a quilonian gale*
Smote, from the front, upon his driving Sail,
thwarted
And heaved the ~~*billows*~~ ~~*reared*~~ *to the sky,*
:
Round the Ship/ laboring in extremity:
Help from her shattered oars in vain she craves;
Then veers the prow, exposing to the waves
Her side; & lo! a surge, to mountain height
Gathering, prepares to burst with its whole weight.
Those hang aloft as if in air, to these
Earth is disclosed between the boiling seas.
Whirl'd on by Notus three encounter shocks,
ree
~~*Th ere Notus drives to perish by the shocks*~~
In the main sea, receiv'd from latent Rocks;
Rocks stretch'd, in dorsal ridge of rugged frame,
a ar
On the deep's surface; Alter s is the name
ree
ree
By which the Italians mark them. Th ere the force
Of Eurus hurries, from an open course,
On straits & shallows, dashes on the strand,
And girds the wreck about with heaps of sand.
Another, in which Lycas & his mate
Faithful Orontes share a common fate,
As his own eyes full plainly can discern,
By a huge wave is swept from prow to stern;
Headlong the pilot falls; thrice whirl'd around,
The Ship is buried in the gulph profound.
boundless
~~*dismal*~~ *eddy*
Amid the ~~*boundless ferment*~~ *a lost few,*
Drowing or drownd, emerge to casual view,

131 The deletion stroke through "billows" was made after an attempt to erase the word.

155 *On waves which planks, & arms, & Trojan wealth*
bestrew.

r
156 *Over the stong-ribb'd pinnace in which sails*
157 *Ilioneus, the hurricane prevails;*
158 *Now conquers Abas, then the ships that hold*
159 *Valiant Achates, & Alethes old;*
160 *The joints all loosning in their sides, they drink*
161 *The hostile brine thro' many a greedy chink.*

[DC MS. 89, 151r]

what strife disturb'd the roaring sea
162 P *Meanwhile,* ~~*how loud t the murmer of the Main,*~~
was
And for what outrages the storm is } *free,*
163 ~~*How fierce the tempest, without check or rein*~~
Ocean
164 *Troubling the* ~~*region*~~ *to its inmost caves,*
Neptune perceived—incensed; &, o'er the waves,
165 ~~*Was known by Neptune, ruler of the waves*~~*:*
Forth looking with a steadfast brow & eye
166 ~~*Incensed he heard & felt, but smooth'd his mien,*~~
Raised from the deep in placid majesty.
167 ~~*And raised above the deep a brow serene;*~~
He saw the Trojan Gallies scattered wide,
168 ~~*Then, looking forth, the Trojan fleet descry'd*~~
The Men they bore oppressed & terrified;
169 ~~*Dispersed & ore the Waters wandering wide,*~~
~~*The*~~ *Waters and*
~~*With*~~ [? ~~*liquid*~~] *& ruinous Heaven*
170 ~~*With sky & waves*~~ *against their peace allied.*
171 *Nor from the Brother was concealed the heat*
172 *Of Juno's anger, & each dark deceit.—*
Eurus he called & Zephyrus; & the pair,
173 ~~*Then having summoned a selected pair*~~*,*
Who at his bidding, quit the fields of Air
174 ~~*Eurus & Zephyrus, O Powers of air*~~*,*
He thus addressed "Upon your birth & kind
175 ~~*Such was the tenor of his speach "on pride*~~
Have ye presumed with confidence so blind
176 x *ancestry* ~~*Of Origin have ye so far relied,*~~
—
177 *As* } *heedless of my Godhead to perplex*
178 *The land with uproar, & the Sea to vex,*
O! winds! thus fiercely
179 *Which by your act* ~~*in this combustion*~~ *heaves!* }
180 *Whom I—but better calm the troubled waves.*
~~*Hereafter not by penalty so slight*~~
~~*Shall ye atone for such offence take flight*~~
181 *Henceforth atonement shall not prove so slight*

170 The revision "Waters and" is probably in the autograph of MW.

For such a trespass; to your king take flight,
And say, that not to <u>*Him*</u> *but unto* <u>*me*</u>
{*th*
Fate ha{*s assigned this watery sovereignty;*
Mine is this trident—his a rocky hold,,
Thy Mansion, Eurus!—vaunting uncontrol'd
P̸ {*re*
Let Eolus the{*ir occupy his hall,*
And in that prison house the winds enthrall."
P *He spake & quicker than the word his will,*
**Felt thro' the Sea, abates each tumid hill,*
Quiets the deep, & silences the shores,
And to a cloudless Heaven the Sun restores.
Cymothoë shoves, with leaning Triton's aid,
The stranded Ships; & from their flinty bed
He with his Trident lifts them; then divides

**This said forthwith he stills both sea & shores*
And to a cloudless sky the Sun restores

[DC MS. 89, 151v]

1st Book

The sluggish heaps of sand, & gently glides,
light s}
Skimming on^*S*}*mooth wheels the level tides.*
{*T*
~~*And*~~ {*thus oft, when a sedition hath ensued*
Arousing all the ignoble multitude,
Straight thro' the Air do stones & torches fly,
With every Missile frenzy can supply;
Then, if a venerable Man step forth,
Strong thro' acknowledged piety & worth,
Hushed at the sight into mute peace/ all stand/
Listening, with eyes & ears at his command;
Their minds to him are subject, & the rage
That burns within their breasts his lenient
words assuage.
So *over*}
~~*Thus*~~ *fell the Sea's whole tumult,*^*awe*} *awed*
Then, when the Sire, casting his eyes abroad,
{*e*
Turns, under open Heaven, his docile Ste{*ads,*
And with his flowing Chariot smoothly speeds.

P *The worn-out Trojans, seeking land where ere*
The nearest coast invites, for Lybia steer.
~~— [?] *Within a long withdrawing bay there lies*~~
There is a bay whose deep retirement hides
~~*A spot concealed from all but searching eyes;*~~
The place where Natures self a port
~~*There nature's self a friendly port provides,*~~

friendly jutting
Framed by a~~n~~ Island's ~~far projecting~~ sides;
Bulwark from which the billows of the Main
Recoil upon themselves, spending their force
{&, in vain.
Vast rocks are here; {*a safe beneath the brows*
Of two heaven-threatening clifs, the floods repose.
{o
Glancing, aloft, in bright theatric sh{*ew*
Woods wave, & gloomily impend below;
Right opposite this pomp of sylvan shade,
Wild crags & lowering rocks a cave have made;
Within, sweet waters gush; & all bestrown
; }
Is the cool floor with seats of living Stone, }
Cell of the Nymphs: no chains, no anchors here
Bind the tired vessels, floating without fear.

[DC MS. 89, 152r]

1st Book
Le~~a~~d by Eneas, in the shelter meet
Seven Ships the scanty relics of his fleet;
The crews, athirst with longings for the land,
Here } { &
* Sand *All* }*disembark,* {[?*or*] *range the wished for* **strand;*
sunny
Or on the ~~grateful~~ shoar their limbs recline,
Heavy with dropping ooze & drenched with brine
~~*All dank, & wasted with the feverish brine.*~~
Achates, from a smitten flint, receives
The spark upon a bed of fostering leaves;
Dry fuel on the natural hearth he lays,
And speedily provokes a mounting blaze.
Then }
[?*Next*] }*forth they bring, not utterly forlorn,*
; }
The needful impliments, & injured corn, }
Bruise it with stones, & by the aid of fire
Prepare the nurlment their frames require.

P *Meanwhile, Æneas mounts a cliff, to gain*
An unobstructed prospect of the Main;
{t
Happy if thence his wis{*hful eyes may mark*
The harass'd Antheus, or some Phrygian bark,
Or Capys, or the guardian sign descry
t } e }
Which, at }*hi* }~~s~~ *stern, Caicus bears on high.*

233–234 Revisions are in the autograph of DW.

249 *No sail appears in sight, nor toiling oar,*
pies
250 *Only he s{ees three Stags upon the shoar;*
Herds are
Behind, whole ~~Herds in order~~ following where these
a
251 *Whole herds, ~~are seen to follow where they~~ lee}d,*
in
And ~~In a~~ long order [~~?~~]
252 ~~*And the*~~ ~~*long troop*~~ ~~*that*~~ *thro the Vallies feed.*
with the *he seized the*
253 *He stops, & ~~seized at once~~ the bow, ~~&~~ store*
swift
254 *Of ~~fleet~~ wing'd Arrows, which Achates bore;*
Leaders to
255 *And first the ~~Chiefs before~~ his shafts have*
bowed
256 *Their heads elate with branching horns, the crowd*
{af
and all the { *frighted drove*
257 *Are stricken next, ~~nor does his hand refrain~~*
~~*are*~~
260 ~~*Till seven, a stag for every Ship are slain.*~~
258 *Fly in confusion to the leafy grove.*
259 *Nor from the weapons does his Hand ~~abstain~~* refrain
[260] *Till seven, a stag for every Ship, are slain,*
261 And with their bulky bodies press the plain.
~~*Then seeks the harbour*~~
262 *Thence to the port he hies divides the spoil;*
ri
263 ~~*And wine presented on Trinacia's soil.*~~

[DC MS. 89, 152[v]]

First B.

And deals out wine which, on Trinacria's soil,
Acestes stored for his departing Guest;
[263] ~~*And wine which good Acestes had e'er while*~~
Then
~~*And*~~*, with these words he sooothes each sorrowing ~~breast~~ breast*
264 ~~*Stored in Trinacria for his parting guest*~~
e {*s*
speaks spak{*e to cheer*
265 ~~*He portions out*~~*, & thus he sooth each sorrowing breast*
~~*Then, thus he speaks to soothe each sorrowing breast*~~

253 Revisions are in the autograph of MW.
257 Revision is in the autograph of JC.
258–[260] Base text is in the autograph of JC.
262–269 Base text is in the autograph of Dora W.
[263]–269 Revisions not in WW's autograph are in MW's, except where noted.
265 Revision "spake to cheer" above line is in Dora W's autograph.

266 P *"O Friends, not unacquainted with your share*
267 *Of misery, e'er doomed these ills to bear!*
worse afflictions
268 *O ye! whom ~~heavier~~ ~~sorrows~~ could not bend* { , / ! }
269 *Jove* *~~God~~ also has for these prepared an end!*
270 *Ø The voices of dread Sylla ye have heard;*
271 *Her belt of rabid mouths your prows have neared* { ; / , }
shunned with peril { *ian*
272 *Ye ~~voyage'd where~~ the ~~inhuman~~ Cyclop* { *s* *~~dwell~~ den;*
Cast off your fears, resume the hearts of men!
273 *~~Resume your courage anxious thought dispel~~*
Hereafter this our present lot may be
274 *~~Yet we may live till this our present doom~~*
A cherished object for pleased memory;
275 *~~Hath shown how sweet a sorrow may become~~*
strange mishaps thro'
276 *Thro' ~~various trials perils manifold~~*
And various we our course to Latium hold
277 *~~To Latium our appointed course we hold~~*
Trojan empire (this to) fate allows
278 *There ~~Fate a settled habitation shows~~*
Shall be revived. Endure with patience wait
279 *~~There we by high permission may repose~~*
280 *~~And Trojan power revive; endure, & wait,~~*
281 *Yourselves reserving for a happier state*
hazards
[276] *Thro' strange mishaps, thro ~~perils~~ manifold*
A
[277] *W* } *nd various, we our course to Latium hold;*
[278] *There Fate a settled habitation shows;*
o
[279] *There Trojan empire~~s~~ (this to* } *Fate allows)*
[280] *Shall be revived.—Endure with patience wait;*
[281] *Yourselves reserving for a happier state.*
—Æneas thus, though sick with weight of care,
{ *u*
282 *~~Even th~~* { *~~is their drooping spirits he sustains~~*
283 Strives by apt words their spirits to repair;
284 *The hope he does not feel his countenance feigns,*
A
285 *W* } *nd, deep within, he smothers his own pains.*

[282] Thus spake Æneas, hope his countenance feigns
The inward bosom
[285] And deep within he smothers his own pains.
286 They seize the quarry and the feast prepare
287 Stripping the ribs the carcass these lay bare,
288/290 Some cut the quivering limbs some tempt the fire
291 Around the spits and caldrons to aspire.

270–281 The autograph is MW's, except where noted.
274–279 Revisions are in the autograph of Dora W.
[276]–285 Autograph not WW's is Dora W's, except where noted.
[285] Revision is in MW's autograph.

[DC MS. 89, 153r]

1st Book

Æ
[282/284] *Thus ~~spake~~ E } neas hope ~~his~~ countenance feigns*
[285] *The ~~inward~~ bosom smothers ~~her~~ own pains*
[286] *~~And now his Followers with busy care~~*
They
[286] *~~Thus~~ seiz~~ed~~ the quarry; for the feast prepare;*
[287] *Part use their skill the carcase to lay bare,*
{ping
[288] *Strip { from off the ribs the dappled hide;*
:
[289] *And part the palpitating flesh divide; }*
[290] *The portions some expose to naked fire*
[291] *Some steep in cauldrons where the flames aspire.*
292 *Not wanting utensils they spread the board*
wasted vigour is
293 *And soon their ~~strength & spirits are~~ restored,*
green turf
294 *While, oer ~~the grass~~ diffused, in genial mood/*
295 *They quaff the mellow wine, nor spare the forest food.*
ask
296 *All hunger thus appeased, they ~~turn~~ ^ in thought*
s, } now
297 *For friends, with long discourse } ~~now~~ vainly sought;*
298 *Hope, fear, & doubt, contend if yet they live,* }
Or
299 *And have endured the last; nor can receive* }
300 *The obsequies a duteous voice might give.* }
301 *Apart, for Lycus mourns the pious Chief;*
302 *For Amicus is touched with silent grief;*
303 *For Gyas, for Cloanthes; & the Crew*
304 *That with Orontes perished in his view.*
305 *So finished their repast, while on the crown*
648 *~~Elsewhere he marks the Stripling who defied~~*
306 *Of heaven stood Jupiter, whence looking down,*
649 *~~Achilles but hath flung his arms aside~~*
307 *He traced the sea where winged vessels glide,*
650 *~~Unhappy Troilus! from the unequal fight~~*
308 *Saw lands, & shores, the Nations scattered wide;*
f }
651 in *~~Now hurried by his steeds in desperate p } light~~*
309 *And ~~from~~ lastly, from that all-commanding height*
652 *~~Behind his empty chariot o'er the plain~~*
{y
310 *He viewed the Lyb { ian realms, with steadfast sight.*
653 *~~Supinely whirled yet grasping still the rein~~*
311 *To him revolving mortal hopes & fears,*

[282/284]–458 Autograph not WW's is MW's, except where noted.
[286]–[287] Revision is in the autograph of DW.
294 Revision is in the autograph of DW.
299 Revision is probably in the autograph of DW.
305–312 The deleted base text, an early draft of Book I, ll. 648–655, appears to have been entered before consecutive work on Book I began.

654 ~~*Along the earth ar/ dragg'd his neck & hair*~~—
312 *Venus, her shining eyes suffused with tears,*
655 ~~*The dust is mark'd by his inverted spear.*~~
313 *Thus sorrowing spake; "O sire! who rul'st the way*
314 *Of Men & Gods with thy eternal sway,—*
And aw'st with
315 ~~*Lord of the*~~ *thunder; what offense, unfit*
316 *For pardon, could my much-lov'd son commit?*
317 *The Trojans what?* ~~*the Trojans to awake*~~ *thine anger to awake*
borne they
318 *That after such dire losses,^ for the sake*
see all the earth world denied
319 *tired* *Of Italy,^* ~~*they roam the world about*~~
^tired
To their hopes & no where may abide
T
320 ~~*From*~~ ~~*t }hat—& from every resting-place shut out*~~
321 *For, that the Romans hence should draw their birth*
322 *As years roll round, even hence &* ~~*rule*~~ *goverth earth*
power
323 *With* ~~*sway*~~ *supreme from Teucer's line restor'd*
324 *Such was—O Father why this change?—thy word.*

[DC MS. 89, 153[v]]

325 *^had perish'd* *From this when Troy* ~~*was withered*~~*, for my grief*
326 *Fates balancing with fates,^ I found relief;*
327 *First Book Like fortune follows: when shall thy decree*
328 *Close, mighty King, this long adversity?*
329 *Antenor, from amid the Grecian hosts*
330 *Escaped, could thrid Illyria's sinuous costs,*
u
331 *Pierce the Lib/rnian realms; oer-climb the fountain*
332 *Of loud Timavus; whence the murmuring mountaing*
333 *A nine-mouthed channel to the torrent yields.*
That
334 ~~*Yet t And*~~ *rolls its headlong sea, a terror to the fields.*
335 *Yet to his Paduan Seats he safely came,*
{whose ear
336 *The City built, {*~~*where*~~ *People* ~~*bore*~~ *his name;*
337 *There hung his Trojan arms, where now he knows*
{e
338 *The consummation of {intire repose.*
{allow'd
339 *But we thy progeny, {aloud to boast*
A } llowed
a }
340 *Of future heaven {—, betrayed {—, our navy lost:*
are
, } {are
341 *Thro' wrath of one } {or driven far from the Italian coast.*

313–403 The cramped spacing of these lines suggests that they were entered later than the surrounding passages of Book I.

342 *Is p{ie / eity thus honour{' / ed {? / , doth thy grace*
343 *Thus in our hands the allotted sceptre place?*
344 *On whom the Sire of Gods & human Kind,*
345 *Half-smiling, turn{'d / s the look that stills the wind,*
346 *And clears the heavens; then, touching with light kiss*
347 *His daughter's lip, he speaks;*
Thy ~~fears~~ griefs dismiss,
348 *And Cytherea these forebodings spare{; / —*
349 *No wavering fates deceive the objects of thy care.*
350 *Lavinian Walls full surely wilt thou see,*
351 *The promised city{; / ,} &, upborne by thee,*
352 *Magnam{n / } in{m / }ous Æneas yet shall range*
353 *The starry heavens, nor doth my purpose change.*
354 *He (since thy soul is troubled) I will raise*
355 *Things from their depths & open fate's dark ways)*
356 *Shall wage dread wars in Italy, abate*
357 *Fierce Nations, build a Town, & rear a State;*
358 *Till three revolving Summers have beheld*
359 *His Latian ~~rule~~ Kingdom, the ~~Rhetu~~ Rutulians quelled.*
360 *But young Ascania{u / }s (Ilus heretofore,*
361 *Name which he held till Ilium was no more,*
362 *Now called Iulus) while the months repeat*
363 *There course, & thirty annual orbs compleat,*
364 *Shall reign, & quit Lavinium {— / } to ~~abide~~ preside*
365 *Oer Albalonga, sternly fortified.*
366 *Here, under Chiefs of this Hectorian race,*
367 *Three hundred years shall empire hold her place;*
368 *Ere Illia, royal Priestess, gives to earth*
369 *From the embrace of Mars, a double birth.*
370 *Then Romulus, the {el / older, proudly drest* *in*
371 *In tawny wolf's-skin, his memorial vest* ✱ *in*
372 *~~Mavortian walls{(/ ,so styled from Mars) shall frame,~~*
373 *~~The people Romans called from his own name.~~ ~~call from his~~ peculiar*
374 *To these I give dominion that shall climb,*
375 *Unchecked by space, uncircumscrib'd by time,*
376 *An empire without end{. / ,} {E / e} ven Juno, driven*
377 *To agitate with fear, earth, sea, & heaven,*
378 *~~At length to better counsel shall incline~~*
With better mind shall for the past atone
379 *~~[?Appreciate] tutelary cares with mine,~~*
Prepared, with me, to cherish as her own
380 *The Romans, lords oer earth,—the nation of the gown.*
381 *So 'tis decreed. As circling times roll on*
382 *P{h / }thia shall fall, Mycenæ shall be won;*

[Left margin, vertical:]
402 *Shall Fury sit, breathing unholy threats*
403 *From his ensanguined mouth, that impotently frets.*

[Right margin, vertical:]
Mavortian walls, his Father's seat, shall frame,
And from himself, the people Romans name

383 *Descendants of Assaracus shall reign*
384 *Oer Argos, subject to the victor's chain:*
em
385 *From a fair st}ock shall Trojan Cæsar rise;*
386 *Ocean may terminate his power—the skies*
;
387 *Can be the only limits of his fame—* } [~~?~~]
388 *A Julius he, inheriting the name*
. F
389 *From great Iulus } f }earless shalt thou greet*
R
390 *The r }uler, when to his celestial seat*
391 *He shall ascend, spoil-laden from the east;*
392 *He, too, a God—to be with vows addressed.*
393 *Then shall a rugged age full long defiled*
394 *With cruel wars, grow placable and mild;*

395 *Then hoary Faith & Vesta shall delight*
396 *To speak their laws; Quirinus will unite*
397 *With his twin brother, to uphold the right.*
398 *Fast shall be closed the iron-bolted gates*
399 *Upon whose dreadful issue Janus waits;*
400 *Within, on high piled arms, & from behind*
401 *With countless links of brazen chains confined,*

[DC MS. 89, 154^{r}]

First B
404 P *This uttered Maia's Son he sends from high*
405 *To embolden Tyrian hospitality;*
406 *Lest haply Dido ignorant of fate*
W
407 *Should chase the w }anderers from her rising state;*
408 *He thro' the azure region works the oars*
y
409 *Of his swift wings, & lights on Li }bian's shores;*
410 *Prompt is he there his mission to fulfil;*
411 *The Tyrians soften, yielding to Jove's will;*
ir
412 *And, above all, the } Queen receives a mind*
413 *Fearless of harm, & to the Trojans kind.*
414 *Æneas much revolving thro' the night*
415 *'Rose with the earliest break of friendly light*
v
416 *Resol }ed to certify by instant quest*
r
417 *Who li }uled the uncultured region, man or beast*
418 *Forthwith he hides beneath a rocky cove*
oershadowed *pendant*
419 *His fleet ~~encompassed~~ by the ~~oerhanging~~ grove*
420 *And brandishing two javelins quits the bay*
421 *Achates sole Companion of his way*
ile *were journeying thus before him stood*
422 *Wh{en they ~~had reached the centre of a wood~~*
; *met within a shady wood*
423 *His mother } ~~suddenly before him stood~~*
424 *The habit of a Virgin did she wear*
425 *Her aspect suitable her gait & air;—*
426 *Armed like a Spartan virgin, or of mien*

in Thrace
427 *Such as^Harpalyce ~~in Thrace~~ is seen*
428 *~~Wea~~ Urging to weariness the fiery horse—*
429 *~~And~~ Outstripping Hebrus in her headlong course.*
430 *Light oer her shoulders had she given the bow*
431 *To hang, her tresses on the wind to flow;*
ith
432 *A huntress w{as bare knee—a knot upbound*
433 *~~Her vest in folds~~*
433 *The folds of that loose vest, which else had swept the ground*
434 *"Ho!" she exclaimd, /their words preventing, "say,*
H
435 *Have you seen some h}untress here astray*
~~With a quiver graced clothed by the spotte~~
436 *One of my sisters with a quiver graced;*
y
437 *Clothed by the spotted li}nx, & o'er the waste*
438 *Pressing the foamy boar with outcry chased?*
439 *Thus venus—thus her son forthwith replied,*
440 *"None of thy Sisters have we here espied,*
teach
441 *None have we* *~~Or~~ heard—; O Virgin, ~~tell~~^~~me~~ ~~by what name~~ in pure grace*
me ~~to~~
to *name thee ~~greeted~~*
442 *Teach ~~Wilt~~* *~~Thou~~ ~~will~~ ~~be~~ ~~styled~~, for no/ ~~of~~ mortal ~~frame~~ face*
443 *Is thi^ne,* *~~Thou art~~; nor bears thy voice a human sound;—*
444 *A Goddess surely, worthy to be owned*
445 *By Phoebus as a Sister; or thy line*
of .—
446 *Is haply ~~from~~ the nymphs, }O Power divine*
Thou propitious and
447 *Be ~~gracious, lighten~~ who/oe'er thou art,*

[DC MS. 89, 154v]

Lighten our labour; *First Book*
tell us
{each *~~part~~*
448 *~~Our trouble~~ t{~~ell~~ ~~us~~ in what clime, what part*
teach roam *{ese wild precincts*
449 *Of earth we ~~wander~~, who th{is ~~forest~~ trace,*
450 *Ignorant alike of person & of place!*
we were
451 *Not as intruders ~~are~~ ~~we~~ come^but tost*
452 *By winds & waters on the savage coast.*
453 *Vouchsafe thy answer; victims oft shall fall*
454 *By this right hand; while on thy name we call!*

[Written vertically in left margin:]
Our ships while struggling other shores to reach
A tempest hurried towards the Lybian beach
Vouchsafe thy answer
Not as intruders come we but were tossed

441–443 Revisions in left margin and over base text are in DW's autograph.
446–449 Revisions are in DW's autograph.
451–454 Revision, written verticallly in left margin, is in the autographs of DW (ll. 451–453) and Dora W (l. 454).

455 *~~Then Ven~~ ~~Then Venus,—such high honour I disclaim~~*
456 *The Tyrian Maids with quivers chase their game*
457 *Wont thus to bear them slung necks behind*
458 *And round their ancles purple buskins bind*
[455] Then Venus, Offerings these which I disclaim;
sylvan
[456] *The Tyrian Maids who chase the ~~forest~~ game*
[457] *Bear thus a quiver slung their necks^behind*
With thus
[458] *~~Thus~~ ~~And~~ purple buskins ~~round~~ their ancles bind,—*
W} a
459 *Learn ~~know~~, w} anderers that a Punic relm you see,*
A}
460 *Tyrians the men a} genor's progeny:*
deem
461 *But Lybian ~~is~~ the soil; the natives are*
a}
462 *Haughty & fierce intracti} ble in war.*
463 *Here Dido reigns, from Tyre compelled to flee*
;}
464 *By an unatural Brother's perfidy,}*
it
465 *Deep was the wrong, nor would aught avail*
.}
466 *Should we do more than skim the doleful tale;}*
M}
467 *Sichæus loved her as his wedded m} ate,*
468 *The richest Lord of the Phœnician State.*
S}
469 *A Virgin s} he when from her Father's hands*
470 *By love induced she past to nuptial bands;*
471 *Unhappy union! for to evil prone,*
472 *Worst of bad men, her Brother held the throne.*
and
473 *Dire fury came among them; ~~for~~ made bold*
B}
474 *b} y that blind appetite, the thirst of gold,*
{ue
475 *~~Wreckless of all forbearance that was d{ ew~~*
476 *To a fond consort he Sichæus slew*
477 *~~Sichæus he ensnared & laid him low~~*
Fell on him unawares & laid him low
478 *~~Before the Alt~~ar with an impious blow.*
scope
479 *His arts concealed the crime, & gave vain ~~hope~~*
480 *In Dido's bosom to a trembling hope.*

He, ~~And~~ feeling not or scorning what was due
gold
To a wife's tender love, Sichæus slew,
Rushed on him unawares & laid him low
Even at the Altar &c

[456]–480 The autograph is Dora W's, except where noted.
[458]–459 Revisions in left margin are in DW's autograph.
461 Revision "deem" is in DW's autograph.
475–478 Revision, written vertically in left margin, is in DW's autograph.

P—

M}
But in a dream appeared the unburied m } *an,*
Lifting a visage wonderous pale and wan;
U } *her*
And u } *rged*^ *to instant flight, & shewed the ground*
Where hoards of ancient treasure might be found,
Needful assistance; by the Vision sway'd,
Dido looks out for fellowship & aid,
: }
They meet who loathe the Tyrant, or who fear; }
And, as some well-trimmed Ships were lying near,
Turn over

[DC MS. 89, 155^{r}]

Second Book 2^{d} *Book*

All breathed in silence and
~~*Deep silence reigned all eyes*~~ *intensely gazed*
the }
When, from his } *lofty couch, his voice Æneas raised,*
{ *And thus* *T* }
{ [? ?] *began; t* } *he task which you impose*
~~*O Queen what you command me to disclose*~~
R }
~~*O Queen*~~ *r* } *evives O Queen*
~~*Opens afresh*~~ *unutterable woes;*
G }
How by the g } *recians Troy was overturned,*
, }
And her power fell— } *to be for ever mourned;*
pitying
Calamities which with a ~~*bursting*~~ *heart*
~~*Troubles which I beheld with bursting heart*~~
I saw,
^ *Of which I formed* ~~*myself*~~ *no common part.*
lamentable { , W } O }
Oh 'twas a ~~*pitiable*~~ *end* { — *w* } *hat o* } *ne*
~~*What Soldier mid the followers of the*~~ *Son*
Of all our foes, Dolopian, Myrmidon,
~~*Of Peleus what obdurate*~~^~~*Myrmidon*~~
Or Soldier bred in
~~*Dolopian or of*~~^ *stern Ulysses' train,*
Such things could utter and
~~*Such tale pursuing could*~~ *from tears refrain?"*
Yet more, from heaven ^now hastes
~~*And hastens now from heaven,*~~ *the dewy night*
And the declining stars to sleep invite
since such strong desire prevails to know
Y }
But ~~*if Th*~~ } ~~*ou wish to trace our various woe*~~

481–488 The autograph is DW's, as is the note "Turn over" under l. 488, which indicates that the translation of Book I continues on 155^{v} (155^{r} contains drafts of Book II, ll. 1–34).

1–34 The autograph is MW's, as is the note at page bottom, indicating that the translation of Book II continues on 163^{r}.

Our wretched fate, & Troy's last overthrow,
~~*And the last agony of Troy to know*~~
16 ~~*And briefly Troy's last agony to know*~~
attempt the theme, tho' in ^ my breast
17 *I will ~~begin, tho sorrow rends my breast~~*
18 ~~*And memory*~~ ~~*shrinks from such*~~ *a* ~~*fearful test*~~
Memory recoils, & shudders at the test.
19 ~~*Worn out by war sustained thro' length of years*~~
The Grecian Chiefs, exhausted of their strength
20 ~~*And forced to raise the sail the Grecian peers*~~
By war protracted to such irksome length,
24 ~~*Construct a monstrous horse with ribs of pine*~~
21 *And from the sche~~me, sieg~~e repulsed; new schemes devised*
23 ~~*Huge fabric of Minerva's art divine*~~
H}
22 *To build a wooden h }orse they of mountain size.*
26 ~~*Vows for a safe return are feigned, free course*~~
Assisted by Minerva's art divine ~~*takes, meanwhile*~~
T}
27 ~~*Free course Gives to*~~ *t }he* ~~*rumour,*~~ ^ ~~*— a chosen force*~~
W}
[24] *They frame the w }ork, & sheathe its ribs with pine;*
28 ~~*By stealth they shut in the capacious horse*~~
[25] *An offering to the Gods—that they may gain*
29 ~~*With weapons line the cavern's inmost gloom*~~
; }
[26] *Their home in safety; this they boldly feign, }*
30 ~~*And fill with armed troops its mighty womb*~~
[27] ~~*And spread the tale abroad meanwhile they hide*~~
31 *In sight of Troy an island lies by fame*
32 *Amply distinguished Tenedos its name*
33 *While Priam reigned in place of thronged resort*
34 ~~*A bay now merely & an unsafe port*~~
[27] *And spread the tale abroad;—meanwhile, they hide*
[28] *Selected Warriors in its gloomy side;*
[29] *Throng the huge concave to its inmost den,*
M}
[30] *And fill that mighty womb with armed m }en.*
I}
[31] *In sight of Troy an i }sland lies, by fame*
[32] *Amply distinguished, Tenedos its name;*
Potent & rich
[33] ~~*Rich*~~, ~~*powerful*~~ *in the time of Priam's sway*
[34] *Now merely for chance keels an unsafe bay.*
Turn over 8 leaves for continuation

[DC MS. 89, 155v]

1st Book

488 *lying near*
489 *~~And o'er the~~ This help they seized; and o'er the water fled,*
490 *With all Pygmalion's wealth,—a Woman at their head.*
The Exiles *reached*
491 *The~~y~~ ^ ~~reached~~ the ~~very~~ spot where soon your eyes*
492 *Shall see the Turrets of New Carthage rise:*
There purchas'd Barca so they ~~tract~~ named the
493 *~~The Fugitives there bought~~ a ~~space of~~ ground,*
From [?it] ~~space~~ the bull's-hide whose thongs had girt it round;
494 *~~As much it as one bull's-hide could compass round~~*
& whither bound
Now say, who are ye, whence, ~~wandering~~
~~Thence Barca named. Now, courteous strangers, say~~
495 *~~Who are you, whence, and what your future way~~*
; T
496 *He ~~deepl~~ answered, deeply sighing, "t o their springs*
497 *Should I trace back these melancholy things*
498 *For you at leisure listening to our woes,*
499 *Vesper, 'mid gathering shadows, to repose*
500 *Might lead the day, before the Tale would close.*
501 *From ancient Troy, if haply ye have heard*
see side *our ships through ~~divers~~ seas*
various
502 *~~That name~~, ~~we come~~: ~~our gallies which~~ had steered*
When by a sudden ~~divers~~ tempest they were toss'd
503 *~~Through sundry seas at length a Tempest toss'd,~~*
504 *Through ~~By chance not rare, upon the Lybian Coast.~~*
505 *Æneas am I: & ~~where'er I go~~ wheresoe'er I go*
t
506 *Carrying T he Gods I rescued from the foe,*
When Troy was overthrown.
507 *~~Attend upon our way~~. A Man you see*
ed above Earth
508 *Famou ~~s~~ ~~in heaven~~ for acts of piety.*
my wished-for resting place;
509 *Italy is ~~the object of my quest—~~*
There does my country lie among a Race
510 *~~My Country where I look for final rest~~*
Sprung from high Jove; the Phrygian Sea I tried
511 *~~Among a race from Jove. The Deep I tried,~~*
G
512 *With twice ten ships which Ida's g rove supplied,*

The name of Troy thro' various seas we steered
Until on Lybian Shores an adverse blast
By chance not rare our shattered vessels cast

488–548 Autograph not WW's is DW's, except where noted.
494–495 Revision is in MW's autograph.
502–504 Revision, written vertically in left margin, is in Dora W's autograph.
508 Revision is in Dora W's autograph.

513 *My Goddess Mother pointing out the way*
nor }
514 * ~~*Fate*~~ } ~~*giving signs that called me to obey*~~
515 *Seven scarcely of that number now are left*
M }
516 *By tempests torn:—m* } *yself unknown, bereft*
517 *And destitute, explore the Lybian Waste;*
518 *Alike from Asia and from Europe chased.*
519 *He spoke, nor haply at this point had closed*
520 *His mournful words; but Venus interposed.*
521 P *Whoeer thou art, I trust, the heavenly Powers/*
! }
522 *Disown thee not, so near the Punic Towers;* }
523 *But hasten to the Queen's imperial Court*
[523] ~~*Proceed Go, let thy footsteps*~~
[523] * ~~*Hence take thy way and seek the royal Court*~~
survive
524 *Thy Friends* ~~*are spared*~~*, their Ships are safe in Port.*

Nor did unwilling Fates oppose their sway;

[DC MS. 89, 156r]

1st Book
525 *Indebted for the shelter which they find*
526 *To altered courses of the rough north wind/:*
527 *Unless* ~~*my P*~~ *fond Parents taught my simple youth*
Deceitful *I announce the*
528 ~~*Vain*~~ *auguries,* ~~*this thou may'st receive as*~~ *truth.*
529 *Behold* ~~*those*~~ *yon twelve fair Swans, a joyous troop!*
530 *Them did the Bird of Jove with threatening swoop*
531/532 *Rout in mid Heaven; but now in order'd train*
533 *They touch, or scarcely fail to touch, the Plain.*
As these ~~*unite*~~
535 *As in recovered union these rejoice,*
And wheel on on *with tuneful*
534 ~~*And wheeled with*~~ ^ *whizzing wings* ~~*& clamorous*~~ *voice*
with their freight thy ships in harbour lie
S }
536 ~~*Even*~~ *s* } *o* ~~*thy ships and friends, once scattered, lie*~~
O } *some* *are* *ing*
537 ~~*Secure*~~*, o* } *r to* ~~*the*~~ *haven's mouth* ^ *draw* ^ *nigh*
every Saill *n*
538 *With* ~~*all their Sails*~~ *full spread, but thou proceed,*
path
539 *And fear no hindrance, where thy* ~~*way*~~ *shall lead*
540 P ✗ *She spake; and as she turned away, all bright*

✗ *This said while turning round she gave to view*
Her neck refulgent with a roseate hew
* *But*
~~*Round*~~ *them journying Venus with a Shroud*
Of Mist enwrapped an undissolving cloud

---

513 The autograph is Dora W's.
514 Deleted line and revision, written vertically in the left margin, is in Dora W's autograph.
521–523 The autograph is MW's.
528 Revisions are in MW's autograph.
535–539 Revisions are in MW's autograph.
540–541 Revision, written vertically in the left margin, is in Dora W's autograph, as is the version of ll. 555–556 below it.

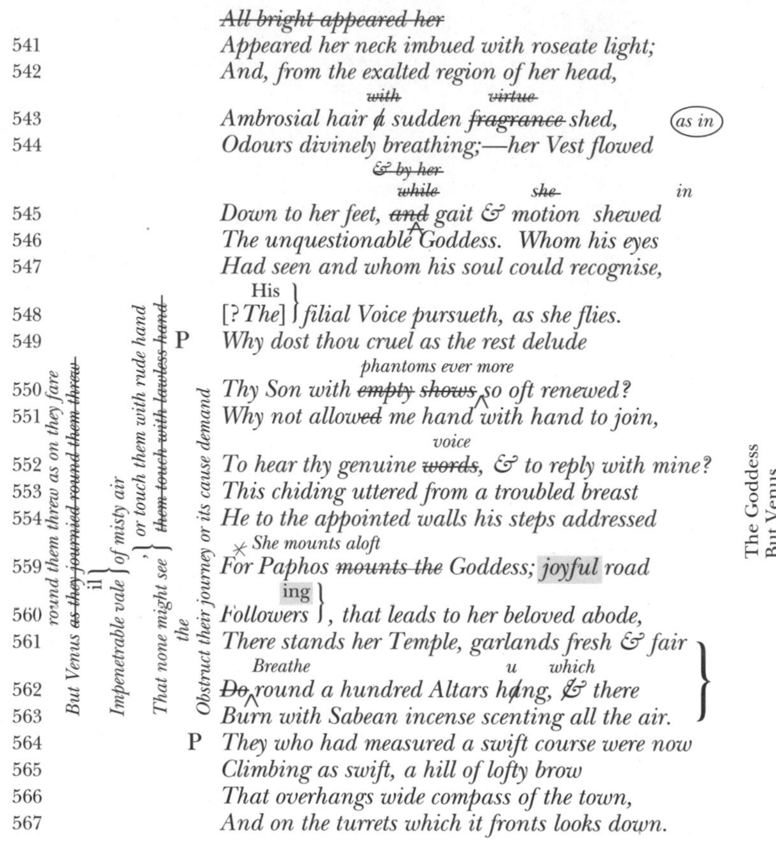

~~All bright appeared her~~
541 *Appeared her neck imbued with roseate light;*
542 *And, from the exalted region of her head,*
with *~~virtue~~*
543 *Ambrosial hair ~~a~~ sudden ~~fragrance~~ shed,* (*as in*)
544 *Odours divinely breathing;—her Vest flowed*
~~& by her~~
~~while~~ *~~she~~* *in*
545 *Down to her feet, ~~and~~ gait & motion shewed*
546 *The unquestionable Goddess. Whom his eyes*
547 *Had seen and whom his soul could recognise,*
His
548 [? *The*] *filial Voice pursueth, as she flies.*
549 P *Why dost thou cruel as the rest delude*
phantoms ever more
550 *Thy Son with ~~empty shows~~ so oft renewed?*
551 *Why not allow~~ed~~ me hand with hand to join,*
voice
552 *To hear thy genuine ~~words~~, & to reply with mine?*
553 *This chiding uttered from a troubled breast*
554 *He to the appointed walls his steps addressed*
But Venus ~~as they journied round them threw~~ round them threw as on they fare
il
Impenetrable vale of misty air
That none might see ~~them touch with lawless hand~~ , or touch them with rude hand
the
Obstruct their journey or its cause demand
× *She mounts aloft*
559 *For Paphos ~~mounts the~~ Goddess; joyful road*
ing
560 *Followers , that leads to her beloved abode,*
561 *There stands her Temple, garlands fresh & fair*
Breathe *u* *which*
562 *~~Do~~ round a hundred Altars h~~a~~ng, ~~&~~ there*
563 *Burn with Sabean incense scenting all the air.*
564 P *They who had measured a swift course were now*
565 *Climbing as swift, a hill of lofty brow*
566 *That overhangs wide compass of the town,*
567 *And on the turrets which it fronts looks down.*

The Goddess
But Venus
× *She, borne aloft, resumed the joyful road*
That leads to Paphos, her beloved abode

---

543 Revisions are in Dora W's autograph. Notation "as in" in right margin, perhaps in DW's autograph, indicates that revisions are to be rejected in favor of the original base text.

545 Revision "while" is in MW's autograph; other revisions are in Dora W's autograph. Notation "in" in right margin, perhaps DW's autograph, indicates that revisions are to be rejected in favor of the original base text.

549–575 Autograph not WW's is MW's, except where noted.

550 Revision is in Dora W's autograph.

551 Deletion in "allowed" is probably by Dora W.

555–558 Revision, written vertically at bottom of left margin, is in Dora W's autograph.

559 Revision is in Dora W's autograph.

559–560 Revision, written vertically in right margin, not WW's is in Dora W's autograph.

562 Revisions are in Dora W's autograph.

[DC MS. 89, 156v]

1st Book

views the city pile on pile ~~rising~~
568 *Æneas ^ ~~wonder-stricken sees the pile~~*
Rising a place of sordid huts erewhile
569 *~~Of the new city cottages erewhile~~*
And as he looks
570 *The gates/ ~~the pavements of~~ the stretching ways,*
571 *The stir, the din, encreasing wonder raise*
572 *The Tyrians work—one Spirit in the whole;*
near ~~*stretch*~~ stretch
573 *These ~~on~~ the walls, these labour to uproll*
[?*pooling*]
574 *Stones for the Citadel with all their might*
structures having marked a ~~chosen~~
575 *These for new ^ ~~mansions fix upon a~~ site*
Entrench the circuit. Some on laws debate
S
576 *~~And grid it with a foss enclose it; s} ome elect~~*
Or choose a Senate for the infant State
~~Grave Men & Fathers worthy of respect~~
577 *~~Laws to ordain or give their dire effect~~;*
Some
578 *~~These~~ dig a haven out, some toil to place*
579 *A ^ Theatre on deep & solid base;*
ew
580 *~~These~~ Some from the rock h{ ue columns to compose*
581 *A goodly ornament for future shows.*

✳ Fresh summer calls the Bees such tasks to ply
Through flowery ~~grounds~~ fields beneath a sunny sky

✳ *work*
~~when~~ the that in fresh *Fresh Summer*
582 ~~*strive*~~ ^ *So bees ~~their tasks in early summer ply~~* *see side*
Thro' *fields* *nny*
583 ~~*Their tasks*~~ *In ~~flowery~~ meads ~~beneath a summer sky~~*
Whe
584 *The }n first they lead their progeny abroad,*
585 *Each fit to undertake his several load;*
produce
586 *Or in a mass the licquid ~~honey~~ blend*
And nectar~~ious~~ hoards the cells
sweet
587 *~~Or~~ with ~~rich~~ nector every cell distend;*
fast
588 *Or, ~~when~~ as home-bound labourers arrive,*
or m
589 *Receive the freight they bring; & f }ustering, drive*
D
590 *The S} rones a sluggard people from the hive;*

568–570 Revisions are in Dora W's autograph.
575 Revisions are in Dora W's autograph.
576 "And" through "enclose" is in MW's autograph; the rest of the line, including revisions, is in Dora W's autograph.
577–617 The autograph is Dora W's, except where noted.

vast
Glows ~~Glows~~ the ~~keen~~ work
591 *~~& work~~* *~~Fervent the scene~~—while time-clad hills & plains*
pure
592 *g(rich* *Scent the ~~sweet~~ honey that rewards their pains.*
pure clear
593 *Oh fortunate!" the Chief Æneas cries"*
As ~~to~~
ile *~~lifts~~*
594 *~~When~~ } on the aspiring town he casts his eyes*
already
595 *Fortunate ye whose walls are free to rise,*
Then strange to tell with mist around him thrown
596 *~~Nor halts he but with mist around him thrown~~*
s } he
597 *In ~~the~~ crowd } mingles, yet is seen by none.*
P
598 *Within the town a central grove displayed*
599 *Its ample texture of delightful shade,*
600 *The storm-vexed Tyrians, newly landed, found*
601 *A hopeful sign while digging there the ground;*
602 *The head of a fierce horse from Earth they drew,*
603 *By Junosself presented to their view;*
604 *Presage of martial fame, & hardy toil*
605 *Bestowed thro' ages on a generous soil*

[DC MS. 89, 157[r]]

1st Book
606 *Sidonian Dido here a Structure high*
607 *Raised to the tutelar~~y~~ Deity,*
Rich
608 *~~Bright~~ with the offerings thro' the temple poured*
609 *And bright with Juno's image there adored;*
~~On steps~~ { , *with steps, the*
610 *High rose { the brazen porch on steps; the beams*
611 *With brass ~~were~~ fastened; & metallic gleams*
612 *Flashed from the valves of brazen doors—forth sent*
While *the resounding*
613 *~~And to & fro~~ on ~~sounding~~ hinges to & fro they went.*
614 *Within this grove Æneas first beheld*
615 *A novel sight by which his fears were quelled;*
616 *Here first gave way to hope so long withstood*
617 *And looked thro' present ill, to future good.*
618 *For while, expectant of the Queen, the stores*
~~far~~
619 *Of that wide spreading Temple he explores;*
620 *Admires the strife of labour; nor forbears* } striving labourers
621 *To ponder oer the lot of noble cares* }
622 *Which the young city for herself prepares;* }

[641] *That to his view the faithful wall presents*
the
~~And thro' his troubles looks to future good~~

618–647 Autograph not WW's is MW's, except where noted.

623 *He meets the wars of Illium, every fight*
624 *In due succession offered to his sight.*
625 *There he beholds Atrides—Priam here—*
C }
626 *And that stern c* } *hief who was to both severe.*
627 *He stopped, & not without a sigh exclaimed,*
By } *h*
628 [? *Of*] } *whom Acates hath not Troy been named?*
629 *What region of the earth but overflows*
the
630 *With us &* ~~*with the*~~ *memorials of our woes?*
631 *Lo Priamus! here also do they raise*
632 *To virtuous deeds fit monuments of praise;*
633 *Tears for the frail estate of human kind* ~~*are* [? *shed*]~~
634 *Are shed & mortal changes touch the mind*
~~*Disperse t*~~ Then banish
~~*Then banish fear Abandon*~~ *fear*
~~*Disperse thy fears*~~ *these walls our acts proclaim* Then banish fear
nor doubt that we shall profit by Dispel thy fears
~~*And we shall find our safety in*~~ *our fame*
635 *Sorrowing He spake, & while the plenteous tear-drops roll,*
He }
636 [? *Then*] } *with an empty picture feeds his soul*
~~*He spake*~~
~~*While*~~ *down his* ~~*manly cheek*~~ ~~*the plenteous teardrops roll*~~
638 *For he beheld the youth of Illiums strain*
{ *thro'*
637 *After the Greeks fast flying* { *oer the plain*
{ *n, oer* } *routed in*
639 *The* { *re saw* } *the Phrygians* ~~*chased & oer*~~ *the war*
640 *Crested Achilles hanging from his carr*

He spake, (nor might the gushing tears controul)
And with an empty picture feeds his Soul.
He saw the Greeks fast flying oe'r the plain
The Trojan youth how in pursuit they strain;
the { *re* / *n* ~~*The*~~ *oe'r the Phrygians routed in the war*
Crested Achilles hanging from his Car

[DC MS. 89, 157v]

Next near }
641 *1st Book* *Then to their* } *view the painted wall presents*
642 *The fate of Resus, & his snow-white tents;*
sleep ~~*drowsy*~~ silent
643 *In the first* ~~*watch*~~ *of* ^ *night betrayed*
i }
644 *To the wide-wasting sword of De* } *omede,*
~~*neighing*~~ fiery horses
645 *Who fro to the camp the* ~~*champing Coursers*~~ ^ *led;*
646 *Ere they from Trojan's states had tasted food*
's }
647 *Or stooped their heads to drink Scamander* } *flood.*

634–635 The heavily revised couplet beginning "Disperse thy fears," although accurately reflecting the Latin original, was omitted from the fair copy manuscripts.

635–641 Revision, written vertically in left margin, is in Dora W's autograph.

he }
~~Unhappy~~ Troilus [?sees] } *next espied* [~~?~~]
The Stripling
648 *~~Elsewhere he marked the Stripling who defied~~*
Flying, his arms now lost or
~~This Stripling whose hath~~ flung ~~his arms~~ aside;
649 *~~Achilles, but hath flung his arms aside~~*
. F }
Ill matched with fierce Achilles; f } *rom the fight*
650 *~~Unhappy Troilus—from the unequal fight~~*
Horses borne
He by his ~~Coursers~~ ~~His steeds are hurrying now~~ in desperate flight
651 *~~Now hurried by his steeds in desperate flight~~*
Cleaves to his empty Chariot, on
652 *~~Behind his empty chariot o'er~~ the plain*
stretched,
653 *Supinely ~~whirled~~, yet grasping still the rein,* { : —
654 *Along the earth are dragg'd his neck & hair:* } , —
655 *The dust is mark'd by his inverted spear.*
656 *Meanwhile, with tresses long & loose, a train*
657 *Of Trojan matrons seek Minerva's fane;*
As on the bear the dedicated veil
658 *~~Mournfully suppliant, they~~ ~~ever~~ ~~bear the veil~~*
They beat their own sad breasts with suppliant wail
en }
659 *~~And beat their bosoms, but in~~* } *~~treaties fail~~.*
n
660 *The ~~obdurate~~ Goddess heeds not offerings, prayers,* ^ *or cries;*
How
661 *And on the ground are fixed her sullen eyes*
incensed whirled ~~Troy~~ amain
662 *Thrice had Achilles ~~hurled the~~ ~~walls around~~,*
e } *pse* }
About Troy wall that } *corse* } *of ~~dragged along the ground;~~ Hector slain,*
663 *~~The vanquished Hector to his chariot bound~~*
~~sword of~~
{ *s now that proffered*
664 *And ~~now is~~ barter* { *ing ~~the~~ corse for* ^ *gold/ :*
What grief the spoils,
665 *~~How is he sadned~~ the chariot to behold!*
!— } *&*
666 *—~~The spoils~~* } *~~&~~* ^ *~~near his friend's dead body stands~~*
And, suppliant, near his Friends dead body stands
undefended hands
667 *Old Priam, stretching forth his unarmed hands!*
Himself 'mid Grecian Chiefs he can espy;
668 *~~Then among Grecian Chieftains he espies~~*
And saw the oriental blazonry
669 *~~Himself comingled; & can recognize~~*
Of swarthy Memnon, & the Host he heads
670 *~~The Eastern host which swarthy Memnon heads~~.*
Lunar
671 *Her ~~moony~~ Shields Penthesilea leads;*

[Marginal, written vertically beside lines 656–662:]
Unhappy Troilus he next espied,
The Stripling's armour lost or flung aside,
Ill matched with fierce Achilles;

648–661 The autograph is DW's, except where noted.
658–659 Revisions are in Dora W's autograph.
661 "How" is perhaps in Dora W's autograph.
662–675 The autograph of the base text is Dora W's; the autograph of the revisions is DW's.

er
672 A~~s~~ zone his } mutilated breast hath bound;
And
673 When } she, exulting on the embattled ground,
674 A Virgin Warrior, with a Virgin train,
675 Dares in the peril to conflict with Men.
676 While on these animated pictures gazed
677 The Dardan Chief, enwrapt, disturb'd, amazed;
678 { With a long retinue of Youth, the Queen
Ascends
679 ~~Approaches~~ the Temple; lovely was her mien; }
680 And her Form beautiful as Earth has seen.

[DC MS. 89, 158r]

1st Book
680 ~~And her Form~~ beautiful ~~as earth has~~
681 Thus, where Eurotas flows, or on the heights
C } Cyn
682 Of A } cimthus, where Diana oft delights
{ s
683 To train her nymphs, and lead~~s~~ the Choir { along,
, } , }
684 Oreads (} in thousands, gathering } ~~)~~ round her throng:
685 Where'er she moves, where'er the Goddess bears
686 Her pendant sheaf of arrows, she appears
687 Far, far above the immortal Company:
688 Latona's breast is thrill'd with silent ecstasy.
689 Even with such lofty bearing Dido pass'd
690 Among the busy crowd;—such looks, she cast
intent
691 Urging the various works, with mind ~~intent~~ ~~whos aim~~
Is ~~To~~ went,
692 ~~On~~ future empire.—Through the porch she ~~went,~~ ~~came~~
Q?to And compass'd round ~~with arm'd~~ attendants, sate
693 ~~And, girt with arm'd Attendants, took her Seat~~
694 Beneath the Temple's dome, upon a throne of State, }
she gave
695 There, laws ~~ordained~~, divided justly there
696 The labour, or, by lot to each assigned his share.
'~~mid~~ turning from the throne a casual glance
697 When, with a numerous concourse at a glance
n } ~~Troop of~~ eager crowd
698 Æneas saw a } ~~Trojan Band~~ advance,
^
T }
~~many t rojans~~ many Trojans
699 In With ~~various Leaders~~, whom the storms of heaven
^

676–712 The autograph is DW's, except where noted.

699 "In" in left margin, in MW's autograph, indicates that the base text, "various Leaders," is to be preferred to the revision.

on other
700 *Had scattered, & ~~to various~~ shores had driven.*
t }
701 *With Antheus & Sergesth } us there appeared.*
b } a } , } follower long endeared
702 *The B } rave Clon } nthes. } ~~Much his heart was chear'd~~*
Joy smote his heart strange
703 *^ ~~But the joy~~ tempered with ~~a fearful~~ awe;*
~~Meanwhile what he beheld~~
704 *That ~~which he looked upon~~ ~~Achates saw~~*
Achates, in like sort, by what he saw ~~was s~~
705 *Both trembled and the hands of both were bent*
Was smitten, |
706 *On instant greeting, but they feared the event.*
707 *Stifling their wish, ~~within t~~ within that cloud involved*
708 *They wait, until the mystery shall be solved,*
709 *What has befallen their Friends; upon what shore*
710 *The Fleet is left; & what they would implore:*
711 *For delegates from every ship they were,*
Temple }
712 *And sought the [?~~Queen~~] } with a clamorous prayer.*
713 *All entered—& leave given, with tranquil breast*
714 *Ilioneus preferred their joint request.*

[DC MS. 89, 158v]

empowered by Jupiter to 1st Book
Jupiter *Oh Queen ~~appointed by high Jove~~ to found*
A hopeful city on this desert ground
717 *Whom he commissions also with the rein*
715 ~~*O Queen ordained this City to erect*~~
718 *Of Justice a proud people to restrain*
716 ~~*Now by whose justice haughty tribes are checked*~~

O Queen, empowered by Jupiter to found
A hopeful City on this desert ground
To whom he gives the curb & guiding rein
Of Justice, a proud people to restrain

wretched
719 *We ^ Trojans rescued from a ~~shattered~~ fleet,*
; }
720 *~~The sport of every wind~~, thy aid entreat, }*
Long tossed thro every sea, ^ ire }
721 *Let at thy voice the unhallowed for } forbear*
722 *To touch our ships, a righteous people spare;*
723 *And on our fortunes look with nearer care!*
724 *We neither seek as plunderers your abodes,* infest violate
our swords ia } your
725 *Nor would ^ molest the ~~Libya} n~~ ^ Household Gods* Nor come to desolate your household Gods
726 *Our spirit tempts us not such course to try,*

713–735 The autograph is MW's, except where noted.
715–719 Revision is in Dora W's autograph, except "empowered by Jupiter to," which is in DW's autograph, as is vertical revision in left margin.
725 Revisions in right margin are in DW's autograph.

raise crests
Nor do the vanquished ~~lift~~ their ~~heads~~ so high.
country by men of
There is a ~~Land~~ ~~Hesperia~~ called ~~by~~ ^ Greece
Hesperia strong in arms
W
~~Old~~, ~~w~~ } ~~arlike~~ ^ ~~&~~ the soil of large encrease
e } no held Men of later fame
held *In Oi } ^ trians ~~tilled~~ it ~~once, but now as fame~~*
Calle it Italia from their Leader's name
~~Reports, a later race have styled the same~~
~~Italia, to preserve their Leaders name~~.
That land we sought; when wrapped in mist arose
O } o }
A } riu } n, helped by every wind that blows;
Dispersed us utterly—on shallows cast;
& gained
And we, we only ~~reached~~ ^ your shores at last.
What race of man is here? Was ever yet
The unnatural which
~~Such barbarous~~ treatment known ~~as~~ we have met?
What country bears with customs that deny,
such
To ship-wrecked men, ~~the~~ ^ hospitality
As S }
~~Which~~ the s } ands offer on the naked beach,
And the first quiet of the land they reach.
Arms were <u>our</u> greeting; yet if ye despise
on
Man and <u>his</u> power look ~~for~~ward & be wise;—
ies. }
The Gods for right & wrong have awful memory }
A man to no one second in the care
Of justice, nor in piety and war,
Ruled over us; if yet Æneas treads
On earth, nor has been summon'd to the shades,
Then no repentance fear if thou take place
Of him, O Queen! } foremost in acts of grace!

Fear no repentance if in acts of grace
gain the
Striving with him thou ~~take the~~ foremost place

[DC MS. 89, 159r]

1st Book *Nor want we in Trinacria towns ~~&~~ & plains*
~~For our support Trinacria also yields~~
Where, sprung from Trojan blood, Acestes reings.
~~Trojan Acestes & his towns & fields~~
Grant leave to draw our ships upon your shores
T } to fit
And t } hence ^ renew their shattered hulks & oars

730–731 Revisions are in Dora W's autograph.
736–764 Autograph is DW's, except where noted.
737 Revisions are in Dora W's autograph.
751–752 Revisions are in Dora W's autograph.

Were *& Chief*
755 *Rhime to be altered* *~~If Fate our Leader~~ ~~& our~~ Friends restored whom now we mourn*
~~To Italy now~~ We to the Italian Coast, with joy would turn
756 *~~Rejoicing shall we seek the Italian Shore~~,*
Should { lie
757 *If Italy { be open to our aim:*
if ~~should~~ welfare
758 *But ~~if~~ our ~~safety~~ be an empty name,*
f }
759 *And thou, best Father of the F }amily*
760 *Of Troy hast perish'd in the Lybian sea,* }
Iulus sank
761 *And young ~~Aiculus lies~~ engulphed with thee,* }
762 *~~Then be it ours at least to seek the home~~*
762 *Then be it ours at least to cross the foam* }
763 *Of the Sicilian Deep, & seek the home* }
764 *Prepared by good Acestes, whence we come.* }
765 —Thus spake Ilioneus; his Friends around
Declared
766 ~~Made thence~~ their sanction with a murmuring sound.
No more done *Dido*
767 *With down-cast looks brief answer^made*
768 *Trojans be fears dismissed anxieties allayed*
769 *The pressure of occasion & a reign* }
exact these rigors, and
770 *Yet new, ~~to such severities~~ constrain;* }
to T }
~~force ask~~ t }he jealous
771 *And to the^vigilance my coasts maintain.* }
T }
772 *The Ænean race, with that heroic t }own*
773 *And widely-blazing war, to whom are they unknown?*
774 *Not so obtuse the Punic breasts we bear;* }
averse } not so
775 *Not so [?] } is Phoebus, ~~nor so~~ far* }
~~when does~~ s }
776 *From Tyrian ramparts ~~does~~^he yoke }his Carr.* }

Not so obtuse
Nor does the giver of the day so far
From this our Tyrian city yoke his Car

777 *But if Hesperia be your wished for bourne*
778 *Or to Trinacrian Shores your prows would turn,*
779 *Then, with all aids that may promote your weal,*
{ e
780 *Ye shall depart, but if desires y { ou feel*
Fixed in this growing realm to share my fate,
781 *~~For fixed abodes within my growing state~~*
781/782 *Wi~~th me to~~ ~~Here fixed to share on equal terms my fate~~*
782 *Yours are the walls which now I elevate.*
~~Return~~ Haste, and
783 *~~Fast~~ ~~Haste to~~ withdraw your gallies from the Sea;*
784 *Trojans^& Tyrians shall be one to me.*
w } too,
785 *~~And~~ W }ould^that, Storm-compelled/ as ye have been,*
786 *The person of your Chief might here be seen!*

767–786 The autograph is Dora W's, except where noted.
774–776 The autograph is MW's.

[DC MS. 89, 159^v]

1st Book

787 *By trusty Servants shall my shores be traced*
to farthe~~r~~st *To ~~the last~~ To farthest*
788 *~~Even to~~ the ^ confines of the Lybian Waste,*
haply, spared by *~~haply~~*
789 *the tempestuous If ~~chance ejected by tempestuous floods~~*
If he the cast away of stormy floods,
790 *~~Some city holds him, or he roams the woods~~*
Wander thro' cities, or in savage woods.
Q
791 P + *Thus did the q }ueen administer relief*
792 *For their dejected hearts; & to the Chief,*
793 *While both were burning with desire to break~~/~~*
794 *From out the darksome cloud, Achates spake.*
795 *"Son of a Goddess what resolves ensue*
From this deliverance whose effects we view?
796 *~~On what is here submitted to thy view~~*
— *,*
797 *All things are safe; } thy fleet & friends restored; }*
798 *Save one whom in our sight the Sea devoured,*
799 *All else respondent to thy Mother's word."*
e
800 *He spake—the circumambiant cloud anon*
urk
801 *Melts & dissolves, the mist } y vale is gone,*
And left Æneas as it passed away ~~The Chief~~ ~~Æneas to display~~
~~day~~ ~~as~~
802 *~~And left in open Air Æneas shone~~*
W
w } ith *standing*
~~Divine~~ [?in] } godlike mien & shoulders ^ in full day;
803 *~~Godlike of mien his Mother had bestowed~~*
{ that same Parent of celestial race }
~~That grace of hair~~ For { on his hair his Mother had bestowed }
shed
804 *~~The Hair which round his Godlike Shoulders flowed~~,*
Diffused around *~~pour'd~~*
her Son *{ ~~Unearthly Had breathed upon his hair~~ surpassing grace }*
805 *Surpassing* *{ [?] grace which was peculiar to a God }*
grace peculiar *{ ~~Upon Diffused around~~ her son }*
806 *to a God* *{ Pour'd [?Distilled] upon her son } the purple light*
807 *Of youth & glorified his eyes made bright*
~~With~~ Like those of heaven with joyance infinite.
808 *~~Of Youth & thro' his eyes a splendor infinite~~*
~~The attribute of Powers that shine forever bright~~
809 *~~That~~ So stood he forth, an unexpected guest,*

pour'd

787–790 The autograph is DW's, except where noted.
788 Revision "to fartherst" in left margin is in Dora W's autograph.
789–790 Revision below the line is in Dora W's autograph.
791–808 The autograph is Dora W's, except where noted.
802 Revisions, excepting "the Chief" and "to display," are in MW's autograph.
803 In revision above the line, "standing" is in MW's autograph, as is the overwriting "with."
804–808 Revisions are in MW's autograph, including vertical revisions in left margin.
805–807 The autograph of the base text is DW's.
809–818 The autograph is MW's, except where noted.

And while all wondered thus the Queen addressed,
He whom you seek am I, Æneas,—flung
y} i}
By storms the Li} by}an solitudes among;
Sole utterable
O ~~Soul~~, who for the un~~speakable~~ |state of Troy
art
Of Troy Art humanly compassionate;
a}
Who not alone h}shelter dost afford
~~the~~ the
To ~~us~~ thin relics of the Grecian sword,
Perpetually exhausted by pursuit
of *~~From~~ dire mischance, of all things destitute,*
them
But in thy purposes with ~~us~~ hast shared
who thus have fared
City & home;—not we, ~~for this regard~~
Not we, nor all the Dardan race that live
Earth ~~O Queen~~ sufficient
Scattered ~~Dispersed~~ throug~~hout the world~~, ~~due~~^thanks can give

[left margin, vertical:] *grace*
And breathing o'er her Son the purple light
Of youth had glorified his eyes made bright

[DC MS. 89, 160r]

1st Book

they the Pious watch with love
The Gods (if ~~powers about us or above~~,
If Justice dwells about us or above)
~~Watching the Righteous, do their course approve~~)
And a mind conscious to itself of right,
Shall, in fit measure, thy deserts requite.
happy ~~blessed~~
What ~~joyful~~ age gave being to such worth?
^blessed
What parents, Dido, brought thee ~~virtuous~~ forth?
While down their channels Rivers seaward flow;
~~Long as the Rivers to the seas shall run~~
While shadowy groves sweep round the mountain's brow,
~~Or mountain shadows travel with the sun~~
~~Heaven feeds the stars thy name shall last~~
While ether feeds the stars whereer be cast
~~Long as blue ether, on its champain vast~~
~~Thy honour & thy praise, where'er my lot be cast~~
~~Shall feed the stars, where'er my lot be cast~~,
Thy lot, whatever land by me be trac'd,
~~Thy name, thy honour, & thy praise, shall last~~
Thy name, thy honour, and thy praise, shall last!
He spake, and turning towards the Trojan Band
Salutes Ilioneus with the better hand,

[left margin, vertical:]
Long as the ~~Rivers~~ to the sea shall flow
Or shadowy groves ~~sweep~~ round the mountains brow

---

813 Revisions are in DW's autograph.
814 Revision "art" is in DW's autograph.
816 Revision is in DW's autograph.
819–822 The autograph of the base text is Dora W's; the autograph of the revisions is DW's.
823–837 Autograph not WW's is DW's.

Sere
836 *And grasps ~~Er~~gestus with the left—then gave*
G
837 ~~*Then gave g reetings to Gyas & Cloanthes brave*~~
[837] Like greetings to the rest, to Gyas brave,
brave Cloanthes
838 And ~~to Cloanthes~~ ~~his tried Friend.~~
Inwardly as~~h~~mazed
839 Sidonian Dido on the Chief had ~~gazed~~ gazed,
i
840 *When first* When first he met her view;—his words like wonder raz zed.
he st~~ood reveal~~ Force pursues
841 *re~~a~~vealed* "What ~~Fortune~~, said She, haunts thee? hath impelld
in thee
842 To these wild shores? ~~in thee~~ have I beheld
on
o
843 That Trojan whom bright [?] Venus, i n the shore
844 Of Phrygian Simois, to ~~Achates~~ Anchises bore?
well do I recall to mind
845 And <u>not by one forgotten is</u> the day ~~shaped~~
846 When to our Sidon Teucer found his way,
847 An Outcast from his native borders driven,
With new realms
848 Who hope~~d new realms~~ to win by aid from Belus given,
the conquering
849 Belus my Father, then ~~successful~~ Lord
newly ravaged
850 Of Cyprus ~~ravaged~~ by his ~~conquering~~ sword.—
851 tale Thenceforth I knew the fate of Troy that rings
852 Earth round—thy name, and the Pelasgian Kings.
Teucer
eu
853 *T ussor himself with liberal tongue would raise*
854 *His adversaries to just heights of praise,*
And vaunt
855 ~~*Vaunting*~~ *a Trojan lineage with fair proof;*
,
856 *Then welcome, noble Strangers ! to our Roof!*

[DC MS. 89, 160v]

1st Book
857 ~~*Tell him I was allow'd to breathe and rest*~~
~~*the ills which on myself have press'd*~~ ~~*wayward*~~
858 ~~*Touched by misfortunes in my own sad breast,*~~
[857] Me too, like fortune after devious strife
860 ~~*I thence have learned to succour the distress'd.*~~
[858] Stay'd in this land, to breathe a calmer life

853–858, 860 Autograph not WW's is DW's.

Me, too, like fortune after devious strife
?884 [?~~Ascanius~~]
Staid in this land—to breathe a calmer life.

859 *From no light ills which on myself have press~~e~~* ' } d
[860] *Pitying I learned to succour the distress~~e~~* ' } d
861 *These words pronounced & mindful to ordain*
862 *Fit sacrifice she issues from the* F } *f ane*
863 *And towards the palace leads Æneas & his train.*
864 *Nor less regardful of his distant friend's,*
865 *To the sea coast she hospitably sends*
866 *Twice ten selected Steers, a hundred Lambs~~,~~*
867 *Swept from the plenteous herbage with their Dams;*
868 *A hundred bristly ridges of huge swine,*
869 *And what the God bestows in sparkling wine.*
870 *But the interior palace doth display*
871 *Its whole magnificence in set array;*
872 *And in the centre of a spacious hall*
Are preparations
873 ~~*Is spread the banquet*~~ *for high festival:*
874 *There gorgeous vestments skillfully enwrought*
875 *With eastern purple; & huge tables—fraught*
876 *With massive argentry; there, carved in gold,*
877 *Thro' long long series, the atchievements bold*
878 *Of Forefathers—each imaged in his place*
879 *From the beginning of the ancient race.*
880 *Æneas, whose parental thoughts obey*
881 *Their natural impulse, brooking no delay,*
882 *Dispatched the prompt Achates to report*
883 *The new events, & lead Ascanius to the Court;*
884 *Ascanius, for on him the Father's mind*
885 *Now rests, as if to that sole care confined;*
886 *And bids him bring, attendant on the boy,*
887 *The richest presents snatched from burning Troy;*
888 *A robe of tissue stiff with shapes expresse* ' } d
889 *In threads of gleaming gold; an upper vest*
890 *Round which acanthus twines its yellow flowers;*
891 *By Argive Helen worn in festal hours;*
892 *Her Mother Ledea's wondrous gift~~s~~, & brought*
æ
893 *To Illium from Mycene—when she sought*
894 *Those unpermitted Nuptials;—thickly set*
895 *With gold & gems, a twofold coronet;*
896 *And sceptre—which Ilione of yore,*
897 *Eldest of Priam's royal Daughters, wore,*
that
that }
898 *And orient pearls on her neck she bore.*

857–900 Beginning with undeleted version of ll. 857–858, "Me, too, . . . calmer life," the autograph is Dora W's, except where noted. This page may have been entered after l. 901ff.

873 Autograph of revision may be DW's.

This to perform Achates speeds his way
To the ships anchored in that peacful Bay.

[DC MS. 89, 161r]

1st Book P

But Cytherea, studious to invent
Arts yet untried, upon new ~~perils~~ {counsels} bent,
Resolves that Cupid, changed in form & face
To young Ascanius, should assume his place;
Present the madning gift {s,} & ~~rouse~~ {kindle} the heat
Of passion ~~kindled~~ at ~~its~~ {the bosom's} inmost seat.
She dreads the ~~Punic craft & glorying~~ {treacherous House and Punic} *tongue;*
By Juno's rancor is her quiet stung:
The calm of night is powerless to remove
These cares, & thus she speaks to winged {L} l ove.

P *"O Son, my strength, my power, {!} who dost despise*
(What save thyself none dare thro' earth & skies)
The joy {Gy} ant-quelling bolts of Jove, I flee
O Son, a suppliant to thy Deity!
What perils meet Æneas in his course, {—}
How Juno's hate with unrelenting force
Pursues thy Brother, {—} this to thee is known;
And oft~~en~~ {times} hast thou made my griefs th~~y~~ {ine} own.
Him now Phœni~~ss~~ {c} ian Dido in soft chains
Of a seductive blandishment detains;
Junonian hospitalities prepared
Such apt occasion that I dread a snare.
Hence, er'e some hostile God can intervene,
Would I by previous [?] wiles inflame the Queen
With passion for Æneas, such strong love
That at my beck, mine only, she shall move.
Hear & assist, {;} {T} t he Father's summons calls
His young Ascanius to the Tyrian walls;
He comes, my dear delight, & costliest things,
Preserved from fire & flood, for presents, brings.

That he may neither ~~know what hope is mine~~
Nor by his presence traverse the design.

~~Momentous [?pondering], much I fear the snare~~
~~Which Juno's hospitality prepare~~

901–952 Autograph not WW's is Dora W's, except where noted.

Him will I take & in close covert keep,
Mid Groves Idalian lulled to gentle sleep.
ras
Or on Cytheas far-sequestered steep.
That he may [?] neither know what hopes are mine hopes
Nor by his presence traverse the design
Do thou/ but for a single night's brief space
—
Dissemble, be that Boy in form & face!
And when inraptured Dido shall receive
Thee to her Arms, & kisses interweave
With many a fond embrace, while joy runs high,
And Goblets crown the proud festivity,
Instil thy subtle poison, & inspire
At every touch an unsuspected fire.

[DC MS. 89, 161v]

1st Book

P *Love, at the word, before his Mother's sight*
Puts off his wings, & walks with proud delight,
u *the gentlest dews*
Like young I llus; but ~~a dewy sleep~~
Of slumber, Venus sheds to circumfuse
~~At the command of Venus falls to steep.~~
steeped
The true Ascanius in ~~a~~ placid rest;
Then wafts him, cherished on her careful breast
~~Whom Venus carries in her fostering breast~~
Through upper air, *G*
~~Wafted on high~~ to an Idalian grove g lade;
A
Where he on soft umaracus is laid,
With breathing flowers embraced & fragrant shade.
But Cupid, following cheerily his guide
\+ *Achates, with the gifts to Carthage hied;*
He reached the Hall where now the Queen reposed
Amid a golden couch, with awnings half enclosed;
The Trojans
y *(* *)—*
Alread , too —Æneas at their head—
On couches lie with purple overspread,
~~Each Trojan occupies his festal bed;~~
time *i* *piled*
Mean~~while~~ on cannisters is ~~heaped~~ the bread,

946–950 Revisions are in DW's autograph.

953–977 The autograph is DW's, except where noted. The difference in her handwriting, especially in ll. 967–977, is probably due to a defective pen.

957–965 Revisions are in the autograph of MW.

~~And for~~ Pellucid water for the hands is born,
~~To lave the hands adroit attendants bring~~
{ borne
~~smooth~~ ~~Pellucid~~ ~~water for and the hands is~~ { ~~for~~
~~With~~ ^ ~~napkins~~ ~~of fine thread,~~ ~~pure water from the spring~~
And ~~with~~ and ~~with~~ napkins of smoo~~th tex~~ture finely shorn.
Within, are fifty handmaids who prepare,
As
~~While~~ they in order stand, the dainty fare,
—fume the household Deities with store
And ~~light~~ ~~the~~ ~~incense breathing fire before~~
Of odorous ~~incense~~; while
~~The houshold Gods; the whilst~~ a hundred more,
Matched with an equal number of like age
P }
But each of manly sex, a docile p } age,
Marshal *with*
~~*Martial*~~ *Arrange the banquet, giving ~~in~~ due grace*
To cup or viand its appointed place.
The Tyrians rushing in, an eager band,
Their painted couches seek, obedient to command.
wonder { the
They gaze in look with ^ on { [? they] Gifts—they gaze
Upon Iulas, dazzled with the rays
That from his ardent countenance are flung,
charmed to hear his simulating tongue
And, ~~cheated by the speech of his dissembling~~ ~~tongue~~
Nor pass unpraised the robe, & veil divine
Round which the yellow flowers & wandering foliage twine.
But chiefly Dido, to the coming ill
v }
Devoted, strives in V }ain her vast desires to fill;
She views the gifts, upon the boy then turns
Insatiable eyes, & gazing burns.
cheated *To ease a Father's cheated love he hung*
Upon Æneas, & around him clung;

[DC MS. 89, 162r]

1st Book
Then sought the Queen, who fixed upon him the whole
That she possessed of look, mind, life, & soul;
And sometimes doth unhappy Dido plant
The Fondling in her bosom, ignorant
— }
How great a God deceives her. He/ } to please
His Acidalian Mother, by degrees

968 "Martial" is in MW's autograph.
975 Revisions are in MW's autograph.
978–1020 The autograph is MW's, except where noted.
982 "cheated" in left margin is in DW's autograph.
985 The "l" in "life" is mistakenly crossed as a "t."

Sichæus
æ
Would sap Siche us; studious to remove
x
The dead/ by influ ~~ence~~ of a living love,
t
Thro' a subsided spirit, dispossess ed
Of amorous passion, thro' a torpid breast.
withdrawn
Now when the viands were removed, & ceased
The first division of the splendid feast;
While round a vacant board the Chiefs reclined,
are brought — they
Huge goblets ~~they bring~~ forth & crown the wine///:
Voices of gladness roll the walls around;
Those gladsome voices from the courts rebound;
From gilded rafters many a blazing light
.
Depends, & torches overcome the night,
— *The minutes fly,—till, as the Queen commands,*
:
A bowl of state is offered to her hands,
Then she, as Belos wont/ & all the line
From Belos, filled it to the brim with wine;
Silence ensued;—"O Jupiter! whose care
Is hospitable dealing, grant my prayer!
Productive be this day of lasting joy
To Tyrians, & these Exiles drive from Troy;—
A Day to
~~May~~ future generations ~~hold it~~ dear!
soul-gladdening
Let Bacchus, donor of ~~exulting~~ chear
Be present; kindly Juno, be thou near!
,
And/ Tyrians ! may your choicest favor wait
Upon this hour, the bond to celebrate!
She spake, & shed an offering on the board,
Then sipped the bowl, whence she the wine had poured;
~~He took~~ And gave to Betus, bidding him take heart;
—
He raised, & , not unequal to his part,
Drank deep, self-drenched from out the brimming gold:
N
Thereafter a like course th'encircling n obles hold.

997 Revisions are in Dora W's autograph.

[DC MS. 89, 162v]

1st Book

P

1021 *Graced with redundant hair, Iopas sings*
to
1022 *The love of Atlas, on resounding strings—*
,
1023 *The labours of the sun;* *the lunar wanderings;—*
;
1024 *Whence human kind, and brute—* *what natural powers*
[?] *;* *.*
1025 *Engender lightning-* */whence the falling showers,*
and that social Twain
1026 *He chaunts Arcturus ~~of the northern Wain~~*
+ *The Bears and Pleiades bedimmed with rain*
1027 *~~The Pleiads moist, the Bears a glittering twain,~~*
W *in winter, shunning Heavens ~~steep~~ steep*
1028 — *Why ~~w linter~~ Suns ~~from Heaven's ethereal~~ ^ heights,*
s.
1029 *Post seaward; what impedes the tardy night .—*
1030 *The learned Song from Tyrian hearers draws*
—
1031 *Loud shouts.* *The Trojans echo the applause.*
1032 But *~~Skilful a varied converse to pursue~~*
~~Still~~ *converse*
1032 *~~And~~, lengthening out the night with ~~topics~~ new;*
1033 *Large draughts of love unhappy Dido drew;*
1034 *Of Priam asked, of Hector o'er & oer—*
1035 *What arms the Son of bright Aurora wore;*
steeds
1036 *What ~~horses~~ those of Diomede;—how great/*
1037 *Achilles—but O Guest! the whole relate; ~~retrace~~*
Retrace the
The
1038 *Retrace Grecian cunning from ~~its th~~ its source,—*
— *—*
1039 *Your own Griefs,* *and your Friends',* *your wander-*
-ing course;
1040 — *For now, till this seventh summer, have you ranged*
sea, or trod
1041 *The ~~waters &~~ ^ the earth, to peace estranged!*

End of the first Book.

× The glittering Bears, and Pleads charged with rain

1021–end of Book I The autograph is DW's.

[DC MS. 89, 163r]

(*continuation from 8 leaves back*

Second Book *while Priam's sway endured;*

33 *Potent & rich ~~in time of Priam's sway,~~*

a bare { *H* / *hold for keels unsafely moored.* ~~*ships*~~

34 *Now ~~merely for chance keels an unsafe bay~~.*

Here did the Greeks, when for their native land

35 ~~*There do the Greeks hide the Greeks secrete themselves, we*~~

them } ~~*thought*~~

[36] We thought ~~had the~~ them sail'd, lurk on the desert strand.

~~*That they*~~ ~~*there not in vain the Greeks*~~

~~*The Greeks sailed thither there concealment sought;*~~

o }

36 ~~*Bound to their native harbours, As we thought;*~~

R }

From ~~itsher~~ long grief at once the ~~land~~ r ealm of

37 *At once from long-protracted grief, all Troy*

,— }

38 *Broke loose, the gates are opened—& with joy*

W }

39 *Th e seek the Dorian camp, & wander oer*

abandond

40 *The spots forsaken, the ~~deserted~~ shore.*

s; }

41 *Here the Dolopian ground~~s~~ its lines present*

42 *And here the dread Achilles pitched his tents;*

along

43 *There lay the ships drawn up ~~upon~~ the coast;*

44 *And here we oft encounterd, host with host.*

M } *the rest*

45 *~~Others~~ m eanwhile^an eye of wonder lift*

~~*Measuring the bulk of that pernicious gift*~~

{ *to*

46 *in* ~~*And I Unwedded Pallas, in that fatal gift*~~

~~*Virgin Pallas*~~ *œ* }

47 *To thee devoted! First, Thyme tes calls*

ingress *thro' disparted*

48 *For its free ~~entrance~~, ~~led within the~~ walls,*

To

{ ~~*And*~~ *within* ; }

{ 49 *Or lodge~~d~~ ~~amid~~ the citadel: —thus he*

y. }

50 *Treacherous, or such the course of destins*

y }

51 *Capi s with some of wiser mind would sweep*

52 *The insidious Grecian offering to the deep,*

it;

53 *Or to the flames subject~~ed~~, or advise*

rfo } *and* } { *vities;*

54 *To penet rate or search the ca nopies.*

- } { *ng*

55 *In to conflicti on judgements break & split*

56 *The crowd, as random thoughts the fancy hit.*

33–100 Autograph is MW's, except where noted.

57 *Down from the Citadel a numerous throng*
58 *Hastes with Laocoon; they sweep along, ~~& he~~*
59 *And he* *The foremoast—crying from afar;*
ould [?minions] !
60 *"What want* } *ye, wretched madmen as ye are,* }
?
61 *Think ye the foe departed,* } *or that e'er*
G
62 *A boon from g* } *recian hands can prove sincere?*
F
63 *Thus do Ye read Ul/ysses? f* } *oes unseen*
M
64 *Lurk in these chambers; or the huge m* } *achine*
65 *Against the ramparts brought, by pouring down*
T
66 *Force from aloft, will seize upon the t* } *own.*
y
67 *Let not a fair pretence m* } *our minds enthrall;*
68 *For me, I fear the G~~reeks~~, & most of all*

[DC MS. 89, 163v]

Second Book

69 *When they are offering gifts." With mighty force,*
70 *This said, he hurled a spear against the Horse;*
71 *It smote the curved ribs, & quivering stood*
:
72 *While groans made answer from the hollow wood;* }
73 *Then, but for loss of mind, & adverse fate,*
75 *We, too, had rushed the den to ~~violate~~, penetrate:*
76 *Streams of Argolic blood our swords had stained,*
T
77 *Troy, t* } *hou might'st yet of stood, & Priam's towers remained!*
an unknown Youth with hand to hand
78 *But lo! ~~with clamor~~ ~~Dardan~~ ~~Shepherds bring~~*
79 *Behind him fastened, whom a clamorous band*
~~An unknown Youth their Captive to the King~~
80/81 *Of Dardan Shepherds to the king hath brought!*
82 *~~The bonds~~ ~~he~~ ~~wears are~~ ~~only~~ ~~what he~~ ~~sought~~*
Even such his scheme when he those chains had sought,
83 *~~Firm is the~~ ~~purpose~~ of ~~his~~ ~~inward thought~~*
A voluntary captive fixed in thought,
84 *Either the City to betray, or meet*
85 *Death, the sure penalty of foiled deceit.*
curious
86 *The^Trojans pouring in deride*
P
87 *And taunt the p* } *risoner with an emulous pride.*
~~see~~ *ians*
88 *~~Now would you know the Greeks~~*
Now see the cunning of the Greeks exprest
of one,
89 *By ~~one~~ ~~man's~~ guilt^~~the~~ an image of the rest.*

[Written vertically in the left margin beside lines 77–87:]
For while in helpless fear so only he eyed
The Phrygians pressing round, what band he cried
Or what wide space of waters now is free

For while *with helpless looks from side to side*
90 ~~For while he stood in helpless fear & eyed~~
Anxiously cast, the Phrygian throng he eyed;
91 ~~And eyed slowly the Phrygians pressing round~~,
"Alas what land, he cries, can now, what sea he cried
W }
92 ~~He cried w }hat land what space of water now is free~~
Can s } c }
93 *~~To~~^offer refuge? what rec }ours }e for me?*
94 *Who mid the Greeks no breathing space can find;*
95 *And whom ye Trojans have to death consigned!*
were we wrought upon; & now with sense
Thus ~~on our minds he wrought~~ &
96 *~~Touched by this lamentation with a sense~~*
touched that checked
97 *Of pity/ ~~that restrained~~ all violence,*
98 *We cheared & urged him boldly to declare*
99 *His origin; what tidings he he may bear;*
what
100 *And in^claims he ventures to confide;*

3d Book
Torment me not Æneas
58 *~~Æneas, why torment me~~? Why this pain*
O cease *refrain*
59 *Given to a buried man? ~~Abstain~~, ~~abstain~~*
And spare this guilty stain.
60 *~~Nor in this sort~~ thy pious hands ~~prophane~~*
61 *Troy brought me forth/ no alien to thy blood*
62 *Nor yields a senseless trunk this sable flood*
63 *Oh fly the cruel land; the greedy shore,*
64 *Forsake with speed for I am Polydore*
65 *~~An iron~~ A flight of iron darts here pierced me through*
thicket
66 *Took life; and into this sharp ~~produce~~ grew!*
67 *Then truly did I stand aghast, cold fear*
68 *Strangling my voice & lifting up my hair.—*

[DC MS. 89, 164r]

3d Book
69 *Erewhile ~~had Pri~~ from Troy had Priam sent by stealth*
70 *This Polydore, and with him store of wealth*
71 *Trusting the Thracian King his Son would rear*
72 *For wretched Priam now gave way to fear;*
ese } s }
73 *Seeing the Town beleaguered. This } alarm }*
74 *Spread to the Thracians King, and when the Arms ~~of Tr~~*
75 *Of Troy were ~~quelle'd he took~~ the ~~Conqueror's side~~*
76 *And the just ~~anger of the Go~~*

Book III, ll. 58–101 Autograph not WW's is DW's.

75 *Of Troy were quelled, to the victorious side*
em }
76 *Of Agamme* }*non he his hope allied*
77 *Breaking through sacred laws without remorse*
78 *Slew Polydore, & seized the gold by force*
79 *What mischief to poor mortals has not thirst*
80 *Of gold created! appetite accursed!* S
81 *Soon as a calmer mind I could recal*
82 *I seek the Chiefs—my Father above all*
83 *Report the omen, and their thoughts demand*
84 *One mind is theirs, to quit the ~~wick~~ impious Land,*
85 *With the first breezes of the South to fly*
86 *Sick of polluted hosptality.*
87 *Forthwith on Polydore our hands bestow*
{ *ld*
88 *A second burial & fresh mo* {*uld upthrow,*
and to his Manes raise beside the mound
89 *Raise ~~Altars to his ghost~~ ~~the tomb around~~,* }
90 *Altars which as they stood in mournful round* }
91 *~~With azure fillets & black cypress bound~~;* }
^ *Cerulean fillets and black cypress bound;*
92 *And with loose hair a customary Band*
93 *Of Trojan women in the circle stand.*
94 { *From cups warm milk and sacred blood we pour* }
~~Thus~~
95 {*Thus ~~And~~ to the tomb the spirit we restore* }
96 { *And with a farewel cry its future rest implore.* }
97 *Then, when the sea grew calm, & gently creeps*
98 *The soft South wind & calls us to the Deeps*
y } *crowd*
99 *The ~~Me~~ Crew draw down our ships; the* } *~~shore they fill~~ the shore;*
: }
100 *The Port We leave* }*~~the Port~~; with cities sprinkled o'er,*
101 *Slowly the Coast recedes, & then is seen no more.*

2^d^ Book

Then *somewhat eased of ~~thus~~*
, }
101 P *And now that fear* }*~~was calmed~~ he thus replied.*
102 *"O King a plain confession shall ensue*
com
103 *On these ~~de~~mands, in all things plain & true.*
104 *And first the tongue that speaks shall not deny*
105 *My origin; a Greek by birth am I.*
106 *Fortune made Sinon wretched; to do more*
er }
107 *And make him false—this lies not in his* } *power.*

Book II, ll. 101–231 Autograph not WW's is MW's.

[DC MS. 89, 164v]

haply
2d *Book* *In converse ~~doubtless~~ ye have heard the name*
108 *~~Perchance in course of common speech the name~~*
109 *~~The~~ Of Palamedes & his glorious fame;*
A Chief with treason falsely charged, & whom
B
110 *~~Hath reached your ears~~. ~~The Chief from P~~ ~~elus sprung~~;*
The Achaians crushed, by a nefarious doom,
111 *~~Whom~~, ~~charged with treachery by a~~ ~~perjured tongue~~*
And now lament when covered with the tomb.
~~And to this war averse~~; ~~the~~ ~~Greeks~~ ~~by heinous doom~~
~~The Achaians crushed a guiltless man, & whom~~
whom they
112 *~~Condemned &^ mourn now~~ ~~covered with the tomb~~*
~~They~~ ~~now deplore when~~ ~~covered with the tomb~~
T
113 *~~Wh~~ ~~to this illustrious Chief by birth allied~~*
His kinsman I, & hither by his side
114 *~~Hither I came while yet in arms untried~~*
Me my poor Father sent, whence first these fields were tried.
115 *~~By my poor father sent to combat by his side~~*
116 *While yet his voice the Grecian chieftains swayed,*
117 *And due respect was to his counsels paid,*
118 *Ere ~~prosperous~~ ~~rule~~ was with his life cut short,*
that high influence
I did not walk
119 *~~Even~~ ~~I too was~~ ~~not~~ ungraced with fair report.*
Ulysses—
120 *~~But when~~ ~~with~~ envy rankling in his breast*
(And these are
121 *~~I speak of~~ things which thousands can attest)*
Thereafter
122 *~~Ulysses~~ turned his subtilty to give*
123 *That fatal injury, & he ceased to live;*
my days
124 *I dragged ~~out life~~ in sorrow & in gloom,*
guiltless
125 *And mourned my ~~blameless~~ friend, indignant*
;
/at his doom,
126 *This inwardly; & yet, not always mute,*
Rashly — sure
127 *^I vowed ~~to make~~ revenge; my ~~just~~ pursuit,*
re
e er the *~~see~~*
128 *If ~~to the~~^ shores of Argos I again ~~should pass~~*
129 *Should see, victorious with my Countrymen.*
threats
130 *Sharp hatred did these open ~~words~~ excite;*
131 *Hence the first breathings of a deadly blight;*
Th
132 *H ence, to appall me, accusations came,*
133 *Which still Ulysses was at work to frame;*
134 *Hence would he scatter daily mid the crowd*
at
135 *Loose hints; su will sustained or disavowed:*

B}   *for instruments*
136 *Meanwhile b* }*eyond himself*^*he looked,* ~~*for aid*~~
And in ~~*dark*~~ *this search of means no respite brooked,*
137 ~~*To his purpose suitable; nor staid*~~
^ *h* *e*}
138 *Till CKalcas his accomplice—but this*} *chain*
foul ^ *appal*
139 *Of* ~~*these*~~ *devices why untwist in vain?*
Why should I linger? ~~*Trojans*~~ *Trojans*
140 ~~*Exhausting thus your patience*~~, *if ye*^*place*
Argive
141 *On the same level all of* ~~*Grecian*~~ *race,*

[DC MS. 89, 165ʳ]

2ᵈ Book

142 *And 'tis enough to know that I am one,*
143 *Punish me;—would Ulysses might look on!*
144/145 *And let the Atridæ hear, rejoiced with what is done!"* }
146 ~~*This*~~ *This stirred us more whose judgements were asleep*
a
their}
147 *To all suspicion of his* } *crimes so deep*
.} *O*}
148 *And craft so fine,* } *o* }*ur questions we renewed;*
149 *And, trembling, thus the fiction he pursued.*
150 ~~*Long*~~ *Oft did the Grecian Host the means prepare*
151 *To flee from Troy, tired with so long a war;*
but
152 *Would they had fled!* ~~*the*~~ *winds as often stopped*
153 *Their going, & the hoisted sails were dropped;*
[157] ~~*So that the*~~
H}
154 *And when this pine-ribbed h* }*orse of monstrou's size*
W}
155 *Stood forth, a finished w* }*ork, before their eyes,*
156 *Then cheifly pealed the storm* ~~*from*~~ *thro' blackened skies:* }
157 *So, that the oracle its aid might lend*
y} *u*}
158 *To quell our doubts, Europe* } *li* }*s we send,*
159 *Who brought the answer of the voice divine*
160 *In these sad words, given from the Delphic shrine.*
161 *"Blood flowed, a Virgin perished to appease the*
162 *The winds when first for Troy ye passed the seas;*
163 *O Grecians! for return across the flood,*
164 *Life must be paid, a sacrifice of blood.*
165 *With this response a universal dread*
166 *Among the shuddering multitude was spread;*
167 *All quaked to think at whom the Fates had aimed*
168 *This sentence, who the victim Phœbus claimed*
169 *Then doth the Ithacan, with tumult loud,*

170 *Bring forth the prophet C {a / ilchas to the crowd;*
171 *Asks what the Gods would have; & some meanwhile*
Discern what end the Mover of the
172 ~~*Presage the crime—the Author of the guile*~~
173 Is compassing; and do not hide from me
174 ~~*In mute reserve the course things to come foresee*~~
The crime, which they in mute reserve foresee.
173 ~~*But do not hide what they behold from me*~~
175 *Ten days refused he still with guarded breath*
176 *To designate the Man— {, } to fix the death;*

[DC MS. 89, 165v]

177 *Second Book The Ithacan~~s~~ still urgent for the deed;*
178 *At last the unwilling v {V} oice announced that I must bleed.*
179 *All gave assent, each happy to be cleard,*
180 *Of {By} one Man's fall, of what himself had feared.*
181 *Now came the accursed day— {;} the salted cates*
182 *Are spread, {,—} the Altar for the victim waits— {;}*
183 *The ~~temple~~ fillets bind my temples. {—} I took flight*
~~*I took flight*~~
184 *Bursting my chains, I own, &, thro' the night,*
185 *Lurked among oozy swamps, & there lay hid*
186 *Till winds might cease their voyage to forbid.*
187 *And now was I compelled at once to part*
188 *With all the dear old longings of the heart;*
C {C / c} hildren
189 *Never to see my c {C} ountry, ~~friends~~, & s {S} ire,*
they perchance will
190 *Whom ^ for this flight require, {;}*
191 *Of them, {—} for this offense of mine, will make*
192 *An expiation, {—} punished for my sake, {.}*
193 *But t {T} hee, by all the p {P} owers who hold their seat*
194 *In heaven~~,~~ & know the truth, do I entreat*
195 *O King! & by whateer may yet remain*
196 *Among mankind of faith without a stain,*
197 *Have pity on my woes, {;} commisserate*
198 *A mind that n'eer deserved this wretched fate!*

Thus tears prevail;
~~Moved by~~ ~~Moved by these tears~~ we spared the Suppliants life,
M }
~~our~~ Pitying the m } an we spare,
~~prompt~~ ~~And kind compassion yield~~ without a strife;
~~Pr~~ He first of all,
E } d }
~~Him~~ e } ven Priam's self, ~~first issues~~ } the commands
To loose his fetters, & unbind his hands;
W }
Then adds these friendly words; "w } hoeer thou be,
; }
P " *Henceforth forget the Grecians, lost to thee, } "*
— } ~~give truly to mine ear~~
We claim thee now, } & let me truly hear
m } first
Who moved the } ~~Greeks~~ this monstrous Horse to rear,
W }
And why? w } as some religious vow the aim?
what use in might
Or for ~~the~~ war this engine ~~did~~ they frame?
aight }
Strait } were these artful words in answer given,
While he upraised his hands, now free, to heaven.

Eternal fires on you I call: , } O ye
And your inviolable Deity!

[DC MS. 89, 166r]

2d Book
less } ! }
Altars & ruthful } swords from which I fled, }
Ye fillets, worn round my devoted head!
Argive sanctions
Be it no crime if ~~sacred duties~~ cease
To awe me, none to hate the men of Greece!
ei }
The law of Country forfie } ting its hold,
Mine be the voice their secrets to unfold!
And ye O Trojans! keep the word ye gave;
Save me, if truth I speak, & Ilium save!
"The Grecian host on Pallas still relied,
~~Thro' the long aid war her aid their hopes supplied.~~
. }
Nor hope had they but what her aid supplied; }
But all things drooped since that ill omened time
In which Ulysses, author of the crime,
l } i }
Was L } eagued with [? th] } mpious Diomede to seize
I }
That i } mage pregnant with your destinies;
e } holy F }
Tore the Palladium from this } ~~sacred~~ f } ane,

Left margin (vertical): *This by No doubtful signs of wrath Tritonia shewed;* / ~~This by no doubtful signs~~ / *The uplifted eyes with flames coruscant glowed,* / ~~it~~ *her Image* / *Soon as they placed* ~~*that image*~~ *in the camp;* / *And trickled o'er its limbs a briny damp,*

Right margin (vertical): *No more done*

228 *The guards who watched the citadel first slain;*
229 *And, fearing not the Goddess, touched the bands*
brow,
230 *Wreathed round her virgin* ~~*head*~~ *with gory hands;*
No more done
232 ~~*So, from the Grecians turned her mind away*~~
failed the Grecians since
231 *Hope ebbed, & strength* ~~*forsook them from*~~ *that day*
them }
From him } the Goddess turned t~~he Goddess~~ her mind away.
233 ~~No doubtful prodigies Tritonia wrought,~~
For when See Side
235 ~~Soon as that image to the Camp was brought~~
234 ~~The uplifted eyes with fires flames coruscant glowd;~~
236 ~~Along the limbs a briny moisture flowed;~~
237 And from the ground the Goddess, (strange to hear!)
~~with~~ Buckler
238 Leapt thrice—, ~~her~~ ~~target~~ graspd and quivering spear.
bade }
239 *Then Calchas bid* } *to stretch* ~~*the*~~ *homeward sail;*
And prophesied that Grecian would
240 ~~*Pergamus stands Argolic*~~ *Arms* ~~*will*~~ *fail;*
we for should
241 *Unless* ~~*He cries*~~, ~~*till for*~~ ^ *new omens* ~~*ye*~~ *repair*
242 *To Argos, thither the Palladium bear*
thence your ~~*crooked ships*~~ *a*
243 ~~*And crossing then in*~~ *And* ~~*having once again*~~ *re-crossed the*
our curved Sea
~~*And thence your curved ships recross the sea*~~
And thence to
244 *Phrygian shores* ~~*Bring back*~~ *a more propitious Deity.*
recross the Sea Fraught with
245 *Fraught They went; but only to return in power*
246 *With favouring Gods, at some unlooked-for hour.*
Horse
247 *commiserate So Calchas read those signs;—the* ~~*Ship*~~ *was built*
~~*the*~~
248 *To calm Minerva, & atone for guilt.*
F }
249 *Compact in strength you see the f* } *abric rise*
250 *A pile stupendous towering to the skies!*

[DC MS. 89, 166v]

2d Book

251 *This was ordained by Calchas* — } *with intent*
vast
252 *That the* ~~*last*~~ ^ *bulk its ingress might prevent,*
253 ~~*Through gate or walls and Ilium ne'er enfold*~~
'e } *in*
And Ilium nea } *r with her walls enfold*
254 *Another safeguard reverenced like the old.*
255 *For if, unawed by Pallas, ye should lift*

239–303 Autograph not WW's is DW's.

A e
~~Your~~ sacrili } gious hand against the Gift,
The Phrygian realm shall perish; (May the Gods
Turn on himself the mischief he forbodes!)
your town ~~it~~
But if ^ it enter, ~~moving~~ by your aid/
Ascending,—
~~Your~~ ~~The~~ ~~City,~~ Asia, then, in arms arrayed
Shall storm the walls of Pelops, & a fate
As dire on our Posterity await.

so
Even ~~thus~~ the arts/ of perjured Sinon gained,
Belief for this &
~~A Prompt belief for~~ all that he had feigned;
were
Thus ~~And~~ ^ they ~~were~~ won by wiles, by tears compelled,
Whom not Tydides, not Achilles quelled;
Who fronted ten years' war with safe disdain;
'Gainst whom a thousand Ships had tried their strength ~~in~~
in vain!

~~To s~~ To speed our fate a thing did now appear,
& of instant .
Yet more momentous, ~~of more urgent~~ fear, }
Laocooen, Priest by Lot to Neptune, stood
Where to his hand a Bull poured forth its blood
;—
Before the Altar, in high offering, slain, }
But M
~~When~~ lo! two Serpents, o'er the tranquil m } ain
Incumbent, roll from Tenedos, & seek
Our coast together (shuddering do I speak.)
Between the waves their elevated ~~crests~~ breasts
Upheaved In circling spires and sanguine crests
flood
Tower o'er the ~~wave~~; the parts that follow sweep,
In folds voluminous & vast, the Deep.
The agitated brine/ with noisy roar
:
Attends their coming, till they touch the shore. }
Sparkle their eyes suffused with blood; and quick
The tongues/ shot forth/ their hissing mouths to lick.
Dispersed with fear, we fly; in close array
o
These move, & towa'rds Laoc[?] } oen point their way; }
But first assault his Sons, their youthful prey.
A
~~Each~~ several Snake in tortuous wreaths engrasps
^ it /
Each slender frame; and, fanging what ~~he~~ clasps,

[DC MS. 89, 167ʳ]

290 2 *Book* *Feeds on the limbs; the Father rushes on;* ~~*arms in his hand*~~*,*
A } *but*
291 *F* } *rms in his hands, for rescue; & anon*
292 *Himself they seize; and coiling round his waist,*
they bind
293 *Their scaly backs,* ~~*have bound*~~ *him, thrice embraced*
294 *With monsterous spires, as with a double Zone;*
295 *And, twice around his neck in tangles thrown,*
its . }
296 *High o'er the Father's head each Serpent lifts his* ^ *own:* }
{ holy
~~*Behold his*~~ { ~~*sacred fillets*~~
297 ~~*The fillets round his brows*~~*, are* ^ *sprinkled oer*
His priestly fillets thus
298 *With sable venom and distained with gore;*
, } *labouring* *s* } *s*
299 *And* } *while his* ^ *hand* } *the knot*~~*ted gyres*~~ *would rend,*
~~The cries he utters~~ ~~wh which~~
he ; }
300 *The* ~~*He utter'd cries that*~~ *to the Heavns ascend,* }
The cries he utters ^
{ *B* *e* }
301 *Loud as a* { *bull—that, wounded by the ax* },
302 *Shook off the uncertain steel, and from the altar breaks,*
303 *To fill with bellowing voice the depth of air!*
Temple slid
304 *But towards the* ~~*citadel*~~ *the hydra pair* ~~*ha*~~
~~Their mission ended~~, and there ~~lay~~
st }
305 ~~*Have slid, & mid*~~ } ~~*the temple*~~ ^ *lie concealed,*
Their work accomplishd ^
ou
306 ~~*Beneath this*~~ *C*~~*r*~~*ouched at Minerva's feet, beneath her orbed shield.*
O }
307 Nor was there o } ne who trembled not with fear }
308 Or Deem'd the expiation too severe, }
For that Laocoon who had hurld— the
For him who hurl'd that sacrilegious spear; }
Whose hand the sacrilegious weapon
For him whose hand the guilty weapon sped;
Now that the sacred offering
~~gift~~ be
But to the Temple let the ~~gift~~ be led;
Strait to the temple earnest
~~Such with the~~ people ~~was~~ the general cry,
So did the people they ~~said~~ said must calm ask with service high
And prayers ~~be offered to her~~ Deity

304–306 "But towards" is in DW's autograph; for rest of passage, autograph not WW's is MW's.

Or deemed the expiation too severe
him whose hand had flung the ~~sacrilegious~~ guilty
For that Laocoon who had hurled the spear;
Had pierced the texture of the Votive Steed,
For him whose hand the guilty weapon sped;
Which to the temple they resolved to lead;
her
But to ~~the~~ temple be this offering led,
There to be lodged ~~with~~ pomp of service high
To please the People now with earnest cry
And supplications; such the general cry.
~~And prayers they said must calm calm her deity.~~
For him whose lance had pierced S
309 *~~Had pierced the fabric of~~ the votive ~~spear~~ s teed,*
T
310 *Which to the t emple they resolved to lead;*
311 *There to be lodged with pomp of service high*
: .
312 *And supplication, such the general cry—*
313 *The Shattering the walls a spacious breach we make;*
314 *We cleave the bulwarks—toil which all partake.*
315 *Some to the feet the rolling wheels apply;*
.
316 *Some round its lofty neck the cables tie,*
317 *The Engine pregnant with our deadly foes*
the ,
318 *Mounts to breach; & ever; as it goes,*

[DC MS. 89, 167v]

Second Book
319 *Boys mixed with maidens chaunt a holy song,*
!
320 [~~?~~] *And press to touch the cords, a happy throng.*
T
321 *The t own it enters thus, & threatening moves along.*
!
322 *My country, glorious Ilium ; & ye towers*
323 *Loved habitation of celestial powers!*
halted ~~at~~ the gate;
324 *Four times it stopped before the gates—a din*
325 *Of armour four times warned us from within;*
D
326 *Yet towards the sacred d ome with reckless mind*
327 *We still press on, & in the place assigned*
G
328 *Lodge the portentous g ift, thro' frenzy blind.*
~~Nor~~ faild ~~now to~~
Nor ~~failed~~ Cassandra—~~also~~ now to scatter, wide
329 P ^~~Cassandra, too, her words was scattering wide~~

309–328 Autograph not WW's is MW's.
329–330 Revisions are in DW's autograph.

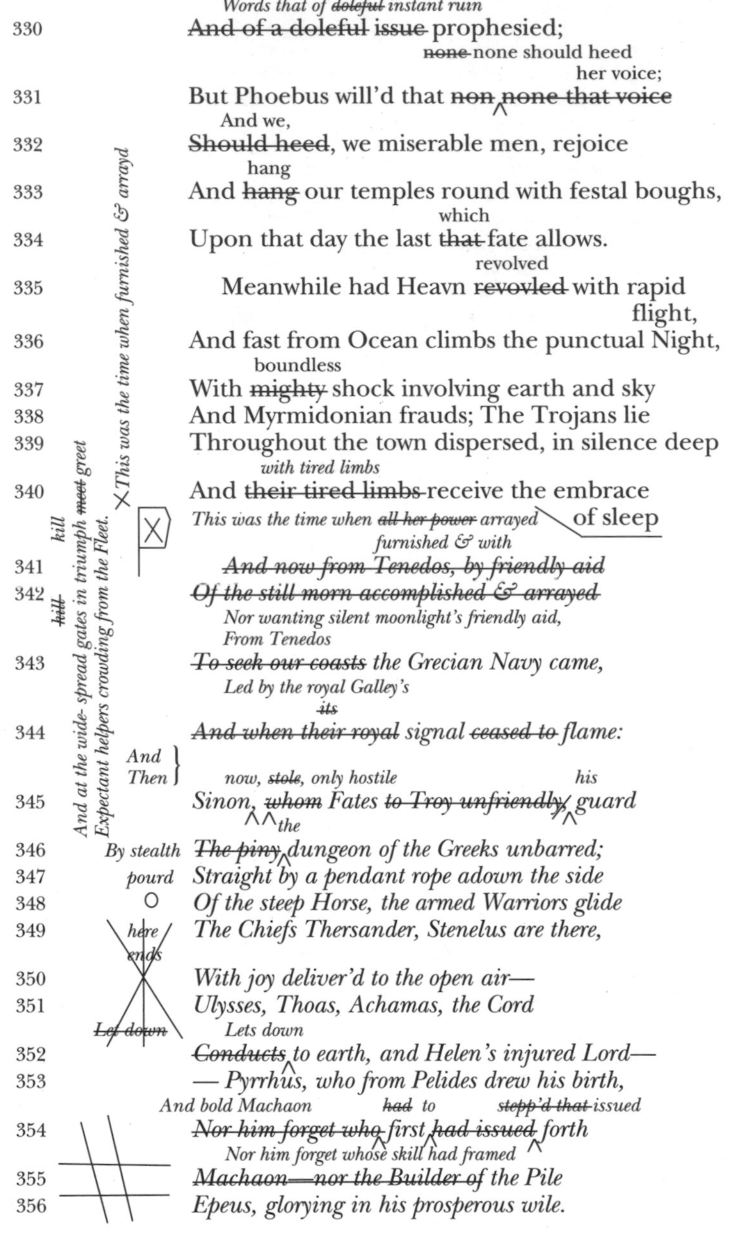

Words that of ~~doleful~~ instant ruin
~~And of a doleful~~ ~~issue~~ prophesied;
~~none~~ none should heed her voice;
But Phoebus will'd that ~~non~~ ~~none that voice~~
And we,
~~Should heed~~, we miserable men, rejoice
hang
And ~~hang~~ our temples round with festal boughs,
which
Upon that day the last ~~that~~ fate allows.
revolved
Meanwhile had Heavn ~~revovled~~ with rapid flight,
And fast from Ocean climbs the punctual Night,
boundless
With ~~mighty~~ shock involving earth and sky
And Myrmidonian frauds; The Trojans lie
Throughout the town dispersed, in silence deep
with tired limbs
And ~~their tired limbs~~ receive the embrace of sleep
This was the time when ~~all her power~~ arrayed
furnished & with
~~And now from Tenedos, by friendly aid~~
~~Of the still morn accomplished & arrayed~~
Nor wanting silent moonlight's friendly aid,
From Tenedos
~~To seek our coasts~~ the Grecian Navy came,
Led by the royal Galley's
~~its~~
~~And when their royal~~ signal ~~ceased to~~ flame:
And Then *now, ~~stole~~, only hostile* *his*
Sinon, ~~whom~~ Fates ~~to Troy unfriendly~~ guard
the
By stealth *~~The piny~~ dungeon of the Greeks unbarred;*
pourd *Straight by a pendant rope adown the side*
Of the steep Horse, the armed Warriors glide
here ends *The Chiefs Thersander, Stenelus are there,*
With joy deliver'd to the open air—
Ulysses, Thoas, Achamas, the Cord
~~Let down~~ *Lets down*
~~Conducts~~ to earth, and Helen's injured Lord—
— Pyrrhus, who from Pelides drew his birth,
And bold Machaon *~~had~~ to* *~~stepp'd that~~ issued*
~~Nor him forget who~~ first ~~had issued~~ forth
Nor him forget whose skill had framed
~~Machaon—nor the Builder of~~ the Pile
Epeus, glorying in his prosperous wile.

[left margin, vertical:] *kill* *~~kill~~* *And at the wide- spread gates in triumph ~~meet~~ greet* / *Expectant helpers crowding from the Fleet.* / *This was the time when furnished & arrayd*

---

340 Autograph of revision is DW's.
341–348 Autograph is MW's, except where noted.
341 Autograph is DW's.
346 "By stealth" and "the" are in DW's autograph.
347–349 "pourd" and "here ends" in left margin in pencil are in DW's autograph; the marginal signals are also in pencil.
349–360 Autograph is DW's.

357 *They rush upon the City that lay still,*
358 *Buried in sleep & wine—the warders kill.* See Side

[DC MS. 89, 168r]

Second Book

It was the earliest hour of slumberous rest,
361 ~~*It was the time in which begins to creep*~~
Gift of the Gods to man with toil oppre {*st* / *ss'd*}
362 ~~*Softly o'er feeble mortals welcome sleep*~~
When present in my dream did Hector rise
363 Boon ~~*Gift of the Gods! when in most doleful guise*~~
364 ~~*Hector amid my dreams appeared to rise*~~ }
365 *And* ^ *stood before* ^ *me with fast streaming eyes.* } ^ *see margin*
A spectacle *how* } ^ ^*sa* } *!* }
370 ~~*Was ever sight*~~ *so* } *pitiably ba* } *d ?* }
371 *How changed from that returning Hector, clad*
glorious spoils Achilles' own proud
372 *In* ^ ~~*all Achilles spoils*~~*,* ~~*his fresh*~~ *attire!*
373 *From Hector, hurling Ship-ward the red Phrygian fire!*
374 *A squall/d beard, hair clotted thick with gore,*
And that same throng of ~~*bleeding*~~ *wounds* — ——— patriot wounds
375 ~~*These signs of injury,*~~ ~~*or highest*~~ *he bore,*
In front of Troy received. And now, methought
376 ~~*And vestiges of many a grisly wound*~~)
~~*That I myself was to a passion*~~ *wrought*
war, }
~~*Gifts of the fight* } *his native walls around.*~~
Of
377 ~~*I gazed upon him to a passion wrought*~~
378 *Of tears, which from my voice this greeting brought.*
379 *O Light of* ~~*the*~~ *Dardan realms! most faithful stay*
To *To* [?] *courage! why this* e } ~~*sad delay*~~ *lingerings of delay?* —
380 ~~*Of Of*~~ *Trojans* ^ ~~*why such lingerings of delay*~~*!*
381 *Where hast thou tarried?* , } ^ *Hector,* ? } *from what coast*
382 *Comest thou,* ; } *long-wished for? that so many lost*
thy kinsmen or & } *loved Compeers*
383 *Thy* ^ *Friends,* ~~*followers, Countrymen*~~ *such travails borne*
~~*Warriors,*~~ *By this* ~~*dejected City*~~ *this afflicted City—we outworn*
384 ~~*By*~~ *Warriors,* ~~*by the city,*~~ ~~*we outworn*~~

[Left margin, vertical, top:]
All else as he'd lifeless corse had lain
What time the Coursers ~~*had*~~ *whirled him o'er the plain*
With thongs, that bound him to the chariot, thrust
Thro' his swoln feet, & black with ~~*sanguinous*~~ *dust*
gory

[Left margin, vertical, bottom:]
fast streaming eyes
Such as he was when horse had striven with horse,
Whirling along the plain his lifeless corse,
The thongs that bound him to the Chariot thrust
Thro' his swoln feet; and black with gory dust
A spectacle how pitiably sad
How changed from that &c

361–456 Autograph not WW's is MW's, except where noted.

361–363 Revision is in DW's autograph, except "Boon" in left margin, which is in MW's autograph.

365–371 Vertical revision, at bottom of left margin, is in DW's autograph; revision at top is MW's.

380 Revision above line is in DW's autograph. Second caret is deleted by erasure.

383 Revision "thy kinsmen or" and ampersand above line are in DW's autograph; "Compeers" above line and "Thy" in left margin are in Dora W's autograph.

384 Revision "Warriors" is in Dora W's autograph; rest of revision is in DW's autograph.

387 Revision above line is in DW's autograph. Revision below line is in Dora W's autograph.

!
385/386 Behold thee? } Why this undeserved disgrace?
~~To~~ Who thus defiled with wounds that honoured face?
{ y
~~And the serene composure of th { at face~~
~~whence these~~ He heard not to detain,
s
387 ~~Why And why keeps every wound~~ } ~~its ghastly place~~?
~~What wounds are these:~~ ^
388 ~~He nought to this—unwilling to detain~~
He nought to this—unwilling to detain
389 One who had asked vain things, with answers vain;
groaning deep,
390 But ~~with deep groan~~, "flee, Goddess-born" he said,
391 "Snatch thyself from these flames around thee spread;
392 Our enemy is master of the walls; d
elevation
393 Down from her ~~height of glory~~ Ilium falls.
Enough for Priam; the long strife is o'er,
394 ~~For more, nor Priam, nor our Country, calls~~
395 Nor does our country ask one effort more.
—
396 Could Pergamus have been defended, } hence,
397 Even from this hand, had issued her defence.
398 Troy, her Penates doth to thee commend,
stores – fates
399 Her sacred ~~the sacred~~ things; let these thy ~~course~~ attend!
400 Sail under their protection for the land
mighty ~~wall~~
401 mighty ~~walls~~ Where ~~potent~~ realms shall grow at thy command.
No more ^ was uttered but his hand he stretched
402 ~~He said, & straight committed to my care~~
came pressing And from the immost sanctuary fetched
403 thither and ~~And from their place of inmost sanctity~~
~~With Vesta brought the fires that may not die~~
404 The consecrated wreathes, the potency
405 Of Vesta, & the fires that may not die.
406 Meantime wild tumults thro' the streets is poured;
though apart & amid thick trees ~~My Father's Mansion stood~~
407 And ~~towards my father's mansion, tho~~' embowered
~~Ap~~art my Fathers mansion ^
408 ~~In shady trees it~~ stood ~~apart~~, the loud alarms
came pressing thither ^ and
409 ~~Thicken~~, ~~& multiplies~~ the clash of arms;

---

388 Revision below line is in DW's autograph.
394 Revision is in Dora W's autograph.
395 Autograph is Dora W's.
401 Revision in left margin is in DW's autograph; revision above line is in Dora W's autograph.
402–403 Revision above line is in Dora W's autograph; revision in left margin, connected with l. 409, is in DW's autograph.
404–405 Autograph is Dora W's.
407 Revisions "though . . . trees" and probably "stood" are in DW's autograph.
408–409 Revision is in DW's autograph.

[DC MS. 89, 168v]

Second Book

410 *Sleep fled,* ; *I climb the roof, & where it rears*
411 *Its loftiest summit, stand with quickened ears;*
412 *As when a fire by raging south winds borne,*
413 *Lights on a billowy sea of ripened corn,*
with
414 *Or rapid torrent sweeps ~~in~~ mountain flood*
415 *The fields, the harvest prostrates, headlong bears the wood;*
416 *High on a rock, the unweeting shepherd, bound*
417 *In blank amazement, listens to the sound:*
was
was ~~is~~ apparent to whom faith ~~is~~ due,
418 *Then ~~perfidy was manifest—the snare~~*
And Grecian plots lie bare to open view.
419 *~~Which by the Greeks contrived lay bare~~*
420 *Above the spacious palace where abode*
i o
421 *Deo phe bus, the flames in triumph rode;*
U
422 *Eu calegon burns next; thro' lurid air*
widening
i en
423 *Sigean Friths reflect a ~~wa nder ing~~ glare;*
424 *Clamor & clangor to the heavens arise,*
425 *The blast of trumpets mixed with vocal cries:*
snatch; weak reason scarcely knows
426 *Arms do I ~~madly seize, with what intent~~*
What aid they promise but my spirit glows;
427 *~~Weak reason knows not, but my soul is bent~~,* ✳
I burn to gather Friends whose firm array
428 *~~A troop to congregate, whose firm array~~*
its
429 *On to the Citadel shall force ~~their~~ way.*
Precipitation works with desperate charms—
430 *~~And to my mind which headlong fury warms~~,*
431 *It seems a lovely thing to die in arms.*

in prompt reply
Said ~~deeply moved~~—tis come—the final hour;
The inevitable close of Dardan power
Hath *Is come:—we have been Trojans—, Ilium was*
And the great name of Troy— ; now all things pass
To Argos:—so wills angry Jupiter

P
Lo ~~Pa~~
432 *But Pantheus, fugitive from Grecian spears,*
Apollo's Priest— his vanquishd Gods he bears
433 *Priest ~~of the sovere~~ign ~~citadel appears,~~*
Phœbus vanquish'd Gods
~~And~~ *~~Priest of Apollo hallowed things he~~ bears,*
And with one hand ~~the other hand~~ his *See Side*
434 *The other* *~~Bears vanquished Gods—his~~ ~~little Grandson leads~~*
The other hand his little Grandson leads
435 *~~And with distract~~ed mind to ~~gain my threshold speeds.~~*
gain
And from the sovereign Fort to gain my my threshold speeds
436 *"Pantheus what hope? which fortress shall we try?*

422 "*Ucalegon*" is written horizontally in left margin.
426–428, 432–433 Revisions are in DW's autograph.
429–430 Revisions are in Dora W's autograph.
434 Revision in left margin is in DW's autograph.

437 *Where plant resistance?" He, in prompt reply,*
~~He in prompt reply & passionately~~
438 *~~Said deeply moved~~ "tis ~~come~~—the final hour,*
~~Thus spake with troubled voice~~
439 *The inevitable close of Dardan power;*
Is come Trojans
440 *~~Trojans we were~~—we have ~~been~~ Ilium was—*
{~~A Town glorious once was Troy~~
{Troy has now fallen do
441 *~~And the great fame of Troy~~—now ^ all things pass* X
~~And the great name of Troy~~
442 *To Argos—so wills angry Jupiter;*
443 *Within the burning t }T own the Grecians domineer.*
444 *Forth from its central stand the enormous Horse*
445 *Pours in continual stream an armed force;*
446 *Sinon insulting leader }Victor aggravates*
hurry thro' the
447 *The flames, & thousands ~~thro' the expanded~~ gates,* X
Thronged, as might seem, with press of all the hosts
448 *~~Press upon thousands—more than voice could name~~*
That ere Mycenæ sent to Phrygian coasts
449 *~~More than from great Mycenæ ever came~~.*
Other with spears in serried files blockade
450 *~~These with thick spears in phalanx set, blockade~~*
es
es;
451 *The passage, }—hangs, with quivering point, the blade,* O
452 *Unsheathed for slaughter—' } scarcely to the foes*
453 *A blind & baffled fight the w }W arders can oppose"*
Urged by these words
454 *~~So Pantheus spake~~; ^ & as the Gods ~~inspire~~*
455 *I rush into the battle, & the fire;*
456 *Where sad Erinnys, where the shock of fight,*

[left margin, vertical:]
Apollo's Priest his
~~Priest of Apollo~~; his vanquish'd Gods he ^ bears *appears he*
hile
And w ith the other hand his Grandson leads
in dismay
He, ~~cold with fear~~, to gain my threshold speeds

[DC MS. 89, 169[r]]

2[d] Book

457 *The roar, the tumult, & the groans, invite;*

437–442 Vertical revision in left margin is in DW's autograph; for base entry see following page).
433–435 Vertical revision, in left margin, is in DW's autograph.
437–438 Revision is in DW's autograph.
440 Revision is in DW's autograph.
441 Revisions "Troy has now fallen" and "do" are in Dora W's autograph; "A Town glorious once was Troy" is in DW's autograph.
447–450 Revision is in Dora W's autograph.
454 Revision is in Dora W's autograph.
456 "where the shock of fight," is in Dora W's autograph.
457–484 Autograph is Dora W's, except where noted.

458 *Ripheus is with me, Epytus the pride*

joins his aid, and ;

459 *Of battles ~~adds his succour~~— to my side*

ani

ni

460 *Flock Dymas, Hypamu s, the moon their guide;*

461 *With young Chorœbus who had lately sought*

a b

462/463 *Our walls by passion for Cassandre w rought;*

464 *He led to Priam an auxiliar train,*

465 *His Son, by wedlock; miserable Man*

~~him a~~ whom a

466 *For ~~whom his~~ raving spouse had prophesied in vain.*

W these collected intent

467 *Whom w hen ^ I saw these ~~thus~~, & ^ ~~bent~~*

468 *To face the strife with deeds of hardiment,*

Champions

469 *I thus began; "O ~~Warriors~~ vainly brave*

470 *If like myself to dare extremes ye crave,*

~~You see Our lost condition is before your sight:~~

471 ~~*Behold our Fate this empire is bereft*~~

~~The Gods to whom this Empire owed its might;~~

~~From shrines and altars, all have taken flight.~~

472/473 ~~*Of all her guardian Gods their altars they have left*~~

You see our lost condition—not a God

Of all the Powers by whom this Empire stood

But hath renounced his Altar. F f led from his abode

Ye would uphold

Fled from his abode a City wrapped in fire

uphold

~~protect~~ a city

Y ~~uphold~~ ^

474 ~~*The city*~~ *y e would aid is wrapped in fire;*

On Die rather, let us rush— ~~combat~~

475 *Go ~~for our choice must be~~ in battle to expire;*

s

476 *At least one safety h hall the vanquished have*

477 *If they no safety seek but in the grave!—*

478 *Thus to their minds was fury added; then,*

er

479 *As Wolves driven forth by hung ar from the den,*

prowl

480 *To ~~hunt~~ amid blind vapours, whom the brood*

481 *Expect, their jaws all parched with thirst for blood,*

482 *Thro' flying darts, thro' pressure of the foe,*

483 *To death, to not uncertain death, we go.*

T midway

T own a ~~central~~ course we bear,

484 *Right thro' the ~~city hold our central way~~*

485 *Aided by +* ~~*Our helpers*~~ *hov'ring darkness, & despair.*

459–460 Revision is probably in DW's autograph.
466 "whom a" may be in DW's autograph.
471–474 Vertical revision in left margin, is in DW's autograph.
474 Revisions above line may be in MW's autograph.
475 Revisions above line may be in MW's autograph.
480 "prowl" is in MW's autograph.
484 Revisions are in MW's autograph, except "T" overwrite.
485–535 Autograph not WW's is MW's, except where noted.

486 P *Can words the havoc of that night express?*
487 *What power of tears may equal the distress?*
488 *An ancient c* {C} *ity sinks & disappears*
489 ~~*A city dominant thro' length of years*~~
490 *~~*Her streets are filled with carnage*~~*; & the abodes*
491 ~~*Of men, the hallowed thresholds of the Gods,*~~
492 ~~*With lifeless trunks are every where endlessly bestrown*~~*:*
493 ~~*Nor do the suffering Trojans bleed alone*~~*;* [*are* ~~*doomed to*~~]
494 *The vanquished sometimes to their hearts recall*
495 *Old virtues, & the conquering Argives fall—*

An ancient city sinks to disappear
X She sinks who ruled {for} thro' ages,—far & near
The unresisting, through the streets, the abodes
Of Men—and hallow'd Temples of the Gods, :
Are fill'd with massacre that takes no heed,
Nor are the Trojans only doom'd to bleed;

[DC MS. 89, 169v]

Second Book

497 ~~*skaith*~~ *skaith* *Sorrow is every where, & fiery* *scathe* {*caith*}
496 *Fear, a* {A} *nguish struggling to be rid of breath,*
498 *And d* {D} *eath still crowding on the s* {S} *hape of d* {D} *eath.*
499 *Androgea* {u} *s, whom a numerous* ~~*train*~~ *force attends*
Was the first Greek we met; he rashly deems us Friends;
First ~~*met us crossed*~~ ~~*our way, he deems us Grecian friends*~~
in ~~*this sort he*~~ *hails* ~~*he*~~
500 ~~*And as a friend thus hails us*~~ *Haste friends!—away*
501 ~~*With these unworthy falterings of delay*~~ ~~*Warri*~~*ors, haste!—*
~~And cries, what sloth retards you?~~
502 *Troy blazes, sacked by others & laid waste;*
503 *And ye come lagging from your ships the last!*
504 *Thus he—& straight* ~~*alarmed by*~~ *mistrusting our replies*
505 *He felt himself begirt with enemies.*
506 *Voice failed, step faultered—at the dire mistake;*
507 *Like o* {O} *ne who, thro' a deeply-tangled brake*
508 *Struggling, hath trod upon a lurking s* {S} *nake;*
509 *And shrunk in terror from the unlooked-for pest*
510 *Lifting his blue-swoln neck & wrathful crest;*
511 *Even so Androgeo* {u} *s, smit with sudden dread,*
512 *Recoils from what he saw, & would have fled;*

Was the first Greek we met; he rashly deems us friends;
~~And cries, "What sloth retards you? Warriors haste!~~
What sloth, he cries, retards you? Warriors, haste!

the troop
513 *Forward* *We rush{ , ~~upon the troop~~—with arms^ surround, : }*
M
514 *The m}en surprized, & ignorant of the ground,*
515 *Subdued by fear, become an easy prey;*
So
516 *~~Thus~~ are we favoured in our first essay.*
517 *With exultation here Corœbus cries;*
bright
518 *Behold O friends how ~~fair~~ our destinies!*
—
519 *Advance, }the road which they point out is plain;*
& bear the insignia of the
520 *Shields let us change, ~~with those whom we have~~ slain,*
Grecians in semblance—
521 *~~Adopt the Grecians bearings~~; wiles are ~~good~~ lawful—who*
To simple valour would restrict a foe?
522 *~~As valour, where a foe must be withstood~~.*
sha *when* ~~This promptly~~
523 *Themselves wi}ll give us arms; ere} this was said,*
s up
524 *The Leader's helmet nod{~~ded~~ on his head,*
i
525 *The emblazoned buckler on his arm is t{ried;*
526 *He fits* *An Argive falchion ~~fitted~~ to his side!*
527 *The like with Rypheus, Dymas; all put on,*
528 *With~~e~~ eager haste, the spoils which they had won.*
529 *Then in the combat mingling, Heaven averse* *Authour*
~~darkness mingling~~ gloom a multitude
530 *Amid the ~~gloom of night~~ ~~the Greeks~~ ^ we pierce,*
And to the shades dismiss them. ^Others
531 *~~Send many to the shades;—some shipward~~ flee,*
532 *Appalled by this imagined treachery;*
Some to the ships some ~~with~~
533 *~~A dastard few would~~^ in the horse would hide—*
Ah who can *Ah what reap they but sorrow who confide*
534 *stand where Heavn* *~~Ah let not living mortal living eer confide~~*
~~Ah~~ ~~tremble~~ if *ir* ~~sanction~~
535 *~~In aught to which the Gods there}countenance~~*
In aught to which *the Gods their sanction* *have denied?*
C
536 Behold Cassandra, Priam's royal c}hild
e
By sacrili}geous men
537 ~~Dragg'd from Minerva's Shrine,~~ with hair all wild;
T
538 *Dragged from Minervas temple! t}owards the skies*

---

530 Revision "darkness mingling" is in Dora W's autograph.
531 Revision is in Dora W's autograph.
533 Revision "Some to the ships" is in Dora W's autograph; "some with" may be in DW's autograph.
536–542 Revisions are in MW's autograph.

[DC MS. 89, 170^r]

lifts
2^d Book *The Virgin ~~raised~~ in vain her glowing eyes*
539 *~~She lifts to Heaven her glowing eyes in vain;~~*
540 *~~Her eyes for manacles the~~ Her eyes—she could no more—for Grecian bands*
~~restrain~~
541 *~~Yet for^her^tender hands have felt the chain~~*
Had rudely manacled her tender hands.
542 *The intolerable sight to madness stung*
543 *Corœbus, & his desperate self he flung*
ruthless foe
544 *For speedy death the ~~embattled Host~~ among!*
545 *We follow, — & with general shock assail*
less hostile throng: here first ;
546 *The ~~ruthful foe~~^but now our efforts fail,*
~~As~~ While F
547 *~~For~~^from the summit of the lofty f ane*
the
548 *Darts, by our people flung, descend amain,*
In miserable heaps their friends are laid;
549 *~~Most wretched slaughter of their friends is made~~*
550 *By shew of Grecian arms/ & crests betrayed.*
551 Wroth for the Virgin rescued, by defeat
552 Provok'd, the Grecians from all quarters meet;
Combating there unite
553 *~~The onset to renew;~~^the brother Kings, ~~&~~*
554 *And thither Ajax all his fierceness brings,*
By the Dolopians followed W
555 ~~Yea the whole host is gathering~~ As w inds fly
556 *To charge from adverse quarters of the sky,*
~~Eurus to conflict~~ ~~While~~
557 *Notus; & Zephyrus ~~& Eurus born~~ ~~and to battle born~~*
~~Insulting Eurus speeds his coursers~~ *while Eurus feeds*
558 *~~Eurus On coursers from the regions of the morn~~*
The strife, exulting on his orient steeds;
559 *Woods roar, ~~the trident where the conflict raves~~*
and foamy Nereus^stirs the waves,
560 *~~By Nereus weilded, into foamy waves,~~*
Rowzed by his trident from
~~Bestirs the waters in~~^their lowest caves.
561 *They also, whomsoe'er thro' shades of night*
a
562 *Our stratu gem had driven to various flight,*

[Left margin, vertical:] *~~Woods roar. The Trident from into foamy waves~~*

543–554 Autograph not WW's is MW's.
556–560 Autograph not WW's is Dora W's, except where noted.
557 Revisions "and to battle borne" on line and "while Eurus feeds" below line are in MW's autograph.
558–559 Revision is in MW's autograph.
559 Vertical revision, in left margin, is in DW's autograph.
560 Revision not WW's is in MW's autograph.
561–581 Autograph not WW's is MW's, except where noted.

{our
~~our borrowed arm~~{~~or they marked~~
563 *Appear ^ ~~by them our bucklers are first known~~* }
the first by ^ whom our shields are known.
564 *The simulating jav'lins they disown*
And mark our utterance of discordant tone. }
their }
565 *~~They mark our speech discordant from our~~ } ~~own~~;* }
fallen *Numbers on numbers bear us down;*
566 *~~By numbers are we overwhelmed~~; & first*
~~sinks~~, falls,
567 *Corœbus ^ him Peneleus hath pierced*
568 *Before Minerva's Altars; next in dust*
Sinks *one*
569 X *virtuous* *Rypheus ~~is laid~~ ^ above all Trojans just*
X righteous above all
570 *And ~~careful of the right~~; but heavenly Powers*
~~accord~~
Ordain by lights *agree*
571 *~~Judge by a rules that~~ ill ~~assort~~ with ours.*
anis F}
572 *Then Dymas, Hyp~~amus~~ ~~by friends~~ are slain by f }riends;*
573 *Nor thee abundant piety defends*
{e
~~round th{y hair~~
falling with the ~~priestly garland fair~~
574 *O Pantheus, ~~his that priestly garland fair~~ in*
~~holy~~ garland wound,
575 *~~Wreath which thy own Apollo bade thee wear~~*
575 *As fits Apollo's Priest, thy brows around.*
eous
{eo
576 *~~A~~ Ashes of Ilium! & ye, dut{ius fires*
577 *Lit for my friends upon their funeral pyres;*
578 *Amid your fall, bear witness to my word,*
~~turns of war, no~~ Grecian
579 *I shunned ^ no ^ hazard of the ~~Grecian~~ sword;*

[DC MS. 89, 170v]

No turns of war, with hand unsparing fought
Second Book *out*
580 *~~Fought with no wish to spare this vital breath~~*

---

563 Revision above line is in Dora W's autograph.
566 Revision above line, except "fallen," is in Dora W's autograph.
570 Revision above line is in Dora W's autograph; "virtuous" in left margin is intended to replace "righteous."
574 Revision "falling with" is in JC's autograph; other revision, above and below line, is in Dora W's autograph.
579 Revision "turns of war, no" is in JC's autograph.
580 Revision "out" is in JC's autograph.

earn'd the death I sought!
581 *And ~~fairly merited~~, had fate so willed, ~~my death~~*
582 Thence am I hurried by the rolling tide
583 *With Iphilus and Pelias ~~by the crowd~~* at my side
One bowed with years;
~~Thence am I torn hurried: Iphilus is bowed~~
~~[?One] slow with years~~
584 *~~With weight of years~~, and Pelias, from a wound*
585 *Given by Ulysses, halts along the ground.*
Abode
586 *New clamours rise, the ~~Seat~~ ~~Seat~~ of Priam calls*
thousands
587 *Besieged by ~~Græcians~~ swarming round the walls;*
how
588 *Concourse ~~as~~ thick! as if throughout the space*
war
589 ∗ *Of the whole City, ~~none~~ in other place*
hushd ~~still~~ no death elsewhere The assailants wield
hushed *above th*
590 *Were ~~silent, no one dying~~ ~~Shield lock'd in shield~~*
~~A shell wise tortoise~~ ~~Above their~~ head shields shell-wise locked in shields
591 ~~Shell-wise the assailing force a covering build;~~
step near ~~to~~ the side
592 Climb step by the ladder ~~as they stand~~
~~Before the~~ ~~Threshold~~ Portal
593 Of the strong ~~entrance~~ daringly applied;
~~Each~~ *weaker* its
594 The ~~The weaker~~ hand ~~the~~ guardian shield presents
595 The right is stretchd to grasp the battlements;
tug
596 The Dardans ~~tug~~ at roof and turrets high
frag
597 Rend para ments off, and with these weapons try
;
598 Life to preserve in such extremity,
599 Roll down the massy rafters, deckd with gold,
Magnific splendors ~~Resplendent~~ splendors *raised by* Kings
600 raised Magnific ~~heritage~~ ~~from~~ ~~lines~~ of old;
601 Others with naked weapons stand prepared
602 In thick array the doors below to guard.
603 A bolder hope inspirits me to lend
My utmost aid P
604 ~~What aid I may~~ the p alace to defend,
afflicted
605 And strengthen the~~se oppressd~~. ~~A Postern Gate~~
From behind

[Left margin, vertical:]
A ∗ *Were hushed, no death elsewhere. The assailants wield*
Above their heads shields shell wise locked in shield;
Climb step by step the ladders near the side
Of the strong ~~side~~ Portal daringly applied;
The weaker hand its guardian shield presents

583–590 Autograph not WW's is JC's, except where noted.
584 Revision is in Dora W's autograph.
587–588 Revision is in Dora W's autograph.
590 Revisions "hushed," "The assailants wield," and "above th," above line, are in Dora W's autograph, as are revisions below line. Revisions "still no death" and "hushd," above line, may be in DW's autograph.
590–594 Vertical revision, in left margin, is in Dora W's autograph, except "A" overwrite.
594 Revision "weaker" is in Dora W's autograph.
600 Revision not WW's is in Dora W's autograph.
604 Revision is in MW's autograph.
605–606 Revisions above and below lines are in MW's autograph.

606 ~~There was that stood from notice separate,~~
{whence
~~From~~ *A gateway opened o* {*n* *a passage blind*
From }
606 ~~And~~ } ~~which ap passage intricate and blind~~
607 The various Mansions of the Palace joined.
608 Unblest Andromeda while Priam reigned
609 Oft, by this way the royal presence gained,
610 A lonely Visitant; this way would tread
611 With young Astyanax, too his Grandsire led.

[DC MS. 89, 171[r]]

2[d] Book *2 Book*

tered
612 ~~*By this seques thoroughfare I clomb*~~
the gate
612 ~~*And reached the very summit of the dome*~~
^ Entering ~~by this~~, I reached the roof where stands
~~*From which the miserable Trojans stand*~~
~~ling~~ The Trojans, hurling their
613 *Hu~~rrying~~ ~~their~~ darts with ineffectual hands*
A }
~~There was~~ a } *Tower ~~created~~ ~~there~~ there was precipitous the scite*
614 ~~*A tower was near upon a lofty*~~ *site* ~~*pr*~~
And the Pile rose to an unrivalled height
615 ~~*Precipitous, itself of matchless height*~~
Frequented station whence in circuit wide
616 ~~*Station whence whosoeer might gaze descried*~~
Troy might be seen ~~in~~ the ~~hostile~~ fleet descried
Argive
617 ~~*(As many wont), all Troy in circuit wide*~~
And all the & sovereign
618 ~~*Beheld*~~ ~~*The*~~ *Achaian camp ~~far spread~~, ~~& Grecian fleet~~) this Tower—*
{ower W}
619 ~~*This t{imber tower w} here timbers walls & beams hid*~~
With irons, grappling where the
~~*There, where the timbers for its*~~ *loftiest floor*
~~Lighted~~ on ~~we shake & rend~~
620 ~~*Had been inserted*~~ ~~*Rested within the walls the point where hook*~~
Pressed with its beams the wall we shake we rend
[619] ~~*And grappling iron easiest fastening took*~~
We join
[620] ~~*With all our might & main to shake & rend*~~

612–625 Autograph of base text is MW's; autograph of revisions is Dora W's, except where noted.
612 Revisions "tered" and "I reached the roof where stands" are in MW's autograph.
613 Revision is in MW's autograph.
618 Revisions "Beheld" and "this Tower—" are in MW's autograph.
619 Revisions on line are in MW's autograph.
620 Revisions on line are in MW's autograph.
[620] Revision is in MW's autograph.
[612]–[625] Autograph is Dora W's.

And in a mass of thundering ruin send [ous]
621 *~~Down doth the Mass with thunder ing voice descend~~*
To crush the Greeks beneath
622 *~~And buries all beneath~~. But numbers press*
623 *To new assault with reckless eagerness*
624 *Weapons & missiles From the ruins grow*
625 *And what the {ir y hasty hands can seize, they throw!*
[612] *Entering th {is e gate I reached the roof where stand*
[613] *The Trojans, hurling darts with ineffectual hand.*
[614] *A Tower th {re ee was, precipitous the scite,*
[615] *And the Pile rose to an unrivalled height;*
[616] *Frequented s {S} tation whence in circuit wide*
[617] *Troy might be seen, the Argive fleet descried,*
[618] *And all the Achaian camp. t {T} his sovereign Tower*
[619] *With irons, grappling where the loftiest floor*
[620] *Pressed with its beams the wall, we shake—we rend—*
[621] *And in a mass of thundering ruin send*
[622] *To crush the Greeks beneath. But numbers press*
[623] *To new assault with reckless eagerness:*
[624] *Weapons & missiles from the ruins grow;*
[625] *And what their hasty hands can seize they throw!*
626 In front stands Pyrrhus glorying in the might
627 Of his own weapons, while his armor bright
628 Casts from the portal gleams of brazen light.
629 So shines a Snake when kindling he hath crept
630 For {th from the winter bed in which he slept,
631 Swoln with a glut of poisonous herbs; but now,
nual
632 Fresh from the shedding of his ~~antient~~ slough,

[DC MS. 89, 171v]

m
633 Glittering with youth warn ^ [?~~glossy~~] with instinctive fires
~~surging~~
634 *2d Book* ~~He coils his burnish'd burnished back in towering gyres~~
He, with raisd breast, involves his back in gyres
635 Darts out his forked tongue and towrd the sun aspires
~~With the~~ Join'd with redoubled
~~phas~~ Periphas
636 ~~Joined in the assault with Perifus~~ comes on
~~Automedon doughty charioteer~~
637 ~~That Chief, redoubtable~~ Automedon,

636–644 Autograph not WW's is Dora W's.
649–652 Autograph is MW's.

To storm the palace, here ~~steeds~~ *Car*
638 *Who drove the Achillean* ^ ~~*Car;*~~ — *the bands*
Sc } *Car*
639 *Of Sy* } *ros next follow hurling fiery brands.*
hath seized an
yrrhus *e labouring* }
640 *P~~hyrr~~us himself* ~~*with*~~ [?] } *axe would cleave*
The ponderous doors or from their hinges heave.
641 ~~*The doors or from their hinges heave,*~~
^ ~~*his iron with persevering stroke*~~ reiterating stroke on stroke
642 *And now* ^ ~~*thro' brazen plate & solid oak*~~
^ *thro' plates of brass & solid* ~~*oak;*~~ oak,
643 *Hath hewed* ~~*an opening with repeated stroke*~~.
A broad mouthed entrance ~~*opening entrance*~~ — to { their / the } inmost seats
644 ~~*A broad mouthed aperture; ;the rent is made*~~
The long drawn courts lie open, the retreats
645 ~~And the long courts appear, retreats amply displayed~~
of Priam and ancestral Kings are bared
~~The House of Priam to its inmost seats~~
~~The House of Priam~~
{ ~~there~~ s }
~~Of Priam~~ or { ~~lies lies open~~ } the retreats
Opens
~~Appears~~ the House of Priam
646 And privacies of an~~tient Kings~~ are bared,
~~And the long~~ courts reveald;
: } armed
647 ~~To instantaneous view;~~ } ~~within~~ the Guard
To instantaneous view; and so the guard ^
648 Stands at the Threshold for defense prepared.—
~~*But tumult spreads*~~
649 *But tumult spreads thro' all the space*
peat *the* *within*
650 *The* ~~*/*~~ *valted roofs re~~sound~~* ~~*with*~~ *mournful din*
Ul } *strange*
651 *lamentations* *Of female You* } *ulations; a* ~~*wild*~~ *vent* ~~*of agony*~~
s }
~~*clamour*~~ } *of agony that*
652 *Of* ~~*agony that*~~ *strikes the starry firmament.*
~~The Matrons~~ Wildering the matrons range the spatious floors
Urgd on by fear distracted as they roam
wide Embrace and print their kisses on [?]
Through the ~~wide~~ chambers of the royal dome
~~Throughout the Matrons~~
trembling
653 The ~~wildering~~ Mothers clasp the doors & fix
~~Enclasp the doors with farewell hold~~
654 Kisses Motherly their last embraces mix
Embrace & print their kisses ~~on~~ the doors
in
655 Pyrrhus, ~~with~~ all his Father's might, dispels
656 Barriers and bolts and living obstacles
. } The are thrown b~~atter'd down~~
657 Force shapes her own clear way; } ~~the~~ doors ~~are thrown~~
~~Fall to the ground, from off their hinges thrown~~

[Left margin, vertical:] The Matrons range with wildering step their floors, / Embrace and print their kisses on the doors.

[Right margin, vertical:] ~~wildering~~ wildly wandering / The Matrons ~~farewell kisses~~ fix / That as they clasp the doors with the { ir / re } embraces mix

705–749 Autograph is Dora W's, except where noted.

658/659 ~~Off from their hinges—gates are battered down;~~
Off from the hinges, gates are batterd down
660 By the inrushing soldiery, who kill
Whom broad
661 ~~The~~ first they meet & the ~~wide~~ area fill.
662 A ~~The~~ foaming river that hath burst its mounds
663 Spreads with like Fury thorough the ravagd grounds
carrying
664 Herds sweeping with their stalls whereer it swells
[663] ~~Flood rushing upon flood in billowing heaps~~
rushing ~~rising~~ ~~over~~ billowy
Flood ~~rushing upon~~ flood in ~~billowy~~ heaps
~~As over~~

[DC MS. 89, 172r]

2d Book *2 Book*

662 Less irresistibly oer dams and mounds
663 Burst by its rage, a foam {y ing River bounds.
664 Herds sweeping with their stalls along the ravag'd grounds.
665 Pyrrhus I saw with slaughter desperate;—
near
666 The two Atridæ ~~at~~ the palace gate
Did I o
667 ~~These eyes~~ behe }ld, and by these eyes were seen
M
668 The hundred Daughters, and the m}other Queen;
669 And hoary headed Priam where he stood
670 Beside the altar, staining with his blood,
671 Fires which himself had hallow'd. Hope had he,
672 None equal hope, of large posterity;
There
673 ~~Of bridal~~ fifty bridal chambers might be told,
674 Superb with trophies and barbaric gold:
lie
675 All, in the pomp, are }levelled with the ground,
676 And where the fire is not, are Grecian Masters found.
O
677 Ask Ye the fate of Priam? o}n that night
~~burnd~~ ~~blazd~~ blazd
678 When captured Ilium ~~burnd~~ before his sight; ar
679 And the foe, bursting through the palace gate,
680 Spread through the privacies of royal state,
681 In vain to tremulous shoulders he restord
682 Arms which had long forgot their antient Lord,
683 And girt upon his side a useless sword;
684 Then thus accoutred forward did he hie,
685 As if to meet the enemy and die.
ie
686 Amid the courts an altar stood in vei}w
687 Of the wide heavns, near which a long-livd laurel grew;

his
And, bending over t{hat great altar, made/
For its Penates an embracing shade.
D
With all her d}aughters throngd, like Doves ~~doves~~ that lie
~~Hecuba with her Daughters as doves fly~~
Cowering, when storms have driven them from the skie,
~~Headlong for a shelter from a stormy place,~~
~~ing with all her Daughters, like Doves~~
~~Throng'd for close consort to that sacred place~~
Hecuba shelters in that sacred place
~~Cleave and~~ the statues of the Gods embrace.
n
Where they}the
But when she saw, in youthful arms arrayed,
Priam himself; what ominous thought she said,
Hangs wretched Spouse this weight on limbs decayd?
~~Put, on these arms, what feelest thou,~~ if we were
And whither wouldst thou ~~hurry~~ hasten? if
More ~~wretched~~ still this succour we might spare
helpless
D
No such d}efenders doth the time demand.
Profitless here would be even Hectors hand

[DC MS. 89, 172v]

2d Book
Retire, this altar ~~will~~ can protect us all,
Or Thou wilt not survive when we must fall."
This to herself; and to the sacred spot
M
She drew the aged m}an to wait their common lot.
But see Polites one of Priam's sons
Charged with the death which he in terror shuns!
The wounded Youth, escaped from Pyrrus, flies
Thro' showers of darts, thro' press of enemies,
Where the long Porticos invite: the space
Of widely vacant courts his footsteps trace.
~~Whom~~ ~~While~~
~~Him~~ Pyrrus/ following near & still more near
Him at the the
Hath caught ~~at~~ with ~~his~~ hand, & presses with ~~his~~ spear.
But, when at length this unremitting flight
Had brought him full before his Father's sight,
He fell & } scarcely prostrate on the ground,
Poured forth his life from many a streaming wound.

726 Horizontal revisions in left margin are in DW's autograph.

Death &
Here ~~aged~~ Priam, scorning self regard
His voice restraind not, nor his anger spar'd;

~~whom no dangers might~~
~~abstain'd not at this sight~~; respect
Then Priam's ~~voice rejecting all controll~~
Let ~~loose in words the passions of the his soul~~
~~Of danger gave free passage to his soul~~
Of ~~danger flying~~ from a soul uncheck'd
Yet shall the Gods, he cries, if Gods there be
such
Who note ~~these~~ acts & care for piety
true
Requite this heinous crime with measure ~~due~~
Nor one reward withhold that is thy due
Who thus t
~~With us~~ a Father's presence has {t} *defil~~l~~ed*
f} C}
And F {f} *orced upon his sight the murder of a c* {C} *hild.*
thus *a*
versed / *~~V Used~~* *Not ~~he~~ Achilles self from whom ~~thy~~ tongue*
~~Used~~ to vain-glorious falsehood, ~~boasts~~ thee [?]
~~Of truth regardless boasts that thou has~~ sprung
~~Delt~~ Dealt with an enemy, my prayers he heard
~~New enmity like this; when I appeared~~
A suppliants rights in Priam he reveared
Gave Hector back to rest within the tomb
And me remitted to my royal home.
M}
This said, the aged m {M} *an a javelin~~g~~ cast*
With weak arm—faltering to the shield it past;
The tinkling shield the harmless point repelled,
Which, to the boss it hung from, barely held.
h S}
Then Pyr^rus, "To my s {S} *ire Pelides bear*
These feats of mine ill relished as they are
Tidings of which I make the messenger.

[DC MS. 89, 173[r]]

2[d] *Book*

To him a faithful history relate 2 *Book*
Of Neoptolemus degenerate;
S}
Now die!" s {S} *o saying to'wa'rds the Altar, thro'*
S}
A Stream of fillial blood the tottering s {S} *ire he drew,*
His left hand locked within the tangled hair
~~dazzling flashing glittering~~
the *~~sword corus corus~~cant in mid*
Raised with ~~his~~ right a brandished sword in air
sword coruscant in ~~mid~~ mid air.
Then to the hilt impelled it thro' his side;—
Thus mid a blazing city Priam died:
Troy falling round him thus he closed his fate;

759 Revision is in MW's autograph.

Once the proud Lord of many an Asian state;
F
Upon the shore lies stretched his mangled f } rame;
B
Head from the shoulders torn, a b } ody without name.
[?Stop]
Then first it was that Horror girt me round
my my
Chill'd ~~the~~ frail heart and all ~~the s~~enses bound;
The image of my Father crossd
~~My Father's image flash'd across~~ my mind;
Perchance in fate with slaughter'd Priam join'd;
Equal in age thus may He breathe out life;
Creusa also, my deserted Wife!
C
The c } hild Iulus left without defence—
And the Whole House laid bare to violence!
Backward I look'd & cast my eyes before,
had faild
My Friends ~~were gone~~ and courage was no more;
All, wearied out had follow'd desperate aims,
stifled ~~stifled~~
Self dash'd to earth ~~or buried~~ in the flames
/ P such
Thus was I left alone, ~~those~~ light my guide
As the conflagrant walls and roofs supplied;
falsehood
When my far-wandering eyesight chanc'd to meet
Helen sequester'd on a lonely seat
Amid the Porch of Vestal. She, through dread
Of Trojan vengeance amply merited,

[DC MS. 89, 173v]

2d Book
Of Grecian punishment, and what the ire
H
Of a deserted h } usband might require,
H
Th } ither had flown, there sate—the common bane
Of ~~Grec~~ Troy and of her country, to obtain
Protection from the altar, or to try
H
What h } ope might spring from trembling secrecy.
Methought my falling Country cried aloud,
And the revenge it seemed to ask, I vowed;
"What shall she visit Sparta once again?
In triumph enter with a royal train?
Consort
Blank ~~Husband~~ and home and Sires and children view;

764 Revision is perhaps in DW's autograph.
834–836 Vertical revision, in left margin, is probably in DW's autograph.

F
779 By Trojan f }emales serv'd a Phrygian retinue
t
780 For this was Priam slain? Troy burn'd }? the shore
781 Of Dardan seas so often drench'd in gore?
782 Not so; for though such victory can claim
783 In its own nature no reward of fame,
784 The punishment that ends the guilty days
W
785 Evn of a w }oman, shall find grateful praise;
786 My Soul at least shall of her weight be eas'd
ashes
787 The ~~Spirits~~ of my Countrymen appeasd.—
Such
788 These words broke forth and in my own despite }
bore
789 Onward I ~~rushd,~~ when through the dreary night }
gracious
790 Appeard my Mother, vested in pure light; }
791 Never till now before me did she shine
792 So much herself so thoroughly divine;
~~as she is wont to move~~
794
793 Goddess | ~~reveald in all the beauty, love~~
A Shape | [?courts] of Jove
795 ~~And Grace~~ ^ ~~familiar to the Powers~~ above.
lifted
796 She ~~seized my bitter hand its wrath~~ ^to ^stay ^
The hand she seiz'd her touch sufficed to
{ is greeting
797 Then And through her roseate mouth th {ese ~~words~~
~~these~~ these ~~words~~ found way
easy way

Goddess revealed in all her beauty love
And majesty as she is wont to move
A shape familiar to the Courts of Jove

798 O Son what pain excites a wrath so blind
all
799 Or ~~How~~ could ~~all~~ thought of me desert thy mind?
Where now is left thy Parent worn with age
801 ~~Wilt thou not first thy nearer task engage~~
800 ~~First~~ ~~First seek a Father left in helpless age?~~
Wilt thou not rather in that search engage

[DC MS. 89, 174[r]]

802 Learn with thine eyes if yet Creusa live?— *2 Book*
803 And if the boy Ascanius still survive?
Them do
804 ~~All these~~ the Greeks environ; that they spare }
805 That swords so long abstain and flames forbear }
806 Is through the intervention of my care. }
807 Not Spartan Helen's beauty so abhorr'd
808 By thee, nor Paris her upbraided Lord
grandeur
809 The ~~Gods of~~ hostile Gods have laid this e~~mpire l~~ow

{s
810 Troy from the Gods recive{ her overthrow.
811 Look! for the impediment of misty shade
812 With which thy mortal sight is overlaid
813 I will disperse; nor thou refuse to hear
Parental n
814 ~~A Parents~~ mandates, ^or resist through fear.
Th}
815 H }ere, where thou see'st block ~~up~~ rolling upon block
con}
816 Mass rent from mass, and dust im }dens'd with smoke
817 In billowy intermixture, Neptune smites
T} es.}
818 The walls, with labouring t }rident disunite }
tearing ~~laying bare~~
819 From their foundation, ~~plucking~~ up as suits
Ilium from her deepest
C} deepest
820 His anger, the Whole c }ity from her^roots
ier}
821 F[?] }cest of all before the Scæan gate Scæan ×
Fiercest / beckoning ~~beckoning~~ to animate
822 Arm'd Juno stands ~~before the Scæan Gate~~ ×
~~Even fiercer shall~~
~~Fiercest of all & beckoning~~
822/823 Beckoning ~~auxiliar tr~~ bands to animate
~~Auxiliar bands and urge them from their~~
823 ~~As they press on full slowly from their fleet;~~
The She}
~~Auxiliar~~ bands & }summon from thei~~r fleet~~ Argive fleet
824 Tritonian Pallas holds her chosen seat
825 High on the Citadel—, look back—see there

Her forces ~~and summons from the Argive fleet~~
Auxiliar bands & summons from their fleet
× The Bands she summons from the Argive fleet

beaming forth {ormy [?~~round~~]
826 Her Ægis ~~casting round~~ a st {[?irring] glare:—
827 The very Father, Jove himself, supplies
sends heaven-born enemies
828 Strength to thei~~r~~ Greeks i~~ncites the Deities~~
M}
829 Against the Dardan arms; m }y Son! take flight!
830 And take close the struggle of this dismal night!
831 I will not quit thy steps whateer betide
832 But to thy Father's house will safely guid:
d}
833 She ceased and m }id in shades her presence
hide

[DC MS. 89, 174v]

2d Book

and Deities
834 Dire faces still appear ~~before my~~ eyes
Advers to her ~~the~~ mighty enemies
835 ~~The mighty Foes of~~ Troy, the adverse Deities

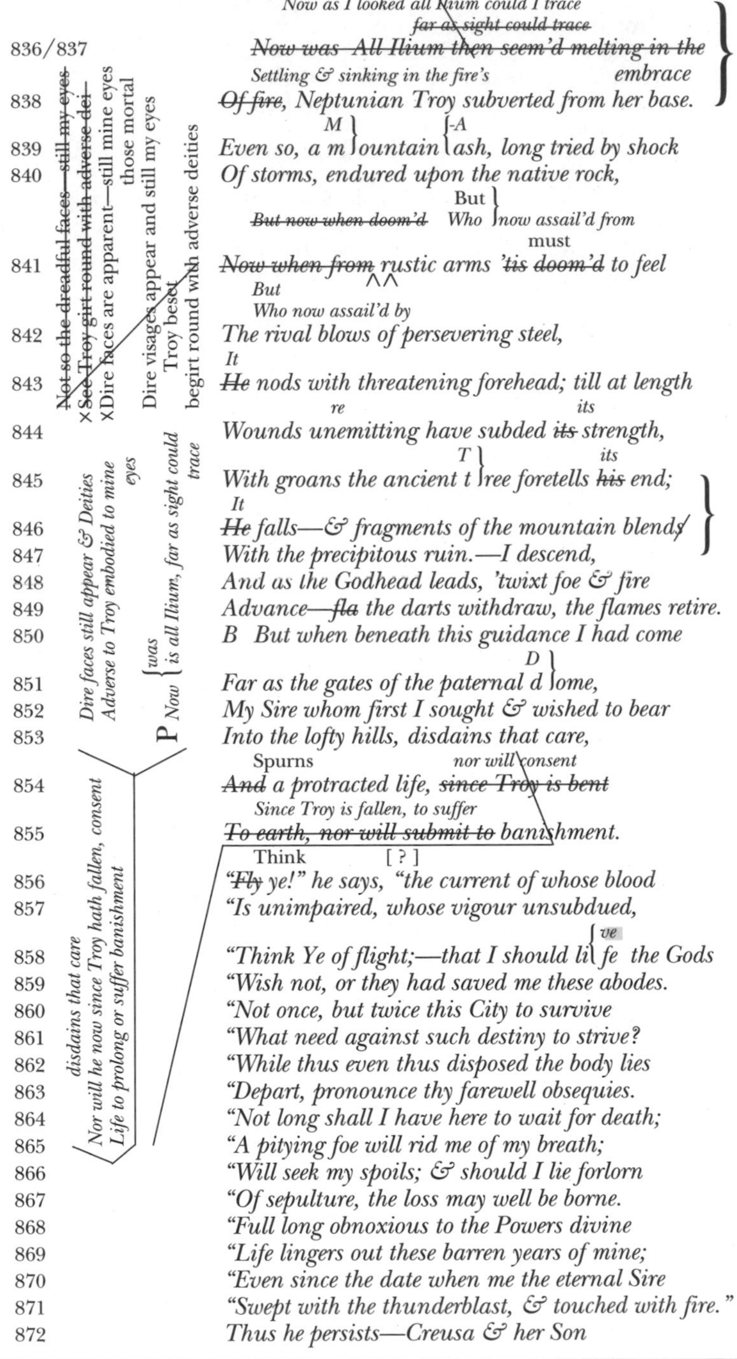

Now as I looked all Ilium could I trace
~~*far as sight could trace*~~
~~*Now was All Ilium then seem'd melting in the*~~
Settling & sinking in the fire's *embrace*
~~*Of fire*~~*, Neptunian Troy subverted from her base.*
M *-A*
Even so, a m ountain ash, long tried by shock
Of storms, endured upon the native rock,
But
~~*But now when doom'd*~~ *Who now assail'd from*
must
~~*Now when from*~~ *rustic arms* ~~*'tis doom'd*~~ *to feel*
But
Who now assail'd by
The rival blows of persevering steel,
It
~~*He*~~ *nods with threatening forehead; till at length*
re *its*
Wounds unemitting have subded ~~*its*~~ *strength,*
T *its*
With groans the ancient t ree foretells ~~*his*~~ *end;*
It
~~*He*~~ *falls—& fragments of the mountain blends*
With the precipitous ruin.—I descend,
And as the Godhead leads, 'twixt foe & fire
Advance—~~*fla*~~ *the darts withdraw, the flames retire.*
B But when beneath this guidance I had come
D
Far as the gates of the paternal d ome,
My Sire whom first I sought & wished to bear
Into the lofty hills, disdains that care,
Spurns *nor will consent*
~~*And*~~ *a protracted life,* ~~*since Troy is bent*~~
Since Troy is fallen, to suffer
~~*To earth, nor will submit to*~~ *banishment.*
Think [?]
"~~*Fly*~~ *ye!" he says, "the current of whose blood*
"Is unimpaired, whose vigour unsubdued,
ve
"Think Ye of flight;—that I should li fe the Gods
"Wish not, or they had saved me these abodes.
"Not once, but twice this City to survive
"What need against such destiny to strive?
"While thus even thus disposed the body lies
"Depart, pronounce thy farewell obsequies.
"Not long shall I have here to wait for death;
"A pitying foe will rid me of my breath;
"Will seek my spoils; & should I lie forlorn
"Of sepulture, the loss may well be borne.
"Full long obnoxious to the Powers divine
"Life lingers out these barren years of mine;
"Even since the date when me the eternal Sire
"Swept with the thunderblast, & touched with fire."
Thus he persists—Creusa & her Son

[Left margin, written vertically:]
~~Not so the dreadful faces—still my eyes~~
× ~~See Troy girt round with adverse dei-~~
× Dire faces are apparent—still mine eyes
those mortal
Dire visages appear and still my eyes
Troy beset
begirt round with adverse deities

Dire faces still appear & Deities
Adverse to Troy embodied to mine
eyes
P *Now* { *was* / *is all Ilium, far as sight could*
trace

disdains that care
Nor will he now since Troy hath fallen, consent
Life to prolong or suffer banishment

836–1079 Autograph not WW's is by MW.

Second the counter-prayer by me begun;
The total house with weeping, deprecate
This weight of wilful impulse given to Fate;
He all unmoved by pleadings & by tears
Guards his resolve & to the spot adheres.

[DC MS. 89, 175r]

I turn to arms death
Second Book ~~I rush~~ ~~to battle~~, death alone
purpose P *"Once more* ~~*to arms*~~, ~~*I covet*~~ ~~*death, the one*~~
object none ⊹ My wish and purpose now, ~~all other~~
Comforter ~~*Remaining hope & chance*~~, *all others gone."*
hast {d
"And ~~*didst*~~ *thou hope*{ *that I could move to find*
"A place of rest, thee Father left behind,
"How could parental lips the guilty thought unbind?
C} H}
"If in so great a ~~*place*~~ *c* }*ity h* }*eaven ordain*
Utter extinction; if thy soul retain
With stedfast longing that abrupt design
Which would to falling Troy add thee & thine,
;—}
That way to death lies open— } *soon will stand*
h
Pyrrus before thee with the reeking brand
{; {H
That drank the blood of Priam{ {*he whose hand*
The }
Her } *Son in presence of the Father slays,*
And at the Altar's base the slaughtered Father lays.
For this, benignant Mother! did'st thou lead
; }
My steps along a way from danger freed? }
M }Men
That I might see remorseless ~~*m*~~} ~~*en*~~ *invade*
; }
The holiest places that these roofs oershade? }
C }
See Father, c }*onsort, Son all tinged & dyed*
, }
With mutual sprinkling }~~*s*~~ *perish side by side?*
; } ! }
Arms bring me, Friends! } *bring Arms:* } *our last hour speaks,—*
It calls the vanquished; cast me on the Greeks!
In rallying combat let us join—not all,
This night, unsolaced by revenge will fall!
{*sumes*
The sword re{[?] *its place, the sheild I bear*
And hurry now to reach the open air;
When on the ground, before the threshold cast
Where
Lo ~~*Behold*~~ *Creusa hath my feet embraced,*
And holding up ~~*Creu*~~ *Iulus, there cleaves fast!*

(Written vertically in the left margin beside lines 880–889:) Once more do arms attract me; death alone / My wish and purpose now, all others gone!

907 *If thou departing be resolved to die,*
908 *Take us thro' all that in thy road may lie;*
909 *But if on arms already tried attend*
H
910 *A single hope,* ~~*let*~~ *then first this h*} *ouse defend;*
911 *On whose protection Sire & Son are thrown;*
W
912 *And I, the w* }*ife that once was called thine own!*
M
913 *Such outcry filled the m* }*ansion; when, behold*
strange portent, &
914 ~~*A prodigy, far*~~ *wonderous to be told!*
915 *All suddenly a luminous crest was seen;*
B
916 *Which, where the b* }*oy Iülus hung between*
917 *The arms of each sad parent, rose & shed,*
lustre
918 *Tapering aloft, its* ^ *from his head!*
919 *Along the hair the lambent flame proceeds*
920 *With harmless touch & round his temples feeds!* *no more done*

[DC MS. 89, 175v]

2 *Book*

921 *In fear we haste, the burning tresses shake*
e
922 *And from the fount the holy fir*{ *es would slake;*
joyfully his hands
923 *But* ~~*glad*~~ ^ *Anchises raised,*
924 *The voice not silent as on heaven he gazed.*
925 P *Almighty* ~~*Almighty*~~ *Jupiter if prayers have power*
seek
926 *To bend thee, look on us, I* ~~*ask*~~ *no more;*
927 *If aught our piety deserve, O deign*
The hope this omen proffers to sustain.
928 ~~*Thy help, nor Father let us sue in vain*~~*,*
secondsecond
~~*Nor Father*~~ ~~*Nor*~~ ~~*let us ask a further*~~ *sign* ~~*in vain*~~
y
929 ~~*Confirm thes*}*ℯ omens & the hope sustain*~~*!*
Nor Father let us ask a second sign in vain.
930 P. *Thus spake the Sire, & scarcely ended, eer*
A peal of sudden thunder
931 ~~*Upon the left it thundered*~~ *loud & clear*
Broke from the left, & shot
932 ~~*Crash of the moment;*~~ ~~*when*~~ ^ *thro' heaven a star*
933 ~~*Shot like torch*~~*. Trailing its torch that sparkled from afar:*
this star, conspicuous sight
934 *Above the roof* ~~*it*~~ ~~*ran the*~~ *s*[?] ~~*sylvan height*~~
y
Ran to be hid on ~~*Id the*~~ *Idas s*{*ilvan height*
935 ~~*Of Ida seeking thro the gloomy night*~~
The long
936 ~~*And its*~~ ^ *way marking with a train of light;*

937 *The furrowy track the distant sky illumes;*
938 *And far & wide are spread sulphureous fumes.*
ris'n *aged*
939 *Up~~rose~~ from earth my ~~conquered~~ Sire implores*
940 *The Deities, the holy star adores, {:}*
am I conquered—now is
941 *"Now, ~~now" he cries in me is~~ ^ no delay;*
942 *"Gods of my Country, where ^ ye lead the way,*
Tis not in me to hesitate or swerve!
943 *~~"I in that course will neither stop, nor swerve~~:*
Ye Powers,
944 *"Preserve my house, ^ this little One preserve!*
945 *"Yours is this augury; & Troy hath still*
946 *"Life in the signs that manifest your will, {:}*
~~can~~
947 *~~"I yield—nor will refuse my Son to be~~*
~~ready~~
948 *~~A willing partner of the way with thee~~*
~~I yield~~
947 *I cannot chuse but yield; & now to t{T}hee*
948 *O Son, a firm associate will I be!*
949 *He spake; & nearer thro' the c{C}ity came,*
950 *Rolling more audibly, the sea of flame:*
951 *"Now give, dear Father, to this neck the freight*
952 *Of thy old age; {—} the burthen will be light*
my
953 *For which ~~these~~ shoulders bend; henceforth one fate,*
954 *~~Henceforth one~~ Evil or good, shall we participate.*

[DC MS. 89, 176r]

Second Book

955 *The Child wi{sha}ll journey tripping at my side;*
956 *Our steps, at distance marked, will be Cer{re}usa's guide; {.}*
957 *My Household! heed these words;—u{U}pon a mound*
958 *(To those who quit the c{C}ity obvious ground)*
959 *A temple, once by Cer{es/[?]} honoured, shows*
960 *Its mouldering front; hard by a cypr{ess/us} grows,*
961 *Thro' ages guarded with religious care. {:}*
962 *Thither, by various roads, let all repair.*
963 *Thou, f{F}ather, take these relics; {!} let thy hand*

of
Bear the Penates to } our native land;
I may not touch them, fresh from deeds of blood,
Till the stream cleanse me with its living flood.
an ample vest
Forthwith^ my shoulders ~~with a vest were~~ clad;
Above the vest a lion's skin was spread;
B
Next came the living b } urthen; fast in mine
His little hand Iulus doth entwine,
~~Cre~~ Following his father with no equal pace;
Creusa treads behind; the darkest ways we trace:
And me, erewhile insensible to harms,
Whom adverse Greeks agglomerate in arms
Moved not, now every breath of air alarms;
All sounds have power to trouble me with fear,
Anxious for whom I lead, & whom I bear.
G igh
Thus, till the g } ates were n { ear, my course I shaped,
And thought the hazards of the time escaped;
When thro' the gloom a noise of feet we hear,
Quick sounds that seemed to press upon the ear;
"Fly," cries my Father looking forth, "O fly!"
They come,—I see their shields & dazzling panoply.
Here in my trepidation was I left,
Through
~~By~~ some unfriendly Power, of mind bereft;
For, whilst I journeyed devious & forlorn,
From/ me, me wretched was Creusa torn;
Whether stopped short by death, or from the road
She wandered, or sank down beneath a load
Of weariness, might proof be sought in vain;
She vanished—ne'er to meet these eyes again.

[DC MS. 89, 176v]

Second Book

Nor did I seek her lost, nor backward turn
My mind, untill we reached the sacred bourne
. A
Of ancient Ceres, } a } ll, even all, save One
Were in the spot assembled; she alone,
As if her melancholy fate disowned
Companion, Son, & husband, no where could be found.
?
Who, man or God from my reproach was free; }
Had desolated Troy a heavier woe for me?

careful
1000 *Mid ~~chosen~~ friends my Sire & Son I place,*
1001 *With the Penates of our Phrygian race,*
1002 *Deep in a winding vale; my footsteps then retrace.* }
1003 *Resolv'd the whole wide city to explore,*
1004 *And face the perils of the night once more.*

[margin, written vertically:] So ~~girt in more refulgent arms~~ I haste / with refulgent arms begirt

girt with {*s—* *I seek*
1005 *So ~~clad in~~ ~~fu~~ arm*{ *~~our~~ ~~towards~~ the walls I haste*
Towards *feet*
1006 *~~And~~ the dark gates thro' which my s~~teps~~ had past;*
ground
1007 *Remeasured where I may the beaten ~~road~~ ~~the beaten ground~~*
1008 *And turn~~ed~~ at every step a searching eye around.*
{*s*
1009 *Horror prevail*{*ed* *on all sides, while with dread*
1010 *The very silence is impregnated!*
F} *M*}
1011 *Fast to my f* } *ather's m* } *an~~sion~~ I repair~~ed~~*
,}
1012 *If haply—* } *haply she had harboured there.*
Seized by the Grecians was *A*}
1013 *~~Greeks rushing in had seized~~ the entire a* }*bode,*
And now *o*}
1014 *~~Save where~~, voracious fire its mastery she* }*wed.*
rolled upward *in flames that*
1015 *~~In flames that~~ by the wind ~~rolled upwards~~, meet;*
the roof;—
1016 *High oer ^ air rages with the heat;*
T}
1017 *Thence to the t* }*owers I pass, where Priam held his seat.* }
{*œ*
1018 *Already Ph*{*enix & Ulysses kept,*
G}
1019 *As chosen g* }*uards, the ~~wealth~~ spoils of Ilium, heaped*
1020 *In Juno's temple, & the wealth that rose*
1021 *Piled on the floors of vacant porticos;*
H}
1022 *Prey torn thro' fire from many a secret h* }*old,*
V} *massy*
1023 *P* }*ests, tables of the Gods, & cups of ~~solid~~ gold;*
round
1024 *And in long order ~~mid~~ these treasures stand*
B} *Y*}
1025 *Matrons & b* }*oys, & y* }*ouths, a trembling band!*
did I
1026 *No Nor spare~~d I then~~ with fearless voice to raise*
1027 *Shouts in the gloom, that filled the streets & ways;*
1028 *And, with re-duplication sad & vain,*
1029 *Creusa called, again & yet again;*
1030 *While thus I prosecute an endless quest,*
S}
1031 *A s* }*hape was seen, unwelcome & unblest;*
S}
1032 *Creusa's s* }*hade appeared before my eyes,*
I}
1033 *Her i* }*mage, but of more than mortal size;*

~~*she to stop my troubles at their source*~~
1034 *Then I, as if the power of life had passed*
1035 *Into my upright hair, stood speechless & aghast.*

[DC MS. 89, 177[r]]

thus }
2[d] *Book* *She spake* } *—to stop my troubles at their source;*
1036 *"Dear Consort why this* ~~*frantic*~~ ~~*course*~~ ~~*pursue*~~
fondly desperate course
1037 ~~*Thus she began*~~, ~~*my trouble to subdue*~~
1038 *Supernal Powers, not doubtfully prepare*
going hence thou wilt
1039 *These issues;* ~~*thou will go but may'st*~~ *not bear*/
with thee; know that
1040 *Creusa* ~~*hence*~~; ~~*controling*~~ *fate denies*
R }
1041 *This fellowship, & this the r* } *uler of the skies.*
1042 *Long wandering's will be thine, no home allowed;*
V }
1043 ~~*And*~~ *v* } *ast the extent of sea that must be ploughed,*
~~*And*~~ *Ere*
1044 ~~*Ere*~~ *mid Hesperian fields where Tiber flows*
~~*will*~~ *tired*
1045 *With gentle current,* ^ *thy* ~~*tired*~~ *keels repose.*
meets *R* } *B* }
1046 *Joy* ~~*waits*~~ *thee there; a r* } *ealm & royal b* } *ride;*
1047 *For loved Creusa let thy tears be dried;*
i }
1048 *I go not where the Myrmy* } *dons abide:*
Derived from Jove
1051 ~~*A Dardan bed*~~, *& raised by thee so high*
a
1052 *Spouse to the offspring of* ~~*the*~~ *Deity;*
M }
1049 *No proud Dolopian m* } *ansion shall I see*
1050 *Nor shall a Grecian Dame be served by me;*
1053 *Far otherwise; upon my native plains*
1054 *Me the great Mother of the Gods detains.*
1055 *Now, fare thee well! protect our son, & prove*
1056 *By tenderness for him, our common love.*
1057 P | *This having said my trouble to subdue,*
; }
1058 | *Into thin air she silently withdrew,* }
1059 *Left me while tears were gushing from their springs,*
tongue
1060 *And on my* ~~*lips*~~ *a thousand hasty things;*
1061 *Thrice with my arms I strove her neck to clasp;*
1062 *Thrice had my hands succeeded in their grasp.*

~~*Only to lose her subtile image light as the*~~
From which the image slipped away, as light
(in) ~~*As the swift winds or sleep when*~~ *taking flight;*
Such was the close & now the night thus spent,
~~*Back to my friends I sped, when thus had worn out night.*~~
F
Back to my f *riends an eager course I bent;*
And here ~~*And here*~~ *a marvellous number I behold*
Of new Associates, concourse manifold!
atrons
Mothers , *& men, & youth that hither hied,*
:
For exile gathering; *& from every side,*
wretched people thronged & multiplied.
The ~~*multitude*~~ ~~*poured*~~ ~~*in, a pitiable tide*~~*!*
Prepared
~~*All bent*~~ *with mind & means their flight to speed*
Across the seas, where I might chuse to lead,
P *Now on the ridge of Ida's summit grey*
Rose Lucifer, prevenient to the day!
— *The Grecians held the gates in close blocade,*
u
Hope was there none of giving fa *rther aid;*
I yielded, took my Father up once more;
F
And sought the mountain with the f *reight I bore. End 2*[d] *Book*

[DC MS. 89, 177[v]]

3rd *Book*

177[v] "3[d] Book" at top center of page is in DW's autograph. Apparently, this space was intended for the opening 101 lines of Book III. Probably because of insufficient space, those lines were never recopied here.

[DC MS. 89, 178r]

~~Amid the Sea there lies~~
3rd Book *In the mid Deep there lies a*
~~There is an Isle, a pleasant~~ spot of earth
{e i
Sacred to her who gave the N{eareads birth
And to Ægean Neptune. Long was toss'd
This then unfruitful ground, & driven from coast to coast
But as it floated o'er the wide-spread Sea
The archer God in filial piety
Between two Sister Islands bound it fast
For man's abode, and to defy the blast.
Thi }
Fur }ther we steer. At length the unruffled place
Received our Vessels in her calm embrace
when
We land—and ~~while~~ the pleasant soil we trod
the
Adored the City of^Delian God.
—} —(} whose brows were
Chief (}Anias, the King, } ~~his temples~~ wreathed around
garland
With ~~sacred~~ laurel^& with fillets bound)/
His sacred Symbols as {'s
~~The King who served~~ Apollo{ ~~as his~~ priest)
;}
Advanced to meet us, from our ships released, }
{h
He recognised Anc{yses; & their hands
Gladly they join, renewing antient Bands
Of hospitality; nor longer waits
The King, but leads us to his friendly gates.
To seek the Temple was my early care,
To whose Divinity I bowed in prayer
Within the reverend Pile of ancient stone;—
"Thymbreus! painful wanderings have we known
to} *U} the e} their*
Grant to} ~~u~~s} weary, dwi} llings of ~~our~~ own!
A City yield, a Progeny insure;
A habitation destined to endure!—
—To us, sad relics of the Grecian sword,
(All that is left of Troy—) another Troy ~~afford~~ accord.
What shall we seek? Whom follow? where abide?
+an augury our course to
Vouchsafe+some trusty omen for our guide
Father, descend; & through our spirits glide!"—
entire
—Then shook, or seemed to shake, the ~~whole~~ abode
A trembling seized the laurels of the God
&} s}
The mountain rock'd—a } sound } with murmuring swell
'd} swell
Rolls } from the Shrine:—upon the ground I fell

102–182 Autograph is DW's.

138 {And / As} *heard the guiding voice our fates foretell*

[DC MS. 89, 178v]

3 Book

Dardans
139 *"Ye patient ~~Dar~~ Trojans! that same Land that bore*
140 *Your first progenitors in days of yore*
141 *That ancient Mother will unfold her breast*
142 *For your return—seek her with faithful quest*
Æ L
143 *So shall the E} noan l} ine command the earth*
144 *As long as future years to future years give birth.*
145 *Thus Phoebus answered, and, forthwith, the Crowd*
146 *Burst into transport vehement & loud:*
147 *All ask what Phoebus wills; and where the bourne*
148 *To which Troy's wandering Race are destined to return.*
149 *Then spake my aged Father, turning o'er*
150 *Traditions handed down from days of yore* X

X *'Give ear," O Chieftains! while my words*
Unfold the hopes this Oracle affords
On the mid sea th

O
153 *"I} n the mid Sea the Cretan Island lies*
154 *Dear to the sovereign Lord of earth & skies*
M
155 *There is the Idean m} ount, & there we trace*
156 *The fountain-head, the cradle of our race.*
157 *A hundred Cities, places of command,*
158 *Rise in the circle of that fruitful land;*
(
159 *Thence to Rhœtean shores, } if things often heard*
)
160 *I faithfully remember, } Tucer steered,*
(*first Progenitor* ( ) *where* *and*
161 } *Our ~~primal Father;~~* } —[? *~~whence~~*]} *~~he~~ chose a spot,*
162 *His Seat of government, when Troy was not;*
housed *While yet the Natives hou~~sed~~sed in vallies deep*
[? *~~housed~~*]
163 *~~Nor then had risen the tutelary Keep~~*
Ere Pergamus had risen, to crown the lofty Steep
164 *~~Of Pergamus;—they dwelt in vallies deep.~~*
f } *~~with~~*
F } *rom Crete we gain'd*
165 *—From Crete came Cybele & all the Train*
All that the Mother of the Gods ordain'd
166 *~~Of Ceremonials which her laws ordain~~;*
167 *The Corybantian Cymbals thence we drew;*
168 *~~To~~The Idean Grove; & faithful Silence, due*
rites { *ous;*
169 *To ~~royal~~ mysteri* { *es and the Lion Pair*
Ruled *from*
170 *~~Yoked~~ by the Goddess to* } *her awful Car.——*
171 *Then^/ haste the Mandate of the Gods obey*
172 *And to the Gno/ssian Realms direct our way;*
173 *But first the Winds propitiate; &, if Jove*

Throne
From his high ~~Seat~~ the enterprize approve,
The third day's light shall bring our happy Fleet *~~shores~~*
~~So near the shores~~ ~~On the third day so near the Coast of~~ Crete,
To [?] safe harbour on the shores of Crete
~~We in her Ports shall lodge, a happy Fleet~~,
He spake; appropriate Victims forth were led
And by his hand upon the Altars bled;
A Bull to soothe the God who rules the Sea—
O
A Bull, o bright Apollo! fell to thee;
doth he smite
A sable Sheep to Hyems next he slew:
purest white
To the soft Zephyrs, one of ~~snow white~~ hue

[DC MS. 89, 179r]

3d Book *~~To the~~*
told *would*
Fame ~~tells~~ ^ that regions may ^ in Crete be found
Bare of the foe deserted tracts of ground,
to recent flight
Left by Idomeneus, ~~who lately chased~~
~~paternal~~ *Driven from those realms his patrimonial right*
~~From his own realm, to distant lands had past~~.
Cheared by a hope those vacant seats to gain
We quit the Ortigian Shore, & scud along the main;
Near *traversed by a rout*
~~By~~ ridgy Naxos, ~~Naxos overswept~~
Of *with* *~~course~~*
~~With~~ madding Bacchanals, our ~~way we kept~~ ^ song & shout
sa
By green Donyia rising o'er the deeps
Olearus & snow-white Parian steeps
Flying with prosperous sail thro' sounds & seas
Starred with the thickly-clustering Cyclades.
Confused & various clamour rises high;
they
"To Crete & to our Ancestors" we cry
with
While Ships & Sailors ~~with~~ each other vie.
ing
Still freshen~~ed~~ from the stern the breezes blow,
speed *Barks they chase wheree'r we go*
And ~~chase~~ ^ the ~~vessels~~ ~~stirring as~~ ^ ~~they go;~~
Till rest is given, ^ upon the ancient shores/
Of the Curetes, to their sails & oars.—

183–201 Autograph not WW's is MW's, except where noted.
198–199 Revisions are in DW's autograph.

* I
202 So with keen hope we trace a circling wall;
and the new City by a name which all
203 ~~The wished-for City Pergamus I call~~
204 Repeat with gladness Pergamus I call
205 ~~And the rejoicing People I exhort~~
The thankful citizens I then exhort
206 To love their hearths, and raise a guardian Fort:
207 The Ships are drawn ashore; with eager hands see margin
S
208 The s ettlers occupy the allotted lands
209 And some prepare for hymeneal bands.
210 I plan our new Abodes, fit laws declare/laws declare
New seats I fix for dwellings but more deadly plague
a sudden ~~corruption tainted the wide corrupted~~ the wide air
plague
211 But now ~~a deadly plague corrupts the air~~ tainted
T piteous were ~~air~~ our limbs
212 Our limbs t o ~~sudden~~ wasting ~~are~~ betrayed
On trees and plants the deadly season preyed.
213 ~~Trees droop'd, & sickened every rising blade~~
214 The men surrender'd their dear lives; or, life ~~remaining~~
feeble
215 Remaining, dragg'd their limbs in ~~weary~~ strife
216 Thereafter Syrius clomb the sultry sky
field
~~Parch'd the herbs every herb to bare sterility~~
218 ~~And forcing earth her produce to deny~~
Parched every herb to bare sterility
217 ~~Parch'd every field to bare ste~~rility.
ly
218 And forced the sick~~ening~~ corn its nurture to deny.
My anxious Sire exhorts ~~now~~
219 ~~My Father urged us then~~ to seek once more
220 The Delian shrine & pardon thence implore
221 Ask of the God to what these sorrows tend
222 ~~How we may~~ Whence we must look for aid, our voyage whither bend.

223 'Twas night, & couch'd upon the dewy ground
224 The weary Animals in sleep were bound
225 When those Penates which my hands had snatchd
226 From burning Troy, while on my bed I watch'd
Appear'd & stood before me
227 Before me stood in vision to my sight
228 Made manifest by copious streams of light.

[Vertical revision, left margin, lines 202–210:]
But pestilence now came & tainted the wide air
To piteous wasting were our limbs betrayed
On trees & plants the deadly season preyed
relinquish'd their dear
The men re~~signed their precious~~ lives or life
Remaining dragged their frames in feeble strife.

[Vertical revision, left margin, lines 211–221:]
The Fleet is drawn ashore; in eager bands
cultivate
The Settlers ~~occupy~~ the allotted lands,
And some for Hymeneal rites prepare;
declare
I plan our new Abodes, fit laws ~~prepare;~~
But pestilence now came ~~to~~ and tainted the wide air

202–251 Autograph not WW's is DW's, except where noted.
211–215 Vertical revision, in left margin, is in MW's autograph.

[DC MS. 89, 179v]

3d Book

Thus did they speak; "we come the delegates
Of Phoebus to foretell thy future fates
~~What from I~~
Things which his Delian tripod to thine ear
Would have announced, thro' us he utters here

Pour'd from the body of the full-orb'd moon
chamber
That thro' the loop-holes of my ~~window~~ shone
Thus they appeared & spake. "Thy future fates
discloses by
Phoebus ~~foretells~~ ~~through~~ ~~us~~, his Delegates
through us to thine ear
Uttering^the ~~very~~ words which ~~to thine ear~~ ~~thou would'st~~ hear
He would impart should'st thou to Delos steer
When Troy was ~~built~~ burnt we cross'd the billowy sea
Faithful Attendants on thy arms, & we
Shall raise to Heaven thy proud Posterity
But thou thy destined wanderings stoutly bear
And for the Mighty, mighty Seats prepare
These thou most leave—Apollo ne'er designed
That thou in Crete a resting place should'st
find
There is a Country styled by Men of Greece
Hesperia—strong in arms—the soil of large increase
Œnotrians held it; men of later fame
Call it Italia from their Leader's name
Our
Thy home is there; there lies the native place
Of Dardanus & Jaseus, whence our race.
Rise then; & to thy aged Father ~~bear~~ speak
{bid
~~Th~~ Indubitable tidings;— {let him seek
The Ausonian Land, & Corithus;—Jove yields
place a}
No ~~rest~~ to us u}mong Dictean fields

Known was each face I looked on seen each head
With fillets bound) while gelid damps oerspread
These trembling limbs) I started from my bed—
And heavenward stretched in prayer my hands supine

Upon the sacred spectacle I gazed
~~Amazed & smitten to my inmost heart~~
And heard the utterance of the Gods amazed
~~By sight & sound (for sleep had here no part;~~
Sleep in this visitation had no share
~~Known was each form I looked on; present were~~
Each face I saw—the fillets round their hair
~~The Deities; & seen the their faces seen & hair~~
Chilled with damp fear I started from my bed;
{hich
Which ~~W{ith fillets bound, while gelid damps oerspread~~
And, & voice
~~Not silent~~ raised my hands^to heaven: then shed
~~These trembling limbs) I started from my bed~~
~~heavenward stretched~~ ~~in prayer~~
~~And stretched toward the heavens my open~~ ~~my hands supine,~~
Upon my hearth, the pure untempered wine
Then}
~~And~~} ~~poured upon the hearth untempered wine~~
A prompt libation for the powers divine.

231–234 Vertical revision, in left margin, is in MW's autograph.
252–279 Autograph is MW's, except where noted.

260 *This rite performed with joy, my Sire I sought,*
261 *Charged with the message which the Gods had brought;*
262 *When I had opened all in order due,*
263 *The truth found easy entrance; for he knew*
Ancestors, the
264 *The double ~~Parents &~~ ambiguous race,*
265 *And owned his new mistake, in person & in place.*
266 *Then he exclaimed, "O Son! severely tried*
fated
267 *In all that Troy is ~~destined~~ to abide,*
268 *This course Cassandra's voice to me made known*
269 *She prophesied of this, & she alone*
270 *~~She c~~ Italia oft she cried, & words outthrew*
271 *Of realms Hesperian to our Nation due.*

[DC MS. 89, 180r]

3d Book *~~Yet how believe that Phrygians ere should~~ gain*
~~A fix'd Abode upon the Hes~~perian plain
272 *But how should Phrygians ~~powe~~ such a power erect*
273 *~~I heard the Prophetess but faith was checkd~~,*
{Whom
{To did Cassandra's sayings then affect?
274 *Now let us yield to Phoebus, & pursue*
happier
275 *The ~~better~~ lot he offers to our view.*
276 *All heard with transport what my Father spake;*
277 *This habitation also we forsake;*
strait
278 *And ~~now~~, a scanty remnant left behind,*
279 *Once more in hollow Ships we court the helpful wind.*
gallies
280 P *But when along the Deep our ~~navy~~ steer'd*
281 *And the last speck of land had disappear'd*
nought was visible
282 *And ~~all that could be seen~~ above around*
Save}
But }
283 *~~Was~~ the blank sky, & ocean without bound*
t}
284 *Then came a tempest-laden cloud T}hat stood*
285 *Right over me, and rouzed the blackening flood*
while around us
286 *The fleet is scattered ~~as the billows~~ rise*
e}
287 *Billows that n}very moment magnifies*
288 *Day fled, & heaven enveloped in a night*
289 *Of stormy rains, is taken from our sight*
their}
290 *By instincts of our} own the clouds are riven*

[Vertical revisions in left margin:]
such power
But how should Phrygians ~~there~~ a realm erect
But how should Phrygians such a power erect
?
How Hesperian shores {All
~~Or~~ reach the ~~Phrygian~~ — [? ~~their~~] faith was check'd
affect
Whom did Cassandra's sayings then affe

272–273 Autograph of base text and revisions, including vertical revisions in left margin, is DW's.
280–285 Autograph is DW's.
286–368 Autograph is MW's.

291 *And prodigal of fire; while we are driven*
292 *Far from the points we aimed at, every bark,*
293 *Errant upon the waters rough & dark*
294 *Even Palenurus owns that night & day*
295 *Thus in each other lost confound his way*
~~we~~ struggle with the gales
296 *Three sunless days ~~the storm our fleet assails~~*
And for three all guidance fails
297 *~~Three~~ starless nights ~~we struggle with the gales~~*
to }
T } came & on } our wistful eyes
298 *~~On~~ t } he fourth day ^ ~~the land so long withdrawn~~*
b }
The far off land then first ~~into welcome~~ } egan to rise
299 *~~From view first rises & begins to dawn~~*
Lifting itself in hills that gently broke
300 *~~To open out the faroff hills & curl the clouds~~*
Upon our view, & rolling clouds of smoke
301 *~~The clouds of silver smoke: our sails we furl;~~*
Sails drop; the Mariners with spring & stoop
302 *~~Rising upon their oars & brisk with hope~~* }
Timed to their oars
303 *~~The mariners~~ ^ the eddying waters scoop* }
304 *The Vessels skim~~s~~ the waves, alive from prow to poop* }
Saved
305 *~~Safe~~ from the perils of the stormy seas*
{We upon
306 *{ I disembark ~~among~~ the Strophedes*
Am } Amid
307 *~~Th long~~ the Ionian waters lie this pair*
308 *Of islands & that Grecian name they bear*
~~Hither with dire Cælena at their head~~
~~For safe retreat the brood of harpies fled~~
~~And there abide sin inhabit since —~~
~~The house of Phineus of that board bereft~~
309 *Th brood of harpies when in fear they left*
doors
310 *The ~~house~~ of Phineus—of that home bereft*
311 *And of their former tables, thither fled*

[DC MS. 89, 180[v]]

312 *There dwell with dire Cælena at their head*
313 *3 Book* *No plague so hidious for impure abuse*
314 *Of upper air did ever Styx produce*
~~with~~ by the
315 *~~When~~* *Stirred ~~with~~ ^ anger ~~by~~ of the Gods to fling*
[?] *her new-born monsterous*
316 *From* *Out ~~of the~~ waves some ~~execrable~~ ^ thing*
317 *Birds they, with virgin faces, crooked claws* }
and never
318 *Of filthy paunch & ~~of in~~satiate maws* }
319 *And pallid mien from hunger without pause* }

X Here lodged in Port ~~we~~ saw the fields oersprread
With goodly herds untended as they fed
Rich Beeves & shaggy goats more wild {than / they they;
~~Large~~ slaughter
Prompt

~~*Here lodged in tranquil harbour we espied*~~
320 ~~*Lo! as we gained the*~~ Port, ~~*the fields oerspred*~~
~~*Rich herds of Cattle roaming far & wide*~~
~~goodly~~
321 ~~*With herds*~~ ~~*& goats*~~ ~~*untended*~~ *as they* ~~*fed*~~
~~*And shaggy goats oer rock, & meadow bed*~~
browzing
~~*And goats that browze the meado*~~
~~*Browzing at large untended as they fled*~~ *fed*
Prompt
322 ~~*Large*~~ *slaughter made, we for the Gods purvey*
323 *And call on Jove himself to share the prey*
along
324 *Then couch by couch* ~~*upon*~~ *the Strand we rear*
dainty
325 *And feast well pleased upon that* ~~*goodly*~~ *chear.*
[320] *Here safe in Port we saw the fields oerspread*
beeves goats
[321] *With* ~~*herds*~~ *&* ~~*flocks*~~ *untended as they fed*
[322] *Prompt slaughter follows, offerings thence we pay*
[323] *And call on Jove himself to share the prey*
[324] *Then couch by couch along the bay we rear*
[325] *And feast well-pleased upon the goodly chear*
326 *But clapping loud their wings the harpy brood*
327 *Rush from the mountain, pounce upon our food*
328 *Pollute the morsels which they fail to seize*
329 *And screaming load with noisome scents the breeze*
330 *Again—but now within a long drawn glade*
331 *Oerhung with rocks & boughs of roughest shade*
332 *We deck our tables & replace the fire*
333 *Upon the altars; but with noises dire*
or
334 *From different points of heaven from blind retreats*
flash
335 *They rush} & hovering oer defile the meats*
336 *"War let them have" I cried & gave command*
337 *To stem the next foul onset arms in hand*
raw
338 *Forthwith the men withdrew} from sight their shields*
339 *And hide their swords where grass a covert yields*
340 *But when the Harpies with loud clang once more*
341 *Gathered & spread upon the curved shore*
342 *From a tall eminence in opon view*
ew
343 *His trumpet sound of charge Mycœnus blue}*
d
344 *Then t}o our swords assault those fowls obscene*
345 *Of generation aqueus & terrene*

[DC MS. 89, 181r]

3 Book

346 *But what avails it, oft repeated blows*
347 *They with inviolable flames oppose*
348 *Baffle the steel & leaving stains behind*
349 *And spoil half-eaten mount upon the wind*
on
350 *Celæna only ~~from~~ a summit high*
nce
351 *Perched & there vented this sad prophesy.*
o *o*
352 *By war descendants of Lam}~~o~~meda}n*
353 *For our slain steers by war would you atone*
354 *Why seek the blameless Harpies to expel*
355 *From regions where by right of birth they dwell*
356 *But learn & fast within your memories hold*
357 *Things which to Phoebus Jupiter foretold*
358 *Phœbus to me & I to you unfold,*
359 *I greatest of the Furies. Ye who strive*
shal
360 *For Italy, in Italy ~~shall~~ arrive* *favouring winds*
{a *~~prospering~~*
361/362 *H{eavens within that wished for land, by leave Of ~~the soothed~~ winds your Navy shall receive*
363 *But do not hope to raise those promised walls*
364 *Ere on your head the curse of hunger falls*
{for
365 *And {ye the slaughter of our herds your doom*
366 *Hath been your very tables to consume*
368 *~~This uttered back she flew to seek the forest's gloom~~*
367 *Gnaw'd and devour'd thro' utter want of food.*
368 *She spake; and, borne on wings, sought refuge in the wood*
a
369 *† The haughty spirits of the men were ~~que}ll'd~~ quail'd*
370 *A shuddering fear thro' every heart prevail'd*
371 *On force of arms no longer they rely*
372 *To daunt whom prayers and vows must pacify*
373 *Whether to Goddesses the Offence were given*
374 *Or they with dire and obscene birds had striven.*

[*Left margin, vertical:* *~~by shud~~ The haughty Spirits of the men were quailed* / *by fear assailed*]

375 *Due Rites or-* *Fit offering made as on the shore he stands*
376 *dain'd* *My Sire Anchises, with uplifted hands*
377 *Invokes the greater Gods Ye powers disarm*
~~Oblation making as the time demands~~
378 *This threat; & from your votaries turn the harm*
~~Invokes the greater Gods while on the shore he stands~~
"~~Ye Powers! annul a threat that teams with fears~~,
~~Avert the ill, and guard your Worshippers~~!"
379 *Then bids to loose the Cables, & unbind*
380 *The willing canvas, to the breeze resign'd.*

367–380 Autograph is DW's.

Where *the Steersman & the south winds urge*
381 P ~~*St*~~ *guides* ~~*Southward, we shoot along the foaming tides*~~
we skim
Our rapid keels, ~~*skim*~~ *the foaming surge*
we skim *e*
382 *we skim* ~~*As the wind urges & the Steersma }n guides*~~

[DC MS. 89, 181v]

3d B
Before us opens
383 ~~*We coast*~~ ~~*Zacinthus,*~~ ^ *midway in the* ~~*deep*~~ *floods/*
Z Zacinthus
384 ~~*Fair island*~~ ^ *shaded with luxuriant woods/*
h *ow* *ext*
385 *Dulicl }ium n { ex & Samè n { ow appears*
os *a*
386 *And Neritus }* ~~*her*~~ *craggy summit rears*
387 *We shun the rocks of Ithica, ill nurse*
stern *her soil*
388 *Of* ~~*dread*~~ *Ul/ysses &* ~~*the land*~~ *we curse*
M *ate* *its vapoury*
389 *Then m }ount Luc { ætæ shews* ~~*his misty*~~ *head*
re
390 *Whe*~~*nce*~~ *from his temple Phoebus strikes with dread*
passing *but*
391 *The Mariner* ~~*now*~~ ~~*fearing*~~ *no mischancee*

Now fear'd to that small City we advance

[?to] that small city
Now feared, to that small city ~~*Now*~~ *feared [?]* ~~*we*~~ *[?* ~~*took*~~*]* ~~*our ships*~~
392 *haul* ~~*We land, &*~~ ^ *to/ards/ the little City advance*
W *ul* *we*
Gladly w } e ~~*hall*~~ *} our }*
393 ~~*The*~~ ^ *stern/ ashore & throw*
out from every
394 *The biting anchor* ~~*to*~~ ^ ~~*confine*~~ ~~*the*~~ *prow*
~~*The un*~~ *reach'd* *e*
395 *Unlook'd-for land thus* ~~*gain'd*~~, *to Jove we rais'd/ e*
e
396 *The votive Altars which with incense blaz { 'd*
illustrating ~~*upon the*~~ *the*
397 *Our Youth* ~~*up*~~ ~~*renew*~~ ^ *Actian Strand* ~~*th*~~
With Trojan games ~~*our*~~ their
398 ~~*The games of Troy*~~ *as in* ~~*their*~~ *native land*
Imbue *eir* *bs*
399 *Besmear th[?] } naked lim[?] } with slippery oil*
400 *And pant for mastery in athletic toil;*
P *Well*
401 ~~*P }ursue How*~~ ^ *pleased so fair a voyage to have shap'd,*
'Mid
402 ~~*But*~~ *Grecian Towns, on every side escaped.*
403 *Sol through his annual round meanwhile had pass'd*

381–382 Autograph of base text is MW's; revisions are in DW's autograph.
383–394 Autograph of base text is MW's, except where noted.
392–394 Revisions are in DW's autograph.
395–535 Autograph not WW's is DW's.

And the sea roughened in the wintry blast;
~~A brazen shield (the same which Abbas wore~~),
[?~~it~~]
High on the Temple gate a brazen shield
~~I took, & hung upon the temple door~~;
I fix'd which mighty Abbas bore
Inscriptive verse declar'd why this was done,
"Arms from the Conquering Greeks & by Æneas" won.
~~The~~
~~On~~ Signal given this friendly port to leave
Contending Oars the ~~briny~~ sparkling waters cleave

Begin here DW
Then, ~~at my~~ word, the Ships ~~unmooring~~ leave their moorings
And with contending oars the waters cleave

Peaks ~~behold~~ in air &
"O Phœac{ian / ea's} ~~airy mountains~~ ~~seen~~ & lost
are seen now
As we proceed;—Epirus ~~next~~ we coast,
a Chaonian harbour won we greet
And ~~safely entering a Chaonian Bay~~
Buthr{otas / [?]} ~~thruo~~ perch'd upon its lofty seat
\+ *~~To high~~ ~~Bu^rotus we direct our way~~*
P. DW *Helenus, Son of Priam, here was Chief*
~~/~~So ran the tale ill fitted for belief

[DC MS. 89, 182r]

Govern'd where Grecian Pyrrhus once had reign'd,
3d B And with the sceptre of the Chief
~~Whose sceptre wielding~~, ~~he therewith~~ had gain'd
Andromache his Spouse, to nuptials led
Once more by one whom Troy had borne & bred.
I long'd to greet him, wish'd to hear his fate
As his own voice the story would relate
Harbour where
So from the ~~Port in which~~ our gallies lay
Right tow'rds the City I pursued my way.
A Grove there was
A Grove *~~And reach'd a Grove~~, where by a streamlet's side*
With the proud name of Simois dignified,
a solemn service paid, ~~as chanced that day~~
S
Andromache, ~~invoking Hector's s hade~~
invoking Hector's shade
(As chanced that day) ~~her solemn offerings paid~~
There did her hands the mournful gifts present
a
Before ~~his~~ Tomb, {—(his / an} empty monument)}

green-sward hallowd by her care
Of living ~~turf,~~ ^ ~~oer which the Mourner bent;~~ }
And ~~two fune~~
~~While~~ two funereal Altars, planted near,
Quicken'd the motion of each falling tear. }
S }
When my approach s }he witness'd, & could see
Phrygian
Our ~~Trojan~~ Arms she shrunk as from a prodigy.
In blank astonishment & terror shook,
: }
While the warm blood her tottering limbs forsook : }
— }
She swoon'd, } & long lay senseless on the ground,
Before these broken words a passage found:
Was that a real shape which met my view?
Son of a Goddess, is thy coming true?
' }
Live }st thou? Or if the light of life be fled
Hector—where is he? This she spake,—then spread
With sounds
SA sound }
~~A voice~~ } of weeping through the Grove and I
A voice
Utter'd these few faint accents in disturb'd reply.
"Fear not to trust thine eyes; I live indeed,
And fraught with trouble is the life I lead.
Fallen from the height where with thy glorious
M }
m }ate
{ ad
Thou stood'st, Andromache, what change h { ath Fate
{ y
To offer, worthy of th { is former state?
Say, did the Gods take pity on thy vows?
Or have they given to Pyrrhus Hector's Spouse?
Then she—with downcast look & voice
subdued
V }
Thrice happy v }irgin, thou of Priam's blood

[DC MS. 89, 182v]

3.d B. *Who in the front of Troy by timely doom*
Didst pour out life before a hostile tomb;
And, slaughter'd thus, wert guarded from the wrong
helpless
Of being swept by lot amid a ~~vanquish'd~~ throng;
O happiest above all who ne'er didst press
A conquering Master's bed in captive wretchedness!
I, since our Ilium fell, have undergone
(Wide waters cross'd) whate'er Achilles' Son

r
463 *Could in the arrogance of bit } th impose*
464 *And faced in servitude a mother's throes.*

e
465 *Thereafter, he at will th { is knot unty'd*
466 *To seek Hermione, a Spartan Bride;*
n
467 *Am } d me to Trojan Helenus he gave—*
S to S
468 —*Captive to captive—if not s } lave too } s } lave.*
469 *Whereat, Orestes with strong love inflamed*
H
470 *Of h } er, now lost, whom as a bride he claim'd,*
471 *And by the Furies driven, in vengeful ire*
Smote
472 ~~*Slew*~~ *Pyrrhus at the Altar of his Sire.* X *Side*
by unexpected blow ~~*arm*~~
473 + *He be } ~~ing~~ an ~~unsuspected~~ ~~blow~~ thus slain* insert onside

When he by this unlook'd for blow was slain
On Helenus devolv'd a part of his domain
Who called

474 *On Helenus devolv'd a part of his domain;*
475 O *Who call'd the neighbouring fields Chaonian ground,*
~~*And gave C Name*~~ ~~*And so he nam'd the region wide around*~~,
476 ~~*Chaonia*~~ *Chaonia named the Region wide around,*
,—
477 O *From Trojan Chaon, } chusing for the site*
ridgy ~~*rocky*~~ *rocky*
478 *Of a new Pergamus yon* ~~*lofty*~~ *height*
;
479 *But thee, a stranger— } in a land unknown—*
480 *What fates have urged? What winds have hither blown?*
481 *Or, say, what God ~~hath~~ upon our Coasts hath thrown?*
the Boy
482 *Survives ^ Ascanius? In his heart*
er
h { is
483 *Doth his lost Mother still retain ~~a~~ part?*
484 *What, Son of great Æneas, brings he forth—*
485 *In emulation of his Father's worth?*
486 *In Priam's Grandchild doth not Hector raise*
487 *High hopes to reach the virtue of past days*
~~*These words*~~ ~~*Then follow'd lamentations long*~~
~~*To this succeeded*~~
488 *Then follow'd sobs & lamentations vain*
489 *But from the City with a numerous train*
490 *Her living consort Helenus descends*
491 *He saw, & ~~glad~~ gave glad greeting to his Friends*

[DC MS. 89, 183r]

492 *3d B And towr'd~~s~~ his hospitable palace leads*
493 *While passion interrupts the speech it feeds.*

gratulate
As we advance I ~~see and~~ note with joy
{ing
Thus dwindl{ed Xanthus & their little Troy
I see in ~~arr~~ haughty state
haughty
Their Pergamus ~~aspiring in proud~~ State
Aspire ~~it~~ ~~*it*~~ ~~as if the Troy~~
^*As if ~~she [?] strove~~ the old to emulate;—*
{ir
And clasp [~~?~~] the threshold of the{ Scæan Gate. }
~~Meanwhile my~~ Follow~~ers share the fresh delight~~
~~Which in my breast these kindred walls excite~~
Nor fails this kindred City to excite
In my Associates unreserv'd delight;

to Italy I bend
end
way
Urg'd by the Gods my ~~course~~ & they portend
o-By every sign they give a happy end

And soon in ample Porticos the King
Receives the Band with earnest welcoming
~~Receives the band with earnest~~ welcoming;
Amid the Hall high festival we hold
~~Whateer of pomp the Palace can afford~~
Refresh'd with viands serv'd in massy gold
~~Shows forth to decorate the festal board~~;
from resplendant goblets
And ~~midst a glad assemblage~~ votive wine
Flows in libation to the Powers divine
Two joyful days thus passed; the southern breeze
Fleet
Once more invites my^ ~~ships~~ to trust the Seas
To Helenus this suit I then prefer;
I}
"Illustrious Trojan! Heaven's i} nterpreter!
o *By prescient Phœbus with his spirit fill'd;*
The harpy queen *Skill'd in the tripod, in the laurel skill'd;*
Skill'd in the stars, and what by voice or wing
Birds to the intelligence of morals bring;
~~I know that to Italy my course~~
T}
Hear and advise! t }o Italy I bend *see Side* O O
~~Speak~~ (for *~~I know that~~* to Italy my course I bend
~~My course & for that aim the Gods~~ portend
Urgd by the Gods who for this aim portend
By every sign they give, a h~~a~~ppy end;
~~the Celæno only~~
The ~~harpy Queen, she only~~, doth presage
A harpy Queen she only
~~The~~ curse of famine in its utmost rage;
O ~~say what~~ I am ~~may are~~ to shun
Now, say, what perils^ first ~~I must eschew;~~
be must I ^
What course for safe deliverance ~~I~~ must run !}
~~To reach the wish'd-for Land what road pursue~~?}
{e
The royal Se{ar ~~the~~ (~~but~~ accustom'd ~~first were~~
P. *He burns (~~the accustom'd~~^victims slain)*

~~Here burn~~
~~Implored the God~~ {ir
523 ~~With prayer, the~~ { ~~favour of the Gods to gain)~~
~~By previous rite~~ [~~?~~]
^ ^Adored the Gods their favour to obtain
524 ~~Unbound the holy~~ *fillets from his sacred head*
And loos'd ~~*the*~~
525 *Then took my hand, &, while a holy dread*
{e
Possess'd m{y ~~*Possess'd my soul*~~ *onward*
526 ~~soul~~*Came over me, her to* ^*the Temple led,*
~~*freely then*~~
527 *Thy Temple, Phœbus!* ~~*then*~~ *from his lip then flow'd*
528 *Communications of the inspiring God.—*

[DC MS. 89, 183v]

ø
~~*Great Son of Venus*~~
529 *3^d B* ~~*Son of a Goddess! doubtless Jo*~~*ve decrees*
No common auspices (this truth is plain)
530 ~~*To guide the Fleet, no common auspices;*~~
~~*the Supreme*~~ *Conduct thee Son of Venus, o'er the Main* }
531 ~~*This order Jove in thy behest ordains*~~ }
~~*Who*~~ *The high behests of* ~~*things*~~ *Jove this course ordain.* }
531 ~~*And And the misfortunes of Fate constrains.*~~
But {ay
~~*Now*~~^*That with* ~~*a*~~ *safer voyage thou m*{*ust reach*
533 *The Ausonian harbour, I will clothe in speech*
fro F}
534 ~~*Few things from*~~ *a Some portions of the future; f* }*ate hath*
hung
535 *Clouds o'er the rest; or Juno binds my tongue.*
536 *And first* <u>that</u> *Italy, whose coasts appear,*
537 *To thy too confident belief, so near,*
open }
538 *With havens* ~~*ready*~~ *for* }*for thy sails, a wide*
distance *rom*
539 *And weary* ~~*region*~~ *doth f* {*or thee divide;*
shall bend the
540 ~~*Beneath*~~ *Trinacrian waves* ~~*thy*~~ *pliant oar*~~*s*~~
~~*Shall*~~ *T* } *through* *a passage must*
541 ~~*Must bend*~~*, & t* } *hou, Ausonian gulph*~~*s*~~^ *explore*
Tread ~~*Trace*~~ *an Isle* *infernal*
542 ~~Trace~~ the ~~*The isle of*~~ *Circe & the* ^~~*Stygian*~~ *pool,*
Before ~~*thy*~~ *rise*
543 ~~*Ere thou a*~~ *City* ~~*raise*~~*, for stedfast rule.*
Cross ere thy
544/545 *Now mark these tokens—soon as thou shalt find*
ø ~~*Side*~~ *br* }
546 *A bulky female of the Br*}*istly kind:*

[Left margin, written vertically:] *o Now be these tokens stored within thy mind / When anxiously reflecting thou shalt find / A bulky*

523–524 Revisions are in MW's autograph.
530–532 Revisions are in MW's autograph.
536–570 Autograph not WW's is MW's.
541–548 Revisions not WW's are in DW's autograph.

By
547 *~~On~~ a sequester'd river's margin laid*
On ground which
548 *~~Where~~ Ilex branches ~~do the ground~~ overshade;*
Ilex
549 *With thirty young-ones couch'd in that recess*
550 *White as the pure white dam whose teats they press.*
551 *There found thy City—on that soil shall close*
552 *All thy solicitudes, in fixed repose*
e ;
553 *Nor dread Ca lœno's threat, the Fates shall clear*
554 *~~The~~ way, & at thy call Apollo interfere*
555 *But shun those lands where our Ionian sea*
556 *Washes the nearest ~~coast~~ shores of Italy*
557 *On all the coasts malignant Greeks abide*
y ave
558 *~~Narycian~~ Nari cian Locrians there, a Town h ad fortified*
559 *~~There dwells~~ Idomenous of Crete ~~girt round~~ hath compassed round*
ldiery the
560 *With so ldiers, on Salentinian ground.*
ere
561 *There w hen Thesalian Phylectetes chose*
A
~~His resting-place~~
562 *His resting-place, the small Petilia rose*
thou shalt stand
563 *But when that sea ~~is cross'd~~ past over, ~~on its strand~~*
~~Altars stand~~
~~The sacrificial For sacrifice erected on its strand~~
564 *Before the Altars kindling on the strand*
565 *While to the Gods are offered up thy vows*
~~in a purple vest enwrap~~
566 *Then ^ cast a purple amice oer thy Brows*
567 *And sacrifice thus cover'd, lest the sight*
~~foe~~
568 *Of any hostile face disturb the rites*
569 *Be this observance kept by thee & thine*
570 *And this to late posterity consign!*

[DC MS. 89, 184r]

571 3d B. *But when by favoring breezes wafted o'er*
572 *Thy Fleet approaches the Sicilian shore*
Straits unfolding by degrees 0 See Bottom Side
'
573 *~~And dense~~ Pelorus ~~gradually throws~~*
Their narrow shun those shores & seas
574 *~~His~~ ^ barriers ~~open to invite thy prows~~*
And to the left thy scourse in safety keep
575 *~~That passage shunn'd—thy course in safety~~ keep*

571–596 Autograph not WW's is DW's, except where noted.
573–578 Revision, written vertically at bottom of left margin, is in MW's autograph.

S}
s}teering that shore along,
576 ~~By veering to the left~~ with ample sweep
577 Erewhile when Earth by violence was rent
578 This ground forsook the Hesperian Continent
579 Nor doubt that power to work such change might lie
Within}
580 Right} the grasp of dark antiquity
where
581 Then flow'd the Sea between & ~~by~~ the force
established
582 Of roaring waves ~~completed~~ the Divorce
~~Yet~~ B} ~~yet to this hour the~~
583 ~~Still b}oils this current through the narrow straits,~~
Still thro' the straits the narrow waters boil
584 ~~And fields & neighbouring Cities separates~~
Dissevering {Town from Town & Soil from Soil
{Right
585 Upon the ~~left~~ the Dogs of Scylla fret
The Left}
586 The Right} by fell Charybdis is beset
Thrice
587 ~~Who~~ tow'rd~~s~~ the bottom of a vast Abyss
588 Down, headlong down the liquid precipice
She as}
589 Sucks ~~in~~ the whirling billows & does} oft
~~Ejects them flung scatter'd through the air~~
aloft
590 Ejecting, sends them into air, aloft
Scylla } pent ~~from~~ within her
591 But [?Sylla]}, ~~Prisoner of a~~ Cavern blind
a
592 Thrusts forth ~~the~~ visage of our human kind
And draws the Ships on rocks: she fair in show
Fair}
593 ~~She} A Woman to the Waist & by that show~~
~~She fair in~~ A Woman to the waist is foul below
594 ~~Draws in the vessels, but her shapes below~~
A huge
595 ~~Is a~~ Sea Beast with Dolphin Tails & bound
596 With water-wolves & Dogs her middle round.
597 But thou against this jeopardy provide
598 Doubling Pachynus with a circuit wide
shapeless may
599 Thus ~~hideous~~ Scylla ~~shall~~ be left unseen
600 Unheard the yelling of the brood marine
601 But above all if Phœbus I revere
602 Not unenlightened an authentic Seer
603 Then Goddess born (on this I could enlarge)
604 Repeating oft and oft the solemn charge)
605 Adore imperial Juno freely wait
on Juno's
606 With gifts ~~upon her~~ Altar~~s~~ supplicate
607 Her potent favour & subdue her hate: X

Thus shalt thou reach Trinacrian limits past
The Italian shore a conqueror at last
Pelorus straits unfolding by degrees
To tempt thy prows, around those shore and seas
And to the left thy ~~course~~ way in safety keep
Steering that coast ~~and~~ a long with ample sweep

And dense Pelorus gradually throws
Its barriers oppen to invite thy prows
That passage shun thy course in safety keep
By steering to the left with ample sweep
Tis said when heaving earth of yore was rent
This ground

Thus ~~shalt~~ thou seek (a conqueror at last)
For ~~Italy~~—Sicilian dangers past
X So shalt thou reach Sicilian limits pass'd
The Italian shore a Conqueror at last
And ~~thus~~ so shalt thou (a Conqueror at last)
Proceed for Italy—Sicilian dangers past

593 Revision is in MW's autograph.
594–595 Revisions "A Woman . . . below" and "A huge" are in MW's autograph.
597–609 Autograph not WW's is MW's.

T}
~~*So will she send t } hee Conqueror at last*~~
~~*To Italy, Trinacrian dangers past*~~ *To Italy (thus conqueror at last)*
A ~~*Conqueror thus*~~ *Shalt thou proceed, Sicilian dangers past*
Thus shalt thou seek (a conqueror at last)
The Italian Shore, Trinacrian Limits past

[DC MS. 89, 184v]

3d Book

The uninstructed from the Cave depart
And quit the Sybil with a murmuring heart

Arriv'd at Cumæ & the sacred flood
Of black Avernus resonant with woods
Thou shalt behold the Sybil where she sits
Within her Cave, rapt in ecstatic fits
And Signs & Characters to leaves commits.
The prophesies which on these Leaves the Maid
Inscribes, are by her hands in order laid
mid secluded
~~*And in*~~ *^ the ^ Cavern* ~~*secluded*~~ *where they fill*
Their several places undisturb'd & still
But if a light wind entering thro' the door
L} R}
Scatter the thin l } eaves on the r } ocky floor
her
~~*She*~~ *to replace* ~~*the*~~ *prophesies will use*
all}
No diligence they } flutter where they chuse
In hopeless disconnection loose & wild
thus
And they who sought for knowledge, ~~*stand*~~ *beguild*
Of her predictions
~~*Without instruction*~~ *from the Cave depart*
a murmuring
And quit the Sybil with ~~*despiteful*~~ *heart*
But thou albeit ill-disposed to wait
And prizing moments at their highest rate
Tho' followers chide & ever & anon
The flattering winds invites thee to be gone
Beg of the moody Prophetess to break
The silent air & for thy guidance speak
disclose
She will foreshow the features of thy doom
The Italian Nations & the wars to come
How to escape from hardships or endure
u}
And make a happy termination sh } re
Enough chains bind the rest or clouds obscure
Go then & high as heaven's ethereal vault
The Trojan name by glorious deeds exalt.
So spake the friendly Seer from hallow'd lips

610–626 Autograph not WW's is DW's.
627–699 Autograph not WW's is MW's.

Then orders presents to our parting Ships
with
Smooth ivory massy gold & ponderous store
Of vases fashioned from the paler ore.
And Dodonæan Cauldrons; nor withholds
k
The golden hauberc } knit in triple folds
o
~~Which Ne~~ That Neoptole } mus erewhile had worn
Nor his resplendant crest which waving plumes adorn
Rich offerings also grace my Fathers hands
Horses, he adds; with Equerries; & bands
Of Rowers & supply of Arms commands

[DC MS. 89, 185r]

3d Book
Meanwhile Anchises bids the Fleet unbind
sei
Its sails for instant see } zure of the wind
addrest
The Interpreter of Phœbus then had { rest
gracious
This ~~parting~~ farewell to his parting guest
Anchises! to celestial honours led
Beloved of Venus, whom she deigned to wed;
Care of the Gods, twice snatch'd from Ilium lost,
Now for Ausonia be these waters cross'd!
~~must thou only~~
Yet only hope to glide along the shores
To which I point; far lies the land from ours
Whither
~~To~~ which } Apollo's voice directs your powers.
Go happy Parent of a pious Son!
No more—I baulk the winds that press thee on.
r less,
~~Evn so~~ No { w ~~to~~ Andromache disturb'd in heart
That parting now we must for ever part,
Embroider'd Vests of golden threads bestows,
u
A Phrygian Tunic o'er Ascania } s throws;
may
And studious that her bounty ~~might~~ become
The occasion, adds rich labours of the loom.
Dear Child! she said, these also, to be kept
As the memorials of my hand, accept.
as ~~the~~ ^ ~~tokens~~ tokens
~~And~~, ~~fare~~ } ~~may be~~, ~~tokens~~ ~~let the~~ { ~~m prove~~
Last gifts of Hectors Consort let them prove
~~In Hector's Consort an enduring~~ love;
tokens
tokens To thee the ~~symbols~~ of ^her stedfast
Take what Andromache at parting gives,

Live happy ye whom race of fortune run
Permits such life—one peril if we shun
Tis but to meet a worse—by you is quiet won.
No seas have ye to measure nor on you
to
Is it imposed Ausonia pursue,
And search for fields still flying from your view
Before your sight a mimic Z anthus flows
By your own hands the Troy that guards you rose
With happier auspices—to stand more free
O

675 *Fair Boy, sole image that for me survives*
676 *Of my Astyanax; in whom his face,*
677 *His eyes are seen, his very hands I trace.*
And } the of
678 *Who* } *now but for obstruction* ~~*from*~~ *the tomb*
679 *His years had open'd into kindred bloom.*
680 *To these, while gushing tears bedew'd my cheek,*
681 *Thus in the farewell moment did I speak*
682 *"Live happy Ye whose race of fortune run*
Permits such life; ×from hard fate undergone
~~*Our fate from labour done*~~
you so to live,
683 *Permits* ~~*such life*~~*,* ~~*our fate*~~ *from labour done*
~~*We to fresh labour pass*~~
684 ~~*To different labour calls*~~*, by you is quiet won.*
~~*We to like fate are call'd*~~ *,* }
685 *No seas have ye to measure not* } *on you*
Ausonia
686 *Is it impos'd* ~~*Hesperia*~~ *to pursue*
687 *And search for fields still flying from the view.*
Before your sight a mimic Xanthus flows
688 ~~*A miniature of Xanthus is display*~~*'d*
The Troy which guards you, by your labour rose
689 ~~*Before you & the Troy your hands hath made*~~
— } far happier, and more free
690 *With* ~~*happier*~~ *auspices,* } *in less degree,*
E } I trust
691 ~~*I trust*~~*,* ~~*e* } *xpos'd*~~ ^to *Grecian enmity.*
Could wish of some avail, from Grecian enmity

[Left margin, written vertically:]
Live happy ye whose race of fortune run
one ~~rest~~ peril if we shun
Permits such life ~~our labours which are shunn'd~~
We meet a worse by
~~Our fate is un-fulfill'd~~ by you is quiet won

[Right margin, written vertically:]
× With happier auspices —to stand more free
(Could ask of more avail) from Grecian enmity

[DC MS. 89, 185^v]

3^d Book

692 *If Tiber ere receive me & the sod*
693 *Of Tiber's meadows by these feet be trod*
re our }
ever I } }
694 *If I* } *destin'd City I behold.*
se } *and*
695 *Our several walls Their* } *neighbouring Towns* ~~*there*~~ *Tribes a kin of old*
He } *& Epirian*
696 ~~*Ep* } *sper Ausonian &*~~ *Hesperian* ^*whose blood came*
lot
697 *From Dardanus whose* ~~*fate*~~ *hath been the same*
698 *Shall make one Troy in spirit. May that care*
699 *To our Descendants pass from heir to heir.—"*

700 *B} N} eneath Ceraunian R} r} ocks our G} g} allies steer*
701 *(No other course finds Italy so near.)*
702 *Meanwhile the S} s} un descends, & o'er the head*
703 *Of every mountain blackening shadows spread.*
704 *Tired of the oar, the Men rejoice when each*
705 *Hath spread his limbs in ease along the beach.*
706 *On the dry margin of the murmuring Deep ~~The~~*
707 *They lie not wanting long the embrace of sleep*

Along the deep our eager Gallies bound
[700] ~~*We coast along Ceraunia*~~*, whence is found*
Near the Ceraunian Peaks from which is found
[701] B — ~~*The shortest*~~ ~~*transit*~~ *to Italian ground* ×*Blank*
passage
[702] *Meanwhile the sun went down, & shadows spread*
[703] *er} Ore} every mountain dark'ned to its head*
[704] *Tired of their Oars the Men no sooner reach*
~~along the beach~~ ~~on the dry beach~~
[705] They stretch *Earth's wish'd for bosom then an}* ~~*their limbs they stretch*~~
They stre~~tch their~~ir limbs beside along the beach
[706] ~~*On the dry margin*~~ ~~*of the*~~ *murmuring Deep*
lay —
They spread The~~y stretch their limbs besi~~de
their limbs beside
[707] *Where wear iness} yness is lost in timely sleep.*

(Left margin, vertical: ~~Ere~~ Ris'n from his Couch ere night with slow ascent / Had found the middle of the firmament / cautious / Prompt Palenurus looks with cautious eyes / To every gust for what it signifies)

~~*Night*~~
708 *Ere She whose Car the Hours had yoked & reined*
709 *Black Night, the middle of her orbit gain'd,*
710 *Up from his couch doth Palenuri u} s rise*
711 *Looks to the wind for what it signifies*
712 *And to each breath of air a watchful ear applies*
713 *N} H} ext all the S} s} tars gliding thro' silent heaven*
watry
714 *The Bears, Arcturus & the* ~~*cluster'd*~~ *Seven*
He notes and ranging wide his
715 ~~*Are noted & his ranging*~~ *eyes behold,*
716 *Magnificent Orion arm'd in gold.*
Assured that all prognostics
717 ~~*When he percie ei} ves that*~~ *all things low & high*
718 *Unite to promise fix'd serenity*
719 *He sends the summons forth our Camp we raise*
720 *Are} Our} gone & every Ship her broadest wings displays*

(Left margin, vertical: And in the Re} freshing dew—)

(Right margin, vertical: And weariness in dwey slumber steep The End)

[705] Earths wish'd for [?–] bosom then along their beach
[706] They spread their limbs beside the murmuring
[706] Their weary limbs beside the murmuring deep
[706] They spread and in the dews of slumber

[700]–[707] Autograph not WW's is DW's.

[DC MS. 89, 186r]

[700] We sail near high Ceraunia, whence is found
[701] The shortest passage to Hesperian ground.
[702] Meanwhile the sun went down & shadows spread
[703] Oer every mountain darken'd to its head
[704] Eased of the~~ir~~ oars upon earth's wish'd for breast
[704] We seek refreshment & prepare for rest:
[705] Nor did indulgent Nature fail to steep
[706] On the dry margin of the murmuring deep
[707] Our weary limbs in the soft dew~~s~~ of sleep.
[708] Ris'n from his couch ere Night with slow ascent
[709] Had measur'd half the vaulted firmament
[710] Prompt Palenurus looks with cautious eyes
[711] To every cloud for what it signifies
{And
[712] {Th to

{*en*
721 *3d Book* *Now wh{ile Aurora reddened in a sky*
722 *From which the Stars had vanish'd, we descry*
723 *The low faint hills of distant Italy*
:
724 *"Italia!" shouts Achates;—* }*round & round*
gratulant gratulant
725 *Italia flies with ~~rapturous~~ rebound,*
726 *From all who see the coast, or hear the happy sound—*
727 *Not slow is Sire Anchises to entwine*
728 *With wreaths a Goblet, which he fill'd with wine;*
729 *Then ~~cried "Ye~~ on the Stern he took his lofty stand,*
730 *And cried, "Ye Deities of Sea & Land*
rule ~~the storms vouchsafe to~~ speed our way
731 *~~Whom the tempestuous elements obey~~*
Through whom the storms are govern'd speed our
732 *~~Vouchsafe a partial wind to smooth the way~~*
^
By breezes docile to your
732 *~~And meet our wishes with your~~ kindliest sway*
With freshening impulse breathe thy wishd wish'd for gales
733 *~~Even as the prayer was uttered freshening gales~~*
And as the Ships press on ~~ready~~ with speedy sails.
734 *~~Dilate the bosom of the swelling~~ sails;*
735 *~~The Port begins to open; & in sight~~*
Opens the Port & peering into sight
736 *Minerva's Temple tops a craggy height*
crowns *~~crowns~~*
peering

[Left margin, written vertically:]
And the port opens as with greedy sails
The Ships press on, and peering into sight

[700]–832 Remainder of Book III material is in the autographs of WW and MW.

[DC MS. 89, 186v]

3.d Book

The Sails are furled by many a busy hand,
st } r
The veering prows are pointed to the l } and
to } semblance
Curved in } ~~the fashion~~ of a bow the haven
east; but with a wave thence driven
Looks to~~wards~~ the ~~waves that from the east are driven~~,
D } s } s } peacefulness
~~Waves that~~ d } isturb } it } ~~not~~; their foamy spray
fence
Breaks upon jutting rocks that guard the bay.
,with gradual
Two towering cliffs extend ~~their arms~~ fall
Their arms into the sea, & frame a wall.
In whose embrace the harbour hidden lies;
And, as its shelter deepens on our eyes,
shore ~~the [?farest]~~ f }
ends *Back from the ~~Port~~ Minerva's temple } lies* .
th across a
Four snow-white Horses grazing the wide fields
Are the first omen which our landing yields
thy tokens bear
Then Sire Anchises—"War ~~thou dost declare~~
the Horse is
O hospitable Land, ~~horses~~ are arm'd for war;
War do these menace, but as, Steed with Steed
Oft joins in friendly Yoke, the sight may breed
Fair hope that peace & concord will succeed.
clanking
To Pallas then in ~~sounding~~ Armour mail'd
Who hail'd us first exulting to be hail'd,
Prayers we address with Phrygian amice veil'd;
H }
And as by h } elenus enjoin'd the fire
On Juno's Altar fumes—to Juno vows aspire.
When we had ceas'd this service to present,
That instant Seaward are our Sail-yards bent,
And we forsake the shore, with cautious dread
Of ground by native Grecians tenanted.
The Bay is quickly reached that draws its name
From proud Tarentum, proud to share the fame
Of Hercules tho' by a dubious claim:
Right opposite we ken the Structure holy
Of the Lacinian Goddess rising slowly,
Next the Caulonian Citadel appear'd
And the Scylacian bay for Shipwrecks fear'd;
Lo, as along the open main we float,
Mount Etna, yet far off! & far remote
Groans of the sea we hear;—deep groans & strokes
Of angry billows beating upon rocks,
And hoarse surf-clamours; while the flood throws up
Sands from the depths of its unsettled cup.

[DC MS. 89, 187[r]]

3.[d] Book ~~My Sire exclaimed Companions,~~ are caught
My Sire exclaimed Companions we
777 ~~Then Sire An~~chises; ~~Doubtless~~ ~~we encroach~~
fleet
By ~~by [?]~~ } flee as ye were taught!
778 ~~On~~ fell Charybdis; ~~with too bold approach~~
doubtless
779 There^are the rocks, ~~and there~~ the dangerous shores
780 Which Helenus denounc'd—away—with straining oars!
M ~~obedien~~t Master
781 obedient Quick, to the left the ~~foremost~~ Galley veers
782 With roaring prow as Palenurus steers.
783 And for the left the band~~s~~ of Rowers strive
784 While every help is caught that winds t~~hat~~ can give
785 The whirlpools dizzy altitudes we scale
the
786 For ghastly sinking when ~~its~~ waters fail
crags ~~and~~ and
787 ×Thrice did the ~~rocks~~ ~~and~~ hollow rocks cry out
Three times we saw the clash—the mutual ~~eddy~~ rout
788 Three times to heavens we saw the waters ~~spout~~ spout
And the sky moisten'd with a briny spout

The hollow rocks thrice gave a fearful cry
Three times we saw the [?] dashing waves fling high
Their foam, dispers'd along a drizzling sky,

790 The flagging wind forsook us with the sun
791 And to Cyclopian shores a darkling course we run.
792 ~~In the capacious haven ships may lie~~
The Port we entered is of ample [~~?~~] size
~~Fearless of winds but Ætna thunders nigh~~
~~Mid the capacious harbour ships may~~
~~Large is the haven, and its waters lie~~
~~Fearless of winds~~
793 ~~Untouch'd by wind~~~~s~~ ~~in still security~~
And unmolested by the winds it lies
794 But all too near is Ætna thundering loud
795 And oftimes casting forth a pitchy cloud
796 Of smoke in whirling convolutions driven
hoary
797 With weight of fiery Embers, high as heavn.
[792] *The Port which now we chance to enter, lies*
[793] *By winds unruffled tho' of ample size*
[794] *But all too near is Etna thundering loud*
[795] *And ofttimes casting up a pitchy cloud*
[796] *Of smoke in whirlling convolution driven*
[797] *With weight of hoary ashes high as heaven*
798 *And globes of flame & sometimes he gives vent*
799 *To rocky fragments from his entrails rent*
800 *And hurls out melting substances that fly*
801 *In thick assemblage & confound the sky*
802 *While groans & lamentations burthensome*
803 *Tell to the air from what a depth they come*
804 *The enormous mass of Etna, so 'tis said,*
805 *On lightening-scorched Enceladus was laid*
806 *And ever pressing on the Giant's frame*
807 *Breathes out from fractured chimneys fitful flame*

[DC MS. 89, 187ᵛ]

3ᵈ Book

808 *And often as he turns his weary side*
809 *Murmuring Trinacria trembles far & wide*
While *ide.*
810 *~~And~~ wreathes of smoke ascend & all the welking/ h igh*
We, through ~~ghout~~ the enwrappd in
811 *~~Cover~~'d thro ~~all that~~ night ~~by w~~oods obscure*
The shock of ~~the~~ those dire
812 *~~Do we those fearful prodigies~~ endure*
~~our eyes~~ might come ~~&~~
813 *Nor could distinguish whence ^the sound ~~might rise~~*
For all the stars to ether's utmost bound
814 *~~Proceeded for the stars of heaven were drown'd~~*
Were hidden or bedimmd N
815 *In widely spreading clouds & n ight withheld ~~the moon~~*
in t
816 *~~In f~~ The Moon, ~~with~~ mist & l owering fogs conceal'd*

[DC MS. 89, 188ᵛ]

i
817 Those left, we harboured o n the joyless coast
harassd long and ~~tossd~~
818 Of Drepanus: here, ~~long by tempests toss'd~~
By storms we
819 ~~My aged~~ Sire Anchises did I lose
And here my Sire Anchises ~~I d~~ did I lose
820 Hellp in my cares and solace of my woes
O ~~best~~ Father
best
821 Here, ~~best~~ of Parent/s best beloved and best
at length ~~parting~~
822 Didst thou desert me ~~needing~~ rest
Didst thou desert me when I needed rest
823 Thou from so many perils saved in vain
Helenus mid ~~many d~~ through mid d doleful strain
824 Not ~~dire Cælæno nor~~ the doleful strain
~~Of Helenus of prophecy foreto~~ld this
825 Fortold their bitter pain;
826 ~~Not dire~~ Celæno;
t Celestial
827 This w rouble, was my last; by heavenly Powers
O Queen O Queen, Have brought me to
828 ~~Propell'd I thence~~ to your friendly shores;
Impelled me thence
O Tyrians! ~~Have thence impelled~~
~~Queen, Then sole speaker~~
S
829 Sole s peaker, thus Æneas did relate
a hush'd audience F
830 To ~~a a mute~~ ears attentive to decrees of f ate,
831 His wandering course remeasured, &, the close

~~When~~ in silence here he
832 Thus reach'd, ~~in silence he~~
his Voice in silence fo~~un~~d repose

[~~?~~]
[819] And here my Sire Anchises did I lose
in
[820] Help ~~of~~ my cares and solace of my woes
H F
[821] O ere, O best p ather best beloved and best
~~Th Didst~~ thou Didst thou desert me when I needed rest.
~~Didst thou desert~~
[822] ~~Me didst Thou quit~~ who long h~~ad needed r~~est,
[823] Thou from so many perils snatchd in vain;
[824] Not Helenus though much in doleful strain
[825] He prophesied, this sorrow did unfold.
is
[826] Not dire Cælæno's ~~Self~~ th e distress foretold.

[829] Sole speaker then Æneas did relate
hush'd
[830] To a ~~mute~~ audience the decrees of Fate
~~wandering~~
[831] His course retraced; and when at the close
[832] Was reachd, in silence here her he found repose
wandering
[831] His wander course remeasured till the close
Now here he found
[832] ~~Was~~ reach'd, ~~and~~ ~~he~~ in silence found repose

[DC MS. 89, 213[v]]

When the abode was reach'd he said this Gate
lowly
The humble dwelling reach'd he said

Which yet by virtue of its Roman name
Which yet by virtue of its roman name
it
1 *This scarcely uttered they advance & straight*
2 *He shews the Altar & Carmental gate*
is the record of
has
3 *Which (such ~~is~~ the ~~story~~) by its roman name*
ancient
4 *Preserves the nymph Carmenta's fame*
W ~~*the glories of the*~~
5 ~~*A prophetess who first the strains divine*~~ [~~?~~]
Who first
[5] ~~*Foretold*~~ *the glories of the Trojan line* ~~*predicted*~~
~~*And*~~ *Predicted and* *l*
6 ~~*Nor left unsung*~~ *the noble Pa lantine.*
ce [*?the*] ~~*grove*~~
7 ~~*Then*~~ ~~[*?shows*]~~ ~~*wood with widely spreading shade*~~

1–46 Autograph not WW's is MW's. These lines are a translation of Book VIII, 337–368.

he
Next *~~Then~~ Next he points^ out an ample sylvan shade*
Which Romulus a fit Assylum made
t
Turns T hence ~~turns~~ & bids Æneus fix his eyes
~~Then pointed where in gloom Lupercal lies~~
Where under a chill rock Lupercal lies
~~Under a rock;—Lycean Pan supplies~~
Named from Lycean Pan in old
~~The name, adopted in~~ Arcadian guise.
Nor left he unobserved the neighbouring wood
Of sacred Argolatum stained with blood.
W G
T here Argus fell, his g uest—the story told
o e
T ~~hey~~ the Tarpi an rock their way they hold,
seek
And to the Capitol now bright with gold.
In those far-distant times a spot forlorn
With brambles choked & rough with savage thorn;
ious
Even then an influence of relig ion awe
The rustics felt subdued by what they saw
The local spirit creeping thro' their blood
Even then they feared the rock they trembled at the wood
~~They trembled at the rock, they feared the wood~~
This grove (said he) this leaf-crown'd hill—some God
H we I
~~Some God~~ h ow named ~~we~~ know not, takes for his abode,
The Arcadians think that Jove himself aloft
remarkd appeared before their
Hath here declared his presence oft & oft
~~here appeared before~~ here before their
Shaking his lurid ægis in their sight
And covering with fierce clouds the stormy height.
~~And gathering round the hill tempestuous light night~~
dismantled
Here also sees two mouldering towns that lie
Mournful remains of buried Ancestry crumbling
Yon ~~ruined fortress~~ mouldering fortress *d* crumbling
~~That citadel did~~ father Janus frame
each from *d*
And Saturn this, ~~both bears the~~ Founder's name .
Conversing thus their onward course they bent
To poor Evander's humble tenement;
Herds range the and the stree native grass
&
~~Spread thro' the~~ Roman forum s^ herds they meet
~~the uncultivated~~ space ~~where they pass~~
æ
And bellowings fill ~~Carina s splendid street~~
bellows ~~there~~ where
Of proud Carinæ ~~wheresoeer~~ they pass
When they had reached the^ house he said, this Gate

faithfully
A
The a rcadians verily believe that oft
They have beheld great Jove himself—aloft
Herds range the Roman forum—in the Street
Of proud Carinæ, bellowing herds they meet

[DC MS. 89, 214r]

C entered plain
38 *This gate c* {*onquering Alcides* ~~*passed;*~~ *his* ~~*simple*~~ *state*
39 *This palace lodged; O guest like him forbear*
humble
40 *To frown on scanty means & ~~scanty~~ fare*
41 *Dare riches to despise; with aim as high*
42 *Mount thou, & train thyself for Deity.*
43 *This said thro' that low door he leads his guest*
44 *The great Æneus to a couch of rest*
45 *There propped he lay on withered leaves, oerspread*
46 *With a bear's skin in Lybian desarts bred.*
[45] There lay the Chief on withered
[35] Herds range the Roman Forum, through the bounds
[36] Of proud Carinæ bellowing resounds—
[35] Herds range the Roman Forum native grass
[36] And proud Carinæ bellows as they pass
the streets
[35] Herds range the Roman Forum in the street
[36] Of proud Carinæ bellowing herds they meet

[DC MS. 89, 218r]

---

476 *Could but the vanquished beat out of their mind*
477 *All hope of safety—safety they might find*

1 *She who to raise lift her heavy eyes had tried*
2 *Faints while the deep wound gurgles at her side*
{*ove*
3 *Thrice on her elbow propp'd she str*{*ives to uphold*
~~*it*~~
4 *Her frame—thrice back on the couch ~~was~~ roll'd*
5 *Then with a wandering eye in heaven's blue round*
6 *She sought the light & groaned when she had found*

484 What, Son of great Æneas brings he forth
485 In emulation of his Father's worth
486 In Priams Grandchild doth not Hector raise
23 ~~*This grove this hill with leafy brow a God*~~
487 High hopes to reach the virtue of past days?
{*I*
24 *How named* {~~*we*~~ *know not takes for his abode*
25 *The Arcadians think that Jove himself, aloft,*
26 *Hath here declared his presence oft & oft*
27 ~~*And oft s*~~

476–477 These lines are from Book II. Autograph is MW's.
1–6 These lines are from Book IV. Autograph is MW's.
484–487 These lines are from Book III.
23–28 These lines are from Book VIII. Autograph is MW's.

27 *Shaking his lu{rid / ring} Egis in their sight*
28 *And gathering round the hill tempestuous night*

1 *Even so bewails, the poplar groves among,*
2 *Sad Philomela her evanish'd y{Y}oung;*
3 *Whom the harsh rustic from the nest hath torn,*
4 *An unfledg'd brood,{;} but on the bough forlorn*
5 *She sits, in mournful darkness, all night long;*
6 *Renews, & still renews, her doleful song,*
7 *And fills the leafy grove, complaing of her wrong.*

1–7 These lines are from *Georgics*, Book IV, 511–515. Autograph is DW's.

DC MS. 101 (with Facing Photographs)

DC MS. 101 consists of five separate items: a handmade notebook, bound in marble boards with a green cloth spine; two notebooks in wrappers, stamped G. Roake, 83 Strand, Bath; a bound exercise book with woodcuts on the wrapper; and a bifolium and a single (a bifolium torn at the fold), identified by Dorothy Wordsworth as "Coleridge's Remarks on Virgil." The first of these items contains a fair copy of *Aeneid*, Books I and II, in Mary Wordsworth's autograph, with revisions by Christopher Wordsworth, Jr., Dorothy Wordsworth, Mary Wordsworth, and William Wordsworth, and a fair copy of *Aeneid*, Book III, lines 409–720, in Dorothy Wordsworth's autograph, with revisions by Dorothy and William Wordsworth. I have designated this manuscript as MS. 101A. The two stamped notebooks contain a fair copy of *Aeneid*, Books I and II—one book per notebook—in Dorothy Wordsworth's autograph, with revisions by Christopher Wordsworth, Jr., and Dorothy and William Wordsworth, and marginal notes by Samuel Taylor Coleridge. Book II is interleaved, and contains a pastcover on 2^{v}. I have designated these two notebooks MS. 101B. The exercise book contains a fair copy of *Aeneid*, Book III, lines 1–816, in Mary Wordsworth's autograph, with revisions by Dorothy, Mary. and William Wordsworth, and a note by Samuel Taylor Coleridge. I have designated it MS. 101C. The final manuscript contains Coleridge's comments on Book I of the translation, drawn up at William Wordsworth's request in April 1824. I have designated it MS. 101D. The manuscripts are described more fully in the Manuscript Census, pages xx–xxi.

The fair copies of Book II in MSS. 101A and 101B contain a number of marginal signals associated with the process of revision undertaken by William Wordsworth and Christopher Wordsworth, Jr., in the summer of 1827. These signals can be found in MS. 101A at lines 33–34, 53–54, 55–56, 99, 101, 167, 195, 200, 202, 324, 461, 476, and 585; in MS. 101B, marginal signals, often in erased pencil, can be found at lines 101, 191, 228, 231, 426, 436, 458, and 605.

Reproduced here is a selection of pages that are too complex or interesting to record in the *apparatus criticus*.

How great a God incumbent o'er her breast
Would fill it with his spirit. He to please

That ... of look, mind, life & soul,
And sometimes doth unhappy Dido fold
The ... in her bosom, ignorant
How great a God deceives her. He, to please
His Acidalian Mother, by degrees
Would steal Sichæus, studious to remove
The dead by influx of a living love
By stealthy entrance of a perilous guest
Troubling a heart that had been long at rest

Now when the viands were withdrawn, & ceas'd
The first diversion of the splendid Feast;
While round a vacant board the Chiefs recline
Huge goblets are brought forth; they crown the wine.
Voices of gladness roll the walls around;
Those gladsome voices from the courts rebound;
From gilded rafters many a blazing light
Depends, & torches overcome the night.
The minutes fly till, as the Queen commands,
A bowl of State is offer'd to her hands:
Then she, as Belus wont & all the Line
From Belus, fill'd it to the brim with wine:
Silence ensued. "O Jupiter! whose care
"Is hospitable Dealing, grant my prayer!

Troubling a heart that long ...

[Book I]

43

[987] *How great a God incumbent oer her breast*
[992] ~~By stealthy entrance of a tyrannous Guest~~
[988] *Would fill it with his spirit. He to please*
[993] ~~Troubling a heart that had been long at~~
[989] *Hi* rest —
984 ~~*Then sought the Queen, who fix'd on him the whole*~~
{ ~~*yet was hers*~~
{ yet was hers
985 ~~*That she possess'd of look, mind, life & soul,*~~
986 ~~*And sometimes doth unhappy Dido plant*~~
987 ~~*The Fondling in her bosom, ignorant*~~
H}
988 ~~*How great a God deceives h er.*~~ *He, to please*
{ ci
989 *His A* {*sedalian Mother, by degrees*
Uproots { *æ*
990 ~~*Would sap*~~ *Sich* {*eus; studious to remove*
991 *The dead by influx of a living love,*
[992] *By stealthy entrance of a* ~~*tyrannous*~~ *guest*
perilous
[993] Troubling a heart that had been long at
992 ~~*Thro' a subsided spirit dispossess'd*~~ rest
Troubling a heart that had been long at rest
993 ~~*Of amorous passion, thro' a torpid breast.*~~
withdrawn
994 *Now when the viands were* ~~*remov'd,*~~ *& ceas'd*
995 *The first division of the splendid Feast;*
996 *While round a vacant board the Chiefs recline*
997 *Huge goblets are brought forth;—they crown the wine.*
998 *Voices of gladness roll the walls around;*
999 *Those gladsome voices from the courts rebound;*
1000 *From gilded rafters many a blazing light*
1001 *Depends, & torches overcome the night,*
1002 *The minutes fly—till, as the Queen commands,*
1003 *A bowl of state is offer'd to her hands:*
{ *u*
1004 *Then She, as Bel* { *as wont & all the Line*
{ *us*
1005 *From Bel* { *as, fill'd it to the brim with wine:*
1006 *Silence ensued. "O Jupiter! whose care*
1007 " *Is hospitable Dealing, grant my prayer!*
[992] By B
[993] Troubling a heart that had been
long at rest

984–1007 Autograph not WW's is MW's, except where noted.
985 Revision is in DW's autograph, over WW's pencil.
989 "s" in "Asedalian" is in pencil.
990 Revision "Uproots" is in pencil.
992–993 Revisions in WW's autograph are in pencil; other revisions are in DW's autograph.

44

"Productive be this day of lasting joy
"To Tyrians, & these Exiles driv'n from Troy;
"A day to future generations dear!
"Let Bacchus, donor of soul-gladdening chear, [gay]
"Be present! kindly Juno, be thou near!
"And Tyrians, may your choicest favours wait
"Upon this hour, the bond to celebrate!"
She spake; & shed an Offering on the board,
Then sipp'd the bowl whence she the wine had pour'd
And gave to Bitias ~~urging the prompt Chief~~ Lord
~~He raised the Bowl & took a long deep draught~~
Then every Chief in turn the beverage quaffed
~~Drank deep, self drench'd from out the brimming gold~~
~~Thereafter a like course the remaining Nobles hold.~~
Graced with redundant hair Iopas sings
The lore of Atlas, to resounding strings—
The labours of the sun; the lunar wanderings:
Whence human kind, & brute; what natural pow'rs
Engender lightning; whence ~~the~~ are falling show'rs.
He chaunts Arcturus, & that ~~social~~ fraternal pain
The glittering Bears, the Pleiads ~~charged~~ fraught with rain;
Why suns in winter, shunning Heaven's steep heights
Post seaward; what impedes the the tardy nights.

[Book I]

44

1008 *" Productive be this day of lasting joy*
1009 *" To Tyrians, & these Exiles driv'n from Troy;*
1010 *" A day to future generations dear!*
quickening
1011 *" Let Bacchus, donor of soul-gladdening chear,*
1012 *" Be present! kindly Juno, be thou near!*
1013 *" And Tyrians, may your choicest favours wait*
1014 *" Upon this hour, the bond to celebrate!"*
1015 *She spake; & shed an Offering on the board,*
1016 *Then sipp'd the bowl whence she the wine had pour'd;*
{ *urging the prompt ~~Chief~~Lord*
{ urging the prompt Lord
1017 *And gave to Belus, ~~bidding him take heart;~~*
{ *He raised the Bowl & took a long deep draught*
{ He rais'd and too the Bowl and
1018 *~~He rais'd—& not unequal to his part,~~*
Then every Chief in tur {*n the beverage quaffed*
{ took a long deep draught
1019 *~~Drank deep, self-drench'd from out the brimming gold:~~*
1020 *~~Thereafter a like course the encircling Nobles hold.~~*
Then every Chief in turn the beverage quaffd
1021 *Graced with redundant hair Iopas sings*
1022 *The lore of Atlas, to resounding strings—*
1023 *The labours of the sun; the lunar wanderings:*
1024 *Whence human Kind, & brute; what natural powr's*
{ *are*
{ are
1025 *Engender lightning; whence ~~the~~ falling show'rs.*
{ *fraternal*
{ fraternal
1026 *He chaunts Arcturus, & that ~~social~~ Twain*
{ *fraught*
{ *the* { fraught
1027 *The glittering Bears,* {*& Pleiads ~~charged~~ with rain;*
1028 *—Why Suns in winter, shunning Heaven's steep heights,*
sea }
1029 *Post on* }*ward; what impedes the tardy nights.*
[1026] He chaunts Arcturus Lord of stormy

hours
[1027] And the twin bears & Peliad fraught
[1011] { soul-quickening
[1027] with { showers

1008–1029 Autograph not WW's is MW's, except where noted.

1011 Revision above line is in pencil.

1017–1027 Revisions in WW's autograph are in pencil, except for "soul-quickening," l. [1011]; other revisions are in DW's autograph.

45

The learned Song from Tyrian healers draws
Loud shouts,—the Trojans echo the applause.
—But, lengthening out the night with converse new,
Large draughts of love unhappy Dido drew;
Of Priam ask'd; of Hector, o'er & o'er—
What Arms the Son of bright Aurora wore;
What ~~Coursers~~ steeds ~~were~~ of Diomed; the car could boast; ~~how great;~~
Among the Leaders of the Grecian Host
~~Achilles,—but, Ulysses, the whole estate,~~
How looked Achilles, their dread Paramount—+
Retrace the Grecian cunning from its source,—
"Your own griefs—& your Friends'; your wand'ring course;
"—For now, till this seventh summer have ye ranged
"The sea, or trod the earth, to peace estranged."

End of the First Book.

Paramount
But nay—the fatal wiles, O Guest, recount
Retrace the Grecian cunning from its source

[Book I]

45

1030 *The learned Song from Tyrian hearers draws*
1031 *Loud shouts,—the Trojans echo the applause.*
1032 *But, lengthening out the night with converse new,*
1033 *Large draughts of love unhappy Dido drew;*
1034 *Of Priam ask'd; of Hector, o'er & o'er—*
1035 *What Arms the Son of bright Aurora wore;*
~~Coursers~~ Steeds the Car
~~Coursers~~ could boast;
1036 *What ~~Horses,~~ } ~~those~~ of Diomed:—~~how great,~~*
Among the Leaders of the Grecian Host
1037 *~~Achilles—"but O Guest! the whole relate;~~* ×
How looked Achilles, their dread Paramount—
1038 *"Retrace the Grecian cunning from its source,—*
1039 *"Your own griefs—& your Friends'—your wand'ring course;*
1040 *"—For now, till this seventh summer have ye ranged*
1041 *"The sea, or trod the earth, to peace estranged!*

What steeds the Car of Diomed
could
Among the Leaders of the Grecian [?bas]
[?]

How looke Achilleis their dre

End of the First Book.

[1037] *Paramount*
[1015] ~~Then sipp'd the Bowl whence she the wine~~
[1037] *But nay—the fatal wiles, O Guest, recount*
~~had pour'd~~
[1038] *Retrace the Grecian cunning from its source*
[1017] ~~And gave to Belus urging the prompt Lord~~
the bowl & took a [?]
[1018] ~~He rais'd [?& ?held]~~ ~~long deep draught~~
[1019] ~~Then every Chief in turn the beverage quaff'd~~
[1018] ~~He [?met] the occasion with a generous draft~~
[1037] ~~How lookd Achilles their dread Paramount~~
[1036] ~~But tell what [?]~~

[1015]–[1019] Revisions are in erased pencil.

1030–end of Book I Autograph not WW's is MW's, except where noted.

1035–1038 Revisions in WW's autograph are in pencil; other revisions are in DW's autograph. On 28[v], in WW's pencil, the following version of l. 1037 is found: "But nay—o gues the the fatal wiles [?recount]"

This said, Laocoon hurl'd with mighty force
A ponderous spear against the monster's side
It smote the curved ribs, & quivering stood
While groans made answer from the scoop'd wood.
We too upon this impulse had not fail'd
Had not by fate & mind adverse fate
Been adverse & our minds infatuate
We, too, had rush'd the den to penetrate,
Streams of Argolic blood our swords had stain'd,
Troy, thou mightst yet have stood, & Priam's tow'rs remain'd.
But lo, an unknown Youth with hand to pen
Behind him fasten'd, whom a boisterous Band
Of Dardan Shepherds to the King had brought,
Dragg'd to the Shore & placed before the King
Such his device when he those chains had sought,
A voluntary captive, fix'd in thought
Either the City to betray, or meet
Death, the sure penalty of foil'd deceit.
The curious Trojans, pouring in, deride
And taunt the Prisoner with an emulous pride.
Now see the cunning of the Greeks exprest
By guilt of One, an image of the rest!
For, while with helpless looks, from side to side
Anxiously cast, the Phrygian throng he eyed,
"Alas! what land," he cries, "can now, what sea
"Can offer refuge? What resource for me?
"Who 'mid the Greeks no breathing-place can find
And whom ye, Trojans, have to death consign'd."
× Of Dardan Swains with clamour hurry
Force with them to the Shore & place before the King

[Book II]

[110] 4 A Chief accused of [?traiter] acts accused [?]
[111] War to dissuade was all his treachery

Laocoon with mighty force
This said, ~~he~~ hurl'd ~~a spear against the Horse~~;
A ponderous spear against the monster Horse
It smote the curved ribs, & quivering stood,
from cavern'd
+ *While groans made answer ~~thro~~' the ~~hollow~~ wood.*
We too upon this impulse had not fate
~~Then, but for loss of mind & adverse fate,~~
Been adverse & our minds infatuate
We, too, had rush'd the den to penetrate;
Streams of Argolic blood our swords had stain'd;
Troy, thou might'st yet have stood, & Priam's towr's remain'd!
~~meanwhile~~ to hand
To hand *But lo! an unknown Youth, with hand ~~to hand~~*
Bound fast boisterous
Behind him ~~fasten'd~~, whom a ~~clamorous~~ Band
~~with loud uproar bring~~
X *~~Of Dardan Shepherds to the King hath brought!~~*
~~Down to the shore & place before the King~~
~~Even~~ such his ~~scheme~~ when he those chains had sought,
device,
A voluntary captive, fix'd in thought
Either the City to betray, or meet
Death, the sure penalty of foil'd deceit.
The curious Trojans, pouring in, deride
And taunt the Prisoner, with an em{u/alous pride.
Now see the cunning of the Greeks exprest
By guilt of One, an image of the rest!
For, while with helpless looks, from side to side
Anxiously cast, the Phrygian throng he ey'd.
"Alas! what land," he cries, "can now, what sea
"Can offer refuge? What resource for me?
"Who 'mid the Greeks no breathing-place can find,
And whom ye, Trojan's, have to death consign'd!"—
[80] X *of Dardan Swains with clamour hurrying*
[81] *Force with them to the shore & place before the King—*

sole sole cause
A Chief for this cause condemn'd to die
That he dissuaded war

[110–111] Revisions are in pencil, as are revisions in left margin.

69–95 Autograph of base text is MW's; revisions not in WW's autograph are in the autograph of CW, Jr.

73 Revision "We too" is in pencil.

79 Revision "Bound fast" is ink over pencil.

'Twas the earliest hour when sweet repose
Gift of the Gods creeps softly on, to close
'Twas the earliest hour of slumberous rest
The eyes of weary mortals. Then arose
Gift of the Gods to man with toil opprest;
Hector, or in my dream appear'd to
When present to my dream did Hector rise
And stood before me with fast-streaming eyes:
Such as he was when horse had striven with horse
Whirling along the plain his lifeless Corse,
The thongs that bound him to the Chariot thrust
Thro' his swoln feet, & black with gory dust.
A spectacle how pitiably sad!
How chang'd from that returning Hector, clad
In glorious spoils, Achilles' own attire!
From Hector hurling shipward the red Phrygian fire!
— A squalid beard, hair clotted thick with gore,
And that same throng of patriot wounds he bore,
In front of Troy receiv'd; & now methought,
That I myself was to a passion wrought
Of tears, which to my voice this greeting brought:
"O Light of Dardan Realms! most faithful stay
To Trojan courage, why these lingerings of delay?
"Hector, so long expected
"Where hast thou tarried, Hector? from what coast
"Com'st thou? long wish'd for! that so many lost
we how faint so many lost
Thy kinsmen or thy friends — such travail borne
"By this afflicted city thy outworn
"These gashes whence
"Behold thee! — Why this undeserv'd disgrace?
"Who thus defil'd with wounds that honor'd face?

Where hast thou tarried Hector? from what coast
Com'st thou long look'd for after thousands lost
Thy kinsmen or thy friends, such travail borne
By desolated Troy how tir'd & worn
Are we who thus behold Thee? how forlorn! Thus gashes whence

After these words

See the

[Book II]

16 It was the earliest hour when sweet repose
Gift of the Gods creeps softly on, to close
361 *~~It was the earliest hour of slumberous~~ rest*
The eyes of weary mortals; then arose
362/363 *~~Gift of the Gods to Man with toil opprest~~;*
Hector, or in my dream appeare'd to
364 *~~When, present to my dream did Hector~~ ^ rise*
365 *And stood before me with fast-streaming eyes:*
366 *Such as he was when horse had striven with horse,*
367 *Whirling along the plain his lifeless Corse,*
bound
368 *The thongs that ^ him to the Chariot thrust*
369 *Thro' his swoln feet, & black with gory dust;—*
370 *A spectacle how pitiably sad!*
371 *How chang'd from that returing Hector, clad*
372 *In glorious spoils, Achilles' own attire!*
373 *From Hector hurling shipward the red Phrygian fire!*
374 *—A squalid beard, hair clotted thick with gore,*
375 *And that same throng of patriot wounds he bore,*
376 *In front of Troy receiv'd; & now, methought,* }
377 *That I myself was to a passion wrought* }
378 *Of tears, which to my voice this greeting brought:* }
379 *"O Light of Dardan Realms! most faithful Stay*
380 *"To Trojan courage, why these lingerings of delay?*

Such as he was when by Pelides slain
Thessalian Coursers whirld him o'er the pla

Hector, so long expected
381 *"~~Where has thou tarried, Hector~~? From what coast*
& we how faint! so many lost
?}
382 *"Com's't thou,*} *~~long wish'd for? That so many lost~~*
383 *"Thy kinsman or thy friends—such travail borne*
~~town,—yet we~~, forlorn,
384 *"~~By this afflicted City—we, outworn~~,*
These gashes whence? { *is*
385/386 *"~~Behold thee!—Why~~ th* { *e undeserv'd disgrace?*
~~calm majestic~~
387 *"<u>Who</u> thus defil'd with wounds ~~that honor'd~~ face?*

After thousand lost
see the end

[382] *Coms't*
[381] *Where hast thou tarried Hector? from what coast*
[382] *Com'st thou long look'd for after thousands* }
[387] *that* } *calm majestic*
[382] *lost*
[383] *Thy kinsmen or thy friends, such travail borne*
[385] *By desolated Troy how tir'd & worn*
[386] *Are we who thus behold Thee? how forlorn! Thes gashes whence?*

361–387 Autograph of base text is MW's; revisions not in WW's autograph are in the autograph of CW, Jr., unless otherwise noted.

366–367 WW, in pencil, has written (vertically, in the left margin) Dryden's translation of this passage.

368 "bound" is in MW's autograph.

382 "see the end," in left margin, is in pencil, and refers to revisions on 51^v and 52^v.

387 Revision "calm majestic," in WW's autograph, is in pencil.

[385] "t" in "tired" is crossed in pencil.

17

He aught to this—unwilling to detain
One, who had ask'd vain things, with answer vain;
But, groaning deep, "Flee, Goddess-born, he said,
"Snatch thyself from these flames around thee spread;
"Our Enemy is master of these walls;
"Down from her elevation Ilium falls.
"Enough for Priam; the long strife is o'er,
"Nor doth our Country ask one effort more.
"Could Pergamus have been defended—hence,
"Even from this hand, had issued her defence;
"Troy her Penates doth to thee commend,
"Her sacred rites—let these the Fates attend!
"Far sailing, seek for these the fated land ~~Sail under their protection for the land~~
"Where mighty walls at length shall ~~realms~~ rise ~~grow~~ at thy command!"
No more was utter'd; but his hand he stretch'd,
And from the inmost Sanctuary fetch'd
The consecrated wreaths, the potency
Of Vesta, & the fires that may not die.
Now, … from street to street
And tho' apart, & mid thick trees embower'd,
My Father's mansion stood, the loud alarms
Came pressing thither, & the clash of arms.
Sleep fled: I climb the roof—&, where it rears
Its loftiest summit, stand with quicken'd ears:

[Book II]

17

au
{o
He n {*aught to this—unwilling to detain*
{,
One {*who had ask'd vain things, with answer vain;*
{*he said*
But, groaning deep, "Flee, Goddess-born, {[?*said he*],
"Snatch thyself from these flames around thee spread;
"Our Enemy is master of these Walls;
"Down from her elevation Ilium falls.
{*or*
"Enough f {*rom Priam; the long strife is o'er,*
"Nor doth our Country ask one effort more.
"Could Pergamus have been defended—hence,
"Even from this hand, had issued her defence;
{*e*
" Troy her Penates doth to the {*commend,*
rites *F*}
" Her sacred ~~stores~~;—let these the f } *ates attend!*
Far sailing, seek for these the fated
"~~Sail under their protection for the Land~~ land
walls at length
"Where mighty ~~Realms~~ shall ~~grow~~ at thy command!"
rise
— No more was utter'd; but his hand he stretch'd,
And from the inmost Sanctuary fetch'd
The consecrated wreaths, the potency
Of Vesta, & the fires that may not die.
Now ~~wild~~ [?~~tumults~~] from street to street
wailings wild {*s*
~~Meantime, wild tumult thro' the street~~ {*~~is pour'd~~;*
are pour'd
And tho' apart, & mid thick trees embower'd,
My Father's mansion stood, the loud alarms
Came pressing thither, & the clash of Arms.
Sleep fled; I climb the roof—&, where it rears
Its loftiest summit, stand with quickened ears:

after thousands lost
Thy kinsmen or thy friends such travel born
By desolated Troy how tired & worn
Are we who thus behold thee, how forlorn

Vertical revision in left margin is of ll. 382–385.

388–411 Autograph of base text is MW's; revisions not in WW's autograph are in the autograph of CW, Jr., unless otherwise noted.

388 Revision "au" is in pencil.

390 Revision is in MW's autograph.

21

—Can words the havoc of that night express?
What power of tears may equal the distress?
An ancient City sinks to disappear;
The kings who ruled for ages. Far & near
Multitudes unresisting thro' streets whose
The unresisting thro' the streets, the abodes
Houses of men & thresholds of the Gods
Of Men, & hallow'd Temples of the Gods,
By [illegible] prostrate
Are fell'd by massacre that takes no heed;
lie dead
Nor are the Trojans only doom'd to bleed;
The Vanquish'd sometimes to their hearts recall
Old virtues, & the conquering Argives fall.
Sorrow is every where, & fiery death,
Fear, Anguish struggling to be rid of breath,
Are every where about above & beneath
And Death still crowding on the shape of Death.
For
Androgeus, whom a numerous Force attends,
Was the first Greek we met: he rashly deems us friends;
"What sloth," he cries, "retards you? Warriors haste!
"Troy blazes, sack'd by others, & laid waste;
"And ye come lagging from your Ships the last!"
Thus he: & strait mistrusting our replies,
He felt himself begirt with enemies:
Voice fail'd—step falter'd at the dire mistake;
Like one, who thro' a deeply-tangled brake
Struggling, hath trod upon a lurking Snake
And shrunk in terror from the unlook'd-for Pest
Lifting his blue-swoln neck & wrathful crest.

[Book II]

P 21

486 *—Can words the havoc of that night express?*
487 *What power of tears may equal the distress?*
to
488 *An ancient City sinks & disappears,/*
489 *She sinks who rul'd for ages.—Far & near*
roads
Multitudes, unresisting thro' streets abodes
Numbers of helpless
490 ~~*The Unresisting, thro' the streets, the abodes*~~
Houses of Men & thresholds of the Gods
491 ~~*Of Men—& hallow'd Temples of the Gods,*~~
~~*swift*~~
By reckless massacre are prostrated
Mow'd down by ruthless massacre
492 ~~*Are fell'd by massacre that takes*~~ *no heed;*
lie dead
493 ~~*Nor are the Trojans only*~~ *doom'd to bleed;*
494 *The Vanquish'd sometimes to their hearts recall*
495 *Old virtues, & the conquering Argives fall.*
497 ~~*Sorrow is every where, & fiery skaith,*~~
Fe
496 *A ar, Anguish struggling to be rid of breath,*
Are every where; about above beneath
498 ~~*And*~~ *Death still crowding on the shape of Death.*
Is
499 *Androgeus, whom a numerous Force attends,*
500 *Was the first Greek we met: he rashly deems us Friends.*
501 *"What sloth," he cries, "retards you? Warriors haste!*
502 *"Troy blazes, sack'd by others, & laid waste;*
503 *"And Ye come lagging from your Ships the last!"*
504 *Thus he: & strait mistrusting our replies,*
505 *He felt himself begirt with enemies:*
—
506 *Voice fail'd—step faulter'd at the dire mistake;*
507 *Like one, who thro' a deeply-tangled brake*
508 *Struggling, hath trod upon a lurking Snake*
509 *And shrunk in terror from the unlook'd-for Pest,*
510 *Lifting his blue-swoln neck & wrathful crest.*

486–510 Base text is in MW's autograph; revisions are in CW, Jr.'s autograph.
486 The "P," signaling a new paragraph, is in pencil.
490 Revision "Numbers of helpless" is in pencil, as is deletion line through "The Unresisting."
492 Revisions "Mow'd down . . . lie dead" and "swift" are in pencil.
492–493 Deletion lines are in pencil.

[Book II]

[381] Full long expected, Hector from what coast

?
[382] Comst Thou! } and We, who after thousands lost,
[383] Thy kindred and thy Friends,—such travail born

[384] By all that breathe in Troy { , — how faint and worn

! us
[385] We, who behold thee; } but why th { y return?
And whence those wounds
[386] These gashes whence? this undeservd disgrace
[387] Who thus Defild that calm majestic face

[381] Where hast thou tarried Hector? from what coast

'
[382] Come } st Thou long-look'd for. After thousands lost
[383] ~~Thy kindred and thy Fr~~ troubles
[383] Of thine & ours after such travail born
[402] No more was utter'd—but with hand outstrech'd
[403] To me he gave the sacred fillets—fetch'd
[404] From the dread covert of ~~their~~ inmost choir
[405] The mighty Vesta and the 'eternal fire

[Book II]

[?403] cates
[461] ~~Which~~
[461] With young Choroebus who intent
[461] ~~With y~~
[461] With young Chorebus who to Troy had sped
[462] By a mad passion for Cassandra led

[381] Where hast thou tarried Hector, from what coast
[382] Com'st Thou l {L} long-look'd for, how, so many lost
labour
[383] Thy kinsmen & thy Friends ~~such travel~~ born
[384] By ~~Troy, do we behold thee? tired & worn—~~
[384] By desolated Troy, do we, outworn
[385/386] Behold these when, th{is / ~~ese wound~~}s undeserv'd disgrace?
[387] {These / Whence} wounds that thus defil that calm majestic face

[381] Where hast thou tarried Hector? from what coast
[382] Comest thou long lookd for?— How, such numbers lost
[383] Thy kindred and thy friends such travel borne
[384] By desolated Troy do we out-worn
[385/386] Behold thee—Whence this undeservd disgrace
[387] These gashes that defile that calm majestic face

[?403, 461–462] WW's pencil; "With y" has been deleted, then erased.
[381–387] The first version of these lines is in WW's pencil.

4 ~~We too, upon this imposture, had [illegible]~~
Been adverse, our mind infatuate
~~We too had risen the door to penetrate~~
~~Left out for [illegible] adverse fate,~~
~~We too, had rush'd the [illegible] to penetrate.~~
Streams of Argolic blood our swords had stain'd
Troy, thou might'st yet have stood, and Priam's Towers remain'd!
~~But lo! an unknown Youth, with hand to hand~~
~~Behind him fasten'd, whom a clamorous Band~~
~~Of Dardan Shepherds to their King had brought!~~
~~Even such his scheme when he was [illegible]~~ sought,
A voluntary captive, fix'd in thought
Either the City to betray, or meet
Death, the sure penalty of foil'd deceit.
The curious Trojans, pouring in, deride
And taunt the Prisoner, with an emulous pride.
Now see the cunning of the Greeks exprest
By guilt of One, ~~an~~ true image of the rest!
For, while with helpless looks, from side to side
Anxiously cast, the Phrygian throng he eyed,
"Alas! what Land," he cries, "can now, what Sea
"Can offer refuge? What resource for me!
"Who 'mid the Greeks no breathing-place can find,
"And whom ye, Trojans, have to death consign'd!"—
Thus were we wrought upon; and now, with sense
Of pity touch'd that check'd all violence,

[Book II]

~~We too, upon this impulse, had not fate~~
4 *Been adverse, & our mind infatuate*
We too had rushed the den to penetrate }
73/74 *~~"Then, but for loss of mind and adverse fate~~,*
75 *~~"We, too, had rush'd the [?den] to penetrate~~:*
76 *"Streams of Argolic blood our swords had stain'd*
77 *"Troy, thou might'st yet have stood, and Priam's Towers remain'd!*

But lo! an
78 P *~~"But lo! an~~ } ~~unknown Youth, with hand to han~~d*
79 *~~"Behind him fasten'd, whom a clamorous Band~~*
80/81 [ ]*~~Dardan Shepherds t[ ] King [ ] brough~~t!*
82 *~~"Even such his scheme when he those~~ chains ~~had~~ sought,* }
83 *"A voluntary captive, fix'd in thought*
84 *"Either the City to betray, or meet*
85 *Death, the sure penalty of foil'd deceit.*
86 *"The curious Trojans, pouring in, deride*
87 *"And taunt the Prisoner, with an emulous pride.*
88 *"Now see the cunning of the Greeks exprest*
true
89 *"By guilt of One, ~~an~~ image of the rest!*
90 *"For, while with helpless looks, from side to side*
91 *"Anxiously cast, the Phrygian throng he ey'd,*
L *S*
92 *"Alas! what l } and," he cries, "can now, what s } ea*
C *W*
93 *"c } an offer refuge? w } hat resource for me?*
94 *"Who 'mid the Greeks no breathing-place can find,*
95 *"And whom ye, Trojans, have to death consign'd!—"*
96 *"Thus were we wrought upon; and now, with sense*
97 *"Of pity touch'd that check'd all violence,*

73–97 The base text is in the autograph of DW; revisions are in the autograph of CW, Jr., except where indicated.

75–80/81 Brackets indicate words that are obscured or partially erased by the wax used to fasten down a pasteover.

78–91 Open quotes at left have been deleted by erasure.

78 "P" in the left margin, in pencil, is WW's signal for a new paragraph. Revisions are in DW's autograph.

92–93 Revisions are in DW's autograph.

16

~~When present~~ to ~~my dream, did Hector rise~~
And stood before me with fast-streaming eyes:
Such as he was when horse had striven with horse,
Whirling along the plain his lifeless Corse,
The thongs that bound him to the Chariot thrust
Through his swoln feet, and black with gory dust;—
A spectacle how piteably sad!
How chang'd from that returning Hector, clad
In glorious spoils, Achilles' own attire!
From Hector hurling ^shipward the red Phrygian fire!
—A squalid beard, hair ~~clotted~~ thick with gore,
And that same throng of patriot wounds he bore,
In front of Troy receiv'd; and now, methought,
That I myself was to a passion wrought
Of tears, which to my voice this greeting brought.
"O Light of Dardan Realms! most faithful Stay
"To Trojan courage, why these lingerings of delay?
"Where hast thou tarried, Hector? ~~From what coast~~
"~~Com'st thou, long waited-for? What so many lost~~ — After thousands looked
"~~Thy kinsmen or thy friends~~ such travail borne
"By this afflicted ~~town~~ we ~~are~~ worn — Now how tir'd and worn
Are we who thus behold thee! how forlorn!
"~~Behold thee. Why this undeserv'd disgrace?~~
These gashes whence? this underserv'd disgrace?
"~~What thus defil'd with wounds that honor'd face?~~"
~~Who thus defiled that calm superb face?~~
He nought to this—unwilling to detain
One, who had ask'd vain things, with answer vain,

[Book II]

16

to }
~~*When present in* } *my dream did Hector rise*~~
And stood before me with fast-streaming eyes:
Such as he was when horse had striven with horse,
C }
Whirling along the plain his lifeless c } *orse,*
The thongs that bound him to the Chariot thrust
Through his swoln feet, and black with gory dust;—
A spectacle how pitiably sad!
How chang'd from that returning Hector, clad
In glorious spoils, Achilles' own attire!
shipward
From Hector hurling^ the red Phrygian fire!
—A squalid beard, ^hair clotted thick with gore,
And that same throng of patriot wounds he bore,
In front of Troy receiv'd; and now, methought, }
That I myself was to a passion wrought }
Of tears, which to my voice this greeting brought. }
"O Light of Dardan Realms! Most faithful Stay
{ *,*
"To Trojan courage { *! why these lingerings of delay?*
"Where hast thou tarried, Hector? ~~*From what co*~~*ast*
look'd After thousands
~~*"Com'st thou, long wish'd-for? That so many*~~ *lost—*
~~*"Thy kinsmen or thy friends—such travail borne*~~*,*
Town how tir'd and worn
"By this afflicted ~~*City*~~*—we* ~~*out*~~*^worn*
Are we who thus behold thee, how forlorn!
~~*"Behold thee! Why this undeserv'd disgrace*~~*?*
These gashes whence? this undeserv'd disgrace?
~~*"Who thus defil'd with wounds that honor'd face*~~*?*
~~Who thus defiled that calm majestic face~~?
{ *o*
He n { *aught to this—unwilling to detain*
One, who had ask'd vain things, with answer vain;

364–389 The autograph of the base text is DW's; revisions not in WW's autograph are in hers.
364 CW, Jr., has revised this line to the reading text on an interleaf, quotation marks omitted.
374 "clotted thick" is written over an illegible erasure.
381–387 CW, Jr., has revised these lines to the reading text on an interleaf.

73
21

Can words the havoc of that night express?
What power of tears may equal the distress?
An ancient City sinks to disappear;
She sinks who rul'd for ages.— Far and near
Multitude
The unresisting through the streets, ~~the abodes~~ roads
Houses of men, and thresholds of
Of men, and hallowed temples of the Gods,
By reckless massacre are prostrated
~~Are fell'd by massacre that takes no heed;~~
Nor are the Trojans only doom'd to bleed;
The Vanquish'd sometimes to their hearts recall
Old virtues, and the conquering Argives fall.
~~Terror is every where, and fiery Skaith,~~
Fear, Anguish struggling to be rid of breath,
Are every where; about, above, beneath
~~And~~ Death still crowding on the shape of Death.
Fi'r Androgeus, whom a numerous Force attends,
Was the first Greek we met: he rashly deems us Friends.
"What sloth," he cries, "retards you? Warriors haste!
"Troy blazes, sack'd by others, and laid waste;
"And ye come lagging from your Ships the last!"
Thus he: and straight mistrusting our replies,
He felt himself begirt with enemies:
Voice fail'd— step faulter'd— at the dire mistake;
Like one, who through a deeply-tangled brake
Struggling, hath trod upon a lurking Snake,
And shrunk in terror from the unlook'd-for Pest
Lifting his blue-swoln neck and wrathful crest.

[Book II]

21

486 *Can words the havoc of that night express?*
487 *What power of tears may equal the distress?*
to ;
488 *An ancient City sinks and* } *disappear* { *s.*
489 *S<u>he</u> sinks who rul'd for ages.—Far and near*
Multitudes *u* roads
490 ~~*The*~~ *Unresisting, throg* } *gh* ~~*the*~~ *streets,* ~~*the abodes*~~
Houses of men and thresholds of
491 ~~*Of Men, and hallow'd Temples of*~~ *the Gods,*
By reckless massacre are prostrated
492 ~~*Are fell'd by massacre that takes no heed*~~*;*
493 *Nor are the Trojans only doom'd to bleed;*
494 *The Vanquish'd sometimes to their hearts recall*
495 *Old virtues, and the conquering Argives fall.*
496 ~~*Sorrow is every-where, and fiery skaith,*~~
497 *Fear, Anguish struggling to be rid of breath,*
Are every where;—about, above, beneath
498 ~~*And*~~ *Death/ still crowding on the shape of Death.*
Is ^
499 *Androgeus, whom a numerous Force attends,*
500 *Was the first Greek we met: he rashly deems us Friends.*
501 *"What sloth," he cries, "retards you? Warriors haste!*
502 *"Troy blazes, sack'd by others, and laid waste;*
Y
503 *"And y* } *e come lagging from your Ships the last!"*
504 *Thus he: and straight mistrusting our replies,*
505 *He felt himself begirt with enemies:*
506 *Voice fail'd—step faulter'd—at the dire mistake;*
,
507 *Like one, who through a deeply-tangled brake*
lurking Snake,
508 ~~Lurking~~ *Struggling, hath trod upon a* { [?*snake*]
^ *P*
509 *And shrunk in terror from the unlook'd-for p* } *est,*
510 *Lifting his blue-swoln neck and wrathful crest.*

486–510 The autograph of the base text is DW's; revisions not in WW's autograph are in hers, except where indicated.

490–492 CW, Jr., has revised these lines to the reading text on the facing interleaf, thus:

~~A passive number~~
passive creatures,
Multitudes, ~~unresisting~~, through streets, roads,
Houses of men, & thresholds of the Gods,
By reckless massacre are prostrated

508 "Lurking" in left margin is in WW's pencil; caret is in pencil.

Our weary limbs in the no untimely sleep
Prompt by the hours ere yet ascending Night
Risen from his couch, ere Night with slow
Had reach'd her orbit to its topmost height
~~Had measured half the vaulted firmament~~
rose and with keen
Prompt Palinurus ~~looks with cautious~~ eyes
~~To every wind~~ for what it signifies;
Looks to the winds
And to each breath of air a watchful ear applies.
Next, all the stars gliding thro' silent Heaven
The Bears, Arcturus, & the watery Seven
He notes; and, ranging wide, his eyes behold
Magnificent Orion armed in gold.
~~Tranquil by his the [illegible] that not a gale will blow~~
~~Assured that all prognostics [illegible]~~
The peace to trouble which all signs foresee,
~~[illegible]~~
He sends the summons forth: our camp we raise,
Are gone; & every Ship her broadest wing displays

- - - - - - - - - - - - - - - - -

We press the bosom of the wished for land,
And, as we lay dispersed along the Strand,
Our bodies we refresh and dewy sleep
Falls upon weary limbs beside the hollow deep

[Book III]

no untimely
707 *Our weary limbs in ~~the soft dew~~ of sleep*
Drawn by the hours ere yet ascending Night
708 *Risen from his couch ere Night with slow*
height
~~Had~~ trackd her orbit to the topmost ~~*ascent*~~
709 ~~*Had measured half the vaulted firmament*~~*,*
rose and with keen
710 *Prompt Palenurus ~~looks with cautious~~ eyes*
~~wind~~
711 ~~*To every cloud*~~ ^ *for what it signifies;*
Looks to the wind
712 *And to each breath of air a watchful ear*
applies.
713 *Next, all the stars gliding thro' silent Heaven*
714 *The Bears, Arcturus, & the watery Seven*
715 *He notes; and, ranging wide, his eyes behold*
716 *Magnificent Orion, armed in gold.*
galc }
Taught by his skill ~~not a~~ that not a wind } will blow
717 ~~*Assured that all prognostics, low & high*~~
The peace to trouble which all signs foreshow
718 ~~*Unite to promise fixed serenity*~~*,*
719 *He sends the summons forth: our Camp*
we raise,
720 *Are gone; & every Ship her broadest wing displays.*

— — — — — — — — — — — — — —

[704] We press the bosom of the wishd for land:
[705] And, as we lay dispersd along the strand,
[706] Our bodies we refresh and dewy sleep
[707] Fell upon weary limbs beside the lulling
deep

[704]–720 Autograph of base text, and of revisions not in WW's autograph, is DW's. "510" and "520," in pencil, are in the autograph of GGW, and hence are not recorded in transcription. These are the corresponding line numbers in Virgil's Latin.

Issues from his couch ~~before the Car of Night~~
~~Driven by the hours had closed [illegible]~~
Driven by the ascending hours [illegible]

~~Meanwhile the sun went down & shadows black~~
~~On every mountain darkened its head,~~
~~Tired of their toil, [illegible]~~
~~Earth's [illegible] along the [illegible]~~
~~They [illegible] beside the [illegible].~~
~~Where weariness is lost in timely sleep~~
~~Ere [illegible]~~
~~Black Night, the middle of her [illegible]ed.~~
~~Up from his couch doth Palinurus rise,~~
~~Listens to the wind for what it signifies~~
~~And [illegible] applies.~~
Next, all the stars gliding through silent heaven,
The Bears, Arcturus, & the clustered Seven
He notes; and, ranging wide, his eyes behold
Magnificent Orion armed in gold.
Assured that all prognostics, low & high,
Unite to promise fixed serenity,
He sends the summons forth: our Camp we raise,
Are gone, & every ship her broadest wing displays
The rowers task allotted to each bar

[Book III]

[708] ~~Risen from his couch before the Car of Nig~~ht
[709] ~~Driv'n by the hours had clomb th ethere~~al
~~heigh~~t
Driven by the ascending hours engulf the Night

[702] ~~*Meanwhile the sun went down & shadows spread*~~
[703] ~~*O'er every mountain, darkened to its head*~~*,*
[704] ~~*Tired of their oars, the men no sooner reach*~~
[705] ~~*Earth's wished-for bosom than along the beach*~~
[706] ~~*They spread their limbs beside the murmur-*~~
~~*-ing Deep*~~
[707] ~~*Where weariness is lost in timely sleep.*~~
[708] ~~*Ere she whose car the Hours had yoked & reined,*~~
[709] ~~*Black Night, the middle of her orbit gained*~~*.*
[710] ~~*Up from his couch doth Palenurus rise*~~*,*
[711] ~~*Looks to the wind for what it signifies*~~
[712] ~~*And to each breath of air a watchful ear*~~
~~*applie*~~*s.*
[713] *Next, all the stars gliding through silent heaven,*
[714] *The Bears, Arcturus, & the clustered Seven*
[715] *He notes; and, ranging wide, his eyes behold*
[716] *Magnificent Orion armed in gold.*
[717] *Assured that all prognostics, low & high,*
[718] *Unite to promise fixed serenity,*
[719] *He sends the summons forth: our Camp we*
raise,
[720] *Are gone, & every Ship her broadest wing*
displays
The rowers task allotted to each
band

---

[702]–[720] Autograph of base text, and of revisions not in WW's autograph, is DW's.

37

"Of my Astyanax,—in whom his face,
"His eyes are seen, his very hands I trace;
"And now, but for obstruction from the tomb,
"His years had open'd into kindred bloom.
"To these, while gushing tears bedew'd my cheek,
"Thus in the farewell moment did I speak;
"Live happy Ye, whose race of fortune run
Permits such life; from trials undergone
"We to the like are call'd; by you is quiet won.
"No seas have Ye to measure; nor on you
"Is it impos'd Ausonia to pursue,
"And search for fields still flying from the view.
"The Xanthus here in miniature—there stands
"A second Troy, the labour of your hands!
"With happier auspices—in less degree
Exposed, I trust, to Grecian enmity.
"If Tiber e'er receive me, & the sod
"Of Tiber's meadows by these feet be trod,

[Book III]

37

[688] ~~Lo Xanthus here in miniature—there stands~~
[689] ~~A second Troy the labour of your hands~~

{ —
676 *"Of my Astyanax {, in whom his face,*
677 *"His eyes are seen, his very hands I trace;*
678 *"And now, but for obstruction from the tomb,*
679 *"His years had open'd into kindred bloom.*
680 *"To these, while gushing tears bedew'd my cheek,*
681 *"Thus in the farewell moment did I speak;*
{ *py*
682 *"Live hap { ap Ye, whose race of fortune run*
;} *trials*
683 *"Permits such life, } from hard ~~fate~~ undergone*
the
684 *"We to ^ like ~~fate~~ are call'd; by you is quiet won.*
on
685 *"No seas have Ye to measure; nor ~~to~~ you*
686 *"Is it impos'd Ausonia to pursue,*
687 *"And search for fields still flying from the view.*
Lo Xanthus here in miniature!—~~there~~ stands
688 ~~*"A miniature Xanthus is display'd*~~
A second Troy, the labour of your hands,
689 ~~*"Before you, & the Troy your hands have made,*~~
690 *"With happier auspices—in less degree*
,}
691 *"Exposed, } I trust, to Grecian enmity.*
~~Mine if it be to sail in Tiber's~~
692 *"If Tiber e're receive me, & the sod* ~~flood~~
693 *"Of Tiber's meadows by these feet be trod,*
[687] ~~And search for fields in [? ? ?]~~
[688] ~~Before your sight a mimic Xanthus~~
~~flows~~
[689] ~~The Troy your made by your own labours~~
~~grows~~
[692] ~~Mine if it be to sail in Tiber's flood~~
[693] ~~And press the sod in Tiber's new [?]~~

676–693 Autograph of base text, and of revisions not in WW's autograph, is MW's. All revisions in WW's autograph are in pencil and have been deleted by erasure.

"If e'er I see our promis'd City rise,
"These neighbouring Nations, bound by ancient ti[es]
[illegible]
"The neighbouring [illegible]
"Hesperian & Epirian, whose blood came
"From Dardanus, whose lot hath been the same
"Shall make one Troy in spirit. May that care
"To our Descendants pass from heir to heir!
We coast the high Ceraunia, whence is found
The shortest transit to Italian ground;
Meanwhile the sun went down, & shadows spre[ad]
O'er every mountain dark'ned to its head.
Tired of their oars the men no sooner reach
Earth's wish'd-for bosom than their limbs they s[tretch]
On the dry margin of the murmuring Deep,
Where weariness is lost in timely sleep.

[Book III]

38 ~~neighbouring~~
[695] ~~These several nations, bound with~~
neigh~~bouring~~
~~If ere I see our promis'd City rise~~
[694] *"If e're I see our promis'd City rise,*
~~These neighbouring Nations bound by antient ties~~
[695] *"These neighbouring Nations bound by ancient ties,*
694 *"~~If e're our destin'd City I behold~~*
695 *"~~The neighbouring Town & Tribes a kin of old~~*
696 *"Hesperian & Epirian, whose blood came*
697 *"From Dardanus, whose lot hath been the same,*
698 *"Shall make one Troy in spirit. May that care*
699 *"To our Descendants pass from heir to heir!*
the high
700 *We coast ~~along~~ Ceraunia, whence is found*
701 *The shortest transit to Italian ground;*
702 *Meanwhile the sun went down, & shadows spread*
703 *Oer every mountain dark'ned to its head.*
704 *Tired of their oars the Men no sooner reach*
{ *a*
705 *Earth's wish'd-for bosom th{en their limbs they stretch*
706 *On the dry margin of the murmuring Deep,*
707 *Where weariness is lost in timely sleep.*
~~These~~
~~neighbouring~~
~~These~~
[695] ~~This [?] neighbouring~~
[694] ~~If ere I see the~~ ~~bound~~
~~bound~~
[695] ~~These neighbouring nations by antient~~
~~[?]~~ ~~ties~~

694–707 Autograph of base text, and of revisions not in WW's autograph, is MW's. All revisions in WW's autograph are in pencil.

APPENDIXES

Appendix I

Wordsworth's Letters to Lord Lonsdale

Between November 9, 1823, and February 17, 1824, Wordsworth corresponded with Lord Lonsdale about his *Aeneid* translation, hoping to solicit his lordship's opinions about it. In the course of this correspondence, the poet explained and defended his methods of translation at great length, especially in the letters of February 5 and 17, 1824. These letters are Wordsworth's most extensive discussion of his methods of translation. They are preserved as part of the Lonsdale Archive in the Cumbria County Records Office, Carlisle, and were first published, without dates and somewhat abridged, in Christopher Wordsworth, Jr.'s *Memoirs of William Wordsworth* (1851). All of the letters are in William Wordsworth's autograph, except the phrase "said he" in the first letter (not reproduced here) and the address of the second, which are in the autograph of Dora Wordsworth. I have here presented only those portions of the letters having directly to do with the translation. The reading text is based on the second edition of *The Letters of William and Dorothy Wordsworth: The Later Years, 1821–1850*, but has been corrected against the manuscripts themselves to reflect more accurately Wordsworth's capitalization and punctuation. In addition, significant substantive revisions, which are regularly omitted in *Later Years*, have here been preserved. Those interested in the full text of these letters should consult *Later Years*, I, 227–254.

Novr 9th [1823]

My Lord,

[. . .] I have just finished a Translation into English Rhyme of the first Æneid. Would your Lordship allow me to send it to you at Cottesmore.[1]— I should be much gratified if you would take the trouble of comparing some passages of it with the original. I have endeavoured to be much more literal than Dryden, or Pitt, who keeps much closer to the original than his Predecessor.—

. . . . ever your Lordships
faithful & obliged Ser[vnt]
W[m] Wordsworth [. . .]

[early December 1823]

The Earl of Lonsdale[2]

My Lord,

Many thanks for your obliging Letter.— I shall be much gratified if you happen to like my Translation, and thankful for any remarks with which you may honor me— I have made so much progress with the 2nd Book, that I defer sending the former 'till that is finished: It takes in many places a high tone of passion, which I would gladly succeed in rendering— When I read Virgil in the original I am moved, but not much so [in *del*] by the translations; and I cannot but think this owing to a defect in the diction; which I have endeavoured to supply, with what success you will erelong be enabled to judge.—[. . .]

Ever My Lord,
most faithfully your obliged
Friend and serv[nt]
W[m] Wordsworth [. . .]

---

[1] Lord Lonsdale's house in Rutland, where he liked to hunt. According to Hugh Owen, in 1796 William Lowther, later Lord Lonsdale, "and his family moved . . . to a house in Cottesmore where he built kennels for a pack of hounds he had bought in 1788. The pack took its name from the village, and William was Master of the famous Cottesmore Hunt from 1788 to 1842." *The Lowther Family* (Chichester, 1990), p. 382.

[2] The autograph is Dora W's, and hence the letter dates from before her departure to London in mid-December 1823.

Rydal Mount 23d Janry
1824

My Lord,

I am quite ashamed of being so long in fulfilling my engagement. But the promises of Poets are like the Perjuries of Lovers,[3] things at which Jove laughs.—At last, however, I have sent off the two first books of my Translations, to be forwarded by Mr Beckett.[4] I hope they will be read by your Lordship with some pleasure, as they have cost me a good deal of pains. Translation is just as to labour what the person who makes the [effort *del*] attempt is inclined to. If he wishes to preserve as much of the original as possible, and that with as little addition of his own as may be, there is no species of composition that costs more pains. A literal Translation of an antient Poet in verse, and particularly in rhyme, is impossible; something must be left out and something added; I have done my best to avoid the one & the other fault. I ought to say a prefatory word about the versification, which will not be found much to the taste of those whose ear is exclusively accommodated to the regularity of Popes Homer. I have run the Couplets freely into each other, much more even than Dryden has done. This variety seems to me to be called for, if any thing of the movement of the Virgilian [metre *del*] versification be transferable to our rhyme Poetry; and independent of this consideration, long Narratives in couplets with the sense closed at the end of each, are to me very wearisome- — I should be grateful for any communication of your Lordships feelings on this part of my labour, or any other. . . .

ever most sincerely
and faithfully your Lordship's
W Wordsworth

Febry 5th [1824]

My Lord,

I am truly obliged by your friendly and frank communication. May I beg that you would add to the favor, by marking with a pencil, [the *del*] some of the passages that are faulty in your view of the case. We seem pretty much of opinion upon the subject of rhyme. Pentameters, where the sense has a close, of some sort,

---

[3]Ovid, *Ars Amatoria*, Book I, 633, "Iuppiter ex alto periuria ridet amantum" ("Jupiter laughs from on high at the perjuries of lovers")—a rare Wordsworthian allusion to Ovid's erotic writings.

[4]John Beckett, M.P., later Right Hon. Sir John Beckett 2nd Bart. (1775–1847), married the Lowthers' fourth daughter, Lady Anne Lowther, in 1817. He was a Leeds banker who served as M.P. for Cockermouth (1818–1821), Haslemere (1826–1832), and, after the Reform Act of 1832, Leeds (1835–1837).

at every two lines, may be rendered in regularly closed couplets; but Hexameters, (especially the Virgilian, that run the lines into each other for a great length) can not.— I have long been persuaded that Milton formed his blank verse, upon the model of the Georgics and the Æneid, and I am so much struck with this resemblance, that I should have attempted Virgil in blank verse;[5] had I not been persuaded, that no [classi *del*] antient Author can be with advantaged be so rendered. Their religion, their warfare, their course of action & feeling, are too remote from modern interest to allow it. We require every possible help and attraction of sound in our language to smooth the way for the admission of things so remote from our present concerns— - My own notion of translation is, then that it cannot be too literal, provided three faults be avoided, <u>baldness</u>, in which I include all that takes from dignity; and <u>strangeness</u> or <u>uncouthness</u> including <u>harshness</u>; and lastly, attempts to convey meanings which as they cannot be given but by languid circumlocutions cannot in fact be said to be given at all. I will trouble you with an instance in which I fear this fault exists. Virgil describing Æneas's voyage, third Book, Verse, 451,[6] says

Hinc sinus Herculei si vera est fama, Tarenti
Cernitur. I render it thus,
Hence we behold the bay that bears the name
Of proud Tarentum, proud to share the fame
Of Hercules, though by a dubious claim;

I was unable to get the meaning with tolerable harmony into fewer words, which are more than to a modern reader perhaps it is worth.——

I feel much at a loss without the assistance of the marks which I have requested, to take an exact measure of your Lordship's feeling with regard to the Diction.— To save you the trouble of reference I will transcribe two passages from [Dray *del*] Dryden; first, from the celebrated appearance of Hector's Ghost, to Æneas, [which ? to Dryden upon this ? ? ? ? through *del*] Æneas thus addresses him.

O Light of Trojans and support of Troy
Thy Fathers Champion, and thy Country's joy,
O long expected by thy friends, from whence
Art thou returned so late for our defense?
Do we behold thee, wearied as we are,
With length of labours, and with toils of war,
After so many funerals of thy own
Art thou restored to thy declining Town?"[7]

---

[5]Two complete blank-verse translations of the *Aeneid* were available to WW: one by Joseph Trapp, published in 1720, which he knew and almost certainly used in preparing his own translation, and the other published by James Beresford in 1794, which STC refers to in his notes to Book I of the translation (see p. 197). WW probably did not consult Beresford.

[6]Actually, Verse 551. In the interleaved copy of the proof sheets of CW, Jr.'s *Memoirs*, owned by EQ and now in the WL, this error is corrected, and it appears in the *Memoirs* themselves so corrected. EQ also supplies a translation of the passage: "literally—hence is discerned the bay of [Tarentum of *inserted*] Hercules, if fame be true—"

[7]An opening quotation mark, probably meant to precede "O Light." has been omitted.

This I think not an unfavorable specimen of Dryden's way of treating the solemnly pathetic passages— Yet surely here is nothing of the cadence of the original, and little of its spirit— The second Verse is not in the original, and ought not to have been in Dryden, for it anticipates the beautiful Hemistich; "Sat[8] patriæ Priamoque datum; by the bye there is the same sort of anticipation in a spirited & harmonious Couplet preceding,

> Such as he was when by Pelides slain
> Thessalian Coursers dragg'd him oer the plain;

This introduction of Pelides here is not in Virgil, because it would have prevented the effect of, "redit exuviae inductus Achillei"[9]— — — There is a striking solemnity in the answer of Pantheus to Ænæas. Venit summa dies, & ineluctabile Tempus

> Dardaniæ, fuimus Troes, fuit Ilium, & ingens
> Gloria Teucrorum[10] &c Dryden thus gives it,
> Then Pantheus, with a groan,
> Troy is no more, and Ilium was a Town,
> The fatal day, the appointed hour is come
> When wrathful Jove's irrevocable Tomb[11]
> Transfers the Trojan state to Grecian hands,
> The fire consumes the Town the foe commands.

My own Translation runs thus, and I quote it because it occurred to my mind immediately on reading your Lordship's observations.—

> Tis come the final hour;
> The inevitable close of Dardan power
> Hath come; we have been Trojans Ilium was
> And the great name of Troy; now all things pass
> To Argos—so wills angry Jupiter
> Amid a burning Town the Grecians domineer.

I cannot say that we have been, and Ilium was are as sonorous words as "fuimus", and "fuit"— but [they *del*] these latter must have been as familiar to the Romans, as the former to ourselves—I should much like to know if your Lordship disapproved of my Translation here—

I have one word to say upon ornament. It was my wish & labour that my Translation should have far more of the genuine ornaments of Virgil than my predecessors. Dryden has been very careless of these, and profuse of his own, which seem to me very rarely to harmonize with those of virgil. As for example, Describing Hector's appearance in the passage above alluded to,

---

[8]A closing quotation mark was probably meant to follow "datum" at the end of the Latin phrase.

[9]In the interleaved *Memoirs*, EQ translates: "who returned arrayed in the spoils of Achilles."

[10]In the interleaved *Memoirs*, EQ translates: "The great & inescapable day of Dardania comes: we [have been *del*] were Trojans, Ilium was, and the mighty glory of the Teucor."

[11]"Tomb" is corrected to "doom" in EQ's interleaved *Memoirs*, and appears so corrected in the *Memoirs* and in all subsequent reprintings of the letter.

"A bloody shroud he seemed, and bathed in tears"—
"I wept to see the visionary man."

again,

"And all the wounds he for his country bore
Now streamed afresh, and with new purple ran.

[And yet, as I sayd before, this seems to be one of the best examples in Dryden's translation *del*]—I feel it however to be too probable, that my Translation, [may *del*] is deficient in ornament, because I must unavoidably have lost many of Virgil's, and have never without reluctance attempted a compensation of my own. Had I [given *del*] taken the liberties of my Predecessors, Dryden especially, I could have translated nine books with the labour that three have cost me.— The third Book being of a humbler Character than either of the former, I have treated with some[12] less scrupulous apprehension, & have interwoven a little of my own; and with permission I will send it erelong for the benefit of your Lordship's observations, which really will be of great service to me if I proceed.— Had I begun the work 15 years ago I should have finished it with pleasure— at present, I fear, it will take more time than I either can or ought to spare. I do not think of going beyond the 4th Book.—

As to the Mss, be so kind as to forward it at your leisure, [to Si *del*] to me at Sir George Beaumonts, Coleorton Hall, near Ashby; whither I am going in about ten days.— May I trouble your Lordship with our respect Compls to Lady Lonsdale

and believe me
your Lordship's faithful
and obliged friend & Servnt
Wm Wordsworth.

Coleorton Hall

near Ashby de La Zouche
17th Febry [1824]

My Lord,

Your Lordships very obliging Letter reached me this morning, having been forwarded from Rydal Mount.— I am sorry to have given you so much trouble; but

---

[12]EQ changed "some" to "rather," with no manuscript authority, and so it appeared in the *Memoirs.*

I attach so much importance to your Lordships judgement, that I was anxious for a clear understanding which could scarcely be effected without a few particulars. May I hope to be favored with them if I have the pleasure of seeing you in the course of next summer. Five minutes conversation will do more than hours of Letter-writing.—

I began my Translation by accident; I continued it with a hope to produce a work which should be to a certain degree affecting, which Drydens is not to me in the least. Dr Johnson has justly remarked that Dryden had little talent for the Pathetic, and the tenderness of Vergil seems to me to escape him.—Vergil's style is an inimitable mixture of the elaborately ornate, and the majestically plain & touching. The former quality is much more difficult to reach [in our language *del*] than the latter, in which whoever fails must fail through want of ability, and not through the imperfections of our language.

In my last I troubled you with a quotation from my own translation, in which I feared a failure; "fuimus" Troes, &c we have been Trojans &c it struck me afterwards that I might have found still [more *del*] stronger instances. —At the close of the 1st Book Dido is described as asking several questions of Æneas,

> Nunc quales Diomedis equi nunc quartus Achillei—

Which Dryden translates (very meanly, I think) thus
"The Steeds of Diomede varied the discourse" &c
My own Translation is probably as faulty upon another principle, [as *del*]

> Of Hector asked—of Priam oer and oer—
> What arms the Son of bright Aurora wore,
> What Horses those of Diomed; how great
> Achilles—but o Queen[13] the whole relate—

These two lines [are *del*] will be deemed, I apprehend, harsh and bald.—So true is Horace's remark "in vitium ducit culpæ fuga[14] &c
with many thanks and a hope to be excused for being so troublesome, I remain,

my Lord
your faithful & obliged Ser^nt
Wm Wordsworth

Sir George & Lady B— are quite well & beg best Comp^ts & wishes—I received the Mss through Mr Beckett—Mrs Wordsworth is much obliged to your Lordships kind offer to frank her Letters— I now take the liberty of enclosing one to my Son for that purpose.

---

[13]WW has mistakenly written "Queen" for "Guest."

[14]*Ars Poetica,* l. 31: "in vitium ducit culpae fuga, si caret arte" (Avoidance of error leads to fault, if skill is lacking).

Appendix II

Coleridge's Notes in DC MS. 101 to *Aeneid,* Book I

In April 1824, at William Wordsworth's request, Samuel Taylor Coleridge drew up a series of notes to Book I of the *Aeneid* translation. The text of these notes, stripped of Coleridge's inaccurate line numbers, is reproduced in the top band, immediately underneath the reading text of the poem. This appendix supplies a photographic reproduction of Coleridge's notes, in order to preserve the symbols and line-number notations not reproduced in the reading text. These symbols and most of the line-number notations also appear at corresponding places in MS. 101B, Dorothy Wordsworth's fair copy of *Aeneid,* Book I, which William had lent to Coleridge. Book I of MS. 101B also contains line numbers, in Coleridge's autograph, at the tops or bottoms of several pages; these are part of an attempt to keep a count of line numbers. As mentioned before, Coleridge's count is inaccurate.

In MS. 101B, the following symbols, apparently in Coleridge's autograph, can be found:

+	In margin, or over particular words, at ll. 5, 46, 54, 74, 81, 88, 89, 142, 277, 355, 437, 509, 512, 514, 621 (here corresponding to a note in Coleridge's autograph at page bottom), 626, 680, and 704.
∞	In margin, at ll. 19, 20.
X	In margin, or over particular words, at ll. 180, 193, 215, 248.

In addition, Coleridge has written line numbers at several places in MS. 101B, sometimes to keep count and sometimes to indicate the presence of a note in MS. 101D. The following line numbers occur in Coleridge's autograph (his count is two lines ahead of the actual number until 327; it is three lines ahead until 400; four lines ahead until 474; six lines ahead until 667; eight lines ahead thereafter): 46, 69, 70, 83, 88, 93, 94, 100, 108, 117, 140, 163, 170, 186, 187, 194, 200, 209, 210, 232, 240, 254, 260, 277, 280, 290, 300, 303, 327, 350, 360, 370, 374, 380, 400, 402, 420, 425, 430, 442, 448, 450, 60 (for 460), 474, 480, 90 (for 490), 498, 500, 511, 522, 530, 40 (for 540), 547, 550, 60 (for 560), 570, 596, 600, 620, 642, 667, 674, 690, 700, 714, 720, 737, 750, 760, 776, 790, 800, 807, 810.

Finally, several words are underlined, apparently by Coleridge, for they seem connected with MS. 101D entries:

l. 28 "train'd" and "wide and far"
l. 48 "inly"
l. 621 "the lot of" (referring to note at page bottom, MS. 101B)

Coleridge's letter to Wordsworth of April 12, 1824, which served as a cover letter for MS. 101D, is written on a single sheet (a bifolium torn in half) of the same paper as MS. 101D (see Manuscript Census, page xxi), folded in half for writing, and folded further for mailing. It is watermarked A COWAN / 1822. A version of the letter, somewhat abridged, was published first in Christopher Wordsworth, Jr.'s *Memoirs of William Wordsworth* (1851), and was republished in *The Collected Letters of Samuel Taylor Coleridge*, edited by E. L. Griggs (who supplied the date), partially in volume V and and fully in VI. The letter reproduced on the following page is based on volume VI, and has been checked against a photostat of the manuscript, which was formerly in the possession of Jonathan Wordsworth.

[Address] W. Wordsworth, Esqre

Dear Wordsworth,

I did not venture to trust your MSS by our common Carrier; and partly the continued Rain, and partly a flush of pharma-copœetic business, prevented either of Mr Gillman's two Pupils going to town with the pacquet on Saturday, and this morning. Dear Dorothy was neither aware of the Crush of unperformed & accumulated Business that ill health & a multitude of time-wasters & [? *del*] requests, I wanted courage to say No to had layed on me—nor of the slowness with which I proceed especially [in any *del*] [where *inserted*] there is any Collating, or turn[ed *del*] [ing *inserted*] from one book to another—

[Thr *del*] Three whole days the going thro' the first book cost me—tho' only to find fault. But I can not find fault, in pen and ink, without thinking [over & *inserted*] over again, and without some sort of an attempt to suggest the alteration—& in so doing how soon an hour is gone—so many half seconds up to half minutes are lost in leaning back on one's chair & looking up in the bodily act of contracting the muscles of the brows & forehead & unconsciously attending to the sensation.—Had I the MSS with me for 5 or 6 months, so as to amuse myself off and on, without any solicitude as to a given day; and could I be persuaded, that if as well done as the nature of the thing [(viz. a translation, Virgil in English) *inserted*] renders possible, it would not raise; but simply—sustain your well-merited fame, for pure diction, where what is not idiom is never other than logically correct; I doubt not, that the inequalities could be removed.– But I am haunted by the apprehension, that I am not feeling or thinking in the same spirit with you, at one time; and at another, too much on the spirit of your writings. Since Milton I know of no Poet, with so many felicities & unforgettable Lines & stanzas as you—and to read therefore page after page without a single brilliant note, depresses me—& I grow peevish with you for having wasted your time on a work so very much below you, that you can not stoop & take. Finally, my conviction is: that you undertook an impossibility: and that there is no medium between a prose Version, and one on the avowed principle of Compensation in the widest sense--/ i.e. manner, Genius, total effect. I confine myself to Virgil when I say this. ——

I must now set to work with all my powers & thoughts to my Leighton, & then to my Logic; and then to my opus maximum! if indeed it shall please God to spare me so long—which I have had too many warnings of late (more than my nearest Friends know of) not to doubt./

N.B. One great Joy, I have in John Coleridges reversionary wind-fall is that it will clap the extinguisher on the Quarterly Schemes, which gave me more pain than I thought fit to express. For to John & his Sister Fanny & to them alone, I have feelings that tell me what the ties of Blood may be—My kind love to Dorothy.

Monday Night, S.T. Coleridge

DC MS. 101D, 1r

Before I commence this revision which had it but been an original poem of yours most cheerfully should I have done I must put you on your guard against the morbid hyper-critical state of my taste to my own grievance & damage. I can only put a mark + to the objections that I feel confident are worth attending to: and —, where I am myself doubtful.

S. T. C.

First Book.

Line.

— 3. A Fugitive of Fate, were it less dubious English, seems to give the sense of fato profugus, urged by propelling fate. By ghastly propelled. A fated Fugitive. —

4. By force supernal.

+ 5. might not "through" be omitted, & the line put in apposition. Stern Juno's unrelenting unforgetting enmity.

+ 8. came. any thing better than flowed. have come might apply to the [illegible] but not to the Alban Sires.

10–14. — This [illegible] should be retranslated.

15.16. — Dryden's seems preferable. Longé applies to the whole, or rather the mouth of the Tiber completes the Italiam. Distant but lying opposite to the Italian Coast, where the Tiber disembogues itself.

+ 18. — 21 — 26 are neither translation or poetry. — Pope, or Hayley, might talk [illegible] an unbounded scope (i.e. no scope at all) to partial hope; but not [illegible] much less in lieu of [illegible] fovetque. — 28 — wide & far. I fear a something ludicrous in this hystero-proteron of a familiar idiom, so barefacedly for rhyme's sake.

p. 3. 48. They set their sails for the open sea, and met the longer or bolder waves [illegible] as the sense by a triplet it might be expressed —

4. 83. + 88 — obscure & reads uncouth. [illegible], my foes, bears far. — 91. [illegible] or scatters: let the corpses [illegible] [illegible] & at all events theirs is unhappy. Virgil avoids this confusion of [illegible] accidents. The corses!

109. — And bear down on the Deep. + unused to spare her tempests. There Eurus, [illegible] Notus, and Africus (the Seaman's Fear!) [illegible] for the storm [illegible] [illegible] —

136 + Help from — [illegible]. Is this a translation of Franguntur remi! — but the She renders the whole description obscure. Is Prow the Nom. or accus. of veers, & is "veer" ever used of a part of a Ship. The Ship may veer; but can the Prow? — I but put the question. — These & these occasion an additional perplexity. — Item. 'The voice may force a metrical effect on" prepares to burst with its whole weight." I do not like the and &c. it produces a pause not intended and removes the instantaneous consequence. — [illegible] [illegible] arenis, you imply in "boiling" — but surely Virgil meant to shew that the storm had driven the fleet shoreward & into shallow water.

142. Encounter a shock received from? As to these lines, however, you construe them otherwise than I should — & I doubt not, better — having studied it. I should not give all the force to Virgil's ab alto that you have done. I should construe it, "from deep water" &c. But the "latentia" seems not a happy epithet in connection with Dorsum immane mari summo. —

DC MS. 101D, 1v

165. &c And for what outrages &c. Not translation, and all this here, incensed — I can scarcely read, as part of a sentence. It sounds to my ear as if I were repeating single words — perceived, incensed, admired, &c — "and terrified" a rhyme to "against their peace allied"!

+ 172, 3/. — so simple in the original, nor was Neptune any stranger to his Sister's Tricks and Tempers. — The heat of anger is not the meaning of Iræ (plural) — nor does doli mean — dark deceit"!

The following Speech is as good as the original — which for the life of me I could never read even at School but as a Tom Thumb Tragedy. The Quos ego. Sed motos. for exquisite vulgarity of boatswain Mutter is incomparable. — Obiter dictum sit: "Godhead" is far too theological & abstract a word.

+ 194. 2d unclouds the Heaven and the Sun restores

200. Ensued? coorta est. This is a very remarkable instance of an inverted Simile. I imagine that Virgil's purpose was to prepare the readers' fancy for land and city imagery & interests.

213. — "Flurry" is very bold; but I think it an improvement.

218. "Nature's self" not Virgilian. I wish, the 3 first lines of this passage, there is a blank, were equal to all the rest. Are [illegible], they do not give the imagery of the original. If I understand the lines, the water splits itself into little coves or sinuses.

244. nutriment.

p. 12 255. 2d He seized the bow, nor lack'd he ample store
Of feather'd shafts, Achates' grievous burden [illegible].

277. + —

281 +. There are unenglishisms here & there in this translation of which I remember no instance in your own poems, one or two in the Descriptive Sketches excepted. Such as the Walter Scott abrupt nudity of the Article. Thus, Trojan Empire (this too Rule allows) —

290–94. Not worth translating; but not well translated — in plain truth, slubbered over, as by rendering the original literally & dis-rhyming your lines, would appear.

303. Why apart? secum, below, means, turned in on himself
? All mourn; and more than all the pious Chief
Him Amycus, him Lycus touch'd with grief
Him Gyas & Cloanthus &c —

315. — Is there other authority for "the way" except the disputed reading in Shakespear & Massinger? We rule our ways.

347. Why half-smiling.

DC MS. 101D, 2[r]

368. It is plain that Virgil means to avoid the trivial name, as one of our old
Poets does in "the fate of ancient Lud"— by the interposition of three words between Lavinum and
Alba. It seems likewise to require a more faithful translation.
370. While Empire hold her place = regnabitur.? Border on the mock-heroic?.
For myself, I wonder at your patience in wading thro' such a stiff
mare mortuum of Dullness! and that of the dullest sort, to wit, History in prosing
narrative prophecy— with so ludicrously anachronical a familiarity of names and
detail— old acquaintance! of the last Platonic sex millennium!—

375— frame walls?— If you wish to strengthen the line, why not— Offspring of Mars,
Mavortian walls shall frame,— + 377— climb? by space? by time— the
unincumscribed in space ~~extent~~ and without bound in time.
unmeasured in extent
In Space unmeasur'd, without bound in time.—

380 Even Juno, she
Whose ~~That~~ wild alarms yet ~~are~~ vex Heaven, Earth & Sea
mad Alarum vexes Earth & Sea— . —383 I don't like; but can
suggest nothing.— Paraphrased is erysthal ~~[illegible]~~, else. The Romans, Lords of all beneath the Sun
That in the Toga were what clad in arms
they were—

424. Rightly translated? Surely, they were boar-spears not javelins:— lato ferro—
and crispans, I imagined, means that play & give of the flexile weapon
likewise. I would suggest that either concealed or some still better word should be put for
hides, or that the whole sentence should be put in the participle absolute,
as the English Reader can not quite free himself from the modern associations with the
word Fleet. The Fleet, concealed beneath the r. c. And overshadowed by the p. g. Two quiv'ring
Spears in hand, he quits the Bay—

428 & q. s.— I am sick of finding fault, the more discomfortably because my
main feeling is that of faulting you for undertaking what compared with the
original is scarcely a possibility, & your name is such that comparison with
Dryden, Pitt, Beresford &c &c stands you in poor stead— nulla gloria praeclaro claudit
But I confess that I cannot read the compressed ~~dignified~~ and sustained yet simple
dignity of Virgilius os habitumque (315 —— 320) & not find the English weak— "is
seen"— suitably (aspect) gait, air— mien—" Arm'd like a Spartan Virgin—:
she in habit and (in Charms)
A Virgin ~~might she [illegible]~~, merely to convey my sense of the
A Spartan Virgin, she— & such her arms—/ climax, 1 2 3—

urge to weariness is scarcely the dictionary meaning (me judice) of fatigat— at all events, not
the poetic force— and the participles ing, ing, kill the rapidity of the movement.
And leaves behind swift Hebrus in her flight— or course or speed
(which, by the bye, with Virgil's pardon, she might have done on a Donkey)

DC MS. 101D, 2ᵛ

441. — Clothed by? 442.. This is one of the sad necessities of rhyme in translation of continuous sentences. "With shrill shouts pressing on the foaming Boar," is quite in the character of an animated enquiry; but to [illegible] on a supplementary description, with entirely changed—.

448 + worthy to be crowned. does not even answer for a rhyme-botch—and does not give the right sense, worthy to be owned by Phœbus as a Sister. The Question is simply Are you Diana or at least one of Diana's Train?—

+ 461 + Slung their necks behind!. V. 7. [illegible] gesture pharetram.

— 465— does not give the force of [illegible] nor the personality of [illegible], which defines the genus intractabile bello.

486. You have convinced me of the necessary injury which the Language must sustain by rhyme translations of Narrative Poems of great length. Where would you have read at [illegible] or in Grasmere Cottage to [illegible] vain scopes to trembling hopes in a room? Were it only for this reason, that it would interfere with your claim to a Regenerator & Jealous Guardian of our Language, I should dissuade the publication. For to you I dare not be insincere— tho' I conjecture, from some of your original Poems (of the more recent, I mean) that our tastes & judgements differ in [illegible] or [illegible] more than formerly— & I am unfeignedly disposed to believe, that the long habit of minute discrimination have over-subtilized my perceptions. I have not composed about 200 verses within the last 18 months— & from the dissatisfaction of they could be read by the most newspaper [illegible] reading other than strongly distinguishable verse, I found them polished almost to sensual effeminacy. You must therefore take my opinions for what they are—

503. & the principles of things, the technical phrase of the [illegible] Poets περὶ ἀρχῶν.

511 — Aeneas I, who wheresoe'er I go carry &c.: super æthera notus earlier— "to the Gods kept my fame." But the whole passage needs to be recomposed— you ~~[illegible]~~ have so diluted the meaning.— I doubt your version of genus ab Jove summo— May it not be part of the answer to the Qui tandem? my kind from highest Jove. i.e. I am Jove's Grandson. — I 515 [illegible] 518.

540. [illegible] strike me as [illegible], there having been no previous division made— but dedere cantus is not with tuneful voice— sent forth the shrill strain, chaunt.— My main objection is that the Imagery of this (in the original obscurely expressed) passage is not distinctly made out in your lines.

549. Vertice = from the exalted region of her head?

590.— Is there authority for scent, except in Perfumers & Snuff shops? I retract the question; but was it not obscure in this place— & with a "while"?

604.— From this line the Translation greatly & very markedly improves, [illegible] has bone & muscle.

DC MS. 101D, 3r

627.– To ponder &c. Destroys the already too obscure [illegible] of [illegible] of [illegible], & thus renders the [illegible] of [illegible] still cruder than Virgil's [illegible] [illegible]– offer'd to his sight, seems likewise slovenly. In my [illegible] Edition it is Atreidas, not Atriden– 632. Achilles' name is [illegible] repeated, I think– & to [illegible] severe ? And pierce to [illegible] Achilles. As the Tear [illegible] his eyes, he [illegible]–.

673.– [illegible] of the [illegible] [illegible] lines should be altered– & the whole passage deserves it. By hurrying over what Virgil makes prominent (Eneas's height of emotion, at this particular point) "his friend" becomes equivocal, p. 8.

? { And close beside his Friend's dead body stands
{ Priam, still suppliant with unweapon'd hands.

696 — Far, far above / too vague for supereminet– & tho' Virgil shows great want of judgement in this outré imitation of Homer, yet still I would give his meaning which your [illegible] submerges.

Where'er she ~~winds her ways~~ threads the dance, the Goddess bears
Her Quiver visible– still, still appears
The ~~[illegible]~~ [illegible] Crescent far above the rest!
Mute Exultation thrills Latona's breast...–

Seems more true to the intention.–

+712. by [illegible] he saw– you would not scarcely write this in a prose note.

720. clamore– with noise just like a parcel of Tars, made their way to the Temple with ~~[illegible]~~ noisy Hail. Virgil wished to contrast the [illegible] [illegible] of inferior officers with the stillness of Eneas & his Staff.

753. care, war, [illegible], shades– rather too confluent?–

776.– an odd line. 798– Cast-away of Floods is this ever applied to the Sea–

811.– Here I think some substitute for humorous should be ventured–

The six first lines of p. 43– [illegible] [illegible] [illegible] [illegible] [illegible] are obscure & run obstructedly. That through twice repeated.– Generally, however, the latter part is done with great spirit.

DC MS. 101D, 3[v]

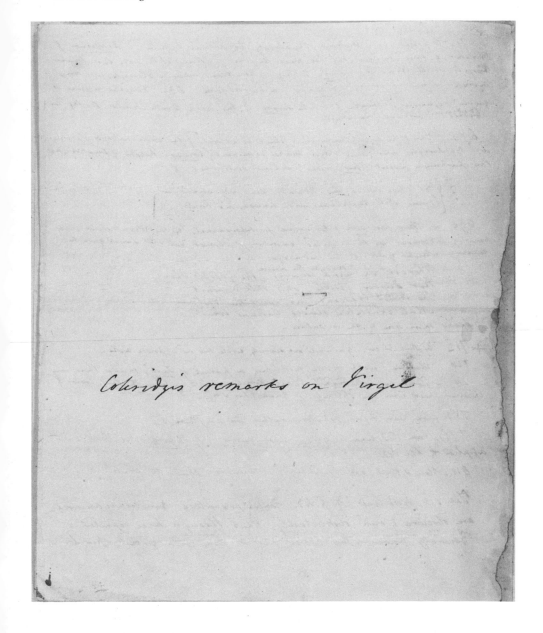

Appendix III

Extract from *Aeneid,* Book I, in *The Philological Museum*

In February 1832, Book I of Wordsworth's *Aeneid* translation, from line 901 to the end, was published in Julius Charles Hare's journal, *The Philological Museum.* It was the only part of the translation to be published in Wordsworth's lifetime, and was republished, with slight variations in punctuation and capitalization, in the editions of Wordsworth's poetry prepared by Henry Reed, William Knight, Edward Dowden, and Thomas Hutchinson; it remained the only published text of the translation until de Selincourt and Darbishire published volume IV of *The Poetical Works* in 1947. Because it was the only authorized version of any part of the poem to be published, and because it was the only remnant of the translation available to the general public for over a century, the *Philological Museum* extract is reprinted here. It is reproduced as it appeared in *The Philological Museum* in 1832, except that line numbers, referring to the corresponding line numbers in the reading text of the present edition, have been added in brackets in the right margin. Hare and *The Philological Museum* are discussed in the introduction to the *Aeneid* translation, pages 170–174.

TRANSLATION OF PART OF THE FIRST BOOK OF THE ÆNEID.

To the Editors of the PHILOLOGICAL MUSEUM.

Your letter reminding me of an expectation I some time since held out to you of allowing some specimens of my translation from the Æneid to be printed in the Philological Museum was not very acceptable: for I had abandoned the thought of ever sending into the world any part of that experiment,—for it was nothing more,—an experiment begun for amusement, and I now think a less fortunate one than when I first named it to you. Having been displeased in modern translations with the additions of incongruous matter, I began to translate with a resolve to keep clear of that fault, by adding nothing; but I became convinced that a spirited translation can scarcely be accomplished in the English language without admitting a principle of compensation. On this point however I do not wish to insist, and merely send the following passage, taken at random, from a wish to comply with your request.

W. W.

But Cytherea, studious to invent
Arts yet untried, upon new counsels bent,
Resolves that Cupid, chang'd in form and face
To young Ascanius, should assume his place;
Present the maddening gifts, and kindle heat
Of passion at the bosom's inmost seat.
She dreads the treacherous house, the double tongue;
She burns, she frets—by Juno's rancour stung;
The calm of night is powerless to remove
These cares, and thus she speaks to wingèd Love:
"O son, my strength, my power! who dost despise
(What, save thyself, none dare through earth and skies)
The giant-quelling bolts of Jove, I flee,
O son, a suppliant to thy deity!
What perils meet Æneas in his course,
How Juno's hate with unrelenting force
Pursues thy brother—this to thee is known;
And oft-times hast thou made my griefs thine own.

Him now the generous Dido by soft chains
Of bland entreaty at her court detains;
Junonian hospitalities prepare
Such apt occasion that I dread a snare.
Hence, ere some hostile God can intervene,
Would I, by previous wiles, inflame the queen
With passion for Æneas, such strong love
That at my beck, mine only, she shall move.
Hear, and assist;—the father's mandate calls
His young Ascanius to the Tyrian walls;
He comes, my dear delight,—and costliest things
Preserv'd from fire and flood for presents brings.
Him will I take, and in close covert keep,
'Mid Groves Idalian, lull'd to gentle sleep,
Or on Cythera's far-sequestered steep,
That he may neither know what hope is mine,
Nor by his presence traverse the design.
Do thou, but for a single night's brief space
Dissemble; be that boy in form and face!
And when enraptured Dido shall receive
Thee to her arms, and kisses interweave
With many a fond embrace, while joy runs high,
And goblets crown the proud festivity,
Instil thy subtle poison, and inspire,
At every touch, an unsuspected fire."
   Love, at the word, before his mother's sight
Puts off his wings, and walks, with proud delight,
Like young Iulus; but the gentlest dews
Of slumber Venus sheds, to circumfuse
The true Ascanius, steep'd in placid rest;
Then wafts him, cherish'd on her careful breast,
Through upper air to an Idalian glade,
Where he on soft *amaracus* is laid,
With breathing flowers embraced, and fragrant shade.
But Cupid, following cheerily his guide
Achates, with the gifts to Carthage hied;
And, as the hall he entered, there, between
The sharers of her golden couch, was seen
Reclin'd in festal pomp the Tyrian queen.
The Trojans too (Æneas at their head)
On couches lie, with purple overspread:
Meantime in cannisters is heap'd the bread,
Pellucid water for the hands is borne,
And napkins of smooth texture, finely shorn.
Within are fifty handmaids, who prepare,
As they in order stand, the dainty fare;
And fume the household deities with store
Of odorous incense; while a hundred more

Match'd with an equal number of like age,
But each of manly sex, a docile page,
Marshal the banquet, giving with due grace
To cup or viand its appointed place.
The Tyrians rushing in, an eager band,
Their painted couches seek, obedient to command.
They look with wonder on the gifts—they gaze
Upon Iulus, dazzled with the rays
That from his ardent countenance are flung,
And charm'd to hear his simulating tongue;
Nor pass unprais'd the robe and veil divine,
Round which the yellow flowers and wandering foliage twine.
But chiefly Dido, to the coming ill
Devoted, strives in vain her vast desires to fill;
She views the gifts; upon the child then turns
Insatiable looks, and gazing burns.
To ease a father's cheated love he hung
Upon Æneas, and around him clung;
Then seeks the queen; with her his arts he tries;
She fastens on the Boy enamour'd eyes,
Clasps in her arms, nor weens (O lot unblest!)
How great a god, incumbent on her breast,
Would fill it with his spirit. He, to please
His Acidalian Mother, by degrees
Blots out Sichæus, studious to remove
The dead, by influx of a living love,
By stealthy entrance of a perilous guest
Troubling a heart that had been long at rest.
Now when the viands were withdrawn, and ceas'd
The first division of the splendid feast,
While round a vacant board the chiefs recline,
Huge goblets are brought forth; they crown the wine;
Voices of gladness roll the walls around;
Those gladsome voices from the courts rebound;
From gilded rafters many a blazing light
Depends, and torches overcome the night.
The minutes fly—till, at the queen's command,
A bowl of state is offered to her hand:
Then she, as Belus wont, and all the line
From Belus, filled it to the brim with wine;
Silence ensued. "O Jupiter, whose care
Is hospitable dealing, grant my prayer!
Productive day be this of lasting joy
To Tyrians, and these Exiles driven from Troy;
A day to future generations dear!
Let Bacchus, donor of soul-quick'ning cheer,
Be present; kindly Juno, be thou near!
And, Tyrians, may your choicest favours wait

Upon this hour, the bond to celebrate!"
She spake and shed an offering on the board;
Then sipp'd the bowl whence she the wine had pour'd
And gave to Bitias, urging the prompt lord;
He rais'd the Bowl, and took a long deep draught;
Then every chief in turn the beverage quaff'd.
   Graced with redundant hair, Iopas sings
The lore of Atlas, to resounding strings,
The labours of the Sun, the lunar wanderings;
Whence human kind, and brute; what natural powers
Engender lightning, whence are falling showers.
He chaunts Arcturus,—that fraternal twain
The glittering Bears,—the Pleiads fraught with rain;
—Why suns in winter, shunning heaven's steep heights
Post seaward,—what impedes the tardy nights.
The learned song from Tyrian hearers draws
Loud shouts,—the Trojans echo the applause.
—But, lengthening out the night with converse new,
Large draughts of love unhappy Dido drew;
Of Priam ask'd, of Hector—o'er and o'er—
What arms the son of bright Aurora wore;—
What steeds the car of Diomed could boast;
Among the leaders of the Grecian host
How look'd Achilles, their dread paramount—
"But nay—the fatal wiles, O guest, recount,
Retrace the Grecian cunning from its source,
Your own grief and your friends'—your wandering course;
For now, till this seventh summer have ye rang'd
The sea, or trod the earth, to peace estrang'd."

College Library